SCOTT FORESMAN

# READING STREET

COMMON CORE ©

## Program Authors

| | |
|---|---|
| Peter Afflerbach | P. David Pearson |
| Camille Blachowicz | Sam Sebesta |
| Candy Dawson Boyd | Deborah Simmons |
| Elena Izquierdo | Susan Watts Taffe |
| Connie Juel | Alfred Tatum |
| Edward Kame'enui | Sharon Vaughn |
| Donald Leu | Karen Kring Wixson |
| Jeanne R. Paratore | |

Glenview, Illinois

Boston, Massachusetts

Chandler, Arizona

Upper Saddle River, New Jersey

ALWAYS LEARNING

PEARSON

*We dedicate Reading Street to*
*Peter Jovanovich.*

*His wisdom, courage,*
*and passion for education*
*are an inspiration to us all.*

Accelerated Reader®

The Acknowledgments page appears in the back of the book immediately following the Oral Vocabulary section and constitutes an extension of this copyright page.

ISBN-13: 978-0-328-72530-4
ISBN-10:     0-328-72530-7
1 2 3 4 5 6 7 8 9 10 V003 16 15 14 13 12

## Program Authors

**Peter Afflerbach, Ph.D.**
Professor; Department of Curriculum and Instruction,
University of Maryland; College Park, Maryland
Areas of Expertise: Common Core State Standards English Language Arts
Work Team, Assessment, and Comprehension

**Camille L. Z. Blachowicz, Ph.D.**
Professor; National College of Education, National-Louis University; Skokie, Illinois
Areas of Expertise: Vocabulary and Comprehension

**Candy Dawson Boyd, Ph.D.**
Professor, School of Education; Saint Mary's College; Moraga, California
Areas of Expertise: Children's Literature and Professional Development

**Elena Izquierdo, Ph.D.**
Associate Professor, University of Texas at El Paso
Area of Expertise: English Language Learners

**Connie Juel, Ph.D.**
Professor of Education; Stanford University; Stanford, California
Areas of Expertise: Phonics, Oral Vocabulary, and Intervention

**Edward J. Kame'enui, Ph.D.**
Dean-Knight Professor of Education and Director, Institute for the Development
of Educational Achievement, and the Center on Teaching and Learning;
College of Education; University of Oregon
Areas of Expertise: Assessment, Intervention, and Progress Monitoring

**Donald J. Leu, Ph.D.**
John and Maria Neag Endowed Chair in Literacy and Technology Board of Directors,
International Reading Association; University of Connecticut; Storrs, Connecticut
Areas of Expertise: Comprehension, Technology, and New Literacies

**Jeanne R. Paratore, Ed.D.**
Professor of Literacy, Language, and Cultural Studies; Boston University School
of Education; Boston, Massachusetts
Areas of Expertise: Intervention and Small Group Instruction

**P. David Pearson, Ph.D.**
Professor of Language, Literacy and Culture, and Human Development;
Graduate School of Education; University of California; Berkeley, California
Areas of Expertise: Common Core State Standards English Language Arts
Work Team, Comprehension

**Sam L. Sebesta, Ph.D.**
Professor Emeritus; Curriculum and Instruction College of Education,
University of Washington; Seattle, Washington
Areas of Expertise: Children's Literature, Reader Response, and Motivation

**Deborah Simmons, Ph.D.**
Professor in the Department of Educational Psychology, College of Education
and Human Development, Texas A&M University
Areas of Expertise: Literacy Development, Phonics, and Intervention

**Susan Watts Taffe, Ph.D.**
Associate Professor and Program Coordinator, Literacy and Second Language Studies,
School of Education; University of Cincinnati; Cincinnati, Ohio
Areas of Expertise: Vocabulary, Comprehension, and New Literacies

**Alfred Tatum, Ph.D.**
Associate Professor and Director, UIC Reading Clinic, University of Illinois at Chicago
Areas of Expertise: Adolescent Literacy, Reader Response, and Motivation

**Sharon Vaughn, Ph.D.**
H. E. Hartfelder/The Southland Corporation Regents Professor;
University of Texas; Austin, Texas
Areas of Expertise: Literacy Development, Intervention, Professional Development,
English Language Learners, Vocabulary, and Small Group Instruction

**Karen Kring Wixson, Ph.D.**
Dean of Education, University of North Carolina, Greensboro
Areas of Expertise: Common Core State Standards English Language Arts Work
Team, Assessment, Small Group Instruction

## Consulting Authors

**Jeff Anderson, M.Ed.**
Author and National Literacy Staff Developer

**Jim Cummins, Ph.D.**
Professor; Department of Curriculum, Teaching and Learning; University of Toronto

**Tahira A. DuPree Chase, Ed.D.**
Director of Curriculum and Instruction, Mt. Vernon City School District, New York

**Lily Wong Fillmore, Ph.D.**
Professor Emerita; Graduate School of Education, University of California, Berkeley

**Georgia Earnest Garcia, Ph.D.**
Professor; Language and Literacy Division, Department of Curriculum and Instruction,
University of Illinois at Urbana-Champaign

**George A. Gonzalez, Ph.D.**
Professor (Retired); School of Education,
University of Texas-Pan American, Edinburg

**Adria Klein, Ph.D.**
Professor Emeritus; School of Education, California State University, San Bernadino

**Lesley Maxwell, M.S., CCC-SLP**
Director of Clinical Education, Clinical Associate Professor; Department of
Communication Sciences and Disorders, MGH Institute of Health Professions

**Valerie Ooka Pang, Ph.D.**
Professor; School of Teacher Education, San Diego State University

**Sally M. Reis, Ph.D.**
Board of Trustees Distinguished Professor; Department of Educational Psychology,
University of Connecticut

**Jon Scieszka, M.F.A.**
Children's Book Author and Founder of GUYS READ, First National Ambassador for
Young People's Literature 2008

**Grant Wiggins, Ed.D.**
President of Authentic Education, coauthor of *Understanding by Design*

# Nurture the love of reading.

Help students learn to read *and* love to read. *Reading Street Common Core* supports reading, writing, and language development. Amazing literature on amazing devices inspires students in a whole new way.

## Literature students love

The best literary and informational text

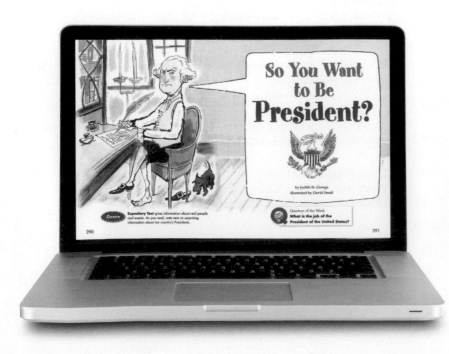

On devices they crave!

Whiteboards, tablets, computers, mobile device

# Build a foundation for reading.

*Reading Street Common Core* helps students develop foundational skills for reading more complex text. Common Core experts helped design the plan. Classroom results prove it works.

## Early Reading Success

*Reading Street* students outperformed their peers by 15 percentile points, even though they started below the comparison students.

## Greater Reading Enjoyment Later

Fourth-grade *Reading Street* students had more positive attitudes toward reading.

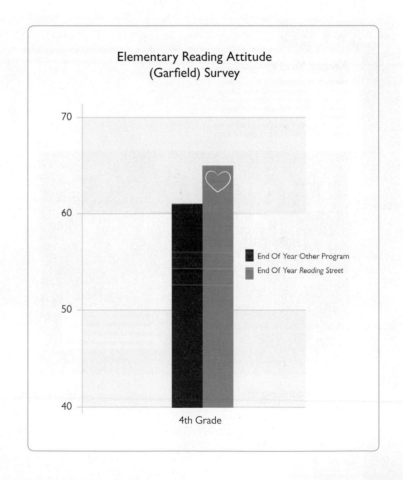

Kindergarten GRADE Total Score

Comparison
Reading Street

Elementary Reading Attitude (Garfield) Survey

End Of Year Other Program
End Of Year Reading Street

"The texts children read provide them with a foundation not just for what they're going to read, but also for what they're going to write and talk about."

Jeanne R. Paratore, Ed.D.
Program Author

# Grow student capacity.

*Reading Street Common Core* builds students' capacity to read complex texts. Zoom in on elements critical to the Common Core State Standards.

 **Zoom in on ©**

## Text-Based Comprehension

Modeling, analysis, and guided practice prepare students for more demanding text.

## Read for Understanding Routine

Routines provide weekly opportunities to develop deep understanding and build higher-order thinking skills through Close Reading.

---

**Routine    Read for Understanding ©**

Deepen understanding by reading the selection multiple times.

1. **First Read**—use the **Access Text** notes to help children clarify understanding.

2. **Second Read**—use the **Close Reading** notes to help children draw knowledge from the text.

## Content Knowledge

Weekly and unit instruction is built around science and social studies concepts. These concepts connect every piece of literature, vocabulary, and writing, allowing students to develop deep knowledge.

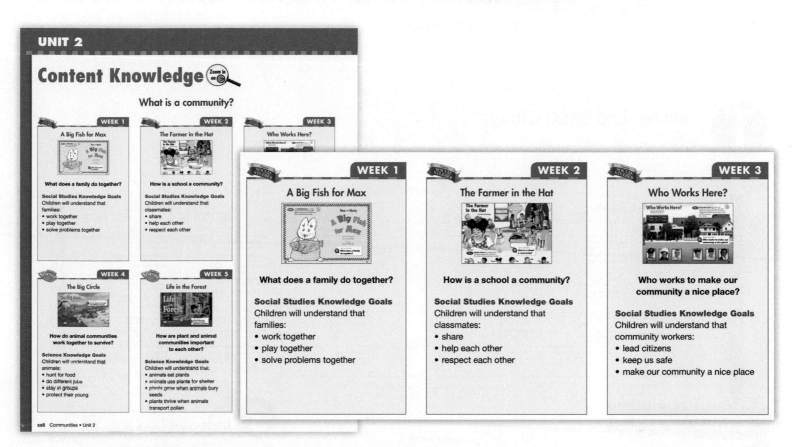

## Writing

Varied writing tasks help students write to inform or explain.

| DAILY | WEEKLY | UNIT |
|---|---|---|
| • 10-minute mini-lessons on writing traits and craft allow students to write in response to their reading<br>• Quick Write routine for writing on demand | • Different writing product each week<br>• Writing mini-lessons and organizational models<br>• Mentor text to exemplify good traits | • One- or two-week Writing Workshops<br>• Writing process lessons<br>     |

# Inspire confidence.

"What do I do in group time?" Follow the simple 3-step plan. *Reading Street Common Core* provides a road map to help you teach with confidence. You'll know exactly where to go and what to do next.

**1** Teacher-Led Small Groups

See how to differentiate instruction day by day.

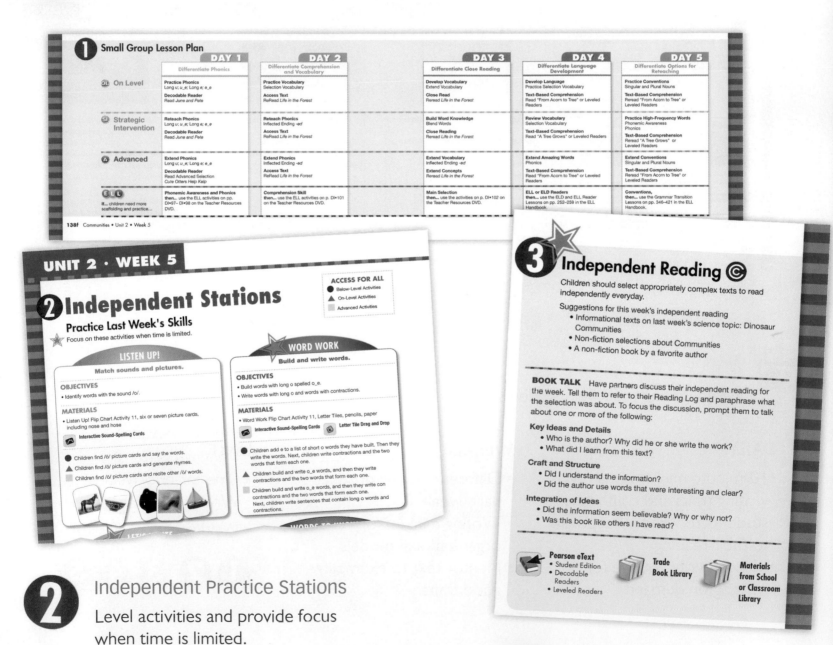

**2** Independent Practice Stations

Level activities and provide focus when time is limited.

**3** Independent Reading

Suggest concept-related reading and partner activities.

Tier 2
Intervention

## Response to Intervention Kit

Tier 2 RTI Kit provides a targeted focus and leveled mini-lessons for individuals and small groups.

Scott Foresman
**Phonemic Awareness**
Teacher's Guide and Student Worktext

• Targeted instruction in phonological and phonemic awareness skills
• Leveled mini-lessons for individual or small-group instruction

Grades 3-6

Scott Foresman
**Response to Intervention Kit**

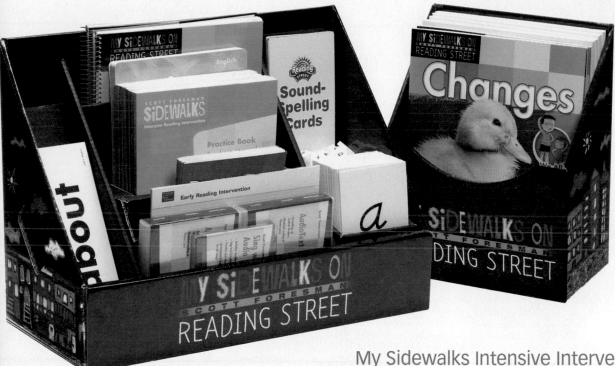

Intensive
Intervention

## My Sidewalks Intensive Intervention

Conceptually related to *Reading Street, My Sidewalks* provides 30 weeks of instruction for struggling readers.

"What we need to do is to increase the support strategies to help students cope with complex text."

**P. David Pearson**
Program Author

# UNIT 4
# One of a Kind

YOU ARE HERE

# UNIT 5
# Cultures

# TABLE OF CONTENTS

# UNIT 2
# Smart Solutions

# UNIT 3
# People and Nature

# One of a Kind

## What does it mean to be unique?

## The Man Who Invented Basketball

BIOGRAPHY

How do talents make someone unique?

**Paired Selection**
**My Turn at Bat: The Story of My Life**
AUTOBIOGRAPHY

## Hottest, Coldest, Highest, Deepest

EXPOSITORY TEXT

What makes nature's record holders unique?

**Paired Selection**
**Paul Bunyan and the Great Lakes**
LEGEND

## Rocks in His Head

BIOGRAPHY

Why is it valuable to have unique Interests?

**Paired Selection**
**Marvelous Marble Mania**
PERSUASIVE TEXT

## America's Champion Swimmer: Gertrude Ederle

BIOGRAPHY

What unique traits does it take to be the first to do something?

**Paired Selection**
**Women Athletes**
ONLINE DIRECTORIES

## Fly, Eagle, Fly!

FOLK TALE

What behaviors are unique to different animals?

**Paired Selection**
**Purple Coyote**
TRICKSTER TALE

# Skills Overview

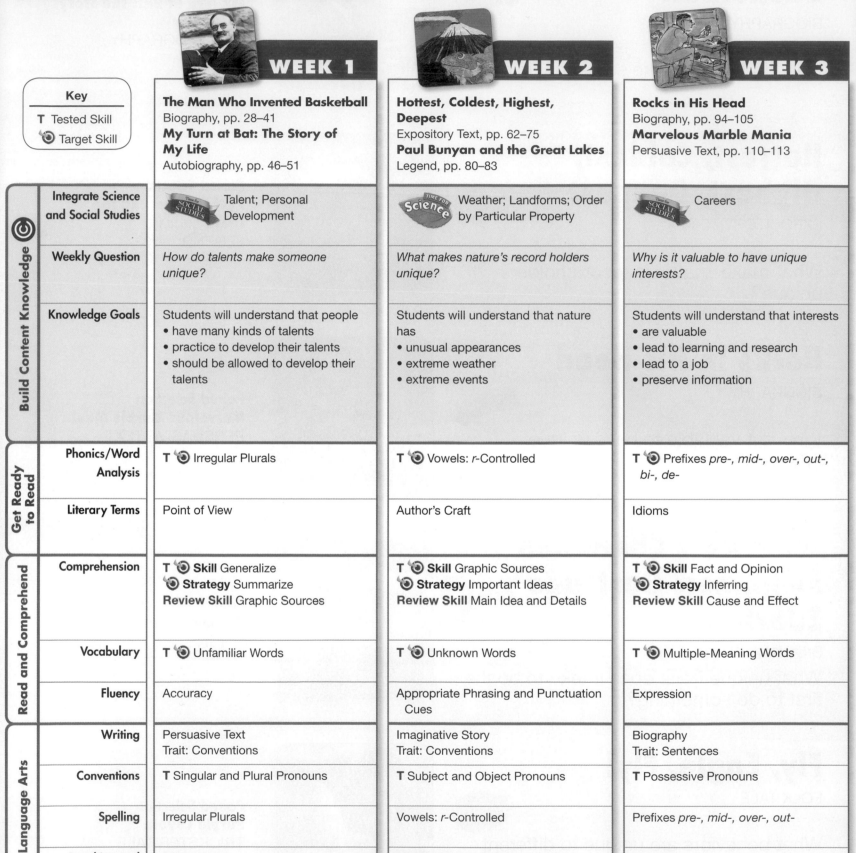

**Key**

T  Tested Skill

🎯  Target Skill

| | | **WEEK 1**<br>**The Man Who Invented Basketball**<br>Biography, pp. 28–41<br>**My Turn at Bat: The Story of My Life**<br>Autobiography, pp. 46–51 | **WEEK 2**<br>**Hottest, Coldest, Highest, Deepest**<br>Expository Text, pp. 62–75<br>**Paul Bunyan and the Great Lakes**<br>Legend, pp. 80–83 | **WEEK 3**<br>**Rocks in His Head**<br>Biography, pp. 94–105<br>**Marvelous Marble Mania**<br>Persuasive Text, pp. 110–113 |
|---|---|---|---|---|
| **Build Content Knowledge** | Integrate Science and Social Studies | *SOCIAL STUDIES* Talent; Personal Development | *TIME FOR Science* Weather; Landforms; Order by Particular Property | *SOCIAL STUDIES* Careers |
| | Weekly Question | *How do talents make someone unique?* | *What makes nature's record holders unique?* | *Why is it valuable to have unique interests?* |
| | Knowledge Goals | Students will understand that people<br>• have many kinds of talents<br>• practice to develop their talents<br>• should be allowed to develop their talents | Students will understand that nature has<br>• unusual appearances<br>• extreme weather<br>• extreme events | Students will understand that interests<br>• are valuable<br>• lead to learning and research<br>• lead to a job<br>• preserve information |
| **Get Ready to Read** | Phonics/Word Analysis | T 🎯 Irregular Plurals | T 🎯 Vowels: *r*-Controlled | T 🎯 Prefixes *pre-, mid-, over-, out-, bi-, de-* |
| | Literary Terms | Point of View | Author's Craft | Idioms |
| **Read and Comprehend** | Comprehension | T 🎯 **Skill** Generalize<br>🎯 **Strategy** Summarize<br>**Review Skill** Graphic Sources | T 🎯 **Skill** Graphic Sources<br>🎯 **Strategy** Important Ideas<br>**Review Skill** Main Idea and Details | T 🎯 **Skill** Fact and Opinion<br>🎯 **Strategy** Inferring<br>**Review Skill** Cause and Effect |
| | Vocabulary | T 🎯 Unfamiliar Words | T 🎯 Unknown Words | T 🎯 Multiple-Meaning Words |
| | Fluency | Accuracy | Appropriate Phrasing and Punctuation Cues | Expression |
| **Language Arts** | Writing | Persuasive Text<br>Trait: Conventions | Imaginative Story<br>Trait: Conventions | Biography<br>Trait: Sentences |
| | Conventions | T Singular and Plural Pronouns | T Subject and Object Pronouns | T Possessive Pronouns |
| | Spelling | Irregular Plurals | Vowels: *r*-Controlled | Prefixes *pre-, mid-, over-, out-* |
| | Speaking and Listening | Presentation | Media Literacy: Weather Forecast | Interview |

**WEEK 4**

 **WEEK 5**

 **WEEK 6**

| WEEK 4 | WEEK 5 | WEEK 6 |
|---|---|---|
| **America's Champion Swimmer: Gertrude Ederle** Biography, pp. 124–139 **Women Athletes** Online Directories, pp. 144–147 | **Fly, Eagle, Fly!** Folk Tale, pp. 158–171 **Purple Coyote** Trickster Tale, pp. 176–181 | **Interactive Review** |
| **SOCIAL STUDIES** Individuals Initiating Change; Heroes; Geography | **Science** Inherited Characteristics; Instincts | **Science** One of a Kind |
| *What unique traits does it take to be the first to do something?* | *What behaviors are unique to different animals?* | *What does it mean to be unique?* |
| Students will understand that being first takes • bravery • imagination • willingness to work hard • determination | Students will understand that some animals • have lures on their heads • blend in with their surroundings • change colors | Connect the Question of the Week to the Big Question |
| Suffixes -er, -or, -ess, -ist | Syllables VCCCV | |
| Word Choice | Sensory Details | |
| **T** 👁 **Skill** Fact and Opinion 👁 **Strategy** Questioning **Review Skill** Generalization | **T** 👁 **Skill** Cause and Effect 👁 **Strategy** Monitor and Clarify **Review Skill** Draw Conclusions | **Review** Unit 4 Target Comprehension Skills and Strategies |
| **T** 👁 Multiple-Meaning Words | **T** 👁 Unknown Words | **Review** Unit 4 Target Vocabulary Skills |
| Appropriate Phrasing | Rate | **Review** Unit 4 Fluency Skills |
| Autobiography Trait: Organization | Writing for Tests: Summary Trait: Word Choice | Quick Write for Fluency |
| **T** Contractions | **T** Prepositions | **Review** Unit 4 Conventions |
| Suffixes -er, -or, -ess, -ist | Syllables VCCCV | **Review** Unit 4 Spelling Patterns |
| Media Literacy: Sportscast | Book Review | |

# Assessment
## 5 Steps to Success on Reading Street

**RIGHT IN YOUR TEACHER'S EDITION**

## Step 1

### Begin the Year

**The Assessment Handbook** provides ideas and support to begin the school year and beyond.

**The Baseline Group Test** helps identify where students are. Use the Baseline Test results to make initial grouping decisions and to differentiate instruction based on ability levels.

### Online Assessment
Save time by using digital assessments. All Reading Street assessments are available on ExamView and in SuccessTracker.

## Step 2

### Every Day

During the day, use these tools to monitor student progress.

- **Corrective Feedback** provides point of use support.

| Corrective feedback | If... students are unable to answer the comprehension questions, then... use the Reteach lesson in *First Stop*. |
|---|---|

- **Monitor Progress** boxes each day check retelling, fluency, and oral vocabulary.

**Don't Wait Until Friday** **MONITOR PROGRESS** **Check Retelling**

If... students have difficulty retelling,
then... use the Retelling Cards/Story Sort to scaffold their retellings.

## Step 3

### Every Week

- **Weekly Assessments** on Day 5 check comprehension and fluency.

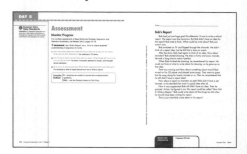

- **Weekly Tests** assess target skills for the week.

- **Fresh Reads** assesses fluency and comprehension as students read a new passage.

- **Reading Street Sleuth** assesses students' ability to find clues in text through close reading.

## Step 4

### Every Unit

- **Unit Benchmark Tests** assess mastery of unit skills: comprehension, vocabulary, phonics, conventions, and writing.

- **Unit Benchmark Tests** provide professional development and support with performance-based assessment.

- **Performance-Based Assessments** assess students' ability to demonstrate text-based comprehension and application of higher-order thinking skills.

## Step 5

### End the Year

- **End-of-Year Benchmark Test** measures student mastery of skills covered in all six units with options for performance-based assessment.

### 5 Steps to Success on Reading Street

1. **Begin the Year**
2. **Every Day**
3. **Every Week**
4. **Every Unit**
5. **End the Year**

#### Digital Assessment

⭐ **SuccessTracker™**

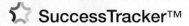
**eStreet Interactive**
www.ReadingStreet.com

# Implementing eStreet Interactive
## Power up your classroom and put time back on your side!

**eSTREET INTERACTIVE**
www.ReadingStreet.com

## Additional Digital Support

**AudioText CD**
**Background Building Audio CD**
**Teacher Resources DVD**

## 1 Plan

Customize your daily plan by clicking, dragging, and posting!

- Online Lesson Planner
- Online Teacher's Edition

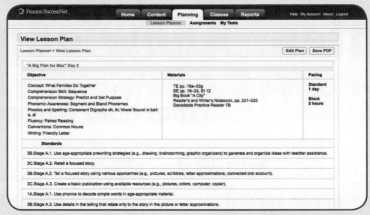

Online Lesson Planner

## 2 Teach

Engage through interactive media!

- Concept Talk Videos
- Letter Tile Drag and Drop
- Envision It! Animations
- Grammar Jammer

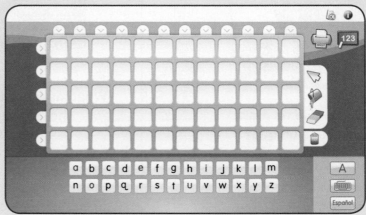

Letter Tile Drag and Drop

## 3 Practice

Motivate through personalized practice activities!

- Story Sort
- Pearson eText
- Journal
- Vocabulary Activities
- Leveled Reader Database

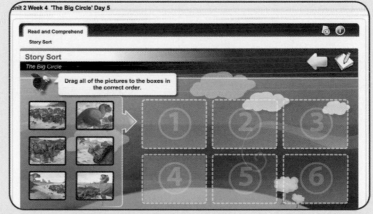

Story Sort

## 4 Manage and Assess

Respond to individual needs!

- Monitor student progress
- Assign
- Prescribe
- Remediate

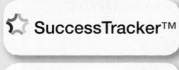
SuccessTracker™

eInstruction® EXAMVIEW® ASSESSMENT SUITE

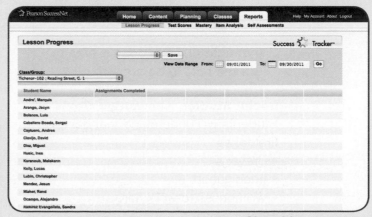

Class Management

# Content Knowledge

Zoom in on ©

## What does it mean to be unique?

### WEEK 1

### The Man Who Invented Basketball

**How do talents make someone unique?**

**Social Studies Knowledge Goals**
Students will understand that people
• have many kinds of talents
• practice to develop their talents
• should be allowed to develop their talents

### WEEK 2

### Hottest, Coldest, Highest, Deepest

**What makes nature's record holders unique?**

**Science Knowledge Goals**
Students will understand that nature has
• unusual appearances
• extreme weather
• extreme events

### WEEK 3

### Rocks in His Head

**Why is it valuable to have unique interests?**

**Social Studies Knowledge Goals**
Students will understand that interests
• are valuable
• lead to learning and research
• lead to a job
• preserve information

### WEEK 4

### America's Champion Swimmer: Gertrude Ederle

**What unique traits does it take to be the first to do something?**

**Social Studies Knowledge Goals**
Students will understand that being first takes
• bravery
• imagination
• willingness to work hard
• determination

### WEEK 5

### Fly, Eagle, Fly!

**What behaviors are unique to different animals?**

**Science Knowledge Goals**
Students will understand that some animals
• have lures on their heads
• blend in with their surroundings
• change colors

## This Week's Target Skills and Strategies

| Target Skills and Strategies | Common Core State Standards for English Language Arts | Indiana Academic Standards for English Language Arts |
|---|---|---|
| **Phonics and Spelling** Skill: Irregular Plurals | CCSS Foundational Skills 3.d. Read grade-appropriate irregularly spelled words. (Also CCSS Language 1.b., CCSS Language 2.e.) | IN 3.1 Students understand the basic features of words. They select letter patterns and know how to translate them into spoken language using phonics, syllables, word parts, and context. They apply this knowledge to achieve fluent oral and silent reading. |
| **Text-Based Comprehension** Skill: Generalize | CCSS Literature 1. Ask and answer questions to demonstrate understanding of a text, referring explicitly to the text as the basis for the answers. | IN 3.3 Students read and respond to a wide variety of significant works of children's literature. |
| Strategy: Summarize | CCSS Literature 2. Recount stories, including fables, folktales, and myths from diverse cultures; determine the central message, lesson, or moral and explain how it is conveyed through key details in the text. | IN 3.3.4 Determine the theme or author's message in fiction and nonfiction text. |
| **Vocabulary** Skill: Unfamiliar Words Strategy: Context Clues | CCSS Language 4. Determine or clarify the meaning of unknown and multiple-meaning word and phrases based on *grade 3 reading and content,* choosing flexibly from a range of strategies. (Also CCSS Language 4.a.) | IN 3.1.6 Use sentence and word context to find the meaning of unknown words. |
| **Fluency** Skill: Accuracy | CCSS Foundational Skills 4. Read with sufficient accuracy and fluency to support comprehension. | IN 3.1.3 Read aloud grade-level-appropriate literary and informational texts fluently and accurately and with appropriate timing, change in voice, and expression. |
| **Listening and Speaking** Presentation | CCSS Speaking/Listening 4. Report on a topic or text, tell a story, or recount an experience with appropriate facts and relevant, descriptive details, speaking clearly at an understandable pace. | The Indiana Academic Standards for Listening and Speaking are not currently assessed on ISTEP+ assessments. Educators and students should implement the Common Core Standards for Speaking and Listening as soon as possible. |
| **Six-Trait Writing** Trait of the Week: Focus/Ideas | CCSS Writing 1.a. Introduce the topic or book they are writing about, state an opinion, and create an organizational structure that lists reasons. (Also CCSS Writing 1.b.) | IN 3.5.6 Write persuasive pieces that ask for an action or response. (Also IN 3.5.7) |
| **Writing** Persuasive Text | CCSS Writing 1.a. Introduce the topic or book they are writing about, state an opinion, and create an organizational structure that lists reasons. (Also CCSS Writing 5.) | IN 3.5.6 Write persuasive pieces that ask for an action or response. |
| **Conventions** Skill: Singular and Plural Pronouns | CCSS Language 1. Demonstrate command of the conventions of standard English grammar and usage when writing or speaking. (Also CCSS Language 1.a.) | IN 3.6.5 Identify and correctly use pronouns, adjectives, compound nouns, and articles in writing. |

## This Week's Cross-Curricular Standards and Resources

### Cross-Curricular Indiana Academic Standards for Social Studies

**Social Studies**
IN 3.1.4 Give examples of people, events and developments that brought important changes to the regions of Indiana.
IN 3.3.7 Describe how climate and the physical characteristics of a region affect the vegetation and animal life living there.

### Reading Street Sleuth

*Street Games*
pp. 44–45

Follow the path to close reading using the Super Sleuth tips:

• Gather Evidence

• Ask Questions

• Make Your Case

• Prove it!

### More Reading in Science and Social Studies

Concept Literacy

Below Level

On Level

Advanced

ELL

ELD

ISBN-13: 978-0-328-73390-3   ISBN-10: 0-328-73390-3

# Your 90-Minute Reading Block

| | Whole Group | Formative Assessment | Small Group | |
|---|---|---|---|---|
| | | How do I make my small groups flexible? | **OL** On Level  **SI** Strategic Intervention  **A** Advanced  What are my other students reading and learning every day in Small Groups? | **Daily Independent Options**  What do my other students do when I lead Small Groups? |
| **DAY 1** | **Content Knowledge** Build Oral Language/Vocabulary **Phonics/Word Analysis** **Read Decodable Reader** **Text-Based Comprehension** **Selection Vocabulary** **Research and Inquiry** Step 1–Identify and Focus Topic **Spelling Pretest** Connect to Phonics/Word Analysis | **Monitor Progress** Check Oral Vocabulary | Differentiate Vocabulary **Build Word Knowledge** **OL** Practice Amazing Words **SI** Reteach Amazing Words **A** Extend Amazing Words **OL SI A** Text-Based Comprehension **Read** *Reading Street Sleuth*, pp. 44–45 or Leveled Readers **A** Inquiry Project **ELL** Access Vocabulary | ⭐ **Independent Reading** Ⓒ Suggestions for this week's independent reading:  • A high-quality magazine article about a favorite sport  • A nonfiction book by a favorite author  • An informational text comparing and contrasting baseball and cricket  **Book Talk** Foster critical reading and discussion skills through independent and close reading.  Students should focus on discussing one or more of the following:  • Key Ideas and Details • Craft and Structure • Integration of Ideas |
| **DAY 2** | **Content Knowledge** Build Oral Language/Vocabulary **Phonics/Word Analysis** **Vocabulary Skill** **Text-Based Comprehension** **Read** Main Selection, using Access Text Notes **Research and Inquiry** Step 2–Navigate/Search **Spelling** Connect to Phonics/Word Analysis | **Monitor Progress** Formative Assessment: Check Word Reading | Differentiate Comprehension **Build Word Knowledge** **OL** Practice Selection Vocabulary **SI** Reteach Selection Vocabulary **A** Extend Selection Vocabulary **OL SI A** Access Text **Read** *The Man Who Invented Basketball* **A** Inquiry Project **ELL** Access Comprehension Skill | |
| **DAY 3** | **Content Knowledge** Build Oral Language/Vocabulary **Phonics/Word Analysis** **Read Decodable Passage** **Text-Based Comprehension** **Read** Main Selection, using Close Reading Notes **Fluency** **Research and Inquiry** Step 3–Analyze Information **Spelling** Connect to Phonics/Word Analysis | **Monitor Progress** Check Retelling | Differentiate Close Reading **OL SI** Reread to Develop Vocabulary **A** Reread to Extend Vocabulary **OL SI A** Close Reading **Read** *The Man Who Invented Basketball* **A** Inquiry Project **ELL** Access Main Selection |  **Pearson eText** • Student Edition • Decodable Readers • Leveled Readers   **Trade Book Library** |
| **DAY 4** | **Content Knowledge** Build Oral Language/Vocabulary **Phonics/Word Analysis** **Read Decodable Passage** **Read Content Area Paired Selection with Genre Focus** **Let's Learn It!** Vocabulary/Fluency/Listening and Speaking **Research and Inquiry** Step 4–Synthesize **Spelling** Connect to Phonics/Word Analysis | **Monitor Progress** Check Fluency | Differentiate Vocabulary **Build Word Knowledge** **OL** Develop Language Using Amazing Words **SI** Review/Discuss Amazing Words **A** Extend Amazing Words and Selection Vocabulary **OL SI A** Text-Based Comprehension **Read** "My Turn at Bat" **A** Inquiry Project **ELL** Access Amazing Words |  **Materials from School or Classroom Library**  **Independent Stations** Practice Last Week's Skills  ⭐ Focus on these activities when time is limited.  ⭐ **Word Wise** **Word Work** ⭐ **Read for Meaning** **Let's Write!** **Words to Know** **Get Fluent** |
| **DAY 5** | **Content Knowledge** Build Oral Language/Vocabulary **Text-Based Comprehension** **Vocabulary Skill** **Phonics/Word Analysis** **Assessment** Fluency, Comprehension **Research and Inquiry** Step 5–Communicate **Spelling Test** Connect to Phonics/Word Analysis | **Monitor Progress** Formative Assessment: Check Oral Vocabulary  **Monitor Progress** Fluency; Comprehension | Differentiate Reteaching **OL** Practice Singular and Plural Pronouns **SI** Review Singular and Plural Pronouns **A** Extend Singular and Plural Pronouns **OL SI A** Text-Based Comprehension **Reread** *Reading Street Sleuth*, pp. 44–45 or Leveled Readers **A** Inquiry Project **ELL** Access Conventions and Writing | |

## Assessment Resources

Common Core Weekly Tests, pp. 91–96

Common Core Fresh Reads for Fluency and Comprehension, pp. 91–96

Common Core Unit 4 Benchmark Test

Common Core Success Tracker, ExamView, and Online Lesson Planner

## Teaching the Common Core State Standards This Week

The Common Core State Standards for English Language Arts are divided into strands for **Reading** (including **Foundational Skills**), **Writing**, **Speaking and Listening**, and **Language**. The chart below shows some of the content you will teach this week, strand by strand. Turn to this week's 5-Day Planner on pages 20d–20e to see how this content is taught each day.

## Reading Strand

- **Phonics/Word Analysis:** Irregular Plurals
- **Text-Based Comprehension:** Generalize; Summarize
- **Fluency:** Accuracy
- **Literary Terms:** Point of View
- **Genre:** Main Selection: Biography; Paired Selection: Autobiography

## Common Core State Standards for English Language Arts

## Writing Strand

- **Writing Mini-Lesson:** Persuasive Text
- **Trait:** Conventions
- **Look Back and Write:** Text Evidence

## Speaking and Listening Strand

- **Content Knowledge:** Build Oral Language
- **Listening and Speaking:** Presentation
- **Research and Inquiry**

## Language Strand

- **Oral Vocabulary: Amazing Words** *mock, idle, potential, ecstatic, thrill, audition, necessary, result, succeed, rise, verge*
- **Vocabulary:** Unfamiliar Words; Context Clues
- **Selection Vocabulary:** *disease, guard, freeze, terrible, study, popular, sports, basketball*
- **Academic Vocabulary:** *presentation, singular pronoun, plural pronoun, point of view, biography, summarize*
- **Conventions:** Singular and Plural Pronouns
- **Spelling:** Irregular Plurals

# Text-Based Comprehension

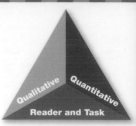

## Text Complexity Measures

Use the rubric to familiarize yourself with the text complexity of *The Man Who Invented Basketball*.

### Bridge to Complex Knowledge

| Quantitative Measures | Lexile | 690L |
|---|---|---|
| | **Average Sentence Length** | 10.26 |
| | **Word Frequency** | 3.62 |

| Qualitative Measures | Levels of Meaning | understand a biography |
|---|---|---|
| | **Structure** | captions; diagrams; map; flash-backs; time line; list; headings |
| | **Language Conventionality and Clarity** | literal; simple sentence structure |
| | **Theme and Knowledge Demands** | a basic understanding of sports in general and especially basketball |

| Reader and Task Suggestions |
|---|
| **FORMATIVE ASSESSMENT** Based on assessment results, use the **Reader and Task Suggestions** in Access Main Selection to scaffold the selection or support independence for students as they read *The Man Who Invented Basketball*. |

| READER AND TASK SUGGESTIONS | |
|---|---|
| **Preparing to Read the Text** | **Leveled Tasks** |
| • Review using context clues to understand unfamiliar words.<br>• Discuss how authors include personal photographs in biographies.<br>• Remind students that they may need to read more slowly and then reread to understand the information contained in graphic organizers. | • **Levels of Meaning • Analysis** If students have difficulty understanding biographies, ask them to identify dates and events in James Naismith's life as they read the selection. Ask if these events really happened or if they were made up.<br>• **Structure** The time line and other graphic organizers may cause difficulty for some students. Ask students to match up the entries on the time line with the events in the selection. |

**Recommended Placement** Both the qualitative and quantitative measures suggest this text should be placed in the Grade 2–3 text complexity band, which is where both the Common Core State Standards and *Scott Foresman Reading Street* have placed it.

# Focus on Common Core State Standards ©

**The Man Who Invented Basketball**

JAMES NAISMITH AND HIS AMAZING GAME

by Edwin Brit Wyckoff

**Genre** **Biography** A biography is the story of a person's life, written by another person. As you read, think about why someone would write about James Naismith.

Question of the Week
**How do talents make someone unique?**

Let's **Think** About Reading!

**Main Selection, pp. 28–41**

**Social Studies in Reading**

**MY TURN AT BAT**
*The Story of My Life*
Ted Williams with John Underwood

**Genre**
**Autobiography**

- An autobiography is the story of a person's life written by the person who lived it.
- Autobiographies are written in the first person, using *I*, *me*, and *my*.
- The events in an autobiography are actual events and experiences in a person's life.
- As you read, think about the difference in point of view between the autobiography and the biography sections of "My Turn at Bat."

Baseball great Ted Williams was born in 1918. His mother, May Venzer, was a Salvation Army worker. She was part Mexican and part French. His father, Samuel Stuart Williams, was a soldier, U.S. marshal, and photographer. He was part Welsh and part Irish.

Their son, Ted, came to have several nicknames, including "Teddy Ballgame," "The Splendid Splinter," and "The Kid."

**Ted recalls his childhood:**

Wilber Wiley was my first real boyhood pal. Wilber had a job delivering the *Evening Tribute*, and when he'd get through about an hour before dark, we'd go to the playground, just the two of us, and hit, hit, hit, and throw, throw, throw.

The playground director was a man named Rodney Luscomb, and Rod Luscomb was my first real hero. I know when I walked up to the rostrum in Cooperstown the day they inducted me into the Hall of Fame Rod Luscomb was one of the people on my mind, one of the people I felt made it possible. That should tell you something about how much a coach can mean to a kid.

I suppose the first strong influence I had to continue in baseball, to make it my life's work, was my coach at Herbert Hoover High in San Diego, a wonderful man named Wos Caldwell.

I'll never forget one day I hit a ball they say went 450 feet, between the right and center fielders. I fell down rounding third—a big skinny kid, all arms and legs—and I got thrown out at home plate.

San Diego was a ballplayer's town, year-round, and by the time I was a pitcher at Herbert Hoover High I was hooked. As a pitcher-outfielder, I batted .583 and .406 my last years in high school, .430 for three years.

**Paired Selection, pp. 46–51**

---

## Text-Based Comprehension

**Generalize**
CCSS Literature 1.

**Summarize**
CCSS Literature 2.

## Fluency

**Accuracy**
CCSS Foundational Skills 4.

## Writing and Conventions

**Trait:** Focus/Ideas
CCSS Writing 1.a., CCSS Writing 1.b.

**Writing Mini-Lesson:** Persuasive Text
CCSS Writing 1.a., CCSS Writing 5.

**Conventions:** Singular and Plural Pronouns
CCSS Language 1.,
CCSS Language 1.a.

## Oral Vocabulary

### Amazing Words

mock                necessary
idle                result
potential           succeed
ecstatic            rise
thrill              verge
audition

CCSS Language 6.

## Selection Vocabulary

**Unfamiliar Words**
CCSS Language 4.

**Context Clues**
CCSS Language 4., Language 4.a.

basketball    guard      study
disease       popular    terrible
freeze        sports

## Phonics and Spelling

**Irregular Plurals**
CCSS Foundational Skills 3.d.,
CCSS Language 1.b.,
CCSS Language 2.e.

wolves        scarves
knives        mice
feet          geese
men           wives
children      elves
women         banjos
sheep         halves
heroes

**Challenge Words**

loaves        potatoes
beliefs       tornadoes
tomatoes

## Listening and Speaking

**Presentation**
CCSS Speaking/Listening 4.

# Preview Your Week

*How do talents make someone unique?*

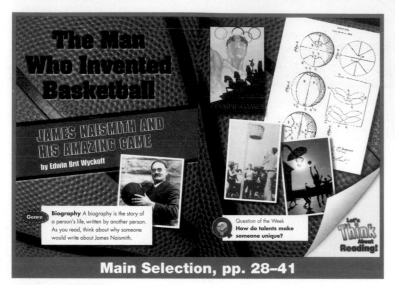

**Main Selection, pp. 28–41**

**Genre:** Biography

 **Vocabulary:** Unfamiliar Words

**Text-Based Comprehension:** Generalize

**Paired Selection, pp. 46–51**

**Social Studies in Reading**

**Genre:** Autobiography

## Build Content Knowledge  Zoom in on ⊙

### KNOWLEDGE GOALS

Students will understand that people

- have many kinds of talents
- practice to develop their talents
- should be allowed to develop their talents

### THIS WEEK'S CONCEPT MAP

Develop a concept-related graphic organizer like the one below over the course of this week.

How talents make someone unique

| Dancing | Running | Kicking | Music |

### BUILD ORAL VOCABULARY

This week, students will acquire the following academic vocabulary/domain-specific words.

**Amazing Words**

| mock | thrill | succeed |
| idle | audition | rise |
| potential | necessary | verge |
| ecstatic | result | |

**OPTIONAL CONCEPT-BASED READING** Use the Digital Path to access readers offering different levels of text complexity.

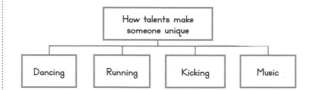
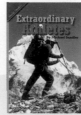

| Concept Literacy | Below-Level | On-Level | Advanced | ELL | ELD |

# This Week's Digital Resources

## eStreet Interactive
www.ReadingStreet.com

### Get Ready to Read

 **Big Question Video** This video introduces students to the Big Question and facilitates discussion of the concept for the unit.

 **Concept Talk Video** Use this video on the Digital Path to build momentum and introduce the weekly concept of talents.

 **Pearson eText** Read the eText of the Student Edition pages on Pearson SuccessNet for comprehension and fluency support.

 **Envision It! Animations** Use this vivid animation on the Digital Path to explain the target comprehension skill, Generalize.

### Read and Comprehend

 **Journal** Use the Word Bank on the Digital Path to have students write sentences using this week's selection vocabulary words.

 **Background Building Audio CD** This audio CD provides helpful background information about talents to help students read and comprehend the weekly texts.

 **Pearson eText** Read the eText of the main selection, *The Man Who Invented Basketball,* and the paired selection, "My Turn at Bat," with audio support on Pearson SuccessNet.

 **Vocabulary Activities** A variety of interactive vocabulary activities on the Digital Path help students practice selection vocabulary and concept-related words.

 **Story Sort** Use the Story Sort Activity on the Digital Path after reading *The Man Who Invented Basketball* to involve students in summarizing.

### Language Arts

 **Grammar Jammer** Select a fascinating animation on the Digital Path to provide an engaging grammar lesson that will capture students' attention.

 **Pearson eText** Find the Student Edition eText of the Let's Write It! and Let's Learn It! pages with audio support on Pearson SuccessNet.

## Additional Resources

 **Teacher Resources DVD-ROM** Use the following resources on the TR DVD or on Pearson SuccessNet throughout the week:

- Amazing Word Cards
- Reader's and Writer's Notebook
- Writing Transparencies
- Daily Fix-It Transparencies
- Scoring Rubrics
- Grammar Transparencies
- ELL Support
- Let's Practice It!
- Graphic Organizers
- Vocabulary Cards

## This Week's Skills

**Phonics/Word Analysis**
Irregular Plurals

**Comprehension**
🔎 **Skill:** Generalize
🔎 **Strategy:** Summarize

**Language**
🔎 **Vocabulary:** Unfamiliar Words
**Conventions:** Singular and Plural Pronouns

**Fluency**
Accuracy

**Writing**
Persuasive Text

# 5-Day Planner

## DAY 1

### Get Ready to Read

**Content Knowledge** 20j
Oral Vocabulary: *mock, idle, potential, ecstatic*

**Monitor Progress**
Check Oral Vocabulary

**Phonics/Word Analysis** 22a
🔎 Irregular Plurals
**READ** Decodable Reader 16A
Reread for Fluency

### Read and Comprehend

**Text-Based Comprehension** 24a
🔎 Generalize
🔎 Summarize

**Fluency** 24–25
Accuracy

**Selection Vocabulary** 25a
*basketball, disease, freeze, guard, popular, sports, study, terrible*

### Language Arts

**Research and Inquiry** 25b
Identify and Focus Topic

**Spelling** 25c
Irregular Plurals, Pretest

**Conventions** 25d
Singular and Plural Pronouns

**Handwriting** 25d
Cursive Letters *G, Y,* and *Q*

**Writing** 25e
Persuasive Text

## DAY 2

### Get Ready to Read

**Content Knowledge** 26a
Oral Vocabulary: *thrill, audition*

**Phonics/Word Analysis** 26c
🔎 Irregular Plurals

**Monitor Progress**
Check Word Reading

**Literary Terms** 26d
Point of View

### Read and Comprehend

**Vocabulary Skill** 26e
🔎 Unfamiliar Words

**Fluency** 26–27
Accuracy

**Text-Based Comprehension** 28–29
**READ** *The Man Who Invented Basketball*—1st Read

### Language Arts

**Research and Inquiry** 35b
Navigate/Search

**Conventions** 35c
Singular and Plural Pronouns

**Spelling** 35c
Irregular Plurals

**Writing** 35d
Persuasive Text

## DAY 3

### Get Ready to Read

**Content Knowledge** 36a
Oral Vocabulary: *necessary, result*

**Word Analysis** 36c
Fluent Word Reading
**DECODE AND READ**
  Decodable Practice Passage 16B

### Read and Comprehend

**Text-Based Comprehension** 36e
Check Understanding
**READ** *The Man Who Invented Basketball*—2nd Read
Monitor Progress Check Retelling

**Fluency** 43b
Accuracy

### Language Arts

**Research and Study Skills** 43c
Dictionary

**Research and Inquiry** 43d
Analyze

**Conventions** 43e
Singular and Plural Pronouns

**Spelling** 43e
Irregular Plurals

**Writing** 45a–45c
Persuasive Text

## DAY 4

### Get Ready to Read

**Content Knowledge** 46a
Oral Vocabulary: *succeed, rise, verge*

**Phonics/Word Analysis** 46c
**Review** Consonant Patterns *wr, kn, st, mb, gn*
Fluent Word Reading
**DECODE AND READ**
  Decodable Practice Passage 16C

### Read and Comprehend

**Genre** 46g
Autobiography
**READ** "My Turn at Bat"
  —Paired Selection

**Fluency** 52–53
Accuracy
Monitor Progress Check Fluency

**Vocabulary Skill** 53a
  Unfamiliar Words

**Listening and Speaking** 53a
Presentation

### Language Arts

**Research and Inquiry** 53b
Synthesize

**Conventions** 53c
Singular and Plural Pronouns

**Spelling** 53c
Irregular Plurals

**Writing** 53d
Persuasive Text

## DAY 5

### Get Ready to Read

**Content Knowledge** 53f
Review Oral Vocabulary
Monitor Progress
Check Oral Vocabulary

### Read and Comprehend

**Text-Based Comprehension** 53h
Review  Generalize

**Vocabulary Skill** 53h
Review  Unfamiliar Words

**Word Analysis** 53i
Review  Irregular Plurals

**Literary Terms** 53i
Review Point of View

**Assessment** 53j, 53l
Monitor Progress
Fluency; Generalize

### Language Arts

**Research and Inquiry** 53n
Communicate

**Spelling** 53o
Irregular Plurals, Test

**Conventions** 53o
Singular and Plural Pronouns

**Writing** 53p
Persuasive Text

**Wrap Up Your Week!** 53p

# Access for All

## What do I do in group time?
It's as easy as 1-2-3!

**1** TEACHER-LED SMALL GROUPS → **2** INDEPENDENT PRACTICE STATIONS → **3** INDEPENDENT READING

## Small Group Time

### Ⓒ Bridge to Common Core

**SKILL DEVELOPMENT**
- Irregular Plurals
- Generalize
- Summarize
- Unfamiliar Words

**DEEP UNDERSTANDING**
**This Week's Knowledge Goals**
Students will understand that people:
- have many kinds of talents
- practice to develop their talents
- should be allowed to develop their talents

## **1** Small Group Lesson Plan

|  | DAY 1 | DAY 2 |
|---|---|---|
|  | **Differentiate Vocabulary** | **Differentiate Comprehension** |
| ⓄⓁ **On-Level** pp. SG•2–SG•6 | **Build Word Knowledge** Practice Amazing Words **Text-Based Comprehension** Read *Reading Street Sleuth,* pp. 44–45 or Leveled Readers | **Build Word Knowledge** Practice Selection Vocabulary **Access Text** Read *The Man Who Invented Basketball* |
| ⓈⒾ **Strategic Intervention** pp. SG•7–SG•11 | **Build Word Knowledge** Reteach Amazing Words Read *Reading Street Sleuth,* pp. 44–45 | **Build Word Knowledge** Reteach Selection Vocabulary **Access Text** Read *The Man Who Invented Basketball* |
| Ⓐ **Advanced** pp. SG•12–SG•16 | **Build Word Knowledge** Extend Amazing Words **Text-Based Comprehension** Read *Reading Street Sleuth,* pp. 44–45 or Leveled Readers | **Build Word Knowledge** Extend Selection Vocabulary **Access Text** Read *The Man Who Invented Basketball* |
| **Independent Inquiry Project** | Identify Questions | Investigate |
| Ⓔ Ⓛ Ⓛ If... students need more scaffolding and practice with... | **Vocabulary, then...** use the activities on DI•17–DI•18 in the Teacher Resources section on SuccessNet. | **the Comprehension Skill, then...** use the activities on page DI•21 in the Teacher Resources section on SuccessNet. |

## Reading Street Sleuth

- Provides access to grade-level text for all students
- Focuses on finding clues in text through close reading
- Builds capacity for complex text

## Build Text-Based Comprehension

*The Man Who Invented Basketball*

### Optional Leveled Readers

| Concept Literacy | Below-Level | On-Level | Advanced | ELL | ELD |

---

## DAY 3

### Differentiate Close Reading

**Reread to Develop Vocabulary**
**Close Reading**
Read *The Man Who Invented Basketball*

**Reread to Develop Vocabulary**
**Close Reading**
Read *The Man Who Invented Basketball*

**Reread to Extend Vocabulary**
**Close Reading**
Read *The Man Who Invented Basketball*

Investigate

**the Main Selection,**
**then...** use the activities on page DI•22 in the Teacher Resources section on SuccessNet.

## DAY 4

### Differentiate Vocabulary

**Build Word Knowledge**
Develop Language Using Amazing Words
**Text-Based Comprehension**
Read "My Turn at Bat"

**Build Word Knowledge**
Review/Discuss Amazing Words
**Text-Based Comprehension**
Read "My Turn at Bat"

**Build Word Knowledge**
Extend Amazing Words and Selection Vocabulary
**Text-Based Comprehension**
Read "My Turn at Bat"

Organize

**Amazing Words,**
**then...** use the Routine on pp. xxxvi–xxxvii in the *ELL Handbook*.

## DAY 5

### Differentiate Reteaching

**Practice Singular and Plural Pronouns**
**Text-Based Comprehension**
Reread *Reading Street Sleuth*, pp. 44–45 or Leveled Readers

**Review Singular and Plural Pronouns**
**Text-Based Comprehension**
Reread *Reading Street Sleuth*, pp. 44–45 or Leveled Readers

**Extend Singular and Plural Pronouns**
**Text-Based Comprehension**
Reread *Reading Street Sleuth*, pp. 44–45 or Leveled Readers

Communicate

**Conventions and Writing,**
**then...** use the Grammar Transition Lessons on pp. 312–386 in the *ELL Handbook*.

## ② Independent Stations

### Practice Last Week's Skills

 Focus on these activities when time is limited.

---

### WORD WISE

**Spell and use words in sentences.**

#### OBJECTIVES
- Spell words with consonant patterns *wr, kn, gn, st,* and *mb.*

#### MATERIALS
- *Word Wise* Flip Chart Activity 16, teacher-made word cards, paper and pencils

 **Letter Tile Drag and Drop**

● Students write one sentence each using words with consonant patterns *wr, kn, gn, st,* and *mb,* and list other words with these patterns.

▲ Students write two sentences each using words with consonant patterns *wr, kn, gn, st,* and *mb,* and list other words with these patterns.

■ Students write three sentences each using words with consonant patterns *wr, kn, gn, st,* and *mb,* and list other words with these patterns.

---

### WORD WORK

**Identify and pronounce words.**

#### OBJECTIVES
- Identify and pronounce words with consonant patterns *wr, kn, gn, st,* and *mb.*

#### MATERIALS
- *Word Work* Flip Chart Activity 16, teacher-made word cards, paper and pencils

 **Letter Tile Drag and Drop**

● Students write a list of one word each with *wr, kn, gn, st,* and *mb,* say each word aloud, and write a rhyming word for each.

▲ Students write a list of two words each with *wr, kn, gn, st,* and *mb,* say each word aloud, and write a rhyming word for each.

■ Students write a list of three words each with *wr, kn, gn, st,* and *mb,* say each word aloud, and write a rhyming word for each.

---

### LET'S WRITE!

**Write to compare and contrast.**

#### OBJECTIVES
- Compare and contrast two animals.

#### MATERIALS
- *Let's Write!* Flip Chart Activity 16, Leveled Readers, paper and pencils

 **Grammar Jammer**

● Students write a sentence comparing two animals and a sentence contrasting them.

▲ Students write two sentences comparing two animals and two sentences contrasting them.

■ Students write and proofread a paragraph comparing and contrasting two animals.

---

### WORDS TO KNOW

**Determine word meanings.**

#### OBJECTIVES
- Identify and define words with prefixes and suffixes.

#### MATERIALS
- *Words to Know* Flip Chart Activity 16, teacher-made word cards, dictionary, paper and pencils

 **Vocabulary Activities**

● Students use a dictionary to find the meaning of four words from the word cards and write a sentence for each. Students circle each word's affix.

▲ Students use a dictionary to find the meaning of six words from the word cards and write a sentence for each. Students circle each word's affix.

■ Students use a dictionary to find the meaning of eight words from the word cards and write a sentence for each.

---

## READ FOR MEANING

### Analyze cause and effect.

#### OBJECTIVES
• Identify cause and effect in nonfiction.

#### MATERIALS
• *Read for Meaning* Flip Chart Activity 16, Leveled Readers, paper and pencils

**Pearson eText**
• Leveled eReaders

**Envision It! Animations**

● Students read a book and write one sentence about an effect and one sentence about what caused the effect.

▲ Students read a book and then draw a two-column chart listing causes and effects.

■ Students read a book and then write a paragraph describing one effect and what caused it.

## GET FLUENT

### GET FLUENT

#### OBJECTIVES
• Read aloud with expression.

#### MATERIALS
• *Get Fluent* Flip Chart Activity 16, Leveled Readers

**Pearson eText**
• Leveled eReaders

● Partners take turns reading with correct expression from a Concept Literacy Reader or a Below-Level Reader.

▲ Partners take turns reading with correct expression from an On-Level Reader.

■ Partners take turns reading with correct expression from an Advanced Reader.

## Manage the Stations
Use these management tools to set up and organize your Practice Stations:

Practice Station Flip Charts

Classroom Management Handbook for Differentiated Instruction Practice Stations, p. 34

## 3 Independent Reading ©

Students should select appropriately complex texts to read and write about independently every day before, during, and after school.

Suggestions for this week's independent reading:
• A high-quality magazine article about a favorite sport
• A nonfiction book by a favorite author
• An informational text comparing and contrasting baseball and cricket

**BOOK TALK** Have partners discuss their independent reading for the week. Tell them to refer to their Reading Logs and paraphrase what each selection was about. Then have students focus on discussing one or more of the following:

**Key Ideas and Details**
• What is the main idea of the text? List details that support it.
• Summarize the events in the text.

**Craft and Structure**
• How is the information in the text organized?
• List the text features. How do they help you understand the text?

**Integration of Ideas**
• Summarize the author's position.
• Does the author support any claims or opinions?

**Pearson eText**
• Student Edition
• Decodable Readers
• Leveled Readers

**Trade Book Library**

**School or Classroom Library**

### Content Knowledge
Oral Vocabulary

### Phonics/Word Analysis
Irregular Plurals

### Text-Based Comprehension
Generalize
Summarize

### Fluency
Accuracy

### Selection Vocabulary

### Research and Inquiry
Identify and Focus Topic

### Spelling
Irregular Plurals

### Conventions
Singular and Plural Pronouns

### Handwriting
Cursive Letters *G, Y, Q*

### Writing
Persuasive Text

## Materials

- Student Edition
- Reader's and Writer's Notebook
- Decodable Reader

## © Bridge to Common Core

**INTEGRATION OF KNOWLEDGE/IDEAS**
This week, students will read, write, and talk about talents.

**Texts This Week**
- "The Myth of Icarus"
- "Batting the Ball"
- "Carlos Catches Sports Fever"
- *The Man Who Invented Basketball*
- "My Turn at Bat"

**Social Studies Knowledge Goals**
Students will understand that people
- have many kinds of talents
- practice to develop their talents
- should be allowed to develop their talents

## Street Rhymes!

Keisha has talent. She plays the violin.
She plays duets with Kimmie, her very gifted twin.
Their teacher sees potential. Their talent truly thrills—
when they play together or practice scales and drills!

- To introduce this week's concept, read aloud the poem several times and ask students to join you.

# Content Knowledge
Zoom in on ©

## Talents

**CONCEPT TALK** To explore the unit concept of One of a Kind, this week students will read, write, and talk about what makes each person unique. Write the Question of the Week on the board, *How do talents make someone unique?*

# Build Oral Language

**TALK ABOUT TALENTS** Have students turn to pp. 20–21 in their Student Editions. Look at each of the photos. Then use the prompts to guide discussion and create a concept map.

- What kind of talent do you think the girl holding the flowers has? (dancing) Let's add *Dancing* to our concept map.
- Could these soccer players have special talents? (Yes, they might run fast or kick really far.) They won't be *idle* for long. Soon they will be running. Let's add *Running* and *Kicking* to our concept map.
- Point out the children playing the instruments. What is their talent? (playing an instrument) Let's add *Music* to our map.
- After discussing the photos, ask: How do talents make someone unique?

**Oral Vocabulary**

Common Core State Standards
Speaking/Listening 1.c. Ask questions to check understanding of information presented, stay on topic, and link their comments to the remarks of others. Also Language 6.

Let's **Talk** About

**Being Unique**

● Share ideas about how special skills and talents make people unique.

● Make and listen to comments about ways people are unique.

● Pose and answer questions about what we can learn from the talents of others.

**READING STREET ONLINE CONCEPT TALK VIDEO** www.ReadingStreet.com

Student Edition, pp. 20–21

**CONNECT TO READING** Tell students that this week they will be reading about people with special talents. Encourage students to add concept-related words to this week's concept map.

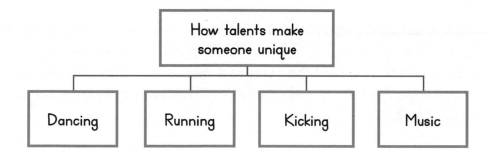

How talents make someone unique

Dancing | Running | Kicking | Music

**eStreet Interactive**
www.ReadingStreet.com

**Pearson eText**
● Student Edition
● Graphic Organizer

**Big Question Video**

**Concept Talk Video**

**ELL**

**Preteach Concepts** Use the Day 1 instruction on ELL Poster 16 to build knowledge, develop concepts, and build oral vocabulary.

**ELL Support** Additional ELL support and modified instruction is provided in the *ELL Handbook* and in the ELL Support lessons found on the *Teacher Resources DVD-ROM.*

*The Man Who Invented Basketball* **20–21**

© **Common Core State Standards**

**Speaking/Listening 1.** Engage effectively in a range of collaborative discussions (one-on-one, in groups, and teacher-led) with diverse partners on grade 3 topics and texts, building on others' ideas and expressing their own clearly. **Language 6.** Acquire and use accurately grade-appropriate conversational, general academic, and domain-specific words and phrases, including those that signal spatial and temporal relationships (e.g., *After dinner that night we went looking for them*).

## Amazing Words

You've learned  1  4  7  words so far.

You'll learn  0  1  1  words this week!

| | |
|---|---|
| mock | necessary |
| idle | result |
| potential | succeed |
| ecstatic | rise |
| thrill | verge |
| audition | |

# Content Knowledge

## Build Oral Vocabulary

**INTRODUCE AMAZING WORDS** "The Myth of Icarus" on p. 21b is about a boy who flies too high. Tell students to listen for this week's Amazing Words—*mock, idle, potential,* and *ecstatic*—as you read the Teacher Read Aloud on p. 21b.

## Amazing Words   Robust Vocabulary Routine

1. **Introduce** Write the word *ecstatic* on the board. Have students say the word aloud with you. In "The Myth of Icarus," Icarus is *ecstatic* about being able to fly. Does the author include any context clues that tell me the meaning of this word? Supply a student-friendly definition. *Ecstatic* means "feeling very happy or excited."

2. **Demonstrate** Have students answer questions to demonstrate understanding. Would winning first prize in a contest make you *ecstatic*?

3. **Apply** Ask students to give a personal example of a time when they felt *ecstatic*.

4. **Display the Word** Run your hand under the syllables *ec-stat-ic* as you read the word. Have students say the word again.

See pp. OV•1 to teach *idle, mock,* and *potential.*

Routines Flip Chart

**AMAZING WORDS AT WORK** Reread "The Myth of Icarus" aloud. As students listen, have them notice how the Amazing Words are used in context. To build oral vocabulary, lead the class in a discussion about the Amazing Words' meanings. Remind students to ask and answer questions with appropriate detail.

Don't Wait Until Friday **MONITOR PROGRESS** **Check Oral Vocabulary**

During discussion, listen for students' use of Amazing Words.

**If...** students are unable to use the Amazing Words in discussion,

**then...** use the Oral Vocabulary Routine in the Routines Flip Chart to demonstrate words in different contexts.

# Teacher Read Aloud

**MODEL FLUENCY** As you read "The Myth of Icarus," model accuracy with smooth, fluent reading.

## The Myth of Icarus

Long ago in Greece, there lived a great architect, inventor, and craftsman named Daedalus. One day, the king got angry with Daedalus and banished him and his son, Icarus, to the island of Crete.

The only way to escape from the island was by sea. The sea was so vast and rough that it seemed to mock their attempts to swim across it. Daedalus and Icarus knew that if they tried to use a boat, they would be arrested.

Daedalus did not want to stay idle forever on Crete. He knew that he had the potential to find a way off the island. Daedalus thought hard about what to do. Finally, he came up with an incredible idea. If he and Icarus could not escape by swimming or using a boat, then they would fly!

Daedalus spent months designing two sets of wings. The wings had to be strong enough to support him and his son on their journey. He collected feathers and sewed them together with string. He held the feathers together on a frame with wax. He added leather straps that would secure the wings on their arms.

Finally, he finished his invention. Daedalus fitted two wings onto his son's strong arms. Then he gave him careful instructions.

He warned, "Icarus, do not fly too low. You must fly high enough so the feathers will not get wet from the sea mist. Damp wings will pull you down, and your arms will tire."

Icarus turned away, ready to fly, but his father stopped him. Daedalus added, "Son, do not fly too high either. The heat of the sun will melt the wax, and the wings will not hold together."

And so, Daedalus and Icarus jumped off a cliff, each wearing a set of wings. They flew miles and miles over the sea. They headed toward the mainland, and their wings drifted on air currents. Their arms did not tire.

The incredible flight thrilled young Icarus. He was ecstatic about his new ability. Before long, he began to ignore his father's warnings. He soared higher and higher. The soft wind blew gently on his face, and the sun warmed his skin. Icarus did not realize that the sun's rays were melting the wax that held his wings together. His wings began to fall apart, and Icarus fell into the sea.

The sea swallowed him, and soon Icarus drowned. Daedalus had lost sight of his son and he reached land alone. Days later, Icarus's wings washed up on the shore. Daedalus realized what had happened, and he cried bitterly, lamenting that his invention had killed his son.

The sea where Icarus died was later named the Icarian Sea. The sea has kept that name to this day, and you can find it near the island of Crete.

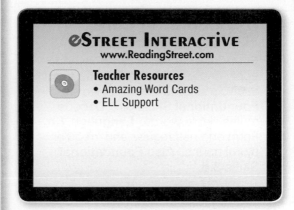

eStreet Interactive
www.ReadingStreet.com
**Teacher Resources**
• Amazing Word Cards
• ELL Support

**ELL Support for Read Aloud** Use the modified Read Aloud on p. DI•19 of the ELL Support lessons on the *Teacher Resources DVD-ROM* to prepare students to listen to "The Myth of Icarus."

**Discuss the Read Aloud** Have small groups of students discuss what they already know about flight. Use the following conversation starters: What kinds of animals are able to fly? What other things have wings? Can people fly the way birds do? What are birds' wings covered with? Share answers with the group.

##  Common Core State Standards

**Foundational Skills 3.** Know and apply grade-level phonics and word analysis skills in decoding words. **Foundational Skills 3.c.** Decode multisyllable words. **Language 1.b.** Form and use regular and irregular plural nouns. **Also Foundational Skills 3.d.**

## Skills Trace

◉ **Irregular Plurals**

**Introduce** U4W1D1

**Practice** U4W1D3; U4W1D4

**Reteach/Review** U4W1D5; U4W2D4

**Assess/Test** Weekly Test U4W1 Benchmark Test U4

**KEY:** U = Unit W = Week D = Day

## Vocabulary Support

You may wish to explain the meanings of these words.

**hooves** the hard part of the foot of horses, cows, sheep, pigs, and some other animals

**geese** tame or wild birds that look like a duck, except have longer necks and are usually larger

**elves** small lively creatures resembling humans

# Word Analysis

## Teach/Model

### ◉ Irregular Plurals

**CONNECT** Write *friends* and *foxes.* Many times you just add *-s* or *-es* to a word to form the plural. *Friends* and *foxes* are two examples. Read these words. Explain that today students will learn to spell and read words that do not fit the regular plural form.

**MODEL** Write *leaves* and *children.* I know that *-ves* is a plural ending for words that end with *-f* or *-fe.* When I see this ending, I work backward to check whether this is a plural word. I cover *-ves* on *leaves* and replace it with *-f* or *-fe.* Cover the *-ves* in *leaves* and replace it with *-f.* If I recognize the new word, I know the first word is the plural of that word. Other words, such as *child,* have plurals that don't follow these rules. I just have to learn them: The plural of *child* is *children.*

**GROUP PRACTICE** Write the words below. Read them together. Identify the singular form of each word and how it changes in the plural form.

| | | | | | |
|---|---|---|---|---|---|
| children | women | wives | men | mice | geese |
| halves | elves | calves | hooves | knives | shelves |

**REVIEW** What do you know about reading irregular plurals? When you recognize an irregular plural, identify the irregular ending *(-ves)* and think of which letters the ending replaces *(-f* or *-fe),* or remember that it is an irregular plural that does not follow a pattern.

## Guide Practice

**MODEL** Have students turn to p. 22 in their Student Editions. Each word is an irregular plural. The first word is *knives.* I know that *-ves* is a plural ending of a word that ends with *-f* or *-fe. Knives* is the plural of *knife.*

**GROUP PRACTICE** For each word in Words I Can Blend, ask for the sound of each letter or word part. Make sure that students identify the correct plural endings. Then have them read the words.

> **Corrective feedback**
> **If...** students have difficulty reading a word,
> **then...** model reading the parts and then the whole word. Then ask students to read it with you.

## Phonics

### Irregular Plurals

Common Core State Standards
Foundational Skills 3.d. Read grade-appropriate irregularly spelled words.
Also Language 1.b.

Envision It! | Sounds to Know

wolves

irregular plurals

READING STREET ONLINE
SOUND-SPELLING CARDS
www.ReadingStreet.com

### Words I Can Blend

**k n i v e s**

**w o m e n**

**g e e s e**

**c h i l d r e n**

**f i s h**

### Sentences I Can Read

1. We used knives to slice the bread.
2. The women fed crumbs to the flock of geese.
3. How many fish did the children catch?

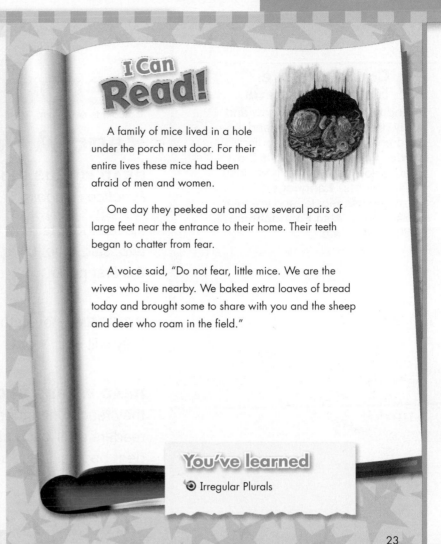

## I Can Read!

A family of mice lived in a hole under the porch next door. For their entire lives these mice had been afraid of men and women.

One day they peeked out and saw several pairs of large feet near the entrance to their home. Their teeth began to chatter from fear.

A voice said, "Do not fear, little mice. We are the wives who live nearby. We baked extra loaves of bread today and brought some to share with you and the sheep and deer who roam in the field."

**You've learned**

Irregular Plurals

22

23

**Student Edition, pp. 22–23**

## Apply

**READ WORDS IN ISOLATION** After students can successfully combine word parts to read the words on p. 22 in their Student Editions, point to words in random order and ask students to read them naturally.

**READ WORDS IN CONTEXT** Have students read each of the sentences on p. 22. Have them identify irregular plural words in the sentences.

**Team Talk** Pair students and have them take turns reading each of the sentences aloud.

**ON THEIR OWN** For additional practice, use *Reader's and Writer's Notebook*, p. 247.

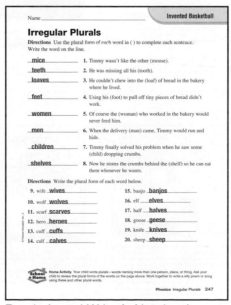

Name _____                    Invented Basketball

**Irregular Plurals**

Directions Use the plural form of each word in ( ) to complete each sentence. Write the word on the line.

mice    1. Timmy wasn't like the other (mouse).
teeth    2. He was missing all his (tooth).
loaves   3. He couldn't chew into the (loaf) of bread in the bakery where he lived.
feet     4. Using his (foot) to pull off tiny pieces of bread didn't work.
women    5. Of course the (woman) who worked in the bakery would never feed him.
men      6. When the delivery (man) came, Timmy would run and hide.
children 7. Timmy finally solved his problem when he saw some (child) dropping crumbs.
shelves  8. Now he stores the crumbs behind the (shelf) so he can eat them whenever he wants.

Directions Write the plural form of each word below.

9. wife  **wives**        15. banjo  **banjos**
10. wolf  **wolves**      16. elf  **elves**
11. scarf  **scarves**    17. half  **halves**
12. hero  **heroes**      18. goose  **geese**
13. cuff  **cuffs**       19. knife  **knives**
14. calf  **calves**      20. sheep  **sheep**

 Home Activity Your child wrote plurals—words naming more than one person, place, or thing. Ask your child to review the plural forms of the words on the page above. Work together to write a silly poem or song using these and other plural words.

Phonics Irregular Plurals  **247**

Reader's and Writer's Notebook, p. 247

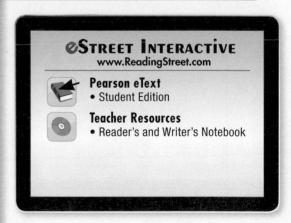

## eStreet Interactive
www.ReadingStreet.com

**Pearson eText**
- Student Edition

**Teacher Resources**
- Reader's and Writer's Notebook

### ELL

**Pronunciation** Assist students with the articulation of phonemes as they blend sounds. Focus on tongue and lip positions when saying words such as *shelves* and *leaves*.

## Common Core State Standards

**Foundational Skills 3.** Know and apply grade-level phonics and word analysis skills in decoding words. **Foundational Skills 3.d.** Read grade-appropriate irregularly spelled words. **Language 1.b.** Form and use regular and irregular plural nouns. **Also Foundational Skills 4., 4.a., 4.b.**

# Decodable Reader 16A

If students need help, then...

## Read *A Party for the Geese*

**READ WORDS IN ISOLATION** Have students turn to p. 1 of *Decodable Practice Readers 3.2.* Have students read each word.

Have students read the high-frequency words *the, a, to, water, of, people, two, said, one, what, where, laughed, was, they, have, their,* and *watched* on the first page.

**PREVIEW** Have students read the title and preview the story. Tell them that they will read words with irregular plurals.

**READ WORDS IN CONTEXT** Pair students for reading and listen as they read. One student begins. Students read the entire story, switching readers after each page. Partners reread the story. This time the other student begins. Make sure that students are monitoring their accuracy when they decode words.

Decodable Practice Reader 16A

| Corrective feedback | **If...** students have difficulty decoding a word, **then...** refer them to the *Sound-Spelling Cards* to identify the word parts. Have them read the word parts individually and then together to say the word. |
|---|---|

- What is the new word?
- Is the new word a word you know?
- Does it make sense in the story?

**CHECK DECODING AND COMPREHENSION** Have students retell the story to include characters, setting, and events. Then have students find words in the story that are irregular plurals. Students should supply *men, women, knives, children, leaves, geese, people, loaves,* and *wolves.*

# Reread for Fluency

**REREAD DECODABLE READER** Have students reread *Decodable Practice Reader 16A* to develop automaticity in decoding words that are irregular plurals.

## Routine | Oral Rereading

1. **Read** Have students read the entire book orally.

2. **Reread** To achieve optimal fluency, students should reread the text three or four times.

3. **Corrective Feedback** Listen as students read. Provide corrective feedback regarding their fluency and decoding.

Routines Flip Chart

**Irregular Plurals**

**Beginning** Write several irregular plural words from the *Decodable Practice Reader* on the board, such as *men, geese, children,* and *leaves.* Point to each word as you say it aloud. Then have students explain the rule for forming each plural word.

**Intermediate** After reading, have students make a T-chart. On the left side of the chart have them list all of the irregular plural words in the *Decodable Practice Reader.* On the right side of the chart have students write the singular form of each word.

**Advanced** After reading the story, have students write a short paragraph that uses 3–4 irregular plural words.

Zoom in on ©

© **Common Core State Standards**

**Literature 1.** Ask and answer questions to demonstrate understanding of a text, refering explicitly to the text as the basis for the answers. **Literature 2.** Recount stories, including fables, folktales, and myths from diverse cultures; determine the central message, lesson, or moral and explain how it is conveyed through key details in the text. **Foundational Skills 4.** Read with sufficient accuracy and fluency to support comprehension. **Speaking/ Listening 2.** Determine the main ideas and supporting details of a text read aloud or information presented in diverse media and formats, including visually, quantitatively, and orally.

## Skills Trace

© Generalize

**Introduce** U3W4D1; U4W1D1; U6W5D1

**Practice** U3W4D2; U3W4D3; U3W5D2; U4W1D2; U4W1D3; U4W1D2; U6W5D2; U6W5D3

**Reteach/Review** U3W4D5; U4W1D5; U6W5D5

**Assess/Test** Weekly Tests U3W4; U4W1; U6W5 Benchmark Tests U4

**KEY:** U = Unit W = Week D = Day

## Comprehension Support

Students may also turn to pp. EI•8 and EI•25 to review the skill and strategy if necessary.

# Text-Based Comprehension

 **Generalize**

**Summarize**

**READ** Remind students of the weekly concept—Talents. Have students read "Batting the Ball" on p. 25.

## MODEL A CLOSE READ

**Think Aloud** When I read, I can sometimes make a statement that is true for many examples. That is called generalizing. When I generalize, I say how things are mostly alike or all alike. Today we're going to read about a girl who loves baseball. **Have students follow along as you read the first two paragraphs of "Batting the Ball."** Can we make a generalization about what we have read so far? One thing we can say is that most third graders have recess. We know this generalization is true because we have recess and so do the third graders in the story.

**TEACH** Have students read p. 25. Explain that the skill of generalizing and the strategy of summarizing are tools they can use to understand the main ideas of a text. Then have them look back at "Batting the Ball" and use a graphic organizer like the one on p. 24 to make generalizations about the passage.

**GUIDE PRACTICE** Have students reread "Batting the Ball," using the call-outs as guides. Then ask volunteers to respond to the questions in the call-outs, citing specific examples from the text to support their answers.

**Skill** School playgrounds have rules to keep children safe.

**Strategy** When Betsy started going to a new school, she found that she was not allowed to play with a hard baseball. She did not understand why she had to play with a soft ball. She played with a baseball anyway, and she got hurt by the hard ball. Then she understood why the teacher only wanted them to use soft balls. She got hurt as a result of her actions, but she also understood the rule better.

**APPLY** Use *Reader's and Writer's Notebook,* p. 248 for additional practice with generalizing.

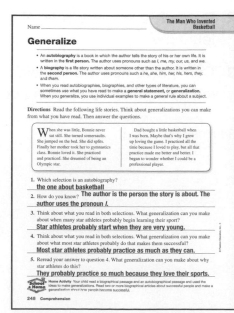

Reader's and Writer's Notebook, p. 248

**Envision It! Skill Strategy**

**Skill**

**Strategy**

**READING STREET ONLINE
ENVISION IT! ANIMATIONS**
www.ReadingStreet.com

### Comprehension Skill

## Generalize

- When you read, you can sometimes make a general statement about what you have read.
- A general statement tells how some things are mostly alike or all alike.
- Use what you learned about generalizing as you read "Batting the Ball." Use the text and a graphic organizer like the one below to make a generalization.

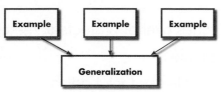

### Comprehension Strategy

## Summarize

Active readers sum up what happens as they read a story. When you sum up, remember to tell only the important events in the order that they happened, maintaining the meaning of the story and what the characters learned. This will help you remember what you are reading.

24

## Batting the Ball

Betsy went to a new school at the beginning of third grade. At recess, Betsy wanted to play baseball. The teacher told Betsy that she could not play with a hard baseball, because someone might get hurt. The playground rule was that only soft balls were allowed.

Betsy laughed. "But I am a baseball player," she said. Betsy did not understand why she could only play with a soft ball.

A few days later, another third-grader brought a hard baseball to school. Betsy was eager to show off her baseball skills. She loved the feel of the bat as it hit the hard ball.

When it was Betsy's turn to bat, she stepped up to home plate. The pitcher threw the ball, and it curved around. The ball hit Betsy in the shoulder and she fell to the ground.

"Ouch!" Betsy cried. The teacher ran over to see what had happened. Betsy stood up, rubbing her shoulder. "I think we should use a soft ball," she said to the teacher.

"What good thinking!" the teacher said, replacing the baseball with a soft ball.

**Skill** Can you make a generalization about school playgrounds using the details from the first paragraph?

**Strategy** Summarize the story. What is the order of events? What are the results of Betsy's actions?

**Your Turn!**

**Need a Review?** See the *Envision It! Handbook* for help with generalizing and summarizing.

**Let's Think About...**
**Ready to Try It?** As you read *The Man Who Invented Basketball*, use what you learned about generalizing and summarizing to understand the text.

25

# Model Fluent Reading

**ACCURACY** Have students listen as you read paragraphs 3 and 4 of "Batting the Ball" with appropriate accuracy. Explain that reading with accuracy means reading every word on the page correctly.

**Routine** Paired Reading

1. **Select a Passage** For "Batting the Ball," use the whole passage.

2. **Reading 1** Students read the entire passage, switching readers at the end of each paragraph.

3. **Reading 2** Partners reread "Batting the Ball."

4. **Reread** For optimal fluency, have partners read three or four times.

5. **Corrective Feedback** Listen as students read. Provide feedback about their accuracy and encourage them to ask questions about unfamiliar words.

Routines Flip Chart

**eStreet Interactive**
www.ReadingStreet.com

**Pearson eText**
• Student Edition

**Envision It! Animations**

**Teacher Resources**
• Reader's and Writer's Notebook

**ELL**

**Compound Words** Have students find a compound word on p. 25. *(baseball, playground)* Write the words on the board. Point to the first part of each word, and then the second part, and have students tell you what they mean. Explain or have students explain how the two words go together and then use each in a sentence.

*The Man Who Invented Basketball* **24–25**

**© Common Core State Standards**

**Writing 7.** Conduct short research projects that build knowledge about a topic. **Language 6.** Acquire and use accurately grade-appropriate conversational, general academic, and domain-specific words and phrases, including those that signal spatial and temporal relationships (e.g., *After dinner that night we went looking for them*). **Also Speaking/ Listening 1., Language 5.b.**

# Selection Vocabulary

Use the following routine to introduce this week's tested selection vocabulary.

**basketball** a game played on a court where two teams try to throw a ball through a raised hoop

**disease** a problem in the body; sickness

**freeze** turn into ice

**guard** a person who watches over or protects something

**popular** liked by many people

**sports** games in which people use their bodies

**study** to spend time learning, usually by reading

**terrible** really bad

**SEE IT/SAY IT** Write *guard.* Scan across the word with your finger as you say it: *guard.*

**HEAR IT** Use the word in a sentence. The crossing *guard* stops cars to let us cross the street.

**DEFINE IT** Elicit definitions from students. How would you tell another student what the word *guard* means? Clarify or give a definition when necessary. Yes, it is a person who protects or defends something or someone. Restate the word in student-friendly terms. The *guard* inside the bank is always alert.

**Team Talk** What do you think a basketball *guard's* responsibility is? Have students form an opinion. Turn and talk to your partner about this. Be prepared to explain your answer. Allow students time to discuss. Ask for examples. Rephrase their examples for usage when necessary or to correct misunderstandings.

**MAKE CONNECTIONS** Have students discuss the word. Have you ever seen a *guard?* Turn and talk to your partner about this. Then be prepared to share. Have students share. Rephrase their ideas for usage when necessary or to correct misunderstandings.

**RECORD** Have students write the word and its meaning.

Continue this routine to introduce the remaining words in this manner.

> **Corrective feedback** | **If...** students are having difficulty understanding, **then...** review the definitions in small groups.

# Research and Inquiry

## Step 1 Identify and Focus Topic

**TEACH** Discuss the Question of the Week: *How do talents make someone unique?* Tell students they will research a talented person. They will present that person's biography to the class on Day 5.

 **MODEL** I'll start by brainstorming a list of questions about people who have special talents. First, I will have to decide on a kind of talent. I love soccer, so I will try to find a person who has a talent for soccer. *Some questions could be Who is the best soccer player in history? Who is the most talented soccer player I can think of? Does that player have a special talent that makes him or her a great player? and What is that talent?*

**GUIDE PRACTICE** After students have brainstormed and formulated open-ended inquiry questions, explain that tomorrow they will conduct library research using their questions. To generate a research plan, help students identify words or phrases that will guide their search for relevant information.

**ON THEIR OWN** Have students work individually, in pairs, or in small groups to write an inquiry question.

## *e*STREET INTERACTIVE
www.ReadingStreet.com

**Teacher Resources**
• Envision It! Pictured Vocabulary Cards
• Tested Vocabulary Cards

## 21st Century Skills
**Internet Guy** *Don Leu*

**Weekly Inquiry Project**

| STEP 1 | Identify and Focus Topic |
|--------|--------------------------|
| STEP 2 | Navigate/Search |
| STEP 3 | Analyze Information |
| STEP 4 | Synthesize |
| STEP 5 | Communicate |

## Academic Vocabulary

**presentation** An individual or group presents information about a particular subject. The information can be given orally or visually.

**ELL**

**Multilingual Vocabulary** Students can apply knowledge of their home languages to acquire new English vocabulary by using the Multilingual Vocabulary Lists (*ELL Handbook,* pp. 433–444).

**ELL**

If... students need more scaffolding and practice with **Vocabulary, then...** use the activities on pp. DI•17–DI•18 in the Teacher Resources section on SuccessNet.

## Day 1 SMALL GROUP TIME • Differentiate Vocabulary, p. SG•1

| **OL** On-Level | **SI** Strategic Intervention | **A** Advanced |
|-----------------|-------------------------------|----------------|
| • **Practice Vocabulary** Amazing Words | • **Reteach Vocabulary** Amazing Words | • **Extend Vocabulary** Amazing Words |
| • **Read** *Reading Street Sleuth,* pp. 44–45 | • **Read** *Reading Street Sleuth,* pp. 44–45 | • **Read** *Reading Street Sleuth,* pp. 44–45 |
| | | • **Introduce** Inquiry Project |

## ⓒ Common Core State Standards

**Language 1.b.** Form and use regular and irregular plural nouns.
**Language 2.e.** Use conventional spelling for high-frequency and other studied words and for adding suffixes to base words (e.g., *sitting, smiled, cries, happiness*). **Also Foundational Skills 3.d., Language 1., 1.a., 1.f., 2.**

# Spelling Pretest

## Irregular Plurals

**INTRODUCE** Remind students that many nouns form the plural by adding *-s* or *-es,* but some do not. Words that do not are called irregular plurals.

**PRETEST** Say each word, read the sentence, and repeat the word.

| | | |
|---|---|---|
| 1. | wolves | Listen to the **wolves** howl in the distance. |
| 2. | knives | Cut the sandwiches with **knives.** |
| 3. | feet | Those shoes hurt my **feet.** |
| 4. | men | The **men** on the rowing team wear uniforms. |
| 5. | children | There are ten **children** on the team. |
| 6. | women | Mom works with five other **women.** |
| 7. | sheep | Did you know that wool comes from **sheep?** |
| 8. | heroes | What would it take for us to be **heroes?** |
| 9. | scarves | Ron lost a hat and two **scarves** this winter. |
| 10. | mice | **Mice,** hamsters, and gerbils make good pets. |
| 11. | geese | The honks of the **geese** were very loud. |
| 12. | wives | How many husbands and **wives** went to the meeting? |
| 13. | elves | The **elves** made shoes for the shoemaker. |
| 14. | banjos | Like fiddles, **banjos** are four-stringed instruments. |
| 15. | halves | All the plates had **halves** of oranges on them. |

### Challenge words

| | | |
|---|---|---|
| 16. | loaves | I can smell the **loaves** of bread baking in the oven. |
| 17. | beliefs | He has strong **beliefs** about adopting pets. |
| 18. | tomatoes | The sauce is made from **tomatoes.** |
| 19. | potatoes | **Potatoes** grow in the ground. |
| 20. | tornadoes | Several **tornadoes** touched down last night. |

**SELF-CORRECT** Have students self-correct their pretests by rewriting misspelled words.

**ON THEIR OWN** Use *Let's Practice It!* p. 217 on the *Teacher Resources DVD-ROM.*

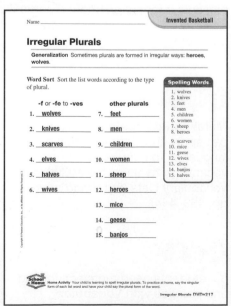

Let's Practice It! TR DVD•217

# Conventions

## Singular and Plural Pronouns

**MAKE CONNECTIONS** To focus attention on singular and plural pronouns, make a class list on the board of all the pronouns students can think of.

**TEACH** Display Grammar Transparency 16, and read aloud the explanation and examples in the box.

**MODEL** Model with item 1. Name or use the correct pronoun.

**GUIDE PRACTICE** Guide students in completing items 3–5. In each item, have students identify the pronoun, tell whether the pronoun is singular or plural, and tell how they know. Record the correct responses on the transparency.

**APPLY** Have students rewrite sentences 6–9 by replacing the underlined word or words with the appropriate pronoun.

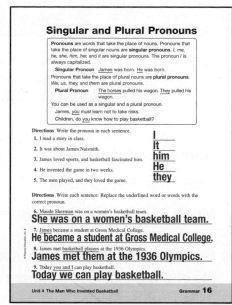

Grammar Transparency 16, TR DVD

**eStreet Interactive**
www.ReadingStreet.com

**Teacher Resources**
• Let's Practice It!
• Grammar Transparency
• Daily Fix-It Transparency

## Daily Fix-It

1. He flyed safly. *(flew; safely)*
2. The world look diffrent from up in the sky. *(looks; different)*

## Academic Vocabulary

A **singular pronoun** is a pronoun that takes the place of a singular noun. Examples are *I, you,* and *him.*

A **plural pronoun** is a pronoun that takes the place of a plural noun. Examples are *we, they,* and *us.*

# Handwriting

**MODEL LETTER FORMATION** Display the lowercase and capital cursive letters *G, Y,* and *Q.* Follow the stroke instructions pictured to model letter formation.

Explain that writing legibly means making letters the correct size, form, and slant. Letters are connected with joining strokes. Model writing this sentence with correct slant and joining strokes: *Go quietly to my room.*

**GUIDE PRACTICE** Have students write these sentences: *Great heroes go on quests. You grew an inch! What was your question?* Circulate around the room, guiding students.

**Irregular Plurals** Tell students that we form some plurals in unexpected ways. Help students memorize the most common irregular plurals.

**Singular and Plural Pronouns** Have students name several singular nouns and several plural nouns. Then have them use each noun orally in a sentence. Ask another student to repeat the sentences, substituting a pronoun for the noun.

## Common Core State Standards

**Writing 1.a.** Introduce the topic or text they are writing about, state an opinion, and create an organizational structure that lists reasons. **Writing 8.** Recall information from experiences or gather information from print and digital sources; take brief notes on sources and sort evidence into provided categories. **Also Writing 1.**

## Bridge to Common Core

### TEXT TYPES AND PURPOSES

This week students write a persuasive essay about their favorite sport or game.

### Opinion Writing

Through reading and discussion, students will gain a deeper understanding of talents. They will use this knowledge from the texts to write and support a persuasive essay.

Through the week, students will improve their range and content of writing through daily mini-lessons.

### 5-Day Plan

| | |
|---|---|
| DAY 1 | Read Like a Writer |
| DAY 2 | Write with Purpose |
| DAY 3 | Logical and Emotional Appeals |
| DAY 4 | Revise: Consolidating with Conjunctions |
| DAY 5 | Proofread for Pronouns and Double Negatives |

### Write Guy by Jeff Anderson

#### What Do You Notice?

When students are examining the model text, ask, "What do you notice?" By giving students the responsibility of commenting on what they find effective in the text, they build self-confidence and often begin to notice features of the writing they might not have otherwise. Eventually they will start trying them in their writing. Relish students' movement toward correctness and beauty.

# Writing

## Persuasive Text

**Mini-Lesson** | **Read Like a Writer**

■ **Introduce** This week you will write a persuasive text. A persuasive text is writing that is intended to convince or persuade the reader.

**Genre** Persuasive Text

**Trait** Focus/Ideas

**Mode** Opinion/Persuasive

■ **Examine Model Text** Let's read an example of a persuasive text about a sport called curling. Have students turn to "Fun on the Ice" on p. 249 of their *Reader's and Writer's Notebook.*

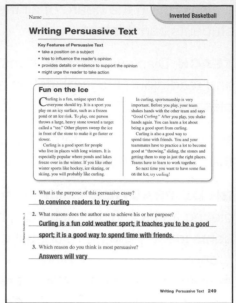

Reader's and Writer's Notebook, p. 249

■ **Key Features** A persuasive text takes a position. The writer's opinion is called a position. Find the writer's position in the first paragraph and circle it. Discuss how that statement helps the reader focus on the text.

The purpose of a persuasive text is to influence the reader's opinion. In each paragraph of this text there is a main idea. The main idea is a reason that you should learn to curl. For each paragraph in the model, have students underline the main idea.

The writer provides details or evidence that support each main idea. For each paragraph have students double underline details that support the main idea.

The writer probably will urge the reader to do something. Which sentences urge the reader to try curling? Have the students underline them.

## Review Key Features

Review the key features of a persuasive text. You might want to post the key features in the classroom for students to reference as they work on their compositions.

### Key Features of Persuasive Text

- takes a position on a subject
- tries to influence the reader's opinion
- provides details or evidence to support the opinion
- might urge the reader to take action

**Routine** | **Quick Write for Fluency** | **Team Talk**

1. **Talk** Have pairs discuss the features of persuasive text.

2. **Write** Each person writes a sentence defining persuasive text.

2. **Share** Partners share their definitions with each other.

Routines Flip Chart

**eStreet Interactive**
www.ReadingStreet.com

**Teacher Resources**
- Reader's and Writer's Notebook
- Let's Practice It!

**ELL**

**Writing Model** Help students understand the writing model by reading it aloud and defining any unfamiliar terms, such as *unique, target,* and *sportsmanship.* Ask students about sports they have played and what they like about those sports.

# Wrap Up Your Day!

✔ **Content Knowledge** Reread "Street Rhymes!" on p. 20j to students. Ask them what they learned today about how talents make someone unique.

✔ **Oral Vocabulary** Have students use the Amazing Words they learned in sentences.

✔ **Homework** Send home this week's Family Times newsletter on *Let's Practice It!* pp. 218–219 on the *Teacher Resources DVD-ROM.*

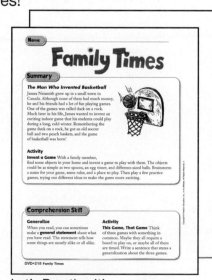

Let's Practice It!
TR DVD•218–219

**Preview
DAY 2**

Tell students that tomorrow they will read about the early life of the man who invented basketball.

### Materials

- Student Edition
- Reader's and Writer's Notebook

---

## Ⓒ Common Core State Standards

**Speaking/Listening 1.** Engage effectively in a range of collaborative discussions (one-on-one, in groups, and teacher-led) with diverse partners on grade 3 topics and texts, building on others' ideas and expressing their own clearly. **Language 6.** Acquire and use accurately grade-appropriate conversational, general academic, and domain-specific words and phrases, including those that signal spatial and temporal relationships (e.g., After dinner that night we went looking for them). **Also Language 5.b.**

# Content Knowledge

## Talents

**EXPAND THE CONCEPT** Remind students of the weekly concept question, *How do talents make someone unique?* Tell students that today they will begin reading *The Man Who Invented Basketball: James Naismith and His Amazing Game.* As they read, encourage students to think about how talent can make someone unique.

## Build Oral Language

**TALK ABOUT SENTENCES AND WORDS** Reread these sentences from the Read Aloud, "The Myth of Icarus."

*The incredible flight thrilled young Icarus. He was ecstatic about his new ability. Before long, he began to ignore his father's warnings.*

- What does *ecstatic* mean? (feeling great joy)
- Why is Icarus feeling ecstatic? (He's discovered a new talent.)
- Why do you think Icarus ignores his father's warnings? (He was excited to be able to fly and it felt wonderful to soar higher and higher.)

**Team Talk** Have students turn to a partner and discuss the following question. Then ask them to share their responses.

- What is the shortest version of these sentences you can make without changing the meaning? (Possible response: Icarus was excited about his new talent of being able to fly, and soon he wasn't listening to his father.)

# Build Oral Vocabulary

**Amazing Words**  **Robust Vocabulary Routine**

1. **Introduce** Write the Amazing Word *thrill* on the board. Have students say it aloud with you. Relate *thrill* to the photographs on pp. 20–21 and "The Myth of Icarus." The boy and girl playing the clarinet and violin might be *thrilled* to play for their relatives. Icarus was *thrilled* by his incredible flight. Have students provide the definition of the word. To *thrill* is "to fill with a shivering, exciting feeling."

2. **Demonstrate** Have students answer questions to demonstrate understanding. In the picture of the dancers, does the girl on the right looked *thrilled*? How can you tell? (No, her head is down and she does not look happy or excited.)

3. **Apply** Have students apply their understanding. What are some antonyms, or words that mean the opposite, of *thrilled*? *(sad, disappointed, bored)*

4. **Display the Word** Point out the initial blend *thr* in *thrill* and have students say the sounds. Then have students read the entire word.

See p. OV•1 to teach *audition.*

Routines Flip Chart

**ADD TO THE CONCEPT MAP** Use the photos on pp. 20–21 and the Read Aloud, "The Myth of Icarus," to discuss how talents can make someone unique and to talk about the Amazing Words *mock, idle, potential,* and *ecstatic.* Add these and other concept-related words to the concept map to develop students' knowledge of the topic. Discuss the following questions. Encourage students to build on others' ideas when they answer.

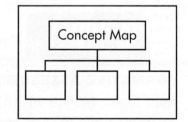

Concept Map

- Do you think Daedalus was *ecstatic* about his invention? Why?
- Why would you describe a beginner at something as someone who has *potential*?
- Why will you never discover your talents if you are *idle*?
- Imagine a girl is trying something for the first time. She makes some mistakes because she has never done it before. How could *mocking* her stop her from finding her talent?

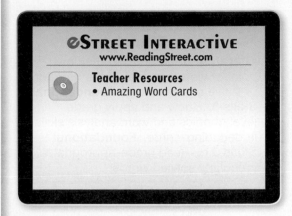

**eSTREET INTERACTIVE**
www.ReadingStreet.com

**Teacher Resources**
• Amazing Word Cards

**Amazing Words**

| | |
|---|---|
| mock | necessary |
| idle | result |
| potential | succeed |
| ecstatic | rise |
| thrill | verge |
| audition | |

## Access for All

 **Advanced**

"The Myth of Icarus" is a Greek myth. Have students look for other Greek myths in the library. Ask them to try to find different versions of the story of Icarus. Have them read and compare the versions and then discuss the similarities and differences with their classmates.

**Cognates** Point out that one of today's Amazing Words has a Spanish cognate. The cognate for *audition* is *audición.*

**Reinforce Vocabulary** Use the Day 2 instruction on ELL Poster 16 to teach selection vocabulary and the weekly concept.

*The Man Who Invented Basketball*  **26b**

**Common Core State Standards**

**Literature 6.** Distinguish their own point of view from that of the narrator or those of characters. **Foundational Skills 3.** Know and apply grade-level phonics and word analysis skills in decoding words. **Foundational Skills 3.d.** Read grade-appropriate irregularly spelled words.

# Word Analysis

## ⊙ Irregular Plurals

**REVIEW** Review irregular plurals, pointing out that some words that end in *-f* or *-fe* form the plural by changing those letters to *-ves.*

**READ WORDS IN ISOLATION** Display these words. Have the class read the words. Then point to the words in random order and ask students to read them quickly.

> **Corrective feedback** | Model reading the word or word parts, and then have students read the words with you.

| | | | |
|---|---|---|---|
| fish | calves | deer | loaves |
| teeth | people | halves | sheep |

**READ WORDS IN CONTEXT** Have the class read these sentences.

**Team Talk** Have pairs take turns reading the sentences naturally.

The **wives** put candles on the **shelves.**

The fall **leaves** crunched under our **feet.**

**Children** in the play were dressed as **mice** and **geese.**

**Don't Wait Until Friday** **MONITOR PROGRESS** **Check Word Reading**

**FORMATIVE ASSESSMENT** Write the following words and have the class read them. Notice which words students miss during the group reading. Call on individuals to read some of the words.

| half | life | strife | hoof | shelf | **Spiral Review** |
|---|---|---|---|---|---|
| hives | fences | curtains | beaches | libraries ◄ | Row 2 reviews words with regular plurals. |
| mice | thieves | scarves | geese | horses ◄ | Row 3 contrasts words with irregular plurals and regular plurals. |

**If...** students cannot read words with irregular plurals at this point,

**then...** use the Day 1 Word Analysis lesson on p. 22a to reteach irregular plurals. Use words from the *Decodable Practice Passages* (or *Reader*). Continue to monitor students' progress using other instructional opportunities during the week. See the Skills Trace on p. 22a.

# Literary Terms

## Point of View

**TEACH** Tell students that *point of view* is a term that describes who is telling a story, or who the narrator is. Explain that there are clues that readers can use to help them figure out the point of view of a story or text. In the first person point of view, which is used in texts such as autobiographies, a person is telling the story of his or her own life. The narrator uses the pronouns *I* and *we.* In the third person point of view, which is used in texts such as biographies, someone else is telling the story of a person's life. The narrator uses the pronouns *he, she, it,* and *they.*

 **Think Aloud** **MODEL** Let's look at "Batting the Ball" on page 25. What is the first pronoun in the story? (she) This tells us that this story is told in the third-person point of view. Do you see an *I* anywhere in the story? (Yes, but it is when Betsy is talking. She is not the narrator of the story.)

**GUIDE PRACTICE** Have students use the first few paragraphs of *The Man Who Invented Basketball* to identify the point of view of the selection. Have students explain how they know whether the selection is a biography or an autobiography.

**ON THEIR OWN** Have students look for examples of first and third person point of view in other selections of their Student Edition.

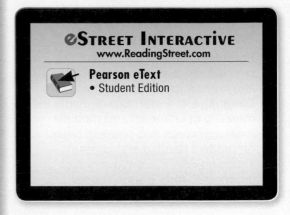

## Academic Vocabulary

**point of view** the perspective from which an author presents the actions and characters of a story

## Common Core State Standards

**Foundational Skills 4.** Read with sufficient accuracy and fluency to support comprehension. **Language 4.** Determine or clarify the meaning of unknown and multiple-meaning words and phrases based on grade 3 reading and content, choosing flexibly from a range of strategies. **Also Foundational Skills 4.c., Language 4.a.**

## Selection Vocabulary

**basketball** a game played on a court where two teams try to throw a ball through a raised hoop

**disease** a problem in the body; sickness

**freeze** turn into ice

**guard** a person who watches over or protects something

**popular** liked by many people

**sports** games in which people use their bodies

**study** to spend time learning, usually by reading

**terrible** really bad

## Bridge to Common Core

### VOCABULARY ACQUISITION AND USE

Students can determine or clarify the meaning of unfamiliar words by using context clues, helping them acquire a broad range of general academic and domain-specific words. By consulting a dictionary or glossary to clarify definitions, they demonstrate the ability to gather vocabulary knowledge on their own.

## Vocabulary Support

Refer students to *Words!* on p. W•7 in the Student Edition for additional practice.

# Vocabulary Skill

## Unfamiliar Words

**READ** Have students read "Carlos Catches Sports Fever" on p. 27. Use the vocabulary skill and strategy as tools to build comprehension.

**TEACH CONTEXT CLUES** Students can use context clues to determine the meanings of unfamiliar words. Content clues are words and sentences around an unfamiliar word that give clues as to its meaning.

**Think Aloud** **MODEL** Write on the board: *Molly studies hard. Every day I see her in the library reading her school books and doing her homework.* In the first sentence, I don't know what the word *studies* means. However, if I keep reading and look for context clues, I can guess. Some context clues I see are *reading her school books* and *doing her homework.* I think that *studying* means "reading and doing schoolwork."

**GUIDE PRACTICE** Write this sentence on the board: *Like Michael Jordan, Carlos had the basketball "disease," but he didn't want a cure!* Have students figure out the meaning of the word *disease* using context clues. If they are having difficulty, explain the meaning of the word *cure.* For additional support, use *Envision It! Pictured Vocabulary Cards* or *Tested Vocabulary Cards.*

**ON THEIR OWN** Have students reread "Carlos Catches Sports Fever" on p. 27. Have them use context clues to determine the meaning of the lesson vocabulary. For additional practice use *Reader's and Writer's Notebook,* p. 250.

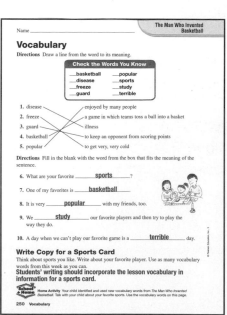

Reader's and Writer's Notebook, p. 250

Common Core State Standards
Language 4.a. Use sentence-level context as a clue to the meaning of a word or phrase. Also Language 4.

## Envision It! Words to Know

basketball

freeze

guard

disease

popular

sports

study

terrible

READING STREET ONLINE
VOCABULARY ACTIVITIES
www.ReadingStreet.com

Vocabulary Strategy for

## Unfamiliar Words

**Context Clues** Unfamiliar words are words you haven't seen before. Context clues in the nearby words and sentences can help you figure out the meaning of these new words. Writers often define or explain unfamiliar words in context to help you understand what you are reading.

1. Read the words and sentences around the word you don't know. Sometimes the author tells you what the word means.

2. If not, use the words and sentences to predict a meaning for the word.

3. Try that meaning in the sentence. Does it make sense?

Read "Carlos Catches Sports Fever" on page 27. Use context clues to help you understand the meanings of the Words to Know.

**Words to Write** Reread "Carlos Catches Sports Fever." Do you have a sport you like to play or watch? Write about the sport you are interested in. Use as many words from the Words to Know list as you can.

## Carlos Catches Sports Fever

Ever since his parents could remember, Carlos had been a sports fanatic. He would study about his favorite players, especially basketball's most popular player: Michael Jordan. Carlos was hoping to become the greatest point guard in the history of the sport. He spent hours practicing shooting hoops in his driveway. Carlos's uncle had installed a pole, basketball hoop, and backboard so that Carlos could play all the time.

Carlos practiced in all kinds of weather, even in January. Carlos just put on extra layers of clothing and extra socks so his toes wouldn't freeze. His mother kept telling him to come inside before he caught a terrible cold. But Carlos didn't want to stop playing. He knew that Michael Jordan had become the best basketball player in history because he was so dedicated to the game. Like Michael Jordan, Carlos had the basketball "disease," but he didn't want a cure!

### Your Turn!

**Need a Review?** For additional help with using context clues to find the meanings of unfamiliar words, see *Words!*

**Ready to Try It?** Read *The Man Who Invented Basketball* on pp. 28–41.

26

27

Student Edition, pp. 26–27

# Reread for Fluency

**ACCURACY** Read the first paragraph of "Carlos Catches Sports Fever" aloud. Tell students that you are going to read carefully, making sure you include all the words on the page.

## Routine | Paired Reading

1. **Select a Passage** For "Carlos Catches Sports Fever," use the whole passage.

2. **Reading 1** Students read the entire passage, switching readers at the end of each paragraph.

3. **Reading 2** Partners reread the passage. This time the other student begins.

4. **Reread** For optimal fluency, have partners read three or four times.

5. **Corrective Feedback** Listen as students read. Provide feedback about their accuracy and encourage them to ask questions about unfamiliar words.

Routines Flip Chart

## eSTREET INTERACTIVE
www.ReadingStreet.com

**Pearson eText**
• Student Edition

**Vocabulary Activities**

**Journal**

**Teacher Resources**
• Envision It! Pictured Vocabulary Cards
• Tested Vocabulary Cards
• Reader's and Writer's Notebook

Zoom in on ©

# Text-Based Comprehension

## Introduce Main Selection

© **Bridge to Common Core**

**CRAFT AND STRUCTURE**

In reading a biography, students assess how point of view affects the content and style of a text. As they preview the selection and prepare to read, students analyze the structure of the selection and how its components relate to each other and the whole when they examine its genre.

**Academic Vocabulary** ©

**biography** the story of a real person's life, written by another person

**Strategy Response Log**

Have students use p. 22 in the *Reader's and Writer's Notebook* to review and use the strategy of summarizing.

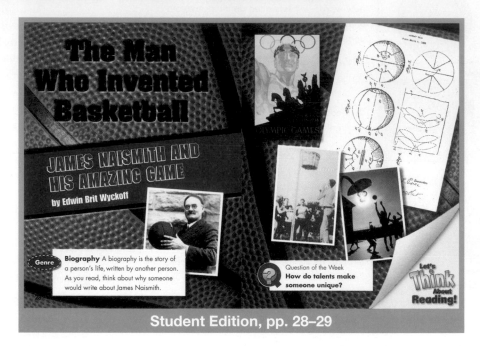

Student Edition, pp. 28–29

**GENRE** Explain that a **biography** is a true story about a real person written by another person. A biography is told in third person (using *he* or *she*). A biography can be the story of a person's entire life, part of a person's life, or of one event. It is usually told in time order. Many biographies use text features such as maps, time lines, headings, photographs, and captions.

**PREVIEW AND PREDICT** Have students preview the title, photographs, and illustrations in *The Man Who Invented Basketball: James Naismith and His Amazing Game.* Have them predict what they will find out as they read.

**PURPOSE** By analyzing *The Man Who Invented Basketball: James Naismith and His Amazing Game,* an informational text, students will gain knowledge of the life of James Naismith and his talent.

# Access Main Selection

| READER AND TASK SUGGESTIONS | |
|---|---|
| **Preparing to Read the Text** | **Leveled Tasks** |
| • Review using context clues to understand unfamiliar words.<br><br>• Discuss how authors include personal photographs in biographies.<br><br>• Remind students that they may need to read more slowly and then reread to understand the information contained in graphic organizers. | • **Levels of Meaning • Analysis** If students have difficulty understanding biographies, ask them to identify dates and events in James Naismith's life as they read the selection. Ask if these events really happened or if they were made up.<br><br>• **Structure** The time line and other graphic organizers may cause difficulty for some students. Ask students to match up the entries on the time line with the events in the selection. |

See Text Complexity Measures for *The Man Who Invented Basketball* on the tab at the beginning of this week.

**READ** Tell students that today they will read *The Man Who Invented Basketball* for the first time. Use the Read for Understanding routine.

## Routine   Read for Understanding ©

Deepen understanding by reading the selection multiple times.

1. **First Read**—if students need support, then use the **Access Text** notes to help them clarify understanding.

2. **Second Read**—Use the **Close Reading** notes to help students draw knowledge from the text.

---

**Day 2   SMALL GROUP TIME • Differentiate Comprehension, p. SG•1**

| OL On-Level | SI Strategic Intervention | A Advanced |
|---|---|---|
| • **Practice** Selection Vocabulary<br>• **Read** *The Man Who Invented Basketball* | • **Reteach** Selection Vocabulary<br>• **Read** *The Man Who Invented Basketball* | • **Extend** Selection Vocabulary<br>• **Read** *The Man Who Invented Basketball*<br>• **Investigate** Inquiry Project |

---

**eSTREET INTERACTIVE**
www.ReadingStreet.com

 **Pearson eText**
  • Student Edition

**AudioText CD**

**Teacher Resources**
  • Reader's and Writer's Notebook

**Background Building Audio CD**

---

## Access for All

**A Advanced**

Have students create a diagram of a basketball court and a list of the rules of the game.

---

**Build Background** To build background, review the selection summary in English (*ELL Handbook*, p. 121). Use the Retelling Cards to provide visual support for the summary. Place English language learners in the groups that correspond to their reading abilities in English.

---

**If...** students need more scaffolding and practice with the **Comprehension Skill, then...** use the activities on p. DI•21 in the Teacher Resources section on SuccessNet.

## Access Text © If students need help, then...

**◎ UNFAMILIAR WORDS** Have students find the word *freeze* on p. 30. Ask them to look at the sentence in which this word is used and the sentences around it for context clues as to its meaning. ("turn into ice")

**(Think Aloud) MODEL** If I didn't know what *freeze* meant, I could look at some of the words around it for clues. The only time a river is solid is when it is ice. What are some other clues? *(winter* and *icy wind)* That makes me think *freeze* means "turn into ice."

**1ST READ**

## Close Reading ©

**EVALUATION • TEXT EVIDENCE** The author helps you make a prediction with clues about what is going to happen later. Identify clues from the text and use them to make a prediction about something that might happen in James's future. (On p. 30, the author says that Uncle Peter wanted James to learn to solve problems by himself. I know from the title that James will invent basketball, so I predict that knowing how to solve problems will help him figure out how to make up rules for basketball.)

**2ND READ**

---

### TOUGH LOVE AND A TOUGH LIFE

Winter in Canada can be very hard. Icy wind sweeps down from the north. Rivers freeze solid. Crossing them can be scary and dangerous.

James Naismith turned eleven in 1872. He was old enough to know where the river near his home became safe, solid ice. But he took a shortcut he had never tried before. His team of horses pulled his wagon onto the frozen river. Their feet pounded the ice. Then one heavy hoof slammed through the sheet of ice. James jumped off the wagon and landed in the water. Grabbing the horses by their reins, he pulled hard. Slowly he forced them to the other side of the river.

James looked around. He saw his uncle Peter Young watching him from behind some trees. But his uncle had not helped him. Uncle Peter wanted James to learn to solve problems by himself and not to take foolish chances. It was a tough lesson.

30

**Let's Think About...**

Read the second paragraph. What do you think the biography will be about? Support your prediction with evidence from the text. **Predict**

Student Edition, p. 30

**ON THEIR OWN** Have students reread pp. 30–31 and use context clues to define other unfamiliar words, such as *disease*. For additional practice, use *Reader's and Writer's Notebook*, p. 254.

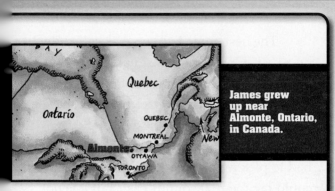

James grew up near Almonte, Ontario, in Canada.

James was born on November 6, 1861, near Almonte, Ontario, which is in Canada. When he was almost nine, his father, John Naismith, came down with deadly typhoid fever. So they would not catch the disease, James, his sister, Annie, and brother, Robbie, were taken to their grandmother's home. A few days later, their father died. Two weeks later, their mother, Margaret, died of the same disease. A short time later, their grandmother Annie Young died of old age.

That left Uncle Peter to take care of the children in Bennie's Corners, near Almonte. The village had a schoolhouse, a blacksmith shop, a store, and lots of other kids to play with.

The children had lots of fun with very little money. When James needed ice skates, he made them. Then he raced out onto the frozen swimming hole like a champion skater.

**Let's Think About...**

How would you describe the early part of James Naismith's childhood? Use information from the text and maintain a logical order. **Summarize**

**2** 31

**Student Edition, p. 31**

# Let's Think About...

❶ I think the biography will be about the life of James Naismith because it names important dates in his life and it tells about something that happened to him as a young boy.

❷ James had a hard early childhood. His father and mother both died of typhoid fever. His grandmother died a short time later.

---

**Common Core State Standards**

**Informational Text 1.** Ask and answer questions to demonstrate understanding of a text, referring explicitly to the text as the basis for the answers. **Also Informational Text 10., Foundational Skills 4.c., Language 4.a.**

## Access for All

**SI Strategic Intervention**

Point out that the first thing mentioned in the text on p. 31 is a birth. Tell students that this is one sign that they are reading a biography. It starts at the very beginning of a person's life.

**A Advanced**

Have students discuss reasons that a biography might begin with an event other than the birth of the subject.

---

Name _____

The Man Who Invented Basketball

**Vocabulary • Unfamiliar Words**

When you are reading, you may find a word you don't know. When this happens, try using **context clues** to figure out the meaning. Look at the words and sentences around the unfamiliar word.

**Directions** Read the following passage about how twins are unique. Then answer the questions below. Look for context clues as you read.

When the new students walked in, everybody stared. The new girls were twins! Everyone thought they would be exactly alike. But as the children got to know the twins, they found out how wrong they had been. Cindy was good at music, but Sandy was terrible. She always sang off key. Sandy was really good at sports, though. As a guard on the basketball team, she kept the other team from making baskets. The twins were alike in one way. They were both popular and well-liked by their classmates.

1. What does *terrible* mean? What sentence is a clue to the meaning?
   Terrible means "not good." The sentence *She always sang off key* is the clue.

2. What are *sports*? What word is a clue?
   games The name of the sport basketball is a clue.

3. What is the goal of a basketball team?
   to score points by making baskets

4. What does a guard on a basketball team do?
   keeps the other team from making baskets

5. What word in the last sentence means the same thing as *popular*?
   well-liked

**Home Activity** Your child used context clues to figure out the meanings of unfamiliar words. Read a biography or character sketch with your child. Stop when you come to an unfamiliar word and ask your child to use context clues to determine the word's meaning.

254 Vocabulary

Reader's and Writer's Notebook, p. 254

## ELL

**Activate Prior Knowledge** Have students work together to make a list of all the words they know that have to do with basketball, such as *court*, *ball*, *hoop*, and *dunk*. Have students teach each other any new words.

## Access Text  If students need help, then...

⊙ **GENERALIZE** Remind students that authors use clue words such as *most, many,* and *all* when they make general statements. Have students identify a generalization in the last paragraph on p. 33.

**(Think Aloud) MODEL** When I look through the paragraph, can I find one of the clue words? (yes, the word *many*) Then I read the sentence: *Hebrew is an ancient language that many ministers study.* Is there a general statement in that sentence? (Yes, "Many ministers study Hebrew" is a general statement.) How are many ministers alike? (Many ministers study Hebrew.)

## Close Reading

**SYNTHESIS • TEXT EVIDENCE** Use your own knowledge and what you learned from the text to make a generalization about James Naismith's brother and his illness. (In paragraph 2 on p. 33, it says that James's brother died because he did not have a doctor nearby. I can make a generalization that when a person gets very sick, it is always important to have a doctor nearby.)

---

**3**

Let's **Think** About...

Can you visualize how to play the game of duck on a rock? **Visualize**

Let's **Think** About...

How do you think James will use duck on a rock years later in his life? **Predict**

**4**

---

The best game in town was called duck on a rock. One player, the guard, would put a rock about the size of his fist on top of a great big rock near the blacksmith shop. The other boys threw stones at the "duck" to knock it off the big rock. If they missed, they had to pick up their stones before the guard could tag them. It sounds easy, but it is not. The pitch could be soft, but it had to be perfectly aimed. When a player missed the duck, there was a lot of running, shouting, and laughing. James would remember duck on a rock years later when it would be very important to him.

James and his friends used this big rock to play their favorite game, duck on a rock.

### THE DROPOUT

James was great at sports. He also worked hard on the family farm. He did not work hard at school, though, and his grades were never very good. He wanted to grow up fast and be a man with a job. When he was fifteen, he left school and worked as a lumberjack.

32

**Student Edition, p. 32**

**ANALYSIS** Summarize what you have learned from reading pp. 32–33 about the work James did and where he went to school. (First, James went to school and worked on the family farm. Then he left school and worked as a lumberjack. Next, he went back to high school and finished quickly. Then he went to McGill University and studied Hebrew and philosophy.)

ON THEIR OWN Have students work in pairs to identify another generalization in the text on pp. 32–33. For additional practice, use *Let's Practice It!* p. 220 on the *Teacher Resources DVD-ROM.*

He cut down trees for almost five years. Then he decided to change his life.

James had a plan. He wanted to go back to high school and finish fast. His next step would be college. In 1883, James entered McGill University in Montreal, Canada.

When James was home for a visit, his brother, Robbie, had a terrible pain in his side. They all thought it was just a stomachache. It was actually a very bad infection. Robbie died a few hours later. A doctor could have helped him. Knowing Robbie might have been saved stayed in James's mind every day of his life.

In 1887, James graduated from McGill University after studying Hebrew and philosophy. Hebrew is an ancient language that many ministers study. Philosophy teaches people to think about life. James had a lot to think about.

Let's **Think** About...

How would you summarize some of the things James had to think about? Support your answer with information from the text.

🔊 Summarize

**5**

33

**Student Edition, p. 33**

Common Core State Standards

**Informational Text 1.** Ask and answer questions to demonstrate understanding of a text, referring explicitly to the text as the basis for the answers. **Informational Text 10.** By the end of the year, read and comprehend informational texts, including history/social studies, science, and technical texts, at the high end of the grades 2–3 text complexity band independently and proficiently.

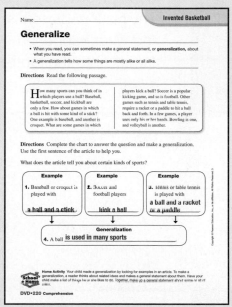

Let's Practice It! TR DVD•220

## Let's Think About...

**3** Yes, I can imagine trying to pick up the stone before the guard can tag me.

**4** James might try to use some of the rules when he invents basketball.

**5** James had to think about helping people. Knowing that his brother Robbie could have been saved stayed in James's mind.

**ELL**

**Summarize** Help students learn to summarize. Read the last paragraph on p. 32 aloud. Ask: What are the most important things to remember from this paragraph? (James was a hard worker but not a good student.) Explain to students that they have just summarized the paragraph.

**Unfamiliar Words** Go through pp. 32–33 with students and have them identify unfamiliar words that were not mentioned in the class activity. If possible, have fluent speakers explain the meanings of the words. Ask students to use each word in a sentence.

*The Man Who Invented Basketball* **33a**

## Access Text © If students need help, then...

**⟳ SUMMARIZE** Remind students that summarizing is retelling the main ideas or events while leaving out unimportant details. Have them summarize important information in the first two paragraphs on p. 34.

**(Think Aloud) MODEL** This section is about how James learned that he could combine studying with fun when he was a student. Some important information to remember is that at first James studied night and day. I can also talk about why his friends said sports had value and what happened when they dragged James onto the football field.

**ON THEIR OWN** Have small groups summarize the last paragraph on p. 34.

## Close Reading ©

**ANALYSIS** What generalization can you make about baseball, field hockey, football, and rugby from the information provided in the story? (Many outdoor games can't be played in cold climates.)

### THE MINISTER PLAYS HARDBALL

For James, the next step was studying to become a minister at McGill's Presbyterian College. There was much to learn, and he studied day and night. His friends tried to get him to play sports. They told him it would sharpen his mind and toughen up his body. He said no and kept on studying.

One day his strong friends dragged him out to the football field. James had so much fun that from then on he found time to study hard and play hard too. He was smaller than the other players, but he was powerful and smart. He learned rugby, which is a very rough game. He loved lacrosse, which can be even rougher.

One Saturday James got two black eyes in a wild game of lacrosse. The next day was Sunday, and he had to give a sermon in the church. James, the student minister, looked out from behind those two black eyes. He may have looked kind of funny, but he finished the sermon he had written.

34

**Let's Think About...**

What words and phrases create a graphic visual image on this page?
**Visualize**

**6**

**Student Edition, p. 34**

**REREAD CHALLENGING TEXT** Have students reread the first three sentences on p. 35 to find out why James would rather talk to teens while teaching them sports than give sermons. Students may need help understanding the benefit of talking to teens during sports or games, and why this might help them live better lives.

**Common Core State Standards**

**Informational Text 1.** Ask and answer questions to demonstrate understanding of a text, referring explicitly to the text as the basis for the answers. **Informational Text 10.** By the end of the year, read and comprehend informational texts, including history/social studies, science, and technical texts, at the high end of the grades 2–3 text complexity band independently and proficiently.

**CHECK PREDICTIONS** Have students look back at the predictions they made earlier and discuss whether they were accurate. Then have students preview the rest of the selection and either adjust their predictions accordingly or make new predictions.

In 1890, James became a Presbyterian minister. But he did not want to give sermons in a church. He thought he could help teens live better lives if he talked to them while teaching them sports. His first sports job was at the International YMCA Training School, which is now Springfield College. So he moved from Canada to Springfield, Massachusetts, in the United States.

**James Naismith believed that the fun and action of sports could improve the lives of young people.**

As a student teacher, James was very good at the job of teaching baseball, field hockey, football, and rugby, which are great games during spring, summer, and fall. Winter was a problem. The men had to come indoors and exercise, which was not much fun. They were so bored that some of them wanted to quit the YMCA training school. James was told to invent an exciting indoor game. It had to be ready in two weeks. That was the deadline.

Let's **Think** About...

Summarize the section "The Minister Plays Hardball." Be sure to maintain the meaning of the section title in your summary.
**Summarize**

**7**

35

If you want to teach this selection in two sessions, stop here.

If you want to continue reading this selection, turn to page 36.

**Access for All**

**SI Strategic Intervention**

Have students work in groups to come up with generalizations about different kinds of sports.

**A Advanced**

Have students work individually to write two generalizations based upon what they have read so far.

**Student Edition, p. 35**

# Let's Think About...

sharpen, toughen, rough, dragged, two black eyes

As a student minister, James learns the value of sports. When he later becomes a minister, he believes he can help teens live better lives if he talks to them while teaching them many sports. He is told to invent a new game that can be played indoors.

**ELL**

**Summarize** Help students take notes about the most important parts of the first paragraph on p. 35. Ask them to use these notes to summarize the paragraph.

*The Man Who Invented Basketball* **35a**

**Common Core State Standards**

**Writing 7.** Conduct short research projects that build knowledge about a topic. **Language 1.** Demonstrate command of the conventions of standard English grammar and usage when writing or speaking. **Language 1.a.** Explain the function of nouns, pronouns, verbs, adjectives, and adverbs in general and their functions in particular sentences. **Language 2.e.** Use conventional spelling for high-frequency and other studied words and for adding suffixes to base words (e.g., *sitting, smiled, cries, happiness*). **Also Writing 8., Language 1.f.**

 **Bridge to Common Core**

### RESEARCH TO BUILD AND PRESENT KNOWLEDGE

On Day 2 of the weeklong research project, students gather relevant information based on their focused questions from Day 1. They consult multiple sources of written information, as well as expert sources, assessing the credibility of each one. This process enables students to develop the capacity to build knowledge on a subject.

# Research and Inquiry

## Step 2 Navigate/Search

**TEACH** Have students generate a research plan for gathering information about their research topic. Encourage them to collect information from multiple sources of written information, including reference texts such as encyclopedias and short biographies. Have them improve the focus of their research as a result of consulting expert sources such as the reference librarian. Tell students to use skimming and scanning techniques to identify important information by looking at text features within reference texts. Headings and bold words might be clues to what kind of information the text will provide. Have students look for other features such as italics, illustrations, captions, or highlighting. Remind students to take notes as they gather information.

 **MODEL** I told the librarian that I wanted to find out about a talented soccer player. We looked in the library catalogue under "soccer" and saw the name "David Beckham." Then the librarian helped me find an encyclopedia entry about David Beckham. She also helped me find a short biography about him.

**GUIDE PRACTICE** Have students continue their review of the text sources they identified. If they are having difficulty finding information about their chosen person, then help them either choose a different subject or use the Internet to broaden their search. Make sure students understand the importance of using valid and reliable sources so that their information is accurate.

**ON THEIR OWN** Remind students that they will be presenting a biography of their subject. Have them make notes about important events in the life of their subject. Remind them to create a Works Cited page as they research, including the author, title, publisher, and publication year for each source used.

# Conventions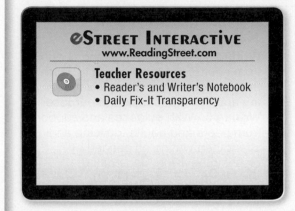

Zoom in on ©

## Singular and Plural Nouns

**TEACH** What is the purpose of pronouns? (They take the place of nouns.) Remind students that the singular pronouns are *I, me, you, he, she, him, her,* and *it.* The plural pronouns are *we, us, you, they,* and *them.* The pronoun *you* can be used as either a singular or a plural pronoun.

**GUIDE PRACTICE** Have students write sentences that use singular pronouns, plural pronouns, or both. If they write a sentence with the pronoun *you,* have them give context clues to identify it as a singular or a plural pronoun.

**ON THEIR OWN** For additional practice, use *Reader's and Writer's Notebook,* p. 251.

# Spelling

## Irregular Plurals

**TEACH** Remind students that many of their spelling words form plurals by changing *f* or *fe* to *ves.* Model how to spell words with these plurals using segmentation and letter sounds. The word *knives* is the plural form of *knife.* When a word ends in *-f* or *-fe,* we change the *-f* or *-fe* to *-ves* to form the plural.

**GUIDE PRACTICE** Have students write each spelling word and say its singular form. Tell them to underline the plural of the words where *-f* or *-fe* was changed to *-ves (wolves, knives, scarves, halves).*

**ON THEIR OWN** For more practice, use *Reader's and Writer's Notebook,* p. 252.

---

**eSTREET INTERACTIVE**
www.ReadingStreet.com

**Teacher Resources**
• Reader's and Writer's Notebook
• Daily Fix-It Transparency

## Daily Fix-It

3. The boy flew high in the sky, and they got in troubel for it.
   *(he; trouble)*
4. Did the boy learn a lessen.
   *(lesson; ?)*

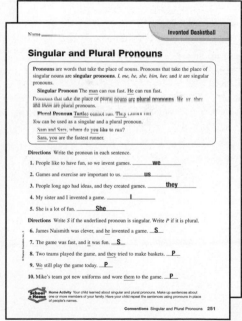

Reader's and Writer's Notebook, pp. 251–252

**Conventions** To provide students with practice on common and plural nouns, use the modified grammar lessons in the *ELL Handbook* and the Grammar Jammer at:
www.ReadingStreet.com

*The Man Who Invented Basketball* **35c**

**Common Core State Standards**

**Writing 4.** With guidance and support from adults, produce writing in which the development and organization are appropriate to task and purpose. **Writing 5.** With guidance and support from peers and adults, develop and strengthen writing as needed by planning, revising, and editing. **Also Writing 1., 1.a., 1.b., 8.**

# Writing

## Persuasive Text

### Writing Trait: Focus/Ideas

**INTRODUCE THE PROMPT** Remind students that the selection they are reading this week, *The Man Who Invented Basketball,* is about a sport. Then explain that they will begin the writing process for a persuasive text about a sport today. Read aloud the writing prompt.

---

### Writing Prompt

---

Write an essay about your favorite sport or game, persuading someone to play it.

---

### SELECT A TOPIC

**Think Aloud** The purpose of a persuasive text is to persuade, or convince. You will try to convince others to try your favorite game or sport. You will give reasons a person would want to play. Let's begin by thinking of a variety of sports and reasons to play them. That information will help you decide what topic you will write about.

**GATHER INFORMATION** Draw a T-chart on the board, and have students name sports and games. List them in the left column. Have students copy this T-chart and work together in pairs to list reasons someone would play the game or sport.

Remind students that they can use the Internet and print resources, as well as their personal experiences, to find information about their sport.

| Game or Sport | Reasons to Play |
|---|---|
| curling | takes concentration; unusual |
| chess | |
| soccer | |

> **Corrective feedback** Circulate around the room as students complete their T-charts. Confer briefly with students who seem to be having trouble. Ask them to talk about how each game is played or the skills needed to play.

## Mini-Lesson | Write with Purpose

■ When you know your purpose for writing, you can identify a main idea and details that will support your purpose. A main idea and details graphic organizer can help you organize your writing. **Display the graphic organizer. Show students that the main idea is related to their purpose for writing. The supporting details are why a person should play the game or sport.**

■ I'm going to write a persuasive text about playing chess. My main idea is that chess is a game everyone should learn. I'll write that in the Main Idea box. Then I'll write reasons in the Supporting Details boxes.

Have students use the graphic organizer on p. 253 of their *Reader's and Writer's Notebook*.

## Routine | Quick Write for Fluency [Team Talk]

1. **Talk** Have pairs discuss how their topics are similar and different.

2. **Write** Have students write one sentence about how the two topics are similar, and another about how they are different.

3. **Share** Have students share what they wrote with the class.

Routines Flip Chart

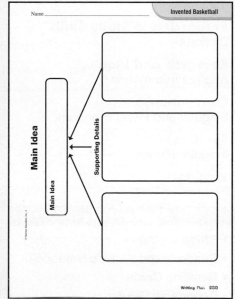

Reader's and Writer's Notebook, p. 253

# Wrap Up Your Day!

✔ **Content Knowledge** Have students discuss what they learned about how basketball was invented.

✔ **Text-Based Comprehension** What generalizations have you made about James Naismith?

**Preview DAY 3**

Tell students that tomorrow they will read more about basketball.

## ⓒ Common Core State Standards

**Speaking/Listening 1.** Engage effectively in a range of collaborative discussions (one-on-one, in groups, and teacher-led) with diverse partners on grade 3 topics and texts, building on others' ideas and expressing their own clearly. **Language 6.** Acquire and use accurately grade-appropriate conversational, general academic, and domain-specific words and phrases, including those that signal spatial and temporal relationships (e.g., *After dinner that night we went looking for them*). **Also Language 5.b.**

# Content Knowledge

## Talents

**EXPAND THE CONCEPT** Remind students of the weekly concept question, *How do talents make someone unique?* Tell students that today they will continue reading *The Man Who Invented Basketball.* Encourage students to think about how thrilling it would be to think up an entirely new sport.

# Build Oral Language

**TALK ABOUT SENTENCES AND WORDS** Reread the first paragraph of Student Edition p. 30.

*Winter in Canada can be very hard. Icy wind sweeps down from the north. Rivers freeze solid. Crossing them can be scary and dangerous.*

- What does *icy* mean? (covered with ice; slippery) *Icy* can also mean "like ice" or "very cold."
- What are some synonyms for the word *icy* the way it is used to describe wind? *(arctic, cold, wintry)*
- What does *scary* mean? (making someone feel afraid)
- What are some synonyms for the word *scary*? *(terrifying, alarming)*
- Why do you think the author chose the words *icy* and *scary*? (Answers will vary.)
- Does the author give a pleasant or unpleasant description of Canadian winters? List words or phrases to support your answer. (unpleasant; "very hard," "icy wind sweeps," "freeze," "scary and dangerous")

**Team Talk** Have students work in pairs to replace words in the sentences without changing meaning.

> **Winter in Canada can be very hard. _____ wind sweeps down from the north. Rivers freeze solid. Crossing them can be _____ and dangerous.**

# Build Oral Vocabulary

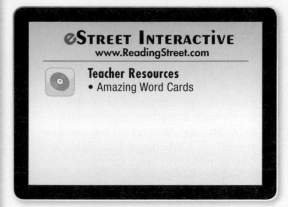
**Amazing Words**     **Robust Vocabulary Routine**

1. **Introduce** Write the word *necessary* on the board. Have students say it with you. Yesterday we learned about James Naismith. He wanted to be a minister, so it was *necessary* for him to go to college. Have students determine a definition of *necessary*. (*Necessary* means "required.")

2. **Demonstrate** Have students answer questions to demonstrate understanding. What is one thing that is *necessary* to be able to play a game of basketball? (a ball)

3. **Apply** Have students apply their understanding. What is one thing it is *necessary* for you to have at school? (a pencil)

4. **Display the Word** Run your hand under the syllables of *nec-es-sar-y* and have students read the word.

See p. OV•1 to teach *result*.

Routines Flip Chart

## Amazing Words

| | |
|---|---|
| mock | necessary |
| idle | result |
| potential | succeed |
| ecstatic | rise |
| thrill | verge |
| audition | |

**ADD TO THE CONCEPT MAP** Discuss the Amazing Words *thrill* and *audition*. Add these and other concept-related words to the concept map. Use the following questions to develop students' understanding of the concept.

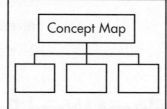

Concept Map

• James Naismith was *thrilled* when he saw that people liked the game of basketball. When is a time when you were *thrilled*?

• You try out for sports teams and *audition* for plays. What are some other kinds of activities for which a person would have to *audition*?

**ELL**

**Expand Vocabulary** Use the Day 3 instruction on ELL Poster 16 to help students expand vocabulary.

**Common Core State Standards**

**Foundational Skills 3.d.** Read grade-appropriate irregularly spelled words. **Foundational Skills 4.b.** Read on-level prose and poetry orally with accuracy, appropriate rate, and expression on successive readings. **Language 1.b.** Form and use regular and irregular plural nouns.

# Word Analysis

## Irregular Plurals

**MODEL WORD SORTING** Write *-f, -fe,* and *other* as heads in a three-column chart. Now we are going to sort words. We'll put words with the plural ending *-ves* and the singular ending *-f* in the first column. Words with the plural ending *-ves* and the singular ending *-fe* will go in the second column. Irregular plurals that don't fit into either of these groups will go in the third column. I will start. Write *shelves* and model how to read it, using the lesson on p. 22a. *Shelves* in the singular form is *shelf,* which ends in *f,* so I will write *shelves* in the first column. Model reading *geese* and *knives* in the same way and writing the words in the correct columns of the chart.

**GUIDE PRACTICE** Use practice words from the activity on p. 26c and other words for the word sort. Point to a word. Have students read the word, identify its parts, and tell where it should be written on the chart.

**Corrective feedback** | For corrective feedback, model reading each word and then telling the singular form of each word.

| -f | -fe | other |
|---|---|---|
| shelves | knives | geese |
| loaves | wives | children |
| leaves | | feet |
| calves | | teeth |
| halves | | mice |

## Fluent Word Reading

**MODEL** Write *feet.* I recognize this as a plural word I know. *Feet* is the plural of the word *foot.*

**GUIDE PRACTICE** Write the words below. Look for word parts you know. When I point to the word, we'll read it together. Allow one second per word part previewing time for the first reading.

| calves | teeth | thieves | knives | people | women |
|---|---|---|---|---|---|

**ON THEIR OWN** Have students read the list above three or four times, until they can read one word per second.

# Decodable Passage 16B

If students need help, then...

## Read *Camping!*

**READ WORDS IN ISOLATION** Have students turn to p. 9 in *Decodable Practice Readers 3.2* and find the first list of words. Each word in this list is an irregular plural. Let's read these words. Be sure that students pronounce each plural word correctly.

**PREVIEW** Have students read the title and preview the story. Tell them that they will read words that are irregular plurals.

**READ WORDS IN CONTEXT** Chorally read the story along with the students. Have students identify words in the story that are irregular plurals. Make sure that students are monitoring their accuracy when they decode words.

**Team Talk** Pair students and have them take turns reading the story aloud to each other. Monitor students as they read to check for proper pronunciation and appropriate pacing.

**eSTREET INTERACTIVE**
www.ReadingStreet.com

**Pearson eText**
• Decodable Reader

## Access for All

**SI** Strategic Intervention

Have students make flash cards for the plural words listed on the chart in the "other" column. Have students practice reading the words until they become fluent.

**A** Advanced

Have students add more plural words to the three-column chart. They may use a dictionary or glossary to check spellings.

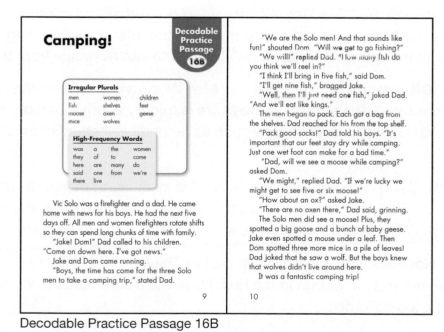

### Camping!

Decodable Practice Passage 16B

**Irregular Plurals**

| men | women | children |
| fish | shelves | feet |
| moose | oxen | geese |
| mice | wolves | |

**High-Frequency Words**

| was | a | the | women |
| they | of | to | come |
| here | are | many | do |
| said | one | from | we're |
| there | live | | |

Vic Solo was a firefighter and a dad. He came home with news for his boys. He had the next five days off. All men and women firefighters rotate shifts so they can spend long chunks of time with family.

"Jake! Dom!" Dad called to his children. "Come on down here. I've got news."

Jake and Dom came running.

"Boys, the time has come for the three Solo men to take a camping trip," stated Dad.

9

"We are the Solo men! And that sounds like fun!" shouted Dom. "Will we get to go fishing?"

"We will!" replied Dad. "How many fish do you think we'll reel in?"

"I think I'll bring in five fish," said Dom.

"I'll get nine fish," bragged Jake.

"Well, then I'll just need one fish," joked Dad. "And we'll eat like kings."

The men began to pack. Each got a bag from the shelves. Dad reached for his from the top shelf.

"Pack good socks!" Dad told his boys. "It's important that our feet stay dry while camping. Just one wet foot can make for a bad time."

"Dad, will we see a moose while camping?" asked Dom.

"We might," replied Dad. "If we're lucky we might get to see five or six moose!"

"How about an ox?" asked Jake.

"There are no oxen there," Dad said, grinning.

The Solo men did see a moose! Plus, they spotted a big goose and a bunch of baby geese. Jake even spotted a mouse under a leaf. Then Dom spotted three more mice in a pile of leaves! Dad joked that he saw a wolf. But the boys knew that wolves didn't live around here.

It was a fantastic camping trip!

10

Decodable Practice Passage 16B

Zoom in on ©

© **Common Core State Standards**

**Informational Text 1.** Ask and answer questions to demonstrate understanding of a text, referring explicitly to the text as the basis for the answers. **Informational Text 2.** Determine the main idea of a text; recount the key details and explain how they support the main idea. **Language 4.a.** Use sentence-level context as a clue to the meaning of a word or phrase.

## Strategy Response Log

Have students revisit the text and use p. 22 in the *Reader's and Writer's Notebook* to summarize the first half of *The Man Who Invented Basketball.*

# Text-Based Comprehension
## Check Understanding

Student Edition, pp. 28–29

**If...** you chose to read *The Man Who Invented Basketball* in two parts, **then...** use the following questions to monitor students' understanding of pp. 28–35 of the selection. Encourage students to cite evidence from the text.

**EVALUATION** How can you tell that *The Man Who Invented Basketball* is not an autobiography? The story of James's life is told by another person, not by himself, and the text uses pronouns such as *he* and *his* instead of *I* and *me.* (p. 30)

**ANALYSIS** Using context clues, figure out the meaning of the word *lumberjack* on p. 32. The next sentence says that James spent five years cutting down trees. A *lumberjack* is someone whose job is to cut down trees.

**RETELL** Have students retell the first part of *The Man Who Invented Basketball,* referring to details in the text. Have them summarize information in the text in a logical order.

> **Corrective feedback** | **If...** students leave out important details,
> **then...** have students look back through the photographs and illustrations in the selection.

**READ** Use the **Access Text** and **Close Reading** notes to finish reading *The Man Who Invented Basketball.*

**If...** you followed the Read for Understanding routine below, **then...** ask students to retell the selection before you reread *The Man Who Invented Basketball.*

**RETELL** Have students retell the first part of *The Man Who Invented Basketball,* referring to details in the text. Have them summarize information in the text in a logical order.

> **Corrective feedback** | **If...** students leave out important details, **then...** have students look back through the photographs and illustrations in the selection.

**READ** Return to p. 34–35 and use the **2nd Read/Close Reading** notes to reread *The Man Who Invented Basketball.*

# Read Main Selection

## Routine    Read for Understanding ©

Deepen understanding by reading the selection multiple times.

1. **First Read**—If students need support, then use the **Access Text** notes to help them clarify understanding.

2. **Second Read**—Use the **Close Reading** notes to help students draw knowledge from the text.

**ELL**

**Check Retelling** To support retelling, review the multilingual summary for *The Man Who Invented Basketball* with the appropriate Retelling Cards to scaffold understanding.

**ELL**

**If...** students need more scaffolding and practice with the **Main Selection, then...** use the activities on p. DI•22 in the Teacher Resources section on SuccessNet.

| **Day 3**  SMALL GROUP TIME • Differentiate Close Reading, p. SG•1 |
|---|

| **OL** On-Level | **SI** Strategic Intervention | **A** Advanced |
|---|---|---|
| • **Reread** to Develop Vocabulary | • **Reread** to Develop Vocabulary | • **Reread** to Extend Vocabulary |
| • **Read** *The Man Who Invented Basketball* | • **Read** *The Man Who Invented Basketball* | • **Read** *The Man Who Invented Basketball* |
| | | • **Investigate** Inquiry Project |

## Access Text © *If students need help, then...*

**GENERALIZE** Have students reread the last sentence of the first paragraph and the first sentence of the second paragraph on p. 37. Ask them which of these sentences is a generalization. (the first one)

**Think Aloud** **MODEL** I look at these two sentences and try to see which tells how several things are alike in one way. The first sentence tells about what many women did, even though the word *many* is not used. The second tells about what one specific woman did. The first sentence is the generalization.

**ON THEIR OWN** Ask students to identify another generalization on pp. 36–37.

## Close Reading ©

### SYNTHESIS • TEXT EVIDENCE

Using information from this selection about football and rugby, make a generalization about outdoor games. Cite details from the text to support your answer. (Paragraph 1 on p. 36 says that games like football and rugby could be risky. So, I can generalize that outdoor games can be dangerous.)

## INVENTING FUN

James struggled with the problem for twelve days. The game had to be fast and fun. It could not be risky, like football or rugby, with teams of men banging into the gym walls.

That good old game from his childhood, duck on a rock, flashed into his head. He remembered how using a soft pitch was the best way to aim for the "duck." James's eyes lit up. He shouted out loud, "I've got it!"

There was no time to invent new gear. Two peach baskets were used as goals. James explained the strange rules. Two teams of men dragged themselves onto the gym floor, grumbling. They took a soccer ball and started playing. The grumbling soon stopped. Cheers and shouts filled the gym. The date was December 21, 1891. Basketball was born. Soon teams formed in gyms all around town.

Let's **Think** About...
What parts of the games and sports James knew well went into basketball?
**Summarize**

8

36

Peach baskets were used as basketball goals before nets.

**Student Edition, p. 36**

**ANALYSIS** How could you use information from the text to summarize the invention of basketball in one or two sentences? (James Naismith invented basketball when he was asked to come up with a game people could play inside in the winter.)

2**ND READ**

**DEVELOP LANGUAGE** Have students reread the third paragraph on p. 37. What does *popular* mean? What other basketball maneuvers might be *popular*?

 **Common Core State Standards**

**Informational Text 10.** By the end of the year, read and comprehend informational texts, including history/social studies, science, and technical texts, at the high end of the grades 2–3 text complexity band independently and proficiently. **Also Informational Text 1., Language 5.b.**

In schools across the United States, students began to play basketball. Women began playing, too.

A young woman named Maude Sherman was on one of the first women's teams. James and Maude soon became friends, and then fell in love. They married on June 20, 1894. James and Maude would have five children together.

In a few years, basketball started being played more like it is played today. The peach baskets had changed to rope baskets. Backboards were added. Dribbling became popular because players were not allowed to hold the ball very long without throwing it. When the ball bounced off the floor as a player raced down the court, it sounded like a fast drumbeat. James thought dribbling was a great idea.

Let's **Think** About...

How were James's first basketball games different from later ones?

 **Summarize**

**9**

37

**Student Edition, p. 37**

### Access for All

 **Strategic Intervention**

To help students summarize, guide them to identify the main idea in different sections of text. Tell students that when they are summarizing shorter pieces of text, the main idea might be the entire summary.

**A** **Advanced**

Have students use the library or Internet to find out more about how early basketball was played and how the game developed.

# Let's Think About...

**8** James used the game of duck on a rock and a soccer ball to help invent the game of basketball.

**9** In his earlier games, James used peach baskets. In the later games, he used rope baskets with backboards. Players were also allowed to dribble in the later games.

**Compound Words** Help students identify compound words on pp. 36–37. *(football, basketball, backboards, drumbeat)* Discuss how to determine meaning by defining the two small words in each word.

*The Man Who Invented Basketball* **37a**

# Access Text  If students need help, then...

◉ **SUMMARIZE** Remind students that a summary is a retelling of information using only the most important facts and the main idea. Have students summarize the information in the last paragraph on p. 38.

(Think Aloud) **MODEL** I only want to include the most important details in my summary. Where James went to school is interesting, but it's more important that he graduated. It's interesting where he worked, but what he did is more important.

# Close Reading

**SYNTHESIS • TEXT EVIDENCE** If I didn't know what the word *products* on p. 39 meant, how could I figure out the word's meaning? What context clues might help me? (One context clue is *ads selling. Products* must be things people sell.)

---

**Let's Think About...**

Were your predictions correct so far? What do you think will happen next in James's life?
**Predict**

10

---

In 1895, James and Maude moved to Denver, Colorado. There James became director of physical education at the largest YMCA in the country.

He was always working on his plan for the future. He remembered his brother dying horribly without help from a doctor. He had seen athletes have terrible accidents. He wanted to be a doctor and help people.

There was no stopping James when he had a plan. He became a student at Gross Medical College in Denver. He would work all day at the YMCA and then study to be a doctor after work and on weekends. James graduated as a medical doctor in 1898. That year he got the job of assistant physical director at the University of Kansas. By 1909 James was working there as a minister, a professor, and a medical doctor.

38

**Student Edition, p. 38**

**ANALYSIS** Help students generate text-based questions by providing the following question stem: In the selection what did James do when _____ ?

**ON THEIR OWN** Have students summarize p. 39.

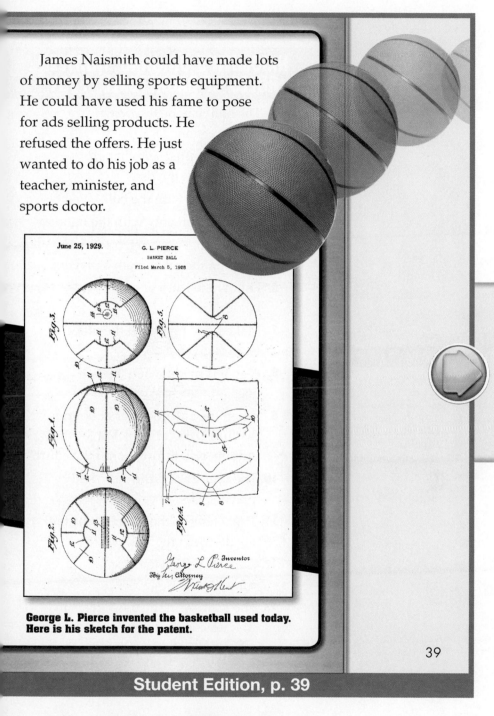

James Naismith could have made lots of money by selling sports equipment. He could have used his fame to pose for ads selling products. He refused the offers. He just wanted to do his job as a teacher, minister, and sports doctor.

June 25, 1929.    G. L. PIERCE
BASKET BALL
Filed March 5, 1928

*P. Inventor*

George L. Pierce invented the basketball used today. Here is his sketch for the patent.

39

**Student Edition, p. 39**

# Let's Think About...

🔵 Yes. I thought James would eventually try to help sick or injured people. I think he will come up with creative ideas on how to treat people.

## Common Core State Standards

**Informational Text 1.** Ask and answer questions to demonstrate understanding of a text, referring explicitly to the text as the basis for the answers. **Also Informational Text 10., Language 4.a.**

## Access for All

**SI Strategic Intervention**

Have students work in pairs to create a one-paragraph summary of James Naismith's life.

## Connect to Social Studies

**The Olympic Games** The Olympics were athletic contests that took place in ancient Greece. The modern Olympic games started in 1896. Basketball became an official game in the Olympics in 1936.

**Cognates** Point out the words *professor* and *doctor* at the bottom of p. 38. There are two Spanish words for *doctor—médico* and the cognate *doctor*. The cognate for *professor* is *profesor*.

## 1ST READ

## Access Text ©  If students need help, then...

**Review USE GRAPHIC SOURCES**
Have students read through the events included on the time line on p. 41. How does this graphic source help us learn about Naismith's life? (It lists the most important events, in order.)

**Think Aloud MODEL** The first thing I see when I examine this time line are dates. In what kind of order are the dates placed? (time order) What information is listed next to each date? (an important event from James Naismith's life)

**ON THEIR OWN** For more practice, use *Let's Practice It!* p. 221 on the *Teacher Resources DVD-ROM.*

**CROSS-TEXT EVALUATION**
**Use a Strategy to Self-Check** How did the Read Aloud, "The Myth of Icarus," help you understand this selection?

Let's **Think** About...

Use the rules to imagine how the game was played in 1891. How was the game different then?
**Visualize**

⑪

40

**Student Edition, p. 40**

### NAISMITH'S ORIGINAL THIRTEEN RULES OF BASKETBALL, 1891

1. The ball may be thrown in any direction.
2. It can be batted with hands, but not with the fist.
3. No running with the ball.
4. Hold the ball only with the hands.
5. No holding, pushing, hitting, or tripping the other team's players.
6. Follow the rules or a foul will be declared.
7. Make three fouls and the other team is given a goal.
8. A goal is made when the ball goes into the basket.
9. When the ball goes out of bounds, the first person to touch it, or the umpire, will throw it onto the court.
10. The umpire is the judge of the players. He can call fouls.
11. The referee is the judge of the ball. He decides on goals.
12. Game time is two fifteen-minute halves.
13. The team with the most goals in that time is the winner.

## 2ND READ

## Close Reading ©

**ANALYSIS** Why might playing duck on a rock not be one of the events included on the time line on p. 41? (It is only a small detail in James's life, not one of the most important events.)

**SYNTHESIS** Summarize the purpose of the list provided on p. 40. (Rules for basketball include how players should handle the ball, what will happen if the rules are not followed, how long the game will last, and how one team can win the game.)

**SYNTHESIS • TEXT EVIDENCE** Using what you learned in this selection, tell how talents can make someone unique. Have students cite examples from the text to support their responses.

**CHECK PREDICTIONS** Have students return to the predictions they made earlier and confirm whether they were accurate.

## TIME LINE

- **1861** Born on November 6, Almonte, Ontario, Canada.

- **1870** Parents die; moves to Bennie's Corners, Ontario.

- **1887** Graduates from McGill University in Montreal, Quebec, Canada.

- **1890** Becomes a Presbyterian minister.

- **1891** Invents basketball; first game is played December 21.

- **1894** Marries Maude Sherman on June 20.

- **1895** Becomes director of physical education at YMCA in Denver, Colorado.

- **1898** Graduates as a medical doctor

- **1909** Is professor, minister, and doctor at the University of Kansas.

- **1917** Helps American soldiers in World War I as a military chaplain.

- **1925** Becomes United States citizen.

- **1936** Is honored at Olympic Games in Berlin, Germany.

- **1939** Dies on November 28 in Lawrence, Kansas.

Let's **Think** About...

Which of the events in the time line are supported by facts and details in the biography?
🔊 **Summarize**

**12**

41

**Student Edition, p. 41**

# Let's Think About...

**11** The game lasted a much shorter time back then.

**12** All events from 1861–1909.

🅒 **Common Core State Standards**

**Informational Text 3.** Describe the relationship between a series of historical events, scientific ideas or concepts, or steps in technical procedures in a text, using language that pertains to time, sequence, and cause/effect. **Informational Text 7.** Use information gained from illustrations (e.g., maps, photographs) and the words in a text to demonstrate understanding of the text (e.g., where, when, why, and how key events occur). **Also Informational Text 10.**

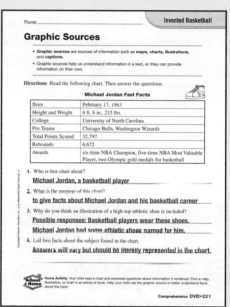

Let's Practice It! TR DVD•221

🅔🅛🅛

**Language Production** Explain to students that a time line is a series of events listed in time order. Tell students that to talk or write about the time line, they will need to be familiar with the following sequence words: *before, after, next, later, first, second,* and *finally.* Explain the meaning of each word and give students an example of how it might be used in relation to the time line. For example: *James was a minister before he invented basketball.* Help students use each sequence word in a sentence.

*The Man Who Invented Basketball* **41a**

Common Core State Standards
Informational Text 1. Ask and answer questions to demonstrate understanding of a text, referring explicitly to the text as the basis for the answers. Also Informational Text 2., Writing 8.

Envision It! Retell

READING STREET ONLINE
STORY SORT
www.ReadingStreet.com

42

## Think Critically

1. On page 36, the author writes about James Naismith coming up with the idea for basketball in only two weeks. Have you ever quickly solved a hard problem? Why was James Naismith's idea for basketball right for the problem?
Text to Self

2. Is the selection written in first or third person? Why was it written that way? How would the selection be different if it were an autobiography instead of a biography? Think Like an Author

3. On page 38, what generalization does the author make about Naismith? What clue word does the author use? Is the generalization well-supported?
Generalize

4. What important events in Naismith's life led to him becoming a teacher and coach? What important events led to him becoming a doctor? Summarize

5. **Look Back and Write** Look back through the selection to find facts and details about the character of James Naismith. Write about the traits that helped him become a success in his life. Provide evidence to support your answer.
Key Ideas and Details • Text Evidence

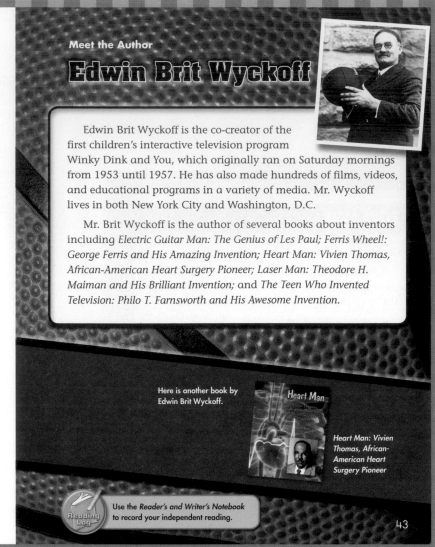

Meet the Author

# Edwin Brit Wyckoff

Edwin Brit Wyckoff is the co-creator of the first children's interactive television program *Winky Dink and You*, which originally ran on Saturday mornings from 1953 until 1957. He has also made hundreds of films, videos, and educational programs in a variety of media. Mr. Wyckoff lives in both New York City and Washington, D.C.

Mr. Brit Wyckoff is the author of several books about inventors including *Electric Guitar Man: The Genius of Les Paul; Ferris Wheel!: George Ferris and His Amazing Invention; Heart Man: Vivien Thomas, African-American Heart Surgery Pioneer; Laser Man: Theodore H. Maiman and His Brilliant Invention;* and *The Teen Who Invented Television: Philo T. Farnsworth and His Awesome Invention.*

Here is another book by Edwin Brit Wyckoff.

*Heart Man: Vivien Thomas, African-American Heart Surgery Pioneer*

Use the *Reader's and Writer's Notebook* to record your independent reading.

43

Student Edition, pp. 42–43

---

Common Core State Standards

Informational Text 1. Ask and answer questions to demonstrate understanding of a text, referring explicitly to the text as the basis for the answers. Also Informational Text 2., 6., Writing 10.

Bridge to Common Core

### RANGE OF READING AND LEVEL OF TEXT COMPLEXITY

To increase students' capacity for reading and comprehending complex texts independently and proficiently, have them read other informational texts by Edwin Brit Wyckoff or about the topic, Talents. After students read closely for a sustained period of time, they should record their reading in their Reading Logs.

# Think Critically

1. **TEXT TO SELF** The idea was right because it was for a game played inside. It was good exercise, but players would not hurt themselves.

2. **THINK LIKE AN AUTHOR** The selection is written in the third person because someone other than Naismith wrote it. An autobiography is written in the first person and uses pronouns *I* and *me*.

3. **GENERALIZE** The generalization is *He was always working on his plan for the future.* It is well supported. The clue word is *always*.

4. **SUMMARIZE** Naismith was great at sports. As a minister, he felt he could help teens if he talked to them while teaching them sports, so he became a teacher and coach. His brother dying young when a doctor could've helped him and seeing hurt athletes led Naismith to become a doctor.

5. **LOOK BACK AND WRITE • TEXT EVIDENCE** To build writing fluency, assign a 10–15 minute time limit.

**eSTREET INTERACTIVE**
www.ReadingStreet.com

**Pearson eText**
• Student Edition

**Story Sort**

## Scoring Rubric  Look Back and Write

**TOP-SCORE RESPONSE** A top-score response uses details from the text to tell about the traits that made James Naismith become a success.

**A top-score response should include:**
• He worked hard all his life.
• He knew how to play hard but fairly.
• He never gave up.

## Retell

Have students work in pairs to retell the selection, using the retelling strip in the Student Edition or the Story Sort as prompts. Monitor students' retellings.

### Scoring Rubric  Expository Retelling

| | 4 | 3 | 2 | 1 |
|---|---|---|---|---|
| **Connections** | Makes connections and generalizes beyond the text | Makes connections to other events, texts, or experiences | Makes a limited connection to another event, text, or experience | Makes no connection to another event, text, or experience |
| **Author's Purpose** | Elaborates on author's purpose | Tells author's purpose with some clarity | Makes some connection to author's purpose | Makes no connection to author's purpose |
| **Topic** | Describes the main topic | Identifies the main topic with some details early in retelling | Identifies the main topic | Retelling has no sense of topic |
| **Important Ideas** | Gives accurate information about events, steps, and ideas using details and key vocabulary | Gives accurate information about events, steps, and ideas with some detail and key vocabulary | Gives limited or inaccurate information about events, steps, and ideas | Gives no information about events, steps, and ideas |
| **Conclusions** | Draws conclusions and makes inferences to generalize beyond the text | Draws conclusions about the text | Is able to tell some learnings about the text | Is unable to draw conclusions or make inferences about the text |

### Plan to Assess Retelling

☑ **This week assess Strategic Intervention students.**
☐ **Week 2** Advanced
☐ **Week 3** Strategic Intervention
☐ **Week 4** On-Level
☐ **Week 5** Assess any students you have not yet checked during this unit.

### Meet the Author

Have students read about author Edwin Brit Wyckoff on p. 43. Ask them how his other books are like *The Man Who Invented Basketball*.

### Read Independently

Have students enter their independent reading into their Reading Logs.

**Don't Wait Until Friday**

## MONITOR PROGRESS  Check Retelling

**If...** students have difficulty retelling,

**then...** use the Retelling Cards/Story Sort to scaffold their retellings.

**Common Core State Standards**

**Foundational Skills 4.** Read with sufficient accuracy and fluency to support comprehension. **Foundational Skills 4.b.** Read on-level prose and poetry orally with accuracy, appropriate rate, and expression on successive readings. **Language 4.d.** Use glossaries or beginning dictionaries, both print and digital, to determine or clarify the precise meaning of key words and phrases.

# Fluency

## Accuracy

**MODEL FLUENT READING** Have students turn to p. 30 in *The Man Who Invented Basketball.* Have students follow along as you read this page. Point out that as you read you are including all the words on the page. Tell students to listen for difficult or unfamiliar words. Remind them that part of reading with accuracy is understanding the meaning of and reading fluently any unfamiliar words.

**GUIDE PRACTICE** Have students follow along as you read the page again. Ask questions to be sure students comprehend the text. Have students reread the page as a group without you until they read with accuracy and make no mistakes. Continue in the same way on p. 31.

| Corrective feedback | **If...** students are having difficulty reading with accuracy, **then...** prompt:<br>• Did you read every word? Where do you see difficult words?<br>• How can you read with better accuracy?<br>• Read the sentence again. Make sure you read carefully and do not miss any words. |
|---|---|

# Reread for Fluency

**Routine** Paired Reading

1. **Select a Passage** For *The Man Who Invented Basketball,* use p. 36.

2. **Reading 1** Students read the entire page, switching readers at the end of the second paragraph.

3. **Reading 2** Partners reread p. 36 of *The Man Who Invented Basketball.* This time the other student begins.

4. **Reread** For optimal fluency, have partners continue to read three or four times.

5. **Corrective Feedback** Listen as students read. Provide feedback about their accuracy and encourage them to ask questions about unfamiliar words.

Routines Flip Chart

# Research and Study Skills

## Dictionary

**TEACH** Ask students what kinds of information they might look up in a dictionary. Students may mention word meanings, syllabication, or pronunciation. Explain to students that they can find print dictionaries in libraries and electronic dictionaries on the Internet or on CD-ROMs in classroom computers. Display a print dictionary and use it to review these concepts:

- Each word defined in a dictionary is called an entry word.
- The **entry words** in a dictionary are organized in alphabetical order so you can quickly and easily find each one.
- The **guide words,** or the two words at the top of every dictionary page, tell the first and last words on that page. You can use your knowledge of alphabetical order to tell which guide words occur before and after the word you are seeking.
- A **pronunciation key** on every spread shows how to say words.
- The parts of an entry might include the word's syllabication and pronunciation, its part of speech or how to use it in a sentence, its definition, and a phrase or sentence showing how to use it in context.

Provide groups with dictionaries. Have groups use the dictionaries to locate the entry words, guide words, and pronunciation key.

**GUIDE PRACTICE** Discuss these questions:

How do you know on which page the word you are looking for will fall? (Look at the guide words at the top of each page and find the two that occur before and after the word for which you are looking.)

Why might the entry words be boldfaced? (to make it easier to tell them apart from their definitions and the other information contained in each entry)

Have students model how they would look up the meaning, syllabication, and pronunciation of an unknown word in the dictionary.

**ON THEIR OWN** Have students review the instructions and complete p. 255 of the *Reader's and Writer's Notebook.*

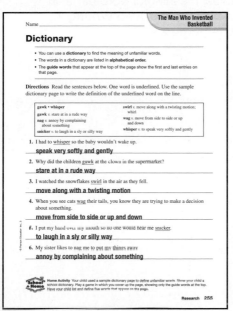

Reader's and Writer's Notebook, p. 255

**Professional Development: What ELL Experts Say about Think-Alouds** "Think-alouds can be particularly informative when used with second-language students. Through this type of dialogue, the teacher can discover not only the types of challenges that students encounter with the text, but also how they deal with such challenges." —Dr. Georgia Earnest García

 **Common Core State Standards**

**Writing 8.** Recall information from experiences or gather information from print and digital sources; take brief notes on sources and sort evidence into provided categories. **Language 1.a.** Explain the function of nouns, pronouns, verbs, adjectives, and adverbs in general and their functions in particular sentences. **Language 2.f.** Use spelling patterns and generalizations (e.g., word families, position-based spellings, syllable patterns, ending rules, meaningful word parts) in writing words. **Also Writing 7., Language 2.e.**

# Research and Inquiry

## Step 3 Analyze Information

**TEACH** Have students follow their research plans to collect information from multiple sources of written information, including reference texts. Tell students that today they will analyze their findings and may have to get more information or change the focus of their original inquiry question.

**Think Aloud** **MODEL** I thought that I had all the information I needed about David Beckham. But when I look at my notes I see that I can't answer my inquiry question *Does that player have a special talent that makes him or her a great player?* I will ask the librarian to help me find out more about David Beckham's talent.

**GUIDE PRACTICE** Remind students that if they have difficulty improving their focus they can ask their reference librarian for guidance. Remind students what they have just learned about time lines. Have students begin a time line about the subject of their biography.

**ON THEIR OWN** Have students evaluate the research they have done so far. Have them determine whether they have enough information to write their biography, and whether they have found enough information to answer their inquiry questions.

# Conventions

## Singular and Plural Pronouns

**REVIEW** Remember, pronouns take the place of nouns. Singular pronouns take the place of singular nouns, and plural pronouns take the place of plural nouns. *You* can be used as either a singular or a plural pronoun. We can use pronouns to avoid repeating a noun. This is one way to make our writing and speaking less wordy.

**CONNECT TO ORAL LANGUAGE** Have the class complete these sentence frames orally.

> The boys can fly.
>
> _____ can fly. (They)
>
> The plane got ready for takeoff.
>
> _____ got ready for takeoff. (It)

**ON THEIR OWN** For additional support, use *Let's Practice It!* p. 222 on the *Teacher Resources DVD-ROM.*

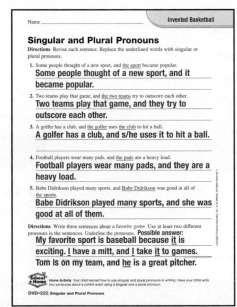

Let's Practice It! TR DVD•222

# Spelling

## Irregular Plurals

**FREQUENTLY MISSPELLED WORDS** The words *clothes* and *want* are often misspelled because the spelling and pronunciation don't quite match. You must memorize these spellings. Have students practice writing the words *clothes* and *want* by completing the following sentences.

> 1. I _____ a new dress. (want)
>
> 2. His _____ were blue. (clothes)
>
> 3. I have to put on my _____. (clothes)
>
> 4. She does not _____ to go for a walk. (want)

**ON THEIR OWN** For additional practice, use *Reader's and Writer's Notebook,* p. 256.

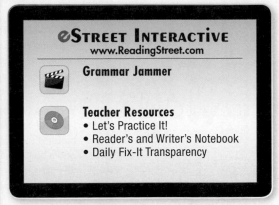

## eStreet Interactive
www.ReadingStreet.com

**Grammar Jammer**

**Teacher Resources**
- Let's Practice It!
- Reader's and Writer's Notebook
- Daily Fix-It Transparency

## Access for All

 **Strategic Intervention**

Have students write ten nouns on index cards, including at least three spelling words. On the other side of each card, have students write the pronouns that can replace the nouns in sentences. Have students work in pairs to quiz each other using the cards.

## Daily Fix-It

5. Childen doesn't have wings, but birds do. *(Children; don't)*

6. Peeple move around with their feets. *(People; feet)*

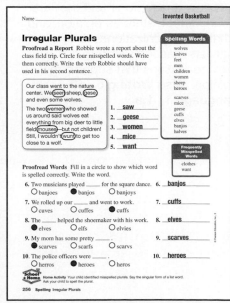

Reader's and Writer's Notebook, p. 256

*The Man Who Invented Basketball* **43e**

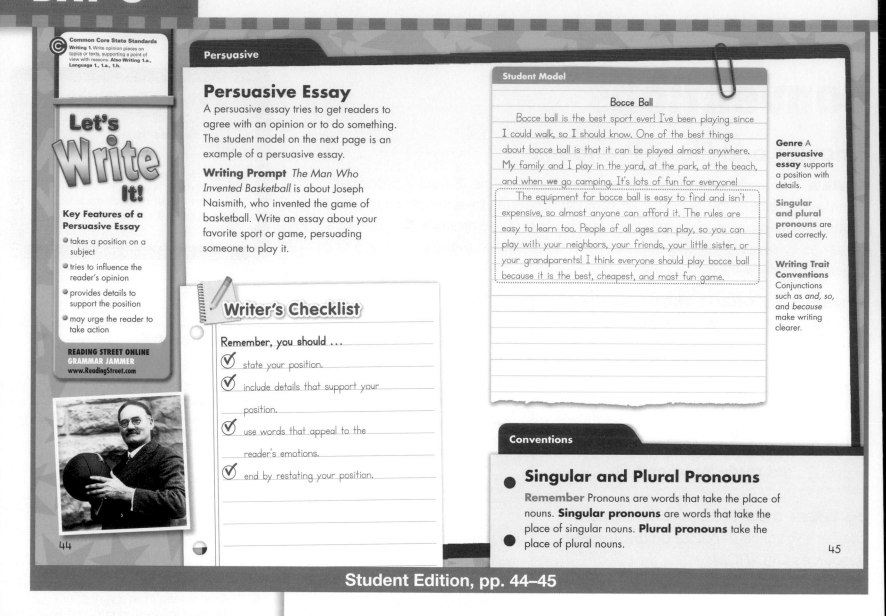

Common Core State Standards
Writing 1. Write opinion pieces on topics or texts, supporting a point of view with reasons. Also Writing 1.a., Language 1., 1.a., 1.h.

## Let's Write it!

**Key Features of a Persuasive Essay**

- takes a position on a subject
- tries to influence the reader's opinion
- provides details to support the position
- may urge the reader to take action

**READING STREET ONLINE**
**GRAMMAR JAMMER**
www.ReadingStreet.com

**Persuasive**

### Persuasive Essay

A persuasive essay tries to get readers to agree with an opinion or to do something. The student model on the next page is an example of a persuasive essay.

**Writing Prompt** *The Man Who Invented Basketball* is about Joseph Naismith, who invented the game of basketball. Write an essay about your favorite sport or game, persuading someone to play it.

### Writer's Checklist

Remember, you should . . .

- ☑ state your position.
- ☑ include details that support your position.
- ☑ use words that appeal to the reader's emotions.
- ☑ end by restating your position.

**Student Model**

#### Bocce Ball

Bocce ball is the best sport ever! I've been playing since I could walk, so I should know. One of the best things about bocce ball is that it can be played almost anywhere. My family and I play in the yard, at the park, at the beach, and when we go camping. It's lots of fun for everyone!

The equipment for bocce ball is easy to find and isn't expensive, so almost anyone can afford it. The rules are easy to learn too. People of all ages can play, so you can play with your neighbors, your friends, your little sister, or your grandparents! I think everyone should play bocce ball because it is the best, cheapest, and most fun game.

**Genre** A **persuasive essay** supports a position with details.

**Singular and plural pronouns** are used correctly.

**Writing Trait Conventions** Conjunctions such as *and, so,* and *because* make writing clearer.

**Conventions**

### Singular and Plural Pronouns

**Remember** Pronouns are words that take the place of nouns. **Singular pronouns** are words that take the place of singular nouns. **Plural pronouns** take the place of plural nouns.

44      45

**Student Edition, pp. 44–45**

## Common Core State Standards

**Writing 1.** Write opinion pieces on topics or texts, supporting a point of view with reasons. **Writing 1.a.** Introduce the topic or text they are writing about, state an opinion, and create an organizational structure that lists reasons. **Writing 1.b.** Provide reasons that support the opinion. **Also Writing 5., 10., Language 1., 1.a.**

## Let's Write It!...

**WRITE A PERSUASIVE TEXT** Use pp. 44–45 in the Student Edition. Direct students to read the key features of a persuasive text, which appear on p. 44. Remind students that they can refer to the information in the Writer's Checklist as they write their own persuasive essays.

Read the student model on p. 45. Point out the key features of a persuasive text in the model.

**CONNECT TO CONVENTIONS** Remind students that singular nouns refer to only one person, place, or thing, so they are replaced with singular pronouns. Plural nouns refer to more than one person, place, or thing, so they are replaced by plural pronouns. Point out the correct use of singular and plural pronouns in the model.

# Writing

## Persuasive Text

### Writer's Craft: Persuasive Elements

**DISPLAY RUBRIC** Display Scoring Rubric 16 from the *Teacher Resources DVD-ROM* and go over the criteria for each trait below each score. Then, using the model in the Student Edition, have student volunteers explain why the model should score a 4 for one of the traits. If a student says that the model should score below 4 for a particular trait, the student should offer support for that response. Remind students that this is the rubric that will be used to evaluate the persuasive text they write.

### Scoring Rubric — Persuasive Text

| | 4 | 3 | 2 | 1 |
|---|---|---|---|---|
| **Focus/Ideas** | Clear statement and support of author's purpose | Mostly clear statement and support of author's purpose | Somewhat clear statement and support of author's purpose | Unclear statement and support of author's purpose |
| **Organization** | Contains clear main idea and details | Contains mostly clear main idea and some details | Main idea somewhat unclear; few details | Unclear main idea; no supporting details |
| **Voice** | Persuasive and knowledgeable | Somewhat persuasive; somewhat knowledgeable | Tries to be persuasive; rarely knowledgeable | Not persuasive; not knowledgeable |
| **Word Choice** | Uses persuasive language | Uses some persuasive language | Uses little persuasive language | Uses no persuasive language |
| **Sentences** | Clear and complete | Mostly clear and complete | Somewhat clear and complete | Unclear and incomplete |
| **Conventions** | Few to no errors in use of singular and plural pronouns | Moderate errors in use of singular and plural pronouns | Several errors in use of singular and plural pronouns | Consistently incorrect use of singular and plural pronouns |

**T-CHART** Have students refer to the T-charts they worked on yesterday. If their charts are not complete, allow additional time for students to finish. Have students work in pairs if they are struggling to complete their charts.

**WRITE** You will be using your charts to write a first draft of your text. While you are writing this draft, don't worry about spelling or grammar. Just put your ideas on paper. You will have a chance later to revise your text.

## Access for All

 **Strategic Intervention**

Have students use a main idea and details chart to analyze the student model.

### ELL

**Connect to Conventions** Give students extra practice with pronouns by having them list nouns they might use in their persuasive texts, such as *team(s), player(s), rules, ball,* or *bat.* Then have them practice replacing these nouns with pronouns in simple sentences. If students use the singular pronoun *he* or *she* to replace a singular noun that names an inanimate object, then say the sentence with the pronoun *it* and have students repeat the sentence after you several times.

## Bridge to Common Core

### RANGE OF WRITING

As students progress through the writing project, they routinely write for a range of tasks, purposes, and audiences. In this lesson, students will focus on writing elements of a persuasive essay, including logical and emotional appeals.

# Writing (Zoom in on ©)

## Persuasive Text

### Mini-Lesson | Logical and Emotional Appeals

■ **Introduce** Today students will focus on writing details that include logical and emotional appeals. Discuss the difference between logical and emotional appeals. A logical appeal gives readers logical reasons or evidence to get them to try the game or sport. For example, playing tennis will help you learn to react quickly. An emotional appeal gives readers emotional reasons to try the game or sport. For example, you'll love hearing people cheer for you. The details you choose to support your main idea should help persuade readers to try your favorite sport or game.

> **A Game of Strategy**
>
> Chess is a game that everyone should learn. It takes skill and strategy. If you are patient enough to learn the rules, you will find it can be exciting and fun.
>
> Chess is good exercise for your brain. Chess is challenging. Each piece on a chessboard can only move a certain way. You have to remember how each piece moves. Also, you have to think about what the other player might do with his or her pieces.
>
> You feel good when you win a game of chess. To win, you play until your opponent's king can't make no moves without being captured. This is called checkmate. You feel proud when you win after a difficult game.
>
> Chess is never boring. Chess can be a quiet game, or it can be a fast game. Some people play a kind of chess called "fast chess," where each player has a short amount of time to make its moves.
>
> Unit 4 The Man Who Invented Basketball    Writing: Model **16A**

Writing Transparency 16A, TR DVD

■ Explain to students that they will refer to their main idea and details charts and other information they have gathered to provide material for their drafts. Students can use their main idea or purpose as the first sentence of their essay. Details should include logical and emotional appeals.

■ Display the Drafting Tips.

### Drafting Tips
✔ Start by looking at your T-chart.

✔ Make sure your draft includes a clear statement of purpose.

✔ Make sure the supporting details or evidence include both logical and emotional appeals.

✔ Don't worry about grammar and mechanics when drafting. You will concentrate on these things during the editing stage.

e**STREET INTERACTIVE**
www.ReadingStreet.com

**Teacher Resources**
• Writing Transparency

**Think Aloud**

**MODEL** I am going to look at my first draft to see whether I have main ideas and supporting details. I will underline each main idea once and the supporting details twice.

Display Transparency 16A. Help students identify the main idea and details of each paragraph of *A Game of Strategy.* Then have students begin their drafts. Have students reread the final paragraph to identify the conclusion about the author's thoughts on the game of chess.

## Routine | Quick Write for Fluency | Team Talk

1. **Talk** Have pairs talk about a time they tried a new game or sport.

2. **Write** Have students write a short paragraph about the experience.

3. **Share** Have each student share his or her paragraph with another student.

Routines Flip Chart

### Access for All

**A** Advanced

Have students make a list of adjectives that describe their sport or game. Then have them rank each adjective according to emotional appeal using a scale of 1 to 10.

# Wrap Up Your Day!

✔ **Content Knowledge** Have students discuss what they learned about the talents James Naismith used to invent basketball.

✔ **Text-Based Comprehension** *What generalizations have you made about why basketball became popular?* Encourage students to cite some examples from the text.

**Preview DAY 4**

Tell students that tomorrow they will read about the life of a famous baseball player.

*The Man Who Invented Basketball* **45c**

## Common Core State Standards

**Speaking/Listening 1.** Engage effectively in a range of collaborative discussions (one-on-one, in groups, and teacher-led) with diverse partners on grade 3 topics and texts, building on others' ideas and expressing their own clearly. **Speaking/Listening 1.c.** Ask questions to check understanding of information presented, stay on topic, and link their comments to the remarks of others. **Also Language 5.b., 6.**

# Content Knowledge

## Talents

**EXPAND THE CONCEPT** Remind students of the weekly concept question, *How do talents make someone unique?* Have students discuss different talents and the ways in which they can make someone unique.

## Build Oral Language

**Team Talk** **TALK ABOUT SENTENCES AND WORDS** Ask students to reread this sentence from Student Edition p. 36.

*Two teams of men dragged themselves onto the gym floor, grumbling.*

- What could the author have written instead of *dragged themselves?* (walked slowly without interest)

- What does *grumbling* mean? (complaining in a quiet, angry way) What are some synonyms for the word *grumbling? (muttering, complaining, moaning)*

- What kind of mood is the author setting by describing the way the men walked onto the gym floor? (The author sets a mood that lacks energy. He is making it clear that the men did not want to play the new game, and that they wanted everyone to know how they felt.)

- Imagine the men were excited to try the new game. How can we change the sentence to give it a different meaning? Have students work in pairs to rewrite the sentence so that it conveys a more energetic, positive mood. (Two teams of men bounded onto the gym floor, cheering.)

# Build Oral Vocabulary

## Amazing Words    Robust Vocabulary Routine

1. **Introduce** Write the Amazing Word *succeed* on the board. Have students say it with you. James Naismith *succeeded* in inventing a new sport. He also *succeeded* in becoming a doctor. Have students determine a definition of *succeed*. (*Succeed* means "to turn out well or to reach a goal.")

2. **Demonstrate** Have students answer questions to demonstrate understanding. Did James Naismith *succeed* at school when he was young? **(no)** Did James Naismith *succeed* in finding a wife? **(yes)** How does a team *succeed* in a game of basketball? **(It scores the most points.)**

3. **Apply** Have students apply their understanding. When a person *succeeds* in finishing high school, what happens? **(He or she graduates.)** When a person *succeeds* in winning a race, what does that mean? **(The person came in first.)** When someone *succeeds* in third grade, into which grade does he or she go next? **(He or she goes into fourth grade.)**

4. **Display the Word** Point out that the first *c* in *succeed* is pronounced /k/ and that the second one is pronounced /s/. Run your hand under the syllables *suc-ceed* and have students say the word.

See p. OV•1 to teach *rise* and *verge*.

Routines Flip Chart

**ADD TO THE CONCEPT MAP** Discuss the Amazing Words *necessary* and *result*. Add these and other concept-related words to the concept map. Use the following questions to develop students' understanding of the concept.

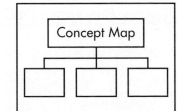

Concept Map

- It was *necessary* for James Naismith to have a good imagination to invent basketball. When is it *necessary* for you to use your imagination?

- James Naismith used his imagination, and the *result* was that he thought up a new sport. If you work hard at a talent that you possess, what might be the *result*?

## Amazing Words

| | |
|---|---|
| mock | necessary |
| idle | result |
| potential | succeed |
| ecstatic | rise |
| thrill | verge |
| audition | |

## Strategy Response Log

Have students complete p. 22 in the *Reader's and Writer's Notebook.* Then have students work in pairs to summarize *The Man Who Invented Basketball.*

**Produce Oral Language** Use the Day 4 instruction on ELL Poster 16 to extend and enrich language.

*The Man Who Invented Basketball*    **46b**

**©** **Common Core State Standards**

**Foundational Skills 3.** Know and apply grade-level phonics and word analysis skills in decoding words. **Foundational Skills 3.d.** Read grade-appropriate irregularly spelled words. **Language 2.e.** Use conventional spelling for high-frequency and other studied words and for adding suffixes to base words (e.g., *sitting, smiled, cries, happiness*). **Also Foundational Skills 3.c.**

Name_____  **Invented Basketball**

**Consonant Patterns *wr, kn, st, mb, gn***

Directions Read each word and identify the consonant pattern with the silent letter. On the lines, write two more words that have the same silent consonant pattern. Underline the consonant pattern in each word you write.
**Sample answers are given.**

1. write    __wring__    __wrap__
2. knight    __knee__    __knowledge__
3. listen    __moisten__    __fasten__
4. thumb    __comb__    __limb__
5. gnaw    __sign__    __design__

Directions Add **wr, kn, st, mb,** or **gn** to complete each word. Use the definitions for help.

6. a ring of flowers or leaves twisted together    __wr__eath
7. a round handle that you turn to let yourself in    door__kn__ob
8. a skilled worker who fixes pipes, sinks, and so on    plu__mb__er
9. to grind together    __gn__ash
10. a plant with purple flowers and a prickly stalk and leaves    thi__st__le
11. to make a musical sound by blowing air through the lips    whi__st__le
12. rough and twisted; bent out of shape    __gn__arled
13. a tiny piece of bread or cake broken from a slice    cru__mb__
14. a fold on a surface that is usually flat    __wr__inkle
15. to hit something with a closed fist    __kn__ock

Home Activity Your child wrote words with consonant patterns wr (write), kn (knight), st (listen), mb (thumb), and gn (gnaw). Play a game in which you and your child each try to write three more words for each consonant pattern. Whoever has more correctly spelled words with the right letter combinations is the winner.

Consonant Patterns wr, kn, st, mb, gn DVD•223

Let's Practice It! TR DVD•223

# Phonics

## Review Consonant Patterns *wr, kn, st, mb, gn*

**REVIEW SOUND-SPELLINGS** Review last week's phonics skill: consonant patterns *wr, kn, st, mb,* and *gn.* Write these words: *write, knight, listen, thumb, gnaw, know, comb, gnats, wrote, gnu, knock,* and *lamb.* We studied the silent consonants in *wr, kn, st, mb, gn.* Let's review by looking at these words. Have students identify the word with the sound /s/. *(listen)* Which consonants stand for /s/ in *listen? (st)* Continue in the same way for the consonants that stand for the following sounds: /n/ *(knight, gnaw, know, gnats, gnu, knock);* /r/ *(wrote);* /m/ *(thumb, comb, lamb).* Tell students that the silent consonants *k* and *g* stand for /n/ when they precede the letter *n.*

> **Corrective feedback** | If students are unable to answer the questions about consonant patterns *wr, kn, st, mb,* and *gn,* refer them to *Sound-Spelling Cards* 40, 42, 43, 48, and 53.

**GUIDE PRACTICE** Display a five-column chart with the headings *wr, kn, st, mb,* and *gn.* Write the following words and help students sort them into the correct columns on the chart: *know, castle, numb, sign, gnats, wrap, knit, glisten, climb, wrist.* Then have students read the words. Ask volunteers to underline the silent consonant in each word.

| wr | kn | st | mb | gn |
|----|----|----|----|----|
| wrap | know | castle | numb | sign |
| wrist | knit | glisten | climb | gnats |

**ON THEIR OWN** For additional practice, use *Let's Practice It!* p. 223 on the *Teacher Resources DVD-ROM.*

# Fluent Word Reading

## Spiral Review

**READ WORDS IN ISOLATION** Display these words. Tell students that they can already decode some words on this list. Explain that they should know other words because they appear often in reading.

Have students read the list three or four times until they can read at the rate of two to three seconds per word.

### Word Reading

| | | | | |
|---|---|---|---|---|
| untrue | replace | dependable | fearless | door |
| sadly | stuck | mistake | disagree | one |
| city | cheerful | echoed | bridge | your |
| the | sensible | have | what | darkness |

**Corrective feedback**

**If...** students have difficulty reading whole words,

**then...** have them use sound-by-sound blending for decodable words or chunking for words that have word parts, or have them say and spell high-frequency words.

**If...** students cannot read fluently at a rate of two to three seconds per word,

**then...** have pairs practice the list until they can read it fluently.

**eStreet Interactive**
www.ReadingStreet.com

**Teacher Resources**
• Let's Practice It!

**Interactive Sound-Spelling Cards**

## Access for All

 **Strategic Intervention**

To assist students having difficulty with silent consonant patterns, have students use crayons to write the words from the review chart on paper. Have students write all letters in each word in black, except for the silent consonant. Have students write the silent consonant in white. Then have students practice reading the words to actually see which consonant in each word should not be pronounced.

## Spiral Review

Review these activities:

• previously taught high-frequency words *the, have, what, door, one, your.*

• prefixes *un-, re-, mis-, dis-;* spellings of *c/s/, ck/k/, ch/k/, dge/j/;* suffixes *-ly, -ful, -ness, -less, -able, -ible*

**Fluent Word Reading** Have students listen to a more fluent reader say the words. Then have them repeat the words.

*The Man Who Invented Basketball* **46d**

 **Common Core State Standards**

**Foundational Skills 3.** Know and apply grade-level phonics and word analysis skills in decoding words. **Foundational Skills 3.d.** Read grade-appropriate irregularly spelled words. **Foundational Skills 4.** Read with sufficient accuracy and fluency to support comprehension. **Also Foundational Skills 4.a., 4.b.**

# Fluent Word Reading

**READ WORDS IN CONTEXT** Display these sentences. Call on individuals to read a sentence. Then randomly point to review words and have students read them. To help you monitor word reading, high-frequency words are underlined and decodable words are italicized.

**MONITOR PROGRESS** Sentence Reading

Your *cheerful* voice *echoed* through the *darkness* and over the bridge.
I have a friend who is *dependable, sensible,* and *fearless.*
The door is *stuck,* so dad will *replace* the hinges.
What one *mistake* did Sara make driving in the city?
I *sadly disagree* with saying things that are *untrue.*

**If...** students are unable to read an underlined high-frequency word,

**then...** read the word for them and spell it, having them echo you.

**If...** students have difficulty reading an italicized decodable word,

**then...** guide them in using sound-by-sound blending or chunking.

# Reread for Fluency

Have students reread the sentences to develop automaticity decoding words.

**Routine** Oral Rereading

1. **Read** Have students read all the sentences orally.

2. **Reread** To achieve optimal fluency, students should reread the sentences three or four times.

3. **Corrective Feedback** Listen as students read. Provide corrective feedback regarding their fluency and decoding.

Routines Flip Chart

# Decodable Passage 16C

If students need help, then...

## Read *Sheep Stampede*

**READ WORDS IN ISOLATION** Have students turn to p. 11 in *Decodable Practice Readers 3.2* and find the first list of words. Each word in this list is an irregular plural. Let's read these words. Be sure that students pronounce each plural word correctly.

**PREVIEW** Have students read the title and preview the story. Tell them that they will read words that are irregular plurals. Make sure that students are monitoring their accuracy when they decode words.

**READ WORDS IN CONTEXT** Chorally read the story along with the students. Have students identify words in the story that are irregular plurals.

**Team Talk** Pair students and have them take turns reading the story aloud to each other. Monitor students as they read to check for proper pronunciation and appropriate pacing.

**eSTREET INTERACTIVE**
www.ReadingStreet.com

**Pearson eText**
• Decodable Reader

## Access for All

**A** Advanced

Have students make a list of the prefixes and suffixes used in the sentences at the top of p. 46e. Have students work with a partner to brainstorm other words that use those same prefixes and suffixes.

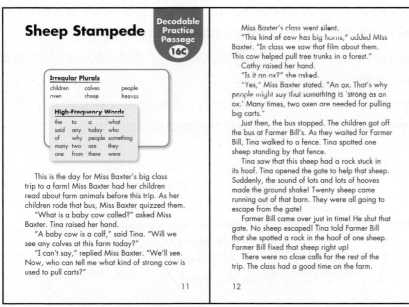

Decodable Practice Passage 16C

# DAY 4

 **Common Core State Standards**

**Informational Text 4.** Determine the meaning of general academic and domain-specific words and phrases in a text relevant to a grade 3 topic or subject area. **Informational Text 6.** Distinguish their own point of view from that of the author of a text.

 **Bridge to Common Core**

**KEY IDEAS AND DETAILS**

As students read and learn about an autobiography, they will analyze how and why individuals, events, and ideas develop and interact over the course of a text. They will determine central ideas or themes of the text, and summarize key supporting details and ideas.

# Social Studies in Reading

## Autobiography

**INTRODUCE** Explain to students that what we read is structured differently, depending on the author's reasons for writing and what kind of information he or she wishes to convey. Different types of texts are called genres. Tell them that autobiography is one type of genre.

**DISCUSS THE GENRE** Discuss with students the difference between biography and autobiography. For example, ask: If I wrote a book about my mother's life, would it be a biography or an autobiography? Why? (biography, because you wrote about her life for her) If you wrote a story about what you did on your summer vacation, would it be a biography or an autobiography? Why? (autobiography, because you wrote about your own life)

**GROUP PRACTICE** On the board, draw a Venn diagram like the one below. Label one side *Biography* and the other *Autobiography.* Have students answer the following questions as you fill in the diagram:

- What do both biographies and autobiographies have in common? (They are both true stories. They are both about real people. They are both stories about a person's life or a special event in a person's life.)

- What is the point of view of a biography? of an autobiography? (third person; first person)

- How can you tell if something is written in the third person or in the first person? (the pronouns *he, she, it, they;* the pronouns *I, we*)

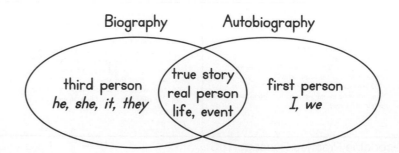

**Team Talk** Have students work in pairs to create a T-chart to discuss and list the pronouns that they would see in an autobiography and a biography. Ask them to share their lists with the class.

**READ** Tell students that they will now read about a story about a famous baseball player that is both a biography and an autobiography. Have the class think about how they will be able to tell which is which.

**eSTREET INTERACTIVE**
www.ReadingStreet.com

**Teacher Resources**
• Graphic Organizer

**ELL**

**Cognates** Point out that both of the genre words have Spanish cognates. The cognate for *biography* is *biografía* and the one for *autobiography* is *autobiografía*.

---

## Day 4  SMALL GROUP TIME • Differentiate Vocabulary, p. SG•1

| **OL** On-Level | **SI** Strategic Intervention | **A** Advanced |
|---|---|---|
| • **Develop** Language Using Amazing Words | • **Review/Discuss** Amazing Words | • **Extend** Amazing Words and Selection Vocabulary |
| • **Read** "My Turn at Bat" | • **Read** "My Turn at Bat" | • **Read** "My Turn at Bat" |
| | | • **Organize** Inquiry Project |

**ELL**

**If...** students need more scaffolding and practice with the **Amazing Words,**
**then...** use the Routine on pp. xxxvi–xxxvii in the *ELL Handbook.*

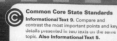

Common Core State Standards
Informational Text 9. Compare and contrast the most important points and key details presented in two texts on the same topic. **Also Informational Text 5.**

## MY TURN AT BAT
### — The Story of My Life —
Ted Williams with John Underwood

**Social Studies in Reading**

### Genre
### Autobiography

● An autobiography is the story of a person's life written by the person who lived it.

● Autobiographies are written in the first person, using *I, me,* and *my.*

● The events in an autobiography are actual events and experiences in a person's life.

● As you read, think about the difference in point of view between the autobiography and the biography sections of "My Turn at Bat."

Baseball great Ted Williams was born in 1918. His mother, May Venzer, was a Salvation Army worker. She was part Mexican and part French. His father, Samuel Stuart Williams, was a soldier, U.S. marshal, and photographer. He was part Welsh and part Irish.

Their son, Ted, came to have several nicknames, including "Teddy Ballgame," "The Splendid Splinter," and "The Kid."

**Ted recalls his childhood:**

Wilber Wiley was my first real boyhood pal. Wilber had a job delivering the *Evening Tribute,* and when he'd get through about an hour before dark, we'd go to the playground, just the two of us, and hit, hit, hit, and throw, throw, throw.

46

The playground director was a man named Rodney Luscomb, and Rod Luscomb was my first real hero. I know when I walked up to the rostrum in Cooperstown the day they inducted me into the Hall of Fame Rod Luscomb was one of the people on my mind, one of the people I felt made it possible. That should tell you something about how much a coach can mean to a kid.

I suppose the first strong influence I had to continue in baseball, to make it my life's work, was my coach at Herbert Hoover High in San Diego, a wonderful man named Wos Caldwell.

I'll never forget one day I hit a ball they say went 450 feet, between the right and center fielders. I fell down rounding third—a big skinny kid, all arms and legs—and I got thrown out at home plate.

San Diego was a ballplayer's town, year-round, and by the time I was a pitcher at Herbert Hoover High I was hooked. As a pitcher-outfielder, I batted .583 and .406 my last years in high school, .430 for three years.

**Let's Think About...**
What words indicate that this section is written in the first person point of view? **Autobiography**

❶

47

**Student Edition, pp. 46–47**

## © Common Core State Standards

**Informational Text 1.** Ask and answer questions to demonstrate understanding of a text, referring explicitly to the text as the basis for the answers. **Informational Text 9.** Compare and contrast the most important points and key details presented in two texts on the same topic. **Informational Text 10.** By the end of the year, read and comprehend informational texts, including history/social studies, science, and technical texts, at the high end of the grades 2–3 text complexity band independently and proficiently. **Also Informational Text 6.**

# Access Text ©

**TEACH Autobiography** Explain that students will be learning the difference between a biography and an autobiography. Have them preview pp. 46–47 of "My Turn at Bat." Remind students that the selection they are reading is an autobiography with several biographical sections. Ask: How can you tell when parts of the selection are biographical? (The word *I* indicates that it is an autobiography. The words *he* and *his* hint that part of it may be a biography.)

**Corrective feedback** | **If...** students are unable to distinguish between the different points of view in the selection, **then...** use the model to help students recognize the difference.

**Think Aloud**

**MODEL** The box at the beginning of the story has someone explaining about Ted Williams's life. It uses the pronouns *he* and *his.* These are not Ted Williams's own words. The next paragraph uses the pronoun *my.* This paragraph is in Ted Williams's own words.

**ON THEIR OWN** Have student pairs write sentences in the first and third person. One sentence should be about the student and the other about the student's partner.

# Close Reading ©

**ANALYSIS** How would you describe what parts of his childhood Ted thinks are most important to recall to tell about his life? (He seems to be talking about the people who had the biggest effect on him and how these people contributed to his later success at baseball.)

**EVALUATION • TEXT EVIDENCE** After reading p. 47, what is a generalization you can make about the effect his coaches had on Ted? (All of his coaches had a positive influence on Ted and helped him achieve great things by inspiring him to work hard and play baseball well.)

# Genre

**LET'S THINK ABOUT...** As you read "My Turn at Bat," use Let's Think About in the Student Edition to help students focus on the features of an autobiography.

❶ the pronouns *I, my,* and *me*

**Language Production** Review baseball terminology with students to help them understand the selection. Words taught could include *diamond, field, center, plate, home, first, second,* and *third,* among others. Draw a baseball diamond on the board and name the positions for students.

# DAY 4

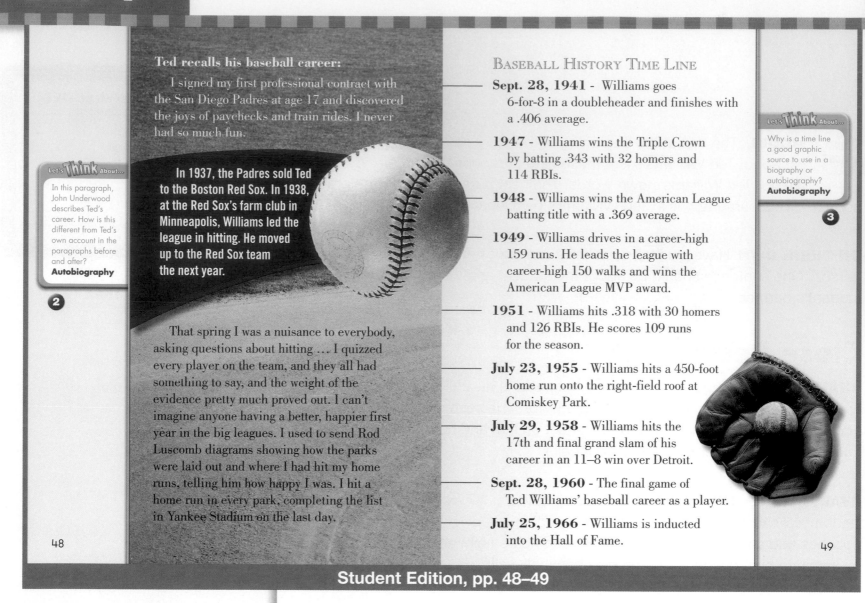

**Ted recalls his baseball career:**

I signed my first professional contract with the San Diego Padres at age 17 and discovered the joys of paychecks and train rides. I never had so much fun.

In 1937, the Padres sold Ted to the Boston Red Sox. In 1938, at the Red Sox's farm club in Minneapolis, Williams led the league in hitting. He moved up to the Red Sox team the next year.

That spring I was a nuisance to everybody, asking questions about hitting ... I quizzed every player on the team, and they all had something to say, and the weight of the evidence pretty much proved out. I can't imagine anyone having a better, happier first year in the big leagues. I used to send Rod Luscomb diagrams showing how the parks were laid out and where I had hit my home runs, telling him how happy I was. I hit a home run in every park, completing the list in Yankee Stadium on the last day.

**Let's Think About...**

In this paragraph, John Underwood describes Ted's career. How is this different from Ted's own account in the paragraphs before and after?
**Autobiography**

❷

**BASEBALL HISTORY TIME LINE**

**Sept. 28, 1941 -** Williams goes 6-for-8 in a doubleheader and finishes with a .406 average.

**1947 -** Williams wins the Triple Crown by batting .343 with 32 homers and 114 RBIs.

**1948 -** Williams wins the American League batting title with a .369 average.

**1949 -** Williams drives in a career-high 159 runs. He leads the league with career-high 150 walks and wins the American League MVP award.

**1951 -** Williams hits .318 with 30 homers and 126 RBIs. He scores 109 runs for the season.

**July 23, 1955 -** Williams hits a 450-foot home run onto the right-field roof at Comiskey Park.

**July 29, 1958 -** Williams hits the 17th and final grand slam of his career in an 11–8 win over Detroit.

**Sept. 28, 1960 -** The final game of Ted Williams' baseball career as a player.

**July 25, 1966 -** Williams is inducted into the Hall of Fame.

**Let's Think About...**

Why is a time line a good graphic source to use in a biography or autobiography?
**Autobiography**

❸

48  49

**Student Edition, pp. 48–49**

## Ⓒ Common Core State Standards

**Informational Text 1.** Ask and answer questions to demonstrate understanding of a text, referring explicitly to the text as the basis for the answers. **Informational Text 6.** Distinguish their own point of view from that of the author of a text. **Informational Text 7.** Use information gained from illustrations (e.g., maps, photographs) and the words in a text to demonstrate understanding of the text (e.g., where, when, why, and how key events occur). **Also Language 3., Language 4.a.**

# Access Text Ⓒ

**TEACH Autobiography** Have students preview pp. 48–49. Ask: What is the point of view in the first paragraph of p. 48? (It is first person point of view.) Who is the author of a text that is told in the first person point of view? (The author is the subject, or the person who is described as *I* in the text.)

**Corrective feedback**  **If...** students are unable to identify and explain first person point of view, **then...** use the model to help explain it.

**Think Aloud** **MODEL** When I tell you about something that has happened to me, I use the first person point of view. "When I was little I flew in a hot air balloon. It was the most fun I ever had." That is me talking about me. If you told the same story, you might say, "When my teacher was little she rode in a hot air balloon. She really liked it." That is third person point of view.

**ON THEIR OWN** Have students begin their own autobiography by writing two sentences about their own childhood.

# Close Reading ©

**SYNTHESIS** Look through pages 48 and 49 and identify any unfamiliar words. Then see if there are any context clues in the sentence in which a word appears or in the sentences nearby. If not, look up the words in a dictionary. Students may identify the words *nuisance* (p. 48; means "an annoyance or inconvenience") or *doubleheader* (p. 49; means "a sporting event with two games or contests").

**EVALUATION • TEXT EVIDENCE** Does the time line cover all of the events in Ted's life from his birth to his death? If not, which events does it cover, and why might it cover only these? Use evidence from the text to support your answer. (It covers only events from a doubleheader game Ted played in 1941 to his induction into the Baseball Hall of Fame in 1966. The title of the time line is "Baseball History Time Line," so the events included on it cover only important events in Ted's baseball career, not all the important events in his life.)

# Genre

**LET'S THINK ABOUT...** features of an autobiography.

❷ John Underwood writes in the third person and uses the pronoun *he.* Also, this paragraph gives only facts about Ted's life, while the parts Ted writes himself also mention his feelings and opinions about the things that were happening in his life at each moment he discusses.

❸ Biographies and autobiographies talk about the most important events in a person's life, and a time line is a good way to show the main things that happened in a person's life in a visual way.

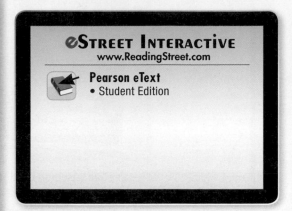

**eSTREET INTERACTIVE**
www.ReadingStreet.com

**Pearson eText**
• Student Edition

## Access for All

**SI** **Strategic Intervention**

If students are having difficulty understanding the different points of view, have them act out sentences written in the different points of view, pointing away from themselves when they are reading a sentence in third person point of view and toward themselves when they are reading a sentence in first person point of view.

**A** **Advanced**

Introduce students to the concept of wide knowledge (omniscience) in third person point of view, or the idea that the narrator knows what all of the characters are thinking and feeling, not just the thoughts and feelings of the main character.

**Practice Pronunciation** Write proper nouns and city names from the story on the board and say them slowly. Have students repeat after you. Then, have students suggest names of other U.S. cities. Write those on the board and have students practice saying them.

In 1941, only his third season in the majors, Williams chased a .400 batting average.

Let's Think About...

How is the point of view in this paragraph different from the point of view in *The Man Who Invented Basketball?* What evidence from the texts supports your answer?

**Autobiography**

❹

Rod Luscomb used to say that in seven years on the playground I never broke a bat hitting a ball incorrectly, that all my bats had the bruises in the same spot, like they were hammered there by a careful carpenter, right on the thick of the hitting surface. That might be an exaggeration, but I believe it is true that when you put in as much time as I did you get results.

A hitter can't just go up there and swing. He's got to think. Listen, when I played I knew the parks, the mounds, the batters' boxes, the backgrounds. I studied the pitchers. I knew what was going on at that plate. It used to kill me to strike out, but when I struck out I knew what it was that got me and what I was going to try to do about it.

50

### Baseball Hall of Fame

A man has to have goals—for a day, for a lifetime—and that was mine, to have people say, "There goes Ted Williams, the greatest hitter who ever lived."

**Ted Williams**

**LF** 1939-1942, 1946-1960
**Class of 1966**

**Theodore Samuel Williams**
**Born:** August 30, 1918, San Diego, CA
**Died:** July 5, 2002, Crystal River, FL
**Bats:** Left  **Throws:** Right

**Played for:** Boston Red Sox
(1939-1942, 1946-1960)
**Elected to Hall of Fame by Baseball Writers:** 1966
282 votes of 302 ballots cast  (93.38%)

**Hitting Stats**

| AVG | G | AB | R | H | HR | RBI | SB | SLG |
|---|---|---|---|---|---|---|---|---|
| .344 | 2292 | 7706 | 1798 | 2654 | 521 | 1839 | 24 | .634 |

Let's Think About...

Using the baseball card on this page, locate facts and details about Ted Williams's life. What other texts might you use to gather information about Ted Williams?

**Autobiography**

❺

Let's Think About...

**Reading Across Texts** How are James Naismith and Ted Williams alike? How are they different?

**Writing Across Texts** Create a Venn diagram to compare and contrast the careers of James Naismith and Ted Williams.

51

**Student Edition, pp. 50–51**

## Common Core State Standards

**Informational Text 1.** Ask and answer questions to demonstrate understanding of a text, referring explicitly to the text as the basis for the answers. **Informational Text 7.** Use information gained from illustrations (e.g., maps, photographs) and the words in a text to demonstrate understanding of the text (e.g., where, when, why, and how key events occur). **Informational Text 9.** Compare and contrast the most important points and key details presented in two texts on the same topic. **Also Informational Text 5., 6.**

# Access Text ©

**TEACH Autobiography** Have students look at the baseball card on p. 51. Ask: In which point of view is the baseball card written? (It is written in third person point of view.) Who is the author of a text that is written in the third person point of view? (someone other than the subject of the text)

**Corrective feedback** | **If...** students are unable to explain third person point of view, **then...** use the model to help explain it.

**MODEL** I think about who is telling the story. I know Ted Williams is not "telling" the baseball card because the pronoun *I* is not used. That means that someone other than Ted Williams wrote the baseball card. So, it is written in the third person point of view.

**ON THEIR OWN** Have students begin a biography of someone they know by writing two sentences about this person, using the third person point of view.

# Close Reading

**ANALYSIS** Is the text to the right of the photo on p. 50 a statement of fact or opinion? How can you tell? (It is a statement of fact because it can be looked up and proved true that Williams chased a .400 batting average in 1941.)

**SYNTHESIS** Summarize the information on Ted Williams's baseball card. (Ted Williams played for the Boston Red Sox. He got voted into the Hall of Fame in 1966.)

# Genre

**LET'S THINK ABOUT...** features of an autobiography.

④ The point of view in this paragraph is the first person point of view. The point of view of *The Man Who Invented Basketball* is the third person. This story uses pronouns such as *I* and *my*. *The Man Who Invented Basketball* uses pronouns such as *he* and *his.*

⑤ Web sites, encyclopedias, biographies

# Reading and Writing Across Texts

Have students make a T-chart listing details about both James Naismith and Ted Williams. Tell them to use the chart to answer the question. Next, have students brainstorm how the careers of James Naismith and Ted Williams were alike and different. Encourage students to use the time lines on p. 41 and p. 49 to answer the question.

**eStreet Interactive**
www.ReadingStreet.com

**Pearson eText**
• Student Edition

**Connect to Social Studies**

**Baseball Begins** The first recorded official baseball game was played in Hoboken, New Jersey, in 1846. The two teams were the Knickerbocker Base Ball Club of New York and the New York Nine. The first professional team played in 1869. The first professional baseball league was founded in 1871.

**Let's Learn It!**

READING STREET ONLINE
ONLINE STUDENT EDITION
www.ReadingStreet.com

## Vocabulary

### Unfamiliar Words

**Context Clues** Use context clues to find the meanings of unfamiliar words while you are reading. The words or sentences around the unfamiliar word may provide its meaning.

**Practice It!** Choose a book from your classroom library or a book you are reading from your school library. Write down any unfamiliar words that you find. Use context clues to determine the meanings of the words. Check the dictionary to see if you are correct.

## Fluency

### Accuracy

It is important to read with accuracy so you can understand the text. Reading each word as it is written on the page makes this possible. Listen to yourself as you read to make sure what you are reading makes sense.

**Practice It!** With a partner, practice reading aloud page 31 from *The Man Who Invented Basketball*. Have your partner make a list of any words you read incorrectly. Look back at each word. Reread the page again. Did your accuracy improve?

## Listening and Speaking

Work productively with others and acknowledge their contributions.

### Presentation

The purpose of oral reports about a topic is to inform. Reports can also be used to entertain, to persuade, or to express an opinion.

**Practice It!** With a group, prepare an oral report on how James Naismith invented basketball. Use the information from the story and outside research. When you present, use photos, sounds, or props to make your report more interesting.

### Tips

**Listeners ...**
- Listen attentively and respond to the topic.
- Think about how visual and sound aids influence the message.

**Speakers ...**
- Determine your purpose for speaking.
- Speak coherently about the topic.

**Teamwork ...**
- Give suggestions that build on others' ideas.
- Ask and answer questions with detail.

52

53

**Student Edition, pp. 52–53**

# Fluency

## Accuracy

**GUIDE PRACTICE** Use the Fluency activity as an assessment tool. Make sure the reading passage is at least 200 words in length. As students read, check their accuracy and attention to punctuation cues.

Don't Wait Until Friday

**MONITOR PROGRESS** Check Fluency

**FORMATIVE ASSESSMENT** As students reread, monitor progress toward their individual fluency goals: Current Goal: 95–105 words correct per minute. End-of-Year Goal: 120 words correct per minute.

**If...** students cannot read fluently at a rate of 95–105 words correct per minute,

**then...** have students practice with text at their independent levels.

# Vocabulary Skill

## ⊙ Unfamiliar Words

**TEACH UNFAMILIAR WORDS • CONTEXT CLUES** Write the following sentences containing unfamiliar words on the board.

> Juanita fumbled the basketball, and it slipped out of her hands and fell to the ground.
>
> Harry had to retrieve the basketball when it bounced out of the court.
>
> Ginny defended the basketball when a player from the other team tried to steal it from her.

**GUIDE PRACTICE** Ask students to use the context clues in each sentence to figure out the meaning of each unfamiliar word.

**ON THEIR OWN** Walk around the room as students are reading on their own and check to make sure that they can understand the context clues in their books.

# Listening and Speaking

## Presentation

**TEACH** Tell students that in order for a presentation to be effective, they must speak coherently about the topic under discussion. Tell them that when they do a presentation, they are trying to communicate specific information that they want their audience to understand and remember. Have students use outside research, photos, sounds, or props to make the reports more interesting. Remind students that formal spoken communication is used for a report.

**GUIDE PRACTICE** Remind students to use good eye contact, speaking rate, volume, enunciation, and the conventions of language to communicate the ideas in their reports. Remind students in the audience to listen attentively to speakers and ask relevant questions and make pertinent comments once speakers are done.

**ON THEIR OWN** Have students give their presentations to the class.

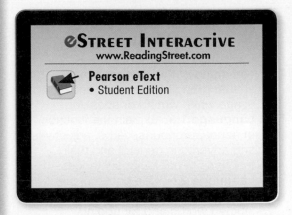

## Presentation

Remind students to use grammatically correct sentences. Tell students that having good posture and using hand gestures and the appropriate facial expressions can also help them communicate during a presentation.

 **Bridge to Common Core**

### PRESENTATION OF KNOWLEDGE/IDEAS

As students present their reports, they should use appropriate phrasing and present their information in an organized fashion so listeners can easily follow along. Students can make strategic use of photos, sounds, props, visual displays and/or graphics to enhance understanding of their presentations.

**Practice Pronunciation** Assist students by modeling the correct pronunciation of the unfamiliar words, having students repeat after you. Pair students with mixed language proficiencies together to practice pronunciation and employ self-correction techniques.

# Research and Inquiry

## Step 4 Synthesize

**TEACH** Have students synthesize their research findings and results. Review how to choose relevant details from a number of sources and organize them logically. Remind students to include the answers to their inquiry questions in their biographies.

**GUIDE PRACTICE** Have students use a word processing program or index cards to prepare for their presentations on Day 5. If students are using index cards, remind them to number the cards so that they can tell what order the cards should be in. If students are using a word processing program, remind them to use a large enough font so that they can read it while standing in front of the class.

**ON THEIR OWN** Have students organize and combine the information they have gathered into a biography. Remind them to complete their presentation notes and any time lines they have started.

# Conventions

## Singular and Plural Pronouns

**TEST PRACTICE** Tell students that important assessments often include questions about singular and plural pronouns. Remind students that a singular pronoun takes the place of a singular noun, while a plural pronoun takes the place of a plural noun.

**ON THEIR OWN** For additional practice, use *Reader's and Writer's Notebook,* p. 257.

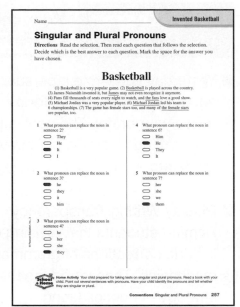

Reader's and Writer's Notebook, p. 257

# Spelling

## Irregular Plurals

**PRACTICE SPELLING STRATEGY**
Remind students of the common spelling strategies to spell new words, such as segmenting words by letter sound, syllables, and word parts. Have them apply these strategies during the following activity. Supply pairs of students with index cards on which the spelling words have been written. Have one student read a word while the other writes it. Then have students switch roles. Have them use the cards to check their spelling and correct any misspelled words.

**ON THEIR OWN** For additional practice, use *Let's Practice It!* p. 224 on the *Teacher Resources DVD-ROM.*

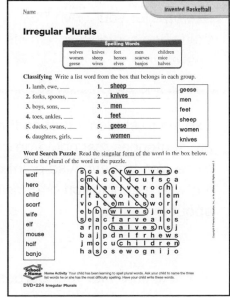

Let's Practice It! TR DVD•224

## eSTREET INTERACTIVE
www.ReadingStreet.com

**Teacher Resources**
• Reader's and Writer's Notebook
• Let's Practice It!
• Daily Fix-It Transparency

## Daily Fix-It

**7.** Do the boys classmates disslike him? *(boy's, dislike)*

**8.** The kids think he is strang, but he like him. *(strange; but they)*

## ⓒ Bridge to Common Core

### CONVENTIONS OF STANDARD ENGLISH

As students identify, form, and use singular and plural pronouns and irregular pronouns, they are demonstrating command of the conventions of standard English. Your guidance will help them use correct grammar, usage, and spelling to convey meaning when they speak and write.

## Common Core State Standards

**Writing 1.c.** Use linking words and phrases (e.g., *because, therefore, since, for example*) to connect opinion and reasons. **Writing 3.d.** Provide a sense of closure. **Writing 5.** With guidance and support from peers and adults, develop and strengthen writing as needed by planning, revising, and editing. **Language 1.h.** Use coordinating and subordinating conjunctions. **Also Writing 1., 10.**

## Write Guy *by Jeff Anderson*

### Adding Without Leaving Readers Hanging

A student might add worthwhile information to his or her writing, but often write sentence fragments. I like to encourage the writer by welcoming the idea and, at the same time, helping students form solid sentences or add dependent parts in order to communicate.

# Writing

## Persuasive Text

| Mini-Lesson | Revise: Consolidating with Conjunctions |

■ Yesterday you wrote a persuasive text about a sport or game. Today you will revise your drafts. The goal is to make your writing clearer, more interesting, and more informative.

■ Display Writing Transparency 16B. Remind students that revising does not include corrections of grammar and mechanics. Then introduce the revising strategy of consolidating.

■ I can see that the first two sentences say, "Chess is good exercise for your brain. Chess is challenging." These two sentences show a cause-and-effect relationship. The cause is "chess is challenging." The effect is "chess is good exercise for your brain." So, I can use the conjunction *because* to combine these two sentences. "Chess is good exercise for your brain because it is challenging."

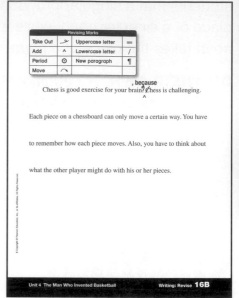

Writing Transparency 16B, TR DVD

Explain to students that as they revise, they should ask themselves if there are sentences that could be combined with conjunctions such as *because, since, yet,* or *until.* Also point out to students that they should end their writing with a conclusion or concluding statement to emphasize their opinion about the game.

### Revising Tips

✔ Make sure that your purpose is clearly stated.

✔ Be sure that you give reasons someone should play the game or sport you chose.

✔ Use conjunctions to combine sentences.

**PEER CONFERENCING • PEER REVISION** Have students switch papers with a partner. As partners read, they should try to complete the sentence *The purpose of this essay is _____.* Then they should list the details that support the purpose. Refer to *First Stop* for more information about peer conferencing.

Have students revise their drafts using the revising strategy and feedback from their partner. Remind students to reread the key features of a persuasive text before they revise.

> **Corrective feedback** | Circulate around the room to monitor students and confer with students as they revise. Remind students who are correcting spelling and capitalization errors that they will have time to edit tomorrow. They should be working on content and flow today.

## Routine    Quick Write for Fluency    Team Talk

1. **Talk** Students talk about what makes their sport or game unique.

2. **Write** Students write two or three sentences about what makes their sport or game unique.

3. **Share** Students share what they wrote with a partner.

Routines Flip Chart

**e STREET INTERACTIVE**
www.ReadingStreet.com

**Teacher Resources**
• Writing Transparency

### Access for All

**SI** Strategic Intervention

If students are having trouble using conjunctions, give them examples of sentences that use *and* and *but* as well as *because, since, yet,* and *until.*

**ELL**

**Support Revising** Have students write conjunctions on self-stick notes and place them at points in their text where they will help with consolidation. Once students have decided which conjunctions to use and where to use them, have them read their texts aloud again.

# Wrap Up Your Day!

✔ **Content Knowledge** *What did you learn about Ted Williams's talents?*

✔ **Oral Vocabulary** Monitor students' oral vocabulary as they respond: *How can talents help a person achieve great things?*

✔ **Text Features** Ask students how the time line and sidebars help them understand the selection.

**Preview DAY 5**

Remind students to think about how people can use their talents to do unique things.

### Materials

- Student Edition
- Weekly Test
- Reader's and Writer's Notebook

## © Bridge to Common Core

### INTEGRATION OF KNOWLEDGE/IDEAS

This week, students have integrated content presented in diverse media and analyzed how different texts address similar topics. They have developed knowledge about talents to expand the unit topic of One of a Kind.

### Social Studies Knowledge Goals

Students have learned that people
- have many kinds of talents
- practice to develop their talents
- should be allowed to develop their talents

# Content Knowledge

## Talents

**REVIEW THE CONCEPT** Have students look back at the reading selections to find examples that best demonstrate how talents make people unique.

## Build Oral Language

**REVIEW AMAZING WORDS** Display and review this week's concept map. Remind students that this week they have learned eleven Amazing Words related to talent. Have students use the Amazing Words and the concept map to answer the Question of the Week, *How do talents make someone unique?*

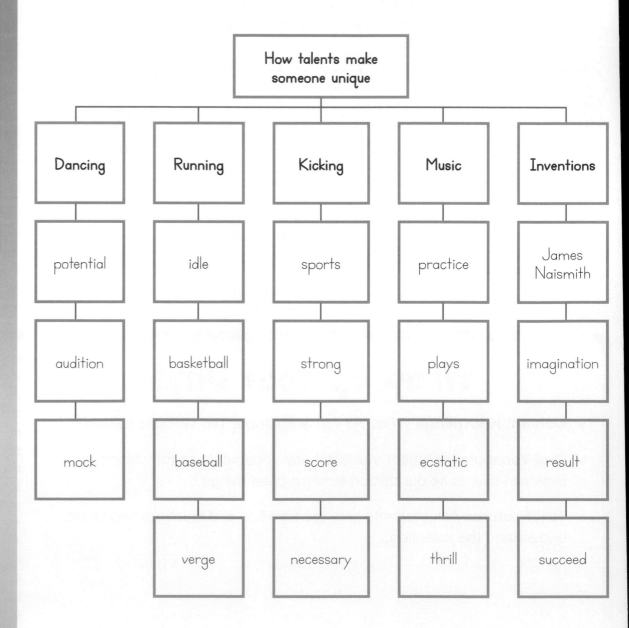

# Build Oral Vocabulary

**Team Talk** **CONNECT TO AMAZING IDEAS** Have pairs of students discuss how the Question of the Week connects to the question for this unit of study, *What does it mean to be unique?* Tell students to use the concept map and what they have learned from this week's discussions and reading selections to form an Amazing Idea—a realization or "big idea" about One of a Kind. Remind partners to pose and answer questions with appropriate detail and to give suggestions that build on each other's ideas. Then ask pairs to share their Amazing Ideas with the class.

Amazing Ideas might include these key concepts:

• There are different kinds of talent.

• People's talents help make them one of a kind.

• People have to practice to develop their talents.

• Everyone should be allowed to develop his or her talents.

**WRITE ABOUT IT** Have students write a few sentences about their Amazing Idea, beginning with "This week I learned . . ."

## Amazing Words

| | |
|---|---|
| mock | necessary |
| idle | result |
| potential | succeed |
| ecstatic | rise |
| thrill | verge |
| audition | |

It's Friday

**MONITOR PROGRESS** **Check Oral Vocabulary**

**FORMATIVE ASSESSMENT** Have individuals use this week's Amazing Words to describe ways people can be one of a kind. Monitor students' abilities to use the Amazing Words and note which words you need to reteach.

**If...** students have difficulty using the Amazing Words,

**then...** reteach using the Oral Vocabuary Routine, pp. 21a, 26b, 36b, 46b, OV•1.

**Check Concepts and Language** Use the Day 5 instructions on ELL Poster 16 to monitor students' understanding of the lesson concept.

Zoom in on ©

© **Common Core State Standards**

**Informational Text 1.** Ask and answer questions to demonstrate understanding of a text, referring explicitly to the text as the basis for the answers. **Informational Text 6.** Distinguish their own point of view from that of the author of a text. **Language 1.b.** Form and use regular and irregular plural nouns. **Language 4.a.** Use sentence-level context as a clue to the meaning of a word or phrase.

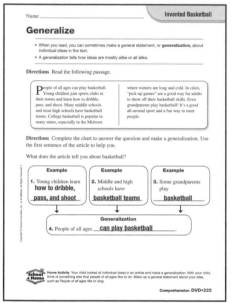

Let's Practice It! TR DVD•225

## Selection Vocabulary

**basketball** a game played on a court where two teams try to throw a ball through a raised hoop

**disease** a problem in the body; sickness

**freeze** turn into ice

**guard** a person who watches over or protects something

**popular** liked by many people

**sports** games in which people use their bodies

**study** to spend time learning, usually by reading

**terrible** really bad

# Text-Based Comprehension

## Review ☉ Generalize

**TEACH** Review the definition of generalizing on p. 24a. Remind students that general statements can have one of the general clue words added without changing the meaning of the sentence. For additional support have students review p. EI•8 on generalizing.

**GUIDE PRACTICE** Have pairs find an example of generalizing in *The Man Who Invented Basketball: James Naismith and His Amazing Game.* Then have them show how one of the generalizing clue words can be inserted into the sentence.

**ON THEIR OWN** For additional practice with generalizing, use *Let's Practice It!* p. 225 on the *Teacher Resources DVD-ROM.*

# Vocabulary Skill

## Review ☉ Unfamiliar Words

**TEACH** Remind students that checking for context clues around an unfamiliar word can often help them figure out what that word means.

**GUIDE PRACTICE** Review with students how to use context clues to figure out the meaning of the word *study*. Write the following sentence on the board: *When I study for a test, I read carefully and look at all my notes.* Have students identify the context clues in the sentence and determine the meaning of *study*.

**ON THEIR OWN** Have students work in pairs to write context sentences using this week's selection vocabulary. Partners can trade sentences and identify the context clues that help them determine each word's meaning.

# Word Analysis

## Review ⟲ Irregular Plurals

**TEACH** Write the following sentences on the board. Have students read each one, first quietly to themselves and then aloud as you track the print.

1. The men stamped their feet in time to the music.
2. You can find the toy elves on those shelves.
3. Wolves will eat deer, field mice, and other prey.
4. The women wore red scarves.
5. Children should not play with knives.

**Team Talk** Have students discuss with a partner which words are simply irregular plurals that they have to memorize and which words form the plural by changing the final *-f* or *-fe* to *-ves.* Then call on individuals to share with the class.

# Literary Terms

## Review Point of View

**TEACH** Have students reread "My Turn at Bat: The Story of My Life" on pp. 46–51. Remind students of the difference between biography and autobiography. Review with them the pronouns used in first person and third person points of view.

**GUIDE PRACTICE** Remind students that the selection contains *both* points of view. Find an example where the point of view changes within the selection. Point it out to students and explain how they can identify the different points of view.

**ON THEIR OWN** As students reread the selection, have them indicate which sections are written in first person and which are written in third person.

**eStreet Interactive**
www.ReadingStreet.com

**Pearson eText**
• Student Edition

**Teacher Resources**
• Let's Practice It!

**Generalize** If students are having difficulty finding a generalization within the selection, help them find examples. Then write a number of both general and specific statements. Have students identify which sentences are generalizations.

**Articulation Tip** In Spanish, plurals are formed by adding *-s* to words ending in a vowel *(madre/madres)* and *-es* to words ending in a consonant *(árbol/árboles).* Spanish speakers may thus add *-es* to any words ending in a consonant. Give students additional practice writing plural endings, especially those formed by adding *-ies* and *-ves.*

## © Common Core State Standards

**Foundational Skills 4.** Read with sufficient accuracy and fluency to support comprehension.
**Foundational Skills 4.a.** Read on-level text with purpose and understanding. **Also Foundational Skills 4.b.**

## Plan to Assess Fluency

☑ **This week assess Advanced students.**

☐ **Week 2** Strategic Intervention

☐ **Week 3** On-Level

☐ **Week 4** Strategic Intervention

☐ **Week 5** Assess any students you have not yet checked during this unit.

Set individual goals for students to enable them to reach the year-end goal.

• Current Goal: 95–105 WCPM

• Year-End Goal: 120 WCPM

# Assessment

## Monitor Progress

**FLUENCY** Make two copies of the fluency passage on p. 53k. As the student reads the text aloud, mark mistakes on your copy. Also mark where the student is at the end of one minute. To check the student's comprehension of the passage, have him or her retell what was read. To figure words correct per minute (WCPM), subtract the number of mistakes from the total number of words read in one minute.

**RATE**

| Corrective feedback | **If...** students cannot read fluently at a rate of 95–105 WCPM, **then...** make sure they practice with text at their independent reading level. Provide additional fluency practice by pairing nonfluent readers with fluent readers. |
| --- | --- |
| | **If...** students already read at 120 WCPM, **then...** have them read a book of their choice independently. |

## ⒺⓁⓁ

**If...** students need more scaffolding and practice with **Conventions and Writing,**

**then...** use the Grammar Transition Lessons on pp. 312–386 in the *ELL Handbook.*

### Day 5 SMALL GROUP TIME • Differentiate Reteaching, p. SG•1

| **OL** On-Level | **SI** Strategic Intervention | **A** Advanced |
| --- | --- | --- |
| • **Practice** Singular and Plural Pronouns | • **Review** Singular and Plural Pronouns | • **Extend** Singular and Plural Pronouns |
| • **Reread** *Reading Street Sleuth,* pp. 44–45 | • **Reread** *Reading Street Sleuth,* pp. 44–45 | • **Reread** *Reading Street Sleuth,* pp. 44–45 |
| | | • **Communicate** Inquiry Project |

Name _____

# Zora the Zebra

Zora was a zebra with only one stripe. Most of the time Zora 13
struggled to hold her head up high. It wasn't easy hearing what the 26
other animals had to say. 31

"A zebra isn't a zebra unless it has at least seven stripes," the 44
other zebras would say. 48

"Zora should change her name to Zero," laughed 56
the mice. 58

"But I would love you if you had no stripe," her mother would say. 72

One day, while the other zebras were drinking from the lake, Zora 84
was standing on a hill. She could see them because their stripes stood 97
out against the light ground. 102

Then Zora noticed something terrible. A pack of wolves was 112
glaring down at the zebras. 117

"Oh no, I must warn them!" Zora cried. 125

She quickly ran down the hill. 131

It was clear that the wolves couldn't see Zora because she only 143
had one stripe. Her color blended well with the ground. 153

"Quick, run for your lives!" Zora shouted. 160

At that moment, the wolves came swooping down the hill. The 171
zebras had a head start and ran to safety. 180

That night, the zebras held a party for Zora. They were sorry for 193
the way they had treated her. "Three cheers for Zora!" they yelled. 205

"Now, this is the kind of attention I like," Zora said. 216

**MONITOR PROGRESS**

• Check Fluency

 **Common Core State Standards**

**Literature 1.** Ask and answer questions to demonstrate understanding of a text, referring explicitly to the text as the basis for the answers. **Literature 10.** By the end of the year, read and comprehend literature, including stories, dramas, and poetry, at the high end of the grades 2–3 text complexity band independently and proficiently.

# Assessment

## Monitor Progress

For a written assessment of Irregular Plurals, Generalize, and Selection Vocabulary, use Weekly Test 16, pp. 91–96.

**GENERALIZE** Use "Wanda's Bad Play" on p. 53m to check students' understanding of generalizing.

1. How does Coach Johnson help Wanda in this story? He helps her identify a skill she is good at and gets her to start thinking about things she can do well instead of focusing on how bad she is at playing baseball.

2. Name two general statements Wanda makes in the story. *I can't tell where a ball is going. I don't catch balls well.*

3. Identify another general statement made in the story and explain how you can tell this is a general statement. *The kids often groaned at her bad plays* is a general statement. I can tell this because it contains the clue word *often.*

---

**Corrective feedback** | **If...** students are unable to answer the comprehension questions,
**then...** use the Reteach lesson in *First Stop.*

---

# Wanda's Bad Play

Wanda raced to catch the baseball in the air. But she wasn't fast enough, and the ball bounced in front of her. When she tried to scoop it up after that, she completely missed it. Other kids on her team groaned loudly at Wanda's bad play. The kids often groaned at her bad plays.

Later, Wanda sat next to Coach Johnson. "I'm an awful baseball player. In fact, the truth is I'm an awful athlete," Wanda said.

"Why do you say that?" asked Coach Johnson.

Wanda thought for an instant and said, "I'd say that for six reasons. First, I don't run very fast. Second, I can't tell where a ball is going. Third, I don't catch balls well. Fourth, I don't throw balls well. Fifth, I don't hit well when I bat. Sixth, when I do hit something, it doesn't go far because I'm not strong. There is only one thing I'm good at. I know baseball rules."

"Hmmm," said Coach Johnson. "I know something else you're good at, Wanda."

Wanda couldn't guess what it was. She asked, "Making lists?"

"Maybe," answered Coach Johnson with a laugh. "But that's not what I was thinking. You're good at analyzing things. That means you are good at thinking about things and figuring out what's right and wrong."

It was Wanda's turn to say, "Hmmm."

Then she asked, "Coach, does that mean I might make a good scientist?"

"Sure," said Coach Johnson. "Or a baseball coach."

Wanda smiled. She liked that idea!

**MONITOR PROGRESS**   • Generalize

## © Common Core State Standards

**Speaking/Listening 1.a.** Come to discussions prepared, having read or studied required material; explicitly draw on that preparation and other information known about the topic to explore ideas under discussion. **Speaking/Listening 3.** Ask and answer questions about information from a speaker, offering appropriate elaboration and detail. **Speaking/Listening 4.** Report on a topic or text, tell a story, or recount an experience with appropriate facts and relevant, descriptive details, speaking clearly at an understandable pace.
**Also Speaking/Listening 1.b., Language 1.a., 1.b., 2.e.**

# Research and Inquiry

## Step 5 Communicate

**PRESENT IDEAS** Have students share their inquiry results by presenting their biographies and giving a brief talk on their research. Have students show the class the time lines they began on Day 3.

**SPEAKING** Remind students how to be good speakers and how to communicate effectively with their audience.

• Respond to relevant questions with appropriate details.

• Speak clearly and loudly.

• Keep eye contact with audience members.

**LISTENING** Review with students these tips for being a good listener.

• Wait until the speaker has finished before raising your hand to ask a relevant question or make a comment.

• Be polite, even if you disagree.

**LISTEN TO IDEAS** Have students listen attentively to the various biographical presentations. Have them make pertinent comments, closely related to the topic.

# Spelling Test

## Irregular Plurals

To administer the spelling test, refer to the directions, words, and sentences on p. 25c.

# Conventions

## Singular and Plural Pronouns

**TEACH** Ask students to explain the difference between singular and plural pronouns. (Singular pronouns replace singular nouns; plural pronouns replace plural nouns.)

**GUIDE PRACTICE** Write the following sentences, with words underlined. Have the class tell you which pronouns replace the underlined words, and whether they are singular or plural.

> <u>A girl</u> saw <u>the boy</u> fly. (*She, him;* singular)
>
> <u>Three girls</u> watched <u>the boy</u> as he flew. (*They, him;* plural and singular)
>
> <u>James</u> cannot fly. (*He;* singular)

**ON THEIR OWN** Read the following sentences: Have students look back at *The Man Who Invented Basketball* to find the correct singular and plural pronouns to complete the sentences. Then have them identify each one as singular or plural. Students should complete *Let's Practice It!* p. 226 on the *Teacher Resources DVD-ROM.*

1. Then _____ raced out onto the frozen swimming hole like a champion skater. *(he)*

2. James would remember duck on a rock years later when _____ would be very important to _____. *(it, him)*

3. _____ thought _____ could help teens live better lives if _____ talked to _____ while teaching _____ sports. *(He, he, he, them, them)*

4. _____ were so bored that some of _____ wanted to quit the YMCA training school. *(They, them)*

**eStreet Interactive**
www.ReadingStreet.com

**Teacher Resources**
• Let's Practice It!
• Daily Fix-It Transparency

## Daily Fix-It

9. The girl worryed about the boy but he was all right. *(worried; boy,)*

10. What a helpfull friend she was. *(helpful; was!)*

Let's Practice It! TR DVD•226

## Teacher Note

**Writing Self-Evaluation** Make copies of the Writing Self-Evaluation Guide on p. 39 of the *Reader's and Writer's Notebook* and hand out to students.

# Writing

## Persuasive Text

**REVIEW REVISING** Remind students that yesterday they revised their essays by combining sentences with conjunctions. Today they will proofread their essays.

### Mini-Lesson  Proofread

#### Proofread for Pronouns and Double Negatives

■ **Teach** When we proofread, we look for errors in spelling, capitalization, punctuation, and grammar. Today we'll make sure we've used pronouns correctly, and we'll eliminate double negatives.

■ **Model** Let's look at the persuasive text we worked on yesterday. Display Transparency 16C. Explain that you will look for errors in spelling, punctuation, and capitalization; and you'll make sure pronouns are used correctly. Then you will eliminate any double negatives. Review the double negative in the sentence *I don't want nothing.* I see a problem. It says *your opponent's king can't make no moves.* I can see that the combination of *can't* and *no* makes a double negative. I'll rewrite this sentence. Continue to point out spelling, capitalization, and punctuation problems. Then have students proofread their own persuasive texts.

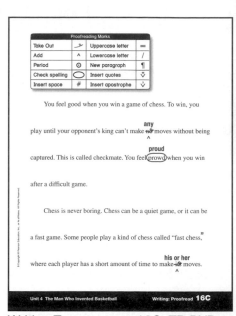

Writing Transparency 16C, TR DVD

**PROOFREAD** Display the Proofreading Tips. Ask students to proofread their compositions, using the Proofreading Tips and paying particular attention to correct use of pronouns. Circulate around the room answering students' questions. When students have finished editing their own work, have pairs proofread one another's persuasive texts.

### Proofreading Tips

✔ Make sure you have used pronouns correctly.

✔ Eliminate any double negatives.

✔ Reread your persuasive text, checking for errors in grammar, spelling, and capitalization.

✔ Use a dictionary to check the spelling of difficult words.

**PRESENT** Have students incorporate revisions and proofreading edits into their persuasive texts to create a final draft.

Give students a choice between presenting their persuasive texts orally as a recording to a small group or to the whole class. When they have finished, each student should complete the Writing Self-Evaluation Guide.

**Routine** | **Quick Write for Fluency** | **Team Talk**

1. **Talk** Pairs talk about a new sport or game they would like to try.

2. **Write** Students write two sentences giving reasons why they want to try the new sport or game.

3. **Share** Students share their reasons aloud with the class.

Routines Flip Chart

# Wrap Up Your Week!

## Talents

How do talents make someone unique?

 This week we explored how talents can make someone unique. In *The Man Who Invented Basketball and* "My Turn at Bat," we learned about the special talents of two people and how they became successful.

**Team Talk** Have students recall their Amazing Ideas about what makes someone unique and use these ideas to help them demonstrate their understanding of the Question of the Week.

Next Week's Concept
## Nature's Record Holders

What makes nature's record holders unique?

**Poster Preview** Prepare students for next week by using Week 2, ELL Poster 17. Read the Poster Talk-Through to introduce the concept and vocabulary. Ask students to identify and describe objects and actions in the art.

**Selection Summary** Send home the summary of *Hottest, Coldest, Highest, Deepest* in English and the students' home languages, if available. They can read the summary with family members.

What makes nature's record holders unique? Tell students that next week they will read about things in nature that set records.

**Preview Next Week**

# Assessment Checkpoints for the Week

## Weekly Assessment

Use pp. 91–96 of *Weekly Tests* to check:

✔  **Phonics/Word Analysis** Irregular Plurals

✔  **Comprehension** Generalize

✔ **Review** **Comprehension** Graphic Sources

✔ **Selection Vocabulary**

| | |
|---|---|
| basketball | popular |
| disease | sports |
| freeze | study |
| guard | terrible |

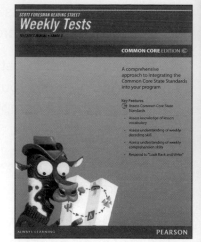

Weekly Tests

## Differentiated Assessment

**A**
Advanced

**OL**
On-Level

**SI**
Strategic
Intervention

Use pp. 91–96 of *Fresh Reads for Fluency and Comprehension* to check:

✔ **Comprehension** Generalize

✔ **Review** **Comprehension** Graphic Sources

✔ **Fluency** Words Correct Per Minute

Fresh Reads for Fluency and Comprehension

## Managing Assessment

Use *Assessment Handbook* for:

**Weekly Assessment Blackline Masters for Monitoring Progress**

✔ **Observation Checklists**

✔ **Record-Keeping Forms**

✔ **Portfolio Assessment**

Assessment Handbook

# TEACHER NOTES

## DAY 1 Differentiate Vocabulary

- **Word Knowledge** Amazing Words
- **Read** "Street Games"
- **Inquiry** Identify Questions

"Street Games"
pp. 44–45

## DAY 2 Differentiate Comprehension

- **Word Knowledge** Selection Vocabulary
- **Access Text** Read *The Man Who Invented Basketball*
- **Inquiry** Investigate

## DAY 3 Differentiate Close Reading

- **Word Knowledge** Develop Vocabulary
- **Close Reading** Read *The Man Who Invented Basketball*
- **Inquiry** Investigate

## DAY 4 Differentiate Vocabulary

- **Word Knowledge** Amazing Words
- **Read** "My Turn at Bat"
- **Inquiry** Organize

## DAY 5 Differentiate Reteaching

- **Conventions** Singular and Plural Pronouns
- **Reread** "Street Games" or Leveled Readers
- **Inquiry** Communicate

Teacher Guides and Student pages can be found in the Leveled Reader Database.

 Place English Language Learners in the groups that correspond to their reading abilities.
**If...** students need scaffolding and practice,
**then...** use the ELL Notes on the instructional pages.

## Independent Practice

**Independent Practice Stations**

See pp. 20h and 20i for Independent Stations.

**Pearson Trade Book Library**

See the Leveled Reader Database for lesson plans and student pages.

**Reading Street Digital Path**

Independent Practice Activities are available in the Digital Path.

**Independent Reading**

See p. 20i for independent reading suggestions.

## Common Core State Standards

**Informational Text 1.** Ask and answer questions to demonstrate understanding of a text, referring explicitly to the text as the basis for the answers. **Foundational Skills 4.** Read with sufficient accuracy and fluency to support comprehension. **Speaking/ Listening 1.** Engage effectively in a range of collaborative discussions (one-on-one, in groups, and teacher led) with diverse partners on grade 3 topics and texts, building on others' ideas and expressing their own clearly. **Language 5.b.** Identify real-life connections between words and their use (e.g., describe people who are *friendly* or *helpful*). **Language 6.** Acquire and use accurately grade-appropriate conversational, general academic, and domain-specific words and phrases, including those that signal spatial and temporal relationships (e.g., *After dinner that night we went looking for them*).

## Independent Reading Options

**Trade Book Library**

### eStreet Interactive
www.ReadingStreet.com

Teacher Guides are available on the Leveled Reader Database.

**If...** students need more scaffolding and practice with **Vocabulary, then...** use the activities on pp. DI•17–DI•18 in the Teacher Resources section on SuccessNet.

## OL On-Level

# ❶ Build Word Knowledge
## Practice Amazing Words

**DEFINE IT** Elicit the definition for the word *idle* from students. Ask: How would you describe *idle* to another student? (Possible response: *Idle* means inactive or to waste time.) Clarify or give a definition when necessary. Continue with the words *potential* and *ecstatic.*

**Team Talk　TALK ABOUT IT** Have pairs of students internalize meanings. Ask: How can you pair the Amazing Words together in a sentence? (Possible response: Kelly felt ecstatic when, in an idle moment, she saw her potential talent as an artist.) Allow time for students to play with the words. Review the concept map with students. Discuss other words they can add to the concept map.

# ❷ Text-Based Comprehension
## Read

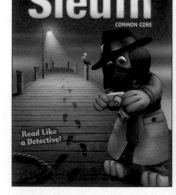

**READ ALOUD "Street Games"** Have partners read "Street Games" from *Reading Street Sleuth* on pp. 44–45.

**ACCESS TEXT** Discuss the Sleuth Work section with students before they work on it. Remind students that they can use these steps with other texts they read.

**Gather Evidence** Talk together about the main idea of the text. Have partners work together to make a list of evidence that supports the main idea. Invite students to share whether the evidence they found is factual or not.

**Ask Questions** Talk together about questions that are based on facts and questions that are based on opinions. Discuss the questions students wrote. Have students identify their questions as factual or opinion based.

**Make Your Case** Remind students that facts can back up opinions. Have students point to the evidence in the text that supports their opinions. If time permits, have students on the same side of the issue rank their reasons from most to least convincing.

 On-Level

# 1 Build Word Knowledge
## Practice Selection Vocabulary

| | | | |
|---|---|---|---|
| basketball | disease | freeze | guard |
| popular | sports | study | terrible |

**DEFINE IT** Discuss the definition for the word *disease* with students. Ask: How would you describe *popular* to another student? (Possible response: *Popular* means something that is liked by many people.) Continue with the remaining words.

**Team Talk** **TALK ABOUT IT** Have pairs use the selection vocabulary in sentences to internalize meaning. Ask: How can you pair the selection vocabulary together in a sentence? (Possible response: In my opinion, basketball is one of the most popular *sports*.) Allow time for students to play with the words and then share their sentences.

# 2 Read
## The Man Who Invented Basketball

If you read *The Man Who Invented Basketball* during whole group time, then use the following instruction.

**ACCESS TEXT** Reread the last paragraph on p. 32 and the first two paragraphs on p. 33. Ask questions to check understanding. Why did James Naismith drop out of high school? (He wanted to grow up fast and get a job.) Why did James later return to high school? (After cutting down trees as a lumberjack for several years, James decided he needed to change his life. His new plan for his life required a high school and college education.)

Have students identify sections from today's reading that they did not completely understand. Reread them aloud and clarify misunderstandings.

If you are reading *The Man Who Invented Basketball* during small group time, then return to pp. 30–35a to guide the reading.

**eSTREET INTERACTIVE**
www.ReadingStreet.com

**Pearson eText**
• Student Edition
• Leveled Reader Database
• *Reading Street Sleuth*

**More Reading for Group Time**

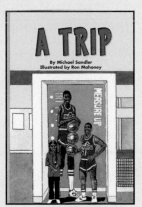

**ON-LEVEL**

**Reviews**
• Generalize
• Summarize
• Selection Vocabulary

Use this suggested Leveled Reader or other text at students' instructional level.

**eSTREET INTERACTIVE**
www.ReadingStreet.com

Use the Leveled Reader Database for lesson plans and student pages for *A Trip*.

**SMALL GROUP TIME**

## Common Core State Standards

**Informational Text 1.** Ask and answer questions to demonstrate understanding of a text, referring explicitly to the text as the basis for the answers. **Informational Text 6.** Distinguish their own point of view from that of the author of a text. **Language 4.** Determine or clarify the meaning of unknown and multiple-meaning words and phrases based on grade 3 reading and content, choosing flexibly from a range of strategies. **Also Language 6.**

## OL On-Level

## ① Build Word Knowledge
### Develop Vocabulary

**REREAD FOR VOCABULARY** Reread the first paragraph on p. 39. Introduce: Let's read this paragraph to find out what *pose* means. To help students understand the word *pose,* ask questions related to the context, such as: Why was James famous? What might James be doing in one of those ads? Have students use a dictionary or thesaurus to find out more information about the word *pose.*

## ② Read
### *The Man Who Invented Basketball*

If you read *The Man Who Invented Basketball* during whole group time, then use the following instruction.

**CLOSE READING** Read pp. 36–37. Have students search though the text to find clues that indicate that the genre of the text is biography. As a class, make a list of the clues. (Someone other than the subject is telling the story. The text uses pronouns such as *he, his,* and *they.* There are dates that tell about important events in James's life, such as December 21, 1891, when he created basketball, and June 20, 1894, when he got married. The events are real, not made up.)

Ask: Why do you think the author chose to write about James Naismith? (Basketball is a very popular sport. Many people would like to know about the life of the person who invented it. James also faced hard challenges and overcame them, so he is a good role model.)

If you are reading *The Man Who Invented Basketball* during small group time, then return to pp. 36–41a to guide the reading.

**If...** students need more scaffolding and practice with the **Main Selection, then...** use the activities on p. DI•22 in the Teacher Resources section on SuccessNet.

**OL** On-Level

# 1 Build Word Knowledge
## Practice Amazing Words

| mock | idle | potential | ecstatic | thrill |
|------|------|-----------|----------|--------|
| audition | necessary | result | succeed | rise |
| verge | | | | |

**Team Talk** **LANGUAGE DEVELOPMENT** Have students practice building more complex sentences. Display a sentence starter and have students add oral phrases or clauses using the Amazing Words. For example: To succeed _____. (To succeed / in an audition / is always a great thrill / and the result of hard work.) Guide students to add at least three phrases or clauses per sentence.

# 2 Read
## "My Turn at Bat"

**BEFORE READING** Read aloud the information about an autobiography on p. 46. Have students preview "My Turn at Bat" and set a purpose for reading. How does an autobiography differ from a biography? (An autobiography uses the words *I, me,* and *my* because the person is telling his or her own story.) Who seems to be telling this story? (Ted Williams)

**DURING READING** Have students read along with you while tracking the print. How is this autobiography organized? (in different sections, starting with Ted Williams's childhood and then describing his career in baseball) How is this autobiography similar to and different from the biography you just read? (Both are about the life and accomplishments of one person, and both are related to sports. The autobiography tells the story from the athlete's point of view. The biography is written by another person and told from that person's point of view.)

**AFTER READING** Have students share their reaction to "My Turn at Bat." Then have them write a conversation between James Naismith and Ted Williams about sports.

**eSTREET INTERACTIVE**
www.ReadingStreet.com

**Pearson eText**
• Student Edition

**SMALL GROUP TIME**

**Independent Reading Options**

**Trade Book Library**

**eSTREET INTERACTIVE**
www.ReadingStreet.com

Teacher Guides are available on the Leveled Reader Database.

## © Common Core State Standards

**Informational Text 2.** Determine the main idea of a text; recount the key details and explain how they support the main idea. **Foundational Skills 4.** Read with sufficient accuracy and fluency to support comprehension. **Writing 2.** Write informative/explanatory texts to examine a topic and convey ideas and information clearly. **Also Writing 10., Language 1.a., 4., 6.**

## More Reading for Group Time

**ON-LEVEL**

**Reviews**
• Generalize
• Summarize
• Selection Vocabulary

Use this suggested Leveled Reader or other text at students' instructional level.

### eSTREET INTERACTIVE
www.ReadingStreet.com

Use the Leveled Reader Database for lesson plans and student pages for *A Trip.*

## OL On-Level

# 1 Build Word Knowledge
## Practice Singular and Plural Pronouns

**IDENTIFY** Choral read the bottom of p. 45 with students and explain that pronouns take the place of nouns in sentences. Some are singular and others are plural. Have partners reread the model persuasive essay to find examples of how the author used singular and plural pronouns. Encourage students to use the student model essay on the same page to practice. Allow time for students to discuss their examples and correct any misunderstandings.

# 2 Text-Based Comprehension
## Read

**REREAD "Street Games"** Have partners reread "Street Games."

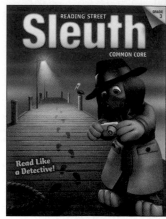

**EXTEND UNDERSTANDING** Talk together about the kinds of games children like to play now and how they compare to street games mentioned in the article.

**PERFORMANCE TASK • Prove It!** Have students work with a partner to write a simple how-to book about a game they play. Encourage students to focus on writing clear, simple instructions. Invite them to add illustrations to their how-to book.

**COMMUNICATE** Have small groups share their how-to books with each other. Invite listeners to ask questions about the games being described in the books.

**SI** Strategic Intervention

# 1 Build Word Knowledge
## Reteach Amazing Words

Repeat the definition of the word. We learned that *idle* means inactive or to waste time. Then use the word in a sentence. My grandmother is always busy and is never idle.

**Team Talk** **TALK ABOUT IT** Have partners take turns using the word *idle* in a sentence. Continue this routine to practice the Amazing Words *ecstatic* and *potential.* Review the concept map with students. Discuss other words they can add to the concept map.

> **Corrective feedback** | **If...** students need more practice with the Amazing Words, **then...** use visuals from the Student Edition or online sources to clarify meaning.

# 2 Text-Based Comprehension
## Read

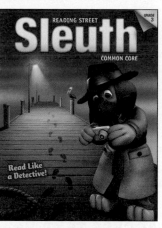

**REREAD "Street Games"** Have students track the print as you read "Street Games" from *Reading Street Sleuth* on pp. 44–45.

**ACCESS TEXT** Discuss the Sleuth Work section with students and provide support as needed as they work on it. Remind students that they can use these steps with other texts they read.

**Gather Evidence** Talk together with students about the main idea of the text. Then work together to make a list of evidence that supports that main idea. Invite students to share whether the evidence they found is factual or not.

**Ask Questions** Have partners work together to write questions. Talk about the kinds of questions students wrote, whether they are factual or opinion based.

**Make Your Case** Remind students that facts can back up their opinions. Have students choose a position and work with a partner on that same position. Have them look for evidence in the text that supports their side of the issue, listing reasons that support their opinion.

**eSTREET INTERACTIVE**
www.ReadingStreet.com
**Pearson eText**
• Student Edition
• Leveled Reader Database
• *Reading Street Sleuth*

**SMALL GROUP TIME**

## More Reading for Group Time

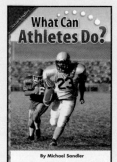

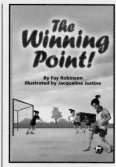

**CONCEPT LITERACY**
**Practice**
Concept Words

**BELOW-LEVEL**
**Reviews**
• Generalize
• Summarize
• Selection Vocabulary

Use these suggested Leveled Readers or other text at students' instructional level.

**eSTREET INTERACTIVE**
www.ReadingStreet.com
Use the Leveled Reader Database for lesson plans and student pages for *What Can Athletes Do?* and *The Winning Point!*

## Strategic Intervention

## Common Core State Standards

**Informational Text 2.** Determine the main idea of a text; recount the key details and explain how they support the main idea. **Foundational Skills 4.** Read with sufficient accuracy and fluency to support comprehension. **Language 4.** Determine or clarify the meaning of unknown and multiple-meaning words and phrases based on grade 3 reading and content, choosing flexibly from a range of strategies. **Also Informational Text 1., Language 5.b., 6.**

# 1 Build Word Knowledge
## Reteach Selection Vocabulary

**DEFINE IT** Describe *freeze* to a friend. Give a definition when necessary. Restate the word in student-friendly terms and clarify meaning with a visual. *Freeze* means to turn into ice. Page 30 shows a river after it freezes.

| | | | |
|---|---|---|---|
| basketball | disease | freeze | guard |
| popular | sports | study | terrible |

**Team Talk** **TALK ABOUT IT** Have you seen water as it freezes? Turn and talk to your partner about this. Allow time for students to discuss. Rephrase students' examples for usage or to correct misunderstandings.

> **Corrective feedback** | **If...** students need more practice with selection vocabulary, **then...** use the *Envision It! Pictured Vocabulary Cards.*

# 2 Read
## *The Man Who Invented Basketball*

If you read *The Man Who Invented Basketball* during whole group time, then use the instruction below.

**ACCESS TEXT** Reread the last paragraph on p. 32 and the first two paragraphs on p. 33. Ask questions to check understanding. What kind of student was James Naismith? (He didn't work hard, and he didn't get good grades.) Why did James drop out of high school? (He wanted to grow up fast and get a job instead.) Why did James return to high school? (His new plan for his life required a high school and college education.) Have students identify sections they did not understand. Reread them aloud. Clarify the meaning of each section to build understanding.

If you are reading *The Man Who Invented Basketball* during small group time, then return to pp. 30–35a to guide the reading.

## Independent Reading Options

**Trade Book Library**

**eStreet Interactive**
www.ReadingStreet.com

Teacher Guides are available on the Leveled Reader Database.

**SI** Strategic Intervention

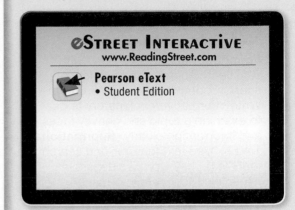

# 1 Build Word Knowledge

## Develop Vocabulary

**REREAD FOR VOCABULARY** Reread the first paragraph on p. 39.
Introduce: Let's read this paragraph to find out what *pose* means. To help students understand the word *pose,* ask questions related to the context, such as: Why was James famous? If James had been in some ads, what would the ads have been selling? If James had been in an ad, what might he be doing?

**Corrective feedback** | **If...** students have difficulty understanding the word *pose,* **then...** have students use a dictionary/thesaurus for more information.

# 2 Read

## *The Man Who Invented Basketball*

If you read *The Man Who Invented Basketball* during whole group time, then use the instruction below.

**CLOSE READING** Read p. 36.
Have students read though the text to find the main ideas. As a class, make a list of these ideas in the order they occur. (James tried to think of a new game. Then he remembered "duck on a rock" from his childhood. He tried out a new game based on the old game. The men liked it and formed teams.)

Now let's use the main ideas we listed to retell what happened in this part of the story. (James struggled hard to think of a new game that would be fun but not risky. Then he remembered how they played "duck on a rock" in his childhood with a soft pitch. He tried out his ideas for a new game based on the old game. At first the men who were playing complained, but soon they were having fun. They began to form teams.)

If you are reading *The Man Who Invented Basketball* during small group time, then return to pp. 36–41a to guide the reading.

**If...** students need more scaffolding and practice with the **Main Selection, then...** use the activities on p. DI•22 in the Teacher Resources section on SuccessNet.

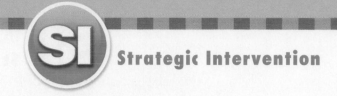

**Strategic Intervention**

## Common Core State Standards

**Foundational Skills 4.** Read with sufficient accuracy and fluency to support comprehension. **Writing 2.** Write informative/explanatory texts to examine a topic and convey ideas and information clearly. **Informational Text 5.** Use text features and search tools (e.g., key words, sidebars, hyperlinks) to locate information relevant to a given topic efficiently. **Also Informational Text 1., 7., 9., Language 1.a., 1.i., 6.**

## 1 Build Word Knowledge
### Review Amazing Words

| | | | | |
|---|---|---|---|---|
| mock | idle | potential | ecstatic | thrill |
| audition | necessary | result | succeed | rise |
| verge | | | | |

**Team Talk** **LANGUAGE DEVELOPMENT** Have pairs of students practice building more complex sentences. Display a sentence starter and have students add oral phrases or clauses using the Amazing Words. Guide students to add at least two phrases or clauses per sentence.

**Corrective feedback** **If...** students have difficulty using Amazing Words orally, **then...** review the meaning of each of the words.

## 2 Read
### "My Turn at Bat"

**BEFORE READING** Read aloud the genre information on p. 46. An autobiography is the story of a person's life written by the person who lived it. Read the rest of the panel. Then have students read the introduction.

**DURING READING** Have students perform a choral reading of the selection. As they read, write each subhead on the board. Subheads can help you locate specific information quickly. How do the subheads organize information in this autobiography? (They divide the autobiography into Ted Williams's childhood, his baseball career, a time line, and his Hall of Fame statistics.)

**AFTER READING** Have students share their reactions to the selection. Then guide them through the Reading Across Texts and Writing Across Texts activities, prompting if necessary.

- Name two athletes you just read about. (James Naismith and Ted Williams)
- How were they alike? How were they different? (Both loved sports. One invented and taught basketball; the other broke records in baseball.)

**ELL**

**If...** students need more scaffolding and practice with **Amazing Words, then...** use the Routine on pp. xxxvi–xxxvii in the *ELL Handbook*.

**SI** Strategic Intervention

# 1 Build Word Knowledge
## Review Singular and Plural Pronouns

**IDENTIFY** Choral read the bottom of p. 45 with students to review singular and plural pronouns. Have partners reread the model persuasive essay on p. 45 to find examples of how the author used singular and plural pronouns. Have students use the student model on that page to practice. Allow time for students to discuss their examples and correct any misunderstandings.

# 2 Text-Based Comprehension
## Read

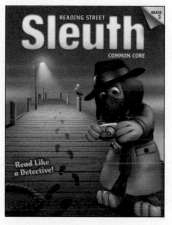

**REREAD "Street Games"** Have partners reread "Street Games" with partners, alternating paragraphs.

**EXTEND UNDERSTANDING** Talk together about students' experiences with playing games mentioned in the article. If students have not experienced playing any of these games, talk together about games students play at recess.

**PERFORMANCE TASK • Prove It!** Have students work with a partner to write a simple how-to book about a game they play. Talk together about the importance of giving instructions in the correct sequential order. Invite students to add illustrations to their how-to book.

**COMMUNICATE** Have small groups share their how-to books with each other. Invite listeners to tell which games they would most like to play and why.

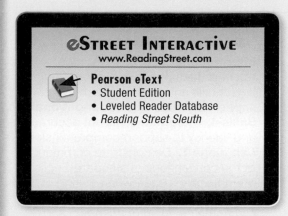

eSTREET INTERACTIVE
www.ReadingStreet.com

Pearson eText
• Student Edition
• Leveled Reader Database
• *Reading Street Sleuth*

**More Reading for Group Time**

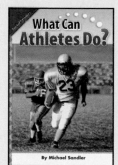

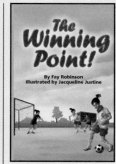

| CONCEPT LITERACY | BELOW-LEVEL |
|---|---|
| **Practice** Concept Words | **Reviews** • Generalize • Summarize • Selection   Vocabulary |

Use these suggested Leveled Readers or other text at students' instructional level.

eSTREET INTERACTIVE
www.ReadingStreet.com

Use the Leveled Reader Database for lesson plans and student pages for *What Can Athletes Do?* and *The Winning Point!*

SMALL GROUP TIME

## Ⓒ Common Core State Standards

**Informational Text 2.** Determine the main idea of a text; recount the key details and explain how they support the main idea. **Foundational Skills 4.** Read with sufficient accuracy and fluency to support comprehension. **Language 1.** Demonstrate command of the conventions of standard English grammar and usage when writing or speaking. **Language 4.** Determine or clarify the meaning of unknown and multiple-meaning words and phrases based on grade 3 reading and content, choosing flexibly from a range of strategies. **Also Informational Text 1., Writing 7., Language 6.**

**Advanced**

## 1 Build Word Knowledge

### Extend Amazing Words

**Team Talk** Have pairs of students define *idle*. Discuss other words or phrases for *idle*. *(inactivity, to waste time, useless)* Continue with *potential* and *ecstatic*.

## 2 Text-Based Comprehension

### Read

**READ "Street Games"** Have students read "Street Games" from *Reading Street Sleuth* on pp. 44–45.

**ACCESS TEXT** Discuss the Sleuth Work section with students before they work on it. Remind students that they can use these steps with other texts they read.

**Gather Evidence** Have students make a list of text evidence that supports the main idea. Invite students to share whether the evidence they found is factual or not.

**Ask Questions** Discuss the questions students wrote. Have students identify their questions as factual or opinion based.

**Make Your Case** Have students choose a position and note evidence in the text that supports their opinions. If time permits, have students rank their reasons from most to least convincing.

## 3 Inquiry: Extend Concepts

**IDENTIFY QUESTIONS** Have students think about questions they have about talents and use these questions to select a favorite athlete. Have them research what special qualities and talents helped their favorite athlete succeed at his or her sport. Throughout the week, they will gather information. On Day 5, they will present what they have learned.

**If...** students need more scaffolding and practice with **Vocabulary, then...** use the activities on pp. DI•17–DI•18 in the Teacher Resources section on SuccessNet.

**A** Advanced

# 1 Build Word Knowledge

## Extend Selection Vocabulary

**Team Talk** Have partners use the selection vocabulary in sentences to internalize their meanings. Have students use as many of the words as they can while making sure the sentence is grammatically correct. (Possible response: I'm a terrible basketball player, but I'm good at several other popular sports.)

| | | |
|---|---|---|
| basketball | disease | freeze |
| popular | sports | study |
| guard | terrible | |

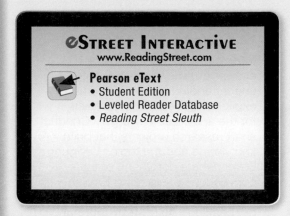
# 2 Read

## *The Man Who Invented Basketball*

If you read *The Man Who Invented Basketball* during whole group time, then use the instruction below.

**ACCESS TEXT** Reread the last paragraph on p. 32 and the first two paragraphs on p. 33. Discuss the personal characteristics and qualities James had that are inferred in this passage about his early life. List them in the order in which they appear in the text.

Ask: What generalizations can you make about James based on this selection? (He was going to live his life his own way and not go along with the crowd, and he was going to accomplish a lot.)

If you are reading *The Man Who Invented Basketball* during small group time, then return to pp. 30–35a to guide the reading.

# 3 Inquiry: Extend Concepts

**INVESTIGATE** Encourage students to use materials at their independent reading levels or student-friendly search engines to identify relevant and credible sites to gather information about athletes. Have students consider how they will present their information.

## More Reading for Group Time

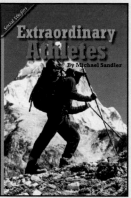

**ADVANCED**

**Reviews**
• Generalize
• Summarize

Use this suggested Leveled Reader or other text at students' instructional level.

Use the Leveled Reader Database for lesson plans and student pages for *Extraordinary Athletes*.

**SMALL GROUP TIME**

**A** Advanced

## © Common Core State Standards

**Informational Text 1.** Ask and answer questions to demonstrate understanding of a text, referring explicitly to the text as the basis for the answers. **Writing 7.** Conduct short research projects that build knowledge about a topic. **Language 1.** Demonstrate command of the conventions of standard English grammar and usage when writing or speaking. **Also Informational Text 3., 6., Writing 4., 6., 10., Speaking/Listening 1., Language 4.a., 6.**

## ① Build Word Knowledge
### Develop Vocabulary

**REREAD FOR VOCABULARY** Reread the label for the graphic on the bottom of p. 39. Let's read this label to find out what *patent* means. Discuss meaning and context with students.

## ② Read
### *The Man Who Invented Basketball*

If you read *The Man Who Invented Basketball* during whole group time, then use the instruction below.

**CLOSE READING** Read pp. 36–39. Have students create a simple time line based on information in the selection. Have them insert only the main idea that corresponds to each date. (Possible responses: Dec. 21, 1891: invents basketball; June 20, 1894: marries Maude Sherman; 1895: becomes director of physical education at YMCA in Denver; 1898: graduates as medical doctor; 1909: working as minister, professor, medical doctor)

Ask: How would you summarize the events in this selection based on your timeline? (James Naismith invented basketball in 1891 based on a childhood game. As its popularity spread, he married one of the first female players. He worked in physical education but, based on his desire to help people, he also became a medical doctor and a minister.)

If you are reading *The Man Who Invented Basketball* during small group time, then return to pp. 36–41a to guide the reading.

## Independent Reading Options

**Trade Book Library**

### *e*STREET INTERACTIVE
www.ReadingStreet.com

Teacher Guides are available on the Leveled Reader Database.

## ③ Inquiry: Extend Concepts

**INVESTIGATE** Provide time for students to investigate their topics in books or online. If necessary, help them locate information that is focused on their topics.

## Ⓔ Ⓛ Ⓛ

**If...** students need more scaffolding and practice with the **Main Selection, then...** use the activities on p. DI•22 in the Teacher Resources section on SuccessNet.

**A** Advanced

## 1 Build Word Knowledge
### Extend Amazing Words and Selection Vocabulary

| | | |
|---|---|---|
| mock | idle | potential |
| ecstatic | thrill | audition |
| necessary | result | succeed |
| rise | verge | |

| | | |
|---|---|---|
| basketball | disease | freeze |
| guard | popular | sports |
| study | terrible | |

**Team Talk** Have students practice building more complex sentences. Display a sentence starter and have students add oral phrases or clauses using the Amazing Words and the selection vocabulary. Guide students to add at least three phrases or clauses per sentence.

## 2 Read
### "My Turn at Bat"

**BEFORE READING** Have students read the panel information on autobiographies on p. 46. Have them use the text features, including the time line and statistics, to set a purpose for reading. Then have students read "My Turn at Bat" on their own.

**DURING READING** As students read, have them find examples of the author's point of view. How is the narrator of an autobiography different from the narrator of a biography? (In an autobiography, the narrator and the subject are the same person.)

**AFTER READING** Have students discuss Reading Across Texts. Then have them complete the Writing Across Texts activity independently.

## 3 Inquiry: Extend Concepts

**ORGANIZE INFORMATION** Provide time for students to organize their information into a format that will effectively communicate their findings to their audience. Provide any necessary materials or computer time.

**SMALL GROUP TIME**

**Independent Reading Options**

**Trade Book Library**

**eSTREET INTERACTIVE**
www.ReadingStreet.com

Teacher Guides are available on the Leveled Reader Database.

## Common Core State Standards

**Foundational Skills 4.** Read with sufficient accuracy and fluency to support comprehension. **Writing 2.** Write informative/explanatory texts to examine a topic and convey ideas and information clearly. **Speaking/Listening 4.** Report on a topic or text, tell a story, or recount an experience with appropriate facts and relevant, descriptive details, speaking clearly at an understandable pace. **Also Language 1.a.**

## More Reading for Group Time

**ADVANCED**

**Reviews**
• Generalize
• Summarize

Use this suggested Leveled Reader or other text at students' instructional level.

### eStreet Interactive
www.ReadingStreet.com

Use the Leveled Reader Database for lesson plans and student pages for *Extraordinary Athletes.*

**A** Advanced

## 1 Build Word Knowledge
### Extend Singular and Plural Pronouns

**IDENTIFY AND EXTEND** Choral read the bottom of p. 45 with students, having them explain the function of singular and plural pronouns. Have partners reread the model persuasive essay to find examples of how the author used singular and plural pronouns. Encourage students to use the student model on the same page to practice. Allow time for students to discuss their examples and correct any misunderstandings.

## 2 Text-Based Comprehension
### Read

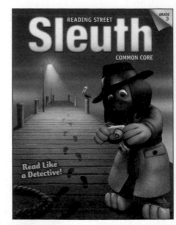

**REREAD "Street Games"** Have partners reread "Street Games." Then have partners discuss what they found to be most interesting about the origins of these street games.

**EXTEND UNDERSTANDING** Talk together about the history of games imitating military exercises. Have students share connections between games they play today and the military.

**PERFORMANCE TASK • Prove It!** Have students work with a partner to write a simple how-to book about a game they play. Remind students to write directions in clear, simple words so readers can easily follow the game. Invite them to add illustrations to their how-to book.

**COMMUNICATE** Have small groups share their how-to books with each other. Invite listeners to ask questions or give suggestions for making the directions even more clear.

## 3 Inquiry: Extend Concepts

**COMMUNICATE** Have students share their inquiry projects on athletes with the rest of the class. Provide the following tips for presenting.

• Match your tone of voice and your pitch to your content.

• Make eye contact with the audience and point to visuals as you speak.

• Use gestures to communicate information (or ideas).

# Indiana Common Core Edition

## This Week's Target Skills and Strategies

| Target Skills and Strategies | © Common Core State Standards for English Language Arts | Indiana Academic Standards for English Language Arts |
|---|---|---|
| **Phonics and Spelling** 🎯 **Skill:** *r*-Controlled Vowels | **CCSS Foundational Skills 3.** Know and apply grade-level phonics and word analysis skills in decoding words. **(Also CCSS Language 2., CCSS Language 2.f.)** | **IN 3.1** Students understand the basic features of words. They select letter patterns and know how to translate them into spoken language using phonics, syllables, word parts, and context. They apply this knowledge to achieve fluent oral and silent reading. |
| **Text-Based Comprehension** 🎯 **Skill:** Graphic Sources | **CCSS Informational Text 7.** Use information gained from illustrations (e.g., maps, photographs), and the words in a text to demonstrate understanding of the text (e.g., where, when, why, and how key events occur). | **IN 3.2.3** Show understanding by identifying answers in the text. |
| 🎯 **Strategy:** Important Ideas | **CCSS Informational Text 2.** Determine the main idea of a text; recount the key details and explain how they support the main idea. **(Also CCSS Informational Text 5.)** | **IN 3.2.5** Distinguish the main idea and supporting details in expository (informational) text. |
| **Vocabulary** 🎯 **Skill:** Unknown Words **Strategy:** Dictionary/Glossary | **CCSS Language 4.** Determine or clarify the meaning of unknown and multiple-meaning word and phrases based on *grade 3 reading and content,* choosing flexibly from a range of strategies. **(Also CCSS Language 4.d.)** | **IN 3.1.7** Use a dictionary to learn the meaning and pronunciation of unknown words. |
| **Fluency** **Skill:** Appropriate Phrasing and Punctuation Cues | **CCSS Foundational Skills 4.** Read with sufficient accuracy and fluency to support comprehension. | **IN 3.1.3** Read aloud grade-level-appropriate literary and informational texts fluently and accurately and with appropriate timing, change in voice, and expression. |
| **Media Literacy** Weather Forecast | **CCSS Speaking/Listening 4.** Report on a topic or text, tell a story, or recount an experience with appropriate facts and relevant, descriptive details, speaking clearly at an understandable pace. | The Indiana Academic Standards for Listening and Speaking are not currently assessed on ISTEP+ assessments. Educators and students should implement the Common Core Standards for Speaking and Listening as soon as possible. |
| **Six-Trait Writing** **Trait of the Week:** Conventions | **CCSS Language 2.** Demonstrate command of the conventions of standard English capitalization, punctuation, and spelling when writing. | **IN 3.6** Students write using Standard English conventions appropriate to this grade level. |
| **Writing** Imaginative Story | **CCSS Writing 3.** Write narratives to develop real or imagined experiences or events using effective technique, descriptive details, and clear event sequences. **(Also CCSS Writing 3.a.)** | **IN 3.5.1** Write narratives. |
| **Conventions** **Skill:** Subject and Object Pronouns | **CCSS Language 1.a.** Explain the function of nouns, pronouns, verbs, adjectives, and adverbs in general and their functions in particular sentences. **(Also CCSS Language 1.f.)** | **IN 3.6.5** Identify and correctly use pronouns, adjectives, compound nouns, and articles in writing. |

## This Week's Cross-Curricular Standards and Resources

### Cross-Curricular Indiana Academic Standards for Social Studies

**Social Studies**
**IN 3.3.6** Explain the basic Earth/sun relationship, including how it influences climate, and identify major climate regions of the United States.
**IN 3.3.7** Describe how climate and the physical characteristics of a region affect the vegetation and animal life living there.

### Reading Street Sleuth

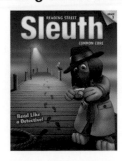

*The Wettest Place on Earth*
pp. 46–47

Follow the path to close reading using the Super Sleuth tips:

• Gather Evidence

• Ask Questions

• Make Your Case

• Prove it!

### More Reading in Science and Social Studies

Concept Literacy

Below Level

On Level

Advanced

ELL

ELD

ISBN-13: 978-0-328-73390-3    ISBN-10: 0-328-73390-3

# Your 90-Minute Reading Block

| | Whole Group | Formative Assessment | Small Group — OL On Level · SI Strategic Intervention · A Advanced | Daily Independent Options |
|---|---|---|---|---|
| | | How do I make my small groups flexible? | What are my other students reading and learning every day in Small Groups? | What do my other students do when I lead Small Groups? |
| **DAY 1** | **Content Knowledge**<br>Build Oral Language/Vocabulary<br>**Phonics/Word Analysis**<br>**Read Decodable Reader**<br>**Text-Based Comprehension**<br>**Selection Vocabulary**<br>**Research and Inquiry**<br>Step 1–Identify and Focus Topic<br>**Spelling Pretest**<br>Connect to Phonics/Word Analysis | **Monitor Progress**<br>Check Oral Vocabulary | Differentiate Vocabulary<br>**Build Word Knowledge**<br>OL Practice Amazing Words<br>SI Reteach Amazing Words<br>A Extend Amazing Words<br>OL SI A **Text-Based Comprehension**<br>Read *Reading Street Sleuth*, pp. 46–47 or Leveled Readers<br>A Inquiry Project<br>ELL Access Vocabulary | ★ **Independent Reading** ©<br>Suggestions for this week's independent reading:<br>• A nonfiction book by a favorite author<br>• A book from the Genius at Work! Great Inventor Biographies series by Edwin Brit Wyckoff<br>• A high-quality magazine article describing a historical sporting event |
| **DAY 2** | **Content Knowledge**<br>Build Oral Language/Vocabulary<br>**Phonics/Word Analysis**<br>**Vocabulary Skill**<br>**Text-Based Comprehension**<br>Read Main Selection, using Access Text Notes<br>**Research and Inquiry**<br>Step 2–Navigate/Search<br>**Spelling**<br>Connect to Phonics/Word Analysis | **Monitor Progress**<br>Formative Assessment: Check Word Reading | Differentiate Comprehension<br>**Build Word Knowledge**<br>OL Practice Selection Vocabulary<br>SI Reteach Selection Vocabulary<br>A Extend Selection Vocabulary<br>OL SI A **Access Text**<br>Read *Hottest, Coldest, Highest, Deepest*<br>A Inquiry Project<br>ELL Access Comprehension Skill | **Book Talk**<br>Foster critical reading and discussion skills through independent and close reading.<br>Students should focus on discussing one or more of the following:<br>• Key Ideas and Details<br>• Craft and Structure<br>• Integration of Ideas |
| **DAY 3** | **Content Knowledge**<br>Build Oral Language/Vocabulary<br>**Phonics/Word Analysis**<br>**Read Decodable Passage**<br>**Text-Based Comprehension**<br>Read Main Selection, using Close Reading Notes<br>**Fluency**<br>**Research and Inquiry**<br>Step 3–Analyze Information<br>**Spelling**<br>Connect to Phonics/Word Analysis | **Monitor Progress**<br>Check Retelling | Differentiate Close Reading<br>OL SI Reread to Develop Vocabulary<br>A Reread to Extend Vocabulary<br>OL SI A Close Reading<br>Read *Hottest, Coldest, Highest, Deepest*<br>A Inquiry Project<br>ELL Access Main Selection |  **Pearson eText**<br>• Student Edition<br>• Decodable Readers<br>• Leveled Readers<br><br> **Trade Book Library**<br><br> **Materials from School or Classroom Library** |
| **DAY 4** | **Content Knowledge**<br>Build Oral Language/Vocabulary<br>**Phonics/Word Analysis**<br>**Read Decodable Passage**<br>**Read Content Area Paired Selection with Genre Focus**<br>**Let's Learn It!**<br>Vocabulary/Fluency/Media Literacy<br>**Research and Inquiry**<br>Step 4–Synthesize<br>**Spelling**<br>Connect to Phonics/Word Analysis | **Monitor Progress**<br>Check Fluency | Differentiate Vocabulary<br>**Build Word Knowledge**<br>OL Develop Language Using Amazing Words<br>SI Review/Discuss Amazing Words<br>A Extend Amazing Words and Selection Vocabulary<br>OL SI A **Text-Based Comprehension**<br>Read "Paul Bunyan and the Great Lakes"<br>A Inquiry Project<br>ELL Access Amazing Words | **Independent Stations**<br>Practice Last Week's Skills<br>★ Focus on these activities when time is limited.<br>**Word Wise**<br>★ **Word Work**<br>**Read for Meaning**<br>★ **Let's Write!**<br>**Words to Know**<br>**Get Fluent** |
| **DAY 5** | **Content Knowledge**<br>Build Oral Language/Vocabulary<br>**Text-Based Comprehension**<br>**Vocabulary Skill**<br>**Phonics/Word Analysis**<br>**Assessment**<br>Fluency, Comprehension<br>**Research and Inquiry**<br>Step 5–Communicate<br>**Spelling Test**<br>Connect to Phonics/Word Analysis | **Monitor Progress**<br>Formative Assessment: Check Oral Vocabulary<br><br>**Monitor Progress**<br>Fluency; Comprehension | Differentiate Reteaching<br>OL Practice Subject and Object Pronouns<br>SI Review Subject and Object Pronouns<br>A Extend Subject and Object Pronouns<br>OL SI A **Text-Based Comprehension**<br>Reread *Reading Street Sleuth*, pp. 46–47 or Leveled Readers<br>A Inquiry Project<br>ELL Access Conventions and Writing | |

## Assessment Resources

Common Core
Weekly Tests, pp. 97–102

Common Core Fresh Reads for Fluency and Comprehension, pp. 97–102

Common Core
Unit 4 Benchmark Test

Common Core Success Tracker, ExamView, and Online Lesson Planner

## Teaching the Common Core State Standards This Week

 The Common Core State Standards for English Language Arts are divided into strands for **Reading** (including **Foundational Skills**), **Writing**, **Speaking and Listening**, and **Language**. The chart below shows some of the content you will teach this week, strand by strand. Turn to this week's 5-Day Planner on pages 54d–54e to see how this content is taught each day.

### Reading Strand

- **Phonics/Word Analysis:** *r*-Controlled Vowels
- **Text-Based Comprehension:** Graphic Sources; Important Ideas
- **Fluency:** Appropriate Phrasing and Punctuation Cues
- **Literary Terms:** Author's Craft
- **Genre:** Main Selection: Expository Text; Paired Selection: Legend

## Common Core State Standards for English Language Arts

### Writing Strand

- **Writing Mini-Lesson:** Imaginative Story
- **Trait:** Conventions
- **Look Back and Write:** Text Evidence

### Speaking and Listening Strand

- **Content Knowledge:** Build Oral Language
- **Media Literacy:** Weather Forecast
- **Research and Inquiry**

### Language Strand

- **Oral Vocabulary: Amazing Words** *evergreens, lumber, competitors, plunged, valuable, champ, sprinter, acrobat, weaken, ranger*
- **Vocabulary:** Unknown Words; Dictionary/Glossary
- **Selection Vocabulary:** *outrun, tides, deserts, waterfalls, peak, average, depth, erupted*
- **Academic Vocabulary:** *r-controlled vowel, graph, author's craft, expository text, punctuation*
- **Conventions:** Subject and Object Pronouns
- **Spelling:** *r*-Controlled Vowels

# Text-Based Comprehension

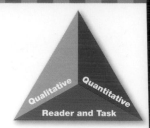

## Text Complexity Measures

Use the rubric to familiarize yourself with the text complexity of *Hottest, Coldest, Highest, Deepest*.

### Bridge to Complex Knowledge

| Quantitative Measures | Lexile | 1000L |
|---|---|---|
| | Average Sentence Length | 14.29 |
| | Word Frequency | 3.39 |

| Qualitative Measures | Levels of Meaning | understand that factual information can be gathered using text, graphs, maps, and images |
|---|---|---|
| | Structure | maps; graphs |
| | Language Conventionality and Clarity | academic language; non-English place names, complex sentence structure |
| | Theme and Knowledge Demands | singular theme; a basic understanding of graphs used for comparison |

| Reader and Task Suggestions | **FORMATIVE ASSESSMENT** Based on assessment results, use the **Reader and Task Suggestions** in Access Main Selection to scaffold the selection or support independence for students as they read *Hottest, Coldest, Highest, Deepest*. |
|---|---|

| READER AND TASK SUGGESTIONS | |
|---|---|
| **Preparing to Read the Text** | **Leveled Tasks** |
| • Review alphabetizing by the first three letters in a word to find words in a dictionary.<br>• Discuss how an author might use maps and charts to deliver factual information.<br>• Remind students that when reading expository text that includes charts and maps, they should read more slowly to understand all of the information the author is providing. | • **Theme and Knowledge Demands** If students have difficulty understanding how the maps on each page relate to the text, have them note where the red dot is on each map and match it to the place mentioned in the text.<br>• **Language Conventionality and Clarity** Students may have difficulty with the academic vocabulary and complex sentences in this selection. Remind students to use context clues, illustrations, and graphic organizers to access the content. |

**Recommended Placement** The quantitative measures suggest this text may be outside the Grade 2–3 text complexity band. The listing of factual information makes the length of some sentences more complex. With scaffolded support, students should be able to access the content of this selection. Students should be encouraged to access the unfamiliar vocabulary using the context clues and images.

# Focus on Common Core State Standards ©

BY STEVE JENKINS

Genre **Expository text** gives information about the real world. Look for numbers and diagrams that help you understand the facts.

Question of the Week
**What makes nature's record holders unique?**

**Main Selection, pp. 62–75**

**Paired Selection, pp. 80–83**

## Text-Based Comprehension

 **Graphic Sources**
CCSS Informational Text 7.

**Important Ideas**
CCSS Informational Text 2.,
CCSS Informational Text 5.

## Fluency

**Appropriate Phrasing and Punctuation Cues**
CCSS Foundational Skills 4.

## Writing and Conventions

**Trait:** Conventions
CCSS Language 2.

**Writing Mini-Lesson:**
Imaginative Story
CCSS Writing 3.a.

**Conventions:** Subject and Object Pronouns
CCSS Language 1.a.,
CCSS Language 1.f.

## Oral Vocabulary

### Amazing Words

| | |
|---|---|
| evergreen | champ |
| lumber | sprinter |
| competitor | acrobat |
| plunge | weaken |
| valuable | ranger |

CCSS Language 6.

## Selection Vocabulary

**Unknown Words**
CCSS Language 4.

**Dictionary/Glossary**
CCSS Language 4.,
CCSS Language 4.d.

| | | |
|---|---|---|
| average | erupted | tides |
| depth | outrun | waterfalls |
| deserts | peak | |

## Phonics and Spelling

**Vowels: *r*-Controlled**
CCSS Language 2.,
CCSS Language 2.f.,
CCSS Foundational Skills 3.

| | |
|---|---|
| third | perfect |
| early | verb |
| world | nerve |
| certain | worm |
| dirty | thirsty |
| herself | workout |
| earth | earn |
| word | |

**Challenge Words**

| | |
|---|---|
| determine | worthwhile |
| commercial | virtual |
| whirlwind | |

## Media Literacy

**Weather Forecast**
CCSS Speaking/Listening 4.

*Hottest, Coldest, Highest, Deepest* **54a**

# Preview Your Week

*What makes nature's record holders unique?*

Main Selection, pp. 62–75

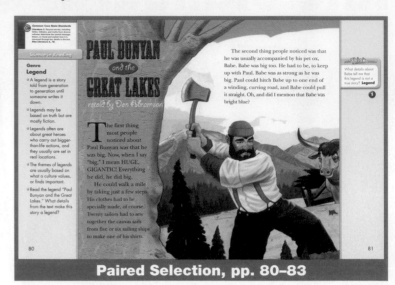

Paired Selection, pp. 80–83

**Genre:** Expository Text

 **Vocabulary:** Unknown Words

**Text-Based Comprehension:** Graphic Sources

**Science in Reading**

**Genre:** Legend

# Build Content Knowledge

 Zoom in on

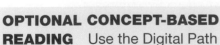

## KNOWLEDGE GOALS

Students will understand that nature has

- unusual appearances
- extreme weather
- extreme events

## THIS WEEK'S CONCEPT MAP

Develop a concept-related graphic organizer like the one below over the course of this week.

What makes nature's record holders unique

Height | Length | Being the most

## BUILD ORAL VOCABULARY

This week, students will acquire the following academic vocabulary/domain-specific words.

### Amazing Words

| | | |
|---|---|---|
| evergreen | valuable | acrobat |
| lumber | champ | weaken |
| competitor | sprinter | ranger |
| plunge | | |

**OPTIONAL CONCEPT-BASED READING** Use the Digital Path to access readers offering different levels of text complexity.

Concept Literacy

Below-Level

On-Level

Advanced

ELL

ELD

# This Week's Digital Resources

## eStreet Interactive
### www.ReadingStreet.com

### Get Ready to Read

 **Concept Talk Video** Use this video on the Digital Path to present and introduce the weekly concept of nature's record holders.

 **Pearson eText** Read the eText of the Student Edition pages on Pearson SuccessNet for comprehension and fluency support.

 **Envision It! Animations** Use this lively animation on the Digital Path to explain the target comprehension skill, Graphic Sources.

### Read and Comprehend

 **Journal** Use the Word Bank on the Digital Path to have students write sentences using this week's selection vocabulary words

 **Background Building Audio CD** This audio CD provides important background information about nature's record holders to help students read and comprehend the weekly texts.

 **Pearson eText** Read the eText of the main selection, *Hottest, Coldest, Highest, Deepest,* and the paired selection, "Paul Bunyan and the Great Lakes," with audio support on Pearson SuccessNet.

 **Vocabulary Activities** A variety of interactive vocabulary activities on the Digital Path help students practice selection vocabulary and concept-related words.

 **Story Sort** Use the Story Sort Activity on the Digital Path after reading *Hottest, Coldest, Highest, Deepest* to involve students in summarizing.

### Language Arts

 **Grammar Jammer** Choose an inviting animation on the Digital Path to provide an engaging grammar lesson that will attract students' attention.

**Pearson eText** Find the Student Edition eText of the Let's Write It! and Let's Learn It! pages with audio support on Pearson SuccessNet.

## Additional Resources

 **Teacher Resources DVD-ROM** Use the following resources on the TR DVD or on Pearson SuccessNet throughout the week:

- Amazing Word Cards
- Reader's and Writer's Notebook
- Writing Transparencies
- Daily Fix-It Transparencies
- Scoring Rubrics
- Grammar Transparencies
- ELL Support
- Let's Practice It!
- Graphic Organizers
- Vocabulary Cards

## This Week's Skills

**Phonics/Word Analysis**
◎ Vowels: *r*-Controlled

**Comprehension**
◎ **Skill:** Graphic Sources
◎ **Strategy:** Important Ideas

**Language**
◎ **Vocabulary:** Unknown Words
**Conventions:** Subject and Object Pronouns

**Fluency**
Appropriate Phrasing and Punctuation Clues

**Writing**
Imaginative Story

# 5-Day Planner

## DAY 1

### Get Ready to Read

**Content Knowledge** 54j
Oral Vocabulary: *evergreen, lumber, competitor, plunge*

> **Monitor Progress**
> Check Oral Vocabulary

**Phonics/Word Analysis** 56a
◎ Vowels: *r*-Controlled
**READ** Decodable Reader 17A
Reread for Fluency

### Read and Comprehend

**Text-Based Comprehension** 58a
◎ Graphic Sources
◎ Important Ideas

**Fluency** 58–59
Appropriate Phrasing

**Selection Vocabulary** 59a
*average, depth, deserts, erupted, outrun, peak, tides, waterfalls*

### Language Arts

**Research and Inquiry** 59b
Identify and Focus Topic

**Spelling** 59c
Vowels: *r*-Controlled, Pretest

**Conventions** 59d
Subject and Object Pronouns

**Handwriting** 59d
Cursive Letters *o, w,* and *b*

**Writing** 59e
Imaginative Story

## DAY 2

### Get Ready to Read

**Content Knowledge** 60a
Oral Vocabulary: *valuable, champ*

**Phonics/Word Analysis** 60c
◎ Vowels: *r*-Controlled

> **Monitor Progress**
> Check Word Reading

**Literary Terms** 60d
Author's Craft

### Read and Comprehend

**Vocabulary Skill** 60e
◎ Unknown Words

**Fluency** 60–61
Appropriate Phrasing

**Text-Based Comprehension** 62–63
**READ** *Hottest, Coldest, Highest, Deepest*—1st Read

### Language Arts

**Research and Inquiry** 69b
Navigate/Search

**Conventions** 69c
Subject and Object Pronouns

**Spelling** 69c
Vowels: *r*-Controlled

**Writing** 69d
Imaginative Story

## DAY 3

### Get Ready to Read

**Content Knowledge** 70a
Oral Vocabulary: *sprinter, acrobat*

**Word Analysis** 70c
Fluent Word Reading
**DECODE AND READ**
Decodable Practice Passage 17B

### Read and Comprehend

**Text-Based Comprehension** 70e
Check Understanding
**READ** *Hottest, Coldest, Highest, Deepest*—2nd Read
Monitor Progress Check Retelling

**Fluency** 77b
Appropriate Phrasing and Punctuation Cues

### Language Arts

**Research and Study Skills** 77c
Bar Graphs

**Research and Inquiry** 77d
Analyze Information

**Conventions** 77e
Subject and Object Pronouns

**Spelling** 77e
Vowels: *r*-Controlled

**Writing** 78–79
Imaginative Story

## DAY 4

### Get Ready to Read

**Content Knowledge** 80a
Oral Vocabulary: *weaken, ranger*

**Phonics/Word Analysis** 80c
**Review** Irregular Plurals
Fluent Word Reading
**DECODE AND READ**
Decodable Practice Passage 17C

### Read and Comprehend

**Genre** 80g
Legend
**READ** "Paul Bunyan and the Great Lakes"—Paired Selection

**Fluency** 84–85
Appropriate Phrasing and Punctuation Cues
Monitor Progress Check Fluency

**Vocabulary Skill** 85a
Unknown Words

**Media Literacy** 85a
Weather Forecast

### Language Arts

**Research and Inquiry** 85b
Synthesize

**Conventions** 85c
Subject and Object Pronouns

**Spelling** 85c
Vowels: *r*-Controlled

**Writing** 85d
Imaginative Story

## DAY 5

### Get Ready to Read

**Content Knowledge** 85f
Review Oral Vocabulary
Monitor Progress
Check Oral Vocabulary

### Read and Comprehend

**Text-Based Comprehension** 85h
Review Graphic Sources

**Vocabulary Skill** 85h
Review Unknown Words

**Word Analysis** 85i
Review Vowels: *r*-Controlled

**Literary Terms** 85i
Review Author's Craft

**Assessment** 85j, 85l
Monitor Progress
Fluency; Graphic Sources

### Language Arts

**Research and Inquiry** 85n
Communicate

**Spelling** 85o
Vowels: *r*-Controlled, Test

**Conventions** 85o
Subject and Object Pronouns

**Writing** 85p
Imaginative Story

**Wrap Up Your Week!** 85q

# Access for All

## What do I do in group time?
It's as easy as 1-2-3!

**1** TEACHER-LED SMALL GROUPS → **2** INDEPENDENT PRACTICE STATIONS → **3** INDEPENDENT READING

## Small Group Time

### Bridge to Common Core

**SKILL DEVELOPMENT**
- Vowels: *r*-Controlled
- Graphic Sources
- Important Ideas
- Unknown Words

**DEEP UNDERSTANDING**
**This Week's Knowledge Goals**
Students will understand that nature has
- unusual appearances
- extreme weather
- extreme events

## 1 Small Group Lesson Plan

| | DAY 1 — Differentiate Vocabulary | DAY 2 — Differentiate Comprehension |
|---|---|---|
| **OL On-Level** pp. SG•18–SG•22 | **Build Word Knowledge** Practice Amazing Words **Text-Based Comprehension** Read *Reading Street Sleuth*, pp. 46–47 or Leveled Readers | **Build Word Knowledge** Practice Selection Vocabulary **Access Text** Read *Hottest, Coldest, Highest, Deepest* |
| **SI Strategic Intervention** pp. SG•23–SG•27 | **Build Word Knowledge** Reteach Amazing Words **Text-Based Comprehension** Read *Reading Street Sleuth*, pp. 46–47 or Leveled Readers | **Build Word Knowledge** Reteach Selection Vocabulary **Access Text** Read *Hottest, Coldest, Highest, Deepest* |
| **A Advanced** pp. SG•28–SG•32 | **Build Word Knowledge** Extend Amazing Words **Text-Based Comprehension** Read *Reading Street Sleuth*, pp. 46–47 or Leveled Readers | **Build Word Knowledge** Extend Selection Vocabulary **Access Text** Read *Hottest, Coldest, Highest, Deepest* |
| **Independent Inquiry Project** | Identify Questions | Investigate |
| **ELL** If... students need more scaffolding and practice with... | **Vocabulary,** then... use the activities on DI•42–DI•43 in the Teacher Resources section on SuccessNet. | **Comprehension Skill,** then... use the activities on page DI•46 in the Teacher Resources section on SuccessNet. |

## Reading Street Sleuth

- Provides access to grade-level text for all students
- Focuses on finding clues in text through close reading
- Builds capacity for complex text

## Build Text-Based Comprehension

*Hottest, Coldest, Highest, Deepest*

### Optional Leveled Readers

| Concept Literacy | Below-Level | On-Level | Advanced | ELL | ELD |
|---|---|---|---|---|---|

| **DAY 3** | **DAY 4** | **DAY 5** |
|---|---|---|
| **Differentiate Close Reading** | **Differentiate Vocabulary** | **Differentiate Reteaching** |
| **Reread to Develop Vocabulary**<br>**Close Reading**<br>Read *Hottest, Coldest, Highest, Deepest* | **Build Word Knowledge**<br>Develop Language Using Amazing Words<br>**Text-Based Comprehension**<br>Read "Paul Bunyan and the Great Lakes" | **Practice Subject and Object Pronouns**<br>**Text-Based Comprehension**<br>Reread *Reading Street Sleuth*, pp. 46–47 or Leveled Readers |
| **Reread to Develop Vocabulary**<br>**Close Reading**<br>Read *Hottest, Coldest, Highest, Deepest* | **Build Word Knowledge**<br>Review/Discuss Amazing Words<br>**Text-Based Comprehension**<br>Read "Paul Bunyan and the Great Lakes" | **Review Subject and Object Pronouns**<br>**Text-Based Comprehension**<br>Reread *Reading Street Sleuth*, pp. 46–47 or Leveled Readers |
| **Reread to Extend Vocabulary**<br>**Close Reading**<br>Read *Hottest, Coldest, Highest, Deepest* | **Build Word Knowledge**<br>Extend Amazing Words and Selection Vocabulary<br>**Text-Based Comprehension**<br>Read "Paul Bunyan and the Great Lakes" | **Extend Subject and Object Pronouns**<br>**Text-Based Comprehension**<br>Reread *Reading Street Sleuth*, pp. 46–47 or Leveled Readers |
| **Investigate** | **Organize** | **Communicate** |
| **Main Selection,**<br>**then...** use the activities on page DI•47 in the Teacher Resources section on SuccessNet. | **Amazing Words,**<br>**then...** use the Routine on pp. xxxvi–xxxvii in the *ELL Handbook*. | **Conventions and Writing,**<br>**then...** use the activities on pp. DI•49–DI•50 in the Teacher Resources section on SuccessNet. |

# ②Independent Stations

## Practice Last Week's Skills

 Focus on these activities when time is limited.

---

## WORD WISE

### Spell and use words in sentences.

**OBJECTIVES**

- Spell irregular plurals.

**MATERIALS**

- *Word Wise* Flip Chart Activity 17, teacher-made word cards, paper and pencils

 **Letter Tile Drag and Drop**

● Students write a sentence for four words with irregular plurals and then write the singular form of each.

▲ Students write a sentence for six words with irregular plurals and then write the singular form of each.

■ Students write a sentence for eight words with irregular plurals and then write the singular form of each.

---

## WORD WORK

### Identify and pronounce words.

**OBJECTIVES**

- Identify and pronounce irregular plurals.

**MATERIALS**

- *Word Work* Flip Chart Activity 17, teacher-made word cards, paper and pencils

 **Letter Tile Drag and Drop**

● Students write and pronounce five words with irregular plurals and then use them in a sentence and read each sentence aloud.

▲ Students write and pronounce seven words with irregular plurals and then use them in a sentence and read each sentence aloud.

■ Students write and pronounce ten words with irregular plurals and then use as many as possible in a paragraph to be read aloud.

---

## LET'S WRITE!

### Write to persuade.

**OBJECTIVES**

- Write persuasive text.

**MATERIALS**

- *Let's Write!* Flip Chart Activity 17, paper and pencils

 **Grammar Jammer**

● Students write a short paragraph that persuades other students to read their favorite book.

▲ Students write two paragraphs persuading other students to read their favorite book.

■ Students write a short three-paragraph essay persuading other students to read their favorite book.

---

## WORDS TO KNOW

### Determine word meanings.

**OBJECTIVES**

- Identify and define unfamiliar words.

**MATERIALS**

- *Words to Know* Flip Chart Activity 17, teacher-made word cards, magazines, paper and pencils

 **Vocabulary Activities**

● Students find three unfamiliar words in a magazine, look up their meanings, and use each in a sentence.

▲ Students find four unfamiliar words in a magazine, look up their meanings, and use each in a sentence.

■ Students find five unfamiliar words, guess their meanings from context, check their answers, and use each word in a sentence.

## READ FOR MEANING

### Use text-based comprehension tools.

#### OBJECTIVES

• Make generalizations based on information presented in the text.

#### MATERIALS

• *Read for Meaning* Flip Chart Activity 17, Leveled Readers, paper and pencils

 **Pearson eText**
• Leveled eReaders

 **Envision It! Animations**

● Students read a book. They write one sentence that makes a generalization and one sentence supporting the generalization.

▲ Students read a book and write a short paragraph that makes a generalization and supports it with facts from the text.

■ Students read a book and write two short paragraphs that make two generalizations and support them with facts from the text.

## GET FLUENT

### Practice fluent reading.

#### OBJECTIVES

• Read aloud with accuracy.

#### MATERIALS

• *Get Fluent* Flip Chart Activity 17, Leveled Readers

 **Pearson eText**
• Leveled eReaders

● Partners read from a Concept Literacy Reader or a Below-Level Reader, practicing accuracy and providing feedback.

▲ Partners read from an On-Level Reader, practicing accuracy and providing feedback.

■ Partners read from an Advanced Reader, practicing accuracy and providing feedback.

## Manage the Stations

Use these management tools to set up and organize your Practice Stations:

Practice Station Flip Charts

Classroom Management Handbook for Differentiated Instruction Practice Stations, p. 35

## 3 Independent Reading ©

Students should select appropriate complex texts to read and write about independently every day before, during, and after school.

Suggestions for this week's independent reading:
• A nonfiction book by a favorite author
• A book from the *Genius at Work! Great Inventor Biographies* series by Edwin Brit Wyckoff
• A high-quality magazine article describing a historical sporting event

**BOOK TALK** Have partners discuss their independent reading for the week. Tell them to refer to their Reading Logs and paraphrase what each selection was about. Then have students focus on discussing one or more of the following:

**Key Ideas and Details**
• What is the main idea of the text? List details that support it.
• Summarize the events in the text.

**Craft and Structure**
• How is the information in the text organized?
• List the text features. How do they help you understand the text?

**Integration of Ideas**
• Make generalizations based on information in the text.
• Provide details to support your generalizations.

 **Pearson eText**
• Student Edition
• Decodable Readers
• Leveled Readers

 **Trade Book Library**

 **School or Classroom Library**

## Ⓒ Bridge to Common Core

**INTEGRATION OF KNOWLEDGE/IDEAS**
This week, students will read, write, and talk about what makes nature's record holders unique.

**Texts This Week**
• "To Climb the Tallest Tree"
• "Largest U.S. Cities"
• "Geography Bee"
• *Hottest, Coldest, Highest, Deepest*
• "Paul Bunyan and the Great Lakes"

**Science Knowledge Goals**
Students will understand that nature has
• unusual appearances
• extreme weather
• extreme events

# Street Rhymes!

Climb the highest mountain.
Sail the deepest sea.
Walk the widest valley.
Tell me what you see.

• To introduce this week's concept, read aloud the poem several times and ask students to join you.

# Content Knowledge

## Nature's Record Holders

**CONCEPT TALK** To further explore the unit concept of One of a Kind, this week students will read, write, and talk about what it means to be unique. Write the Question of the Week on the board, *What makes nature's record holders unique?*

# Build Oral Language

**TALK ABOUT NATURE'S RECORD HOLDERS** Have students turn to pp. 54–55 in their Student Editions. Look at each of the photos. Then use the prompts to guide discussion and create a concept map.

• What is unusual about the iceberg? **(It is very tall.)** What else is unusual about the iceberg? **(It is in a very cold climate.)** The most extreme climates are either very hot or very cold. Let's add *Height* and *Being the most* to our map.

• What is unusual about the rattlesnake? **(It is very long.)** This kind of snake is one of the longest in Texas. Something that is very long, like a river or a snake, can be an extreme in nature. Let's add *Length* to the concept map.

Common Core State Standards
Language 6. Acquire and use accurately grade-appropriate conversational, general academic, and domain-specific words and phrases, including those that signal spatial and temporal relationships (e.g., *After dinner that night we went looking for them*). Also Speaking/Listening 1.c.

**Oral Vocabulary**

You've learned
**1 5 8**
Amazing Words ⭐
so far this year!

## Let's Talk About

### Nature's Record Holders

- Ask relevant questions about nature's record holders.
- Comment on nature's unique environments.
- Offer suggestions for how we might protect unique places in nature.

**READING STREET ONLINE**
**CONCEPT TALK VIDEO**
www.ReadingStreet.com

54                                            55

**Student Edition, pp. 54–55**

**CONNECT TO READING** Tell students that this week they will be reading about extremes in nature, including real places and in a legend. Throughout the week, encourage students to add concept-related words to this week's concept map.

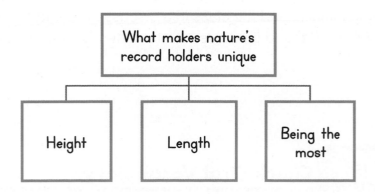

What makes nature's record holders unique

| Height | Length | Being the most |

## eSTREET INTERACTIVE
www.ReadingStreet.com

**Pearson eText**
• Student Edition

**Concept Talk Video**

 **ELL**

**Preteach Concepts** Use the Day 1 instruction on ELL Poster 17 to build knowledge, develop concepts, and build oral vocabulary.

**ELL Support** Additional ELL support and modified instruction is provided in the *ELL Handbook* and in the ELL Support lessons found on the *Teacher Resources DVD-ROM*.

## Amazing Words

You've learned **1 5 8** words so far.

You'll learn **0 1 0** words this week!

| | |
|---|---|
| evergreen | champ |
| lumber | sprinter |
| competitor | acrobat |
| plunge | weaken |
| valuable | ranger |

# Content Knowledge

## Build Oral Vocabulary

**INTRODUCE AMAZING WORDS** "To Climb the Tallest Tree" on p. 55b tells how Stephen Sillett climbed the tallest tree in the world. Tell students to listen for this week's Amazing Words—*evergreen, lumber, competitor,* and *plunge*— as you read the Teacher Read Aloud on p. 55b.

## Amazing Words    Robust Vocabulary Routine

1. **Introduce** Write the word *evergreen* on the board. Have students say the word aloud with you. In "To Climb the Tallest Tree," we learn that redwood trees are *evergreens.* Supply a student-friendly definition. *Evergreen* means having green leaves all year round.

2. **Demonstrate** Have students answer questions to demonstrate understanding. Do *evergreen* trees lose their leaves? (no) Are pine trees, which keep their leaves all year, *evergreens?* (yes)

3. **Apply** Ask students to give a sentence using *evergreen.*

4. **Display the Word** Run your hand under the syllables *e-ver-green* as you read the word.

See p. OV•2 to teach *lumber, competitor,* and *plunge.*

Routines Flip Chart

**AMAZING WORDS AT WORK** Reread "To Climb the Tallest Tree" aloud. As students listen, have them notice how the Amazing Words are used in context. To build oral vocabulary, lead the class in a discussion about the meanings of the Amazing Words. Remind students to listen attentively and make pertinent comments.

**MONITOR PROGRESS** Check Oral Vocabulary

During discussion, listen for students' use of Amazing Words.

**If...** students are unable to use the Amazing Words in discussion,

**then...** use the Oral Vocabulary Routine in the Routines Flip Chart to demonstrate words in different contexts.

# Teacher Read Aloud

**MODEL FLUENCY** As you read "To Climb the Tallest Tree," model appropriate phrasing by grouping words in a meaningful way and paying attention to punctuation cues.

# To Climb the Tallest Tree

Stephen Sillett loves trees. He loves to study trees. He loves to climb trees. In the summer of 2006, he climbed the tallest tree in the world because he wanted to measure just how high it is.

Sillett, a university professor, lives in California, near a forest where redwood trees grow. The tallest trees in the world are redwoods. They are one of nature's giants. Some stand over 350 feet tall and are still growing.

How can these trees grow so tall? The rich soil in the redwood forest helps the trees grow. The weather helps too. Redwoods are evergreens, which means that they keep their leaves all year. In the winter, rain falls often in the redwood forest, so the trees get plenty of water. In the summer, they get water from the thick fog that covers their leaves.

A long time ago, there were many more redwoods. These giant trees usually live for thousands of years. But about 40 years ago, people started to cut down the tallest redwoods to use them for lumber. Sillett wanted to find the tallest tree that was still standing.

Sillett looked all over the redwood forest. He went to an area he had never been to before. There were plenty of tall redwoods in that part of the forest. But which one was the tallest? He found several competitors, but chose one that looked tallest to him. But to find out if that tree really was the tallest, he would have to climb to the top.

The tree wasn't easy to climb. In fact, it took longer than Sillett thought. First, he had to wait until nesting season was over. A rare bird builds its nest in the redwoods' branches. Sillett did not want to disturb the nests. So he waited until the baby birds hatched and grew strong enough to fly.

Then, Sillett had to find a way to climb the tree's giant trunk. The first branch was hundreds of feet above the ground! How would he get up there to step on it? Sillett tied a large bolt to the end of a rope and used a crossbow to shoot the rope over the branch. The rope caught on the branch. The bolt sailed over the branch and then plunged to the ground. Sillett hammered the bolt into another tree. Then, he climbed the rope up to the lowest branch.

From there, he still had a long way to go. But Sillett was determined to reach the top. When he did, he dropped down a long measuring tape. He was right! At a little over 379 feet high, that tree IS the tallest one on Earth.

That redwood was named Hyperion after a famous giant in Greek stories. Sillett wants people to know about Hyperion. He wants people to save nature's giants and help keep them growing strong.

**ELL Support for Read Aloud** Use the modified Read Aloud on p. DI•44 of the ELL Support lessons on the *Teacher Resources* DVD-ROM to prepare students to listen to "To Climb the Tallest Tree."

**Support Listening Comprehension** Have small groups of students discuss what they already know about redwood trees. How are these trees different from other trees? What makes them so different and where do they grow? Why are there fewer redwoods today than long ago? Share answers with the group. Use pictures from the Student Edition to provide visual support.

**Common Core State Standards**

**Foundational Skills 3.** Know and apply grade-level phonics and word analysis skills in decoding words.

## Skills Trace

**Vowels: *r*-Controlled** /èr/ spelled *ir, er, ur, ear, or*; /är/ spelled *ar*, and /ôr/ spelled *or, ore, oar*

**Introduce/Teach** U4W2D1

**Practice** U4W2D3, U4W2D4

**Reteach/Review** U4W2D5, U4W3D4

**Assess/Test** Weekly Test U4W2 Benchmark Test U4

**KEY:** U=Unit   W=Week   D=Day

## Vocabulary Support

You may wish to explain the meanings of these words.

**boar** a male pig or hog

**curtain** a window covering made from fabric

# Phonics

## Teach/Model

### Vowels: *r*-Controlled

**CONNECT** Connect today's lesson to previously learned sound-spellings *r* and *wr*. Write *rocket* and *writing.* You can read words like these already. They both begin with the /r/ sound. Today you'll learn to spell and read words with /èr/ spelled *ir, er, ur, ear, or*; /är/ spelled *ar*; and /ôr/ spelled *or, ore, oar.*

**MODEL** Write *earth.* I see that this word has the letters *ear* that spell the sound /èr/. This is how I blend this word. Point to each spelling as you say its sound. Then blend the word: /er/ /th/, *earth.* Follow this procedure to model *third, verb, market, normal,* and *soaring.*

**GROUP PRACTICE** Continue the process. This time have students blend with you. Remind them that the letter *r* changes the sound of a vowel or vowels in a syllable.

| | | | | |
|---|---|---|---|---|
| third | heard | forth | large | store |
| boar | party | curtain | word | germ |

**REVIEW** What do you know about reading these words? (When you see the letter *r* plus a vowel or vowels, it makes one sound.)

## Guide Practice

**MODEL** Have students turn to p. 56 in their Student Editions. Each word on this page has the vowel sound /èr/, /är/, or /ôr/. The first word is *ferment.* I hear /èr/ in the first syllable. In *ferment,* /èr/ is spelled *er.*

**GROUP PRACTICE** For each word in Words I Can Blend, ask for the sound of each letter or group of letters. Make sure that students identify the correct sounds for the *r*-controlled vowels. Then have them blend the words.

> **Corrective feedback**
>
> **If...** students have difficulty blending a word,
> **then...** model blending the word. Then have students blend it with you.

**Phonics**

## 🔊 r-Controlled Vowels

**Words I Can Blend**

f e r m e n t

c a r p o o l

c i r c u s

p u r c h a s e

s u p p o r t

### Sentences I Can Read

1. We saw the bread ferment when we watched it rise.
2. Our group will carpool to the circus.
3. This purchase will support a good cause.

**Envision It!** Sounds to Know

fern · er

pearls · ear

girl · ir

score · ore

artist · ar

orchestra · or

worm · or

curtains · ur

**READING STREET ONLINE**
SOUND-SPELLING CARDS
www.ReadingStreet.com

56

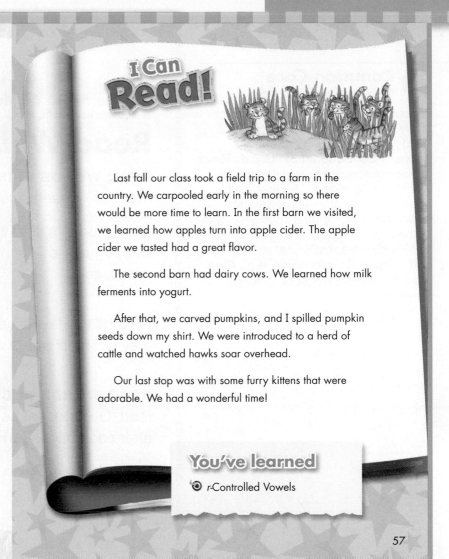

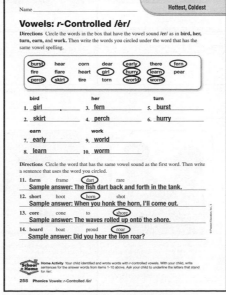

**I Can Read!**

Last fall our class took a field trip to a farm in the country. We carpooled early in the morning so there would be more time to learn. In the first barn we visited, we learned how apples turn into apple cider. The apple cider we tasted had a great flavor.

The second barn had dairy cows. We learned how milk ferments into yogurt.

After that, we carved pumpkins, and I spilled pumpkin seeds down my shirt. We were introduced to a herd of cattle and watched hawks soar overhead.

Our last stop was with some furry kittens that were adorable. We had a wonderful time!

**You've learned**
🔊 r-Controlled Vowels

57

**Student Edition, pp. 56–57**

## Apply

**READ WORDS IN ISOLATION** After students can successfully segment and blend the words on p. 56 in their Student Editions, point to words in random order and ask students to read them naturally.

**READ WORDS IN CONTEXT** Have students read each of the sentences on p. 56. Have them identify words in the sentences that have the *r*-controlled vowel sounds /ėr/, /är/, and /ôr/.

**Team Talk** Pair students and have them take turns reading each of the sentences aloud.

**ON THEIR OWN** For additional practice, use *Reader's and Writer's Notebook*, p. 258.

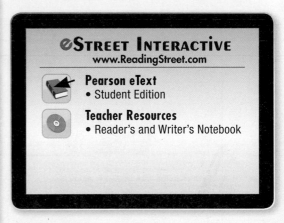

Reader's and Writer's Notebook,
p. 258

**eSTREET INTERACTIVE**
www.ReadingStreet.com

**Pearson eText**
• Student Edition

**Teacher Resources**
• Reader's and Writer's Notebook

**ELL**

**Contrastive Analysis Chart** See also the Contrastive Analysis Chart in *First Stop*.

**Language Transfer** Many languages do not have a sound like /ėr/. Therefore, many students for whom English is not the home language may have trouble pronouncing words such as *dirt* or *fern*. Help students practice saying and writing words with the same pronunciation, such as *her, bird*, and *turn*.

## Common Core State Standards

**Foundational Skills 3.** Know and apply grade-level phonics and word analysis skills in decoding words. **Foundational Skills 3.d.** Read grade-appropriate irregularly spelled words. **Language 6.** Acquire and use accurately grade-appropriate conversational, general academic, and domain-specific words and phrases, including those that signal spatial and temporal relationships (e.g., *After dinner that night we went looking for them*).

# Decodable Reader 17A

If students need help, then...

## Read *Whirling Girl*

**READ WORDS IN ISOLATION** Have students turn to p. 13 of *Decodable Practice Readers 3.2.* Have students read each word.

Have students read the high-frequency words *from, the, one, was, to, what, who, of, put, could, do, into, were, wanting, you, said, they,* and *have* on the first page.

**PREVIEW** Have students read the title and preview the story. Tell them that they will read words with the *r*-controlled vowel sounds /er/, /är/, and /ôr/.

**READ WORDS IN CONTEXT** Pair students for reading and listen as they read. One student begins. Students read the entire story, switching readers after each page. Partners reread the story. This time the other student begins.

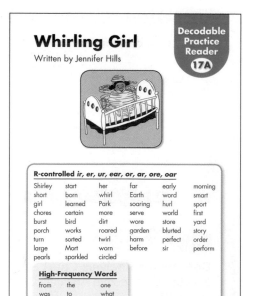

Decodable Practice Reader 17A

**Corrective feedback** | **If...** students have difficulty decoding a word, **then...** refer them to the *Sound-Spelling Cards* to identify the sounds in the word. Then prompt them to blend the word.

- What is the new word?
- Is the new word a word you know?
- Does it make sense in the story?

**CHECK DECODING AND COMPREHENSION** Have students retell the story to include characters, setting, and events. Then have students find words in the story that have *r*-controlled vowels. Students should supply *Shirley, start, her, far, early, morning, short, born, whirl, Earth, word, smart, girl, learned, Park, soaring, hurl, sport, chores, certain, more, serve, world, first, burst, bird, dirt, wore, store, yard, porch, works, roared, garden, blurted, story, sorted, twirl, turn, harm, perfect, order, large, Mort, worn, before, sir, perform, pearls, sparkled,* and *circled.*

# Reread for Fluency

**REREAD DECODABLE READER** Have students reread *Decodable Practice Reader 17A* to develop automaticity decoding words with *r*-controlled vowels.

**Routine** Oral Rereading

1. **Read** Have students read the entire book orally.

2. **Reread** To achieve optimal fluency, students should reread the text three or four times.

3. **Corrective Feedback** Listen as students read. Provide corrective feedback regarding their fluency and decoding.

Routines Flip Chart

## Academic Vocabulary ©

An *r*-controlled vowel is a vowel followed by the letter *r*. The *r* influences the sound of the vowel, which is neither long nor short (*bark, girl, term, fur*).

## ELL

**r-Controlled Vowels**

**Beginning** Choose several words with the *r*-controlled vowel sound /ėr/, such as *bird, her,* and *pearls,* from the *Decodable Practice Reader,* and write them on the board. Point to each word as you say it aloud. Then underline the letters that spell the sound /ėr/ in each word. Have students repeat the words with you. Do the same for words with /är/ and /ôr/.

**Intermediate** Remind students that the letter *r* and the vowel it controls must be in the same syllable. Write several multisyllable words with the *r*-controlled vowel sound from the *Decodable Practice Reader,* such as *morning, soaring,* and *certain.* Have students divide each word into syllables and then blend them to read the entire word.

**Advanced** After reading the story, have students choose 4 or 5 words with the *r*-controlled vowel sound and write a sentence for each word.

*Hottest, Coldest, Highest, Deepest* **57b**

Zoom in on ©

## Skills Trace

© **Graphic Sources**

**Introduce** U3W3D1; U4W2D1; U6W3D1

**Practice** U3W3D2; U3W3D3; U4W1D3; U4W2D2; U4W2D3; U6W3D2; U6W3D3

**Reteach/Review** U3W3D5; U4W2D5; U6W3D5

**Assess/Test** Weekly Tests U3W3; U4W2; U6W3 Benchmark Tests

**KEY:** U=Unit   W=Week   D=Day

## Academic Vocabulary ©

**graph** a pictorial representation of data that shows how any one piece of information compares to other pieces

## Comprehension Support

Students may also turn to pp. EI•10 and EI•11 to review the skill and strategy if necessary.

# Text-Based Comprehension

## ⊙ Graphic Sources
## ⊙ Important Ideas

**READ** Remind students of the weekly concept—Nature's Record Holders. Have students read "Largest U.S. Cities" on p. 59.

### MODEL A CLOSE READ

**Think Aloud** As I read "Largest U.S. Cities," I look for information in the type, photos, and the bar graph to identify the important ideas. The type size and color for the title of the article, as well as the photos, captions, and graph, show me that an important idea is that the U.S. has four very large cities. Have students follow along as you read the second paragraph aloud. This paragraph tells us the four largest cities in the United States in order of size. I can see that information visually in the bar graph at the bottom of the page. I can see at a glance that New York has the most people living in it, because the bar for New York is the longest one.

**TEACH** Have students read p. 58. Explain that the skill of using graphic sources and the strategy of important ideas are tools they can use to help them integrate information and ideas. Review the bulleted items and explanations on p. 58. Have students make their own graphs of the information to apply their understanding of graphic sources.

**GUIDE PRACTICE** Have students reread "Largest U.S. Cities" using the callouts as guides. Then ask volunteers to respond to the questions in the callouts, citing specific examples from the text to support their answers.

**Strategy** The U.S. has four large cities. The names of the cities are New York, Los Angeles, Chicago, and Houston. **Skill** New York City has a population much larger than any other city in the United States.

**APPLY** Use *Reader's and Writer's Notebook* p. 259 for additional practice with graphic sources.

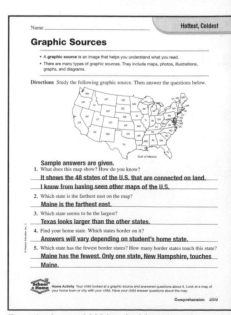

Reader's and Writer's Notebook, p. 259

**Envision It!** Skill Strategy

**Skill**

Graphic Sources

**Strategy**

Important Ideas

**THINK**

READING STREET ONLINE
ENVISION IT! ANIMATIONS
www.ReadingStreet.com

### Comprehension Skill

## ◉ Graphic Sources

- Graphic sources are ways of showing information visually, or in a way you can see.

- Charts, diagrams, maps, and graphs are examples of graphic sources, or features.

- Graphic sources can help you predict what the reading will be about.

- Use what you learned about graphic sources to read "Largest U.S. Cities." Then use the text and the bar graph to make a new graph showing how the population of New York City compares to Los Angeles, Chicago, and Houston combined.

### Comprehension Strategy

## ◉ Important Ideas

Before you read a selection or story, look for the important ideas in titles, topic sentences, key words, charts, or photos and other illustrations. While you read, stop and ask, "What is this text all about?" Important ideas summarize a selection or tell what it is all about. Try to find the most important idea in each paragraph and verify your predictions.

# Largest
## U.S. Cities

New York

Los Angeles

Chicago

Houston

Millions of people in the United States live in cities. The number of people who live in a city is called its population.

The U.S. city with the most people living in it is New York City. Los Angeles, California, comes in second. Chicago, Illinois, is the third largest city with Houston, Texas, closely following. New York City, however, has almost as many people as Los Angeles, Chicago, and Houston put together!

**Strategy** What are two important ideas in the text?

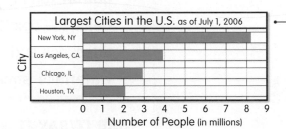

**Largest Cities in the U.S.** as of July 1, 2006

| City | 0 | 1 | 2 | 3 | 4 | 5 | 6 | 7 | 8 | 9 |
|------|---|---|---|---|---|---|---|---|---|---|
| New York, NY | | | | | | | | | | |
| Los Angeles, CA | | | | | | | | | | |
| Chicago, IL | | | | | | | | | | |
| Houston, TX | | | | | | | | | | |

Number of People (in millions)

**Skill** Look at the bar graph. What facts can you learn from the graph?

**Your Turn!**

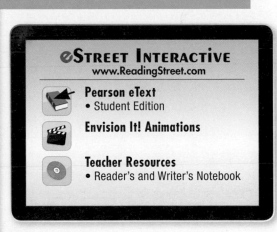

⏸ **Need a Review?** See the *Envision It! Handbook* for help with graphic sources and important ideas.

▶ **Ready to Try It?** As you read *Hottest, Coldest, Highest, Deepest*, use what you learned about graphic sources and important ideas.

58

59

**Student Edition, pp. 58–59**

# Model Fluent Reading

**APPROPRIATE PHRASING** Have students listen as you read the second paragraph of "Largest U.S. Cities" with appropriate phrasing. Explain that punctuation marks help to divide sentences into phrases, and the pause for a period is longer than the pause for a comma.

**Routine** Oral Rereading

1. **Read** Have students read paragraph 2 of "Largest U.S. Cities" orally.

2. **Reread** To achieve optimal fluency, students should reread the text three or four times.

3. **Corrective Feedback** Have students read aloud without you. Provide feedback about their phrasing, helping students to group phrases by pausing at punctuation marks.

Routines Flip Chart

**eSTREET INTERACTIVE**
www.ReadingStreet.com

**Pearson eText**
- Student Edition

**Envision It! Animations**

**Teacher Resources**
- Reader's and Writer's Notebook

**Common Core State Standards**

**Foundational Skills 3.** Know and apply grade-level phonics and word analysis skills in decoding words. **Language 4.** Determine or clarify the meaning of unknown and multiple-meaning word and phrases based on grade 3 reading and content, choosing flexibly from a range of strategies.

# Selection Vocabulary

Use the following routine to introduce this week's tested selection vocabulary.

**average** the quantity found by dividing the sum of all quantities by the number of quantities

**depth** the distance from the top to the bottom

**deserts** dry, sandy regions without water and trees

**erupted** burst out

**outrun** run faster than someone or something else

**peak** the pointed top of a mountain or hill

**tides** rise and fall of the ocean's waters about every twelve hours

**waterfalls** streams of water that fall from a high place

**SEE IT/SAY IT** Write *erupted.* Scan across the word with your finger as you say it: *e-rupt-ed.*

**HEAR IT** Use the word in a sentence. I read about a volcano that *erupted* in Hawaii.

**DEFINE IT** Elicit definitions from students. How would you describe to another student what *erupted* means? Clarify or give a definition when necessary. Yes, it means "to burst out" or "break through." Restate the meaning of the word in student-friendly terms. So, *erupted* is to explode suddenly.

**Team Talk** What danger could people who live close to a volcano that *erupts* experience? Turn and talk to your partner about this. Be prepared to explain your answer. Allow students time to discuss. Ask for examples. Rephrase their examples for usage when necessary or to correct misunderstandings.

**MAKE CONNECTIONS** Have students discuss the word. Have you ever seen a volcano *erupt* in person or on TV? Turn and talk to your partner about this. Then be prepared to share. Have students share. Rephrase their ideas for usage when necessary or to correct misunderstandings.

**RECORD** Have students write the word and its meaning.

Continue this routine to introduce the remaining words in this manner.

> **Corrective feedback**  |  **If...** students are having difficulty understanding, **then...** review the definitions in small groups.

# Research and Inquiry

## Step 1 Identify and Focus Topic

**TEACH** Discuss the Question of the Week: *What makes nature's record holders unique?* Tell students they will research some of nature's record holders and what makes them unique. They will present their articles to the class on Day 5.

**Think Aloud** **MODEL** I'll start by brainstorming a list of questions about people or places that hold records. I know many athletes have set records. There are also cities that have the tallest buildings or the most people. Some possible questions could be *Who are the fastest runners in the world? What are the tallest buildings?* and *Who has written the most books?*

**GUIDE PRACTICE** After students have brainstormed inquiry questions, explain that tomorrow they will conduct online research using their questions. Help students identify keywords that will guide their search.

**ON THEIR OWN** Have students work individually, in pairs, or in small groups to write an inquiry question.

**eSTREET INTERACTIVE**
www.ReadingStreet.com

**Teacher Resources**
• Envision It! Pictured Vocabulary Cards
• Tested Vocabulary Cards

### 21st Century Skills
**Internet Guy** *Don Leu*

**Weekly Inquiry Project**

| STEP 1 | Identify and Focus Topic |
|--------|--------------------------|
| STEP 2 | Navigate/Search |
| STEP 3 | Analyze Information |
| STEP 4 | Synthesize |
| STEP 5 | Communicate |

**ELL**

**Multilingual Vocabulary** Students can apply knowledge of their home languages to acquire new English vocabulary by using the Multilingual Vocabulary Lists (*ELL Handbook* pp. 433–444).

**ELL**

**If...** students need more scaffolding and practice with **Vocabulary, then...** use the activities on pp. DI•42–DI•43 in the Teacher Resources section on SuccessNet.

---

## Day 1 SMALL GROUP TIME • Differentiate Vocabulary, p. SG•17

| OL On-Level | SI Strategic Intervention | A Advanced |
|-------------|---------------------------|------------|
| • **Practice Vocabulary** Amazing Words<br>• **Read** *Reading Street Sleuth,* pp. 46–47 | • **Reteach Vocabulary** Amazing Words<br>• **Read** *Reading Street Sleuth,* pp. 46–47 | • **Extend Vocabulary** Amazing Words<br>• **Read** *Reading Street Sleuth,* pp. 46–47<br>• **Introduce** Inquiry Project |

## Common Core State Standards

**Speaking/Listening 6.** Speak in complete sentences when appropriate to task and situation in order to provide requested detail or clarification. **Language 1.a.** Explain the function of nouns, pronouns, verbs, adjectives, and adverbs in general and their functions in particular sentences. **Language 2.** Demonstrate command of the conventions of standard English capitalization, punctuation, and spelling when writing. **Language 2.f.** Use spelling patterns and generalizations (e.g., word families, position-based spellings, syllable patterns, ending rules, meaningful word parts) in writing words. **Also Language 1.f.**

# Spelling Pretest

## Vowels: *r*-Controlled

**INTRODUCE** Tell students to think of words with the *r*-controlled vowel sound /èr/ spelled *ir, er, ur, ear,* and *or*.

**PRETEST** Say each word, read the sentence, and repeat the word.

| | | |
|---|---|---|
| 1. | third | I am **third** in line behind Shawn and Lea. |
| 2. | early | It's better to be **early** than late. |
| 3. | world | Where in the **world** are we? |
| 4. | certain | I'm **certain** you called me. |
| 5. | dirty | The rug is **dirty** so we will clean it. |
| 6. | herself | Dana saw **herself** in the mirror. |
| 7. | earth | We planted some seeds in the **earth.** |
| 8. | word | Look up that **word** in the dictionary. |
| 9. | perfect | Dale got a **perfect** score in the game. |
| 10. | verb | Every sentence has a **verb.** |
| 11. | nerve | **Nerve** endings let us feel things. |
| 12. | worm | I found a **worm** in the garden. |
| 13. | thirsty | Drink water if you are **thirsty.** |
| 14. | workout | The gym is a place for a **workout.** |
| 15. | earn | If you work, you **earn** money. |

### Challenge words

| | | |
|---|---|---|
| 16. | determine | I must **determine** whether I need a coat today. |
| 17. | commercial | That **commercial** was selling cereal. |
| 18. | whirlwind | A **whirlwind** stirred up dust in the desert. |
| 19. | worthwhile | It is **worthwhile** to read that book. |
| 20. | virtual | Jake and Tim finished the race in a **virtual** tie. |

**SELF-CORRECT** Have students self-correct their pretests by rewriting misspelled words.

**ON THEIR OWN** Use *Let's Practice It!* p. 227 on the *Teacher Resources DVD-ROM.*

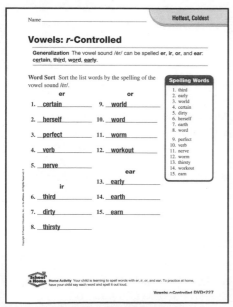

Let's Practice It! TR DVD•227

# Conventions

## Subject and Object Pronouns

**MAKE CONNECTIONS** To focus attention on subject and object pronouns, have student volunteers write sentences on the board about something they recently did with a friend. Have them circle the subject and any objects in each sentence.

**TEACH** Display Grammar Transparency 17, and read aloud the explanation and examples in the box. Point out the subject pronouns *I, you, he, she, it, we,* and *they* and the object pronouns *me, you, him, her, it, us,* and *them.*

**MODEL** Model identifying *they* as a subject pronoun in sentence 1 and *them* as an object pronoun in sentence 2. Apply the rules for using subject pronouns and object pronouns to show how you identified each one.

**GUIDE PRACTICE** Guide students to complete items 3–5. Record the correct responses on the transparency.

**APPLY** Have students read sentences 6–10 on the transparency and write the subject or object pronoun to complete each sentence correctly.

Grammar Transparency 17, TR DVD

# Handwriting

**MODEL LETTER FORMATION AND SPACING** Display the lowercase cursive letters *o, w,* and *b.* Follow the stroke instruction pictured to model letter formation.

Explain that writing legibly means that letters are evenly spaced. The sidestrokes that join letters are not too long or too short, and there is more space between words than between the letters in a word. Model writing this sentence with proper letter spacing: *The bunny borrowed a burrow.*

**GUIDE PRACTICE** Have students write this sentence: *The burro wore a bow on its brow.* Circulate around the room, guiding students.

## Daily Fix-It

1. Some of the worst weather in the world is in antarctica. *(world; Antarctica)*
2. The days is freezing there even in summer. *(are; freezing)*

## Academic Vocabulary

A **subject pronoun** is a pronoun that is used as the subject of a sentence.

An **object pronoun** is a pronoun that is used after an action verb or as the object of a preposition.

**ELL**

**Language Production: Subject and Object Pronouns** Model statements using subject and object pronouns while demonstrating their meaning. For example, say: I (point to yourself) give him (point to a boy) this pencil. He (point to the boy) gives me (point to yourself) the pencil. Have students repeat and then create their own statements.

**Handwriting: Homographs** To provide practice in handwriting lowercase cursive *o, w,* and *b* and to extend language opportunities with homographs, have students write two sentences using *bow* (/bō/) and *bow* (/bou/).

*Hottest, Coldest, Highest, Deepest* **59d**

## Bridge to Common Core

### TEXT TYPES AND PURPOSES

#### Imaginative Story

This week students write an imaginative story in which one character tells a riddle to another.

#### Narrative Writing

Through reading and discussion, students will gain a deeper understanding of what it means to be unique. They will use this knowledge from the texts to write and support imaginative stories.

Through the week, students will improve their range and content of writing through daily mini-lessons.

### 5-Day Plan

| | |
|---|---|
| **DAY 1** | Read Like a Writer |
| **DAY 2** | Developing a Story Sequence Chart |
| **DAY 3** | Writer's Craft: Dialogue |
| **DAY 4** | Revise: Consolidating |
| **DAY 5** | Proofread for Subject and Object Pronouns |

---

**Write Guy** *by Jeff Anderson*

#### Two Words: Subject, Verb!

Let's help students gain confidence in composing sentences. Guide partners as they make up fun two-word sentences. *Rex howled! Kathy giggled. Lions growl.* Then let the students continue creating sentences, checking to make sure each includes a subject and verb. Another activity is to challenge students to find favorite sentences in books, and then whittle them down to the simple subject and verb. This paves the way for grammar to support students' writing.

---

# Writing

## Imaginative Story

**Mini-Lesson** **Read Like a Writer**

■ **Introduce** This week you will write an imaginative story. An imaginative story is a fictional story about events that did not really happen. You will use your imagination to write the story.

| | |
|---|---|
| **Prompt** | Write an imaginative story in which one character tells a riddle to another. |
| **Trait** | Conventions |
| **Mode** | Narrative |

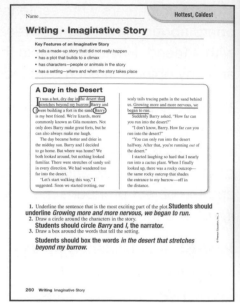

Reader's and Writer's Notebook, p. 260

■ **Examine Model Text** Let's read an example of an imaginative story in which one character tells a riddle to another. Have students read "A Day in the Desert" on p. 260 of their *Reader's and Writer's Notebook*.

■ **Key Features** An imaginative story has a plot. The action in the story builds to an exciting, sometimes tense point. That point is called the climax. Have students underline the sentence that is the climax of the story. *(Growing more and more nervous, we began to run.)*

An imaginative story has characters, or the people or animals in the story. Have students draw a circle around the characters in the story. *(Barry* and the narrator, *I)* Then have them talk about what they know about the characters in the story.

An imaginative story has a setting, which is the place and time where the story takes place. Have students draw a box around the words that tell the setting. *(the desert that stretches beyond my burrow)*

## Review Key Features

Review the key features of an imaginative story with students. You may want to post the key features in the classroom for students to refer to as they work on their imaginative stories.

### Key Features of an Imaginative Story

- tells a story that did not really happen
- has a plot that builds to a climax
- has characters—people or animals in the story
- has a setting—where and when the story takes place

**Routine** **Quick Write for Fluency** **Team Talk**

1. **Talk** Have small groups take several minutes to discuss the features of an imaginative story.

2. **Write** Each student writes a short description of an imaginative story.

3. **Share** Group members read their descriptions to each other.

Routines Flip Chart

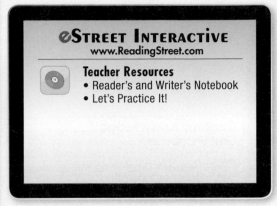

**eSTREET INTERACTIVE**
www.ReadingStreet.com

**Teacher Resources**
- Reader's and Writer's Notebook
- Let's Practice It!

**Read Like a Writer** Read the writing model aloud, and help students understand it. Point out that it is an imaginative story, which is a fictional story about events that did not really happen. Use a picture to explain the riddle if students do not understand the concept of "halfway in, then out." Ask students what kind of setting they would like to use in a story and have them describe it.

# Wrap Up Your Day!

✔ **Content Knowledge** Reread "Street Rhymes!" on p. 54j to students. Ask them what they learned this week about record holders in nature.

✔ **Oral Vocabulary** Have students use the Amazing Words they learned in context sentences.

✔ **Homework** Send home this week's Family Times newsletter on *Let's Practice It!* pp. 228–229 on the *Teacher Resources DVD-ROM*.

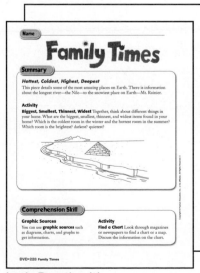

Let's Practice It!
TR DVD•228–229

**Preview DAY 2**

Tell students that tomorrow they will read about places in nature that are the hottest, coldest, deepest, and highest.

### Materials

- Student Edition
- Reader's and Writer's Notebook

## Common Core State Standards

**Writing 3.c.** Use temporal words and phrases to signal event order. **Speaking/Listening 1.a.** Come to discussions prepared, having read or studied required material; explicitly draw on that preparation and other information known about the topic to explore ideas under discussion. **Speaking/ Listening 6.** Speak in complete sentences when appropriate to task and situation in order to provide requested detail or clarification. **Language 6.** Acquire and use accurately grade-appropriate conversational, general academic, and domain-specific words and phrases, including those that signal spatial and temporal relationships (e.g., *After dinner that night we went looking for them*).

# Content Knowledge

## Nature's Record Holders

**EXPAND THE CONCEPT** Remind students of the weekly concept question, *What makes nature's record holders unique?* Tell students that today they will begin reading *Hottest, Coldest, Highest, Deepest.* As they read, encourage students to think about some of nature's record holders and what makes them stand out.

# Build Oral Language

**TALK ABOUT SENTENCES AND WORDS** Reread a sentence from the Read Aloud, "To Climb the Tallest Tree."

*But about 40 years ago, people started to cut down the tallest redwoods to use them for lumber.*

- What does *use them for lumber* mean? (cut trees into boards)
- Why would people cut down the tallest redwoods? (They would produce the most wood.)
- Why do you think the author included this information in the article? (to show why redwoods are disappearing)

**Team Talk** Have students turn to a partner and discuss the following question. Then ask them to share their responses.

- How can you reorganize the sentence while keeping the meaning the same? (Possible response: People started to cut down the tallest redwoods for lumber about 40 years ago.)

# Build Oral Vocabulary

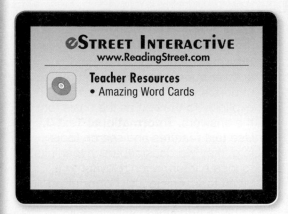

## Amazing Words

### Robust Vocabulary Routine

1. **Introduce** Write the Amazing Word *valuable* on the board. Have students say it aloud with you. Relate *valuable* to the Read Aloud, "To Climb the Tallest Tree." A redwood tree can live to be thousands of years old and grow over 300 feet tall. What makes it *valuable?* Have students determine the definition of the word. *Valuable* means useful or worth a great deal of money.

2. **Demonstrate** Have students answer questions to demonstrate understanding. Is climbing a tree a *valuable* way to measure it? What is something *valuable* to wear on your feet when you are in an area where rattlesnakes live?

3. **Apply** Have students apply their understanding. What is a synonym for *valuable? (expensive, useful)*

4. **Display the Word** Run your hand under the word as you emphasize the syllables in *val-u-a-ble.* Have students say the word.

See pp. OV•2 to teach *champ.*

Routines Flip Chart

## Amazing Words

| | |
|---|---|
| evergreen | champ |
| lumber | sprinter |
| competitor | acrobat |
| plunge | weaken |
| valuable | ranger |

**ADD TO THE CONCEPT MAP** Use the photos on pp. 54–55 and the Read Aloud, "To Climb the Tallest Tree," to talk about the Amazing Words—*evergreen, lumber, competitor,* and *plunge.* Add the words to the concept map to develop students' knowledge of the topic. Discuss the following questions. Remind students to listen attentively to other students and to answer with appropriate detail. Encourage students to build on others' ideas when they answer.

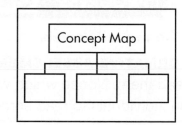

Concept Map

• A record holder in nature can have the most of something—a lake with the most water, or a tree that can make the most *lumber*. What else could make a record holder in nature?

• Why could an *evergreen* hold a record for the oldest tree?

• As a *competitor* in a running match, would you run as fast as you can run, or would you run slowly?

**ELL**

**Reinforce Vocabulary** Use the Day 2 instruction on ELL Poster 17 to teach lesson vocabulary and the lesson concept.

**Common Core State Standards**

**Informational Text 1.** Ask and answer questions to demonstrate understanding of a text, referring explicitly to the text as the basis for the answers. **Informational Text 5.** Use text features and search tools (e.g., key words, sidebars, hyperlinks) to locate information relevant to a given topic efficiently. **Foundational Skills 3.** Know and apply grade-level phonics and word analysis skills in decoding words.

# Phonics

## Vowels: *r*-Controlled

**REVIEW** Review *r*-controlled vowels using *Sound-Spelling Cards* 55, 62, 67, 72, 87, 91, 92, 93, and 104.

**READ WORDS IN ISOLATION** Display these words. Have the class read the words. Then point to the words in random order and ask students to read them quickly.

| | | |
|---|---|---|
| shirt | heard | word |
| permit | fur | carpool |
| confirm | former | |

**Corrective feedback** | Model blending decodable words and then ask students to blend them with you.

**READ WORDS IN CONTEXT** Display these sentences. Have the class read the sentences.

The **worm burrowed** into the **earth.**

**Were** you **first** in line at the **car wash?**

This **morning** we talked about **current** events.

Don't Wait Until Friday

**MONITOR PROGRESS** **Check Word Reading**

### *r*-Controlled Vowels

**FORMATIVE ASSESSMENT** Write the following words and have the class read them. Notice which words students miss during the group reading. Call on individuals to read some of the words.

| mirth | merge | work | early | | **Spiral Review** |
|---|---|---|---|---|---|
| shrunk | switch | speckled | spendthrift | | Row 2 reviews words with /a/, /e/, /i/, /o/, /u/. |
| purple | birdbath | energy | herself | backyard | Row 3 contrasts words with spellings of /ėr/ and /är/, and /a/, /e/, /i/, /o/, /u/. |

**If...** students cannot read words with *r*-controlled vowels at this point,

**then...** use the Day 1 Blending Strategy routine on p. 56a to reteach *r*-controlled vowels. Use words from the *Decodable Practice Passages* (or Reader). Continue to monitor students' progress using other instructional opportunities during the week. See the Skills Trace on p. 56a.

# Literary Terms

## Author's Craft

**TEACH** Explain to students that authors make choices when they write, including choices about what words to use. Authors may use superlatives—words that show something is the best or the most in a group, such as the hottest or coldest—to help readers understand ideas. These words also help to get readers' attention.

**MODEL** Let's look at "Largest U.S. Cities." What word showing that something is the most can you find in the title? *(Largest)* What does it tell us about the topic of the article? (The article will be about the cities in the U.S. that have the most people.)

**GUIDE PRACTICE** Direct students to look at pp. 64–65 of *Hottest, Coldest, Highest, Deepest.* Have students identify the superlatives the author uses to grab the reader's attention.

**ON THEIR OWN** Have students skim the pages of *Hottest, Coldest, Highest, Deepest* and list the boldfaced words the author chose to use to show that something is the best or the most.

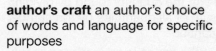

**Academic Vocabulary** ©

**author's craft** an author's choice of words and language for specific purposes

**Common Core State Standards**

**Foundational Skills 3.** Know and apply grade-level phonics and word analysis skills in decoding words. **Foundational Skills 4.** Read with sufficient accuracy and fluency to support comprehension. **Language 4.d.** Use glossaries or beginning dictionaries, both print and digital, to determine or clarify the precise meaning of key words and phrases. **Also Language 4.**

## Selection Vocabulary

**average** the quantity found by dividing the sum of all quantities by the number of quantities

**depth** the distance from the top to the bottom

**deserts** dry, sandy regions without water and trees

**erupted** burst out

**outrun** run faster than someone or something else

**peak** the pointed top of a mountain or hill

**tides** rise and fall of the ocean's waters about every twelve hours

**waterfalls** streams of water that fall from a high place

 **Bridge to Common Core**

### VOCABULARY ACQUISITION AND USE

Using a dictionary or glossary to look up the meaning of unknown words helps students determine the meanings of unfamiliar words and enables them to acquire a broad range of academic and domain-specific words. By consulting a dictionary or glossary to clarify definitions, they demonstrate the ability to gather vocabulary knowledge on their own.

## Vocabulary Support

Refer students to *Words!* on p. W•14 in the Student Edition for additional practice.

# Vocabulary Skill

##  Unknown Words

**READ** Have students read "Geography Bee" on p. 61. Use the vocabulary skill and strategy as tools to build comprehension.

**TEACH DICTIONARY/GLOSSARY** Tell students that when they encounter an unknown word, they can use a dictionary or glossary to look up the meaning. Explain that a dictionary or glossary provides definitions that help students understand the meanings of unknown words.

**Think Aloud** **MODEL** Write on the board: *Which volcano has erupted the most times?* I need help to figure out the meaning of *erupted* in this sentence, so I will use a dictionary or glossary. A glossary is usually part of a book, while a dictionary is a separate book of words and definitions. When I look up *erupt* in a dictionary, I see that it means "to burst out" or "to throw forth lava, water, gases, or other material." Now I understand the question about the volcano.

**GUIDE PRACTICE** Write on the board: *We can measure the depth of the box with a ruler to see if it will fit on the shelf.* Have students determine the meaning of *depth* using context clues. If they are unable to use context clues to define *depth,* then have them look up the word in a dictionary or glossary. For additional support, use *Envision It! Pictured Vocabulary Cards* or *Tested Vocabulary Cards.*

**ON THEIR OWN** Reread "Geography Bee" on p. 61. Have students use a dictionary or glossary to list the definitions for the lesson vocabulary. For additional practice use *Reader's and Writer's Notebook* p. 261.

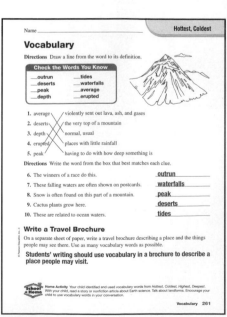

Reader's and Writer's Notebook, p. 261

Common Core State Standards
Language 4.d. Use glossaries or beginning dictionaries, both print and digital, to determine or clarify the precise meaning of key words and phrases. Also Language 4.

**Envision It!** Words to Know

erupted

outrun

tides

average
depth
deserts
peak
waterfalls

**READING STREET ONLINE
VOCABULARY ACTIVITIES**
www.ReadingStreet.com

60

Vocabulary Strategy for

## ⊙ Unknown Words

**Dictionary/Glossary** You can use a dictionary or glossary to find the meaning of an unknown word. The words in a dictionary or glossary are in alphabetical order.

Follow these steps with *deepest, deserts,* and *depth* from "Geography Bee."

**1.** Turn to the section for the words' first letter in the glossary or dictionary.

**2.** Look at the first three letters in the word. Put them in alphabetical order, and then find and read the entry for each word.

**3.** Decide which meaning you think fits in the sentence if there is more than one meaning listed.

**4.** Try that meaning in the sentence to see if it makes sense.

Read "Geography Bee" on page 61. Use the glossary or a dictionary to help you find the meanings of other unknown words.

**Words to Write** Reread "Geography Bee." Write four geography bee questions about your state. Then find and write the answers. Use words from the Words to Know list.

## Geography Bee

Have you heard of a geography bee? You probably know what a spelling bee is. In a spelling bee, people take turns spelling difficult words. The person who spells the most words correctly wins. In a geography bee, people answer questions about places on Earth.

The questions in a geography bee will never have a yes or no answer. For example, this question would not be used in a geography bee: Can a person outrun the tides at the Bay of Fundy?

To answer the questions in a geography bee, you must know facts about continents, countries, states, and physical features of the world, such as deserts or oceans.

Here are some sample questions for you to try: When was the last time Mount St. Helens erupted? What is the hottest spot on Earth? Which is the highest of all the waterfalls on Earth? Which mountain peak is the tallest in the world? What is the average summer temperature at the South Pole? What is the depth of the deepest point of Marianas Trench?

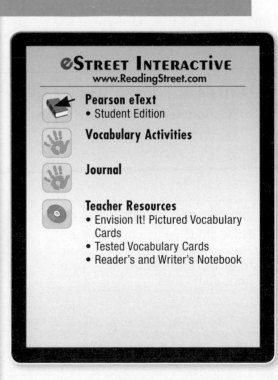

**Your Turn!**

⏸ **Need a Review?** For additional help with using a dictionary or glossary to find unknown words, see *Words!*

▶ **Ready to Try It?** Read *Hottest, Coldest, Highest, Deepest* on pp. 62–75.

61

**Student Edition, pp. 60–61**

# Reread for Fluency

**APPROPRIATE PHRASING** Read the first paragraph of "Geography Bee" aloud, pausing after end punctuation and commas. Tell students that when they read words in groups, they should make a short pause after a comma and a longer pause after punctuation at the end of a sentence.

**Routine** Oral Rereading

**1. Read** Have students read the first paragraph of "Geography Bee" orally.

**2. Reread** To achieve optimal fluency, students should reread the text three or four times.

**3. Corrective Feedback** Have students read aloud without you. Provide feedback about their phrasing, helping students to group phrases by pausing at punctuation marks.

Routines Flip Chart

## eSTREET INTERACTIVE
www.ReadingStreet.com

**Pearson eText**
• Student Edition

**Vocabulary Activities**

**Journal**

**Teacher Resources**
• Envision It! Pictured Vocabulary Cards
• Tested Vocabulary Cards
• Reader's and Writer's Notebook

Zoom in on

 **Common Core State Standards**

**Informational Text 7.** Use information gained from illustrations (e.g., maps, photographs), and the words in a text to demonstrate understanding of the text (e.g., where, when, why, and how key events occur). **Informational Text 10.** By the end of the year, read and comprehend informational texts, including history/social studies, science, and technical texts, at the high end of the grades 2–3 text complexity band independently and proficiently. **Foundational Skills 4.a.** Read on-level text with purpose and understanding.

 **Bridge to Common Core**

### CRAFT AND STRUCTURE

Students analyze the structure of an expository text and how its components relate to each other and the whole. Prior to reading, they use text features to help them preview and predict what they will learn about and to better understand the text.

## Academic Vocabulary

**expository text** informational writing that explains an object, idea, or theme

## Strategy Response Log

Have students use p. 23 in the *Reader's and Writer's Notebook* to review and use the strategy of important ideas.

# Text-Based Comprehension

## Introduce Main Selection

Student Edition, pp. 62–63

**GENRE** Explain that **expository text** tells about real people or events and gives information about things. Its purpose is to explain what a person, event, or thing is like. Expository texts often include text features such as boldfaced words, subheads, charts, graphs, photos, and maps to help readers better understand the topic.

**PREVIEW AND PREDICT** Prior to reading have students locate and preview the title, illustrations, boldfaced words, maps, charts, diagrams, and graphs for *Hottest, Coldest, Highest, Deepest.* Ask them to predict what they will learn about as they read. Remind them that they can check and verify their predictions when they read.

**PURPOSE** By analyzing *Hottest, Coldest, Highest, Deepest,* an expository text, students will gain knowledge of nature's record holders.

# Access Main Selection

| READER AND TASK SUGGESTIONS | |
|---|---|
| **Preparing to Read the Text** | **Leveled Tasks** |
| • Review alphabetizing by the first three letters in a word to find words in a dictionary.<br><br>• Discuss how an author might use maps and charts to deliver factual information.<br><br>• Remind students that when reading expository text that includes charts and maps, they should read more slowly to understand all of the information the author is providing. | • **Theme and Knowledge Demands** If students have difficulty understanding how the maps on each page relate to the text, have them note where the red dot is on each map and match it to the place mentioned in the text.<br><br>• **Language Conventionality and Clarity** Students may have difficulty with the academic vocabulary and complex sentences in this selection. Remind students to use context clues, illustrations, and graphic organizers to access the content. |

See Text Complexity Measures for *Hottest, Coldest, Highest, Deepest* on the tab at the beginning of this week.

**READ** Tell students that today they will read *Hottest, Coldest, Highest, Deepest* for the first time. Use the Read for Understanding routine.

## Routine | Read for Understanding

Deepen understanding by reading the selection multiple times.

1. **First Read**—If students need support, then use the **Access Text** note to help them clarify understanding.

2. **Second Read**—Use the **Close Reading** notes to help students draw knowledge from the text.

## Day 2 | SMALL GROUP TIME • Differentiate Comprehension, p. SG•17

| OL On-Level | SI Strategic Intervention | A Advanced |
|---|---|---|
| • **Practice** Selection Vocabulary<br><br>• **Read** *Hottest, Coldest, Highest, Deepest* | • **Reteach** Selection Vocabulary<br><br>• **Read** *Hottest, Coldest, Highest, Deepest* | • **Extend** Selection Vocabulary<br><br>• **Read** *Hottest, Coldest, Highest, Deepest*<br><br>• **Investigate** Inquiry Project |

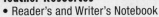

**eSTREET INTERACTIVE**
www.ReadingStreet.com

 **Pearson eText**
• Student Edition

 **AudioText CD**

 **Teacher Resources**
• Reader's and Writer's Notebook

**Background Building Audio CD**

### Access for All

**A** Advanced

Have students make a list of the kinds of records that people want to know about (sports, weather, etc.).

**Build Background** To build background, review the selection summary in English (*ELL Handbook* p. 127). Use the Retelling Cards to provide visual support for the summary.

If... students need more scaffolding and practice with the **Comprehension Skill, then...** use the activities on p. DI•46 in the Teacher Resources section on SuccessNet.

## 1ST READ

## Access Text © If students need help, then...

**⊚ IMPORTANT IDEAS** Have students look at the first sentence on p. 65. Tell them to think about the important ideas as they read. Remind them that important ideas also will be in titles, captions, or different type.

**(Think Aloud) MODEL** I see that the rest of the sentences tell about other rivers that are not as long as the Nile. The fact that the Nile is the longest river in the world is an important idea in the selection.

**ON THEIR OWN** Have students reread pp. 64–65 to find other clues that the first sentence on p. 65 is an important idea in the book.

I f you could visit any spot on Earth, where would you go? What if you wanted to see some of the most amazing natural wonders in the world?

There are deserts that haven't seen rain for hundreds of years and jungles where it pours almost every day. There are places so cold that even in the summer it's below freezing and spots where it's often hot enough to cook an egg on the ground. There are mountains many miles high and ocean trenches that are even deeper. You can find rivers thousands of miles long and waterfalls thousands of feet high.

Where are the very hottest and coldest, windiest and snowiest, highest and deepest places on Earth? Travel the world and visit the planet's record holders.

64

**Student Edition, p. 64**

## 2ND READ

## Close Reading ©

**ANALYSIS • TEXT EVIDENCE** Read the sentences on page 65. The first sentence contains an important idea about the Nile. What other important idea can you find in that text? (The second sentence on p. 65 tells us that the Amazon River is mightier than the Nile "because it carries half of all the river water in the world." It's not the longest river, but it is important too.)

**ANALYSIS** Why do you think the author begins the article with two questions? (I think he's trying to get our attention. His questions made me want to read the article to find answers to the questions.)

**DEVELOP LANGUAGE** Have students reread the second paragraph on page 64. What does *trenches* mean? Where else might you find trenches?

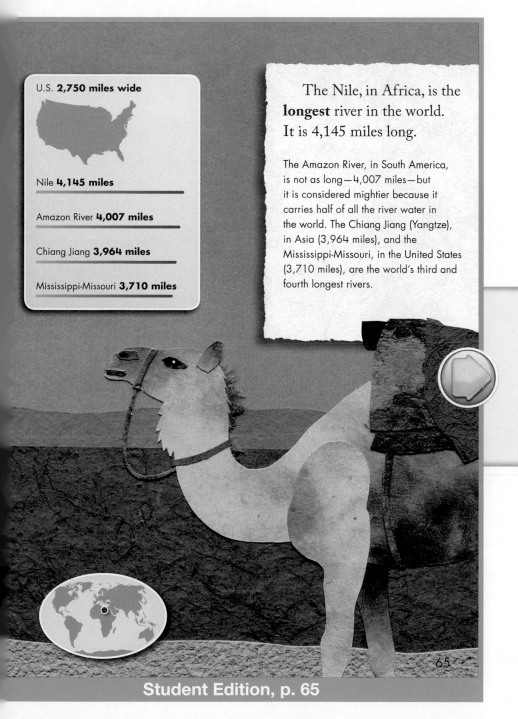

U.S. **2,750 miles wide**

Nile **4,145 miles**

Amazon River **4,007 miles**

Chiang Jiang **3,964 miles**

Mississippi-Missouri **3,710 miles**

The Nile, in Africa, is the **longest** river in the world. It is 4,145 miles long.

The Amazon River, in South America, is not as long—4,007 miles—but it is considered mightier because it carries half of all the river water in the world. The Chiang Jiang (Yangtze), in Asia (3,964 miles), and the Mississippi-Missouri, in the United States (3,710 miles), are the world's third and fourth longest rivers.

65

**Student Edition, p. 65**

**INFERENCE** Look at the chart on page 65. Why do you think the author compares the world's longest rivers with the width of the United States? (I think he's trying to help us understand just how long these rivers really are by comparing them to something we're familiar with, the size of this country.)

 **Common Core State Standards**

**Informational Text 2.** Determine the main idea of a text; recount the key details and explain how they support the main idea. **Informational Text 5.** Use text features and search tools (e.g., key words, sidebars, hyperlinks) to locate information relevant to a given topic efficiently. **Foundational Skills 4.a.** Read on-level text with purpose and understanding.

**Access for All**

**(A) Advanced**

Ask students to find out more information about the Nile and the Amazon. Then have them make a T-chart showing how the two rivers are alike and different. Have them use the chart to explain what makes the Amazon the mightiest river even though the Nile is the longest river.

**ELL**

**Activate Background Knowledge** Define *extreme* (having or being very much of something) and explain that p. 64 tells us about many different places on Earth that are extreme, including deserts that get no rain and very rainy jungles. Partner students and ask pairs to find more examples of extreme places on p. 64. Have partners share one idea with the group.

**Text Features** Use newspaper headlines to explain the concept of using text features such as bigger or darker type to show important ideas. Then page through the selection with students and have them find examples of bigger or darker type to show important ideas.

*Hottest, Coldest, Highest, Deepest* **65a**

**1ST READ**

## Access Text © If students need help, then...

**Review** © **MAIN IDEA AND DETAILS**

Have students read about Lake Baikal and Lake Superior on p. 66. Then ask students to identify the main idea on the page.

**Think Aloud** **MODEL** I see that the topic of the page is two lakes that are record holders. Lake Baikal is the oldest and deepest lake, while Lake Superior is the largest freshwater lake. The main idea is that even though Lake Superior is larger, Lake Baikal is the deepest lake and has more water.

**2ND READ**

## Close Reading ©

**SYNTHESIS • TEXT EVIDENCE**

What is an important detail that supports the main idea on page 67? (An important detail is that Mauna Kea is 33,476 feet tall.)

**ANALYSIS** Why do you think the author chose to emphasize the words *oldest* and *deepest* on page 66? (These words make the reader think of the most of something. They jump out as if to say, "I'm important.")

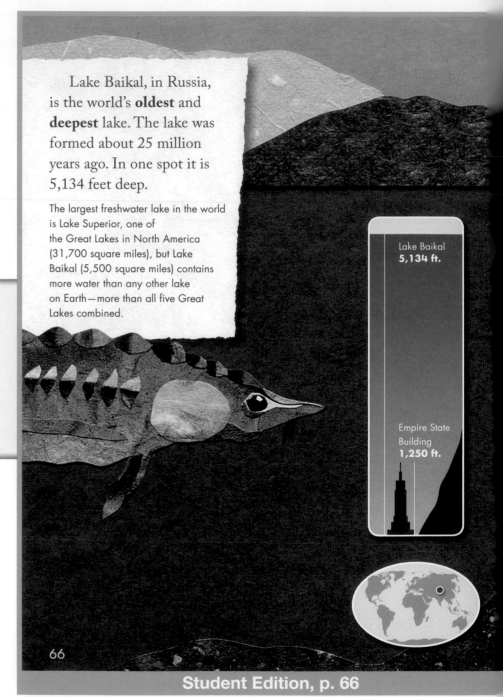

Lake Baikal, in Russia, is the world's **oldest** and **deepest** lake. The lake was formed about 25 million years ago. In one spot it is 5,134 feet deep.

The largest freshwater lake in the world is Lake Superior, one of the Great Lakes in North America (31,700 square miles), but Lake Baikal (5,500 square miles) contains more water than any other lake on Earth—more than all five Great Lakes combined.

Lake Baikal 5,134 ft.

Empire State Building 1,250 ft.

66

**Student Edition, p. 66**

**ON THEIR OWN** Ask students to identify the topic of p. 67 and then use supporting details to identify the main idea. For additional practice with main idea and details, use *Let's Practice It!* p. 231 on the *Teacher Resources DVD-ROM.*

Mount Everest is the **highest** mountain in the world. Its peak is 29,028 feet above sea level.

Mount Everest is considered the **highest** mountain—above sea level—in the world, but it's not really the **tallest**. Measured from its base on the floor of the ocean, Mauna Kea, in Hawaii, is 33,476 feet tall. Only the top 13,796 feet of Mauna Kea are above sea level.

67

**Student Edition, p. 67**

**EVALUATE • TEXT EVIDENCE** Look at the three oval maps of the world on pages 66 and 67. Of the three places mentioned in the text (Lake Baikal, Mount Everest, and Mauna Kea), which two are located nearest to each other? (I can tell from the map on p. 66 and the top map on p. 67 that Lake Baikal and Mount Everest are the nearest. The dots marking their locations are on the same continent. Mauna Kea is far away from them.)

**Common Core State Standards**

**Informational Text 1.** Ask and answer questions to demonstrate understanding of a text, referring explicitly to the text as the basis for the answers. **Also Informational Text 2., 7.**

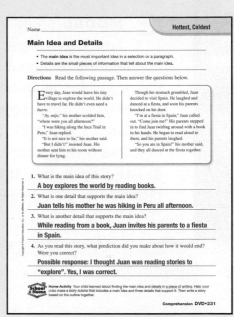

Let's Practice It! TR DVD•231

**Connect to Science**
**Measuring Mauna Kea**
Explain that we use investigations to learn about the natural world. Ask students to discuss what challenges scientists might have had as they measured Mauna Kea.

**E L L**

**Vocabulary: Adjectives** Write on the board: *oldest.* Explain that *oldest* is an adjective, or a word that tells more about something. Ask what small word they see in *oldest (old).* Explain that adding -est to a word shows that something is the most, so oldest means "most old." Model adding -est to *deep, high,* and *cold* and have students explain what each new word means.

**Important Ideas** Ask students to name the boldfaced words on pp. 66 and 67, which show important ideas (*oldest, deepest, highest, tallest*). Then have them use each word in a sentence.

*Hottest, Coldest, Highest, Deepest* **67a**

## Access Text © *If students need help, then...*

**⊙ GRAPHIC SOURCES** Have students read p. 68. Ask them to use the text and chart to decide if there is anywhere in the United States that can reach a temperature nearly as hot as Al Aziziyah.

**(Think Aloud) MODEL** I read that Al Aziziyah can reach a temperature of 136°F and that the temperature in Death Valley, California, once reached 134.6°F. The two thermometers show the temperatures 136°F and 134.6°F. I can see that Death Valley can be nearly as hot as Al Aziziyah, the hottest spot on the planet.

**ON THEIR OWN** Have students look at the other thermometers and labels. Ask why the author might have chosen to include those facts. For additional practice with graphic sources, use *Let's Practice It!* p. 230 on the *Teacher Resources DVD-ROM.*

The **hottest** spot on the planet is Al Aziziyah, Libya, in the Sahara, where a temperature of over 136°F has been recorded.

The hottest temperature ever recorded in the United States is 134.6°F, in Death Valley, California.

136°F
134.6°F

98.6°F
Body temp.

68°F
Room temp.

32°F
Water freezes

68

**Student Edition, p. 68**

## Close Reading ©

**ANALYSIS • TEXT EVIDENCE** How can you use graphic sources to find that the hottest and coldest spots in the world are on different continents? **(You can look at the maps on pp. 68 and 69 and see that the dot showing where each place is located is on a different continent on each of the maps.)**

**ANALYSIS • TEXT EVIDENCE** What is an important detail supporting the main idea that Vostok, Antarctica, is the coldest place on the planet? **(An important detail, in paragraph 1 on p. 69, is that the temperature once reached 129°F below zero there.)**

**CHECK PREDICTIONS** Have students look back at the predictions they made earlier and discuss whether they were accurate. Then have students preview the rest of the selection and either adjust their predictions accordingly or make new predictions.

The **coldest** place on the planet is Vostok, Antarctica. A temperature of 129°F below zero was recorded there.

It is so cold at the South Pole that the average summer temperature is −58°F. The coldest temperature ever recorded in the United States is −80°F, at Prospect Creek Camp, Alaska.

The **wettest** place on Earth is Tutunendo, Colombia, where an average of 463 inches of rain falls every year.

Mount Wai-ale-ale, on the island of Kauai in Hawaii, has the most rainy days—350 a year. On the island of La Réunion, in the Indian Ocean, more than 61 inches of rain fell in a single day.

69

**Student Edition, p. 69**

If you want to teach this selection in two sessions, stop here.

If you want to continue reading this selection, turn to page 70.

**REREAD CHALLENGING TEXT** Have partners take turns rereading the paragraphs on pp. 68–69 to practice reading numbers fluently. Students may need help reading the special symbols and characters used in temperatures.

© **Common Core State Standards**
**Informational Text 2.** Determine the main idea of a text; recount the key details and explain how they support the main idea. **Informational Text 6.** Distinguish their own point of view from that of the author of a text. **Informational Text 7.** Use information gained from illustrations (e.g., maps, photographs) and the words in a text to demonstrate understanding of the text (e.g., where, when, why, and how key events occur). **Also Language 4.**

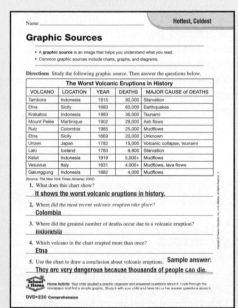

Let's Practice It! TR DVD•230

## Access for All

**SI Strategic Intervention**

Display the sentence *The wettest place on Earth is Tutunendo, Colombia, but the rainiest place is Mount Wai-ale-ale.* Explain that the author shows on p. 69 that the *wettest* place on Earth is different from the *rainiest* place. Have students discuss how this might be possible.

**ELL**

**Formal and Informal Language** Explain that *recorded* is a formal way to say that information was written down to use at a later time. Provide examples: *The teacher recorded the students' grades. The nurse recorded my temperature on the chart.*

**Bridge to Common Core**

### RESEARCH TO BUILD AND PRESENT KNOWLEDGE

Students create research plans and begin to gather relevant information about their topics. They conduct Internet searches, consulting multiple digital sources, assessing the credibility of each one. This process enables students to demonstrate an understanding of the subject under investigation.

# Research and Inquiry

## Step 2 Navigate/Search

**TEACH** Have students generate a research plan for gathering information about their topics. Suggest students conduct an Internet search using their inquiry questions and the keywords they identified. Tell them to skim and scan each site for information that helps answer their inquiry question or leads them to specific information that will be useful. Boldfaced or italicized words may be clues to the kind of information the Web site will provide. Have students also look for charts, graphs, and highlighted text. Have students take notes as they research.

 **Think Aloud**

**MODEL** When I conducted a search on *fastest runners,* I realized that I might want to know the fastest runner for different races. The person who runs the fastest 50-yard dash probably wouldn't win a marathon. I will look at different races to see who set records for different events. I will pay attention to captions and boldfaced words to help me find important information.

**GUIDE PRACTICE** Have students review Web sites they identified. Remind them that they should look at several sites and make sure that the information about a record holder is the same on all the sites. Explain that while this is a good process to follow whenever they do Internet research, it is especially important when they are dealing with record holders, since record holders may change over time. There also may be disagreements about who or what really holds the record.

**ON THEIR OWN** Have students continue their review of Web sites, taking notes as they find relevant information.

# Conventions

## Subject and Object Pronouns

**TEACH** Write *He and I said hello to her* on the board. Ask students to identify the subjects of the sentence. (*He* and *I*) Remind students that a pronoun used as the subject of a sentence is called a subject pronoun. Have students identify the object pronoun in the sentence. (*her*) Remind them that object pronouns are used after action verbs or as objects of prepositions.

**GUIDE PRACTICE** Have students create a sentence with a proper noun as the subject and then replace it with a subject pronoun. Then have them say a sentence with a noun in the predicate and replace it with an object pronoun.

**ON THEIR OWN** For additional practice, use *Reader's and Writer's Notebook* p. 262.

# Spelling

## Vowels: *r*-Controlled

**TEACH** Remind students that the sound /ėr/ has several spellings. It may be spelled *ir, er, ur, ear,* and *or.*

**GUIDE PRACTICE** Have students write each spelling word on the board and underline the sound /ėr/ spelled *ir, er, ur, ear,* or *or.*

**ON THEIR OWN** For additional practice, use *Reader's and Writer's Notebook* p. 263.

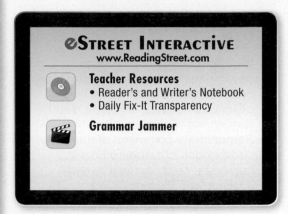

**eStreet Interactive**
www.ReadingStreet.com

**Teacher Resources**
• Reader's and Writer's Notebook
• Daily Fix-It Transparency

**Grammar Jammer**

## Daily Fix-It

3. Terry and me read about Mt. everest. *(I; Everest)*
4. Its the highest mountain on erth. *(It's; earth or Earth)*

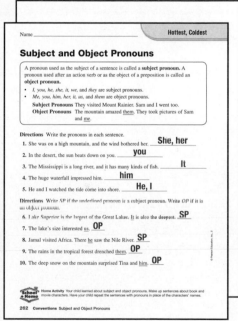

Reader's and Writer's Notebook, pp. 262–263

**Conventions** To provide students with practice using subject and object pronouns, use the modified grammar lessons in the *ELL Handbook* and Grammar Jammer online at www.ReadingStreet.com

**Language Transfer: Gender-Neutral Pronouns** English learners may incorrectly use masculine or feminine personal pronouns because nouns in their home languages have genders. If this happens, say the sentence with the gender-neutral pronoun *it,* and have students repeat after you several times.

*Hottest, Coldest, Highest, Deepest* **69c**

## Common Core State Standards

**Writing 3.** Write narratives to develop real or imagined experiences or events using effective technique, descriptive details, and clear event sequences. **Language 2.** Demonstrate command of the conventions of standard English capitalization, punctuation, and spelling when writing. **Also Writing 3.a., 3.d.**

# Writing

## Imaginative Story

### Writer's Craft: Generating Ideas

**INTRODUCE THE PROMPT** Review the key features of an imaginative story. Remind students that they should think about these features as they plan their writing. Then explain that they will begin the writing process for an imaginative story today. Read aloud the reading prompt.

---

### Writing Prompt

Write an imaginative story in which one character tells a riddle to another.

---

### SELECT A TOPIC

**Think Aloud** To help choose a topic, let's make a chart and list possible settings for a story on one side and what might happen in each setting on the other side. **Display a T-chart.** We read about some extreme places on earth in *Hottest, Coldest, Highest, Deepest.* Yesterday we read "A Day in the Desert," about a pair of lizards in the desert. I'm going to start the chart with that. **Add the information to the T-chart.** Ask students to name other settings and story lines that might happen in each setting. Remind them that because this will be an imaginative story, the story line does not have to be something that could actually happen.

| Setting | Story Line |
|---|---|
| desert | getting lost |
| highest mountain | climbing it |
| river | nearly going over a waterfall |

Also remind students that they will need to include a riddle in their story. Explain that a riddle is a statement or question that describes something in an unusual way and therefore takes some thought to understand. People usually have to figure something out in order to understand or answer a riddle. Refer to the riddle in "A Day in the Desert."

**Corrective feedback** Circulate around the room as students use the chart to select a setting and story line to write about. If students are having trouble deciding, suggest they picture each setting and choose the story line they would find most exciting to write about. Then remind them to think of a riddle that they will be able to use in their story.

**eSTREET INTERACTIVE**
www.ReadingStreet.com

**Teacher Resources**
• Reader's and Writer's Notebook
• Graphic Organizer

## Mini-Lesson  Developing a Story Sequence Chart

■ A story sequence chart helps you organize your story. It also helps you organize the events. I'm going to write about sailing on the Nile River. **Write *the Nile River with waterfall* in the Setting box.**

■ For my characters, I think I'll create a family. There will be a mother, a father, and two girls. **Enter this information in the Characters box.**

■ In the Events boxes, write the main events of the story that will lead up to a climax. First, the family will be sailing down the Nile River. Next, the girls will share riddles. Then they will realize that they are quickly approaching a waterfall. Last, they will all work together to get their boat to shore.

Have students begin their own story sequence charts using the form on p. 264 of their *Reader's and Writer's Notebook.*

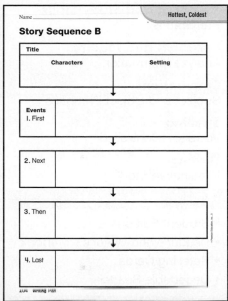

Reader's and Writer's Notebook, p. 264

## Routine  Quick Write for Fluency  Team Talk

**1. Talk** Have partners discuss the settings they selected.

**2. Write** Each student writes two sentences describing his or her setting.

**3. Share** Partners read their descriptions to each other. Then each partner asks the other a question about his or her setting.

Routines Flip Chart

# Wrap Up Your Day!

✔ **Content Knowledge** What did you learn about places in nature that hold records?

✔ **Text-Based Comprehension** What is the hottest temperature ever recorded in the United States? Where was it recorded?

## Preview DAY 3

Tell students that tomorrow they will read more about other places in nature that hold records.

## ⓒ Common Core State Standards

**Speaking/Listening 1.c.** Ask questions to check understanding of information presented, stay on topic, and link their comments to the remarks of others. **Language 6.** Acquire and use accurately grade-appropriate conversational, general academic, and domain-specific words and phrases, including those that signal spatial and temporal relationships (e.g., *After dinner that night we went looking for them*).

# Content Knowledge

## Nature's Record Holders

**EXPAND THE CONCEPT** Remind students of the weekly concept question, *What makes nature's record holders unique?* Discuss how the question relates to *Hottest, Coldest, Highest, Deepest.* Encourage students to think about some of nature's amazing record holders.

## Build Oral Language

**TALK ABOUT SENTENCES AND WORDS** Reread a sentence from Student Edition p. 64 of *Hottest, Coldest, Highest, Deepest.*

*There are deserts that haven't seen rain for hundreds of years and jungles where it pours almost every day.*

• What does *deserts* mean? (dry, sandy regions without water and trees)
• What does *haven't seen rain* mean? (Rain has not fallen there.)
• What do deserts and jungles have in common? (extreme weather conditions)

**Team Talk** Have students work with a partner to create one sentence for each idea in the original sentence. Use the following sentence frames.

> **There are deserts that** _____ _____.
> **There are jungles where** _____ _____.

# Build Oral Vocabulary

**Amazing Words**    **Robust Vocabulary Routine**

1. **Introduce** Write the word *sprinter* on the board. Have students say it with you. Yesterday, we read about the hottest place on the planet, where a temperature of over 136°F would certainly affect a *sprinter's* speed. Have students determine a definition of *sprinter*. (A *sprinter* is a runner who is fast in short races.)

2. **Demonstrate** Have students answer questions to demonstrate understanding. What kind of animals are fast *sprinters*? (cheetahs, lions, horses, zebras, rabbits, giraffes)

3. **Apply** Have students apply their understanding. Where might you see a *sprinter* running? (at a track meet, in the Olympics)

4. **Display the Word** Run your hand under the syllables *sprint-er* as you read the word. Have students say the word.

See p. OV•2 to teach *acrobat*.

Routines Flip Chart

### Amazing Words

| | |
|---|---|
| evergreen | champ |
| lumber | sprinter |
| competitor | acrobat |
| plunge | weaken |
| valuable | ranger |

**ADD TO THE CONCEPT MAP** Discuss the Amazing Words *valuable* and *champ*. Add these words and other concept-related words to the concept map. Use the following questions to develop students' understanding of the concept. Have students ask and answer questions with appropriate detail and give suggestions based on the ideas of others.

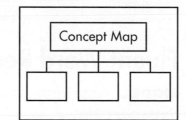

Concept Map

• How can rain be *valuable* for a farmer's crops?

• How could a *champ* help protect the wildlife along the Amazon River?

• Would very hot temperatures be *valuable* for an athlete?

**Professional Development: What ELL Experts Say About Sheltered Instruction** "English language learners benefit when teachers shelter, or make comprehensible, their literacy instruction. Sheltered techniques include using consistent, simplified, clearly enunciated, and slower-paced oral language to explain literacy concepts or activities."
—Dr. Georgia Ernest García

**Expand Vocabulary** Use the Day 3 instruction on ELL Poster 17 to help students expand vocabulary.

**Common Core State Standards**

**Foundational Skills 3.** Know and apply grade-level phonics and word analysis skills in decoding words. **Foundational Skills 3.d.** Read grade-appropriate irregularly spelled words.

# Phonics

**MODEL WORD SORTING** Write /ėr/, /är/, and /ôr/ as headings on a three-column chart. Now we are going to sort words. We'll sort words with the *r*-controlled vowel sounds /ėr/, /är/, and /ôr/ into the columns on the chart. I will start. Write *burn* and model how to read it, using the blending strategy on p. 56a. *Burn* has the sounds /b/ /ėr/ /n/ with /ėr/ spelled *ur,* so I will write *burn* in the column under /ėr/. Model sorting *park* (/är/) and *chore* (/ôr/) in the same way.

**GUIDE PRACTICE** Use the practice words from the activities on p. 56a for the word sort. Point to a word. Have students read the word, identify the *r*-controlled vowel sound in the word, and tell where it should be written on the chart.

> **Corrective feedback** | For corrective feedback, model tracking each word and reading it.

| /ėr/ | /är/ | /ôr/ |
|------|------|------|
| burn | park | chore |
| third | large | forth |
| heard | party | store |
| curtain | | boar |
| word | | |
| germ | | |

# Fluent Word Reading

**MODEL** Write *birth.* I know the sounds for *b, ir,* and *th.* Blend them and read the word *birth.*

**GUIDE PRACTICE** Write the words below. Say the sounds in your head for each spelling you see. When I point to the word, we'll read it together. Allow one second per sound previewing time for the first reading.

| whirl | learn | carver | porch | dirty | storm |

**ON THEIR OWN** Have students read the list above three or four times, until they can read one word per second.

# Decodable Passage 17B

If students need help, then...

## Read *Mom's Purse*

**READ WORDS IN ISOLATION** Have students turn to p. 21 in *Decodable Practice Readers 3.2* and find the first list of words. Each word in this list has an *r*-controlled vowel sound. Let's blend and read these words. Be sure that students identify the correct vowel sound in each word.

**PREVIEW** Have students read the title and preview the story. Tell them that they will read words with the vowel sounds /ėr/, /är/, or /ôr/.

**READ WORDS IN CONTEXT** Chorally read the story along with the students. Have students identify words in the story that have the vowel sounds /ėr/, /är/, or /ôr/.

**Team Talk** Pair students and have them take turns reading the story aloud to each other. Monitor students as they read to check for proper pronunciation and appropriate pacing.

**eStreet Interactive**
www.ReadingStreet.com

**Pearson eText**
• Decodable Reader

## Access for All

**A** **Advanced**
Have students write sentences using the pairs of words *third, heard; store, boar;* and *large, party.*

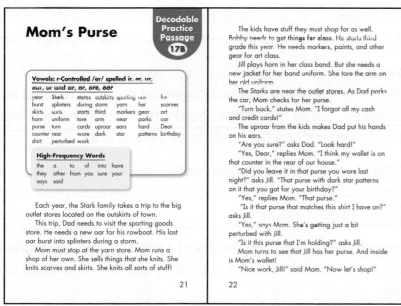

Decodable Practice Passage 17B

Zoom in on ©

© **Common Core State Standards**
**Informational Text 5.** Use text features and search tools (e.g., key words, sidebars, hyperlinks) to locate information relevant to a given topic efficiently. **Informational Text 7.** Use information gained from illustrations (e.g., maps, photographs) and the words in a text to demonstrate understanding of the text (e.g., where, when, why, and how key events occur). **Language 4.** Determine or clarify the meaning of unknown and multiple-meaning words and phrases based on grade 3 reading and content, choosing flexibly from a range of strategies. **Language 4.d.** Use glossaries or beginning dictionaries, both print and digital, to determine or clarify the precise meaning of key words and phrases.

## Strategy Response Log

Have students list 2 or 3 important ideas presented in *Hottest, Coldest, Highest, Deepest* on p. 23 in the *Reader's and Writer's Notebook.*

# Text-Based Comprehension
## Check Understanding

**Student Edition, pp. 62–63**

**If...** you chose to read *Hottest, Coldest, Highest, Deepest* in two parts,

**then...** use the following questions to monitor students' understanding of pp. 62–69 of the selection. Encourage students to cite evidence from the text.

**EVALUATION** Why does the graph on page 68 show body and room temperatures and the temperature at which water freezes? (It lets the reader compare those temperatures to the temperatures in Al Aziziyah and Death Valley. It makes it easier to understand how hot those places are.)

**ANALYSIS** The word *base* has several meanings. Use a dictionary or glossary to define the word *base* as it is used on page 67. (On p. 67, the word *base* means the lowest part, or bottom.)

**RETELL** Have students retell the details of *Hottest, Coldest, Highest, Deepest* through p. 69. Encourage students to use the boldfaced words in their retellings.

> **Corrective feedback**
> **If...** the students leave out important details,
> **then...** have students look back through the illustrations in the selection.

**READ** Use the Read for Understanding routine to finish reading *Hottest, Coldest, Highest, Deepest.*

**If...** you followed the Read for Understanding routine below,

**then...** ask students to retell the selection before you reread *Hottest, Coldest, Highest, Deepest.*

**RETELL** Have students retell the details of *Hottest, Coldest, Highest, Deepest* through p. 69. Encourage students to use the boldfaced words in their retellings.

> **Corrective feedback**
>
> **If...** the students leave out important details,
>
> **then...** have students look back through the illustrations in the selection.

**READ** Return to p. 62–63 and use the **2nd Read/Close Reading** notes to reread *Hottest, Coldest, Highest, Deepest.*

# Read Main Selection

**Routine**    **Read for Understanding** ©

Deepen understanding by reading the selection multiple times.

1. **First Read**—If students need support, use the **Access Text** notes to help them clarify understanding.

2. **Second Read**—Use the **Close Reading** notes to help students draw knowledge from the text.

---

**Day 3**   **SMALL GROUP TIME • Differentiate Close Reading, p. SG•17**

| **OL** On-Level | **SI** Strategic Intervention | **A** Advanced |
|---|---|---|
| • **Reread** to Develop Vocabulary | • **Reread** to Develop Vocabulary | • **Reread** to Extend Vocabulary |
| • **Read** *Hottest, Coldest, Highest, Deepest* | • **Read** *Hottest, Coldest, Highest, Deepest* | • **Read** *Hottest, Coldest, Highest, Deepest* |
| | | • **Investigate** Inquiry Project |

**ELL**

**Check Retelling** To support retelling, review the multilingual summary for *Hottest, Coldest, Highest, Deepest* with the appropriate Retelling Cards to scaffold understanding.

**ELL**

**If...** students need more scaffolding and practice with the **Main Selection,**

**then...** use the activities on p. DI•47 in the Teacher Resources section on SuccessNet.

*Hottest, Coldest, Highest, Deepest*    **70f**

## Access Text © If students need help, then...

**⊚ UNKNOWN WORDS** Have students use a dictionary or glossary to determine the meaning, pronunciation, and syllabication of the word *current* at the end of p. 71, paragraph 2.

**(Think Aloud) MODEL** I see two meanings for *current* in a dictionary: "a flow of water, electricity, air, or any fluid" and "of or about the present time." Since the passage says "a narrow, strong air current," I know it's the first definition. The word has two syllables, stressing the first, and it is pronounced kėr-ənt.

The **driest** place is the Atacama Desert, in Chile, where no rain has fallen for the last 400 years.

Any place that receives less than 10 inches of precipitation a year is considered a desert. The driest place in the United States is Death Valley, California, where only about 1½ inches of rain fall every year.

— **72 in.** Adult man

— **10 in.** Desert precipitation

— **1½ in.** Death Valley average annual precipitation

70

**Student Edition, p. 70**

## Close Reading ©

**ANALYSIS • TEXT EVIDENCE** Use context clues to tell the meaning of the word *annual* in the chart on page 70. (The chart shows that Death Valley receives 1 1/2 inches of average annual precipitation. The text says that only about 1 1/2 inches of rain fall every year in Death Valley. *Annual* must mean "every year." The dictionary says that *annual* means "happening every year or yearly.")

**ON THEIR OWN** Have students use a dictionary to figure out the meaning, pronunciation, and syllabication of the word *peaks* on p. 71, paragraph 2. For additional practice, use *Reader's and Writer's Notebook,* p. 265.

The **windiest** spot on Earth is atop Mount Washington, in New Hampshire. A wind speed of 231 miles per hour has been recorded there.

It is also very windy near the tops of the world's highest mountains, the Himalayas. Many of these peaks are tall enough to reach the jet stream, a narrow, strong air current that is found above 28,000 feet.

71

**Student Edition, p. 71**

**SYNTHESIS** What would be a challenge to people living in the Atacama Desert? Why? (Finding drinking water would be a serious challenge in the Atacama Desert because no rain falls there.)

Ⓒ **Common Core State Standards**

**Informational Text 5.** Use text features and search tools (e.g., key words, sidebars, hyperlinks) to locate information relevant to a given topic efficiently. **Language 4.** Determine or clarify the meaning of unknown and multiple-meaning words and phrases based on grade 3 reading and content, choosing flexibly from a range of strategies.

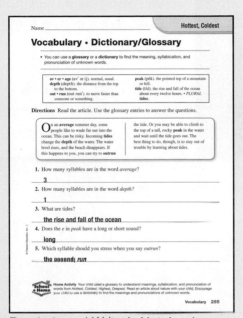

**Reader's and Writer's Notebook,** p. 265

 **Connect to Science**

**Life in the Desert** The Atacama Desert is so dry that few things can live there. In some portions of the desert, there are not even any insects. In some areas, moisture collects from fog, allowing plants to grow.

**ELL**

**Vocabulary: Unknown Words** After reviewing the meaning of *precipitation*, have partners ask and answer these questions using the word: *What is one kind of precipitation? What is another kind of precipitation? Does a desert have much precipitation?*

*Hottest, Coldest, Highest, Deepest* **71a**

## 1ST READ

## Access Text © If students need help, then...

**☺ IMPORTANT IDEAS** Remind students to pause to find the important idea in each paragraph as they read. Have them find the important idea on p. 72.

**(Think Aloud) MODEL** I notice the word *highest* is in bold type. That makes it stand out and look important. The text says that Angel Falls is the world's highest waterfall. I need to read on, however, to be sure if that is the important idea of the page.

## 2ND READ

## Close Reading ©

**SYNTHESIS** Why might the author have boldfaced two words on the bottom half of page 73? (Sangay is the world's most active volcano. If the author only boldfaced *active,* the sentence would not make its point clearly.)

**EVALUATION • TEXT EVIDENCE** Have volcanic eruptions existed throughout modern times? Use evidence from the text to support your answer. (Yes, on the bottom half of p. 73 the author says that volcanoes, including Mount Etna, have been erupting regularly since 1500 B.C.)

The world's **highest** waterfall is Angel Falls, in Venezuela. It is 3,212 feet high.

Angel Falls is more than seventeen times higher than Niagara Falls (180 feet), in New York State. Victoria Falls, in Zimbabwe, Africa, carries more water than any other waterfall. It is 355 feet high.

Angel Falls
3,212 ft.

Victoria Falls
355 ft.

Empire State Building
1,250 ft.

Niagara Falls
180 ft.

72

**Student Edition, p. 72**

**N THEIR OWN** Have students read the rest of the page and decide if
Angel Falls being the highest waterfall is the important idea on the page.
Have them explain their reasoning.

The **deepest** spot in the ocean is the Marianas Trench, in the Philippines. It is 36,202 feet deep.

The average depth of the world's oceans is about 3 miles, or 16,000 feet. The lowest spot on dry land is the shore of the Dead Sea, 1,100 feet below sea level.

The world's **most active** volcano is Sangay, in Ecuador. Since 1937 it has erupted once every 24 hours on average. It once erupted more than 400 times in a single day.

Other very active volcanoes include Colima, in Mexico (it has erupted regularly since 1560); Aso, in Japan (erupting since 533); and Mount Etna, in Italy (erupting regularly since 1500 B.C.).

73

**Student Edition, p. 73**

**ANALYSIS** Help students generate text-based questions by providing the following question stem: In the selection, where _____?

## Common Core State Standards

**Informational Text 2.** Determine the main idea of a text; recount the key details and explain how they support the main idea. **Informational Text 7.** Use information gained from illustrations (e.g., maps, photographs) and the words in a text to demonstrate understanding of the text (e.g., where, when, why, and how key events occur).

## Access for All

**SI** Strategic Intervention

Help students to understand the details about waterfalls on p. 72 by explaining the phrase "carries more water." (A waterfall is measured not just by how high it is, but by how much water falls from the top to the bottom of the waterfall.)

## Connect to Science
**Animal Adaptations**

Explain that some animals are uniquely adapted to living in or near waterfalls. An example is Australia's waterfall frog, whose tadpoles attach themselves by the mouth to rocks in fast-flowing streams.

## ELL

**Vocabulary: Compound Words** Use the illustration on p. 72 to review that *waterfall* is a compound word made of two smaller words, *water* and *fall.* Say, A waterfall is water that falls. Then provide the compound words *airplane, flashlight, bedroom,* and *mailbox.* Have students use the smaller words to explain the meaning of the compound words.

1ST READ

## Access Text © If students need help, then...

**⊙ GRAPHIC SOURCES** Have students use the text and graph on p. 75 to explain how showing the height of an adult man helps us to understand how much snow falls on Mount Rainier.

**(Think Aloud) MODEL** On the graph, I see that 100 feet of snow, which is 1,200 inches, fell on Mount Rainier in one year. I also see the figure of a six-foot-tall man. I know that 100 feet is a lot taller than a six-foot man. This fact helps us understand how high 100 feet is.

**ON THEIR OWN** Have students explain how a graphic source can show an important idea on p. 74.

### CROSS-TEXT EVALUATION
**Use a Strategy to Self-Check** How did "Largest U.S. Cities" on p. 59 help you understand this selection?

The **most extreme tides** occur in the Bay of Fundy, in Nova Scotia, Canada. There the water level rises and falls more than 50 feet every 6 hours.

The tide here comes in so fast that it can overtake a person trying to outrun it.

74

**Student Edition, p. 74**

2ND READ

## Close Reading ©

**ANALYSIS • TEXT EVIDENCE** What is the main idea of *Hottest, Coldest, Highest, Deepest*? What details support that idea? (The main idea is that there are places on Earth that hold records for being extreme. The author tells about many places with extremes, such as Mount Rainier, on p. 75, which once got more than 100 feet of snow in a year; and a volcano in Ecuador, on p. 73, that once erupted 400 times in a single day.)

**SYNTHESIS • TEXT EVIDENCE** Using what you learned in this selection, tell what makes nature's record holders unique. Have students cite examples from the text to support their responses.

**CHECK PREDICTIONS** Have students return to the predictions they made earlier and confirm whether they were accurate.

100 ft.
Mt. Rainier record
1-year snowfall

The **snowiest** place on Earth is Mount Rainier, in Washington State. One year, more than 1,200 inches of snow fell there.

Mount Rainier is covered in snow the whole year. Some of the snow has formed glaciers, masses of ice that slowly move down the mountain under their own weight.

6 ft.
Adult man

3 ft.
Typical annual
New York City
snowfall

75

**Student Edition, p. 75**

**SYNTHESIS** What do you think is the cause of the dry climate in the Atacama Desert and Death Valley? (I think that it's the lack of precipitation throughout those areas.)

 **Common Core State Standards**

**Informational Text 1.** Ask and answer questions to demonstrate understanding of a text, referring explicitly to the text as the basis for the answers. **Informational Text 2.** Determine the main idea of a text; recount the key details and explain how they support the main idea. **Informational Text 7.** Use information gained from illustrations (e.g., maps, photographs) and the words in a text to demonstrate understanding of the text (e.g., where, when, why, and how key events occur). **Also Informational Text 3.**

## Access for All

 **Strategic Intervention**

Have students work in pairs to explain how graphic sources help them identify the main idea and an important detail on p. 75. Have one student look for boldfaced words and another look at type sizes on the page.

 **Advanced**

Explain that the Mi'kmaq people of North America believed the tides in the Bay of Fundy were caused by a giant whale splashing in the water. Have students discuss how this concept could explain a place with extreme tides.

 **Connect to Science**

**Glaciers on the Move**

Explain that the surface of the Earth can be changed by glaciers like the ones at Mount Rainier. Glaciers slide over the rock on which they lie, and one of the Mount Rainier glaciers was once measured moving as fast as 29 inches per day.

**Monitor Comprehension** Read aloud the first sentence on p. 74. Model using the reading strategy of monitor and clarify by saying: I wonder what *most extreme tides* are. The sentence doesn't give me a clue. I will read on to find the answer. Read the second and third sentences and then ask students to use the information to explain what an extreme tide is.

Common Core State Standards
Informational Text 1. Ask and answer questions to demonstrate understanding of a text, referring explicitly to the text as the basis for the answers. Also Informational Text 2., 5., Writing 8.

**Envision It!** Retell

READING STREET ONLINE
STORY SORT
www.ReadingStreet.com

76

## Think Critically

1. Which environment would you most like to visit? In which environment would you most like to live? Explain your answers. **Text to World**

2. Why did the author show a man and the Empire State Building on some of the pages? How were these graphic features helpful in locating facts from the selection? **Think Like an Author**

3. Which graphic source from the selection was most helpful to you? How was it helpful? **Graphic Sources**

4. How does the selection's title help you understand the most important ideas on each page? **Important Ideas**

5. **Look Back and Write** Mount Everest is the highest mountain, but Mauna Kea is the tallest mountain. Look back at page 67. Write the reason that the tallest and the highest mountain are not the same. Provide evidence to support your answer.

**Key Ideas and Details • Text Evidence**

### Meet the Author and Illustrator
# STEVE JENKINS

Steve Jenkins has always liked science and art. As a child he kept spiders and lizards and liked to draw and paint. His father was a scientist. "We did a lot of projects together," he said. "We wrote a little book about animals."

In his books, Mr. Jenkins tries to make science fun. "Kids have a natural interest in animals and things like volcanoes," he said. He wrote *Hottest, Coldest, Highest, Deepest* partly because his son was always asking him those kinds of questions.

The pictures in Mr. Jenkins's books are not drawings or paintings. They are called collages. His collages are made by cutting different kinds of paper and pasting them in layers.

Read more books by Steve Jenkins.

*The Top of the World: Climbing Mount Everest*

*What Do You Do With a Tail Like This?*

Use the *Reader's and Writer's Notebook* to record your independent reading.

77

---

## Common Core State Standards

**Informational Text 1.** Ask and answer questions to demonstrate understanding of a text, referring explicitly to the text as the basis for the answers. **Also Informational Text 2., 5., 6., Writing 2.a., 2.b.**

### Bridge to Common Core

**RANGE OF READING AND LEVEL OF TEXT COMPLEXITY**

To increase students' capacity for reading and comprehending complex texts independently and proficiently, have them read other informational texts by Steve Jenkins or about the science topic, nature's record holders. After students read closely for a sustained period of time, they should record their reading in their Reading Logs.

# Think Critically

1. **TEXT TO WORLD** I would most like to visit Mount Everest and I would most like to live near Mauna Kea in Hawaii.

2. **THINK LIKE AN AUTHOR** The author showed a man and the Empire State Building to compare the size of things he wrote about to things we already know. The graphic features include pictures and labels and are placed next to the text that explains them, so its easy to find what you're looking for.

3. **GRAPHIC SOURCES** The graphic on p. 72 was most helpful because it compared the heights of the waterfalls to the height of the Empire State Building.

4. **IMPORTANT IDEAS** The selection's title helps me to understand the most important ideas on each page because it reminds me that the text is about places that are the most extreme in nature.

5. **LOOK BACK AND WRITE • TEXT EVIDENCE** To build writing fluency, assign a 10–15 minute time limit.

## Scoring Rubric | Look Back and Write

**TOP-SCORE RESPONSE** A top-score response uses details to tell why the highest mountain is not the same as the tallest mountain.

**A top-score response should include:**

• Mount Everest is highest because its peak is 29,028 feet above sea level.

• Mauna Kea is tallest because it is 33,476 feet tall when measured from its base to its top.

• Mauna Kea is taller than Mount Everest because if both mountains started at the same place, Mauna Kea would tower over Mount Everest.

# Retell

Have students work in pairs to retell the selection, using the retelling strip in the Student Edition or the Story Sort as prompts.

## Scoring Rubric | Expository Retelling

| | 4 | 3 | 2 | 1 |
|---|---|---|---|---|
| Connections | Makes connections and generalizes beyond the text | Makes connections to other events, texts, or experiences | Makes a limited connection to another event, text, or experience | Makes no connection to another event, text, or experience |
| Author's Purpose | Elaborates on author's purpose | Tells author's purpose with some clarity | Makes some connection to author's purpose | Makes no connection to author's purpose |
| Topic | Describes the main topic | Identifies the main topic with some details early in retelling | Identifies the main topic | Retelling has no sense of topic |
| Important Ideas | Gives accurate information about events, steps, and ideas using details and key vocabulary | Gives accurate information about events, steps, and ideas with some detail and key vocabulary | Gives limited or inaccurate information about events, steps, and ideas | Gives no information about events, steps, and ideas |
| Conclusions | Draws conclusions and makes inferences to generalize beyond the text | Draws conclusions about the text | Is able to tell some learnings about the text | Is unable to draw conclusions or make inferences about the text |

**Don't Wait Until Friday**

## MONITOR PROGRESS | Check Retelling

**If...** students have difficulty retelling,

**then...** use the Retelling Cards/Story Sort to scaffold their retellings.

## Plan to Assess Retelling

☐ **Week 1** Strategic Intervention

☑ **This week assess Advanced students.**

☐ **Week 3** Strategic Intervention

☐ **Week 4** On-Level

☐ **Week 5** Assess any students you have not yet checked during this unit.

## Meet the Author

Have students read about author Steve Jenkins on p. 77. Ask them why he decided to write *Hottest, Coldest, Highest, Deepest.*

## Read Independently

Have students enter their independent reading into their Reading Logs.

**Common Core State Standards**

**Informational Text 7.** Use information gained from illustrations (e.g., maps, photographs), and the words in a text to demonstrate understanding of the text (e.g., where, when, why, and how key events occur). **Foundational Skills 4.** Read with sufficient accuracy and fluency to support comprehension. **Foundational Skills 4.a** Read on-level text with purpose and understanding.

# Fluency

## Appropriate Phrasing and Punctuation Cues

**MODEL FLUENT READING** Have students turn to p. 68 of *Hottest, Coldest, Highest, Deepest.* Have students follow along as you read the page. Tell them to listen as you make a short pause for commas that separate place names, such as Al Aziziyah, Libya. Point out that you also pause at commas used to group words into phrases that tell where the places are, such as "in Death Valley, California." Explain that you will make a short pause at the commas and a longer pause at the periods so you can read with appropriate phrasing.

**GUIDE PRACTICE** Have students follow along as you read the page again. Then have them reread the page as a group without you until they read with appropriate phrasing, grouping words as needed. Ask questions to be sure that they comprehend the text. Continue in the same way with p. 69.

| Corrective feedback | **If...** students are having difficulty reading with correct phrasing, **then...** prompt them as follows: |
|---|---|
| | • Where can we break up this sentence? Which words are related? |
| | • Read the sentence again. Pause after each group of words. |
| | • Tell me the sentence. Now read it with pauses after each group of words. |

# Reread for Fluency

**Routine** Oral Rereading

1. **Read** Have students read p. 70 of *Hottest, Coldest, Highest, Deepest* orally.

2. **Reread** To achieve optimal fluency, students should reread the text three or four times.

3. **Corrective Feedback** Have students read aloud without you. Provide feedback about their phrasing, helping students to group phrases by pausing at punctuation cues. Listen for appropriate phrasing.

Routines Flip Chart

# Research and Study Skills

## Bar Graphs

**TEACH** Ask students where they are likely to see bar graphs as they read. Students may mention textbooks, newspapers, or magazines. Display a bar graph and use it to review these terms:

- A graph shows data, or information, in visual form. A special kind of graph, called a bar graph, uses bars to compare numbers or amounts.
- Bar graphs usually show numbers rounded to the nearest ten or hundred, rather than exact numbers.
- Bar graphs have a title that tells what the graph is about.
- The horizontal and vertical lines of the graph are called axes. One axis has a scale of numbers or amounts.

**GUIDE PRACTICE** Discuss these questions:

How can you compare things with a bar graph without looking at the numbers? (You can compare the lengths of the bars.)

How can you find information in a bar graph? (First, read the label to see what the bar represents. Then see what number is near the end of the bar.)

Have students tell what is being compared in the bar graph you displayed. Direct their attention to the labels on the axes. Then ask questions specific to the information in the graph.

**ON THEIR OWN** Have students review and complete p. 266 of the *Reader's and Writer's Notebook.*

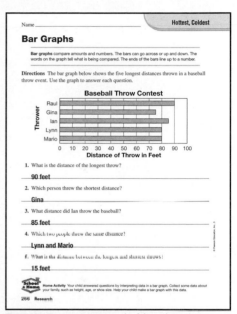

Reader's and Writer's Notebook, p. 266

**Graphs** Help students create a simple bar graph. List the colors *red, yellow, blue, pink, green,* and *purple* on the board and have students vote for their favorite of these colors. Then have students put the information into bar graph form with number of students on the vertical axis and colors on the horizontal axis. Ask students questions they can answer using the information on their graphs: *Which color is the students' favorite? How many students like the color green? Do more students like pink or purple best?*

*Hottest, Coldest, Highest, Deepest* **77c**

 **Common Core State Standards**

**Writing 8.** Recall information from experiences or gather information from print and digital sources; take brief notes on sources and sort evidence into provided categories.
**Language 1.a.** Explain the function of nouns, pronouns, verbs, adjectives, and adverbs in general and their functions in particular sentences.
**Language 1.f.** Ensure subject-verb and pronoun-antecedent agreement.
**Also Language 2.e., 2.f.**

# Research and Inquiry

## Step 3 Analyze Information

**TEACH** Tell students that today they will analyze their research findings and may want to change the focus of their original inquiry question.

**Think Aloud** **MODEL** Originally I thought it would be easy to discover the fastest runner on Earth. However, when I researched the question, I discovered that there are many people who are the fastest. I also realized it is interesting to find out how these runners got to be so fast. I think I am going to focus on how runners who set records train. Now my inquiry question is *How do runners get fast enough to set records?* I can talk with my neighbor who runs on the track team in high school.

**GUIDE PRACTICE** Have students analyze their findings. They may need to refocus their inquiry question to better fit the information they found. Explain to students that if they have difficulty improving their focus, they can ask a reference librarian or a local expert for guidance.

Remind students that they can use a graphic source, such as a bar graph, to provide a visual representation of their findings.

**ON THEIR OWN** Pair students to evaluate research findings. Ask partners to consider if the research opened any new avenues of inquiry that should be addressed.

# Conventions

## Subject and Object Pronouns

**REVIEW** Remind students that this week they learned about subject and object pronouns:

• A subject pronoun is used as the subject of a sentence. *I, you, he, she, it, we,* and *they* are subject pronouns.

• An object pronoun is used after an action verb or as the object of a preposition. *Me, you, him, her, it, us,* and *them* are object pronouns.

**CONNECT TO ORAL LANGUAGE** Have the class use pronouns to complete these sentence frames orally.

---

_____ used a thermometer to measure the temperature.

Look at the tallest peaks. Scientists measure _____.

---

**ON THEIR OWN** For additional support, use *Let's Practice It!* p. 232 on the *Teacher Resources DVD-ROM.*

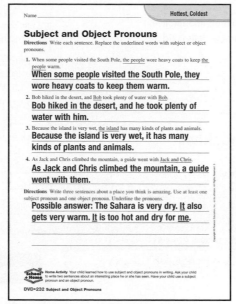

Let's Practice It! TR DVD•232

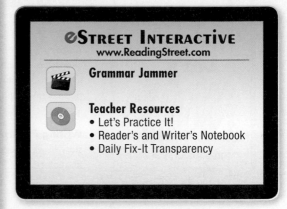

eSTREET INTERACTIVE
www.ReadingStreet.com

**Grammar Jammer**

**Teacher Resources**
• Let's Practice It!
• Reader's and Writer's Notebook
• Daily Fix-It Transparency

## Daily Fix-It

5. Mr. Jackson showed Tracy and I a picture of cammels in the desert. *(me; camels)*

6. Sand were blowing in the dessert like a snowstorm. *(was; desert)*

---

# Spelling

## Vowels: *r*-Controlled

**FREQUENTLY MISSPELLED WORDS** Students often misspell the words *another, brother,* and *heard* because they have the same sound spelled different ways. I'm going to read a sentence. Choose the correct word to complete the sentence and write it correctly.

1. May I have _____ piece of pizza, please? (another)

2. I didn't see lightning, but I _____ thunder. (heard)

3. Lauren is my sister, and Sean is my _____. (brother)

**ON THEIR OWN** For additional practice, use *Reader's and Writer's Notebook,* p. 267.

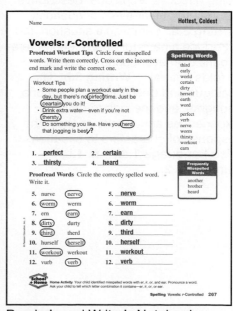

Reader's and Writer's Notebook, p. 267

*Hottest, Coldest, Highest, Deepest*  **77e**

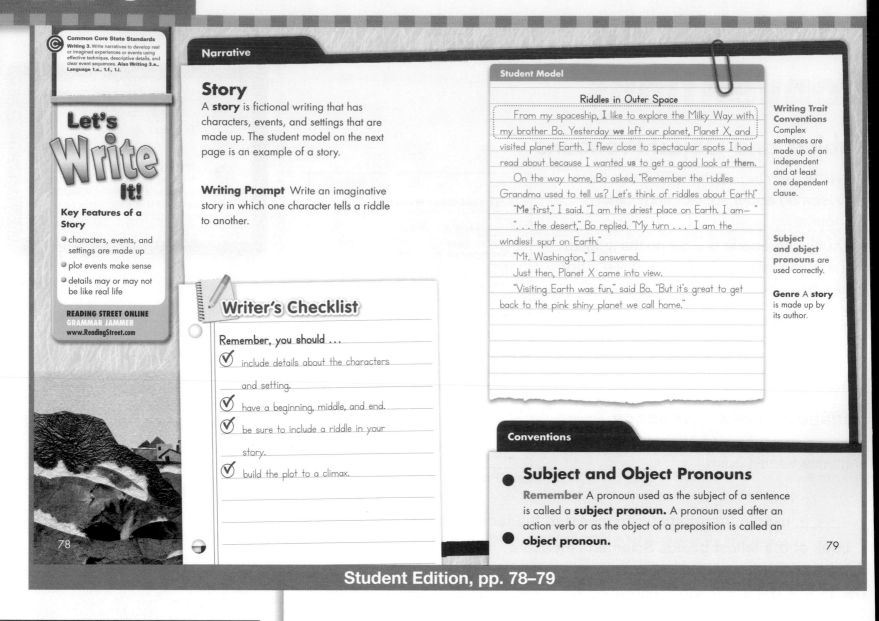

Common Core State Standards
Writing 3. Write narratives to develop real or imagined experiences or events using effective technique, descriptive details, and clear event sequences. Also Writing 3.a., Language 1.a., 1.f., 1.i.

## Let's Write It!

**Key Features of a Story**

- characters, events, and settings are made up
- plot events make sense
- details may or may not be like real life

**READING STREET ONLINE**
**GRAMMAR JAMMER**
www.ReadingStreet.com

### Narrative

## Story

A **story** is fictional writing that has characters, events, and settings that are made up. The student model on the next page is an example of a story.

**Writing Prompt** Write an imaginative story in which one character tells a riddle to another.

### Writer's Checklist

Remember, you should . . .

☑ include details about the characters and setting.

☑ have a beginning, middle, and end.

☑ be sure to include a riddle in your story.

☑ build the plot to a climax.

### Student Model

#### Riddles in Outer Space

From my spaceship, I like to explore the Milky Way with my brother Bo. Yesterday **we** left our planet, Planet X, and visited planet Earth. I flew close to spectacular spots I had read about because I wanted **us** to get a good look at them.

On the way home, Bo asked, "Remember the riddles Grandma used to tell us? Let's think of riddles about Earth!"

"Me first," I said. "I am the driest place on Earth. I am— "

". . . the desert," Bo replied. "My turn . . . I am the windiest spot on Earth."

"Mt. Washington," I answered.

Just then, Planet X came into view.

"Visiting Earth was fun," said Bo. "But it's great to get back to the pink shiny planet we call home."

**Writing Trait Conventions**
Complex sentences are made up of an independent and at least one dependent clause.

**Subject and object pronouns** are used correctly.

**Genre** A **story** is made up by its author.

### Conventions

- **Subject and Object Pronouns**

  **Remember** A pronoun used as the subject of a sentence is called a **subject pronoun.** A pronoun used after an action verb or as the object of a preposition is called an
- **object pronoun.**

78    79

**Student Edition, pp. 78–79**

## Common Core State Standards

**Writing 3.** Write narratives to develop real or imagined experiences or events using effective technique, descriptive details, and clear event sequences. **Writing 3.a.** Establish a situation and introduce a narrator and/or characters; organize an event sequence that unfolds naturally. **Writing 3.b.** Use dialogue and descriptions of actions, thoughts, and feelings to develop experiences and events or show the response of characters to situations. **Also Language 1.a., 1.f., 1.i., Language 2.**

## Let's Write It!

**WRITE AN IMAGINATIVE STORY** Use pp. 78–79 in the Student Edition. Direct students to read the key features of a story, which appear on p. 78. Remind students that they can refer to the information in the Writer's Checklist as they write their own imaginative story.

Read the student model on p. 79. Point out the characters, setting, and plot in the model.

**CONNECT TO CONVENTIONS** Remind students that subject pronouns are used as subjects of sentences and object pronouns are used after action verbs or as objects of prepositions. Point out the correct use of subject and object pronouns in the model.

# Writing

## Imaginative Story

### Writer's Craft: Dialogue

**DISPLAY RUBRIC** Display Scoring Rubric 17 from the *Teacher Resources DVD–ROM* and review the criteria for each trait under each score. Then, using the student writing model in the Student Edition, choose students to explain whether the model should score a 4 for each of the traits and why. If a student suggests that the model should score below 4 for a particular trait, the student should provide support for that response. Remind students that this is the rubric that will be used to evaluate the imaginative stories they will begin writing.

### Access for All

**SI Strategic Intervention**

Have pairs of students complete a story sequence chart based on the student model on p. 79 of the Student Edition. Then have them compare it to their own story sequence charts. Ask them to decide if their charts will help them write a composition with the same qualities as the model. Monitor their discussion and provide feedback.

## Scoring Rubric — Imaginative Story

| | 4 | 3 | 2 | 1 |
|---|---|---|---|---|
| **Focus/Ideas** | Vivid story, well-developed characters, detailed setting, plot building to climax | Story with adequate characters, setting, and plot development | Story lacks focus, developed characters, detailed setting, and plot development | No focus or development of characters, setting, or plot |
| **Organization** | Clear beginning, middle, and end; clear sequence of events | Beginning, middle, and end; able to follow sequence of events | Unclear beginning, middle, and end; unclear sequence of events | No beginning, middle, or end; no sequence of events |
| **Voice** | Effective use of dialogue helps develop characters | Some effective use of dialogue | Dialogue often flat and ineffective | No dialogue used |
| **Word Choice** | Strong use of vivid, precise words | Some use of precise words | Few precise words | Vague, general words |
| **Sentences** | Clear sentences of various lengths and types; strong variety of beginnings | Sentences of a few lengths and types; variety of beginnings | Sentences of similar length and type; weak variety of beginnings | No attempt at sentences of various lengths and types; no variety of beginnings |
| **Conventions** | Few, if any, errors; correct use of subject and object pronouns | Several minor errors; correct use of subject and object pronouns | Many errors; a few errors in use of subject and object pronouns | Numerous errors; incorrect use of subject and object pronouns |

**STORY SEQUENCE CHARTS** Have students refer to the story sequence charts they worked on yesterday. If their charts are not complete, allow time for them to generate ideas to complete their story lines.

**WRITE** You will be using your story sequence charts as you write the draft of your imaginative story. When you are drafting, don't worry if your composition does not sound exactly as you want it to. You will have a chance to revise it tomorrow.

**Understanding the Rubric** Read the rubric aloud and help students understand it. Then focus on the score 4. Ask students to explain in their own words what qualities a score 4 story has.

## Common Core State Standards

**Writing 3.b.** Use dialogue and descriptions of actions, thoughts, and feelings to develop experiences and events or show the response of characters to situations. **Language 2.** Demonstrate command of the conventions of standard English capitalization, punctuation, and spelling when writing. **Language 2.c.** Use commas and quotation marks in dialogue. **Also Foundational Skills 4., 4.a., 4.b.**

### RANGE OF WRITING

As students progress through the writing project, they routinely write for a range of tasks, purposes, and audiences. In this lesson, they learn to write dialogue for their drafts of an imaginative story, and to include details about their characters and setting.

# Writing

## Imaginative Story

### Mini-Lesson  Writer's Craft: Dialogue

■ **Introduce** Explain to students that dialogue between characters can make a story more interesting and lively to read. Dialogue should sound similar to natural speech, or the way people speak. Because students' stories must include a riddle that one character tells another, it's a good idea to write the riddle as dialogue. Students may include other dialogue if they like.

Display the Drafting Tips for students. Remind them that the focus of drafting is to get their ideas down in an organized way. Then display Writing Transparency 17A.

### Drafting Tips

✔ To get started, review your story sequence chart.

✔ Make sure to include details about your characters and setting and to build your events up to a climax.

✔ Don't worry about grammar and mechanics when drafting. You'll concentrate on them during the proofreading stage.

**Think Aloud** **MODEL** I'm going to write the first paragraph of my imaginative story. It will describe the setting in detail. When I draft, I develop my story line. I don't worry about revising or proofreading because those tasks come later. I'll refer to my story sequence chart to make sure I include all the elements of a good imaginative story: characters, a setting, and events that build up to a climax.

Explain the process of drafting using the Writing Transparency. Direct students to use the Drafting Tips to guide them in writing their drafts. Remind them to include dialogue in their stories.

#### The Riddle of the River

My family and I were cruising down the mighty Nile River one day. The sun was hot overhead, and thick green rainforest lined the river's banks. We had been sailing for days.

My big sister Gloria was drawing a picture of the river and the trees. "Hey, Maria," she asked. "What always runs but never walks?" Gloria and me like to kid each other sometimes.

"I don't know, Gloria, I said. "what always runs but never walks?"

"A river!"

I groaned. Then I hurd a rumble off in the distance. We continued floating down the river. The rumble grew louder and louder.

"Hey, Gloria," I asked. "What suddenly stops running and falls down?"

"I don't know, Maria. What suddenly stops running and falls down?"

"A river, when it's about to go over a waterfall!"

The river was flowing fast now. The waterfall had become a roar. My family lunged into action. Mom steered the boat straight toward the west shore. Gloria and I paddled madly to help speed it along. Dad grabbed a rope and stood ready at the stern.

Although it seemed like forever, it probably took just a few minutes. We approached the shore close enough for Dad to loop the rope around a branch and tie the boat tight. We were safe!

Unit 4 Hottest, Coldest, Highest, Deepest          Writing: Model **17A**

Writing Transparency 17A, TR DVD

## Writing Trait: Conventions

Discuss the importance of using conventions in writing. Good writers follow the rules for writing. Following rules helps your readers understand what you have written. For instance, a capital letter signals the beginning of a sentence. Quotation marks are used to show someone is speaking.

Display the following example and review ways students should write dialogue: "This book is about riddles," said Maria.

- Start dialogue with a capital letter and end with the proper punctuation mark.
- Use quotation marks to signify when someone is speaking.
- Indent dialogue for a new paragraph when a new person is speaking.

### Routine | Quick Write for Fluency | Team Talk

1. **Talk** Pairs talk about the characters in their stories.

2. **Write** Each student writes a brief paragraph describing his or her characters, using subject and object pronouns correctly.

3. **Share** Partners check each other's writing for the correct use of subject and object pronouns. Then each partner asks the other a question about his or her characters.

Routines Flip Chart

**eStreet Interactive**
www.ReadingStreet.com

**Teacher Resources**
• Writing Transparency

### Access for All

**SI** Strategic Intervention

If students are having difficulty thinking of a riddle to include in their stories, provide books of riddles or examples downloaded from the Internet.

# Wrap Up Your Day!

✔ **Content Knowledge** *What makes the places you read about unique?*

✔ **Text-Based Comprehension** *How did the graphic sources help you to clarify the information?* Have students give examples.

**Preview DAY 4**

Tell students that tomorrow they will read about an American legend.

### Materials

- Student Edition
- Reader's and Writer's Notebook
- Decodable Reader

## © Common Core State Standards

**Speaking/Listening 1.** Engage effectively in a range of collaborative discussions (one-on-one, in groups, and teacher-led) with diverse partners on grade 3 topics and texts, building on others' ideas and expressing their own clearly. **Speaking/Listening 1.c.** Ask questions to check understanding of information presented, stay on topic, and link their comments to the remarks of others. **Language 6.** Acquire and use accurately grade-appropriate conversational, general academic, and domain-specific words and phrases, including those that signal spatial and temporal relationships (e.g., *After dinner that night we went looking for them*).

# Content Knowledge

## Nature's Record Holders

**EXPAND THE CONCEPT** Remind students of the weekly concept question, *What makes nature's record holders unique?* Have students discuss ways in which some of nature's record holders have affected our lives.

## Build Oral Language

**Team Talk** **TALK ABOUT SENTENCES AND WORDS** Ask students to reread paragraph 2 on Student Edition p. 70.

- What other words could we use in place of *precipitation?* (rain, drizzle, hail, sleet, snow)

- Remind students that they can always use a dictionary to find the meaning of an unknown or unfamiliar word. Have students work with a partner to find the meaning of *precipitation* in a classroom dictionary. To extend the activity, have partners take turns using *precipitation* in a sentence.

# Build Oral Vocabulary

## Amazing Words — Robust Vocabulary Routine

1. **Introduce** Write the Amazing Word *weaken* on the board. Have students say it with you. Yesterday, we read that the snowiest place on Earth is Mount Rainier. How might all that snow *weaken* a person who tried to climb Mount Rainier? Have students determine a definition of *weaken*. (To *weaken* something means to take away some of its power.)

2. **Demonstrate** Have students answer questions to demonstrate understanding. What things might *weaken* a tree? (lack of water, damage from insects)

3. **Apply** Have students apply their understanding. Which of these things might *weaken* the roof of a house: high winds or a butterfly?

4. **Display the Word** Run your hand under the word as you emphasize the syllables in *weak-en*. Have students say the word.

See p. OV•2 to teach *ranger*.

Routines Flip Chart

---

**ADD TO THE CONCEPT MAP** Discuss the Amazing Words *sprinter* and *acrobat*. Add these and other concept- related words to the concept map. Use the following questions to develop students' understanding of the concept. Remind students to ask and answer questions with appropriate detail and to build on other students' answers.

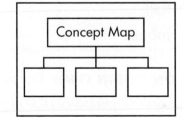

Concept Map

- Picture a *sprinter* trying to outrun the Bay of Fundy. Did you ever have to run away from something very quickly?

- A person who skis from the top of Mount Rainier has to be quite an *acrobat*. Do you know anyone who is a good *acrobat*?

**eSTREET INTERACTIVE**
www.ReadingStreet.com

**Teacher Resources**
- Amazing Word Cards
- Reader's and Writer's Notebook

## Amazing Words

| | |
|---|---|
| evergreen | champ |
| lumber | sprinter |
| competitor | acrobat |
| plunge | weaken |
| valuable | ranger |

## Strategy Response Log

Have students complete p. 23 in the *Reader's and Writer's Notebook*. Then have students summarize the important ideas that they found in the selection.

**Vocabulary: Activate Prior Knowledge** Use photos from the Internet or magazines to show images of forest or park rangers. Use them to discuss with students what a ranger does, including keeping people and animals safe, fighting fires, educating the public, and looking for people who are lost.

**Produce Oral Language** Use the Day 4 instruction on ELL Poster 17 to extend and enrich language.

**Common Core State Standards**

**Foundational Skills 3.** Know and apply grade-level phonics and word analysis skills in decoding words. **Foundational Skills 3.d.** Read grade-appropriate irregularly spelled words.

# Word Analysis

## Review Irregular Plurals

**REVIEW IRREGULAR PLURALS** To review last week's word analysis skill, write *children, people, teeth,* and *leaves.* You studied words like these last week. What do you know about words like these, which have irregular plural forms? (The plurals are not formed by simply adding an *-s* or *-es* to the base word.) Have students read the word *children.* What is the singular form of *children?* *(child)* of *people?* *(person)* Continue in the same way for *teeth (tooth)* and *leaves (leaf).*

> **Corrective feedback** | If students are unable to answer the questions about irregular plurals, refer them to *Sound-Spelling Card* 140.

**GUIDE PRACTICE** Display a three-column chart with the heads *Singular Form; -f, -fe* to *-ves;* and *Irregular Plural.* Write the singular forms of the words in the first column. We will work together to place irregular plurals of words in the chart. Listen as I say the singular form of each word. Then you say the plural form and tell me which column to write in. Write each word in the appropriate column. Then have students read the words.

| Singular Form | *-f, -fe* to *-ves* | Irregular Plural |
|---|---|---|
| life | lives | |
| sheep | | sheep |
| half | halves | |
| mouse | | mice |

**ON THEIR OWN** For additional practice, use *Let's Practice It!* p. 233 on the *Teacher Resources DVD-ROM.*

---

Name _____        Hottest, Coldest

**Irregular Plurals**

- To form the plural of most words, add *s* or *es*.
- Some words have **irregular plurals** that do not follow this rule.
- One common type of irregular plural is to change the *f* in the singular word to *v*, then add *s* or *es*.

**Directions** Change the *f* in the singular word to *v*, then add *s* or *es* to form the plural. Write the plural form on the line.

1. dwarf __dwarves__    5. loaf __loaves__
2. leaf __leaves__    6. scarf __scarves__
3. knife __knives__    7. life __lives__
4. hoof __hooves__

**Directions** Each sentence has an underlined word that takes an irregular plural. Write the irregular plural of the underlined word on the line. Use the box to help you.

| children | geese | mice | sheep | teeth | men | women |

__teeth__    8. You should brush your <u>tooth</u> twice every day.

__children__    9. There are roles for seven <u>child</u> in *The Sound of Music.*

__sheep__    10. You have to shear <u>sheep</u> to get their wool.

__mice__    11. Cats chase <u>mouse</u> even when they aren't hungry.

__women__    12. Many <u>woman</u> have been elected to the U.S. Congress.

__geese__    13. Many Europeans eat <u>goose</u> instead of turkeys at the holidays.

__men__    14. <u>Man</u> in traditional Scottish dress wear kilts, or skirts.

**Home Activity** Your child wrote words with irregular plurals (mouse, mice), including words that change from *f* to *v* (scarf, scarves). Leaf through the dictionary with your child. Find more words that have irregular plurals and challenge your child to spell them correctly.

Irregular Plurals DVD•233

Let's Practice It! TR DVD•233

# Fluent Word Reading

## Spiral Review

**READ WORDS IN ISOLATION** Display these words. Tell students that they can already decode some words on this list. Explain that they should know other words because they appear often in reading.

Have students read the list three or four times until they can read at the rate of two to three seconds per word.

### Word Reading

| | | | | |
|---|---|---|---|---|
| illness | were | wren | cheerful | very |
| whistled | sadly | come | crumb | where |
| your | have | sensible | want | done |
| to | who | signs | dependable | know |

**Corrective feedback**

**If...** students have difficulty reading whole words,

**then...** have them use sound-by-sound blending for decodable words or chunking for words that have word parts, or have them say and spell high-frequency words.

**If...** students cannot read fluently at a rate of two to three seconds per word,

**then...** have pairs practice the list until they can read it fluently.

**eSTREET INTERACTIVE**
www.ReadingStreet.com

Teacher Resources
• Let's Practice It!

Interactive Sound-Spelling Cards

## Access for All

 **Strategic Intervention**

To assist students having difficulty with irregular plurals, write the following words on separate cards: *tooth, teeth, mouse, mice, life, lives, person, people, sheep, sheep.* Shuffle the cards and place them face down in rows. Have students play a memory game by choosing two cards. If the singular and plural forms match, students keep them. If not, they put them back in the same place. You may wish to include additional pairs of words to make the game more challenging.

## Spiral Review

These activities review

• previously taught high-frequency words *were, very, come, where, your, have, want, done, to, who.*

• consonant patterns *(wr, kn, gn, st, mb)*; suffixes *(-ly, -ful, -ness, -less, -able, -ible).*

**Practice Pronunciation** Have students say words with silent letters until they become comfortable saying them as one sound.

*Hottest, Coldest, Highest, Deepest* **80d**

**Common Core State Standards**

**Foundational Skills 3.** Know and apply grade-level phonics and word analysis skills in decoding words. **Foundational Skills 3.d.** Read grade-appropriate irregularly spelled words. **Foundational Skills 4.** Read with sufficient accuracy and fluency to support comprehension. **Foundational Skills 4.c.** Use context to confirm or self-correct word recognition and understanding, rereading as necessary.

# Fluent Word Reading

**READ WORDS IN CONTEXT** Display these sentences. Call on individuals to read a sentence. Then randomly point to review words and have students read them. To help you monitor word reading, high-frequency words are underlined and decodable words are italicized.

## MONITOR PROGRESS | Sentence Reading

The *cheerful wren whistled* a happy song.
It is not *sensible* to come when you have an *illness*.
Do you *know* someone who is very *dependable*?
*Sadly* there wasn't a *crumb* left when we were done.
Where do you want your *signs* to go?

**If...** students are unable to read an underlined high-frequency word,

**then...** read the word for them and spell it, having them echo you.

**If...** students have difficulty reading an italicized decodable word,

**then...** guide them in using sound-by-sound blending or chunking.

# Reread for Fluency

Have students reread the sentences to develop automaticity decoding words.

### Routine | Oral Rereading

1. **Read** Have students read all the sentences orally.

2. **Reread** To achieve optimal fluency, students should reread the sentences three or four times.

3. **Corrective Feedback** Listen as students read. Provide corrective feedback regarding their fluency and decoding.

Routines Flip Chart

# Decodable Passage 17C

If students need help, then...

## Read *Thursday's Roaring Storm*

**READ WORDS IN ISOLATION** Have students turn to p. 23 in *Decodable Practice Readers 3.2* and find the first list of words. Each word in this list has the *r*-controlled vowel sounds /ėr/, /är/, or /ôr/. Let's blend and read these words. Be sure that students identify the correct vowel sound in each word.

Next, have students read the high-frequency words.

**PREVIEW** Have students read the title and preview the story. Tell them that they will read words with *r*-controlled vowels.

**READ WORDS IN CONTEXT** Chorally read the story along with the students. Have students identify words in the story that have the *r*-controlled vowel sounds /ėr/, /är/, and /ôr/. Monitor students as they read to check for proper pronunciation and appropriate pacing.

**Team Talk** Pair students and have them take turns reading the story aloud to each other. Make sure that students are monitoring their accuracy when they decode words.

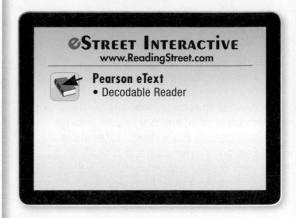

**eStreet Interactive**
www.ReadingStreet.com

**Pearson eText**
• Decodable Reader

### Access for All

**A Advanced**
Have students write definitions of the words with suffixes found in the sentences on p. 80e. Invite them to add some additional words with suffixes, and their definitions, to the list.

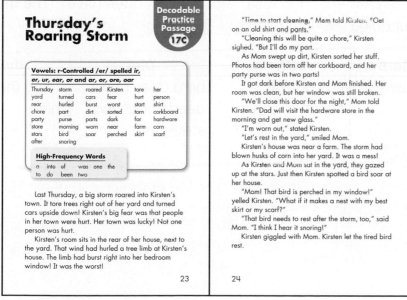

Decodable Practice Passage 17C

## © Common Core State Standards

**Literature 2.** Recount stories, including fables, folktales, and myths from diverse cultures; determine the central message, lesson, or moral and explain how it is conveyed through key details in the text. **Literature 3.** Describe characters in a story (e.g., their traits, motivations, or feelings) and explain how their actions contribute to the sequence of events.

## © Bridge to Common Core

### KEY IDEAS AND DETAILS

Students will read a legend, using key supporting details and main ideas to determine its central themes and understand the genre. Students will analyze how and why characters, events, and ideas develop over the course of the text.

# Science in Reading

## Legend

**INTRODUCE** Remind students that authors structure texts differently depending on their reasons and purposes for writing. A genre is a type of writing. Explain that legends constitute a genre.

**DISCUSS THE GENRE** Ask students what legends, such as stories about Johnny Appleseed or Robin Hood, they can recall. Explain: A legend is an old story, passed down over the years, about the great deeds of a hero. Legends are similar to myths because they concern amazing events from the past. Unlike myths, however, legends may be based on historical facts. Like fictional stories, legends have characters, a plot, a setting, and a theme. Let's look at each of these parts of a legend.

**GROUP PRACTICE** Display a chart like the one below. Ask students to think about legends they know. Ask:

• What are characters in a legend like? (They are often very brave or very strong.)

• Where do legends take place? (They take place in real times in history.)

• What kind of things happen in a legend? (The character does good deeds. The character shows how strong he or she is.)

• What type of theme, or "big idea," do legends, often have? (The theme is often about doing the right thing.)

| characters | setting | plot | theme |
|---|---|---|---|
| very brave or strong | real time in history | hero does good deeds or shows strength | doing the right thing |

**eStreet Interactive**
www.ReadingStreet.com

**Teacher Resources**
• Graphic Organizer

**Team Talk** Have students paraphrase the theme in a legend they know. Then have students work in pairs to discuss the difference between a legend and a story about animal characters.

**READ** Tell students that they will read a legend about a hero who was very big and strong. Have the class think about why it would be interesting to read about a person who is bigger and stronger than other people.

---

**Day 4** SMALL GROUP TIME • Differentiate Vocabulary, p. SG•17

| **OL On-Level** | **SI Strategic Intervention** | **A Advanced** |
|---|---|---|
| • **Develop** Language Using Amazing Words | • **Review/Discuss** Amazing Words | • **Extend** Amazing Words and Selection Vocabulary |
| • **Read** "Paul Bunyan and the Great Lakes" | • **Read** "Paul Bunyan and the Great Lakes" | • **Read** "Paul Bunyan and the Great Lakes" |
| | | • **Organize** Inquiry Project |

**ELL**

**If...** students need more scaffolding and practice with the **Amazing Words,**
**then...** use the Routine on pp. xxxvi–xxxvii in the *ELL Handbook.*

**Common Core State Standards**
Literature 2. Recount stories, including fables, folktales, and myths from diverse cultures; determine the central message, lesson, or moral and explain how it is conveyed through key details in the text. Also Literature 3., 10.

**Science in Reading**

### Genre
### Legend

- A legend is a story told from generation to generation until someone writes it down.
- Legends may be based on truth but are mostly fiction.
- Legends often are about great heroes who carry out bigger-than-life actions, and they usually are set in real locations.
- The themes of legends are usually based on what a culture values, or finds important.
- Read the legend "Paul Bunyan and the Great Lakes." What details from the text make this story a legend?

# PAUL BUNYAN
## and the
# GREAT LAKES
*retold by Don Abramson*

The first thing most people noticed about Paul Bunyan was that he was big. Now, when I say "big," I mean HUGE, GIGANTIC! Everything he did, he did big.

He could walk a mile by taking just a few steps. His clothes had to be specially made, of course. Twenty tailors had to sew together the canvas sails from five or six sailing ships to make one of his shirts.

The second thing people noticed was that he was usually accompanied by his pet ox, Babe. Babe was big too. He had to be, to keep up with Paul. Babe was as strong as he was big. Paul could hitch Babe up to one end of a winding, curving road, and Babe could pull it straight. Oh, and did I mention that Babe was bright blue?

Let's Think About...
What details about Babe tell me that this legend is not a true story? **Legend**

**1**

80

81

**Student Edition, pp. 80–81**

---

© **Common Core State Standards**

**Literature 2.** Recount stories, including fables, folktales, and myths from diverse cultures; determine the central message, lesson, or moral and explain how it is conveyed through key details in the text. **Also Literature 3., 10.**

# Access Text ©

**TEACH Legend** Have students preview "Paul Bunyan and the Great Lakes" on pp. 80–83. Have them look at the title, illustrations, and words written in capital letters. Then ask: How is Paul Bunyan a typical hero of a legend? Where might this story take place?

| Corrective feedback | **If...** students are unable to explain that Paul Bunyan is a typical legendary hero because he is very big and strong, and that the setting is a real place with trees and mountains, **then...** use the model to guide students in understanding legends. |
|---|---|

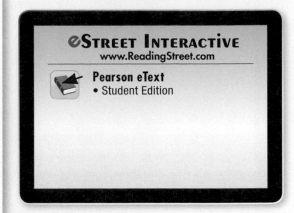

**Think Aloud** **MODEL** When I preview the story, I see that the title mentions a real place, the Great Lakes. The pictures show a person who is very big swinging an axe and digging a big hole. I also see that the author put the words *huge, gigantic,* and *big* in capital letters. I think Paul Bunyan is a typical hero of a legend because he is very big and strong, and that the setting is the Great Lakes.

**ON THEIR OWN** Have students look back at the chart from p. 80g and use it to predict the plot of "Paul Bunyan and the Great Lakes."

# Close Reading ©

**EVALUATION** Why might the author have chosen to use capital letters for the words *huge* and *gigantic?* (The story is about a gigantic character, so he chose to make those words bigger.)

**ANALYSIS** Why does the author start the story by telling us the first thing most people noticed about Paul Bunyan was that he was big? (Paul Bunyan's size is an important idea in the story, so the author starts by telling us about it.)

# Genre

**LET'S THINK ABOUT...** As you read "Paul Bunyan and the Great Lakes," use Let's Think About in the Student Edition to help students focus on the features of a legend.

Babe is so big and strong, he can pull a road straight; Babe is bright blue.

## Access for All

**SI Strategic Intervention**
Students may have difficulty understanding the difference between legends and other kinds of short stories. Explain that legends contain some sort of historical truth, where general short stories need not do this. The legend of Paul Bunyan probably comes from stories of the feats of real lumberjacks, who valued strength and speed at their work.

**A Advanced**
Have students conduct an Internet search using the keywords *Paul Bunyan* and *origin* to learn how the legend might have begun. Explain that *origin* means a "place where something comes from."

**Monitor Comprehension** To check comprehension, have students respond to questions about parts of the text, such as: How did Paul Bunyan walk a mile? How did Paul and Babe make a curving road straight?

Babe wasn't just a pet. He was a working animal. That was useful because Paul was a lumberjack. Paul decided to hire a crew of lumberjacks. He had to build a lumber camp to give his crew a place to live. He found a nice spot and set the men to building, using lumber they had cut down themselves.

A camp needs a good supply of drinking water, so Paul dug out a huge reservoir to catch rainwater and to hold water from a number of rivers that emptied into it. People called it Lake Ontario, after some Native American words that mean "great lake." That worked fine for a while, but Babe could drink half the lake himself every morning before breakfast. So Paul dug another reservoir, and then another. They were also given Native American names: Lake Erie and Lake Huron.

Paul's lumber camp was growing too, and he had more men and more animals than ever before. So he dug Lake Michigan and then, finally, Lake Superior. Now he had a really good water supply.

As I said, Paul did everything BIG!

Let's **Think** About...
What is the setting of this legend? **Legend**

**2**

Let's **Think** About...
According to this legend, how were the Great Lakes made? **Legend**

**3**

Let's **Think** About...
What is the theme of the story? What details support the theme? **Legend**

**4**

Let's **Think** About...
**Reading Across Texts** *Hottest, Coldest, Highest, Deepest* tells interesting facts about real places on Earth. How is this legend about Paul Bunyan similar and different?

**Writing Across Texts** Choose one place described in *Hottest, Coldest, Highest, Deepest.* Make up a short story in which Paul Bunyan makes the amazing feature of that setting.

82

83

**Student Edition, pp. 82–83**

## Common Core State Standards

**Literature 2.** Recount stories, including fables, folktales, and myths from diverse cultures; determine the central message, lesson, or moral and explain how it is conveyed through key details in the text. **Literature 10.** By the end of the year, read and comprehend literature, including stories, dramas, and poetry, at the high end of the grades 2–3 text complexity band independently and proficiently. **Writing 3.a.** Establish a situation and introduce a narrator and/or characters; organize an event sequence that unfolds naturally. **Also Writing 3.d.**

# Access Text ©

**TEACH Legend** Remind students that the plot of a legend usually tells about the hero's good deeds or strength. Ask: How is the plot of "Paul Bunyan and the Great Lakes" typical of a legend?

**Corrective feedback**

**If...** students are unable to explain that the story's plot is typical of a legend because it shows Paul Bunyan using his impossibly great strength,

**then...** use the model to guide students in understanding the elements of a legend.

**Think Aloud**

**MODEL** I know that the plot is the series of events in a story, so to think about how the plot is typical of a legend, I look at the things that happen in the story. Paul is digging reservoirs, or places to hold water, the size of some of the largest lakes in the world. This plot is typical of a legend, because it shows how Paul Bunyan uses his unusual strength.

**ON THEIR OWN** Have students review the characteristics of a legend's theme and discuss how the theme of "Paul Bunyan and the Great Lakes" is typical of a legend.

## Close Reading ©

**EVALUATION** What was the effect of Paul Bunyan's decision to dig reservoirs for drinking water? (The effect was that the Great Lakes were formed.)

**SYNTHESIS** What details support the idea that Paul needed to dig more and more reservoirs? (The facts that Babe the ox could drink half the lake and that the lumber camp was growing are supporting details.)

## Genre

**LET'S THINK ABOUT...** features of a legend.

- The setting is the Great Lakes area.

- According to the legend, the Great Lakes were created when Paul Bunyan wanted to dig reservoirs to catch drinking water for his crew of lumberjacks and Babe, his ox.

- The theme is that everything Paul Bunyan does is big. The descriptions of how each lake was dug support the theme.

## Reading and Writing Across Texts

Have students create a Venn diagram listing the similarities and differences between the Paul Bunyan legend and *Hottest, Coldest, Highest, Deepest*. Suggest that they use the information they identified in their diagrams as they craft their short stories. Remind students that their short story should have an imaginative plot, a description of the chosen setting, and a theme. Encourage them to work in pairs to brainstorm the different parts of their story before they begin to write. Their stories should build to a dramatic climax before the resolution.

**eSTREET INTERACTIVE**
www.ReadingStreet.com

**Pearson eText**
• Student Edition

**Teacher Resources**
• Graphic Organizer

**Connect to Science**

**Great Lakes Formation**
Explain that the Great Lakes were actually formed during the Ice Age. Glaciers moving over the area carved out deep basins, forming lakes when the glaciers melted.

### Access for All

**SI Strategic Intervention**

To help students organize their writing, provide a graphic organizer with spaces to plan the beginning, middle, and end of the story before students begin to write.

**A Advanced**

Have students research differences between lumberjacks from the past and modern loggers who use sophisticated equipment in their work.

**Discuss Writing** Partner students to orally rehearse their stories before they begin to write.

## Let's Learn It!

READING STREET ONLINE
ONLINE STUDENT EDITION
www.ReadingStreet.com

## Vocabulary

### Unknown Words

**Dictionary/Glossary** You can use a dictionary or glossary to look up the definition of unknown words. Find out how to pronounce the word by using the pronunciation key and looking at each syllable.

**Practice It!** Find two or three unknown words from *Hottest, Coldest, Highest, Deepest*. Look up their definitions, syllable divisions, and pronunciations in a dictionary or glossary. Rewrite each definition in your own words.

## Fluency

### Appropriate Phrasing

Remember to pause when you come to a comma, a dash, and before and after reading information in parentheses.

**Practice It!** With your partner, practice reading *Hottest, Coldest, Highest, Deepest*, page 66. Remember to pause for a comma, a dash, and before and after information in parentheses.

## Media Literacy

Work productively and follow etiquette for conversation.

### Weather Forecast

In a weather forecast, an announcer tells about the weather in an area and the expected weather for the next few days.

**Practice It!** Prepare a weather forecast for a TV news program. Use newspapers, Web sites, and TV and radio broadcasts for ideas. Include elements unique to TV in your presentation. Then discuss how communication changes when moving from one genre of media to another.

### Tips

**Listening ...**
• Listen to identify the speaker's credibility and effectiveness.

**Speaking ...**
• Make eye contact with your audience by looking at the camera.
• Speak clearly and loudly.

**Teamwork ...**
• Ask and answer questions about communication and digital media.

84

85

**Student Edition, pp. 84–85**

# Fluency

## Appropriate Phrasing and Punctuation Cues

**GUIDE PRACTICE** Use the Student Edition activity as an assessment tool. As students read aloud with partners, walk around to make sure their phrasing is appropriate and that they use punctuation marks as guides for grouping words together.

**Don't Wait Until Friday**

## MONITOR PROGRESS Check Fluency

**FORMATIVE ASSESSMENT** As students reread, monitor their progress toward their individual fluency goals.

Current Goal: 95–105 words correct per minute.

End-of-Year Goal: 120 words correct per minute.

**If...** students cannot read fluently at a rate of 95–105 words correct per minute,

**then...** have students practice with text at their independent levels.

# Vocabulary Skill

## ⊙ Unknown Words

**TEACH UNKNOWN WORDS • DICTIONARY/GLOSSARY** Remind students that the main selection tells about the most extreme tides. Model using a dictionary or the glossary to look up the meaning, syllabication, and pronunciation of the word *extreme*. Explain: A dictionary or glossary shows how to divide a word into syllables. The pronunciation guide shows how to say each syllable and which syllable to stress when you say the word.

**GUIDE PRACTICE** Have students select another word from the main selection with two or more syllables and look up its meaning, syllabication, and pronunciation. Point out the pronunciation key to help students with phonetic spellings.

**ON THEIR OWN** Walk around the room as students look up the words in a dictionary or glossary. Check to make sure students understand the meaning and pronunciation of each word.

# Media Literacy

## Weather Forecast

**TEACH** Encourage classmates to think about the ways weather forecasters on television get an audience's attention. They should also think about the differences among forecasts in different media such as television, the Internet, newspapers, or radio. Suggest that students use current weather patterns as a guide for their forecast. Remind students to begin with a catchy or interesting statement. They can then share today's weather report, and the weather forecast for tonight and tomorrow. They may wish to include a 3-, 5-, or 7-day extended forecast.

**GUIDE PRACTICE** Partner students to rehearse their forecasts together. Remind them to speak loudly and clearly and at a rate slow enough for their listeners to understand the words, while making eye contact with the audience.

**ON THEIR OWN** Have students deliver their weather forecasts to the class. Remind students to listen attentively and to make sure their questions or comments relate directly to the subject. For an alternative presentation, have students record their forecasts and use the audio for their presentation.

eStreet Interactive
www.ReadingStreet.com

**Pearson eText**
• Student Edition

## Weather Forecast

Remind students that a specialized vocabulary is used in weather forecasts. Encourage students to check the pronunciation of words such as *precipitation* before they rehearse their forecasts.

ⓒ **Bridge to Common Core**

**PRESENTATION OF KNOWLEDGE/ IDEAS**

As students present their weather forecasts, they should adapt their speech to emulate a TV meteorologist who is communicating with at-home viewers. They should use appropriate phrasing, speak loudly and clearly, and present information in an organized fashion. Students can make strategic use of digital media and/ or visual displays by presenting their weather data on computer or posterboard versions of maps, radar images, bar graphs, and other graphics.

**Use Content-Area Vocabulary** Ask partners to work together to use content-area words in a sentence.

**Ⓒ Common Core State Standards**

**Writing 8.** Recall information from experiences or gather information from print and digital sources; take brief notes on sources and sort evidence into provided categories. **Language 1.a.** Explain the function of nouns, pronouns, verbs, adjectives, and adverbs in general and their functions in particular sentences. **Language 2.f.** Use spelling patterns and generalizations (e.g., word families, position-based spellings, syllable patterns, ending rules, meaningful word parts) in writing words.
**Also Language 2.g.**

# Research and Inquiry

## Step 4  Synthesize

**TEACH** Have students synthesize their research findings and results. Remind students that an article about a record holder should include both a main idea, stating the record, and details that include comparisons between the record holder and others competing for that record or other records. Suggest that these comparisons can be represented visually and labeled in a graphic source such as a bar graph or chart to show the results of their research.

**GUIDE PRACTICE** Review how to choose relevant information from a number of sources and organize it logically into an article, using this week's readings as examples. Make sure students use captions to clearly identify factual information.

**ON THEIR OWN** Have students review and organize their notes to write their articles. Remind them that their article should include facts and details that support their main idea.

# Conventions

## Subject and Object Pronouns

**TEST PRACTICE** Remind students that grammar skills, such as the correct use of subject and object pronouns, are often assessed on important tests. Help students recall that subject pronouns are used as subjects of sentences and object pronouns are used after action verbs or as objects of prepositions.

**ON THEIR OWN** For additional practice, use *Reader's and Writer's Notebook,* p. 268.

Reader's and Writer's Notebook, p. 268

# Spelling

## Vowels: *r*-Controlled

**PRACTICE SPELLING STRATEGY** Supply pairs of students with index cards on which the spelling words have been written. Have one student read a word while the other writes it. Then have students switch roles. Use the cards to check your spelling and correct any misspelled words.

**ON THEIR OWN** For additional practice, use *Let's Practice It!* p. 234 on the *Teacher Resources DVD-ROM.*

Let's Practice It! TR DVD•234

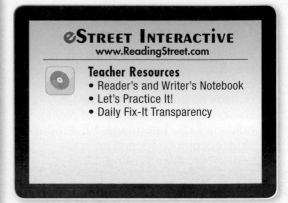

## Daily Fix-It

7. Is Africas river the longest in the world. *(Africa's; world?)*

8. Many unusuall animals lives there. *(unusual; live)*

## Access for All

Ⓐ **Advanced**

Have students write the spelling words in sentences rather than in isolation.

## © Bridge to Common Core

**CONVENTIONS OF STANDARD ENGLISH**

As students identify and use subject and object pronouns, they are demonstrating command of the conventions of standard English. Your guidance will help them use correct grammar, usage, and spelling to convey meaning when they speak and write.

**Common Core State Standards**

**Writing 3.a.** Establish a situation and introduce a narrator and/or characters; organize an event sequence that unfolds naturally. **Language 1.h.** Use coordinating and subordinating conjunctions. **Language 1.i.** Produce simple, compound, and complex sentences. **Also Writing 3.c., Language 2.**

**Write Guy** *by Jeff Anderson*
### Writers Write!

Student writers succeed in classrooms where they write. Simple, isn't it? Are you trying to meet some mandate or standard with such blinders on that you're forgetting daily writing? Students need to read every day and to write every day. Teachers do not need to read and assess everything that students write.

# Writing

## Imaginative Story

**Mini-Lesson** | **Revise: Consolidating**

■ Yesterday we wrote an imaginative story with one character telling a riddle to another. Today we will revise our drafts. The goal is to make your writing clearer, more interesting, and more informative.

■ Display Writing Transparency 17B. Remind students that revising does not include corrections of grammar and mechanics. Tell them that this will be done during the lesson as they proofread their work. Then introduce the revising strategy of consolidating.

| Revising Marks | | | |
|---|---|---|---|
| Take Out | ⟿ | Uppercase letter | = |
| Add | ^ | Lowercase letter | / |
| Period | ⊙ | New paragraph | ¶ |
| Move | ⌒ | | |

I groaned. Then I hurd a rumble off in the distance. ~~We~~ **As**
continued floating down the river. ~~The~~ rumble grew louder and
louder.

"Hey, Gloria," I asked. "What suddenly stops running and falls down?"

"I don't know, Maria. What suddenly stops running and falls down?"

    "A river, when it's about to go over a waterfall!"
The river was flowing fast now. ~~The~~ waterfall had become a **, and**
roar. My family lunged into action.

Unit 4 Hottest, Coldest, Highest, Deepest          Writing: Revise **17B**

Writing Transparency 17B, TR DVD

■ Short, simple sentences sound choppy and dull. To make my writing more interesting to read, I'll look for places where I can combine ideas into longer sentences. These two sentences can be one complex sentence: *We continued floating down the river. The rumble grew louder and louder.* I'll combine them like this: *As we continued floating down the river, the rumble grew louder and louder.* These two sentences also sound short and choppy: *The river was flowing fast now. The waterfall had become a roar.* I'll combine them into one compound sentence: *The river was flowing fast now, and the waterfall had become a roar.* Reread your imaginative story for places where you might make simple sentences into compound or complex sentences.

Display and review the Revising Tips. Tell students to use the tips as they revise their stories.

### Revising Tips
✔ Be sure the story has details about characters and setting.

✔ Be sure the events are told in order and build to a climax.

✔ Vary sentences by combining ideas into compound or complex sentences.

**eSTREET INTERACTIVE**
www.ReadingStreet.com

**Teacher Resources**
• Writing Transparency

**PEER CONFERENCING • PEER REVISION** Have pairs exchange papers for peer revision. Tell students to write compliments and suggestions directly on their partner's draft. Tell students that their questions should focus on where their partner could revise by combining simple sentences. Have students revise their stories. They should use the comments their partners made during peer conferencing as well as the key features of a story to guide their revision. Be sure that students are using the revising strategy of consolidating.

**Corrective feedback** | Circulate around the room to monitor students and confer with them as they revise. Remind students who are correcting errors that they will have time to edit tomorrow. They should be working on their story line and sentence variety today.

## Routine    Quick Write for Fluency    Team Talk

1. **Talk** Pairs discuss their favorite places described in *Hottest, Coldest, Highest, Deepest.*

2. **Write** Each student writes a brief explanation of why he or she would like to visit the place from the selection.

3. **Share** Partners read their explanations to each other. Then each checks the other's writing for descriptive details.

Routines Flip Chart

**ELL**

**Revising Sentences** Help students hear English sentence variety. Read aloud short, choppy sentences and then complex and compound sentences. Then have students read aloud their own sentences. Guide them to decide if the sentences need to be revised.

# Wrap Up Your Day!

✔ **Content Knowledge** Have students discuss why Paul Bunyan was unique.

✔ **Oral Vocabulary** Monitor students' use of oral vocabulary as they respond to this question: *Why do you think Paul Bunyan was a champ at chopping lumber?*

✔ **Text Features** Discuss how focusing on words in bold print helps students understand text.

**Preview DAY 5**

Remind students to think about record holders in nature.

### Materials

- Student Edition
- Weekly Test
- Reader's and Writer's Notebook
- Amazing Word Cards

---

## © Bridge to Common Core

**INTEGRATION OF KNOWLEDGE/IDEAS**

This week, students have integrated content presented in diverse media and analyzed how different texts address similar topics. They have developed knowledge about nature's record holders to expand the unit topic of One of a Kind.

**Science Knowledge Goals**

Students have learned that nature has

- unusual appearances
- extreme weather
- extreme events

# Content Knowledge

## Nature's Record Holders

**REVIEW THE CONCEPT** Have students look back at the reading selections to find examples that best demonstrate how different places and features in nature are unique.

## Build Oral Language

**REVIEW AMAZING WORDS** Display and review this week's concept map. Remind students that this week they have learned ten Amazing Words related to nature's record holders. Have students use the Amazing Words and the concept map to answer the Question of the Week, *What makes nature's record holders unique?*

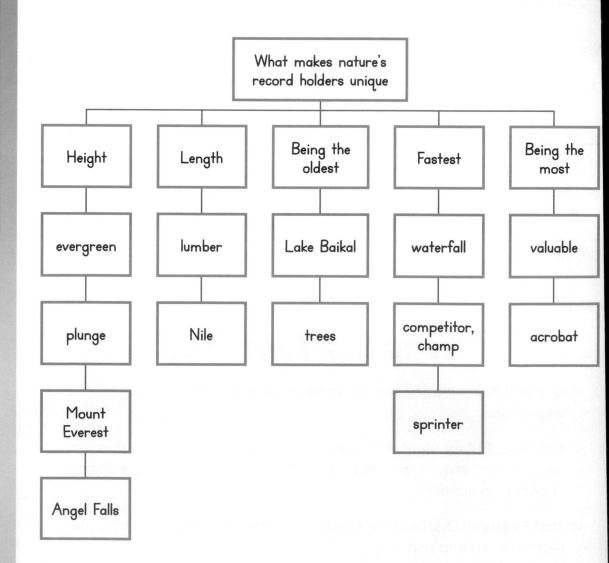

# Build Oral Vocabulary

**Team Talk** **CONNECT TO AMAZING IDEAS** Have pairs of students discuss how the Question of the Week connects to the question for this unit of study: *What does it mean to be unique?* Tell students to use the concept map and what they have learned from this week's discussions and reading selections to form an Amazing Idea—a realization or "big idea" about One of a Kind. Remind partners to pose and answer questions with appropriate detail and to give suggestions that build on each other's ideas. Then ask pairs to share their Amazing Ideas with the class.

Amazing Ideas might include these key concepts:

• Something that is unique might be the best or have the most of something.

• Length, age, and height are some ways to measure being unique in nature.

**WRITE ABOUT IT** Have students write a few sentences about their Amazing Idea, beginning with "This week I learned . . ."

**eStreet Interactive**
www.ReadingStreet.com

Concept Talk Video

Teacher Resources
• Amazing Word Cards

Story Sort

## Amazing Words

| | |
|---|---|
| evergreen | champ |
| lumber | sprinter |
| competitor | acrobat |
| plunge | weaken |
| valuable | ranger |

It's Friday

## MONITOR PROGRESS  Check Oral Vocabulary

**FORMATIVE ASSESSMENT** Have individuals use this week's Amazing Words to describe things that are unique. Monitor students' abilities to use the Amazing Words and note which words you need to reteach.

**If...** students have difficulty using the Amazing Words,

**then...** reteach using the Oral Vocabuary Routine, pp. 55a, 60b, 70b, 80b, OV•2.

**Concept Map** Work with students to add new words to the concept map.

# DAY 5

## © Common Core State Standards

**Informational Text 7.** Use information gained from illustrations (e.g., maps, photographs) and the words in a text to demonstrate understanding of the text (e.g., where, when, why, and how key events occur). **Language 4.** Determine or clarify the meaning of unknown and multiple-meaning words and phrases based on grade 3 reading and content, choosing flexibly from a range of strategies. **Foundational Skills 3.** Know and apply grade-level phonics and word analysis skills in decoding words.

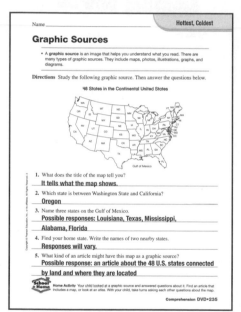

Let's Practice It! TR DVD•235

## Selection Vocabulary

**average** the quantity found by dividing the sum of all quantities by the number of quantities

**depth** the distance from the top to the bottom

**deserts** dry, sandy regions without water and trees

**erupted** burst out

**outrun** run faster than someone or something else

**peak** the pointed top of a mountain or hill

**tides** rise and fall of the ocean's waters about every twelve hours

**waterfalls** streams of water that fall from a high place

85h   One of a Kind • Unit 4 • Week 2

# Text-Based Comprehension

## Review ⊙ Graphic Sources

**TEACH** Review the definition of graphic sources on p. 58. Remind students that graphic sources show information visually and can include charts, diagrams, maps, and graphs. For additional support have students review pp. EI•10–EI•11 on graphic sources.

**GUIDE PRACTICE** Have student pairs find an example of two different graphic sources in *Hottest, Coldest, Highest, Deepest*. Then have pairs explain how the source helps readers to understand the information on the page.

**ON THEIR OWN** For additional practice with graphic sources, use *Let's Practice It!* p. 235 on the *Teacher Resources DVD-ROM*.

# Vocabulary Skill

## Review ⊙ Unknown Words

**TEACH** Remind students to use a dictionary or glossary to help them understand the meanings of words they do not know.

**GUIDE PRACTICE** Review with students how to find the correct meaning of *average* using a dictionary or glossary. Explain that there may be more than one definition for the word.

**ON THEIR OWN** Have students work with partners to write context sentences using this week's lesson vocabulary words. Partners can trade sentences and identify the context clues that help them determine each word's meaning.

# Phonics

## Review ↻ Vowels: *r*-Controlled

**TEACH** Write the following sentences on the board. Have students read each one, first quietly to themselves and then aloud as you track the print.

1. Ben was thirsty from his workout.
2. José came in first with a perfect score.
3. The old curtains are dirty, but still worth saving.
4. The squirrel burrowed into the earth.
5. It took some nerve to park the big car.

**Team Talk** Have pairs of students identify and circle the words with the sound /ėr/, /är/, or /ôr/. Then call on individuals to share with the class.

# Literary Terms

## Review Author's Craft

**TEACH** Have students reread pp. 72–74 of *Hottest, Coldest, Deepest, Highest*. Remind students that superlatives, or words that show something is the best in a group, help readers to understand ideas.

**GUIDE PRACTICE** Direct students' attention to the text at the top of p. 73. Have students name two sentences that show something is the best or the most. Then ask students to find another sentence on the page that shows something is the best or the most. Guide a discussion of why the author chose those words to describe the *deepest* spot in the ocean, *lowest* spot on dry land, and *most active* volcano.

**ON THEIR OWN** Have students make a T-chart with the following headings: *Superlatives with* -est; *Superlatives with* most. Ask them to list examples of each from the selection.

eSTREET INTERACTIVE
www.ReadingStreet.com

Pearson eText
• Student Edition

Teacher Resources
• Let's Practice It!

**Author's Craft** Point out the phrase *most active volcano* and explain that we use *most* to form a superlative for a long word, usually an adjective. We add *-est* to form a superlative for a short word. Provide the following words and have students give the superlative: *big (biggest), short (shortest), exciting (most exciting), expensive (most expensive)*.

*Hottest, Coldest, Highest, Deepest* **85i**

**Common Core State Standards**

**Informational Text 1.** Ask and answer questions to demonstrate understanding of a text, referring explicitly to the text as the basis for the answers. **Foundational Skills 4.** Read with sufficient accuracy and fluency to support comprehension. **Foundational Skills 4.a.** Read on-level text with purpose and understanding.

## Plan to Assess Fluency

☐ **Week 1** Advanced

☑ **This week assess Strategic Intervention students.**

☐ **Week 3** On-Level

☐ **Week 4** Strategic Intervention

☐ **Week 5** Assess any students you have not yet checked during this unit.

Set individual goals for students to enable them to reach the year-end goal.

• Current Goal: 95–105 WCPM

• Year-End Goal: 120 WCPM

# Assessment

## Monitor Progress

**FLUENCY** Make two copies of the fluency passage on p. 85k. As the student reads the text aloud, mark mistakes on your copy. Also mark where the student is at the end of one minute. To check the student's comprehension of the passage, have him or her retell what was read. To figure words correct per minute (WCPM), subtract the number of mistakes from the total number of words read in one minute.

### RATE

| Corrective feedback | **If...** students cannot read fluently at a rate of 95–105 WCPM, **then...** make sure they practice with text at their independent reading level. Provide additional fluency practice by pairing nonfluent readers with fluent readers. **If...** students already read at 120 WCPM, **then...** have them read a book of their choice independently. |
| --- | --- |

**ELL**

**If...** students need more scaffolding and practice with **Conventions and Writing,** **then...** use the activities on pp. DI•49–DI• 50 in the Teacher Resources section on SuccessNet.

**Day 5** **SMALL GROUP TIME • Differentiate Reteaching, p. SG•17**

| **OL** On-Level | **SI** Strategic Intervention | **A** Advanced |
| --- | --- | --- |
| • **Practice** Subject and Object Pronouns | • **Review** Subject and Object Pronouns | • **Extend** Subject and Object Pronouns |
| • **Reread** *Reading Street Sleuth,* pp. 46–47 | • **Reread** *Reading Street Sleuth,* pp. 46–47 | • **Reread** *Reading Street Sleuth,* pp. 46–47 |
| | | • **Communicate** Inquiry Project |

Name _____

# Ring of Fire

One special area of Earth is known as the Ring of Fire. It is the          15

land areas that surround the Pacific Ocean. The edges of Asia, North          27

America, Central America, and South America are a part of the Ring.          39

This area contains 75 percent of the world's volcanoes.          48

Earth's top layer is made up of plates, or layers of land. These          61

plates move. The largest plate in the world is the Pacific Plate. It is          75

located under the Pacific Ocean. When the plates collide into one          86

another, there can be trouble. The collision may cause an earthquake.          97

Ocean tides may rise very high during earthquakes too.          106

When one plate slides under another plate, melted rock called          116

magma may rise to Earth's surface. This causes volcanoes to erupt.          127

On May 18, 1980, a volcano in Washington called Mount St. Helens          139

erupted. Thousands of animals died because they could not outrun the          150

melted rock rushing from the volcano.          156

Before Mount St. Helens erupted, its peak was 9,677 feet          166

high. After the eruption, its height was 8,363 feet. The volcano lost          178

1,314 feet when the top of the mountain blew off during the eruption.          191

Scientists are always looking for ways to warn people well ahead          202

of a volcano's eruption or an earthquake. It is important to save lives.          215

**MONITOR PROGRESS**          • Check Fluency

**Common Core State Standards**

**Informational Text 7.** Use information gained from illustrations (e.g., maps, photographs) and the words in a text to demonstrate understanding of the text (e.g., where, when, why, and how key events occur).

# Assessment

## Monitor Progress

For a written assessment of *r*-Controlled Vowels, Graphic Sources, and Selection Vocabulary, use Weekly Test 17, pp. 97–102.

**◉ GRAPHIC SOURCES** Use "The Texas 8000 Patch" on p. 85m to check students' understanding of graphic sources.

**1.** Which mountain did Sylvia climb first? When? (She climbed Bush Mountain first on October 12, 2007.)

**2.** What other mountains must Sylvia climb after she completes her climb of Mt. Livermore? (Shumard Peak, Bartlett Peak, and El Capitan)

**3.** How many times has she climbed with Maria Perez? (twice)

> **Corrective feedback** | **If...** students are unable to answer the comprehension questions,
> **then...** use the Reteach lesson in *First Stop*.

Name _____

# The Texas 8000 Patch

The newest members of the Texas Climbers Club were excited. This morning they were going to hike up Mt. Livermore, the fifth highest mountain in Texas. Mt. Livermore is one of Texas's seven mountains that reach more than 8,000 feet high. The club calls those mountains the Texas 8000.

"When we reach the peak of Mt. Livermore, I'll have only three more of the Texas 8000 left to climb," said Sylvia.

"When you've done that, you'll get a patch exactly like this," said Maria.

Maria pointed to a colorful patch sewn on her hiking vest. The patch had the phrase "Texas 8000" and a picture of a mountaintop on it. Maria is a leader of the club. She has climbed all the Texas 8000 mountains more than once. Like other leaders, she can sign members' cards to show that they have climbed each of the Texas 8000 mountains.

As the group started their hike, Sylvia looked at Maria's Texas 8000 patch one more time. She couldn't wait to get hers!

| The Texas 8000: Sylvia's Climbs | | | | |
|---|---|---|---|---|
| **Mountain** | **County** | **Height** | **Date Climbed** | **Leader's Name** |
| Guadalupe Peak | Culberson | 8,749 feet | Dec. 15, 2008 | Maria Perez |
| Bush Mountain | Culberson | 8,631 feet | Oct. 12, 2007 | Maria Perez |
| Shumard Peak | Culberson | 8,615 feet | | |
| Bartlett Peak | Culberson | 8,508 feet | | |
| Mt. Livermore | Jeff Davis | 8,368 feet | | |
| Hunter Peak | Culberson | 8,368 feet | April 26, 2008 | David Keltner |
| El Capitan | Culberson | 8,085 feet | | |

**MONITOR PROGRESS**    • **Graphic Sources**

 **Common Core State Standards**

**Speaking/Listening 1.a.** Come to discussions prepared, having read or studied required material; explicitly draw on that preparation and other information known about the topic to explore ideas under discussion. **Speaking/Listening 3.** Ask and answer questions about information from a speaker, offering appropriate elaboration and detail. **Language 1.a.** Explain the function of nouns, pronouns, verbs, adjectives, and adverbs in general and their functions in particular sentences. **Language 2.** Demonstrate command of the conventions of standard English capitalization, punctuation, and spelling when writing. **Language 2.f.** Use spelling patterns and generalizations (e.g., word families, position-based spellings, syllable patterns, ending rules, meaningful word parts) in writing words.

# Research and Inquiry

## Step 5 Communicate

**PRESENT IDEAS** Have students share their inquiry results in small groups by presenting their articles, giving a brief talk on their research and answering discussion questions. Have students display the graphic sources they created.

**SPEAKING** Remind students how to be good speakers and how to communicate effectively with their audience.

• Respond to relevant questions with appropriate detail.

• Speak slowly, clearly, and loudly.

• Keep eye contact with audience members.

**LISTENING** Review with students these tips for being a good listener.

• Wait until the speaker has finished before raising your hand to ask a relevant question or make pertinent comments.

• Be polite, even if you disagree.

**LISTEN TO IDEAS** Have students listen attentively to the various presentations. Have them make pertinent comments, closely related to the topic.

# Spelling Test

## Vowels: *r*-Controlled

To administer the spelling test, refer to the directions, words, and sentences on p. 59c.

# Conventions

## Subject and Object Pronouns

**MORE PRACTICE** Remind students that the subject pronouns *I, you, he, she, it, we,* and *they* are used as subjects of sentences. The object pronouns *me, you, him, her, it, us,* and *them* are used after action verbs or as objects of prepositions.

**GUIDE PRACTICE** Have students come to the front of the room and demonstrate giving books to each another while the rest of the class writes sentences using the appropriate subject and object pronouns. Include different possibilities, and challenge students to come up with different ways of expressing them. For example:

> **She gives the book to him.**
>
> **He gives the book to her.**
>
> **She and he give the books to them.**

**ON THEIR OWN** Write these sentences on the board. Have students copy the sentences, substituting the correct subject or object pronoun for the underlined words. Students should complete *Let's Practice It!* p. 236 on the *Teacher Resources DVD-ROM.*

**1.** <u>Steve Jenkins</u> wrote this book about extreme places. *(He)*

**2.** <u>Some deserts</u> have not seen rain for hundreds of years. *(They)*

**3.** The tide in the Bay of Fundy can overtake <u>a man</u>. *(him)*

**4.** <u>The Amazon River</u> contains half of the world's river water. *(It)*

**5.** These natural wonders really amaze <u>you and me</u>. *(us)*

**eSTREET INTERACTIVE**
www.ReadingStreet.com

**Teacher Resources**
• Let's Practice It!
• Daily Fix-It Transparency

## Daily Fix-It

**9.** The clime up the mountain was too hard for Joe and she. *(climb; her)*

**10.** She sliped and hurt her self. *(slipped; herself)*

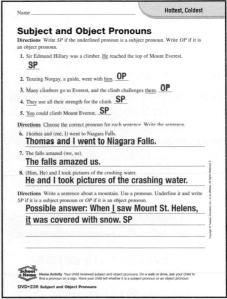

Name _____    Hottest, Coldest

**Subject and Object Pronouns**
Directions Write *SP* if the underlined pronoun is a subject pronoun. Write *OP* if it is an object pronoun.

1. Sir Edmund Hillary was a climber. <u>He</u> reached the top of Mount Everest.
**SP**

2. Tenzing Norgay, a guide, went with <u>him</u>. **OP**

3. Many climbers go to Everest, and the climb challenges <u>them</u>. **OP**

4. <u>They</u> use all their strength for the climb. **SP**

5. <u>You</u> could climb Mount Everest. **SP**

Directions Choose the correct pronoun for each sentence. Write the sentence.

6. Thomas and (me, I) went to Niagara Falls.
**Thomas and I went to Niagara Falls.**

7. The falls amazed (we, us).
**The falls amazed us.**

8. (Him, He) and I took pictures of the crashing water.
**He and I took pictures of the crashing water.**

Directions Write a sentence about a mountain. Use a pronoun. Underline it and write *SP* if it is a subject pronoun or *OP* if it is an object pronoun.
**Possible answer: When I saw Mount St. Helens, it was covered with snow. SP**

School + Home **Home Activity** Your child reviewed subject and object pronouns. On a walk or drive, ask your child to find a pronoun on a sign. Have your child tell whether it is a subject pronoun or an object pronoun.
DVD•236 Subject and Object Pronouns

Let's Practice It! TR DVD•236

## Teacher Note

**Writing Self-Evaluation** Make copies of the Writing Self-Evaluation Guide on p. 39 of the *Reader's and Writer's Notebook* and hand out to students.

### Ⓒ Bridge to Common Core

**PRODUCTION AND DISTRIBUTION OF WRITING**

Over the course of the week, students have developed and strengthened their drafts through planning, revising, rewriting, and proofreading. The final drafts are imaginative stories in which the organization and style are appropriate to the purpose and audience.

# Writing  Zoom in on Ⓒ

## Imaginative Story

**REVIEW REVISING** Remind students that yesterday they revised their imaginative stories, paying particular attention to combining ideas into compound and complex sentences. Today they will proofread their imaginative stories.

### Mini-Lesson   Proofread

**Proofread for Subject and Object Pronouns**

■ **Teach** When we proofread, we look closely at our work, searching for errors in mechanics such as spelling, capitalization, punctuation, and grammar. Today we will focus on making sure subject and object pronouns are used correctly.

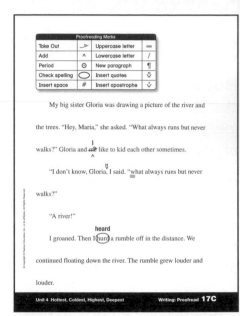

Writing Transparency 17C, TR DVD

■ **Model** Let's look at part of the story we revised yesterday. Display Writing Transparency 17C. Explain that you will look for errors in the use of subject and object pronouns. I see a problem in the fourth sentence: *Gloria and me like to kid each other sometimes. Gloria and me* is the subject of the sentence, so the subject pronoun *I* should be used: *Gloria and I.* Point out the quotation mark missing after *Gloria,* the lowercase *what* in the second paragraph, and the misspelled word *hurd* in the fourth paragraph. Tell students they should reread their stories a number of times, each time looking for errors in punctuation, capitalization, spelling, and grammar.

**WRITING PROCESS** Display the Proofreading Tips. Ask students to proofread their stories, using the Proofreading Tips and paying particular attention to subject and object pronouns. Circulate around the room answering students' questions. When students have finished editing their own work, have pairs proofread one another's imaginative stories.

### Proofreading Tips

✔ Be sure subject and object pronouns are used correctly.

✔ Check for punctuation and capitalization, especially with dialogue.

✔ Check for correct spelling.

✔ Check for correct grammar.

**eSTREET INTERACTIVE**
www.ReadingStreet.com

**Teacher Resources**
• Writing Transparency
• Reader's and Writer's Notebook

**PRESENT** Give students options for presenting: a recording (oral presentation) or a poster. For each option, students should illustrate their stories on posterboard. For an oral presentation, students should read their stories aloud to the class and explain the poster art. For a poster presentation, students should attach their stories to the poster and display it in the room. When students have finished, have each complete a Writing Self-Evaluation form.

## Routine · Quick Write for Fluency · Team Talk

1. **Talk** Pairs discuss what they learned about writing an imaginative story this week.

2. **Write** Each student writes a few sentences explaining what he or she learned.

3. **Share** Partners read each other's sentences and ask each other questions about what they learned.

Routines Flip Chart

**Academic Vocabulary** ©

**Punctuation** includes marks, such as commas and periods, which are used to organize writing.

# Wrap Up Your Week!

## Nature's Record Holders

What makes nature's record holders unique?

**Think Aloud** In *Hottest, Coldest, Highest, Deepest* and in "Paul Bunyan and the Great Lakes," we learned what makes someone or something unique.

**Team Talk** Have students recall their Amazing Ideas about one of a kind and use these ideas to help them demonstrate their understanding of the Question of the Week.

Next Week's Concept
## Unique Interests

Why is it valuable to have unique interests?

**ELL**

**Poster Preview** Prepare students for next week by using Week 3 ELL Poster 18. Read the Talk-Through to introduce the concept and vocabulary.

**Selection Summary** Send home the summary of *Rocks in His Head,* in English and in the students' home languages, if available. Students can read the summary with family members.

Why is it valuable to have unique interests? Next week you will read about where one man's interest in rocks took him.

**Preview Next Week**

*Hottest, Coldest, Highest, Deepest* **85q**

# Assessment Checkpoints for the Week

## Weekly Assessment

Use pp. 97–102 of *Weekly Tests* to check:

✔ 👁 **Phonics** Vowels: *r*-Controlled

✔ 👁 **Comprehension** Graphic Sources

✔ **Review** **Comprehension** Main Idea and Details

✔ 👁 **Selection Vocabulary**

| | | |
|---|---|---|
| average | erupted | tides |
| depth | outrun | waterfalls |
| deserts | peak | |

Weekly Tests

## Differentiated Assessment

**Advanced**

Use pp. 97–102 of *Fresh Reads for Fluency and Comprehension* to check:

✔ 👁 **Comprehension** Graphic Sources

✔ **Review** **Comprehension** Main Idea and Details

**On-Level**

✔ **Fluency** Words Correct Per Minute

**SI**
**Strategic**
**Intervention**

Fresh Reads for Fluency and Comprehension

## Managing Assessment

Use *Assessment Handbook* for:

✔ **Weekly Assessment Blackline Masters for Monitoring Progress**

✔ **Observation Checklists**

✔ **Record-Keeping Forms**

✔ **Portfolio Assessment**

Assessment Handbook

# TEACHER NOTES

## DAY 1 Differentiate Vocabulary

- **Word Knowledge** Amazing Words
- **Read** "The Wettest Place on Earth"
- **Inquiry** Identify Questions

"The Wettest Place on Earth"
pp. 46–47

## DAY 2 Differentiate Comprehension

- **Word Knowledge** Selection Vocabulary
- **Access Text** Read *Hottest, Coldest, Highest, Deepest*
- **Inquiry** Investigate

## DAY 3 Differentiate Close Reading

- **Word Knowledge** Develop Vocabulary
- **Close Reading** Read *Hottest, Coldest, Highest, Deepest*
- **Inquiry** Investigate

## DAY 4 Differentiate Vocabulary

- **Word Knowledge** Amazing Words
- **Read** "Paul Bunyan and the Great Lakes"
- **Inquiry** Organize

## DAY 5 Differentiate Reteaching

- **Conventions** Subject and Object Pronouns
- **Reread** "The Wettest Place on Earth" or Leveled Readers
- **Inquiry** Communicate

Teacher Guides and Student pages can be found in the Leveled Reader Database.

 Place English Language Learners in the groups that correspond to their reading abilities.
**If...** students need scaffolding and practice,
**then...** use the ELL Notes on the instructional pages.

## Independent Practice

**Independent Practice Stations**

See pp. 54h and 54i for Independent Stations.

**Pearson Trade Book Library**

See the Leveled Reader Database for lesson plans and student pages.

**Reading Street Digital Path**

Independent Practice Activities are available in the Digital Path.

**Independent Reading**

See p. 54i for independent reading suggestions.

**On-Level**

## Common Core State Standards

**Literature 1.** Ask and answer questions to demonstrate understanding of a text, referring explicitly to the text as the basis for the answers. **Foundational Skills 4.** Read with sufficient accuracy and fluency to support comprehension. **Language 4.** Determine or clarify the meaning of unknown and multiple-meaning words and phrases based on grade 3 reading and content, choosing flexibly from a range of strategies.

### Independent Reading Options

**Trade Book Library**

**eStreet Interactive**
www.ReadingStreet.com

Teacher Guides are available on the Leveled Reader Database.

**If...** students need more scaffolding and practice with **Vocabulary,** **then...** use the activities on pp. DI•42–DI•43 in the Teacher Resources section on SuccessNet.

# ① Build Word Knowledge
## Practice Amazing Words

**DEFINE IT** Elicit the definition for the word *competitor* from students. Ask: How would you describe a competitor to another student? (Possible response: a rival, or a person who competes) Clarify or give a definition when necessary. Continue with the words *evergreen* and *plunge.*

**Team Talk** **TALK ABOUT IT** Have pairs internalize meanings. Ask: How can you pair the Amazing Words together in a sentence? (Possible response: Competitors in the race plunged into the lake near the evergreen forest.) Allow time for students to play with the words. Review the concept map with students. Discuss other words they can add to the concept map.

# ② Text-Based Comprehension
## Read

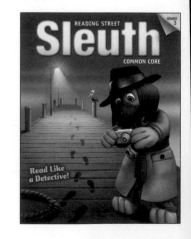

**READ ALOUD "The Wettest Place on Earth"** Have partners read "The Wettest Place on Earth" from *Reading Street Sleuth* on pp. 46–47.

**ACCESS TEXT** Discuss the Sleuth Work section with students before they work on it. Remind students that they can use these steps with other texts they read.

**Gather Evidence** Talk together about using a T-chart to note facts and opinions. Remind students that facts can be proven true. Have partners make a T-chart that lists the facts and opinions of the story.

**Ask Questions** Talk together about revisiting the text to form questions. Remind students that not all questions can be answered by the text. Have students share their questions and talk about how they might get the answers to their questions.

**Make Your Case** Have partners make a list of the best ways to explore a new area. Encourage partners to list reasons that support their ideas. Encourage students to make connections with their own experiences of exploring a new place.

**On-Level**

# 1 Build Word Knowledge
## Practice Selection Vocabulary

| average | depth | deserts | erupted |
|---------|-------|---------|---------|
| outrun | peak | tides | waterfalls |

**DEFINE IT** Discuss the definition for the word *peak* with students. Ask: How would you describe *peak* to another student? (Possible response: the top of the mountain.) Continue with the remaining words.

**Team Talk** **TALK ABOUT IT** Have pairs use the selection vocabulary in sentences to internalize meaning. Ask: How can you pair the selection vocabulary together in a sentence? (Possible response: The average temperature on mountain peaks is extremely low.) Allow time for students to play with the words and then share their sentences.

# 2 Read
## *Hottest, Coldest, Highest, Deepest*

If you read *Hottest, Coldest, Highest, Deepest* during whole group time, then use the following instruction.

**ACCESS TEXT** Reread the text and graphic box on p. 66. Ask questions to check understanding. How are the two lakes in this selection compared? (by their depth, measured in feet; and by their size, measured in square miles) How can Lake Baikal contain more water than Lake Superior, the larger of the two lakes? (Lake Baikal is much deeper than Lake Superior.)

Have students identify sections from today's reading that they did not completely understand. Reread them aloud and clarify misunderstandings.

If you are reading *Hottest, Coldest, Highest, Deepest* during small group time, then return to pp. 64–69a to guide the reading.

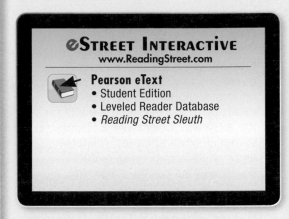

**eSTREET INTERACTIVE**
www.ReadingStreet.com

**Pearson eText**
• Student Edition
• Leveled Reader Database
• *Reading Street Sleuth*

**SMALL GROUP TIME**

**More Reading for Group Time**

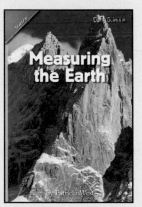

**ON-LEVEL**

**Reviews**
• Graphic Sources
• Important Ideas
• Selection Vocabulary

Use this suggested Leveled Reader or other text at students' instructional level.

**eSTREET INTERACTIVE**
www.ReadingStreet.com

Use the Leveled Reader Database for lesson plans and student pages for *Measuring the Earth*.

**On-Level**

## ① Build Word Knowledge
### Develop Vocabulary

**REREAD FOR VOCABULARY** Reread the second paragraph on p. 70. Introduce: Let's read this paragraph to find out what *precipitation* means. To help students understand the word *precipitation,* ask questions related to the context, such as: What is being measured? What kinds of regions get the least amount of precipitation? Have students use online sources to find out more information about precipitation.

## ② Read
### *Hottest, Coldest, Highest, Deepest*

If you read *Hottest, Coldest, Highest, Deepest* during whole group time, then use the following instruction.

**CLOSE READING** Read pp. 72–73. Have students list the most important ideas in the text. (The world's highest waterfall is Angel Falls in Venezuela; the deepest spot in an ocean is in the Marianas Trench in the Philippines; the world's most active volcano is Sangay in Ecuador.)

Ask: How does the graphic chart on p. 72 help you understand a main idea on that page? (Looking at the graphic makes it easier to compare the waterfalls. I can see how high Angel Falls really is by comparing it with the Empire State Building, which I am already familiar with.)

If you are reading *Hottest, Coldest, Highest, Deepest* during small group time, then return to pp. 70–75a to guide the reading.

**If...** students need more scaffolding and practice with the **Main Selection, then...** use the activities on p. DI•47 in the Teacher Resources section on SuccessNet.

**On-Level**

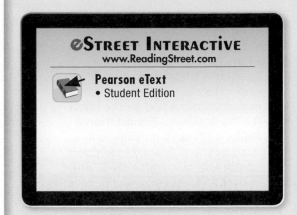

*e*STREET INTERACTIVE
www.ReadingStreet.com

**Pearson eText**
• Student Edition

# 1 Build Word Knowledge
## Practice Amazing Words

| | | | | |
|---|---|---|---|---|
| evergreen | champ | lumber | sprinter | competitor |
| acrobat | plunge | weaken | valuable | ranger |

**Team Talk** **LANGUAGE DEVELOPMENT** Have partners practice building more complex sentences. Display a sentence starter and have students add oral phrases or clauses using the Amazing Words. For example: The ranger _____. (The ranger pointed out the evergreen trees / explaining that they were valuable resources / for lumber, / but disease can weaken them.) Guide students to add at least three phrases or clauses per sentence.

# 2 Read
## "Paul Bunyan and the Great Lakes"

**BEFORE READING** Read aloud the information on p. 80. Have students preview "Paul Bunyan and the Great Lakes" and set a purpose for reading. Based on the pictures, how is this legend about the Great Lakes different from the expository text you just read? (The legend is not real. It seems to be about a giant digging a lake. The selection I just read is nonfiction. It gives interesting facts instead of telling a funny story.)

**DURING READING** Have students read along with you.

• According to this legend, how did the Great Lakes form? (Paul Bunyan dug them out for his ox and his lumberjack crew to drink from.)

• Paul Bunyan, the ox, and the Great Lakes all share what quality? (They are all amazingly large.)

**AFTER READING** Have students share their reaction to "Paul Bunyan and the Great Lakes." Then have them work in small groups or pairs to create a legend about a natural feature in your community.

**SMALL GROUP TIME**

**Independent Reading Options**

**Trade Book Library**

*e*STREET INTERACTIVE
www.ReadingStreet.com

Teacher Guides are available on the Leveled Reader Database.

## Common Core State Standards

**Literature 1.** Ask and answer questions to demonstrate understanding of a text, referring explicitly to the text as the basis for the answers. **Foundational Skills 4.** Read with sufficient accuracy and fluency to support comprehension. **Writing 3.** Write narratives to develop real or imagined experiences or events using effective technique, descriptive details, and clear event sequences. **Language 4.** Determine or clarify the meaning of unknown and multiple-meaning words and phrases based on grade 3 reading and content, choosing flexibly from a range of strategies.

## More Reading for Group Time

**ON-LEVEL**

**Reviews**
• Graphic Sources
• Important Ideas
• Selection Vocabulary

Use this suggested Leveled Reader or other text at students' instructional level.

### eSTREET INTERACTIVE
www.ReadingStreet.com

Use the Leveled Reader Database for lesson plans and student pages for *Measuring the Earth*.

## On-Level

# ① Build Word Knowledge
## Practice Subject and Object Pronouns

**IDENTIFY** Choral read the bottom of p. 79 with students and discuss subject and object pronouns, giving them a couple of subject/object examples, such as *I/me* and *she/her*. Have partners reread the model story to find examples of how the author used subject and object pronouns. Encourage students to use the student model story on the same page to practice. Allow time for students to discuss their examples and correct any misunderstandings.

# ② Text-Based Comprehension
## Read

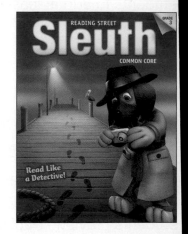

**REREAD "The Wettest Place on Earth"** Have partners reread "The Wettest Place on Earth."

**EXTEND UNDERSTANDING** Talk together about the amount of rain Wai-ale-ale receives in a year. Have students compare this to an estimate of the amount of rain their community gets in a year. Encourage students to follow up with rainfall research for their community.

**PERFORMANCE TASK • Prove It!** Have students imagine what the driest place on Earth might be like. The hottest? The coldest? The highest? Ask students to imagine they could travel to a weather record-holding location somewhere on the planet. Have them draw a picture of what it might look like there, and write a paragraph telling what it might be like to be there in person. Encourage students to do basic research before beginning their paragraph so they may incorporate both facts and opinions.

**COMMUNICATE** Have pairs share their paragraphs. Invite listeners to point out both facts and opinions in the paragraph.

**Strategic Intervention**

# 1 Build Word Knowledge

## Reteach Amazing Words

Repeat the definition of the word. We learned that a competitor is a person who competes in something. Then use the word in a sentence. All of the competitors in the race gathered at the starting line.

**Team Talk** **TALK ABOUT IT** Have pairs take turns using the word *competitor* in a sentence. Continue this routine to practice the Amazing Words *evergreen* and *plunge*. Review the concept map with students. Discuss other words they can add to the concept map.

> **Corrective feedback** | **If...** students need more practice with the Amazing Words, **then...** use visuals from the Student Edition or online sources to clarify meaning.

# 2 Text-Based Comprehension

## Read

**REREAD "The Wettest Place on Earth"** Have students track the print as you read "The Wettest Place on Earth" from *Reading Street Sleuth* on pp. 46–47.

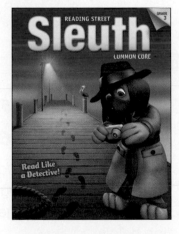

**ACCESS TEXT** Discuss the Sleuth Work section with students and provide support as needed as they work on it. Remind students that they can use these steps with other texts they read.

**Gather Evidence** Talk together about the difference between facts and opinions. Remind students that facts can be proved to be true. Ask students to create a T-chart with the headings "Facts" and "Opinions." Have partners work together to list facts and opinions they find in the story.

**Ask Questions** Talk together about the idea that not all questions can be answered by the text. Have students share their questions. Discuss how students might get answers to their questions.

**Make Your Case** Talk together about experiences students have had with exploring new places. Have partners make a list of the best ways to explore a new area and reasons that support those ideas.

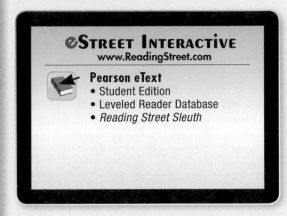

**eStreet Interactive**
www.ReadingStreet.com

**Pearson eText**
• Student Edition
• Leveled Reader Database
• *Reading Street Sleuth*

**SMALL GROUP TIME**

## More Reading for Group Time

**CONCEPT LITERACY**
**Practice**
Concept Words

**BELOW-LEVEL**
**Reviews**
• Graphic Sources
• Important Ideas
• Selection Vocabulary

Use these suggested Leveled Readers or other text at students' instructional level.

**eStreet Interactive**
www.ReadingStreet.com

Use the Leveled Reader Database for lesson plans and student pages for *Extremes* and *How to Measure the Weather*.

**SI** Strategic Intervention

# 1 Build Word Knowledge
## Reteach Selection Vocabulary

**DEFINE IT** Describe *peak* to a friend. Give a definition when necessary. Restate the word in student-friendly terms and clarify meaning with a visual. *Peak* means the top of a mountain or hill. Page 67 shows the peak of a mountain.

| | | | |
|---|---|---|---|
| average | depth | deserts | erupted |
| outrun | peak | tides | waterfalls |

**Team Talk** **TALK ABOUT IT** Have you seen a mountain peak? Turn and talk to your partner about this. Allow time for students to discuss. Ask for examples. Rephrase students' examples for usage when necessary or to correct misunderstandings. Continue with the remaining words.

**Corrective feedback** | **If...** students need more practice with selection vocabulary, **then...** use the *Envision It! Pictured Vocabulary Cards*.

# 2 Read

## *Hottest, Coldest, Highest, Deepest*

If you read *Hottest, Coldest, Highest, Deepest* during whole group time, then use the instruction below.

**ACCESS TEXT** Reread the text and graphic box on p. 66. Ask questions to check understanding. Which of the two lakes is deeper? (Lake Baikal) Which of the two lakes is larger when measured in square miles? (Lake Superior) How can Lake Baikal contain more water than Lake Superior? (because Lake Baikal is so much deeper than Lake Superior)

Have students identify sections they did not understand. Reread them aloud. Clarify the meaning of each section to build understanding.

If you are reading *Hottest, Coldest, Highest, Deepest* during small group time, then return to pp. 64–69a to guide the reading.

## Independent Reading Options

**Trade Book Library**

**eSTREET INTERACTIVE**
www.ReadingStreet.com

Teacher Guides are available on the Leveled Reader Database.

**SI** Strategic Intervention

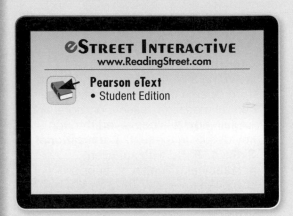

# 1 Build Word Knowledge

## Develop Vocabulary

**REREAD FOR VOCABULARY** Reread the second paragraph on p. 70. Introduce: Let's read this paragraph to find out what *precipitation* means. To help students understand the word *precipitation*, ask questions related to the context, such as: What is being measured? What happens when there is very little rain? What places get the least amount of precipitation?

| Corrective feedback | **If...** students have difficulty understanding the word *precipitation*, **then...** guide students to use online sources to find more information. |
| --- | --- |

# 2 Read

## *Hottest, Coldest, Highest, Deepest*

If you read *Hottest, Coldest, Highest, Deepest* during whole group time, then use the instruction below.

**CLOSE READING** Read aloud pp. 72–73. Have students search through the text to find the important comparisons being made in this selection. Have them use the bold print as a guide. As a class, make a list of the comparisons on the board. (highest waterfall, deepest spot in the ocean, most active volcano)

Now let's use the comparisons we listed to summarize the important ideas in the text. (The world's highest waterfall is Angel Falls in Venezuela. The deepest spot in an ocean is in the Marianas Trench in the Philippines. The world's most active volcano is Sangay in Ecuador.)

If you are reading *Hottest, Coldest, Highest, Deepest* during small group time, then return to pp. 70–75a to guide the reading.

**SMALL GROUP TIME**

**If...** students need more scaffolding and practice with the **Main Selection, then...** use the activities on p. DI•47 in the Teacher Resources section on SuccessNet.

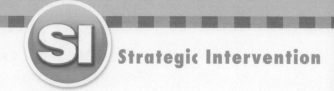

## Common Core State Standards

**Literature 2.** Recount stories, including fables, folktales, and myths from diverse cultures; determine the central message, lesson, or moral and explain how it is conveyed through key details in the text. **Foundational Skills 4.** Read with sufficient accuracy and fluency to support comprehension. **Writing 3.** Write narratives to develop real or imagined experiences or events using effective technique, descriptive details, and clear event sequences. **Language 1.f.** Ensure subject-verb and pronoun-antecedent agreement. **Language 2.** Demonstrate command of the conventions of standard English capitalization, punctuation, and spelling when writing.

# 1 Build Word Knowledge
## Review Amazing Words

| evergreen | champ | lumber | sprinter | competitor |
|-----------|-------|--------|----------|------------|
| acrobat | plunge | weaken | valuable | ranger |

**Team Talk** **LANGUAGE DEVELOPMENT** Have partners practice building more complex sentences. Display a sentence starter and have students add oral phrases or clauses using the Amazing Words. For example: The sprinter was a _____. (The sprinter was a champ, / but she weakened / and suddenly plunged to the ground before the finish line.) Guide students to add at least two phrases or clauses per sentence.

**Corrective feedback** | **If...** students have difficulty using Amazing Words orally, **then...** review the meaning of each of the words.

# 2 Read
## "Paul Bunyan and the Great Lakes"

**BEFORE READING** Read aloud the information about legends on p. 80. A legend is a story from the past. Usually it is told from generation to generation until one person writes it down. Legends often explain something from history or culture. This legend will tell about the Great Lakes. Read the rest of the panel on p. 80. Then have students read the introduction.

**DURING READING** Have students perform a choral reading of the selection. As they read, write each of the legend's exaggerations on the board. In what way are things in this legend made to seem extreme? (Everything is made to seem big.)

**AFTER READING** Have students share their reactions to the selection. Then guide them through the Reading Across Texts and Writing Across Texts activities, prompting if necessary. What are both selections about? (They are both about extremes in nature.)

## ELL

**If...** students need more scaffolding and practice with **Amazing Words, then...** use the Routine on pp. xxxvi–xxxvii in the *ELL Handbook*.

**Strategic Intervention**

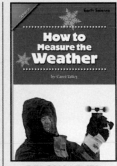

**eSTREET INTERACTIVE**
www.ReadingStreet.com

**Pearson eText**
• Student Edition
• Leveled Reader Database
• *Reading Street Sleuth*

# 1 Build Word Knowledge

## Review Subject and Object Pronouns

**IDENTIFY** Choral read the bottom of p. 79 with students to review subject and object pronouns. Have partners reread the model story on p. 79 to find examples of how the author used subject and object pronouns. Have students use the student model story on that page to practice. Allow time for students to discuss their examples and correct any misunderstandings.

# 2 Text-Based Comprehension

## Read

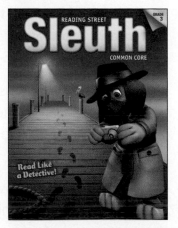

**REREAD "The Wettest Place on Earth"** Have partners reread "The Wettest Place on Earth," alternating paragraphs.

**EXTEND UNDERSTANDING** Talk together about the author's use of descriptive words to help readers visualize Olivia's experience. Have students point out examples of descriptive language that helped them to visualize the story's setting.

**PERFORMANCE TASK • Prove It!** Have students imagine what the driest place on Earth might be like. The hottest? The coldest? The highest? Ask students to imagine they could travel to a weather record-holding location somewhere on the planet. Have them draw a picture of what it might look like there and write a paragraph telling what it might be like to be there in person. Remind students how the author used descriptive language to paint a picture. Encourage students to add both descriptive language and factual evidence to their paragraphs.

**COMMUNICATE** Have pairs share their paragraphs. Encourage listeners to restate descriptive language that helped them visualize the setting.

**More Reading for Group Time**

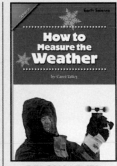

| CONCEPT LITERACY | BELOW-LEVEL |
|---|---|
| **Practice** | **Reviews** |
| Concept Words | • Graphic Sources |
| | • Important Ideas |
| | • Selection Vocabulary |

Use these suggested Leveled Readers or other text at students' instructional level.

**eSTREET INTERACTIVE**
www.ReadingStreet.com

Use the Leveled Reader Database for lesson plans and student pages for *Extremes* and *How to Measure the Weather.*

**SMALL GROUP TIME**

**A** Advanced

## 1 Build Word Knowledge

### Extend Amazing Words

**Team Talk** Have pairs of students define *competitor.* What are some synonyms for *competitor?* *(contender, rival)* How is *contender* different from the word *competitor?* (*Contender* can mean someone who has a good chance to win.) Continue with *evergreen* and *plunge.*

## 2 Text-Based Comprehension

### Read

**READ "The Wettest Place on Earth"** Have partners read "The Wettest Place on Earth" from *Reading Street Sleuth* on pp. 46–47.

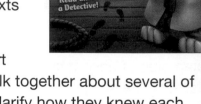

**ACCESS TEXT** Discuss the Sleuth Work section with students before they work on it. Remind students that they can use these steps with other texts they read.

**Gather Evidence** Have students make a T-chart that lists facts and opinions found in the story. Talk together about several of the opinions students identified. Have students clarify how they knew each was an opinion and not a fact.

**Ask Questions** Talk together about revisiting the text to form questions. Have students share their questions and identify the section of text that triggered that question to be asked. Discuss how students might get answers to their questions.

**Make Your Case** Encourage students to make connections with their own experiences of exploring a new place. Have students list their opinions about the best ways to explore a new area. Encourage students to list reasons that support those ideas.

## 3 Inquiry: Extend Concepts

**IDENTIFY QUESTIONS** Have students think about questions they have about unique features in nature and use these questions to select a particular natural feature to study. Have them create a poster that explains and describes the feature. Throughout the week, they will gather information. On Day 5, they will present what they have learned.

 Advanced

# 1 Build Word Knowledge

## Extend Selection Vocabulary

**Team Talk** Have partners use the selection vocabulary in sentences to internalize their meanings. Have students use as many of the words as they can while making sure the sentence is grammatically correct. (Possible response: The average yearly rainfall in deserts and on mountain peaks is extremely low.) Continue with additional selection vocabulary words.

| | | |
|---|---|---|
| average | depth | deserts |
| erupted | outrun | peak |
| tides | waterfalls | |

# 2 Read

## *Hottest, Coldest, Highest, Deepest*

If you read *Hottest, Coldest, Highest, Deepest* during whole group time, then use the instruction below.

**ACCESS TEXT** Reread the text and graphic box on p. 66. Discuss similarities and differences in the information provided in the expository text and the graphic box. (The detail about Lake Baikal being 5,134 feet deep is presented in both the text on the page and the graphic box; the detail about the height of the Empire State Building is presented only in the graphic box.) Ask: Why do you think the author includes the information about the Empire State Building in the graphic box? (Having something you are familiar with allows you to make a quick comparison.)

If you are reading *Hottest, Coldest, Highest, Deepest* during small group time, then return to pp. 64–69a to guide the reading.

# 3 Inquiry: Extend Concepts

**INVESTIGATE** Encourage students to use materials at their independent reading levels or student-friendly search engines to identify relevant and credible sites to gather information about natural features. Have students consider how they will present their information.

## More Reading for Group Time

**ADVANCED**

**Reviews**
• Graphic Sources
• Important Ideas

Use this suggested Leveled Reader or other text at students' instructional level.

**eSTREET INTERACTIVE**
www.ReadingStreet.com

Use the Leveled Reader Database for lesson plans and student pages for *Largest, Fastest, Lightest, Longest*.

SMALL GROUP TIME

**A** Advanced

## Common Core State Standards

**Literature 2.** Recount stories, including fables, folktales, and myths from diverse cultures; determine the central message, lesson, or moral and explain how it is conveyed through key details in the text. **Informational Text 5.** Use text features and search tools (e.g., key words, sidebars, hyperlinks) to locate information relevant to a given topic efficiently. **Informational Text 7.** Use information gained from illustrations (e.g., maps, photographs) and the words in a text to demonstrate understanding of the text (e.g., where, when, why, and how key events occur). **Also Language 4.**

## Independent Reading Options

**Trade Book Library**

### eSTREET INTERACTIVE
www.ReadingStreet.com

Teacher Guides are available on the Leveled Reader Database.

**ELL**

**If...** students need more scaffolding and practice with the **Main Selection, then...** use the activities on p. DI•47 in the Teacher Resources section on SuccessNet.

**SG•30**  One of a Kind • Unit 4 • Week 2

## 1 Build Word Knowledge
### Develop Vocabulary

**REREAD FOR VOCABULARY** Reread the second paragraph on p. 70. Let's read this paragraph to find out what *precipitation* means. Discuss meaning and context with students.

## 2 Read
### *Hottest, Coldest, Highest, Deepest*

If you read *Hottest, Coldest, Highest, Deepest* during whole group time, then use the instruction below.

**CLOSE READING** Read pp. 72–73. Have students create a T-chart with the heads "Text Features" and "Purpose." Have them examine the page to find and list the features the author uses to present information. Then have them indicate what the author's purpose is for each feature. (bold print: signals main ideas about nature's record holders; graphic box: helps reader quickly make comparisons among waterfalls; maps: help reader quickly locate each record holder globally; illustrations: provide descriptive detail to help reader visualize nature's record holders)

Ask: Why do you think the author uses several different features to present the information? (The author can present a lot of information quickly and in a small space by using these features. He also really wants to attract the reader's attention with a variety of kinds of features.) What can you conclude about the author's overall purpose in writing the article? (He wants to both inform and to entertain the reader.)

If you are reading *Hottest, Coldest, Highest, Deepest* during small group time, then return to pp. 70–75a to guide the reading.

## 3 Inquiry: Extend Concepts

**INVESTIGATE** Provide time for students to investigate their natural features in books or online. If necessary, help them locate information that is focused on their topics.

 **Advanced**

# 1 Build Word Knowledge
## Extend Amazing Words and Selection Vocabulary

| | | |
|---|---|---|
| evergreen | champ | lumber |
| sprinter | competitor | acrobat |
| plunge | weaken | valuable |
| ranger | | |

| | | |
|---|---|---|
| average | depth | deserts |
| erupted | outrun | peak |
| tides | waterfalls | |

**Team Talk** **LANGUAGE DEVELOPMENT** Have partners practice building more complex sentences. Display a sentence starter and have students add oral phrases or clauses using the Amazing Words and the selection vocabulary.

# 2 Read
## "Paul Bunyan and the Great Lakes"

**BEFORE READING** Have students read aloud the panel information on legends on p. 80 and ask them to set a purpose for reading. Then direct students to read "Paul Bunyan and the Great Lakes" on their own.

**DURING READING** Point out that a legendary character sometimes has the same qualities as ordinary people—but in greater quantities. How is Paul Bunyan different from an ordinary man? (He is physically bigger and stronger in every way.) How are his actions legendary? (They are big and impressive like him.)

**AFTER READING** Lead a discussion of Reading Across Texts. Then have students do Writing Across Texts independently.

# 3 Inquiry: Extend Concepts

**ORGANIZE INFORMATION** Provide time for students to organize their information into a format that will effectively communicate their findings to their audience. Provide any necessary materials or computer time.

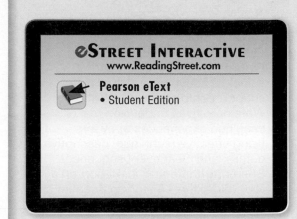

**eSTREET INTERACTIVE**
www.ReadingStreet.com

**Pearson eText**
• Student Edition

**SMALL GROUP TIME**

**Independent Reading Options**

**Trade Book Library**

**eSTREET INTERACTIVE**
www.ReadingStreet.com

Teacher Guides are available on the Leveled Reader Database.

## A Advanced

### Common Core State Standards

**Foundational Skills 4.** Read with sufficient accuracy and fluency to support comprehension. **Writing 3.** Write narratives to develop real or imagined experiences or events using effective technique, descriptive details, and clear event sequences. **Speaking/Listening 4.** Report on a topic or text, tell a story, or recount an experience with appropriate facts and relevant, descriptive details, speaking clearly at an understandable pace.

## ① Build Word Knowledge

### Extend Subject and Object Pronouns

**IDENTIFY AND EXTEND** Choral read the bottom of p. 79 with students and have them explain subject and object pronouns, encouraging them to provide sample sentences, such as *She and I are best friends*. Have partners reread the model story to find examples of how the author used subject and object pronouns. Encourage students to use the student model story on the same page to practice. Allow time for students to discuss their examples and correct any misunderstandings.

## ② Text-Based Comprehension

### Read

**REREAD "The Wettest Place on Earth"** Have partners reread the selection. Have partners discuss whether they would like to visit Wai-ale-ale or not. Have them back up their opinions with convincing reasons.

**EXTEND UNDERSTANDING** Talk together about why humans decide to take dangerous journeys, such as hiking up Wai-ale-ale. Have students share their opinions about making such journeys.

**PERFORMANCE TASK • Prove It!** Have students imagine what the driest place on Earth might be like. The hottest? The coldest? The highest? Ask students to imagine they could travel to a weather record-holding location somewhere on the planet. Have them draw a picture of what it might look like there, and write a paragraph telling what it might be like to be there in person. Encourage students to research the setting for their paragraph, incorporating both facts and opinions into their writing.

**COMMUNICATE** Have pairs share their paragraphs. Invite listeners to ask the writer questions about the setting.

### More Reading for Group Time

**ADVANCED**

**Reviews**
- Graphic Sources
- Important Ideas

Use this suggested Leveled Reader or other text at students' instructional level.

**eSTREET INTERACTIVE**
www.ReadingStreet.com

Use the Leveled Reader Database for lesson plans and student pages for *Largest, Fastest, Lightest, Longest*.

## ③ Inquiry: Extend Concepts

**COMMUNICATE** Have students share their inquiry projects on natural features with the rest of the class. Provide tips for presenting.

# Indiana Common Core Edition

## This Week's Target Skills and Strategies

| Target Skills and Strategies | © Common Core State Standards for English Language Arts | Indiana Academic Standards for English Language Arts |
|---|---|---|
| **Phonics and Spelling** 🔊 Skill: Prefixes *pre-, mid-, over-, out-, bi-, de-* | **CCSS Foundational Skills 3.a.** Identify and know the meaning of the most common prefixes and derivational suffixes. **(Also CCSS Language 2.f.)** | **IN 3.1.8** Use knowledge of prefixes and suffixes to determine the meaning of words. |
| **Text-Based Comprehension** 🔊 Skill: Fact and Opinion | **CCSS Informational Text 1.** Ask and answer questions to demonstrate understanding of a text, referring explicitly to the text as the basis for the answers. **(Also CCSS Informational Text 3.)** | **IN 3.2.2** Ask questions and support answers by connecting prior knowledge with literal information from the text. **(Also IN 3.2.3)** |
| 🔊 Strategy: Inferring | **CCSS Informational Text 1.** Ask and answer questions to demonstrate understanding of a text, referring explicitly to the text as the basis for the answers. **(Also CCSS Informational Text 6.)** | **IN 3.2.2** Ask questions and support answers by connecting prior knowledge with literal information from the text. **(Also IN 3.2.3)** |
| **Vocabulary** 🔊 Skill: Multiple-Meaning Words **Strategy:** Context Clues | **CCSS Language 4.** Determine or clarify the meaning of unknown and multiple-meaning word and phrases based on *grade 3 reading and content,* choosing flexibly from a range of strategies. **(Also CCSS Language 4.a.)** | **IN 3.1.6** Use sentence and word context to find the meaning of unknown words. **(Also IN 3.1.9)** |
| **Fluency** **Skill:** Expression | **CCSS Foundational Skills 4.b.** Read on-level prose and poetry orally with accuracy, appropriate rate, and expression on successive readings. **(Also CCSS Foundational Skills 4.)** | **IN 3.1.3** Read aloud grade-level-appropriate literary and informational texts fluently and accurately and with appropriate timing, change in voice, and expression. |
| **Listening and Speaking** Interview | **CCSS Speaking/Listening 1.b.** Follow agreed-upon rules for discussions (e.g., gaining the floor in respectful ways, listening to others with care, speaking one at a time about the topics and texts under discussion). | The Indiana Academic Standards for Listening and Speaking are not currently assessed on ISTEP+ assessments. Educators and students should implement the Common Core Standards for Speaking and Listening as soon as possible. |
| **Six-Trait Writing** **Trait of the Week:** Sentences | **CCSS Language 1.i.** Produce simple, compound, and complex sentences. | **IN 3.6.2** Write correctly complete sentences of statement, command, question, or exclamation, with final punctuation. |
| **Writing** Biography | **CCSS Writing 2.** Write informative/explanatory texts to examine a topic and convey ideas and information clearly. **(Also CCSS Writing 2.a.)** | **IN 3.5.2** Write descriptive pieces about people, places, things, or experiences. **(Also IN 3.5.7)** |
| **Conventions** **Skill:** Possessive Pronouns | **CCSS Language 1.a.** Explain the function of nouns, pronouns, verbs, adjectives, and adverbs in general and their functions in particular sentences. | **IN 3.6.5** Identify and correctly use pronouns, adjectives, compound nouns, and articles in writing. |

## This Week's Cross-Curricular Standards and Resources

### Cross-Curricular Indiana Academic Standards for Science and Social Studies

**Science**
**IN 3.2.1** Examine the physical properties of rock samples and sort them into categories based on size using simple tools such as sieves.
**IN 3.2.2** Observe the detailed characteristics of rocks and minerals. Identify rocks as being composed of different combinations of minerals.

**Social Studies**
**IN 3.4.2** Give examples of goods and services provided by local business and industry.

### Reading Street Sleuth

*Rocks and More Rocks*
pp. 48–49

Follow the path to close reading using the Super Sleuth tips:

• Gather Evidence

• Ask Questions

• Make Your Case

• Prove it!

### More Reading in Science and Social Studies

Concept Literacy

Below Level

On Level

Advanced

ELL

ELD

ISBN-13: 978-0-328-73390-3   ISBN-10: 0-328-73390-3

# Your 90-Minute Reading Block

| | Whole Group | Formative Assessment | Small Group  OL On Level  SI Strategic Intervention  A Advanced | Daily Independent Options |
|---|---|---|---|---|
| | | How do I make my small groups flexible? | What are my other students reading and learning every day in Small Groups? | What do my other students do when I lead Small Groups? |
| **DAY 1** | **Content Knowledge**  Build Oral Language/Vocabulary  **Phonics/Word Analysis**  **Read Decodable Reader**  **Text-Based Comprehension**  **Selection Vocabulary**  **Research and Inquiry**  Step 1–Identify and Focus Topic  **Spelling Pretest**  Connect to Phonics/Word Analysis | **Monitor Progress**  Check Oral Vocabulary | Differentiate Vocabulary  **Build Word Knowledge**  OL Practice Amazing Words  SI Reteach Amazing Words  A Extend Amazing Words  OL SI A **Text-Based Comprehension**  Read *Reading Street Sleuth*, pp. 48–49 or Leveled Readers  A Inquiry Project  ELL Access Vocabulary | ★ **Independent Reading** ©  Suggestions for this week's independent reading:  • Another book by Steve Jenkins, such as *Down, Down, Down: A Journey to the Bottom of the Sea*  • A magazine article about climbing the world's highest mountain  • A Native American legend |
| **DAY 2** | **Content Knowledge**  Build Oral Language/Vocabulary  **Phonics/Word Analysis**  **Vocabulary Skill**  **Text-Based Comprehension**  Read Main Selection, using Access Text Notes  **Research and Inquiry**  Step 2–Navigate/Search  **Spelling**  Connect to Phonics/Word Analysis | **Monitor Progress**  Formative Assessment:  Check Word Reading | Differentiate Comprehension  **Build Word Knowledge**  OL Practice Selection Vocabulary  SI Reteach Selection Vocabulary  A Extend Selection Vocabulary  OL SI A **Access Text**  Read *Rocks in His Head*  A Inquiry Project  ELL Access Comprehension Skill | **Book Talk**  Foster critical reading and discussion skills through independent and close reading.  Students should focus on discussing one or more of the following:  • Key Ideas and Details  • Craft and Structure  • Integration of Ideas |
| **DAY 3** | **Content Knowledge**  Build Oral Language/Vocabulary  **Phonics/Word Analysis**  **Read Decodable Passage**  **Text-Based Comprehension**  Read Main Selection, using Close Reading Notes  **Fluency**  **Research and Inquiry**  Step 3–Analyze Information  **Spelling**  Connect to Phonics/Word Analysis | **Monitor Progress**  Check Retelling | Differentiate Close Reading  OL SI **Reread to Develop Vocabulary**  A **Reread to Extend Vocabulary**  OL SI A **Close Reading**  Read *Rocks in His Head*  A Inquiry Project  ELL Access Main Selection |  **Pearson eText**  • Student Edition  • Decodable Readers  • Leveled Readers   **Trade Book Library** |
| **DAY 4** | **Content Knowledge**  Build Oral Language/Vocabulary  **Phonics/Word Analysis**  **Read Decodable Passage**  **Read Content Area Paired Selection with Genre Focus**  **Let's Learn It!**  Vocabulary/Fluency/Listening and Speaking  **Research and Inquiry**  Step 4–Synthesize  **Spelling**  Connect to Phonics/Word Analysis | **Monitor Progress**  Check Fluency | Differentiate Vocabulary  **Build Word Knowledge**  OL Develop Language Using Amazing Words  SI Review/Discuss Amazing Words  A Extend Amazing Words and Selection Vocabulary  OL SI A **Text-Based Comprehension**  Read "Marvelous Marble Mania"  A Inquiry Project  ELL Access Amazing Words |  **Materials from School or Classroom Library**  **Independent Stations**  Practice Last Week's Skills  ★ Focus on these activities when time is limited.  **Word Wise**  **Word Work**  ★ **Read for Meaning**  **Let's Write!**  ★ **Words to Know**  **Get Fluent** |
| **DAY 5** | **Content Knowledge**  Build Oral Language/Vocabulary  **Text-Based Comprehension**  **Vocabulary Skill**  **Phonics/Word Analysis**  **Assessment**  Fluency, Comprehension  **Research and Inquiry**  Step 5–Communicate  **Spelling Test**  Connect to Phonics/Word Analysis | **Monitor Progress**  Formative Assessment:  Check Oral Vocabulary  **Monitor Progress**  Fluency; Comprehension | Differentiate Reteaching  OL **Practice Possessive Pronouns**  SI **Review Possessive Pronouns**  A **Extend Possessive Pronouns**  OL SI A **Text-Based Comprehension**  Reread *Reading Street Sleuth*, pp. 48–49 or Leveled Readers  A Inquiry Project  ELL Access Conventions and Writing | |

## Assessment Resources

Common Core  Weekly Tests, pp. 103–108

Common Core Fresh Reads for Fluency and Comprehension, pp. 103–108

Common Core  Unit 4 Benchmark Test

Common Core Success Tracker,  ExamView, and Online Lesson Planner

## Teaching the Common Core State Standards This Week

The Common Core State Standards for English Language Arts are divided into strands for **Reading** (including **Foundational Skills**), **Writing**, **Speaking and Listening**, and **Language**. The chart below shows some of the content you will teach this week, strand by strand. Turn to this week's 5-Day Planner on pages 86d–86e to see how this content is taught each day.

## Reading Strand

- **Phonics/Word Analysis:** Prefixes *pre-*, *mid-*, *over-*, *out-*, *bi-*, *de-*
- **Text-Based Comprehension:** Fact and Opinion; Inferring
- **Fluency:** Expression

- **Literary Terms:** Idioms
- **Genre:** Main Selection: Biography; Paired Selection: Persuasive Text

## Common Core State Standards for English Language Arts

## Writing Strand

- **Writing Mini-Lesson:** Biography
- **Trait:** Sentences
- **Look Back and Write:** Text Evidence

## Speaking and Listening Strand

- **Content Knowledge:** Build Oral Language
- **Listening and Speaking:** Interview
- **Research and Inquiry**

## Language Strand

- **Oral Vocabulary: Amazing Words** *hobby*, *project*, *leftover*, *murmur*, *ancestor*, *ornament*, *descendant*, *forge*, *compartment*
- **Vocabulary:** Multiple-Meaning Words; Context Clues
- **Selection Vocabulary:** *stamps, spare, chores, attic, labeled, customers, board*

- **Academic Vocabulary:** *fact, opinion, biography, possessive pronoun, idiom, problem and solution*
- **Conventions:** Possessive Pronouns
- **Spelling:** Prefixes *pre-*, *mid-*, *over-*, *out-*, *bi-*, *de-*

# Text-Based Comprehension

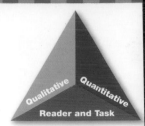

## Text Complexity Measures

Use the rubric to familiarize yourself with the text complexity of *Rocks in His Head*.

## Bridge to Complex Knowledge

| Quantitative Measures | Lexile | 720L |
|---|---|---|
| | Average Sentence Length | 11.44 |
| | Word Frequency | 3.71 |

| Qualitative Measures | Levels of Meaning | understand biographies; some double meaning phrases |
|---|---|---|
| | Structure | simple structure; events in order chronologically |
| | Language Conventionality and Clarity | natural, conversational language; some academic language |
| | Theme and Knowledge Demands | a basic understanding of museums and the concept of collecting |

| Reader and Task Suggestions | **FORMATIVE ASSESSMENT** Based on assessment results, use the **Reader and Task Suggestions** in Access Main Selection to scaffold the selection or support independence for students as they read *Rocks in His Head*. |
|---|---|

| READER AND TASK SUGGESTIONS | |
|---|---|
| **Preparing to Read the Text** | **Leveled Tasks** |
| • Review strategies for understanding multiple-meaning words.<br>• Discuss the features of a biography.<br>• Remind students to adjust their reading rate as needed when they encounter unfamiliar concepts and vocabulary. | • **Levels of Meaning • Analysis** If students don't understand the double meaning of the phrase "rocks in his head," have them use context clues from the first paragraph on p. 101 to understand one nonliteral meaning.<br>• **Language Conventionality and Clarity** Students may find the natural, conversational language of the selection easy to follow. Have students identify quotes from the text that give clues to the personality of the main character. |

**Recommended Placement** Both the qualitative and quantitative measures suggest this text should be placed in the Grade 2–3 text complexity band, which is where both the Common Core State Standards and *Scott Foresman Reading Street* have placed it.

# Focus on Common Core State Standards ©

**Main Selection, pp. 94–105**

**Paired Selection, pp. 110–113**

## Text-Based Comprehension

**Fact and Opinion**
CCSS Informational Text 1.,
CCSS Informational Text 3.

**Inferring**
CCSS Informational Text 1.,
CCSS Informational Text 6.

## Fluency

**Expression**
CCSS Foundational Skills 4.

## Writing and Conventions

**Trait:** Sentences
CCSS Language 1.i.

**Writing Mini-Lesson:** Biography
CCSS Writing 2., CCSS Writing 2.a.

**Conventions:** Possessive Pronouns
CCSS Language 1.a.

## Oral Vocabulary

### Amazing Words

| | |
|---|---|
| hobby | ornament |
| project | descendant |
| leftover | forge |
| murmur | compartment |
| ancestor | |

CCSS Language 6.

## Selection Vocabulary

**Multiple-Meaning Words**
CCSS Language 4.

**Context Clues**
CCSS Language 4.,
CCSS Language 4.a.

| | | |
|---|---|---|
| attic | customer | spare |
| board | labeled | stamps |
| chores | | |

## Phonics and Spelling

**Prefixes** *pre-, mid-, over-, out-, bi-, de-*
CCSS Foundational Skills 3.a.,
CCSS Language 2.f.

| | |
|---|---|
| prepaid | pretest |
| midnight | midpoint |
| overflow | outgoing |
| outdoors | overtime |
| outline | overdue |
| overgrown | outside |
| prefix | outfield |
| Midwest | |

**Challenge Words**

| | |
|---|---|
| precaution | overweight |
| prediction | prehistoric |
| midsection | |

## Listening and Speaking

**Interview**
CCSS Speaking/Listening 1.b.

# Preview Your Week

*Why is it valuable to have unique interests?*

**Main Selection, pp. 94–105**

**Paired Selection, pp. 110–113**

**Genre:** Biography

 **Vocabulary:** Multiple-Meaning Words

 **Text-Based Comprehension:** Fact and Opinion

**Social Studies in Reading**

**Genre:** Persuasive Text

## Build Content Knowledge (Zoom in on ©)

Time for SOCIAL STUDIES

### KNOWLEDGE GOALS
Students will understand that interests

- are valuable
- lead to learning and research
- lead to a job
- preserve information

### THIS WEEK'S CONCEPT MAP
Develop a concept-related graphic organizer like the one below over the course of this week.

The value of unique interests
- Research
- Knowledge
- Information

### BUILD ORAL VOCABULARY
This week, students will acquire the following academic vocabulary/domain-specific words.

**Amazing Words**

| hobby | murmur | descendant |
| project | ancestor | forge |
| leftover | ornament | compartment |

**OPTIONAL CONCEPT-BASED READING** Use the Digital Path to access readers offering different levels of text complexity.

Concept Literacy

Below-Level

On-Level

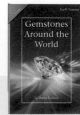
Advanced

ELL

ELD

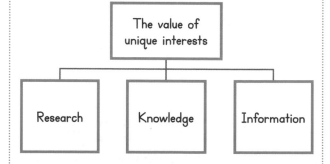

# This Week's Digital Resources

## eStreet Interactive
www.ReadingStreet.com

### Get Ready to Read

 **Concept Talk Video** Use this video on the Digital Path to introduce and familiarize students with the weekly concept of unique interests.

 **Pearson eText** Read the eText of the Student Edition pages on Pearson SuccessNet for comprehension and fluency support.

 **Envision It! Animations** Use this colorful animation on the Digital Path to explain the target comprehension skill, Fact and Opinion.

### Read and Comprehend

 **Journal** Use the Word Bank on the Digital Path to have students write sentences using this week's selection vocabulary words.

 **Background Building Audio CD** This audio CD provides essential background information about unique interests to help students read and comprehend the weekly texts.

 **Pearson eText** Read the eText of the main selection, *Rocks in His Head,* and the paired selection, "Marvelous Marble Mania," with audio support on Pearson SuccessNet.

 **Vocabulary Activities** A variety of interactive vocabulary activities on the Digital Path help students practice selection vocabulary and concept-related words.

### Story Sort

 **Story Sort** Use the Story Sort Activity on the Digital Path after reading *Rocks in His Head* to involve students in summarizing.

### Language Arts

 **Grammar Jammer** Find a useful animation on the Digital Path to provide an engaging grammar lesson that will capture students' attention.

**Pearson eText** Find the Student Edition eText of the Let's Write It! and Let's Learn It! pages with audio support on Pearson SuccessNet.

## Additional Resources

 **Teacher Resources DVD-ROM** Use the following resources on the TR DVD or on Pearson SuccessNet throughout the week:

- Amazing Word Cards
- Reader's and Writer's Notebook
- Writing Transparencies
- Daily Fix-It Transparencies
- Scoring Rubrics
- Grammar Transparencies
- ELL Support
- Let's Practice It!
- Graphic Organizers
- Vocabulary Cards

## This Week's Skills

**Phonics/Word Analysis**
Prefixes *pre-, mid-, over-, out-, bi-, de-*

**Comprehension**
◉ **Skill:** Fact and Opinion
◉ **Strategy:** Inferring

**Language**
◉ **Vocabulary:** Multiple-Meaning Words
**Conventions:** Possessive Pronouns

**Fluency**
Expression

**Writing**
Biography

# 5-Day Planner

## DAY 1

### Get Ready to Read

**Content Knowledge** 86j
Oral Vocabulary: *hobby, project, leftover, murmur*

> **Monitor Progress**
> Check Oral Vocabulary

**Phonics/Word Analysis** 88a
◉ *pre-, mid-, over-, out-, bi-, de-*
**READ** Decodable Reader 18A
Reread for Fluency

### Read and Comprehend

**Text-Based Comprehension** 90a
◉ Fact and Opinion
◉ Inferring

**Fluency** 90–91
Expression

**Selection Vocabulary** 91a
*attic, board, chores, customer, labeled, spare, stamps*

### Language Arts

**Research and Inquiry** 91b
Identify and Focus Topic

**Spelling** 91c
Prefixes *pre-, mid-, over-, out-*, Pretest

**Conventions** 91d
Possessive Pronouns

**Handwriting** 91d
Cursive Letters *v* and *z*

**Writing** 91e
Biography

## DAY 2

### Get Ready to Read

**Content Knowledge** 92a
Oral Vocabulary: *ancestor*

**Phonics/Word Analysis** 92c
◉ Prefixes *pre-, mid-, over-, out-, bi-, de-*

> **Monitor Progress**
> Check Word Reading

**Literary Terms** 92d
Idioms

### Read and Comprehend

**Vocabulary Skill** 92e
◉ Multiple-Meaning Words

**Fluency** 92–93
Expression

**Text-Based Comprehension** 94–95
**READ** *Rocks in His Head*—1st Read

### Language Arts

**Research and Inquiry** 99b
Navigate/Search

**Conventions** 99c
Possessive Pronouns

**Spelling** 99c
Prefixes *pre-, mid-, over-, out-*

**Writing** 99d
Biography

## DAY 3

### Get Ready to Read

**Content Knowledge** 100a
Oral Vocabulary: *ornament, descendant*

**Word Analysis** 100c
Fluent Word Reading
**DECODE AND READ**
Decodable Practice Passage 18B

### Read and Comprehend

**Text-Based Comprehension** 100e
Check Understanding
**READ** *Rocks in His Head*—2nd Read
> **Monitor Progress** Check Retelling

**Fluency** 107b
Expression

### Language Arts

**Research and Study Skills** 107c
Online Information

**Research and Inquiry** 107d
Analyze Information

**Conventions** 107e
Possessive Pronouns

**Spelling** 107e
Prefixes *pre-, mid-, over-, out-*

**Writing** 109a–109c
Biography

## DAY 4

### Get Ready to Read

**Content Knowledge** 110a
Oral Vocabulary: *forge, compartment*

**Phonics/Word Analysis** 110c
Review Vowels: *r*-Controlled
Fluent Word Reading
**DECODE AND READ**
Decodable Practice Passage 18C

### Read and Comprehend

**Genre** 110g
Persuasive Text
**READ** "Marvelous Marble Mania"
—Paired Selection

**Fluency** 114–115
Expression
> **Monitor Progress** Check Fluency

**Vocabulary Skill** 115a
Multiple-Meaning Words

**Listening and Speaking** 115a
Interview

### Language Arts

**Research and Inquiry** 115b
Synthesize

**Conventions** 115c
Possessive Pronouns

**Spelling** 115c
Prefixes *pre-, mid-, over-, out-*

**Writing** 115d
Biography

## DAY 5

### Get Ready to Read

**Content Knowledge** 115f
Review Oral Vocabulary
> **Monitor Progress**
> Check Oral Vocabulary

### Read and Comprehend

**Text-Based Comprehension** 115h
Review Fact and Opinion

**Vocabulary Skill** 115h
Review Multiple-Meaning Words

**Word Analysis** 115i
Review Prefixes *pre-, mid-, over-, out-, bi-, de-*

**Literary Terms** 115i
Review Idioms

**Assessment** 115j, 115l
> **Monitor Progress**
> Fluency; Fact and Opinion

### Language Arts

**Research and Inquiry** 115n
Communicate

**Spelling** 115o
Prefixes *pre-, mid-, over-, out-* Test

**Conventions** 115o
Possessive Pronouns

**Writing** 115p
Biography

**Wrap Up Your Week!** 115q

# Access for All

## What do I do in group time?
It's as easy as 1-2-3!

**1** TEACHER-LED SMALL GROUPS → **2** INDEPENDENT PRACTICE STATIONS → **3** INDEPENDENT READING

## Small Group Time

### © Bridge to Common Core

**SKILL DEVELOPMENT**
- Prefixes *pre-, mid-, over-, out-, bi-, de-*
- *Fact and Opinion*
- Inferring
- Multiple-Meaning Words

**DEEP UNDERSTANDING**

**This Week's Knowledge Goals**
Students will understand that interests
- are valuable
- lead to learning and research
- lead to a job
- preserve information

## **1** Small Group Lesson Plan

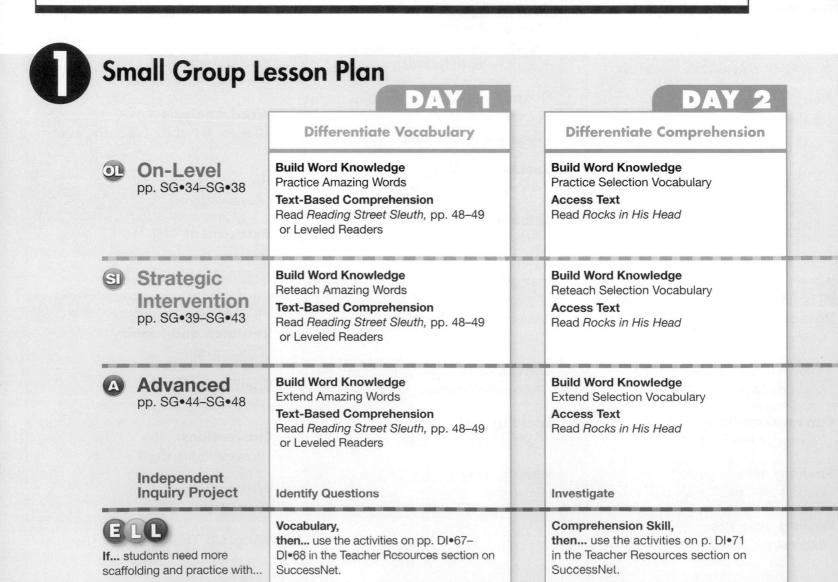

|  | DAY 1 Differentiate Vocabulary | DAY 2 Differentiate Comprehension |
|---|---|---|
| **OL On-Level** pp. SG•34–SG•38 | **Build Word Knowledge** Practice Amazing Words **Text-Based Comprehension** Read *Reading Street Sleuth*, pp. 48–49 or Leveled Readers | **Build Word Knowledge** Practice Selection Vocabulary **Access Text** Read *Rocks in His Head* |
| **SI Strategic Intervention** pp. SG•39–SG•43 | **Build Word Knowledge** Reteach Amazing Words **Text-Based Comprehension** Read *Reading Street Sleuth*, pp. 48–49 or Leveled Readers | **Build Word Knowledge** Reteach Selection Vocabulary **Access Text** Read *Rocks in His Head* |
| **A Advanced** pp. SG•44–SG•48 | **Build Word Knowledge** Extend Amazing Words **Text-Based Comprehension** Read *Reading Street Sleuth*, pp. 48–49 or Leveled Readers | **Build Word Knowledge** Extend Selection Vocabulary **Access Text** Read *Rocks in His Head* |
| **Independent Inquiry Project** | Identify Questions | Investigate |
| **ELL** If... students need more scaffolding and practice with... | **Vocabulary,** then... use the activities on pp. DI•67–DI•68 in the Teacher Resources section on SuccessNet. | **Comprehension Skill,** then... use the activities on p. DI•71 in the Teacher Resources section on SuccessNet. |

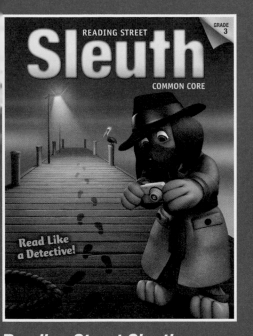

## Reading Street Sleuth

- Provides access to grade-level text for all students
- Focuses on finding clues in text through close reading
- Builds capacity for complex text

## Build Text-Based Comprehension

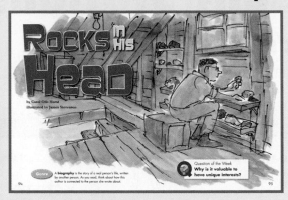

*Rocks in His Head*

## Optional Leveled Readers

| Concept Literacy | Below-Level | On-Level | Advanced | ELL | ELD |

| **DAY 3** | **DAY 4** | **DAY 5** |
|---|---|---|
| **Differentiate Close Reading** | **Differentiate Vocabulary** | **Differentiate Reteaching** |
| **Reread to Develop Vocabulary**<br>**Close Reading**<br>Read *Rocks in His Head* | **Build Word Knowledge**<br>Develop Language Using Amazing Words<br>**Text-Based Comprehension**<br>Read "Marvelous Marble Mania" | **Practice Possessive Pronouns**<br>**Text-Based Comprehension**<br>Reread *Reading Street Sleuth*, pp. 48–49 or Leveled Readers |
| **Reread to Develop Vocabulary**<br>**Close Reading**<br>Read *Rocks in His Head* | **Build Word Knowledge**<br>Review/Discuss Amazing Words<br>**Text-Based Comprehension**<br>Read "Marvelous Marble Mania" | **Review Possessive Pronouns**<br>**Text-Based Comprehension**<br>Reread *Reading Street Sleuth*, pp. 48–49 or Leveled Readers |
| **Reread to Extend Vocabulary**<br>**Close Reading**<br>Read *Rocks in His Head* | **Build Word Knowledge**<br>Extend Amazing Words and Selection Vocabulary<br>**Text-Based Comprehension**<br>Read "Marvelous Marble Mania" | **Extend Possessive Pronouns**<br>**Text-Based Comprehension**<br>Reread *Reading Street Sleuth*, pp. 48–49 or Leveled Readers |
| **Investigate** | **Organize** | **Communicate** |
| **Main Selection,**<br>**then...** use the activities on p. DI•72 in the Teacher Resources section on SuccessNet. | **Amazing Words,**<br>**then...** use the Routine on pp. xxxvi–xxxvii in the *ELL Handbook*. | **Conventions and Writing,**<br>**then...** use the Grammar Transition Lessons on pp. 312–386 in the *ELL Handbook*. |

# Independent Stations

## Practice Last Week's Skills

 Focus on these activities when time is limited.

## WORD WISE

### Spell and use words in sentences.

**OBJECTIVES**

- Spell words with *r*-controlled vowels /èr/ spelled *ir, er, ur, ear,* and *or;* /är/ *ar;* and /ôr/ *or, ore,* and *oar.*

**MATERIALS**

- *Word Wise Flip* Chart Activity 18, word cards, paper and pencils

 **Letter Tile Drag and Drop**

- ● Students choose five words from word cards, write a sentence for each, and list other words with similar spellings.

- ▲ Students choose seven words from word cards, write a sentence for each, and list other words with similar spellings.

- ■ Students choose nine words from word cards, write a sentence for each, and list two words with similar spellings for each word.

## WORD WORK

### Identify and pronounce words.

**OBJECTIVES**

- Identify and pronounce words with *r*-controlled vowels /èr/ spelled *ir, er, ur, ear,* and *or;* /är/ *ar;* and /ôr/ *or, ore,* and *oar.*

**MATERIALS**

- *Word Work* Flip Chart Activity 18, word cards, paper and pencils

**Letter Tile Drag and Drop**

- ● Students write and pronounce eight words with *r*-controlled vowels. They should circle the vowels and the *r* that create the *r*-sound.

- ▲ Students write and pronounce ten words with *r*-controlled vowels. They should circle the vowels and the *r* that create the *r*-sound.

- ■ Students write and pronounce twelve words with *r*-controlled vowels. They should circle the vowels and the *r* that create the *r*-sound.

## LET'S WRITE!

### Write in a genre or style.

**OBJECTIVES**

- Write an imaginative story.

**MATERIALS**

- *Let's Write!* Flip Chart Activity 18, magazines, paper and pencils

 **Grammar Jammer**

- ● Students choose a picture from a magazine and write a short, imaginative story to go with it.

- ▲ Students choose a picture from a magazine and use correct punctuation and capitalization to write a short, imaginative story to go with it.

- ■ Students choose a picture from a magazine and use complex sentences to write a short, imaginative story to go with it.

## WORDS TO KNOW

### Determine word meanings.

**OBJECTIVES**

- Identify the meanings of unknown words.

**MATERIALS**

- *Words to Know* Flip Chart Activity 18, newspapers, paper and pencils

 **Vocabulary Activities**

- ● Students find three unknown words in a newspaper. They look up the meanings and write a sentence for each word.

- ▲ Students find five unknown words in a newspaper. They look up the meanings and write a sentence for each word.

- ■ Students find seven unknown words in a newspaper. They look up the meanings and write a paragraph using each word.

## Manage the Stations

Use these management tools to set up and organize your Practice Stations:

Practice Station Flip Charts

Classroom Management Handbook for Differentiated Instruction Practice Stations, p. 36

---

## READ FOR MEANING

### Analyze graphic sources.

#### OBJECTIVES

• Identify graphic sources and the information they present.

#### MATERIALS

• *Read for Meaning* Flip Chart Activity 18, Leveled Readers, paper and pencils

**Pearson eText**
• Leveled eReaders

**Envision It! Animations**

● Students locate a graphic source in a book and write a sentence telling the information that it gives.

▲ Students choose two graphic sources from a book and write sentences describing the information that each source gives.

■ Students choose two graphic sources from a book and write a short paragraph describing the information that each source gives.

---

## GET FLUENT

### Practice fluent reading.

#### OBJECTIVES

• Use punctuation cues and read aloud with appropriate phrasing.

#### MATERIALS

• *Get Fluent* Flip Chart Activity 18, Leveled Readers

**Pearson eText**
• Leveled eReaders

● Partners practice reading with appropriate phrasing from a Concept Literacy Reader or a Below-Level Reader.

▲ Partners practice reading with appropriate phrasing from an On-Level Reader.

■ Partners practice reading with appropriate phrasing from an Advanced Reader.

---

## 3 Independent Reading ©

Students should select appropriately complex texts to read and write about independently every day before, during, and after school.

Suggestions for this week's independent reading:
• Another book by Steve Jenkins, such as *Down, Down, Down. A Journey to the Bottom of the Sea*
• A magazine article about climbing the world's highest mountain
• A Native American legend

---

**BOOK TALK** Have partners discuss their independent reading for the week. Tell them to refer to their Reading Logs and paraphrase what each selection was about. Then have students focus on discussing one or more of the following:

**Key Ideas and Details**
• What are some of the important ideas in the text? How do you know?
• Summarize the events in the text.

**Craft and Structure**
• How is the information in the text organized?
• What information is presented in any graphic sources in the text?

**Integration of Ideas**
• Describe the important ideas in the legend.
• Provide details that allowed you to identify the ideas as important.

---

**Pearson eText**
• Student Edition
• Decodable Readers
• Leveled Readers

**Trade Book Library**

**School or Classroom Library**

**Content Knowledge**
Oral Vocabulary

**Phonics/Word Analysis**
◉ Prefixes *pre-, mid-, over-, out-, bi-, de-*

**Text-Based Comprehension**
◉ Fact and Opinion
◉ Inferring

**Fluency**
Expression

**Selection Vocabulary**

**Research and Inquiry**
Identify and Focus Topic

**Spelling**
Prefixes *pre-, mid-, over-, out-*

**Conventions**
Possessive Pronouns

**Handwriting**
Cursive Letters *v* and *z*

**Writing**
Biography

### Materials

• Student Edition
• Reader's and Writer's Notebook
• Amazing Word Cards
• Decodable Reader

### © Bridge to Common Core

**INTEGRATION OF KNOWLEDGE/IDEAS**
This week, students will read, write, and talk about why it is valuable to have unique interests.

**Texts This Week**
• "Picture Perfect"
• "Looking at Rocks"
• "More Than a Hobby"
• *Rocks in His Head*
• "Marvelous Marble Mania"

**Social Studies Knowledge Goals**
Students will understand that interests
• are valuable
• lead to learning and research
• lead to a job
• preserve information

## Street Rhymes!

Cook or cycle, bowl, or paint,
fish or ride a bike—
stamp collecting, flying kites—
What hobbies do you like?

• To introduce this week's concept, read aloud the poem several times and ask students to join you.

# Content Knowledge  Zoom in on ©

## Unique Interests

**CONCEPT TALK** To further explore the unit concept of One of a Kind, this week students will read, write, and talk about what it means to be unique. Write the Question of the Week on the board, *Why is it valuable to have unique interests?*

## Build Oral Language

**TALK ABOUT UNIQUE INTERESTS** Have students turn to pp. 86–87 in their Student Editions. Look at each of the photos. Then use the prompts to guide discussion and create a concept map.

• Why is the boy using a magnifying glass? (He is studying the leaf very closely.) Studying plants is a popular *hobby.* People gather details, or do research, about the things that interest them. Let's add *Research* to our concept map.

• Why are the boy and girl looking at pictures in a book? (They are identifying the shells that they have collected.) People who have unique interests gain special knowledge about their subjects. Let's add *Knowledge* to our concept map.

• What kind of information are the girls organizing for their *project?* (They are organizing a family history.) People with unique interests often organize information about their interests. Let's add *Information* to the concept map.

• After discussing the photos, ask: Why is it valuable to have unique interests?

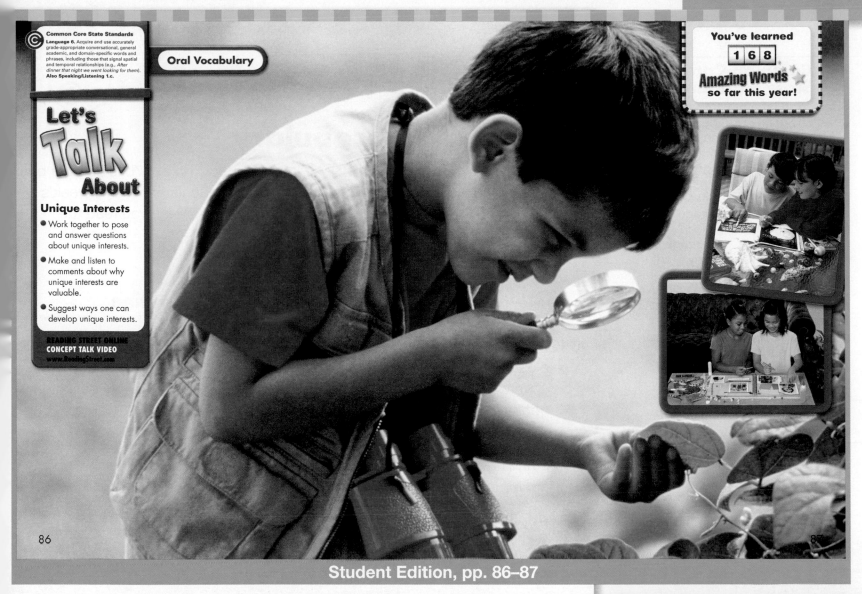

Common Core State Standards
Language 6. Acquire and use accurately grade-appropriate conversational, general academic, and domain-specific words and phrases, including those that signal spatial and temporal relationships (e.g., *After dinner that night we went looking for them).* Also Speaking/Listening 1.c.

**Oral Vocabulary**

## Let's Talk About

### Unique Interests

- Work together to pose and answer questions about unique interests.
- Make and listen to comments about why unique interests are valuable.
- Suggest ways one can develop unique interests.

**READING STREET ONLINE
CONCEPT TALK VIDEO**
www.ReadingStreet.com

You've learned

**1 6 8**

**Amazing Words** ★ so far this year!

86

87

Student Edition, pp. 86–87

**CONNECT TO READING** Tell students that this week they will be reading about a man who has a unique interest in rocks. Encourage students to add concept-related words to this week's concept map.

```
        The value of unique
              interests

   Research    Knowledge    Information
```

 **eStreet Interactive**
www.ReadingStreet.com

**Pearson eText**
• Student Edition

**Concept Talk Video**

**ELL**

**Preteach Concepts** Use the Day 1 instruction on ELL Poster 18 to build knowledge, develop concepts, and build oral vocabulary.

**ELL Support** Additional ELL support and modified instruction are provided in the *ELL Handbook* and in the ELL Support lessons found on the *Teacher Resources DVD-ROM.*

*Rocks in His Head* **86–87**

**Common Core State Standards**

**Speaking/Listening 1.c.** Ask questions to check understanding of information presented, stay on topic, and link their comments to the remarks of others. **Language 4.** Determine or clarify the meaning of unknown and multiple-meaning words and phrases based on grade 3 reading and content, choosing flexibly from a range of strategies. **Language 6.** Acquire and use accurately grade-appropriate conversational, general academic, and domain-specific words and phrases, including those that signal spatial and temporal relationships (e.g., *After dinner that night we went looking for them*).

## Amazing Words

You've learned **1 6 8** words so far.

You'll learn **0 0 9** words this week!

| | |
|---|---|
| hobby | ornament |
| project | descendant |
| leftover | forge |
| murmur | compartment |
| ancestor | |

# Content Knowledge

## Build Oral Vocabulary

**INTRODUCE AMAZING WORDS** "Picture Perfect" on p. 87b is about a boy with a unique interest in photography. Tell students to listen for this week's Amazing Words—*hobby, project, leftover,* and *murmur*—as you read the Teacher Read Aloud on p. 87b.

### Amazing Words       Robust Vocabulary Routine

1. **Introduce** Write the word *hobby* on the board. Have students say the word aloud with you. In "Picture Perfect," Sammy's *hobby* begins when he discovers that he loves to take pictures. Supply a student-friendly definition. A *hobby* is something a person likes to do a lot in his or her free time.

2. **Demonstrate** Have students answer questions to demonstrate understanding. Does Sammy earn money with his *hobby*? What special tools or equipment does Sammy use for his *hobby*?

3. **Apply** Ask students to give a personal example of a *hobby*.

4. **Display the Word** Run your hand under the syllables *hob-by* as you read the word. Have students say the word again.

See p. OV•3 to teach *project, leftover,* and *murmur.*

Routines Flip Chart

**AMAZING WORDS AT WORK** Reread "Picture Perfect" aloud. As students listen, have them notice how the Amazing Words are used in context. To build oral vocabulary, lead the class in a discussion about the Amazing Words' meanings. Remind students to listen attentively, ask relevant questions, and make pertinent comments.

 **MONITOR PROGRESS** Check Oral Vocabulary

During discussion, listen for students' use of Amazing Words.

**If...** students are unable to use the Amazing Words in discussion,

**then...** use the Oral Vocabulary Routine in the Routines Flip Chart to demonstrate words in different contexts.

# Teacher Read Aloud

**MODEL FLUENCY** As you read "Picture Perfect," model appropriate expression by adjusting your voice to demonstrate a lively, fluent reader.

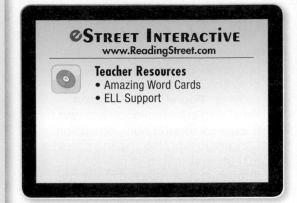

## Picture Perfect

It was Grandpa Jay who first got Sammy hooked on taking pictures. When Sammy was barely two years old, Grandpa Jay held a digital camera up to Sammy's face and said, "Hey there, Sam my man. Push this camera button right here!" Sammy had always liked pushing things, so he happily obeyed. The camera clicked, taking a close-up picture of Grandpa Jay's fuzzy gray beard. Sammy laughed at the hilarious picture. And voilà! A hobby was born.

By the time Sammy was five, his parents had given him a small disposable camera to take with him wherever he went. Sammy kept the camera in his backpack and whipped it out whenever he wanted to remember a special moment.

By age nine, Sammy owned a digital camera and a film camera. He loved taking pictures of anyone and anything: his family and friends, his dog Maxine and his hamster Chuck, his one-story house, his street with the funny cracked sidewalks, his parents' orange car, and his school—Roosevelt Elementary. Sammy took pictures up close and from far away. He printed them in color and in black and white. He even took pictures while running, jumping, and standing on his head.

Once when Sammy was at a family picnic, he heard his cousin murmur, "Why do you take so many pictures?"

"Because," said Sammy, "the camera helps me remember stuff. Photographs are like memories that stay around forever."

That evening, Sammy found out that his family would soon be hosting a huge birthday party for Grandpa Jay. Sammy knew immediately what he was going to give his grandfather as a present—a photo album of family memories. Sammy started on his new project by going through all of the photos he'd ever taken. There were so many pictures to choose from! One showed his dad and his brother eating leftover Thanksgiving turkey in some silly pajamas. Another showed his mom laughing as she tried to skateboard down the street. There were pictures from every celebration and every major event that Sammy could remember.

Finally, when Grandpa Jay's birthday arrived, Sammy eagerly brought out the album. "This is for you!" he said, giving the book to his surprised grandfather. As Grandpa Jay opened the cover, the first picture he saw was the one of his fuzzy gray beard. Grandpa Jay burst out laughing and hugged his grandson.

"I thought that this would be a way to remember the special things we've all done together as a family," Sammy said. "Just like now!" And with that, Sammy quickly pulled out his camera and snapped a photo of his smiling grandfather. "I'll save that picture for the next album! I know there are going to be a whole lot more to come!"

**ELL Support for Read Aloud** Use the modified Read Aloud on p. DI•69 of the ELL Support lessons on the *Teacher Resources DVD-ROM* to prepare students to listen to "Picture Perfect."

**Support Listening Comprehension** To increase understanding of the academic vocabulary heard in the Read Aloud, use visuals to support understanding of words children may not know, such as *digital camera, disposable camera, film camera, photographs,* and *photo album.*

###  Common Core State Standards

**Foundational Skills 3.a.** Identify and know the meaning of the most common prefixes and derivational suffixes. **Foundational Skills 4.** Read with sufficient accuracy and fluency to support comprehension. **Language 2.f.** Use spelling patterns and generalizations (e.g., word families, position-based spellings, syllable patterns, ending rules, meaningful word parts) in writing words.

### Skills Trace

🎯 Prefixes *pre-, mid-, over-, out-, bi-, de-*

**Introduce** U4W3D1
**Practice** U4W3D3; U4W3D4
**Reteach/Review** U4W3D5; U4W4D4
**Assess/Test** Weekly Test U4W3
Benchmark Test U4
**KEY:** U=Unit   W=Week   D=Day

### Vocabulary Support

You may wish to explain the meanings of these words.

**biped** an animal with two feet

**dethrone** to remove from power

# Word Analysis

## Teach/Model

### 🎯 Prefixes *pre-, mid-, over-, out-, bi-, de-*

**CONNECT** Connect today's lesson to previously learned prefixes *un-* and *re-*. Write *unfit* and *renew*. Read these words. You already know that a prefix changes the meaning of the base word. Today you'll learn to spell and read words with other prefixes.

**MODEL** Write *midpoint*. *Midpoint* is a two-syllable word formed from the prefix *mid-* and the base word *point*. I know that *mid-* means "middle." *Point* means "a certain position." *Midpoint* means "in the middle position."

Write *bicycle, preview, deconstruct, overwork,* and *outfield.* Model how to read and define each word by looking for the base word and the prefix (*bi-* means "two"; *pre-* means "before" or "in front of"; *de-* can mean "to do the opposite of"; "down" or "lower"; or "to take away or remove"; *over-* means "too much" or "above"; and *out-* can mean "to the greatest extent").

**GROUP PRACTICE** Continue the process. This time have students read the words with you. Identify the prefix in each word and how it changes the meaning of the base word.

| | | | | | |
|---|---|---|---|---|---|
| pretreat | outstanding | overtime | biped | midsection | dethrone |
| preheat | bifocals | overreach | bimonthly | midweek | outdone |

**REVIEW** What do you know about reading words with prefixes? When you see a word with a prefix, identify the prefix and the base word and then read the whole word.

## Guide Practice

**MODEL** Have students turn to p. 88 in their Student Editions. Each word on this page has a prefix. The first word is *midway*. I see the prefix *mid-* and the base word *way*. I put them together and read the word: *midway*. *Midway* means "in the middle of something."

**GROUP PRACTICE** For each word in Words I Can Blend, ask for the prefix and the base word. Make sure that students identify the correct word parts. Then have them put the parts together and read the words.

> **Corrective feedback** | **If...** students have difficulty reading a word,
> **then...** model reading the parts and then the whole word, and then ask students to read it with you.

**Envision It!** | Prefixes to Know

outfielder
out-

overgrown
prefix over-

midnight
prefix mid-

defrost
prefix de-

bicycle
prefix bi-

preschool
prefix pre-

READING STREET ONLINE
SOUND-SPELLING CARDS
www.ReadingStreet.com

**Phonics**

## Affixes: Prefixes pre-, mid-, over-, out-, bi-, de-

### Words I Can Blend

midway
preheated
decomposed
outweigh
overheard
bimonthly

### Sentences I Can Read

1. Midway through the recipe, I preheated the oven.

2. The decomposed leaves outweigh the freshly fallen leaves.

3. I overheard that our bimonthly meeting was canceled.

88

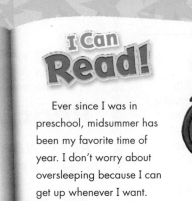

## I Can Read!

Ever since I was in preschool, midsummer has been my favorite time of year. I don't worry about oversleeping because I can get up whenever I want.

I ride my bicycle from midmorning through midafternoon. Mom calls me in at midday to eat lunch and drink some water. She wants to make sure I don't get dehydrated.

My biggest challenge is trying to outrun my dog when we race with each other. Mom says summer is when I outgrow most of my clothes. All that fresh air is good for me.

### You've learned

Prefixes pre-, mid-, over-, out-, bi-, de-

89

**Student Edition, pp. 88–89**

## Apply

**READ WORDS IN ISOLATION** After students can successfully combine the word parts to read the words on p. 88 in their Student Editions, point to words in random order and ask students to read them naturally.

**READ WORDS IN CONTEXT** Have students read each of the sentences on p. 88. Have them identify words in the sentences that have prefixes.

**Team Talk** Pair students and have them take turns reading each sentence aloud.

Chorally read the I Can Read! passage on p. 89 with students.

**ON THEIR OWN** For additional practice, use the *Reader's and Writer's Notebook*, p. 269.

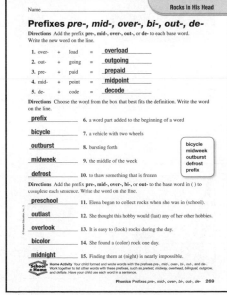

Name _____                    Rocks in His Head

**Prefixes pre-, mid-, over-, bi-, out-, de-**

Directions Add the prefix pre-, mid-, over-, out-, or de- to each base word. Write the new word on the line.

1. over- + load = overload
2. out- + going = outgoing
3. pre- + paid = prepaid
4. mid- + point = midpoint
5. de- + code = decode

Directions Choose the word from the box that best fits the definition. Write the word on the line.

prefix      6. a word part added to the beginning of a word
bicycle     7. a vehicle with two wheels
outburst    8. bursting forth
midweek     9. the middle of the week
defrost     10. to thaw something that is frozen

bicycle
midweek
outburst
defrost
prefix

Directions Add the prefix pre-, mid-, over-, bi-, or out- to the base word in ( ) to complete each sentence. Write the word on the line.

preschool   11. Elena began to collect rocks when she was in (school).
outlast     12. She thought this hobby would (last) any of her other hobbies.
overlook    13. It is easy to (look) rocks during the day.
bicolor     14. She found a (color) rock one day.
midnight    15. Finding them at (night) is nearly impossible.

School + Home Home Activity Your child formed and wrote words with the prefixes pre-, mid-, over-, bi-, out-, and de-. Work together to list other words with these prefixes, such as pretest, midway, overhead, bilingual, outgrow, and deflate. Have your child use each word in a sentence.

Phonics Prefixes pre-, mid-, over, bi-, out-, de-    269

Reader's and Writer's Notebook, p. 269

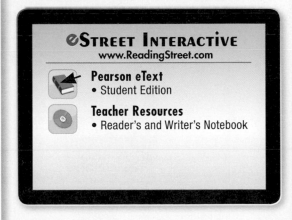

## eSTREET INTERACTIVE
www.ReadingStreet.com

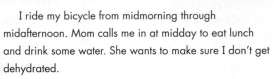

**Pearson eText**
• Student Edition

**Teacher Resources**
• Reader's and Writer's Notebook

## ELL

**Formal and Informal Language** Explain to students that all prefixes cannot be placed in front of all base words. To be sure that a prefix can be paired with a base word, tell students to check the word with the prefix in the dictionary.

**Contrastive Analysis Chart** See also the Contrastive Analysis Chart in *First Stop.*

*Rocks in His Head* **88–89**

# Decodable Reader 18A

If students need help, then…

## Read *Midsummer Fun*

**READ WORDS IN ISOLATION** Have students turn to p. 25 of *Decodable Practice Readers 3.2.* Have students read each word.

Have students read the high-frequency words *do, you, have, a, to, of, what, are, the, pull, into, two, water, your, ones, they,* and *want* on the first page.

**PREVIEW** Have students read the title and preview the story. Tell them that they will read words with the prefixes *pre-, mid-, over-, out-, bi-,* and *de-.*

**READ WORDS IN CONTEXT** Pair students for reading and listen as they read. One student begins. Students read the entire story, switching readers after each page. Partners reread the story. This time the other student begins.

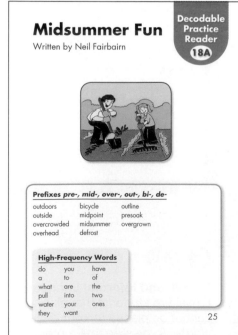

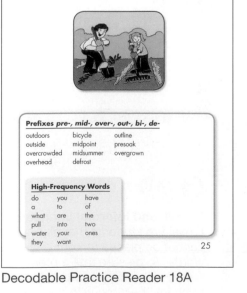

Decodable Practice Reader 18A

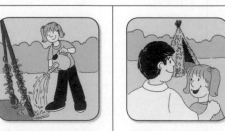

| Corrective feedback | **If...** students have difficulty decoding a word, **then...** refer them to the *Sound-Spelling Cards* to identify the word parts. Have them read the word parts individually and then together to say the word. |
|---|---|

- What is the new word?
- Is the new word a word you know?
- Does it make sense in the story?

**CHECK DECODING AND COMPREHENSION** Have students retell the story to include characters, setting, and events. Then have students find words in the story that have the prefixes *pre-*, *mid-*, *over-*, *out-*, *bi-*, and *de-*. Students should supply *outdoors, bicycle, outline, outside, midpoint, presoak, overcrowded, midsummer, overgrown, overhead,* and *defrost*.

# Reread for Fluency

**REREAD DECODABLE READER** Have students reread *Decodable Practice Reader 18A* to develop automaticity decoding words with prefixes.

**Routine** **Oral Rereading**

1. **Read** Have students read the entire book orally.

2. **Reread** To achieve optimal fluency, students should reread the text three or four times.

3. **Corrective Feedback** Listen as students read. Provide corrective feedback regarding their fluency and decoding.

Routines Flip Chart

**Leveled Support: Prefixes**

**Beginning** Write several words with prefixes from the *Decodable Practice Reader,* such as *outdoors, bicycle,* and *midsummer.* Point to each word as you say it aloud. Then cover the prefix in each word and have students read aloud the base word. Cover the base word and have students read aloud the prefix. Finally, have students read aloud the entire word with you.

**Intermediate** Write the prefixes *mid-, out-,* and *pre-* in one column and the words *way, soak, doors, read, point,* and *did* in a second column. Have students take turns drawing a line from a prefix to a base word to make the words *midway, presoak, outdoors, preread, midpoint,* and *outdid.*

**Advanced** After reading the story, have students choose four or five words with prefixes from the story. Have students write each word and draw a line between the prefix and the base word. Then have students write a sentence with the base word and another sentence with the entire word.

Zoom in on ⊙

### Common Core State Standards

**Informational Text 1.** Ask and answer questions to demonstrate understanding of a text, referring explicitly to the text as the basis for the answers. **Informational Text 3.** Describe the relationship between a series of historical events, scientific ideas or concepts, or steps in technical procedures in a text, using language that pertains to time, sequence, and cause/ effect. **Informational Text 6.** Distinguish their own point of view from that of the author of a text. **Foundational Skills 4.b.** Read on-level prose and poetry orally with accuracy, appropriate rate, and expression on successive readings.

## Skills Trace

⊙ **Fact and Opinion**

**Introduce** U4W3D1; U4W4D1; U6W1D1

**Practice** U1W4D2; U1W4D3; U4W3D2; U4W3D3; U4W4D2; U4W4D3; U6W1D2; U6W1D3; U6W3D3

**Reteach/Review** U4W3D5; U4W4D5; U6W1D5

**Assess/Test** Weekly Tests U4W3; U4W4; U6W1 Benchmark Tests U4

**KEY:** U=Unit  W=Week  D=Day

## Academic Vocabulary ⊙

**fact** a statement that can be proved true or false

**opinion** a statement of someone's judgment, belief, or way of thinking about something

## Comprehension Support

Students may also turn to pp. EI•7 and EI•20 to review the skill and strategy if necessary.

# Text-Based Comprehension

## ⊙ Fact and Opinion
## ⊙ Inferring

**READ** Remind students of the weekly concept—Unique Interests. Have students read "Looking at Rocks" on p. 91.

### MODEL A CLOSE READ

**Think Aloud** I see that the first paragraph of "Looking at Rocks" has a fact in the last line. Have students follow along as you read the first paragraph. I can check in a reference book to verify the information. The first sentence says that looking at rocks is fun and interesting. I know that people don't agree on what is fun or interesting, so this is an opinion. When I read in the text that scientists study rocks to learn about people from long ago, I didn't understand. But then I realized that the author was referring to archaeologists, who dig up places where people once lived. They might find rocks that people used to make things, which would teach the scientists about those people.

**TEACH** Have students read p. 90. Explain that the skill of fact and opinion and the strategy of inferring are tools they can use to better understand a text. Review the bulleted items and explanations on p. 90. Then have students use a graphic organizer like the one on p. 90 and draw conclusions about statements of fact and opinion from the passage.

**GUIDE PRACTICE** Have students reread "Looking at Rocks" using the callouts as guides. Then ask volunteers to respond to the questions in the callouts, citing specific examples from the text to support their answers.

**Skill** Looking at rocks is fun and interesting; *fun, interesting*
**Strategy** by telling them which rocks work better than others.

**APPLY** Use *Reader's and Writer's Notebook,* p. 270 for additional practice with fact and opinion.

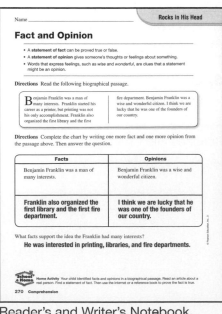

Reader's and Writer's Notebook, p. 270

Common Core State Standards
Informational Text 1. Ask and answer questions to demonstrate understanding of a text, referring explicitly to the text as the basis for the answers.

**Envision It!** Skill Strategy

**Skill**

Fact and Opinion

**Strategy**

Inferring

READING STREET ONLINE
ENVISION IT! ANIMATIONS
www.ReadingStreet.com

**Comprehension Skill**

## 🎯 Fact and Opinion

- A statement of fact can be proved true or false.

- A statement of opinion gives someone's thoughts or feelings about something. An opinion cannot be proved true or false.

- Use what you learned about fact and opinion and the chart below as you read "Looking at Rocks." Then choose one fact from your chart. Use a reference source to prove the statement of fact true or false.

| Facts | Opinions |
|-------|----------|
|       |          |
|       |          |

**Comprehension Strategy**

## 🎯 Inferring

When you infer, you combine your background knowledge with ideas in the text to come up with your own idea about what the author is trying to present. Active readers infer the ideas, morals, lessons, and themes of a written work.

# LOOKING AT ROCKS

Looking at rocks is fun and interesting. Some rocks look the same all over. They are made of one thing. However, most rocks do not look the same all over. Some have different colors. Some have sparkles. Others have shiny spots. The colors and sparkles and shine come from the different materials mixed together in the rock.

**Skill** What opinion is expressed in this paragraph? What words tell you that it is an opinion?

If you like looking at rocks, you can get a job working with rocks when you grow up. Some scientists look at rocks to find out about people from long ago. Other scientists look at rocks to find oil. Some rock scientists help builders make buildings safe. Others try to predict when an earthquake will happen or a volcano will erupt.

**Strategy** How do you think rock scientists can help builders make safe buildings?

Rocks can tell us many things. Take a look!

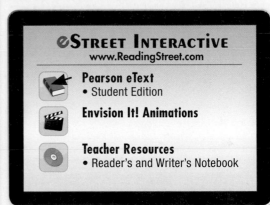

**Your Turn!**

⏸ **Need a Review?** See the *Envision It! Handbook* for help with fact and opinion and inferring.

▶ **Ready to Try It?** As you read *Rocks in His Head*, use what you've learned about fact and opinion and inferring to understand the text.

90

91

**Student Edition, pp. 90–91**

# Model Fluent Reading

**EXPRESSION** Have students listen as you read paragraph 1 of "Looking at Rocks" with appropriate expression. Explain that you will adjust your voice level to stress important words and phrases.

**Routine** Oral Rereading

1. **Read** Have students read paragraph 1 of "Looking at Rocks" orally.

2. **Reread** To achieve optimal fluency, students should reread the text three or four times.

3. **Corrective Feedback** Have students read aloud without you. Provide feedback about their expression and encourage them to adjust their voice level to stress important words and phrases. Listen for use of appropriate expression. To achieve optimal fluency, students should reread the text three to four times.

Routines Flip Chart

**eSTREET INTERACTIVE**
www.ReadingStreet.com

**Pearson eText**
- Student Edition

**Envision It! Animations**

**Teacher Resources**
- Reader's and Writer's Notebook

 **Common Core State Standards**

**Foundational Skills 4.** Read with sufficient accuracy and fluency to support comprehension. **Writing 7.** Conduct short research projects that build knowledge about a topic. **Language 4.** Determine or clarify the meaning of unknown and multiple-meaning words and phrases based on grade 3 reading and content, choosing flexibly from a range of strategies. **Language 4.a.** Use sentence-level context as a clue to the meaning of a word or phrase. **Also Language 5., 6.**

# Selection Vocabulary

Use the following routine to introduce this week's tested selection vocabulary.

> **attic** the space in a house just below the roof and above the other rooms
>
> **board** a group of people who manage something
>
> **chores** small tasks or easy jobs that you have to do regularly
>
> **customer** someone who buys goods or services
>
> **labeled** put or wrote a label on something
>
> **spare** extra
>
> **stamps** small pieces of paper with glue on the back for mailing letters and packages

**SEE IT/SAY IT** Write *customer.* Scan across the word with your finger as you say it: *cus-to-mer.*

**HEAR IT** Use the word in a sentence. The *customer* had to stand in line a long time.

**DEFINE IT** Elicit definitions from students. How would you describe to another student what *customer* means? Clarify or give a definition when necessary. Yes, it means "someone who buys things or services." Restate the meaning of the word in student-friendly terms. So, *customer* means a person who buys something.

**Team Talk** Is it important to be a smart *customer?* Turn and talk to your partner about this. Be prepared to explain your answer. Allow students time to discuss. Ask for examples. Rephrase their examples for usage when necessary or to correct misunderstandings.

**MAKE CONNECTIONS** Have students discuss the word. Have you ever been a *customer?* Turn and talk to your partner about this. Then be prepared to share. Have students share. Rephrase their ideas for usage when necessary or to correct misunderstandings.

**RECORD** Have students write the word and its meaning.

Continue this routine to introduce the remaining words in this manner.

> **Corrective feedback** | **If...** students are having difficulty understanding, **then...** review the definitions in small groups.

# Research and Inquiry

## Step 1 Identify and Focus Topic

**TEACH** Discuss the Question of the Week: *Why is it valuable to have unique interests?* Tell students they will research some unique interests and why they are valuable. They will present their informational articles to the class on Day 5.

**Think Aloud** **MODEL** I'll start by brainstorming a list of questions about unique interests. I have read many biographies, or stories of people's lives that are written by other people, that feature people with many different interests. My own unique interest is playing the guitar, so I'll choose that as my topic for research. Some possible questions could be *Is learning to play a musical instrument, such as a guitar, a valuable interest for someone to pursue? Is it difficult to learn to play the guitar? What makes playing the guitar enjoyable?*

**GUIDE PRACTICE** After students have brainstormed inquiry questions, explain that tomorrow they will conduct online research using their questions. Help students identify keywords that will help their search.

**ON THEIR OWN** Have students work individually, in pairs, or in small groups to write an inquiry question.

---

## 21st Century Skills
**Internet Guy** *Don Leu*

**Weekly Inquiry Project**

| STEP 1 | Identify and Focus Topic |
|--------|--------------------------|
| STEP 2 | Navigate/Search |
| STEP 3 | Analyze Information |
| STEP 4 | Synthesize |
| STEP 5 | Communicate |

## Academic Vocabulary

**biography** a story of a real person's life, written by another person

 **ELL**

**Multilingual Vocabulary** Students can apply knowledge of their home languages to acquire new English vocabulary by using the Multilingual Vocabulary Lists (*ELL Handbook,* pp. 433–444).

**ELL**

**If...** students need more scaffolding and practice with **Vocabulary, then...** use the activities on pp. DI•67–DI•68 in the Teacher Resources section on SuccessNet.

---

| **Day 1** | **SMALL GROUP TIME • Differentiate Vocabulary, p. SG•33** |
|-----------|-----------------------------------------------------------|

| **OL On-Level** | **SI Strategic Intervention** | **A Advanced** |
|-----------------|-------------------------------|----------------|
| • **Practice Vocabulary** Amazing Words | • **Reteach Vocabulary** Amazing Words | • **Extend Vocabulary** Amazing Words |
| • **Read** *Reading Street Sleuth,* pp. 48–49 | • **Read** *Reading Street Sleuth,* pp. 48–49 | • **Read** *Reading Street Sleuth,* pp. 48–49 |
| | | • **Introduce** Inquiry Project |

**Common Core State Standards**

**Language 1.a.** Explain the function of nouns, pronouns, verbs, adjectives, and adverbs in general and their functions in particular sentences.

**Language 2.f.** Use spelling patterns and generalizations (e.g., word families, position-based spellings, syllable patterns, ending rules, meaningful word parts) in writing words.

# Spelling Pretest

## Prefixes *pre-, mid-, over-, out-*

**INTRODUCE** Tell students to think of words with prefixes, such as *pre-* (preview), *mid-* (midway), *over-* (overthrow), and *out-* (outlast).

**PRETEST** Say each word, read the sentence, and repeat the word.

| | | |
|---|---|---|
| 1. | **prepaid** | Avoid box office lines with **prepaid** theater tickets. |
| 2. | **midnight** | It's 11:58 p.m., two minutes to **midnight.** |
| 3. | **overflow** | Don't let the bathtub **overflow.** |
| 4. | **outdoors** | We go **outdoors** to ride our bikes. |
| 5. | **outline** | Draw the **outline** of the picture first. |
| 6. | **overgrown** | The garden is **overgrown** with weeds. |
| 7. | **prefix** | A **prefix** is part of a word. |
| 8. | **Midwest** | Sarah lives in the **Midwest.** |
| 9. | **pretest** | Use today's **pretest** to study for the test. |
| 10. | **midpoint** | Mark the **midpoint** of the line. |
| 11. | **outgoing** | My friend is very friendly and **outgoing.** |
| 12. | **overtime** | Dad has to work **overtime.** |
| 13. | **overdue** | The library books are **overdue.** |
| 14. | **outside** | I ride my bike **outside** in the park. |
| 15. | **outfield** | The player in the **outfield** caught the ball. |

### Challenge words

| | | |
|---|---|---|
| 16. | **precaution** | Hank approached the cliff's edge with **precaution.** |
| 17. | **prediction** | We did not believe the fortune teller's **prediction.** |
| 18. | **midsection** | Your belly button is at the **midsection** of your body. |
| 19. | **overweight** | That fat dog is **overweight.** |
| 20. | **prehistoric** | The scientist studied **prehistoric** dinosaur bones. |

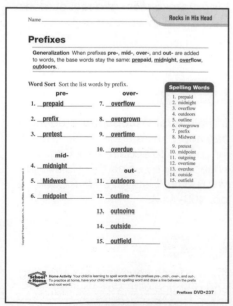

Let's Practice It! TR DVD•237

**SELF-CORRECT** Have students self-correct their pretests by rewriting misspelled words.

**ON THEIR OWN** Use *Let's Practice It!* page 237 on the *Teacher Resources DVD-ROM.*

# Conventions

## Possessive Pronouns

**MAKE CONNECTIONS** Have volunteers write sentences that describe their pets on the board. After completing this activity, have students identify any possessive pronouns in the sentences.

**TEACH** Display Grammar Transparency 18, and read aloud the explanation and examples in the box. Point out the possessive pronouns, *your* and *mine,* in the sample sentence.

**MODEL** Model writing the correct form of the possessive pronoun to complete numbers 1 and 2. Explain that you look for the word that shows ownership to identify possessive pronouns.

**GUIDE PRACTICE** Guide students to complete items 3–5. Record the correct responses on the transparency.

**APPLY** Have students read sentences 6–9 on the transparency and replace the underlined words with a possessive pronoun to rewrite each sentence.

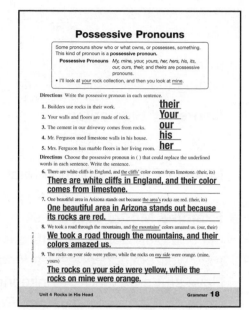

### Possessive Pronouns

Some pronouns show who or what owns, or possesses, something. This kind of pronoun is a **possessive pronoun.**

**Possessive Pronouns** *My, mine, your, yours, her, hers, his, its, our, ours, their,* and *theirs* are possessive pronouns.

• I'll look at your rock collection, and then you look at mine.

**Directions** Write the possessive pronoun in each sentence.

1. Builders use rocks in their work.  **their**
2. Your walls and floors are made of rock.  **Your**
3. The cement in our driveway comes from rocks.  **our**
4. Mr. Ferguson used limestone walls in his house.  **his**
5. Mrs. Ferguson has marble floors in her living room.  **her**

**Directions** Choose the possessive pronoun in ( ) that could replace the underlined words in each sentence. Write the sentence.

6. There are white cliffs in England, and the cliffs' color comes from limestone. (their, its)
   **There are white cliffs in England, and their color comes from limestone.**
7. One beautiful area in Arizona stands out because the area's rocks are red. (their, its)
   **One beautiful area in Arizona stands out because its rocks are red.**
8. We took a road through the mountains, and the mountains' colors amazed us. (our, their)
   **We took a road through the mountains, and their colors amazed us.**
9. The rocks on your side were yellow, while the rocks on my side were orange. (mine, yours)
   **The rocks on your side were yellow, while the rocks on mine were orange.**

Unit 4 Rocks in His Head                Grammar **18**

Grammar Transparency 18, TR DVD

# Handwriting

**MODEL LETTER FORMATION AND SIZE** Display lowercase cursive letters *v* and *z.* Follow the stroke instructions pictured to model letter formation.

Explain that writing legibly means letters are the correct size, cursive strokes are joined together, and there is correct spacing between letters and words. The descenders touch the line below and sidestrokes are correct. Model writing this sentence with proper letter size and joining strokes: *Zach and Vera drive their van to the zoo.* Point out how sidestrokes change the beginning stroke of the following letter.

**GUIDE PRACTICE** Have students write these phrases: *invite a zebra, veer and zigzag.* Circulate around the room, guiding students.

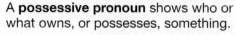

## Daily Fix-It

1. Colin and him find rocks in many places out doors. *(he; outdoors)*
2. The rocks in my poket has gold flecks. *(pocket, have)*

## Academic Vocabulary

A **possessive pronoun** shows who or what owns, or possesses, something.

**Language Production: Possessive Pronouns** Hold up a common classroom item, such as a pen, and identify it as *my pen.* Then pass the pen and call on students to repeat these phrases: *his pen, her pen, their pen, our pen.* Write each phrase and ask volunteers to underline the possessive pronoun and read it aloud.

**Handwriting** To provide practice in handwriting *v* and *z* and to extend language opportunities, have students complete the following sentence frame by naming their favorite zoo animals: *I like to visit the _____ when I visit the zoo.*

## Common Core State Standards

**Writing 2.** Write informative/ explanatory texts to examine a topic and convey ideas and information clearly. **Writing 2.a.** Introduce a topic and group related information together; include illustrations when useful to aiding comprehension.

## Bridge to Common Core

### TEXT TYPES AND PURPOSES

**Biography**

This week students write a biography of someone who has unique interests.

**Informative/Explanatory Writing**

Through reading and discussion, students will gain a deeper understanding of why it is valuable to have unique interests. They will use this knowledge from the texts to write and support a biography.

Through the week, students will improve their range and content of writing through daily mini-lessons.

### 5-Day Plan

| DAY 1 | Read Like a Writer |
|---|---|
| DAY 2 | Developing a Story Sequence Chart |
| DAY 3 | Writing Trait: Sentences |
| DAY 4 | Revise: Consolidating |
| DAY 5 | Proofread for Possessive Pronouns |

**Write Guy** *by Jeff Anderson*

**Details, Details**

Ask students to notice details in mentor text—but not just any details. Rather than pointing out many details, select a detail that is beyond the obvious. With guidance, students can learn how to include *details that matter* rather than obvious details or simply longer and longer lists of details.

# Writing

## Biography

**Mini-Lesson** | **Read Like a Writer**

■ **Introduce** This week you will write a biography. A biography is nonfiction writing that tells about the life of a real person.

**Genre**     Biography

**Trait**     Sentences

**Mode**     Expository/Informative/Explanatory

■ **Examine Model Text** Let's read an example of a biography that introduces us to a man who collects one-of-a-kind bicycles. Have students read "A Tinkering Man's Collection" on p. 271 of their *Reader's and Writer's Notebook*.

■ **Key Features** Find the person this biography tells about and circle his or her name. Point out that biographies use words such as *he* or *she*. Tell students to underline examples of *he* in each paragraph and tell who this pronoun represents. (Uncle Stefan)

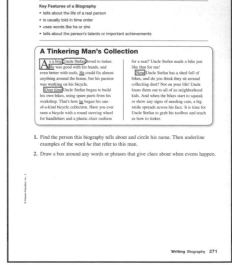

Reader's and Writer's Notebook, p. 271

Events in a biography are usually told in time order. Direct students to the start of each paragraph and have them draw a box around any words or phrases that give clues about time order.

Biographies tell about a person's talents or achievements. What talent does Uncle Stefan have? (He tinkers.) Have students summarize what Uncle Stefan achieved with this talent.

## Review Key Features

Review the key features of a biography with students. You may want to post the key features in the classroom for students to refer to as they work on their compositions.

**Key Features of a Biography**
- tells about the life of a real person
- is usually told in time order
- uses words such as *he* or *she*
- tells about the person's talents or important achievements

**Routine** | **Quick Write for Fluency** | **Team Talk**

**1. Talk** Have pairs discuss the key features of a biography.

**2. Write** Each student writes a few sentences defining a biography.

**3. Share** Partners read their sentences aloud to one another.

Routines Flip Chart

**ELL**

**Examine the Model** Read the writing model aloud and help students understand it. Point out that this model is a biography, which means it tells about the life of a real person and about events that really happened. Have students work in groups. Ask each student to name a friend or family member who collects something. Then ask the student to dictate a sentence about this person's collection. Call on group members to summarize what they have heard.

# Wrap Up Your Day!

✔ **Content Knowledge** Reread "Street Rhymes!" on p. 86j to students. Ask them what they learned this week about having unique interests.

✔ **Oral Vocabulary** Have students use the Amazing Words they learned in context sentences.

✔ **Homework** Send home this week's Family Times newsletter on *Let's Practice It!* pp. 238–239 on the *Teacher Resources DVD-ROM*.

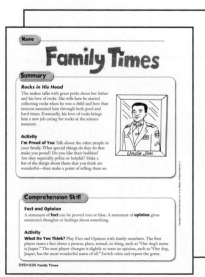

Let's Practice It!
TR DVD•238–239

Preview
DAY 2

Tell students that tomorrow they will read about a rock collector.

### Materials

- Student Edition
- Reader's and Writer's Notebook

© **Common Core State Standards**

**Foundational Skills 3.** Know and apply grade-level phonics and word analysis skills in decoding words.
**Language 6.** Acquire and use accurately grade-appropriate conversational, general academic, and domain-specific words and phrases, including those that signal spatial and temporal relationships (e.g., *After dinner that night we went looking for them*).

# Content Knowledge

## Unique Interests

**EXPAND THE CONCEPT** Remind students of the weekly concept question, *Why is it valuable to have unique interests?* Tell students that today they will begin reading *Rocks in His Head.* As they read, encourage students to think about why it is valuable for people to have unique interests.

## Build Oral Language

**TALK ABOUT SENTENCES AND WORDS** Reread a sentence from the Read Aloud, "Picture Perfect."

*Sammy laughed at the hilarious picture. And voilà! A hobby was born.*

- What does *hobby* mean? (a favorite thing one likes to do)
- What does "A hobby was born" mean? (started a new hobby)
- Why does the author tell us that "Sammy laughed at the hilarious picture"? (to show that Sammy started the hobby because taking pictures was fun)

**Team Talk** Have students turn to a partner and discuss the following question. Then ask them to share their responses.

- What is the shortest version of these sentences you can make without changing the basic meaning? (Possible response: A hobby was born when Sammy laughed at the picture.)

# Build Oral Vocabulary

## Amazing Words  Robust Vocabulary Routine

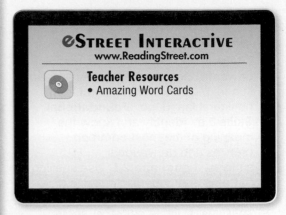
1. **Introduce** Write the Amazing Word *ancestor* on the board. Have students say it aloud with you. Relate *ancestor* to the photographs on pp. 86–87 and "Picture Perfect." The girls are putting pictures of their *ancestors* in a scrapbook. Who might some of these *ancestors* be? (grandparents, parents) Who is Sammy's *ancestor*? (his grandfather) Have students determine the definition of the word *ancestor*. (An *ancestor* is a relative from a past time.)

2. **Demonstrate** Have students answer questions to demonstrate understanding. Is your great-grandmother your *ancestor*? (yes) Is your father's best friend your *ancestor*? (no) Can your brother or sister be your *ancestor*? (no)

3. **Apply** Have students apply their understanding. If you and an *ancestor* were together, which of you would be older? (the ancestor)

4. **Display the Word** Write *ancestor* on the board. Run your hand under the syllables *an-ces-tor* as you read the word.

Routines Flip Chart

## Amazing Words

| | |
|---|---|
| hobby | ornament |
| project | descendant |
| leftover | forge |
| murmur | compartment |
| ancestor | |

**ADD TO THE CONCEPT MAP** Use the photos on pp. 86–87 and the Read Aloud, "Picture Perfect," to discuss why unique interests are valuable and to talk about the Amazing Words *hobby, murmur, project,* and *leftover.* Add these and other concept-related words to the concept map to develop students' knowledge of the topic. Discuss the photos and vocabulary to generate questions about the topic.

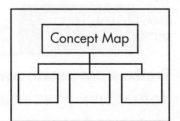

Concept Map

• What *hobby* interests you?

• What might you *murmur* to an artist whose *project* you admire?

• What might be the unique interest of someone who knows how to create a wonderful dinner from *leftover* food?

**Reinforce Vocabulary** Use the Day 2 instruction on ELL Poster 18 to teach lesson vocabulary and the lesson concept.

**Common Core State Standards**

**Literature 4.** Determine the meaning of words and phrases as they are used in a text, distinguishing literal from nonliteral language. **Foundational Skills 3.a.** Identify and know the meaning of the most common prefixes and derivational suffixes. **Language 2.f.** Use spelling patterns and generalizations (e.g., word families, position-based spellings, syllable patterns, ending rules, meaningful word parts) in writing words.

# Word Analysis

## Prefixes *pre-, mid-, over-, out-, bi-, de-*

**REVIEW** Review the prefixes *pre-, mid-, over-, out-, bi-,* and *de-,* pointing out that prefixes are added to the beginning of base words.

**READ WORDS IN ISOLATION** Display these words. Have the class read the words. Then point to the words in random order and ask students to read them quickly.

| | | | |
|---|---|---|---|
| outdid | overjoyed | biweekly | derail |
| preview | midway | outcast | preheat |

**Corrective feedback** | Model blending decodable words and then ask students to blend them with you.

**READ WORDS IN CONTEXT** Display these sentences. Have the class read the sentences.

**Team Talk** Have pairs take turns reading the sentences naturally.

Kate played **outfield** in the **preseason** games.

Layla **departed** for school on her **bicycle.**

Chris was **overcome** by the heat at the **midpoint** of the race.

 Don't Wait Until Friday

**MONITOR PROGRESS** Check Word Reading

Prefixes *pre-, mid-, over-, out-, bi-, de-*

**FORMATIVE ASSESSMENT** Write the following words and have the class read them. Notice which words students miss during the group reading. Call on individuals to read some of the words.

| history | happy | turn | fiction | **Spiral Review** |
|---|---|---|---|---|
| prehistory | unhappy | return | nonfiction ← | Row 2 reviews words with prefixes *pre-, un-, re-, non-*. |
| prehistoric | unhappily | returnable | nonfictional ← | Row 3 contrasts words with prefixes and suffixes. |

**If...** students cannot read words with prefixes at this point,

**then...** use the Day 1 Word Analysis lesson on p. 88a to reteach prefixes. Use words from the *Decodable Practice Passages* (or Reader). Continue to monitor students' progress using other instructional opportunities during the week. See the Skills Trace on p. 88a.

# Literary Terms

## Idioms

**TEACH** Tell students that an idiom is a playful use of language that is frequently found in both fiction and nonfiction. An idiom is a figure of speech that contains more than one word and that has a meaning and a use totally its own. The literal meanings of the words do not explain the meaning of the expression.

**Think Aloud** **MODEL** Let's look at "More Than a Hobby" on p. 93. The fourth paragraph ends with the statement *You are on your way.* What does the idiom "on your way" mean? **(becoming successful)** You have to learn the meaning of idioms; they usually can't be figured out by using the literal meanings of the words in the expression.

**GUIDE PRACTICE** Find an example of an idiom in *Rocks in His Head*. Explain what the idiom means.

**ON THEIR OWN** Have students look for examples of idioms in other selections in their Student Edition.

**eStreet Interactive**
www.ReadingStreet.com

**Pearson eText**
• Student Edition

## Academic Vocabulary

**idiom** a figure of speech that has a meaning separate from the literal meaning of the expression

**problem and solution** a text pattern that shows the development of a problem and one or more solutions to the problem

**Common Core State Standards**

**Foundational Skills 4.b.** Read on-level prose and poetry orally with accuracy, appropriate rate, and expression on successive readings. **Language 4.** Determine or clarify the meaning of unknown and multiple-meaning words and phrases based on grade 3 reading and content, choosing flexibly from a range of strategies. **Language 4.a.** Use sentence-level context as a clue to the meaning of a word or phrase.

## Selection Vocabulary

**attic** the space in a house just below the roof and above the other rooms

**board** a group of people who manage something

**chores** small tasks or easy jobs that you have to do regularly

**customer** someone who buys goods or services

**labeled** put or wrote a label on something

**spare** extra

**stamps** small pieces of paper with glue on the back for mailing letters and packages

 **Bridge to Common Core**

### VOCABULARY ACQUISITION AND USE

Students can determine or clarify the meanings of unfamiliar words by using context clues, which enables them to acquire a broad range of general academic and domain-specific words. By consulting a dictionary or glossary to clarify definitions, they demonstrate the ability to gather vocabulary knowledge on their own.

## Selection Vocabulary

Refer students to *Words!* on p. W•10 in the Student Edition for additional practice.

# Vocabulary Skill

## 🎯 Multiple-Meaning Words

**READ** Have students read "More Than a Hobby" on p. 93. Use the vocabulary skill and strategy as tools to build comprehension.

**TEACH CONTEXT CLUES** Tell students that when they encounter a multiple-meaning word, they should use context clues to determine the meaning. Explain how context clues can help students determine the correct meaning of a multiple-meaning word.

*Think Aloud* **MODEL** Write on the board: *My father replaced the flat tire on our car with the spare tire that he keeps in the trunk.* I know that *spare* can mean "thin," but this meaning doesn't make sense in the sentence. The meaning "extra" does make sense, though, so in this sentence, *spare* means "extra," or "ready when needed."

**GUIDE PRACTICE** Write this sentence on the board: *There are so many stamps on the envelope that there's hardly any space to write the address.* Have students determine the meaning of *stamps* using context clues. For additional support, use the *Envision It! Pictured Vocabulary Cards* or *Tested Vocabulary Cards.*

**ON THEIR OWN** Reread "More Than a Hobby" on p. 93. Have students use context clues to list the definitions for the lesson vocabulary. For additional practice, use *Reader's and Writer's Notebook,* p. 272.

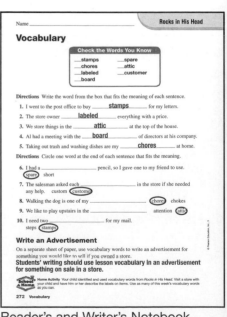

Reader's and Writer's Notebook, p. 272

Common Core State Standards
Language 4.a. Use sentence-level context as a clue to the meaning of a word or phrase. Also Language 4.

## Envision It! Words to Know

chores

labeled

stamps

attic
board
customer
spare

**READING STREET ONLINE
VOCABULARY ACTIVITIES**
www.ReadingStreet.com

### Vocabulary Strategy for
## 🎯 Multiple-Meaning Words

**Context Clues** You may read a word you know but whose meaning does not make sense in the sentence. The word may have more than one meaning. For example, *bug* means "an insect" and "to annoy."

**1.** Try the meaning of the word that you know. Does it make sense in the sentence?

**2.** If it does not make sense, perhaps it has another meaning. Can you figure out another meaning from the context?

**3.** Try the new meaning in the sentence. Does it make sense?

Read "More Than a Hobby" on page 93. Look for words that might have more than one meaning. Remember to use nearby words to figure out the correct meaning.

**Words to Write** Reread "More Than a Hobby." What kind of shop would you like to open? Write about your shop. Use words from the Words to Know list in your answer.

## More Than a Hobby

It starts out as a hobby. As a child, you collect stamps or toy cars or rocks. At first, collecting is an activity you do in your spare time or after doing your chores.

Perhaps you collect a few rocks here and a few rocks there. Then one day you realize that the shelves in your room are bulging with rocks. So you move them to the basement or the attic where there is more space.

As you get older, you learn more about rocks, and you talk with other rock collectors. You begin to think *Maybe this isn't just a hobby.*

*Could it be a business?*

So you open a rock shop. Every rock in the shop is labeled with information about the rock and how much it costs. This really impresses your very first customer, so he buys several rocks. You are on your way.

Over time, your small business grows large, and you become the chairman of the board. And it all started with a hobby.

### Your Turn!

⏸ **Need a Review?** For additional help with context clues and multiple-meaning words, see *Words!*

▶ **Ready to Try It?** Read *Rocks in His Head* on pp. 94–105.

92

93

**Student Edition, pp. 92–93**

---

# Reread for Fluency

**EXPRESSION** Read paragraph 3 of "More Than a Hobby" aloud, keeping your expression slow and steady and using changes of voice level for emphasis. Use a rising pitch to emphasize the question. Tell students that you are reading the passage with expression, paying special attention to new vocabulary.

### Routine | Oral Rereading

1. **Read** Have students read paragraph 3 of "More Than a Hobby" orally.

2. **Reread** To achieve optimal fluency, students should reread the text three or four times.

3. **Corrective Feedback** Have students read aloud without you. Provide feedback about their expression and encourage them to adjust their pitch for the appropriate expression. Have students reread three to four times.

Routines Flip Chart

### eStreet Interactive
www.ReadingStreet.com

**Pearson eText**
• Student Edition

**Vocabulary Activities**

**Journal**

**Teacher Resources**
• Envision It! Pictured Vocabulary Cards
• Tested Vocabulary Cards
• Reader's and Writer's Notebook

Zoom in on ©

## © Common Core State Standards

**Foundational Skills 3.** Know and apply grade-level phonics and word analysis skills in decoding words. **Foundational Skills 4.a.** Read on-level text with purpose and understanding. **Language 6.** Acquire and use accurately grade-appropriate conversational, general academic, and domain-specific words and phrases, including those that signal spatial and temporal relationships (e.g., *After dinner that night we went looking for them*).

## © Bridge to Common Core

### CRAFT AND STRUCTURE

Students analyze the structure of the selection and how its components relate to each other and the whole when they examine its genre. As they set a purpose for reading and preview the selection, they come to see how point of view shapes the content and style of the text.

### Academic Vocabulary ©

**biography** nonfiction writing that tells the story of a real person's life

### Strategy Response Log

Have students use the Strategy Response Log on p. 24 in the *Reader's and Writer's Notebook* to review the characteristics of biographies. As they read, have them look for characteristics of the genre.

# Text-Based Comprehension

## Introduce Main Selection

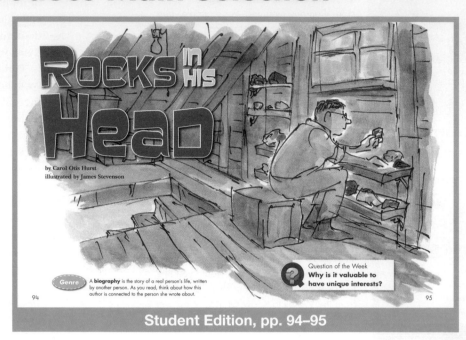

Student Edition, pp. 94–95

**GENRE** Explain that a **biography** tells the story of a real person's life, talents, or achievements. The story is usually told in chronological order. An autobiography is written by the person whose life is described and uses words such as *I* and *me*. A biography is written by someone else and uses words such as *he, she, him,* and *her.*

**PREVIEW AND PREDICT** Have students preview the title and the illustrations in *Rocks in His Head.* Ask them to predict what they think the selection will be about as they read.

**PURPOSE** By analyzing *Rocks in His Head,* an expository text, students will gain knowledge of why it is valuable to have unique interests.

# Access Main Selection

| READER AND TASK SUGGESTIONS | |
|---|---|
| **Preparing to Read the Text** | **Leveled Tasks** |
| • Review strategies for understanding multiple-meaning words.<br>• Discuss the features of a biography.<br>• Remind students to adjust their reading rate as needed when they encounter unfamiliar concepts and vocabulary. | • **Levels of Meaning • Analysis** If students don't understand the double meaning of the phrase "rocks in his head," have them use context clues from the first paragraph on p. 101 to understand one nonliteral meaning.<br>• **Language Conventionality and Clarity** Students may find the natural, conversational language of the selection easy to follow. Have students identify quotes from the text that give clues to the personality of the main character. |

See Text Complexity Measures for *Rocks in His Head* on the tab at the beginning of this week.

**READ** Tell students that today they will read *Rocks in His Head* for the first time. Use the Read for Understanding routine.

**Routine** **Read for Understanding**

Deepen understanding by reading the selection multiple times.

1. **First Read**—If students need support, use the **Access Text** notes to help them clarify understanding.

2. **Second Read**—Use the **Close Reading** notes to help students draw knowledge from the text.

## Access for All

**SI** Strategic Intervention

Work with students to set a purpose for reading, or if time permits, have students work with partners to set purposes.

**A** Advanced

Have students investigate different ways people might pursue the hobby of rock collecting. Have them report their findings to the class.

 **ELL**

**Build Background** To build background, review the selection summary in English (*ELL Handbook*, p. 133). Use the Retelling Cards to provide visual support for the summary.

**Day 2** **SMALL GROUP TIME • Differentiate Comprehension, p. SG•33**

| **OL** On-Level | **SI** Strategic Intervention | **A** Advanced |
|---|---|---|
| • **Practice** Selection Vocabulary<br>• **Read** *Rocks in His Head* | • **Reteach** Selection Vocabulary<br>• **Read** *Rocks in His Head* | • **Extend** Selection Vocabulary<br>• **Read** *Rocks in His Head*<br>• **Investigate** Inquiry Project |

 **ELL**

**If...** students need more scaffolding and practice with the **Comprehension Skill, then...** use the activities on p. DI•71 in the Teacher Resources section on SuccessNet.

## Access Text © If students need help, then...

**⊙ FACT AND OPINION** Write these sentences on the board. Have students determine which is a fact and which is an opinion: *They called the station the Antler Filling Station.* (fact) *I've got rocks in my head, I guess.* (opinion)

**(Think Aloud) MODEL** I can check whether the first sentence is a fact by looking it up in local records. It is a fact because it can be proved true or false.

The word *guess* in the second sentence tells me that it's an opinion. An opinion is someone's judgment or belief. It cannot be proved true or false.

**ON THEIR OWN** Have students reread pp. 96–97 to find more statements of fact. For additional practice, see *Let's Practice It!* p. 240 on the *Teacher Resources DVD-ROM.*

## Close Reading ©

**CONTEXT CLUES • TEXT EVIDENCE**
Use context clues to figure out the meaning of the word *quarries* on p. 96, paragraph 1. (The narrator says his father walked around old quarries when he was looking for rocks. *Quarries,* then, must be places in the landscape that are filled with rocks, like mines, or pits where workers dig out valuable minerals. That definition works in the sentence.)

Some people collect stamps. Some people collect coins or dolls or bottle caps. When he was a boy, my father collected rocks. When he wasn't doing chores at home or learning at school, he'd walk along stone walls and around old quarries, looking for rocks. People said he had rocks in his pockets and rocks in his head. He didn't mind. It was usually true.

When people asked what he wanted to be when he grew up, he'd say, "Something to do with rocks, I think."

"There's no money in rocks," someone said.

"Probably not," said my father.

When he grew up, my father decided to open a gas station. (People called them filling stations then.) My grandfather helped him build one on Armory Street in Springfield, Massachusetts.

They called the station the Antler Filling Station. My father carefully painted the name right over the doorway.

Inside the filling station was a desk with a cash drawer (which my father usually forgot to lock) and a table for his chess set.

96

**Student Edition, p. 96**

**DEVELOP LANGUAGE** Have students reread the third paragraph on page 97. *What are minerals? Where might you expect to find minerals?*

My father built narrow wooden shelves on the back wall and painted them white. People said, "What are those shelves for?"

He said, "I've got rocks in my head, I guess."

Then, one by one, he placed his rocks and minerals on those shelves. He carefully labeled each rock to show what kind it was and where it had come from.

In those days lots of rich people had automobiles, but then Henry Ford came out with the Model T.

That was a car many people could afford. My father had taken one apart and put it back together again and again until he knew every inch of the Model T. He thought that anyone who had spare parts for the Model T and could repair it so that it drove like new would do a good business. He bought some parts from dealers and found some parts in junkyards.

97

**Student Edition, p. 97**

**INFERENCE** When the father was young, he wanted a job that had "something to do with rocks," but when he grew up, he opened a gas station. *What does this tell you about the father's decision about his career?* (The father probably realized that he couldn't support a family by collecting rocks. He based his choice on what was most practical.)

---

 **Common Core State Standards**

**Informational Text 1.** Ask and answer questions to demonstrate understanding of a text, referring explicitly to the text as the basis for the answers. **Informational Text 3.** Describe the relationship between a series of historical events, scientific ideas or concepts, or steps in technical procedures in a text, using language that pertains to time, sequence, and cause/effect. **Language 4.** Determine or clarify the meaning of unknown and multiple-meaning words and phrases based on grade 3 reading and content, choosing flexibly from a range of strategies. **Also Informational Text 6., Language 5.a.**

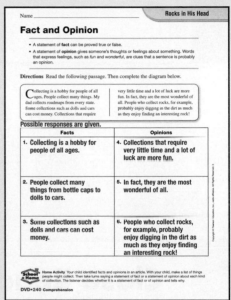

Let's Practice It! TR DVD•240

 **Connect to Social Studies**

**From Hobby to Career** How do the people who say, "I love my job" find this out? An enjoyable way to try out an interest is to take it on as a hobby. Students who love learning about rocks, earth science, or the environment, for example, can turn an interest into a career as a geologist, a researcher, or "green" designer.

**Idioms** Explain that the expression *rocks in his head* means "he has no common sense." Ask when students might use this idiom.

*Rocks in His Head* **97a**

**1ST READ**

## Access Text © If students need help, then...

**Review CAUSE AND EFFECT**
Remind students that there can be more than one cause, or reason, for something to happen. Ask students to identify *why* people came to the filling station.

**Think Aloud** **MODEL** When there are no clue words to help me figure out causes, I ask myself questions. Why did this happen? What are the reasons this happened? One effect may have several causes. To make sure I find all the causes, I look at the entire paragraph.

**ON THEIR OWN** Have students reread pp. 98–99 to find more cause-and-effect relationships. For additional practice with cause and effect, see *Let's Practice It!* p. 241 on the *Teacher Resources DVD-ROM*.

**2ND READ**

## Close Reading ©

**ANALYSIS • TEXT EVIDENCE**
Identify a cause-and-effect relationship that has one cause and more than one effect. (On p. 99, it says the stock market fell. This cause had several effects. Bad times came; people couldn't afford to buy new cars or fix old ones, and the narrator's father had time to play chess and go rock hunting.)

**ANALYSIS** Based on this text, what is a positive meaning for the idiom "rocks in his head"? (It has the positive meaning that the narrator's father thinks about rocks all the time and they are very important to him.)

---

The pile of Model T parts sat just to the left of the lift. Soon, that pile of parts was bigger than the filling station.

People said, "If you think people are going to buy that junk, you've got rocks in your head."

"Maybe I have," he said. "Maybe I have."

But people did come to buy that junk. They came to buy gas, and they came to play chess, and they came to look at the rocks.

TURQUOISE    AZURITE    MALACHITE

For a while my father was too busy for the chess games. He was pumping gas, changing tires, and fixing Model Ts.

"Where did you get this one?" a customer would say, holding up a rock.

"Found it in a slag pile in New Hampshire," he'd say. Or, "Traded for it with a fella from Nevada. Gave him some garnets from Connecticut."

"People in Nevada and Connecticut collect rocks like you do?" people would ask.

"Lots of folks have rocks in their heads," said my father. He'd dig into his pocket and take out a rock. "Take a look at this one."

98

**CHECK PREDICTIONS** Have students look back at the predictions they made earlier and discuss whether they were accurate. Then have students preview the rest of the selection and either adjust their predictions accordingly or make new predictions.

Then the stock market fell. At first, people didn't think it would matter much to my father. After all, he had no money in the stock market.

"I may have rocks in my head," he said, "but I think bad times are coming."

And bad times did come. People couldn't afford to buy new cars or fix their old ones.

When business was slow, my father would play chess with some of his customers. When business was very slow, my grandfather would mind the filling station, and we'd pile as many of us kids as would fit into our Model T, and we'd hunt for more rocks with my father.

99

**Student Edition, p. 99**

If you want to teach this selection in two sessions, stop here.

If you want to continue reading this selection, turn to p. 100–101.

**ANALYSIS** Use context clues and a dictionary to find the meaning of the word *mind* on p. 99. (The narrator's father goes rock hunting when business is slow. Then the grandfather "would mind the filling station." So *mind* must mean "take care of" or "watch over" as it is used in this sentence.)

Common Core State Standards

**Informational Text 3.** Describe the relationship between a series of historical events, scientific ideas or concepts, or steps in technical procedures in a text, using language that pertains to time, sequence, and cause/effect. **Also Foundational Skills 3., 4.a., Language 3.b., 4.a.**

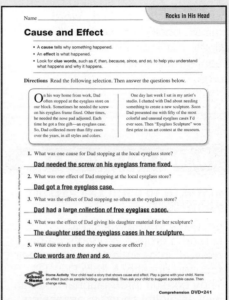

Name _____  Rocks in His Head

**Cause and Effect**

• A **cause** tells why something happened.
• An **effect** is what happened.
• Look for **clue words**, such as *if, then, because, since,* and *so,* to help you understand what happens and why it happens.

**Directions** Read the following selection. Then answer the questions below.

On his way home from work, Dad often stopped at the eyeglass store on our block. Sometimes he needed the screw on his eyeglass frame fixed. Other times, he needed the nose pad adjusted. Each time he got a free gift—an eyeglass case. So, Dad collected more than fifty cases over the years, in all styles and colors.

One day last week I sat in my artist's studio. I chatted with Dad about needing something to create a new sculpture. Soon Dad presented me with fifty of the most colorful and unusual eyeglass cases I'd ever seen. Then "Eyeglass Sculpture" won first prize in an art contest at the museum.

1. What was one cause for Dad stopping at the local eyeglass store?
**Dad needed the screw on his eyeglass frame fixed.**

2. What was one effect of Dad stopping at the local eyeglass store?
**Dad got a free eyeglass case.**

3. What was the effect of Dad stopping so often at the eyeglass store?
**Dad had a large collection of free eyeglass cases.**

4. What was the effect of Dad giving his daughter material for her sculpture?
**The daughter used the eyeglass cases in her sculpture.**

5. What clue words in the story show cause or effect?
**Clue words are *then* and *so.***

School Home **Home Activity** Your child read a story that shows cause and effect. Play a game with your child. Name an effect (such as people holding up umbrellas). Then ask your child to suggest a possible cause. Then change roles.

Comprehension DVD•241

Let's Practice It! TR DVD•241

ELL

**Clarify** Focus students' attention on the father's explanation of where he got the rock, on p. 98: "Found it …" This is an example of informal English in which the subject pronoun (*I,* in this case) is dropped. Restate the sentence in formal English: "I found it …" Then ask students to restate the other sentences in the paragraph in formal English, using subject pronouns.

*Rocks in His Head* **99a**

**Informational Text 5.** Use text features and search tools (e.g., key words, sidebars, hyperlinks) to locate information relevant to a given topic efficiently. **Foundational Skills 3.a.** Identify and know the meaning of the most common prefixes and derivational suffixes. **Language 1.a.** Explain the function of nouns, pronouns, verbs, adjectives, and adverbs in general and their functions in particular sentences. **Language 2.f.** Use spelling patterns and generalizations (e.g., word families, position-based spellings, syllable patterns, ending rules, meaningful word parts) in writing words.

© **Bridge to Common Core**

### RESEARCH TO BUILD AND PRESENT KNOWLEDGE

On Day 2 of the weeklong research project, students gather relevant information based on their focused questions from Day 1. They consult informational texts as well as digital sources, assessing the credibility of each one, and conduct interviews with experts. This process enables students to develop the capacity to build knowledge on a subject through research.

# Research and Inquiry

**Step 2** Navigate/Search

**TEACH** Have students generate a research plan for gathering information about their topic. Suggest that students search the Internet using their inquiry questions and keywords. Tell them to skim and scan each article entry or site for information that helps answer their inquiry question or leads them to specific information that will be useful. Bolded or italicized words may be clues to what kind of information the article or Web site will provide. Have students look for other features, such as headings, illustrations, captions, or highlighting. Encourage students to make on-site inspections to further their research, such as visiting a pertinent classroom and visiting an expert. Remind students to take notes as they gather information.

**Think Aloud** **MODEL** I used the keywords *learning to play musical instrument* to look for information about how learning to play a musical instrument is a valuable interest. I found information about learning how to play instruments, but this didn't help to answer my question. I decided to widen my search by the keywords *musical hobby* and *benefits*. This led me to more useful information such as health benefits and social benefits. To further my research, I decided to go to a music class where I could interview the musicians and inspect social benefits on-site. Everyone seemed to enjoy being at the music class and performing music together.

**GUIDE PRACTICE** Have students continue their review of Web sites and encyclopedia entries they identified, and encourage them to make on-site inspections and conduct interviews with experts. As students take notes from Web sites, advise them to be alert to additional key words that might lead them to more specific information. Explain that when such words or terms are underlined on a Web site, they can click on those words to go to a Web page that contains more detailed information.

**ON THEIR OWN** Have students create a Works-Cited page. They should write down the author, title, publisher, and publication year for each source used. For Web sites, they should record the Web addresses, authors, and the dates the Web sites were last updated.

# Conventions

## Possessive Pronouns

**TEACH** Write this sentence on the board: *That dog is Madison's dog.* Point out that the possessive pronoun *hers* could replace the phrase *Madison's dog* because *hers* takes the place of a person's name and what she owns.

**GUIDE PRACTICE** Have students suggest words or phrases that are the equivalent of the following possessive pronouns.

| | | | |
|---|---|---|---|
| my | mine | our | ours |
| your | yours | your | yours |
| his, her, its | his, hers, its | their | theirs |

**ON THEIR OWN** For additional practice, use *Reader's and Writer's Notebook,* p. 273.

# Spelling

## Prefixes *pre-, mid-, over-, out-*

**TEACH** Remind students that their spelling words have prefixes. Model how to spell *midnight.* First I spell the prefix. Write *mid.* Then I spell the base word. Write *night.* I write both parts together to spell *midnight.* Tell students that they may also be able to divide the word by syllables to spell it, as in the case of *midnight.*

**GUIDE PRACTICE** Write the spelling words on the board. Have students write each spelling word and underline the prefix.

**ON THEIR OWN** For additional practice, use *Reader's and Writer's Notebook,* p. 274.

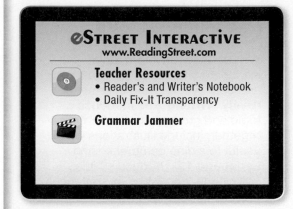

eSTREET INTERACTIVE
www.ReadingStreet.com

**Teacher Resources**
• Reader's and Writer's Notebook
• Daily Fix-It Transparency

**Grammar Jammer**

## Daily Fix-It

3. The strangeest rocks are her's. *(strangest; hers)*

4. Didnt she find them in the Middwest? *(Didn't; Midwest)*

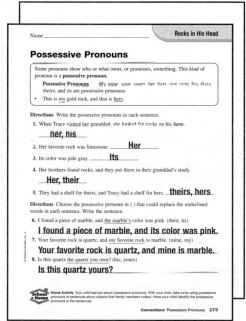

Reader's and Writer's Notebook, pp. 273–274

 **ELL**

**Conventions** To provide students with practice on possessive pronouns, use the modified grammar lessons in the *ELL Handbook* and the Grammar Jammer! online at: www.ReadingStreet.com

© **Common Core State Standards**

**Writing 2.** Write informative/explanatory texts to examine a topic and convey ideas and information clearly. **Writing 2.a.** Introduce a topic and group related information together; include illustrations when useful to aiding comprehension. **Language 1.i.** Produce simple, compound, and complex sentences.

# Writing

## Biography

**Writer's Craft: Sequence**

**INTRODUCE THE PROMPT** Remind students that the selection they'll be reading this week, *Rocks in His Head,* is an example of a biography. Review with students that biographies are a type of expository writing that tell about events in the life of a real person, and that these events are usually told in time order. Remind students to think about these features as they plan their writing. Then explain that they will begin the writing process for a biography today. Read aloud the writing prompt.

**Writing Prompt**

Think about a friend or family member who has an interesting collection. Now write a short biography of that person's life.

**SELECT A TOPIC**

**Think Aloud** To help choose a topic, I will make a chart. Since I'm writing a biography of someone with an interesting collection, I'll make a list of people I know who have collections. **Display a T-chart.** I will write the person's name and what they collect on a list. The first person I'll list is my friend Tom. Tom has a collection of bottle caps that dates back about 40 years. **Continue** modeling by filling in the chart with the name of each person and what they collect, such as *Cousin Don's collection of mystery novels,* and *Great-Grandma's sock puppet collection.*

**GATHER INFORMATION** Remind students that they can conduct personal interviews to gather more information about their friend or family member and his or her collection.

| Person's Name | What They Collect |
| --- | --- |
| Tom | bottle cap collection |
| Cousin Don | collection of mystery novels |
| Great-Grandma | sock puppet collection |

**Corrective feedback** Circulate around the room, providing assistance and corrective feedback to students as they complete their T-charts. Confer briefly with students who are having difficulty selecting a person to write about. Ask these students to recall stories they've heard about people they know who have collections. Suggest they look at home photographs to get ideas of people to write about.

## Mini-Lesson | Developing a Story Sequence Chart

▪ A story sequence chart helps show the order in which events take place. I can use it to help me write my biography in time order.

▪ In the *Beginning* box I will include details about Great-Grandma's life as a young woman.

▪ In the *Middle* box I will include information about how Great-Grandma's sock puppet collection started.

▪ Finally, in the *End* box, I will write about Great-Grandma's sock puppets in the present day.

Have students begin their own story sequence charts using the form on p. 275 of their *Reader's and Writer's Notebook*.

## Routine | Quick Write for Fluency    `Team Talk`

1. **Talk** Pairs discuss the person they will write about.

2. **Write** Each student writes a sentence about that person's collection.

3. **Share** Partners read their sentence to one another.

Routines Flip Chart

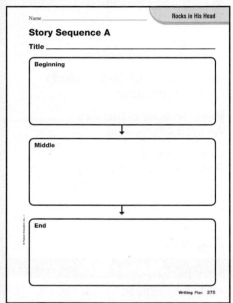

eSTREET INTERACTIVE
www.ReadingStreet.com

**Teacher Resources**
- Reader's and Writer's Notebook
- Graphic Organizer

Reader's and Writer's Notebook,
p. 275

# Wrap Up Your Day!

✔ **Content Knowledge** *What did you learn about collecting rocks?*

✔ **Text-Based Comprehension** *How were you able to determine what is a fact and what is an opinion in this section?*

### Preview DAY 3

Tell students that tomorrow they will read more about how the father continues his interest in rocks.

### Materials

- Student Edition
- Reader's and Writer's Notebook
- Retelling Cards
- Decodable Reader

### Common Core State Standards

**Speaking/Listening 1.c.** Ask questions to check understanding of information presented, stay on topic, and link their comments to the remarks of others. **Language 6.** Acquire and use accurately grade-appropriate conversational, general academic, and domain-specific words and phrases, including those that signal spatial and temporal relationships (e.g., *After dinner that night we went looking for them*).

# Content Knowledge

## Unique Interests

**EXPAND THE CONCEPT** Remind students of the weekly concept question, *Why is it valuable to have unique interests?* Discuss how the question relates to collecting rocks. Encourage students to think about how having a hobby can add enjoyment and satisfaction to a person's everyday life.

# Build Oral Language

**TALK ABOUT SENTENCES AND WORDS** Reread a sentence from Student Edition p. 97.

*He carefully labeled each rock to show what kind it was and where it had come from.*

- What does *labeled* mean? (to put or write a label on something)
- What would he write on the label? (He would describe what kind of rock or mineral it was and where it came from.)
- Why would he put this information about each rock and mineral on a label? (so the people who looked at them would know what they were and where they came from)

**Team Talk** Have students work with a partner to create one sentence for each idea in the original sentence. Use the following sentence frames.

**He carefully labeled** _____ _____. **He wanted to show what** _____ _____ _____.

**He wanted to show where** _____ _____ _____ _____.

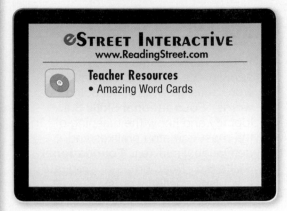
# Build Oral Vocabulary

## Amazing Words

### Robust Vocabulary Routine

1. **Introduce** Write the word *ornament* on the board. Have students say it with you. Yesterday, we read that rocks can be interesting *ornaments* when they are displayed on shelves. Have students determine a definition of *ornament*. (An *ornament* is an item used for decoration.)

2. **Demonstrate** Have students answer questions to demonstrate understanding. What is an *ornament* that you might hang on your front door? (a wreath)

3. **Apply** Have students apply their understanding. What are some *ornaments* that people wear? (scarves, necklaces, bracelets, earrings)

4. **Display the Word** Rewrite *or-na-ment* on the board. Run your hand under the syllables as you read the word. Have students say the word.

See p. OV•3 to teach *descendant.*

Routines Flip Chart

## Amazing Words

| | |
|---|---|
| hobby | ornament |
| project | descendant |
| leftover | forge |
| murmur | compartment |
| ancestor | |

**ADD TO THE CONCEPT MAP** Discuss the Amazing Word *ancestor.* Add this and other concept-related words to the concept map. Use the following questions to develop students' understanding of the concept. Add words generated in the discussion to the concept map.

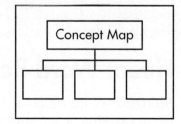

Concept Map

• What are some ways that people honor their *ancestors?*

• The narrator's grandfather helped to build a gas station for his son. What are some ways that people's *ancestors* affect their lives?

**Expand Vocabulary** Use the Day 3 instruction on ELL Poster 18 to help students expand vocabulary.

### Common Core State Standards

**Foundational Skills 3.** Know and apply grade-level phonics and word analysis skills in decoding words. **Foundational Skills 3.a.** Identify and know the meaning of the most common prefixes and derivational suffixes. **Foundational Skills 3.d.** Read grade-appropriate irregularly spelled words.
**Language 2.f.** Use spelling patterns and generalizations (e.g., word families, position-based spellings, syllable patterns, ending rules, meaningful word parts) in writing words.

# Word Analysis

## Prefixes *pre-, mid-, over-, out-, bi-, de-*

**MODEL WORD SORTING** Write *pre-, mid-, over-, out-, bi-,* and *de-* as heads on a six-column chart. Now we are going to sort words by prefixes. At the top of each column is a prefix. Words with the prefix *pre-* will go in that column. Words with the other prefixes will go in those columns. I will start. Write *midnight* and model how to read it, using the Word Analysis lesson on p. 88a. *Midnight* is made up of the base word *night* and the prefix *mid-*, so I will write *midnight* in the second column. Model reading *outside* and *pretest* in the same way.

**GUIDE PRACTICE** Use the practice words from the activity on p. 88a for the word sort. Point to a word. Have students read the word, identify its parts, and tell where it should be written on the chart.

**Corrective feedback** For corrective feedback, model reading the base word and then the prefix.

| pre- | mid- | over- | out- | bi- | de- |
| --- | --- | --- | --- | --- | --- |
| pretreat | midsection | overtime | outstanding | biped | dethrone |
| preheat | midweek | overreach | outdone | bifocals | |
| | | | | bimonthly | |

## Fluent Word Reading

**MODEL** Write *biplane.* I know the prefix *bi-*. I know the base word *plane*. I put them together and read the word *biplane.*

**GUIDE PRACTICE** Write the words below. Look for word parts you know. When I point to the word, we'll read it together. Allow one second per word part previewing time for the first reading.

**midsection  overweight  outburst  preteen  bisection  deactivate**

**ON THEIR OWN** Have students read the list above three or four times, until they can read one word per second.

# Decodable Passage 18B
f students need help, then...

## Read *A Midsummer Visit*

**READ WORDS IN ISOLATION** Have students turn to p. 33 in *Decodable Practice Readers 3.2* and find the first list of words. Each word in this list has a prefix. Let's decode and read these words. Be sure that students identify the prefix in each word.

Next, have students read the high-frequency words.

**PREVIEW** Have students read the title and preview the story. Tell them that they will read words with the prefixes *pre-, mid-, over-, out-, bi-,* and *de-.*

**READ WORDS IN CONTEXT** Chorally read the story along with students. Have students identify words in the story that have the prefixes *pre-, mid-, over-, out-, bi-,* and *de-.* Make sure that students are monitoring their accuracy when they decode words.

**Team Talk** Pair students and have them take turns reading the story aloud to each other. Monitor students as they read to check for proper pronunciation and appropriate pacing.

**eStreet Interactive**
www.ReadingStreet.com

 **Pearson eText**
• Decodable Reader

---

## Access for All

**Ⓐ Advanced**

Have students come up with their own words with prefixes to add to the chart.

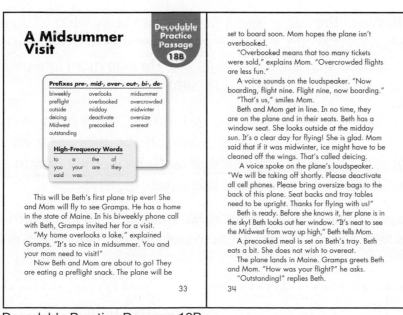

### A Midsummer Visit

**Decodable Practice Passage 18B**

**Prefixes pre-, mid-, over-, out-, bi-, de-**

| | | |
|---|---|---|
| biweekly | overlooks | midsummer |
| preflight | overbooked | overcrowded |
| outside | midday | midwinter |
| deicing | deactivate | oversize |
| Midwest | precooked | overeat |
| outstanding | | |

**High-Frequency Words**

| | | | |
|---|---|---|---|
| to | a | the | of |
| you | your | are | they |
| said | was | | |

This will be Beth's first plane trip ever! She and Mom will fly to see Gramps. He has a home in the state of Maine. In his biweekly phone call with Beth, Gramps invited her for a visit.

"My home overlooks a lake," explained Gramps. "It's so nice in midsummer. You and your mom need to visit!"

Now Beth and Mom are about to go! They are eating a preflight snack. The plane will be set to board soon. Mom hopes the plane isn't overbooked.

"Overbooked means that too many tickets were sold," explains Mom. "Overcrowded flights are less fun."

A voice sounds on the loudspeaker. "Now boarding, flight nine. Flight nine, now boarding."

"That's us," smiles Mom.

Beth and Mom get in line. In no time, they are on the plane and in their seats. Beth has a window seat. She looks outside at the midday sun. It's a clear day for flying! She is glad. Mom said that if it was midwinter, ice might have to be cleaned off the wings. That's called deicing.

A voice spoke on the plane's loudspeaker. "We will be taking off shortly. Please deactivate all cell phones. Please bring oversize bags to the back of this plane. Seat backs and tray tables need to be upright. Thanks for flying with us!"

Beth is ready. Before she knows it, her plane is in the sky! Beth looks out her window. "It's neat to see the Midwest from way up high," Beth tells Mom.

A precooked meal is set on Beth's tray. Beth eats a bit. She does not wish to overeat.

The plane lands in Maine. Gramps greets Beth and Mom. "How was your flight?" he asks.

"Outstanding!" replies Beth.

33    34

Decodable Practice Passage 18B

Zoom in on ©

© **Common Core State Standards**

**Informational Text 3.** Describe the relationship between a series of historical events, scientific ideas or concepts, or steps in technical procedures in a text, using language that pertains to time, sequence, and cause/effect. **Informational Text 6.** Distinguish their own point of view from that of the author of a text. **Foundational Skills 4.** Read with sufficient accuracy and fluency to support comprehension. **Foundational Skills 4.a.** Read on-level text with purpose and understanding. **Also Informational Text 1., 5., Language 2.f., 4.**

## Strategy Response Log

Have students revisit p. 24 in the *Reader's and Writer's Notebook* to add additional information about biographies.

# Text-Based Comprehension
## Check Understanding

**Student Edition, pp. 94–95**

**If...** you chose to read *Rocks in His Head* in two parts,

**then...** use the following questions to monitor students' understanding of the selection. Encourage students to cite evidence from the text.

**INFERENCE** When the father was a boy, he said he wanted to do something with rocks when he grew up, even though people told him "there's no money in rocks." What does that tell you about him? **He was more interested in his hobby than in earning a lot of money. (p. 96)**

**ANALYSIS** After the father opened his gas station, more people started buying automobiles. Write one fact and one opinion about what he did to take advantage of the new trend. **Statement of fact—he learned how to repair automobiles; Opinion—he was smart and clever. (p. 97)**

**RETELL** Have students retell *Rocks in His Head,* pp. 96–99, referring to details in the text. Encourage students to use the text features to guide their retellings.

> **Corrective feedback** | **If...** the students leave out important details,
> **then...** have students look back through the illustrations in the selection.

**READ** Use the **Access Text** and **Close Reading** notes to finish reading *Rocks in His Head.*

**If...** you followed the Read for Understanding routine below,

**then...** ask students to retell the selection before you reread *Rocks in His Head*.

**RETELL** Have students retell *Rocks in His Head,* pp. 96–99, referring to details in the text. Encourage students to use the text features to guide their retellings.

> **Corrective feedback** | **If...** students leave out important details,
> **then...** have students look back through the illustrations in the selection.

**READ** Return to p. 96–97 and use the **2nd Read/Close Reading** notes to reread *Rocks in His Head.*

# Read Main Selection

**Routine** **Read for Understanding** ©

Deepen understanding by reading the selection multiple times.

1. **First Read**—If students need support, use the **Access Text** notes to help them clarify understanding.

2. **Second Read**—Use the **Close Reading** notes to help students draw knowledge from the text.

**Check Retelling** To support retelling, review the multilingual summary for *Rocks in His Head* with the appropriate Retelling Cards to scaffold understanding.

**Day 3** **SMALL GROUP TIME • Differentiate Close Reading, p. SG•33**

| **OL** On-Level | **SI** Strategic Intervention | **A** Advanced |
|---|---|---|
| • **Reread** to Develop Vocabulary | • **Reread** to Develop Vocabulary | • **Reread** to Extend Vocabulary |
| • **Read** *Rocks in His Head* | • **Read** *Rocks in His Head* | • **Read** *Rocks in His Head* |
| | | • **Investigate** Inquiry Project |

**If...** students need more scaffolding and practice with the **Main Selection,**
**then...** use the activities on p. DI•72 in the Teacher Resources section on SuccessNet.

## Access Text © If students need help, then...

**◉ INFERRING** Have students read p. 100. Then ask them what they can infer about the father based on the way he moved his rock collection.

**(Think Aloud) MODEL** I see in the text that the father carefully wrapped and packed every rock. He also built shelves for the rocks. I know that when people are very attached to something, they treat it with great care. I can infer, then, that the father's rock collection was very important to him.

## Close Reading ©

**ANALYSIS • TEXT EVIDENCE** The narrator says "Then people stopped coming for gas." What conclusion can you draw about the father's filling station from this statement of fact? Support your answer with textual evidence. (I can conclude that the father's filling station is no longer doing well. The statement of fact says that people stopped coming for gas. In order for a filling station to do well, people need to buy gas.)

He had to build more shelves for the rocks, up the west wall of the station.

Then people stopped coming for gas. They stopped coming to play chess, and they even stopped coming to look at the rocks and minerals. They were all too busy looking for work.

One day my father picked up the chess set and carefully packed it in a big box. He took down each mineral, wrapped it in newspaper, and carefully placed it in a wooden box.

When his friends came with a truck to help us move, they said, "Watch out for those wooden boxes. He's got rocks in his boxes, now."

"Yessir," said my father. "That's just what I got in there. Take a look at this one."

The house we moved to was old and falling apart. My father said he'd have it fixed up in no time.

But before he started in on the repairs, we had to take those rocks up to the attic, where he'd already built tiny little wooden shelves.

My father did fix up the old house, and after he finished each repair, he went up to the attic with his rocks. He spent a lot of time reading about rocks, too.

100

**Student Edition, p. 100**

**ANALYSIS** Help students generate text-based questions by providing the following question stem: In the selection, what did the narrator's father do when _____?

**ON THEIR OWN** Have students use a graphic organizer to list text clues and background knowledge for making another inference.

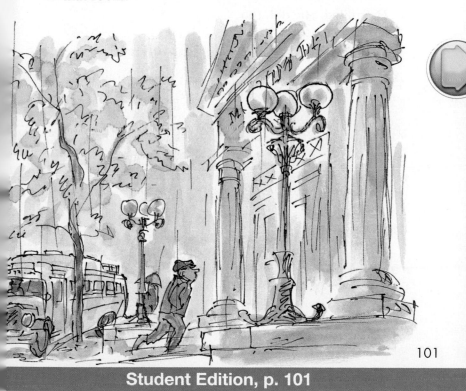

"If you think those rocks are ever going to do you any good," said my mother, "you've got rocks in your head."

"Maybe I have," said my father. "Maybe I have." He reached into his pocket. "Take a look at this one."

My father spent a lot of time looking for any job he could find. Most jobs lasted only a day or two.

On rainy days when my father could find no other work, he'd take the bus to the science museum. They had a whole room full of glass cases containing many rocks. Sometimes he'd spend the whole day in that room.

101

**Student Edition, p. 101**

**ANALYSIS • TEXT EVIDENCE** What would cause the father to go to the science museum? Find examples in the text. (In the last paragraph on p. 101, it says that when it was rainy and he couldn't find any work to do for the day, he would take the bus to the museum.)

## Common Core State Standards

**Informational Text 7.** Use information gained from illustrations (e.g., maps, photographs) and the words in a text to demonstrate understanding of the text (e.g., where, when, why, and how key events occur). **Informational Text 8.** Describe the logical connection between particular sentences and paragraphs in a text (e.g., comparison, cause/effect, first/second/third in a sequence). **Foundational Skills 3.** Know and apply grade-level phonics and word analysis skills in decoding words. **Also Informational Text 1., 3., 6.**

## Access for All

**SI Strategic Intervention**

Tell students that they can use text features such as illustrations to help them figure out the meaning of unknown words. Have them practice with several words from the text, such as *museum*.

**A Advanced**

Have students gather information about ways people in your community can collect, see, or study special rocks. Have them report on places and events such as local parks with rock features or museum offerings, including exhibits, lectures, and educational programs.

## ELL

**Sequence** Help students understand the sequence of events on p.100 by looking for clue words. *(then, one day, before, after)* Explain that readers can look for clue words such as *before* or *after* to better understand the order in which things happen. Have students create their own sentences using sequence words.

*Rocks in His Head* **101a**

# Access Text © If students need help, then...

👁 **INFERRING** Have students read the last paragraph on p. 103. Ask students to draw a conclusion based on the fact that the father opens the mineral cases and scrubs some of the rocks with toothbrushes.

**Think Aloud** **MODEL** I read that the father scrubs some of the rocks until they sparkle. If someone spends that much time and care cleaning something, then that must mean the person cares about it. I can conclude that the father cares a lot about these rocks and wants them to look their best.

# Close Reading ©

**ANALYSIS • TEXT EVIDENCE** Find a statement of fact on page 103. How do you know that it is a statement of fact? (In the first paragraph on p. 103, the author says, *"These rocks have come from all over the world."* This is a statement of fact. A museum keeps records about the objects it displays, so it can be proved that they come from all over the world.)

One afternoon he looked up to see a lady standing beside him. "I've seen you here before," she said.

"I come here a lot," he said. "I guess I've got rocks in my head."

"Tell me what you're looking for," she said.

"I'm looking for rocks that are better than mine," he said.

"How many did you find?" she asked.

"Ten," he said.

The lady looked around at the hundreds of rocks, in all those glass cases. "Only ten?"

"Maybe eleven," he said.

He smiled. She did, too.

102

**Student Edition, p. 102**

**ON THEIR OWN** Have students reread pp. 102–103 to look for other facts they can draw conclusions about. Have them support their assertions with textual evidence.

 **Common Core State Standards**

**Informational Text 3.** Describe the relationship between a series of historical events, scientific ideas or concepts, or steps in technical procedures in a text, using language that pertains to time, sequence, and cause/effect. **Informational Text 8.** Describe the logical connection between particular sentences and paragraphs in a text (e.g., comparison, cause/effect, first/second/third in a sequence).

"You *have* got rocks in your head," she said. "I'm Grace Johnson, the director of this museum. These rocks have come from all over the world."

"So have mine," said my father. He reached into his pocket. "Take a look at this one," he said.

"Did you study rocks at college?" she asked.

"Couldn't afford to go to college," he said.

"Let me see the rest of your rocks," she said.

Mrs. Johnson got out her big Packard touring car, and my father got in. They drove to our house.

"Where are the rocks?" she asked.

"Up here," said my father, leading the way to the attic. "Watch your step."

Two hours later Mrs. Johnson said, "I can't hire you as a mineralogist. The board won't allow it. But I need a night janitor at the museum. Will you take the job?"

"Will I be cleaning rocks?" he asked.

"Sometimes," she said.

So my father took the job as night janitor at the museum. Before he went home, he'd open some of the mineral cases and scrub some of the rocks with a toothbrush until they sparkled like diamonds.

103

**Student Edition, p. 103**

**EVALUATION** What examples can you give from the selection that demonstrate the key differences between a biography and an autobiography? (It is written about the narrator's father—and it is told in chronological order using words such as *he* and *his*. An autobiography is written by the person it is about and uses words such as *I* and *me*.)

## Access for All

**SI** Strategic Intervention

Tell students that to determine the causes, or reasons, something happens, they should look at the entire passage, both before and after the effect is mentioned.

**A** Advanced

The author quotes her father throughout the biography, and he often repeats the same phrases. Have students use a T-chart to track the father's repetition of certain phrases such as "rocks in my head" or "Take a look at this one." Ask students to discuss how these quotations help to give an impression of the father's character.

 **ELL**

**Multisyllabic Words** Tell students that if they come to a long word they don't know, such as *mineralogist*, they can look for meaningful word parts that they recognize, such as *mineral*. Help students think of words they know that have similar word parts. For example, a *biologist* studies *biology*, so a *mineralogist* studies *minerals*. Have students determine if this meaning makes sense in the sentence.

*Rocks in His Head* **103a**

## Access Text © If students need help, then...

### MULTIPLE-MEANING WORDS

Have students use context to determine the meaning of *rocks* on p. 104.

**Think Aloud** **MODEL** When I look up *rock* in a dictionary, I see it can mean "stone" or "move side to side." This selection is about a father who collects stones. So *rocks* means "stones" here.

**ON THEIR OWN** Have students use context clues and a dictionary to find the meaning of *board* on p. 104. For additional practice, use *Reader's and Writer's Notebook,* p. 276.

### CROSS-TEXT EVALUATION

**Use a Strategy to Self-Check** How did the Read Aloud, "Picture Perfect" help you to understand this selection?

---

Mrs. Johnson came in early for work one morning and saw him carefully writing a new label for one of the rocks.

"What are you doing?" she asked.

"One rock was labeled wrong," he said. "I fixed it."

Mrs. Johnson smiled. "I've been talking to the board of directors. They know that I need a person here who knows as much about rocks as you do."

"What about the college education?" he asked.

She said, "I told them I need somebody with rocks in his head and rocks in his pockets. Are you it?"

"Maybe I am," said my father. "Maybe I am."

He reached into his pocket and took out a rock. "Take a look at this one," he said.

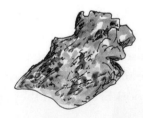

104

**Student Edition, p. 104**

## Close Reading ©

**ANALYSIS • TEXT EVIDENCE** Use context clues and a dictionary to tell the meaning of the word *pick* in the tongue twister on page 105. (In this tongue twister, the text says that Peter Piper is gathering peppers. Therefore, the meaning of *pick* is "to pluck from a plant.")

**SYNTHESIS • TEXT EVIDENCE** Using what you learned in this selection, explain the value of having unique interests. Have students cite examples from the text to support their responses.

**CHECK PREDICTIONS** Have students return to the predictions they made earlier and confirm whether they were accurate.

---

**Talent with a Twist of the Tongue**

The phrase "rocks in his head" is a play on words. Tongue twisters are also a type of word play. People all around the world enjoy these playful verses and they exist in every language. Below are three well-known tongue twisters. As you read, think about what makes this language playful.

**Try to say these three tongue twisters as fast as you can:**

She sells sea shells by the sea shore.
The shells she sells are surely seashells.
So if she sells shells on the seashore,
I'm sure she sells seashore shells.

Peter Piper picked a peck of pickled peppers.
Did Peter Piper pick a peck of pickled peppers?
If Peter Piper picked a peck of pickled peppers,
where's the peck of pickled peppers Peter Piper picked?

How much wood would a woodchuck chuck
if a woodchuck could chuck wood?
He would chuck, he would, as much as he could,
and chuck as much wood as a woodchuck would
if a woodchuck could chuck wood.

105

**Student Edition, p. 105**

**REREAD CHALLENGING TEXT** Have students reread p. 105 to practice reading tongue twisters fluently. Students may need to start out slowly before they're able to read at an appropriate rate.

---

**Common Core State Standards**

**Informational Text 7.** Use information gained from illustrations (e.g., maps, photographs) and the words in a text to demonstrate understanding of the text (e.g., where, when, why, and how key events occur). **Informational Text 9.** Compare and contrast the most important points and key details presented in two texts on the same topic. **Language 4.** Determine or clarify the meaning of unknown and multiple-meaning word and phrases based on grade 3 reading and content, choosing flexibly from a range of strategies. **Language 5.** Demonstrate understanding of word relationships and nuances in word meanings. **Also Informational Text 3.**

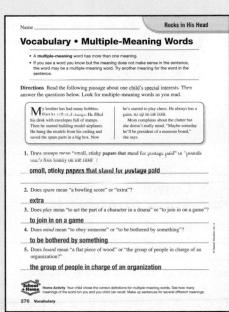

Reader's and Writer's Notebook, p. 276

**Monitor Understanding** Reading aloud the first four paragraphs on p. 104, ask: Why do you think Mrs. Johnson was happy? (She knew she had found someone who was very knowledgeable about rocks. She saw that the father had known a rock was mislabeled.)

*Rocks in His Head* **105a**

Common Core State Standards
Informational Text 1. Ask and answer questions to demonstrate understanding of a text, referring explicitly to the text as the basis for the answers. Also Informational Text 2., Writing 8.

**Envision It!** Retell

READING STREET ONLINE
STORY SORT
www.ReadingStreet.com

106

## Think Critically

1. What is the difference in point of view between a biography and autobiography? How is this biography different from the autobiography by Ted Williams? Text to Text

2. The author tells you that her father has rocks in his head. Is she making fun of him? Is she proud of him? How can you tell? Think Like an Author

3. What facts did you learn about the jobs the author's father had? Which job do you think the father liked best? Why? Which job would you like best? Why?
   Fact and Opinion

4. Using facts and details from this selection, what can you infer about the people who work in museums? How has this information changed your view of people and things that are unique?
   Inferring

5. **Look Back and Write** Look back at pages 96–98. Use facts and details from the selection to write what the father collected and why. Provide evidence to support your answer.
   Key Ideas and Details • Text Evidence

### Meet the Author and the Illustrator

## Carol Otis Hurst

*Rocks in His Head* was **Carol Otis Hurst's** first book. It is the true story of her father. "He collected rocks from the time he was a small boy. He kept at it throughout his life, not caring that others thought it was a waste of time." Ms. Hurst says her father loved to learn new things. "He'd be thrilled to think kids at school were reading a story about him."

## James Stevenson

**James Stevenson** has written and illustrated more than one hundred children's books. More than thirty of them have won awards.

He wrote his first children's book with his eight-year-old son. "Tell me a story and we'll make a book," he told his son James. "He stood at my desk and told a story. I wrote it down and then did the pictures." They called the book *If I Owned a Candy Factory*. It was published in 1968.

**Read more books about unique people.**

*Beethoven Lives Upstairs* by Barbara Nichol

*Snowflake Bentley* by Jacqueline Briggs Martin

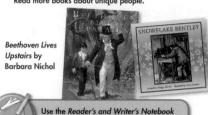

Use the *Reader's and Writer's Notebook* to record your independent reading.

107

---

**Student Edition, pp. 106–107**

---

**Common Core State Standards**

**Informational Text 1.** Ask and answer questions to demonstrate understanding of a text, referring explicitly to the text as the basis for the answers. **Also Informational Text 2., 3., 6., Writing 2., 2.a., 2.b., 9., Language 1.i., 5.a.**

### Bridge to Common Core

**RANGE OF READING AND LEVEL OF TEXT COMPLEXITY**

To increase students' capacity for reading and comprehending complex texts independently and proficiently, have them read other informational texts by Carol Otis Hurst or about the social studies topic, Unique Interests. After students read closely for a sustained period of time, they should record their reading in their Reading Logs.

## Think Critically

1. **TEXT TO TEXT** An autobiography is written by the subject himself or herself. A biography is written by someone else about the subject. This biography uses the pronoun *he* to refer to the subject. The autobiography of Ted Williams uses the pronoun *I*.

2. **THINK LIKE AN AUTHOR** The author is proud of her father. She admires the way he learned all about the Model T and describes how Grace Johnson was impressed by his knowledge about rocks.

3. **FACT AND OPINION** Students should identify their responses as statements of facts or opinions.

4. **INFERRING** Students should back up their responses with examples from the selection.

5. **LOOK BACK AND WRITE • TEXT EVIDENCE** To build writing fluency, assign a 10–15 minute time limit.

## Scoring Rubric  Look Back and Write

**TOP-SCORE RESPONSE** A top-score response uses details from the story to tell about what the father collected and why.

**A top-score response should include:**

• The father collected rocks for many years.

• He liked to look at rocks, talk about them, and trade them.

• He enjoyed reading about rocks and studying them.

# Retell

Have students work in pairs to retell the selection, using the retelling strip in the Student Edition or the Story Sort as prompts. Monitor students' retellings.

## Scoring Rubric  Expository Retelling

|  | 4 | 3 | 2 | 1 |
|---|---|---|---|---|
| **Connections** | Makes connections and generalizes beyond the text | Makes connections to other events, texts, or experiences | Makes a limited connection to another event, text, or experience | Makes no connection to another event, text, or experience |
| **Author's Purpose** | Elaborates on author's purpose | Tells author's purpose with some clarity | Makes some connection to author's purpose | Makes no connection to author's purpose |
| **Topic** | Describes the main topic | Identifies the main topic with some details early in retelling | Identifies the main topic | Retelling has no sense of topic |
| **Important Ideas** | Gives accurate information about events, steps, and ideas using details and key vocabulary | Gives accurate information about events, steps, and ideas with some detail and key vocabulary | Gives limited or inaccurate information about events, steps, and ideas | Gives no information about events, steps, and ideas |
| **Conclusions** | Draws conclusions and makes inferences to generalize beyond the text | Draws conclusions about the text | Is able to tell some learnings about the text | Is unable to draw conclusions or make inferences about the text |

**Don't Wait Until Friday**

## MONITOR PROGRESS  Check Retelling

**If...** students have difficulty retelling,

**then...** use the Retelling Cards/Story Sort to scaffold their retellings.

## Plan to Assess Retelling

☐ **Week 1** Strategic Intervention

☐ **Week 2** Advanced

☑ **This week assess Strategic Intervention students.**

☐ **Week 4** On-Level

☐ **Week 5** Assess any students you have not yet checked during this unit.

## Meet the Author

Have students read about author Carol Otis Hurst on p. 107. Ask them how she expresses her pride in her father's unique interest.

## Read Independently

Have students enter their independent reading into their Reading Logs.

**Common Core State Standards**

**Informational Text 5.** Use text features and search tools (e.g., key words, sidebars, hyperlinks) to locate information relevant to a given topic efficiently. **Foundational Skills 4.** Read with sufficient accuracy and fluency to support comprehension. **Foundational Skills 4.a.** Read on-level text with purpose and understanding. **Writing 8.** Recall information from experiences or gather information from print and digital sources; take brief notes on sources and sort evidence into provided categories.

# Fluency

## Expression

**MODEL FLUENT READING** Have students turn to p. 98 of *Rocks in His Head.* Have students follow along as you read this page. Tell them to listen to the expression of your voice as you read the words that different characters say. Adjust your voice level to stress important words and phrases.

**GUIDE PRACTICE** Have students follow along as you read the page again. Then have them reread the page as a group without you until they read with the right expression and with no mistakes. Ask questions to be sure students comprehend the text. Continue in the same way on p. 99.

| Corrective feedback | **If...** students are having difficulty reading with the right expression, <br>**then...** prompt: <br>• Which word is a problem? Let's read it together. <br>• Read the sentence again to be sure you understand it. <br>• Tell me the sentence. Now read it as if you are speaking to me. |
| --- | --- |

# Reread for Fluency

**Routine** Oral Rereading

1. **Read** Have students read p. 101 of *Rocks in His Head* orally.

2. **Reread** To achieve optimal fluency, students should reread the text three or four times.

3. **Corrective Feedback** Have students read aloud without you. Provide feedback about their expression and encourage them to adjust their voice level to stress important words and phrases. Listen for use of appropriate expression. Have students reread three to four times.

Routines Flip Chart

# Research and Study Skills

## Online Information

**TEACH** If available, have students display the results of Web research they have done. Tell students that they can use information they get from the Web in many of the same ways they would use information from reference books. Review with students how to explore Web sites.

- Enter keywords in a search engine to find Web sites devoted to the research topic.

  Many Web sites contain online directories. An online directory is a kind of table of contents of Web sites on a particular topic. Often this table of contents is a list of links accompanied by descriptions of what can be found on the site.

- Clicking on a link in an online directory brings up the new Web site.

- It's important to evaluate the reliability of a Web site for research by paying attention to the ending of the Web site's "address," or URL. Sites that end in *.gov* are hosted by the government. Sites ending in *.edu* are hosted by schools. Sites for museums and libraries usually end in *.org*.

**GUIDE PRACTICE** Discuss these questions:

How do you begin an online search for information? (by entering keywords into a search engine)

Where will you find an online directory? How do you use it? (Online directories are found on Web sites. To use an online directory, click on the links provided.)

**ON THEIR OWN** Have students review and complete p. 277 of the *Reader's and Writer's Notebook*.

eStreet INTERACTIVE
www.ReadingStreet.com

**Teacher Resources**
- Reader's and Writer's Notebook

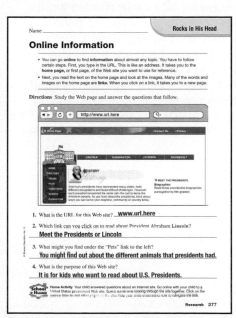

Reader's and Writer's Notebook, p. 277

**Professional Development: What ELL Experts Say About Reading Strategies** "Beginning English language learners benefit from the repeated readings of predictable texts with illustrations, especially when the teacher has provided a brief preview of each text to introduce the topic of the story and preview new vocabulary." —Dr. Georgia Earnest García

## Common Core State Standards

**Writing 8.** Recall information from experiences or gather information from print and digital sources; take brief notes on sources and sort evidence into provided categories. **Language 1.a.** Explain the function of nouns, pronouns, verbs, adjectives, and adverbs in general and their functions in particular sentences. **Language 1.f.** Ensure subject-verb and pronoun-antecedent agreement. **Language 2.e.** Use conventional spelling for high-frequency and other studied words and for adding suffixes to base words (e.g., *sitting, smiled, cries, happiness*). **Language 2.f.** Use spelling patterns and generalizations (e.g., word families, position-based spellings, syllable patterns, ending rules, meaningful word parts) in writing words. **Also Foundational Skills 4.a.**

# Research and Inquiry

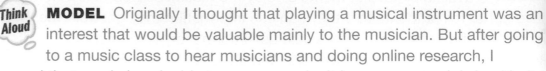

**Step 3** Analyze Information

**TEACH** Tell students that today they will analyze their findings and may need to change the focus of their original inquiry question.

**MODEL** Originally I thought that playing a musical instrument was an interest that would be valuable mainly to the musician. But after going to a music class to hear musicians and doing online research, I learned that music is valuable to many people. It improves people's health, it relaxes people, and it can provide social interaction. I will refocus my inquiry question to include information from my research. Now my inquiry question is *Is playing a musical instrument an interest that is valuable to the community as well as to the musician?*

**GUIDE PRACTICE** Have students analyze their findings. They may need to refocus their inquiry question to better fit the information they found. Remind students that if they have difficulty improving their focus they can ask a reference librarian or a local expert for guidance.

**ON THEIR OWN** Have students summarize their research for a partner. Partners should discuss each other's findings and evaluate the focus of their inquiry questions.

# Conventions

## Possessive Pronouns

**REVIEW** Remind students that this week they learned about possessive pronouns:

- Pronouns are words that take the place of nouns.
- Pronouns that show who or what owns, or possesses, something are called possessive pronouns, such as *his, hers,* and *theirs.*

**CONNECT TO ORAL LANGUAGE** Have the class replace the underlined word or phrase with the correct possessive pronoun and read the new sentence aloud.

Let's Practice It! TR DVD•242

<u>Jamal's</u> sculpture is finished.

<u>Kaya's sculpture</u> is on view in the school library.

**ON THEIR OWN** For additional support, use *Let's Practice It!* p. 242 on the *Teacher Resources DVD-ROM.*

# Spelling

## Prefixes *pre-, mid-, over-, out-*

**FREQUENTLY MISSPELLED WORDS** Students often misspell the word *outside.* The words *midnight, outgoing,* and *overdue* are also difficult to spell. I'm going to read a sentence. Choose the correct word to complete the sentence and then write it correctly.

1. Noon and _____ look the same on a clock. (midnight)
2. We took our sled _____ after the first snowfall. (outside)
3. The actor had an _____ personality. (outgoing)
4. Some stores charge fees for _____ payments. (overdue)

**ON THEIR OWN** For additional practice, use *Reader's and Writer's Notebook,* p. 278.

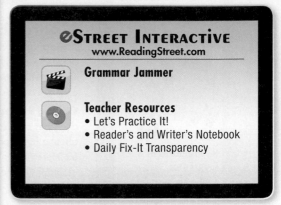

**eSTREET INTERACTIVE**
www.ReadingStreet.com

**Grammar Jammer**

**Teacher Resources**
- Let's Practice It!
- Reader's and Writer's Notebook
- Daily Fix-It Transparency

## Access for All

**SI Strategic Intervention**

Provide students with a list of possessive pronouns. Have students work in pairs to find and write examples of possessive pronouns in the main selection or other grade-appropriate texts.

## Daily Fix-It

5. That black rock of theirs's is unnown to me. *(theirs; unknown)*
6. The yellow rock was found in the camp ground by Juan and he. *(campground; him)*

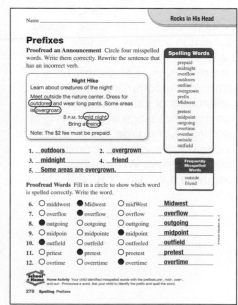

Reader's and Writer's Notebook, p. 278

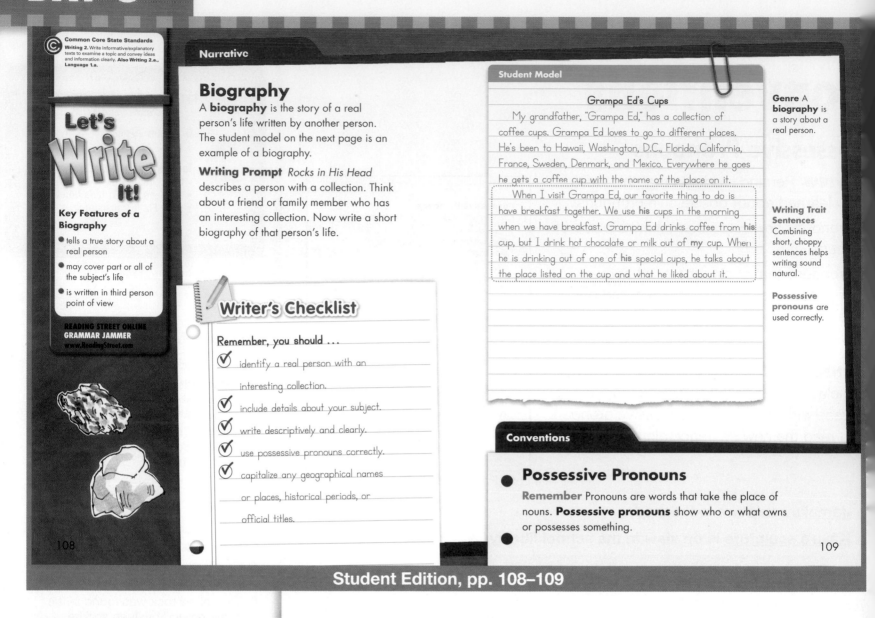

Common Core State Standards
Writing 2. Write informative/explanatory texts to examine a topic and convey ideas and information clearly. Also Writing 2.a., Language 1.a.

## Let's

# Write It!

**Key Features of a Biography**

- tells a true story about a real person
- may cover part or all of the subject's life
- is written in third person point of view

**READING STREET ONLINE
GRAMMAR JAMMER**
www.ReadingStreet.com

### Narrative

## Biography

A **biography** is the story of a real person's life written by another person. The student model on the next page is an example of a biography.

**Writing Prompt** *Rocks in His Head* describes a person with a collection. Think about a friend or family member who has an interesting collection. Now write a short biography of that person's life.

### Writer's Checklist

Remember, you should . . .

✓ identify a real person with an interesting collection.

✓ include details about your subject.

✓ write descriptively and clearly.

✓ use possessive pronouns correctly.

✓ capitalize any geographical names or places, historical periods, or official titles.

**Student Model**

#### Grampa Ed's Cups

My grandfather, "Grampa Ed," has a collection of coffee cups. Grampa Ed loves to go to different places. He's been to Hawaii, Washington, D.C., Florida, California, France, Sweden, Denmark, and Mexico. Everywhere he goes he gets a coffee cup with the name of the place on it.

When I visit Grampa Ed, our favorite thing to do is have breakfast together. We use his cups in the morning when we have breakfast. Grampa Ed drinks coffee from his cup, but I drink hot chocolate or milk out of my cup. When he is drinking out of one of his special cups, he talks about the place listed on the cup and what he liked about it.

**Genre** A **biography** is a story about a real person.

**Writing Trait Sentences** Combining short, choppy sentences helps writing sound natural.

**Possessive pronouns** are used correctly.

### Conventions

## Possessive Pronouns

**Remember** Pronouns are words that take the place of nouns. **Possessive pronouns** show who or what owns or possesses something.

108

109

**Student Edition, pp. 108–109**

---

## Common Core State Standards

**Writing 2.** Write informative/explanatory texts to examine a topic and convey ideas and information clearly. **Writing 2.a.** Introduce a topic and group related information together; include illustrations when useful to aiding comprehension. **Language 1.** Demonstrate command of the conventions of standard English grammar and usage when writing or speaking. **Language 1.i.** Produce simple, compound, and complex sentences. **Also Writing 2.b., Language 1.a., 1.c., 1.h., 2.a.**

# Let's Write It!

**WRITE A BIOGRAPHY** Use pp. 108–109 in the Student Edition. Direct students to read the key features of a biography that appear on p. 108. Remind students that they can refer to the information in the Writer's Checklist as they write their own biographies.

Read the student model on p. 109. Point out compound and complex sentences and the possessive pronouns in the model.

**CONNECT TO CONVENTIONS** Remind students that a possessive pronoun shows who or what owns, or possesses, something. Point out the correct use of possessive pronouns in the model.

# Writing

## Biography

### Writing Trait: Sentences

**DISPLAY RUBRIC** Display Scoring Rubric 18 from the *Teacher Resources DVD-ROM* and go over the criteria for each trait under each score. Then, using the student writing model in the Student Edition, choose students to explain why the model should score a 4 for one of the traits. If a student offers that the model should score below 4 for a particular trait, the student should offer support for that response. Remind students that this is the rubric that will be used to evaluate the biographies they will begin writing today.

## Scoring Rubric — Biography

| | **4** | **3** | **2** | **1** |
|---|---|---|---|---|
| **Focus/Ideas** | Well-developed characters, setting, and events | Developed characters, setting, and events | Underdeveloped characters, setting, and events | Undeveloped characters, setting, and events |
| **Organization** | Clear sequence of events | Able to follow sequence of events | Unclear sequence of events | No sequence of events |
| **Voice** | Clear interest in talents and important events in subject's life | Some interest in talents and important events in subject's life | Little interest in talents and important events in subject's life | No interest in talents and important events in subject's life |
| **Word Choice** | Strong use of vivid words | Adequate use of vivid words | Weak use of vivid words | No use of vivid words |
| **Sentences** | Clear sentences of various lengths and types; strong variety of sentence beginnings | Sentences of a few lengths and types; variety of sentence beginnings | Sentences of similar length and type; weak variety of sentence beginnings | No attempt at sentences of various lengths and types; no variety of sentence beginnings |
| **Conventions** | Few, if any, errors; strong use of possessive pronouns | Several minor errors; adequate use of possessive pronouns | Many errors; weak use of possessive pronouns | Numerous errors; no or incorrect use of possessive pronouns |

**STORY SEQUENCE CHARTS** Have students refer to the story sequence charts they worked on yesterday. If their charts are not yet complete, allow students additional time to plan the beginning, middle, and end events of their biography.

**WRITE** You will be using your story sequence charts as you write the draft of your biography. When you are drafting, don't worry if your biography does not sound exactly as you would like. You will have a chance to revise it tomorrow.

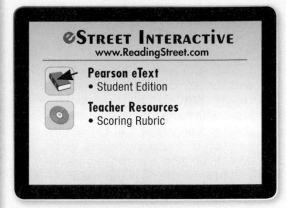

## eSTREET INTERACTIVE
www.ReadingStreet.com

**Pearson eText**
• Student Edition

**Teacher Resources**
• Scoring Rubric

---

### Access for All

**A** Advanced

Have students expand their story sequence charts by including a list of transition words or phrases that will help them later on to connect the events listed in the chart.

---

**Story Sequence Charts** Have students verbalize each section of information on their story sequence chart before they write. Use sentence frames to help, such as the following: *My biography is about _____. It takes place in _____. This person collects _____.*

## Common Core State Standards

**Writing 2.** Write informative/ explanatory texts to examine a topic and convey ideas and information clearly. **Writing 2.b.** Develop the topic with facts, definitions, and details. **Language 1.a.** Explain the function of nouns, pronouns, verbs, adjectives, and adverbs in general and their functions in particular sentences. **Language 1.i.** Produce simple, compound, and complex sentences. **Also Language 1.h.**

## Bridge to Common Core

### RANGE OF WRITING

As students progress through the writing project, they begin to adapt the form and content of their writing for a particular purpose. In this lesson, they learn to write different kinds of sentences to give their writing more texture and to make it more interesting.

# Writing

## Biography

### Mini-Lesson | Writing Trait: Sentences

■ **Introduce** Explain to students that good writing has a natural flow. Different kinds of sentences and sentences of different lengths give writing texture and make it more interesting. Remind students of the three sentence types: declarative, interrogative, and exclamatory. Explain that students can use all three sentence types as they write their drafts. Also, they can write both short and long sentences. Display the Drafting Tips for students. Remind them that the focus of drafting is to get their ideas down in an organized way. Then display Writing Transparency 18A.

### Socks, or Puppets, or Both?

When my Great-Grandma was a young woman, she loved to knit. She was great at knitting socks. She was a fast knitter. Her designs were beautiful.

What if a sock was old? She never threw it out! "Waste not, want not" is her motto. That's how she began a sock-puppet collection—she made it herself. She would sew eyes, ears, and a nose onto hers old sock and give it new life. over time, Great-Grandma created a "family" of more than thirty sock puppetts.

My brother and me love to stage puppet shows with Great-Grandma's sock puppets whenever we visit.

Unit 4 Rocks in His Head          Writing: Model **18A**

Writing Transparency 18A, TR DVD

### Drafting Tips

✔ To get started, review your story sequence chart.

✔ Write paragraphs that tell events in time order.

✔ Include sentences of varying types and lengths.

**Think Aloud** **MODEL** Now I will write my draft. I will use information I put in my story sequence chart to help me. In the *Beginning* box I might write *When my Great-Grandma was a young woman, she loved to knit*. This is how I want to start my biography. As I write, I will remember that I can include both telling and asking sentences to tell my story. I can also use short sentences and long sentences. I won't worry about revising or proof-reading as I write because I will have time to do those tasks after I get my ideas down.

Direct students to use the Drafting Tips to guide them in writing their drafts. Remind them to write sentences that tell about their subject's talents or important achievements.

**eSTREET INTERACTIVE**
www.ReadingStreet.com

**Teacher Resources**
• Writing Transparency

**Routine** | **Quick Write for Fluency** | **Team Talk**

1. **Talk** Have pairs talk about the talents or important achievements of the person they chose to write about.

2. **Write** Each person writes a sentence about the person using a possessive pronoun.

3. **Share** Partners check each other's sentences for correct use of possessive pronouns.

Routines Flip Chart

## Access for All

**SI** Strategic Intervention

Make sure students understand the difference between a sentence and a sentence fragment. List several sentence fragments and have students complete sentences from them. When they are finished, have them tell what was needed to make the sentence complete.

# Wrap Up Your Day!

✔ **Content Knowledge** Have students discuss how the father in this selection was able to stick to his interests.

✔ **Text-Based Comprehension** *What statements of opinion were made about the father in this selection?*

**Preview DAY 4**

Tell students that tomorrow they will read about marbles.

*Rocks in His Head* **109c**

### Materials

- Student Edition
- Reader's and Writer's Notebook
- Decodable Reader

## Common Core State Standards

**Speaking/Listening 1.c.** Ask questions to check understanding of information presented, stay on topic, and link their comments to the remarks of others. **Language 6.** Acquire and use accurately grade-appropriate conversational, general academic, and domain-specific words and phrases, including those that signal spatial and temporal relationships (e.g., *After dinner that night we went looking for them*).

# Content Knowledge

## Unique Interests

**EXPAND THE CONCEPT** Remind students of the weekly concept question, *Why is it valuable to have unique interests?* Have students discuss ways in which unique interests can affect our lives in positive ways.

# Build Oral Language

**Team Talk** **TALK ABOUT SENTENCES AND WORDS** Ask students to reread the first paragraph on Student Edition p. 104.

*Mrs. Johnson came in early for work one morning and saw him carefully writing a new label for one of the rocks.*

- What does *carefully* mean? (to do something cautiously and with attention)
- What are some antonyms for *carefully*? (*carelessly, sloppily, inattentively*)
- How can we rewrite this sentence while still keeping the same meaning? (Possible response: He was carefully writing a new label for one of the rocks when Mrs. Johnson came in early one morning.)
- Have pairs make a list of multiple-meaning words from the sentence along with each word's various meanings. Then have students write sentences that use each word with its different meanings.

# Build Oral Vocabulary

## Amazing Words

### Robust Vocabulary Routine

**1. Introduce** Write the word *compartment* on the board. Have students say it aloud with you. We read about the glass cases at the science museum where rocks were stored in *compartments.* Why do you think museums store things in *compartments?* (Compartments keep things organized.) Have students supply a definition. (A *compartment* is a small section of something such as a box or drawer.)

**2. Demonstrate** Have students answer questions to demonstrate understanding. What *compartments* did the narrator's father use for storing rocks? (shelves, his pockets)

**3. Apply** Have students apply their understanding. What are some things you have that you could store in *compartments?* (socks, shoes, collections, sports equipment)

**4. Display the Word** Run your hand under the syllables *com-part-ment* as you say the word.

See p. OV•3 to teach *forge.*

Routines Flip Chart

**ADD TO THE CONCEPT MAP** Discuss the Amazing Words *ornament* and *descendant*. Add these and other concept-related words to the concept map. Use the following questions to develop students' understanding of the concept. Add words generated in discussion to the concept map.

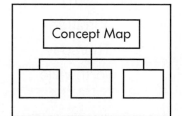

- Why do you think people enjoy *ornament* collecting? What do they do with the *ornaments?*

- What is a type of *ornament* that people may pass along to their children and other *descendants?*

**eStreet Interactive**
www.ReadingStreet.com

**Teacher Resources**
- Amazing Word Cards
- Reader's and Writer's Notebook

## Amazing Words

| | |
|---|---|
| hobby | ornament |
| murmur | descendant |
| project | forge |
| leftover | compartment |
| ancestor | |

## Strategy Response Log

Have students review the characteristics of a biography on p. 24 of the *Reader's and Writer's Notebook*. Then have them compare *Rocks in His Head* to another example of a biography that they have read or know about.

**Cognates** Point out that *compartment,* one of today's Amazing Words, has a Spanish cognate, *compartimiento.*

**Produce Oral Language** Use the Day 4 instruction on ELL Poster 18 to extend and enrich language.

## Common Core State Standards

**Foundational Skills 3.** Know and apply grade-level phonics and word analysis skills in decoding words.
**Foundational Skills 4.** Read with sufficient accuracy and fluency to support comprehension.

# Phonics

## Review Vowels: *r*-Controlled

**REVIEW SOUND-SPELLINGS** To review last week's phonics skill, write *star, purpose, birth,* and *board.* You studied words like these last week. What do you know about words like these that have *r*-controlled vowel sounds? (The *r* changes the sound of the preceding vowel.) Have students identify the letters that spell the *r*-controlled vowel sound in each word. What letters stand for the *r*-controlled vowel in *star*? *(ar)* In *purpose*? *(ur)* Continue in the same way for *birth (ir)* and *board (oar).*

> **Corrective feedback** | If students are unable to answer the questions about *r*-controlled vowels, refer them to *Sound-Spelling Cards* 55, 62, 67, 72, 87, 91, 92, 93 and 104.

**GUIDE PRACTICE** Display a three-column chart with the heads /ėr/, /är/, and /ôr/. We will work together to place words with *r*-controlled vowel sounds in the chart. Listen as I say each word. Words with the *r*-controlled vowel sound /ėr/ as in *worm* will go in the first column. Words with the *r*-controlled vowel sound /är/ as in *farm* will go in the second column. Words with the *r*-controlled vowel sound /ôr/ as in *corn* will go in the third column. Write each word in the appropriate column. Then have students read the words and ask volunteers to underline the letters that spell the *r*-controlled vowel sound in each word.

| /ėr/ | /är/ | /ôr/ |
|---|---|---|
| verb | carbon | former |
| furniture | marketplace | boredom |
| Thursday | shark | soaring |
| worthwhile | backyard | corner |

**ON THEIR OWN** For additional practice, use *Let's Practice It!* p. 243 on the *Teacher Resources DVD-ROM.*

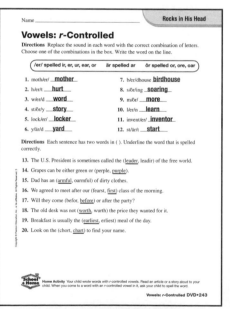

Let's Practice It! TR DVD•243

# Fluent Word Reading

## Spiral Review

**READ WORDS IN ISOLATION** Display these words. Tell students that they can already decode some words on this list. Explain that they should know other words because they appear often in reading.

Have students read the list three or four times until they can read at the rate of two to three seconds per word.

### Word Reading

| | | | | |
|---|---|---|---|---|
| men | climbing | said | leaves | what |
| the | knives | listen | whistled | two |
| done | laughed | people | have | children |
| to | a | where | geese | signs |

**Corrective feedback**

**If...** students have difficulty reading whole words,
**then...** have them use sound-by-sound blending for decodable words or chunking for words that have word parts, or have them say and spell high-frequency words.

**If...** students cannot read fluently at a rate of two to three seconds per word,
**then...** have pairs practice the list until they can read it fluently.

**eSTREET INTERACTIVE**
www.ReadingStreet.com

**Teacher Resources**
• Let's Practice It!
• Graphic Organizer

**Interactive Sound-Spelling Cards**

## Access for All

**SI** Strategic Intervention

To assist students having difficulty with the *r*-controlled vowels /ėr/, /är/, and /ôr/, focus on only one *r*-controlled vowel at a time. Write words with /ėr/ spelled *ir, er, ur, ear,* and *or* on separate cards. Have students sort the words by the *r*-controlled vowel spelling and then read all the words. Repeat with /är/ words spelled *ar* and /ôr/ words spelled *or, ore,* and *oar.*

## Spiral Review

These activities review

• previously taught high-frequency words *said, what, the, two, done, laughed, people, have, to, a, where.*

• irregular plurals; consonant patterns *wr, kn, gn, st, mb.*

**Pronunciation** Have students say the words with consonant patterns *wr, kn, gn, st, mb.* Listen carefully to make sure that they do not pronounce the silent letters.

*Rocks in His Head* **110d**

**Common Core State Standards**

**Foundational Skills 3.a.** Identify and know the meaning of the most common prefixes and derivational suffixes. **Foundational Skills 3.d.** Read grade-appropriate irregularly spelled words. **Foundational Skills 4.** Read with sufficient accuracy and fluency to support comprehension. **Foundational Skills 4.c.** Use context to confirm or self-correct word recognition and understanding, rereading as necessary.

# Fluent Word Reading

**READ WORDS IN CONTEXT** Display these sentences. Call on individuals to read a sentence. Then randomly point to review words and have students read them. To help you monitor word reading, high-frequency words are underlined and decodable words are italicized.

**MONITOR PROGRESS** Sentence Reading

The *children* underlined laughed when some *geese* honked.

Jim *whistled* to the two *men climbing* the cliff.

They put *signs* where people can see them.

What have you done with the *knives*?

"*Listen* to the *leaves* in the trees," a girl said.

**If...** students are unable to read an underlined high-frequency word,

**then...** read the word for them and spell it, having them echo you.

**If...** students have difficulty reading an italicized decodable word,

**then...** guide them in using sound-by-sound blending or chunking.

# Reread for Fluency

Have students reread the sentences to develop automaticity decoding words.

**Routine** Oral Rereading

1. **Read** Have students read all the sentences orally.

2. **Reread** To achieve optimal fluency, students should reread the sentences three or four times.

3. **Corrective Feedback** Listen as students read. Provide corrective feedback regarding their fluency and decoding.

Routines Flip Chart

# Decodable Passage 18C

f students need help, then...

## Read *Spelling Bee*

**READ WORDS IN ISOLATION** Have students turn to p. 35 in *Decodable Practice Readers 3.2* and find the first list of words. Each word in this list has a prefix. Let's decode and read these words. Be sure that students identify the prefix in each word. Next, have students read the high-frequency words.

**PREVIEW** Have students read the title and preview the story. Tell them that they will read words with the prefixes *pre-, mid-, over-, out-, bi-,* and *de-*. Make sure that students are monitoring their accuracy when they decode words.

**READ WORDS IN CONTEXT** Chorally read the story along with the students. Have students identify words in the story that have the prefixes *pre-, mid-, over-, out-, bi-,* and *de-*.

**Team Talk** Pair students and have them take turns reading the story aloud to each other. Monitor students as they read to check for proper pronunciation and appropriate pacing.

**eStreet Interactive**
www.ReadingStreet.com

**Pearson eText**
• Decodable Reader

### Access for All

**A** Advanced

Have students write their own sentences that use words with silent letters. They can use words from p. 110e or choose other words they know.

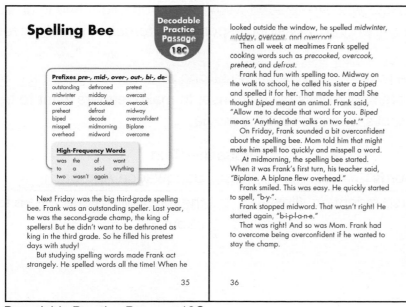

Decodable Practice Passage 18C

**Common Core State Standards**

**Informational Text 1.** Ask and answer questions to demonstrate understanding of a text, referring explicitly to the text as the basis for the answers. **Informational Text 6.** Distinguish their own point of view from that of the author of a text. **Language 4.** Determine or clarify the meaning of unknown and multiple-meaning words and phrases based on grade 3 reading and content, choosing flexibly from a range of strategies. **Language 5.** Demonstrate understanding of word relationships and nuances in word meanings.

 **Bridge to Common Core**

### KEY IDEAS AND DETAILS

Analyzing the language of a persuasive article will lead students to read closely and critically to determine the author's purpose. They will differentiate between what the text says explicitly and what it infers. They will analyze how the text is structured to persuade the reader.

# Social Studies in Reading

## Persuasive Text

**INTRODUCE** Explain to students that what we read is structured differently depending on the author's reasons for writing and what kind of information he or she wishes to convey. Different types of texts are called *genres*. Tell students that persuasive text is one type of genre.

**DISCUSS THE GENRE** Discuss with students the different purposes authors have for writing. Explain: A movie review is written to persuade the reader to agree with the reviewer, but it might also entertain and inform the reader. Authors present facts and details to support their opinions. As a reader, you will get the most out of a text by asking yourself what the author's purpose is in presenting the facts and details. Explain that two clues that signal persuasive text are the author's use of "loaded words," or words that have strong emotional appeal, and the bandwagon approach, an appeal to the desire to be part of the "in" group.

**GROUP PRACTICE** Display a T-chart like the one below. Ask the following questions. Encourage students to answer questions with appropriate detail.

- What are some negative "loaded words" that you might find in an advertisement for a cell phone? **Possible responses:** *cheap, poor reception, flimsy*

- What are some positive "loaded words" that you might find in an advertisement for a cell phone? **Possible responses:** *affordable, excellent reception, sturdy*

- "This is the movie everyone will be talking about!" Why might a movie review use this statement? **Possible response:** to make readers want to be part of the group that's talking about the movie

### Persuasive Text

| "Loaded Words" | Bandwagon Approach |
|---|---|
| cheap, limited reception, flimsy | the movie everyone will be talking about |

**Team Talk** Have students work in pairs to discuss and brainstorm examples of "loaded language" and the bandwagon approach that they've seen in TV ads or in persuasive text. Ask them to share their examples with the class.

**READ** Tell students that they will now read a persuasive text about the game of marbles. Have the class think about the author's purpose for writing the article.

**eStreet Interactive**
www.ReadingStreet.com

**Teacher Resources**
• Graphic Organizer

---

**ELL**

**Cognates** The Spanish word *persuasivo* may be familiar to Spanish speakers as the cognate for *persuasive*.

**ELL**

**If...** students need more scaffolding and practice with the **Amazing Words,**
**then...** use the Routine on pp. xxxvi–xxxvii in the *ELL Handbook*.

---

## Day 4 SMALL GROUP TIME • Differentiate Vocabulary, p. SG•33

| **OL** On-Level | **SI** Strategic Intervention | **A** Advanced |
|---|---|---|
| • **Develop** Language Using Amazing Words | • **Review/Discuss** Amazing Words | • **Extend** Amazing Words and Selection Vocabulary |
| • **Read** "Marvelous Marble Mania" | • **Read** "Marvelous Marble Mania" | • **Read** "Marvelous Marble Mania" |
| | | • **Organize** Inquiry Project |

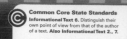

Common Core State Standards
Informational Text 6. Distinguish their own point of view from that of the author of a text. Also Informational Text 2., 7.

## Social Studies in Reading

### Genre
**Persuasive Text**

- When an author's purpose is to persuade, the text will have facts or opinions to convince you to think or do something.
- An author can use "loaded words," or strong, opinionated words.
- The "bandwagon approach" is used to convince the reader that a large number of people are doing something and you should do it too.
- Read the article, "Marvelous Marble Mania." As you read, look for loaded words and the bandwagon approach.

110

# Marvelous Marble Mania

### by Robert Kausal

Look in your closet. Is it over filled with games that you never play anymore? Every year toy-makers come out with hundreds of new games. Many of these games can be fun to play for a few days, or weeks, but then the game pieces get scattered around the house, the batteries run down, or they just get super boring.

Sometimes the best games are the ones that have been around the longest. That's because they are fun, challenging, and easy to learn.

## Knuckle Down . . . . . . . . . . . . . .

One of the oldest and most popular games in the world is played with marbles. You might be surprised to learn that marbles have been around for thousands of years. Children in Egypt played with marbles as far back as 4000 B.C.E.! Back then marbles were made out of clay. Today, most marbles are made of glass. Games with these multi-colored balls are played in places like Australia, India, Turkey, and yes, even the United States.

> **Here are some terms people use when playing marbles:**
>
> - **Keepsies:** You get to keep all of the marbles you win. Also called "playing for keeps."
> - **Knuckle down:** When you begin a game, you touch your shooting knuckle to the ground.
> - **Mibs:** These are the target marbles in a game.
> - **Quitsies:** When you allow an opponent to quit the game whenever he or she wants. You can also call "No Quitsies."
> - **Elephant Stomps:** Allows a player to smash his or her marble into the ground, making it difficult to knock out.

Let's **Think** About...

What persuasive device is the author using in this paragraph? Support your answer with evidence from the text. Persuasive Text

111

**Student Edition, pp. 110–111**

---

## Common Core State Standards

**Informational Text 1.** Ask and answer questions to demonstrate understanding of a text, referring explicitly to the text as the basis for the answers. **Informational Text 2.** Determine the main idea of a text; recount the key details and explain how they support the main idea. **Informational Text 6.** Distinguish their own point of view from that of the author of a text. **Also Informational Text 3., 7., Language 4., 5.**

## Access Text ©

**TEACH Persuasive Text** Have students preview "Marvelous Marble Mania" on pp. 110–111 and ask them to look for examples of persuasive devices. Then ask: Why do you think the author uses the word *marvelous* in the title of the article? (to show he really likes marbles)

> **Corrective feedback**
>
> **If...** students are unable to explain why the author uses the word *marvelous* in the title,
>
> **then...** use the model to guide students in analyzing "loaded words."

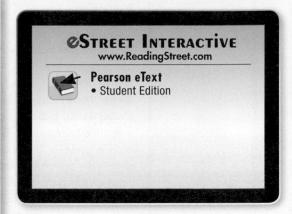

**MODEL** The author could have left out the adjective *marvelous* in the title, but he had a reason for using it. What is a synonym for *marvelous? (wonderful)* This is a strong word. I think that the author uses this "loaded word" to persuade readers to agree with his opinion of the game of marbles.

**ON THEIR OWN** Have students reread pp. 110–111 to look for other examples of persuasive text. Have students tell what the author is trying to persuade the reader to think.

# Close Reading

**EVALUATION** Does page 110 provide mostly statements of fact or statements of opinion? How do you know? (The page provides mostly statements of opinion. Only one statement of fact is provided: *Every year toy-makers come out with hundreds of new games.* This is a statement of fact because it can be proved true or false. The other statements can't be proved.)

**SYNTHESIS • TEXT EVIDENCE** On page 111, the author provides some facts about the game of marbles. What do you think is the author's purpose in providing these facts? Support your response with evidence from the text. (The author may want to convince the reader that the game of marbles is a lot of fun. He does this in the second sentence by saying that people around the world have been playing it for a very long time.)

# Genre

**LET'S THINK ABOUT...** As you read "Marvelous Marble Mania," use Let's Think About in the Student Edition to help students focus on the features of a persuasive text.

The author is using the bandwagon approach by emphasizing that the game has been played for thousands of years and that it is still played in countries all around the world.

**Access for All**

 **Strategic Intervention**

Before reading, have students preview the text features, such as the glossary box on p. 111 and the drawings and photographs on p. 113. Ask students to discuss what they know about playing the game of marbles.

**"Loaded Words"** Help students understand that words with strong connotations are words that create an emotional response in the reader. Provide these examples for students and have them give a "thumbs up" or "thumbs down" sign to show their reactions: *skinny/slim, tall/looming, odd/unique.* Ask students to give other examples of "loaded words."

## Keepsies

Marbles are popular all over the world. That's because there are hundreds of games you can play with them. Some really fun games are Poison, Boss Out, Cherry Pit, Ringer, Nine Holes, and Black Snake. In the United States, kids and adults play Ringer in marble tournaments. The goal with most marble games is to "knuckle down" and shoot your opponents marbles out of the ring. It takes a lot of skill, but if you practice enough, you can play for keeps, or keepsies.

## Don't Lose Your Marbles

Another reason that marbles are popular is because of their brilliant beauty. Marbles come in all colors, designs, and sizes. One handmade marble from the 1800s can be worth thousands of dollars! People still make handmade marbles today, but most are made by machine. Once you start collecting marbles, you will be amazed by how unique and beautiful they are. So what are you waiting for? Join the millions of people around the world who play marbles. It is fun, challenging, and easy to learn. And who knows, maybe some day your marbles will be worth lots of money too.

**Let's Think About...**
Does the author use any "loaded words" in this paragraph? What is he trying to get you to think or do? **Persuasive Text**
❷

112

## How to Play the Game Ringers

Thirteen mibs are arranged in the middle of a circle. The goal of the game is to shoot from outside the circle and knock the marbles out of the ring. If you knock out a mib and your marble is still in the circle, you can keep shooting. If your shooter goes outside the circle, you lose your turn. The first player to knock out seven mibs wins.

**Let's Think About...**
Summarize how to play Ringers, explaining the game in logical order in five or six steps. Then follow the directions when you play! **Persuasive Text**
❸

**Let's Think About...**
Look at the illustrations. How should you arrange the marbles? **Persuasive Text**
❹

**Let's Think About...**
**Reading Across Texts** What would a rock collection, like the one in *Rocks in His Head*, have in common with a marble collection?

**Writing Across Texts** Write a letter to a friend telling why you want to collect rocks or marbles, and why your friend should too.

113

**Student Edition, pp. 112–113**

---

## © Common Core State Standards

**Informational Text 8.** Describe the logical connection between particular sentences and paragraphs in a text (e.g., comparison, cause/effect, first/second/third in a sequence). **Informational Text 9.** Compare and contrast the most important points and key details presented in two texts on the same topic. **Language 4.** Determine or clarify the meaning of unknown and multiple-meaning words and phrases based on grade 3 reading and content, choosing flexibly from a range of strategies. **Also Informational Text 1., 3., 6., Foundational Skills 3.**

# Access Text ©

**TEACH Persuasive Text** Have students list two examples of the bandwagon approach from p. 112. Then ask: What is the author trying to persuade the reader to think or do? (play and collect marbles) How is the selection about rocks and the one about marbles alike?

**Corrective feedback**

**If...** students have difficulty identifying examples, **then...** model identifying text clues that signal the bandwagon approach.

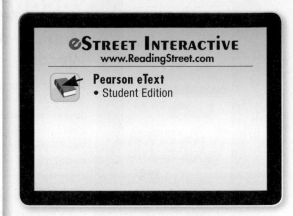

**Think Aloud** **MODEL** The first sentence on page 112 says *Marbles are popular all over the world.* Based on this information, do you think lots of people enjoy playing marbles? **(yes)** I think the author wants me to think that I would enjoy playing marbles because so many other people enjoy the game.

**ON THEIR OWN** Have students reread the page and look for another example of the bandwagon approach. Ask them to explain what the author wants them to think or do.

# Close Reading

**ANALYSIS** Why do you think the author includes information about how beautiful and valuable marbles can be? **(The author wants to appeal to readers who might be more interested in collecting marbles than in playing games with them.)**

**ANALYSIS • TEXT EVIDENCE** The author writes that marbles are popular all over the world. Is the popularity of marbles a cause or an effect? Use evidence from the text to support your answer. **(It is an effect. In paragraph 1 on p. 112, the author says that marbles are popular all over the world *because* there are hundreds of games people can play with them.)**

# Genre

**LET'S THINK ABOUT...** features of persuasive text.

 "Loaded words" include *hundreds, popular, really fun.* He is trying to make the reader want to play marbles.

First, 13 mibs are arranged in the middle of a circle. Then players try to shoot from outside the circle to knock the marbles out of the ring. If a player knocks out a mib and their marble is still in the circle, they can keep playing. If the shooter lands outside the circle, then you lose a turn. To win, a player has to be the first to knock 7 mibs out of the circle.

You should arrange the marbles in the shape of an X.

# Reading and Writing Across Texts

Have students create a concept web with either *Rocks* or *Marbles* in the center circle. Students can brainstorm details about each to add to the outer circles. Have students use their concept maps to list reasons why rocks and marbles are a good thing to collect. Remind them to use information from the two selections. Then have them use the list to write their letter.

## Access for All

**SI Strategic Intervention**
Point out that the clue word *because* in the second sentence on p. 112 indicates the cause that, or reason why, marbles are so popular.

**A Advanced**
Have students look for another reason the author gives for why marbles are popular. Ask them to write a sentence that states the two causes of the popularity of marbles.

**Graphic Organizer** Provide support to students when creating a concept web. Help them choose the key terms for their webs, and then work together to add details.

*Rocks in His Head* **113a**

### Let's Learn It!

READING STREET ONLINE
ONLINE STUDENT EDITION
www.ReadingStreet.com

## Vocabulary

### Multiple-Meaning Words

**Context Clues** Multiple-meaning words are words that are spelled the same but have different meanings. Use context clues by looking at the words around a multiple-meaning word to figure out its meaning in the sentence.

**Practice It!** Make a list of four multiple-meaning words. Use each word in a sentence. Exchange papers with a partner and use context clues to figure out the meanings of the four words.

## Fluency

### Expression

Reading with expression makes a story more exciting. Stressing words differently, saying some words with more feeling than others, or changing your tone of voice for dialogue makes the story lively.

**Practice It!** With your partner, read aloud page 96. How should your tone of voice be different when reading dialogue than when reading a regular paragraph?

## Listening and Speaking

Speak clearly and make eye contact with your subject.

### Interview

In an interview, one person asks another person questions. Use formal language and remember to speak clearly, coherently, and with expression during an interview.

**Practice It!** Work in pairs to prepare an interview to present to the class. You might want to pretend the person being interviewed has an interesting job, and a reporter will interview him or her for a newspaper article. Prepare questions and conduct your interview in front of the class.

### Tips

**Listening ...**
- Try to anticipate what the speaker will say next.
- Ask relevant questions in response.

**Speaking ...**
- Speak clearly and distinctly.
- Use possessive pronouns correctly.

**Teamwork ...**
- Ask and answer questions with detail.
- Make the interview sound like a natural conversation.

114        115

**Student Edition, pp. 114–115**

---

# Fluency

## Expression

**GUIDE PRACTICE** Use the Student Edition activity as an assessment tool. As students read aloud with partners, walk around to make sure their expression is appropriate.

Don't Wait Until Friday

**MONITOR PROGRESS** Check Fluency

**FORMATIVE ASSESSMENT** As students reread, monitor their progress toward their individual fluency goals.

Current Goal: 95–105 words correct per minute.

End-of-Year Goal: 120 words correct per minute.

**If...** students cannot read fluently at a rate of 95–105 words correct per minute,

**then...** have students practice with text at their independent levels.

# Vocabulary Skill

## ⊙ Multiple-Meaning Words

**TEACH MULTIPLE-MEANING WORDS • CONTEXT CLUES** Write the following sentence on the board.

*The postal worker said I need to put more stamps on this envelope.*

Point out to students that they can determine the correct meaning of *stamps* in the sentence by looking at the words around it.

**GUIDE PRACTICE** Tell students to be sure to use context clues in the sentences they write for their multiple-meaning words.

**ON THEIR OWN** Walk around the room as students work with partners to check that students identify the correct meanings.

# Listening and Speaking

## Interview

**TEACH** Tell students that in order for an interview to be successful, everyone must work together. Have partners brainstorm jobs and topics that might be discussed during an interview for an article. One partner can pretend to hold the job and the other can conduct the interview.

**GUIDE PRACTICE** Remind interviewers to face the person they are interviewing, use eye contact, and speak clearly and coherently. Tell them to wait for questions to be answered before asking the next question. They should listen to the answer so that their next question follows logically. Have students restate these instructions prior to following them. If needed, have students give these instructions again to their partner.

**ON THEIR OWN** Have students conduct the interview with their partners.

## Interviewing

**Rehearsal Tips**

- Look at the person you are interviewing.
- Ask questions in a logical order.
- Make sure each answer is completed before you ask the next question.
- Express interest in answers as they are given.

**©** Bridge to Common Core

### COMPREHENSION AND COLLABORATION

As students prepare for their interviews, they collaborate with other students, building on others' ideas and expressing their own clearly and persuasively. They evaluate their partners' points of view, reasoning, and use of evidence and rhetoric.

**Practice Pronunciation** Assist pairs of students by modeling the correct pronunciation of the words from a glossary, then having students repeat after you. Pair students with mixed language proficiencies together to practice pronunciation and employ self-corrective techniques.

*Rocks in His Head* **115a**

**Common Core State Standards**

**Foundational Skills 4.b.** Read on-level prose and poetry orally with accuracy, appropriate rate, and expression on successive readings. **Writing 2.** Write informative/explanatory texts to examine a topic and convey ideas and information clearly. **Writing 8.** Recall information from experiences or gather information from print and digital sources; take brief notes on sources and sort evidence into provided categories. **Also Language 1.a., 2.f.**

# Research and Inquiry

## Step 4 Synthesize

**TEACH** Have students synthesize their research findings and results. Suggest that students create a Web directory to show the online sources they used for their research. Review how to choose relevant information from a number of sources and organize it logically. Explain to students that when writing exactly what a research source says, they must use quotation marks and cite the source in their informational article in order to avoid plagiarism, or copying someone's idea and trying to pass it off as original. If they are explaining what the research source said in their own words, or paraphrasing, then they do not need to use quotations marks, but must still cite the source.

**GUIDE PRACTICE** Have students use a word-processing program or poster-board to prepare for their presentations on Day 5. Remind students to include multiple sources of valid and reliable oral and written information in their informational articles. Check to see that students have prepared a works-cited page that includes the author, title, publisher, and publication year for each source they use.

**ON THEIR OWN** Have students organize their research findings in the form of an informational article. Then have them plan their presentations.

# Conventions

## Possessive Pronouns

**TEST PRACTICE** Remind students that grammar skills, such as possessive pronouns, are often assessed on important tests. Recall that possessive pronouns show who or what owns, or possesses, something.

**ON THEIR OWN** For additional practice, use *Reader's and Writer's Notebook*, p. 279.

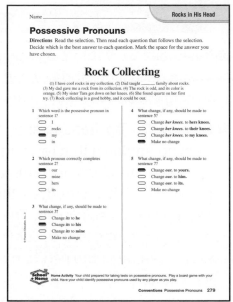

Reader's and Writer's Notebook, p. 279

# Spelling

## Prefixes *pre-, mid-, over-, out-*

**PRACTICE SPELLING STRATEGY**
Remind students that words with prefixes in this lesson are easier to spell if the student keeps the base word in mind. Have students segment or divide each word by its prefix and base word in their mind before spelling the word. Remind them to use the letter sounds to help them spell each word part.

**ON THEIR OWN** For additional practice, use *Let's Practice It!* p. 244 on the *Teacher Resources DVD-ROM*.

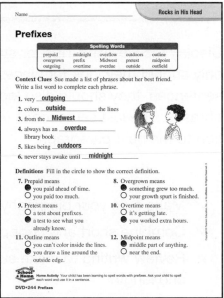

Let's Practice It! TR DVD•244

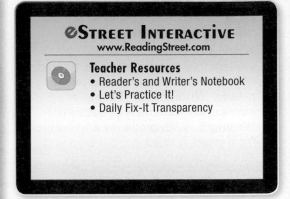

**eSTREET INTERACTIVE**
www.ReadingStreet.com

**Teacher Resources**
- Reader's and Writer's Notebook
- Let's Practice It!
- Daily Fix-It Transparency

## Daily Fix-It

7. Hers green rock was finded in South America. *(Her; found)*

8. Rob and them displayed the rocks in Ms. Shaws room. *(they; Shaw's)*

### © Bridge to Common Core

**CONVENTIONS OF STANDARD ENGLISH**

As students identify, form, and use possessive pronouns, they are demonstrating command of the conventions of standard English. Your guidance will help them use correct grammar, usage, and spelling to convey meaning when they speak and write.

## Common Core State Standards

**Writing 2.** Write informative/explanatory texts to examine a topic and convey ideas and information clearly. **Writing 2.d.** Provide a concluding statement or section. **Writing 5.** With guidance and support from peers and adults, develop and strengthen writing as needed by planning, revising, and editing. **Language 3.** Use knowledge of language and its conventions when writing, speaking, reading, or listening. **Also Language 1.h., 1.i.**

## Write Guy *by Jeff Anderson*

**Teaching Trait-by-Trait: Focus**

In a writing conference, choose one aspect of a students' draft, not many things. This will help the student more than trying to think about multiple writing traits at once. Maybe there is one skill at this student's growing edge of knowledge that I can help him improve. I'd hate to see that lost in a swarm of my other comments.

# Writing Zoom in on

## Biography

**Mini-Lesson**  **Revise: Consolidating**

■ Yesterday we wrote biographies about someone we know who has an interesting collection. Today we will revise our drafts. The goal is to make your writing clearer, more interesting, and more informative.

■ Display Writing Transparency 18B. Remind students that revising does not include corrections of grammar and mechanics. Then introduce the revising strategy of consolidating. The two short sentences at the end of our first paragraph can be combined to make one long sentence.

■ When you revise, ask yourself *Do my sentences sound short, choppy, or awkward?* The revising strategy of consolidating can be used to combine these types of sentences. Reread your biography for places you can combine sentences for clarity.

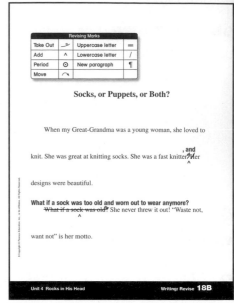

Writing Transparency 18B, TR DVD

Display the Revising Tips for students. Tell students that as they revise, not only should they look for places where they can combine short and choppy sentences, they should also look for places to add transition words and phrases. The last sentence in every paragraph should offer a smooth transition to the next paragraph.

### Revising Tips

✔ Make sure your biography is told in time order.

✔ Combine short and choppy sentences.

✔ Review writing to make sure it shows a variety of sentence types and length.

**eSTREET INTERACTIVE**
www.ReadingStreet.com

**Teacher Resources**
• Writing Transparency

**PEER CONFERENCING • PEER REVISION** Have partners exchange papers and read aloud each other's biographies. Remind students to listen for sentences that sound short or choppy, as well as sentences that all begin with the same word or phrase. Have partners review their lists and discuss ways to revise language for clarity.

Have students revise their biographies. They should use the lists they wrote during Peer Revision as well as the key features of biographies to guide their revision. Check to make sure students are using the revising strategy of consolidating.

**Corrective feedback** | Circulate around the room to monitor and confer with students as they revise. Remind students who are correcting grammatical errors that they will have time to proofread tomorrow. They should be working on clarifying ideas and language today.

**Routine**    **Quick Write for Fluency**    Team Talk

1. **Talk** Have pairs discuss how the dad in *Rocks in His Head* is one of a kind.

2. **Write** Each student writes a paragraph that gives information about the father.

3. **Share** Partners read and check each other's paragraphs for examples of the dad's talents and achievements.

Routines Flip Chart

**E L L**

**Support Revising** Call on a volunteer and give him or her several commands, such as: *Stand up. Raise your hands. Walk three steps forward. Turn around. Walk back.* Discuss with students how you can combine these short, choppy sentences to make a longer sentence. Call on students to combine sentences orally. Write example sentences on the board and choral read them together.

# Wrap Up Your Day!

✔ **Content Knowledge** Have students discuss what they learned through the riddles and explanations.

✔ **Oral Vocabulary** Monitor students' use of oral vocabulary as they respond to this question: *What hobbies are featured in the illustrations?*

✔ **Text Features** Discuss how the illustrations help students understand text.

**Preview DAY 5**

Remind students to think about why it's important to have unique interests.

### Materials

- Student Edition
- Weekly Test
- Reader's and Writer's Notebook

## Bridge to Common Core

**INTEGRATION OF KNOWLEDGE/IDEAS**

This week, students have integrated content presented in diverse media and analyzed how different texts address similar topics. They have developed knowledge about unique interests to expand the unit topic of One of a Kind.

**Social Studies Knowledge Goals**

Students have learned that interests

- are valuable
- lead to learning and research
- lead to a job
- preserve information

# Content Knowledge

## Unique Interests

**REVIEW THE CONCEPT** Have students look back at the reading selections to find examples that best demonstrate why it is valuable to have unique interests.

## Build Oral Language

**REVIEW AMAZING WORDS** Display and review this week's concept map. Remind students that this week they have learned nine Amazing Words related to unique interests. Have students use the Amazing Words and the concept map to answer the Question of the Week, *Why is it valuable to have unique interests?* Be sure their answers include appropriate detail.

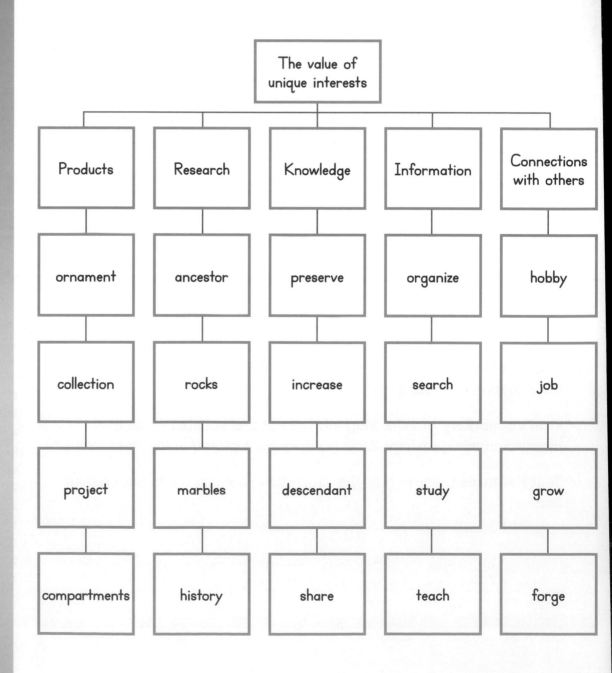

The value of unique interests

| Products | Research | Knowledge | Information | Connections with others |
|---|---|---|---|---|
| ornament | ancestor | preserve | organize | hobby |
| collection | rocks | increase | search | job |
| project | marbles | descendant | study | grow |
| compartments | history | share | teach | forge |

# Build Oral Vocabulary

**Team Talk** **CONNECT TO AMAZING IDEAS** Have pairs of students discuss how the Question of the Week connects to the question for this unit of study: *What does it mean to be unique?* Tell students to use the concept map and what they have learned from this week's discussions and reading selections to form an Amazing Idea—a realization or "big idea" about One of a Kind. Remind partners to answer questions with appropriate detail and to give suggestions that build on each other's ideas. Then ask pairs to share their Amazing Ideas with the class.

Amazing Ideas might include these key concepts:

• Unique interests help you grow as a person.

• People have a variety of interests.

• People express their interests and talents in creative ways, including artwork, writing, and collecting items.

**WRITE ABOUT IT** Have students write a few sentences about their Amazing Idea, beginning with "This week I learned . . ."

## Amazing Words

| | |
|---|---|
| hobby | ornament |
| murmur | descendant |
| project | compartment |
| leftover | forge |
| ancestor | |

**It's Friday**

## MONITOR PROGRESS  Check Oral Vocabulary

**FORMATIVE ASSESSMENT** Have individuals use this week's Amazing Words to describe unique interests. Monitor students' abilities to use the Amazing Words and note which words you need to reteach.

**If...** students have difficulty using the Amazing Words,

**then...** reteach using the Oral Vocabulary Routine, pp. 87a, 92b, 100b, 110b, OV•3.

**ELL**

**Check Concepts and Language** Use the Day 5 instruction on ELL Poster 18 to monitor students' understanding of the lesson concept.

**Concept Map** Work with students to add new words to the concept map.

*Rocks in His Head* **115g**

Zoom in on

**Common Core State Standards**

**Informational Text 3.** Describe the relationship between a series of historical events, scientific ideas or concepts, or steps in technical procedures in a text, using language that pertains to time, sequence, and cause/effect. **Foundational Skills 3.a.** Identify and know the meaning of the most common prefixes and derivational suffixes. **Language 4.** Determine or clarify the meaning of unknown and multiple-meaning words and phrases based on grade 3 reading and content, choosing flexibly from a range of strategies. **Also Language 2.f., 4.a.**

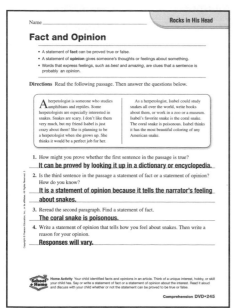

Let's Practice It! TR DVD•245

## Selection Vocabulary

**attic** the space in a house just below the roof and above the other rooms

**board** a group of people who manage something

**chores** small tasks or easy jobs that you have to do regularly

**customer** someone who buys goods or services

**labeled** put or wrote a label on something

**spare** extra

**stamps** small pieces of paper with glue on the back for mailing letters and packages

# Text-Based Comprehension

## Review ⊙ Fact and Opinion

**TEACH** Review the definitions of statements of fact and statements of opinion on p. 90. Remind students that statements of fact can be proved true or false and that statements of opinion give someone's thoughts or feelings about something. For additional support have students review p. EI•7 on fact and opinion.

**GUIDE PRACTICE** Have partners identify the facts and opinions and evaluate whether or not they can be proved. Have student pairs find an example of a statement of fact in *Rocks in His Head.* Then have pairs tell whether their statement of fact is correct.

**ON THEIR OWN** For additional practice, use *Let's Practice It!* p. 245 on the *Teacher Resources DVD-ROM.*

# Vocabulary Skill

## Review ⊙ Multiple-Meaning Words

**TEACH** Remind students that multiple-meaning words have more than one meaning. Context clues can help readers understand which meaning of the word makes sense in the sentence.

**GUIDE PRACTICE** Review with students how to find the correct meaning of *board* in this sentence: *The board of directors will meet tomorrow.* Ask students to point out the context clues that help them define the word.

**ON THEIR OWN** Have students work with partners to write context sentences using this week's lesson vocabulary words *stamps* and *spare*. Partners can trade sentences and identify the context clues that help them determine each word's meaning.

# Word Analysis

**Review**  Prefixes *pre-, mid-, over-, out-, bi-, de-*

**TEACH** Write the following sentences on the board. Have students read each one, first quietly to themselves and then aloud as you track the print.

**GUIDE PRACTICE**

1. We are at the midpoint of our bicycle trip.
2. The view from this scenic overlook is outstanding.
3. Use binoculars to see the outfield.
4. Our midsummer vacation is overdue.
5. We had to prepay to depart on our trip.

**Team Talk** Have students work with a partner to identify and underline the prefixes in the words. Then point to underlined words at random and have the group read them together.

# Literary Terms

## Review Idioms

**TEACH** Remind students that idioms are a type of word play frequently found in both fiction and nonfiction. An idiom is a figure of speech that contains more than one word and that has a meaning and a use totally its own. The literal meanings of the words do not explain the meaning of the expression.

**GUIDE PRACTICE** Point out the idiom *There's no money in rocks* from p. 96 of *Rocks in His Head*. Discuss the meaning of the idiom and have students find and explain other examples of idioms on pp. 97–99.

**ON THEIR OWN** Have students make a T-chart with the headings *Idiom* and *Meaning*. Ask them to list examples of idioms from the selection in the first column and write the explanations in the second column.

**ELL**

**Fact and Opinion** If students have trouble distinguishing fact from opinion, advise them to consider how they could find out whether each statement is true or false. For example, they might consult a reference book or ask an expert. Tell students that if a statement can be proved true or false, it is a fact. Provide sentence frames to help students respond: *This statement is a _____ (fact/opinion) because _____.*

**Articulation Tip** Speakers of monosyllabic languages such as Cantonese, Hmong, Khmer, Korean, and Vietnamese may have difficulty understanding that multisyllabic words are single words. Help students practice saying and writing words with prefixes as single words.

## Common Core State Standards

**Foundational Skills 4.** Read with sufficient accuracy and fluency to support comprehension. **Foundational Skills 4.a.** Read on-level text with purpose and understanding. **Foundational Skills 4.c.** Use context to confirm or self-correct word recognition and understanding, rereading as necessary.

## Plan to Assess Fluency

☐ **Week 1** Advanced

☐ **Week 2** Strategic Intervention

☑ **This week assess On-Level students.**

☐ **Week 4** Strategic Intervention

☐ **Week 5** Assess any students you have not yet checked during this unit.

Set individual goals for students to enable them to reach the year-end goal.

- Current Goal: 95–105 WCPM
- Year-End Goal: 120 WCPM

# Assessment

## Monitor Progress

**FLUENCY** Make two copies of the fluency passage on p. 115k. As the student reads the text aloud, mark mistakes on your copy. Also mark where the student is at the end of one minute. To check the student's comprehension of the passage, have him or her retell what was read. To figure words correct per minute (WCPM), subtract the number of mistakes from the total number of words read in one minute.

### RATE

| Corrective feedback | **If...** students cannot read fluently at a rate of 95–105 WCPM, **then...** make sure they practice with text at their independent reading level. Provide additional fluency practice by pairing nonfluent readers with fluent readers. |
|---|---|
| | **If...** students already read at 120 WCPM, **then...** have them read a book of their choice independently. |

---

**ELL**

**If...** students need more scaffolding and practice with **Conventions and Writing,** **then...** use the Grammar Transition Lessons on pp. 312–386 in the ELL Handbook.

## Day 5 SMALL GROUP TIME • Differentiate Reteaching, p. SG•33

| **OL** On-Level | **SI** Strategic Intervention | **A** Advanced |
|---|---|---|
| • **Practice** Possessive Pronouns | • **Review** Possessive Pronouns | • **Extend** Possessive Pronouns |
| • **Reread** *Reading Street Sleuth,* pp. 48–49 | • **Reread** *Reading Street Sleuth,* pp. 48–49 | • **Reread** *Reading Street Sleuth,* pp. 48–49 |
| | | • **Communicate** Inquiry Project |

Name _____

# Mona's Stamp Collection

| | |
|---|---:|
| It was midday when Mona had finished her chores. | 9 |
| "Where are you going?" asked her friend Jules. | 17 |
| "I'm going to Stone's Stamp Store to see if I can trade this dinosaur | 31 |
| stamp for a cartoon stamp," she answered. | 38 |
| "Who are you mailing the stamp to?" Jules asked. | 47 |
| "No one. I collect stamps," Mona replied. | 54 |
| "Why?" Jules said in a puzzled voice. | 61 |
| "It's fun to collect stamps. They're small and easy to keep," | 72 |
| Mona explained. | 74 |
| "Can I come with you?" Jules asked. | 81 |
| "Sure," Mona said. | 84 |
| Mona and Jules entered the stamp store. There were racks of | 95 |
| stamps on overhead shelves. The racks were labeled with names from | 106 |
| around the world. | 109 |
| "Hi, Mr. Stone. I found this stamp in my attic," Mona started to | 122 |
| explain, "and I was wondering if I might trade it for a cartoon stamp." | 136 |
| Mr. Stone looked at the stamp carefully. "Do you know what you | 148 |
| have here?" he asked. | 152 |
| "An old prehistoric dinosaur standing in an overgrown grass | 161 |
| field," Mona answered. | 164 |
| "This is a one-of-a-kind stamp. It's worth quite a bit of money," | 176 |
| Mr. Stone explained. | 179 |
| "Does this mean I can have the cartoon stamp?" Mona asked. | 190 |
| "No, this means you can have a *hundred* cartoon stamps," | 200 |
| Mr. Stone laughed. | 203 |

**MONITOR PROGRESS** • Check Fluency

**Common Core State Standards**

**Informational Text 1.** Ask and answer questions to demonstrate understanding of a text, referring explicitly to the text as the basis for the answers. **Informational Text 3.** Describe the relationship between a series of historical events, scientific ideas or concepts, or steps in technical procedures in a text, using language that pertains to time, sequence, and cause/effect. **Foundational Skills 4.** Read with sufficient accuracy and fluency to support comprehension. **Foundational Skills 4.c.** Use context to confirm or self-correct word recognition and understanding, rereading as necessary.

# Assessment

## Monitor Progress

For a written assessment of Prefixes, Fact and Opinion, and Selection Vocabulary, use Weekly Test 18, pp. 103–108.

**FACT AND OPINION** Use "Coyotes" on p. 115m to check students' understanding of fact and opinion.

1. Is the following sentence a fact or an opinion? *Coyotes are the most amazing animals in America!* How do you know whether it is a fact or opinion? (Opinion; the speaker is making a judgment about coyotes. It cannot be proved true or false.)

2. What conclusion can you draw from the following fact? *Now coyotes roam all over the United States, except Hawaii.* (The coyotes don't live in Hawaii because it is an island. They are unable to swim across the ocean to get there.)

3. State two facts from this passage. (Coyotes originally lived in the Great Plains area. Although they like to eat meat, coyotes can eat many things.)

> **Corrective feedback** | **If...** students are unable to answer the comprehension questions,
> **then...** use the Reteach lesson in *First Stop.*

Name _____

## Coyotes

What do you know about coyotes? Did you realize that they might be your neighbors? They probably are, even if you happen to live in a city.

Coyotes are the most amazing animals in America! They are wild dogs, similar to wolves. But unlike wolves, they can live near where people live.

People often think that humans moved into coyote territory. That is sometimes true, but not always. Coyotes originally lived in the Great Plains area. That includes states from North Dakota down to Texas. Now coyotes roam all over the entire United States, except Hawaii. That means coyotes moved into human territory.

In addition, coyotes have proven that they can survive almost anywhere, including in big cities and suburbs. Although they like to eat meat, coyotes can eat many things: sandwiches, grass, garbage, and more. That is why they can live just about anywhere.

If a coyote is not the most amazing animal in America, it is certainly one of the smartest! Being smart is one reason coyotes can live around people. Part of being smart means they usually stay away from humans. However, coyotes are starting to show themselves more. That may be because there are more of them. It also may be because coyotes are not as afraid of people as they used to be.

A coyote is not a pet. If you happen to see a coyote once in a while on your street and in a park, remember that it is a wild animal. Stay away!

**MONITOR PROGRESS**     • Fact and Opinion

 **Common Core State Standards**

**Speaking/Listening 1.a.** Come to discussions prepared, having read or studied required material; explicitly draw on that preparation and other information known about the topic to explore ideas under discussion. **Speaking/Listening 4.** Report on a topic or text, tell a story, or recount an experience with appropriate facts and relevant, descriptive details, speaking clearly at an understandable pace. **Language 1.a.** Explain the function of nouns, pronouns, verbs, adjectives, and adverbs in general and their functions in particular sentences. **Language 6.** Acquire and use accurately grade-appropriate conversational, general academic, and domain-specific words and phrases, including those that signal spatial and temporal relationships (e.g., *After dinner that night we went looking for them*). **Also Speaking/Listening 3., Language 2.f.**

# Research and Inquiry

## Step 5 Communicate

**PRESENT IDEAS** Have students share their inquiry results by presenting their information and giving a brief talk on their research.

**SPEAKING** Remind students how to be good speakers and how to communicate effectively with their audience.

• Respond to relevant questions with appropriate details.

• Speak clearly and loudly, with appropriate rate, volume, and enunciation.

• Keep eye contact with audience members.

**LISTENING** Remind students of these tips for being a good listener.

• Wait until the speaker has finished before raising your hand to ask a relevant question.

• Be polite, even if you disagree.

**LISTEN TO IDEAS** Have students listen attentively to the various presentations and talks. Have them make pertinent comments, closely related to the topic.

# Spelling Test

## Prefixes *pre-, mid-, over-, out-*

To administer the spelling test, refer to the directions, words, and sentences on p. 91c.

# Conventions

## Possessive Pronouns

**MORE PRACTICE** Remind students that a possessive pronoun shows who or what owns, or possesses, something.

**GUIDE PRACTICE** Write the following words. Have students tell which possessive pronouns would be used with each word or phrase.

| Tanya | my cap | the girl's book | the boy's skates |
|---|---|---|---|
| Mr. North | Mount Shasta | Sandra's room | Dan and Matt |

**ON THEIR OWN** Write these sentences. Have students look back in *Rocks in His Head* to find the correct possessive pronouns to fill in the blanks. Students should complete *Let's Practice It!* p. 246 on the *Teacher Resources DVD-ROM.*

1. "You *have* got rocks in _____ head," she said. (your)

2. "Probably not," said _____ father. (my)

3. He'd dig into _____ pocket and take out a rock. (his)

4. People couldn't afford to buy new cars or fix _____ old ones. (their)

5. "I'm looking for rocks that are better than _____," he said. (mine)

**Teacher Resources**
• Let's Practice It!
• Daily Fix-It Transparency

## Daily Fix-It

9. The small rock is mine and the big one is your. *(mine,; yours)*

10. Can we put them both in the disply case. *(display; case?)*

Let's Practice It! TR DVD•246

**Common Core State Standards**

**Writing 2.** Write informative/explanatory texts to examine a topic and convey ideas and information clearly. **Language 1.a.** Explain the function of nouns, pronouns, verbs, adjectives, and adverbs in general and their functions in particular sentences. **Language 2.** Demonstrate command of the conventions of standard English capitalization, punctuation, and spelling when writing.

## Teacher Note

**Writing Self-Evaluation** Make copies of the Writing Self-Evaluation Guide on p. 39 of the *Reader's and Writer's Notebook* and hand out to students.

 **Bridge to Common Core**

### PRODUCTION AND DISTRIBUTION OF WRITING

Over the course of the week, students have developed and strengthened their drafts through planning, revising, editing, and rewriting. The final drafts are clear and coherent biographies in which the organization and style are appropriate to the purpose and audience.

# Writing Zoom in on ©

## Biography

**REVIEW REVISING** Remind students that yesterday they revised their biographies, paying particular attention to combining short and choppy sentences to create smooth, flowing language. Today they will proofread their compositions.

### Mini-Lesson | Proofread

**Proofread for Possessive Pronouns**

■ **Teach** When we proofread, we look closely at our work, searching for errors in mechanics. Today we will look for spelling, capitalization, and punctuation problems in the revised drafts, but first we will make sure that possessive pronouns are used correctly.

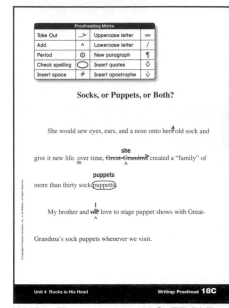

Writing Transparency 18C, TR DVD

■ **Model** Let's look at the last two paragraphs from our revised biographies. Display Writing Transparency 18C. Explain that you will look for errors in the use of possessive pronouns. I see a problem in the first sentence here. We need the possessive pronoun *her* to show that Great-Grandma owns the old sock, and here we have *hers*. Since what Great-Grandma owns, an old sock, is still part of the sentence, we need to use *her* instead of *hers*. Explain to students that they should reread their biographies a number of times. Have them look for different types of errors with each reading: spelling, punctuation, capitalization, and grammar.

**PROOFREAD** Ask students to proofread their compositions, using the Proofreading Tips and paying particular attention to possessive pronouns. Remind students to capitalize any geographical names or places as well as any historical periods. Circulate around the room answering students' questions. When students have finished editing their own work, have pairs proofread one another's biography.

### Proofreading Tips

✔ Be sure that you use possessive pronouns correctly.

✔ Use a dictionary or computer spell checker to check for correct spelling of difficult words.

✔ Be sure that your different sentence types end with the correct punctuation.

**eSTREET INTERACTIVE**
www.ReadingStreet.com

**Teacher Resources**
• Writing Transparency
• Reader's and Writer's Notebook

**PRESENT** Give students two options for presenting their work: an oral presentation or a decorative copy of their finished work to give to the person they wrote about. When students have finished, have each complete a Writing Self-Evaluation form.

**Routine** **Quick Write for Fluency** | Team Talk |

**1. Talk** Pairs discuss what they learned about interesting collections this week.

**2. Write** Each student writes two sentences summarizing what they learned.

**3. Share** Partners read their sentences to one another.

Routines Flip Chart

# Wrap Up Your Week!

## Unique Interests

Why is it valuable to have unique interests?

**Think Aloud** In *Rocks in His Head* and "Marvelous Marble Mania," we learned that having unique interests can be useful and valuable.

**Team Talk** Have students recall their Amazing Ideas about one of a kind and use these ideas to help them demonstrate their understanding of the Question of the Week.

Next Week's Concept
## Unique Traits

What unique traits does it take to be the first to do something?

**Poster Preview** Prepare students for next week by using Week 4 ELL Poster 19. Read the Talk-Through to introduce the concept and vocabulary.

**Selection Summary** Send home the summary of next week's selection, *America's Champion Swimmer: Gertrude Ederle,* in English and students' home languages, if available in the *ELL Handbook.*

What unique traits does it take to be the first to do something? Tell students that next week they will be reading a story about a champion swimmer.

**Preview Next Week**

# Assessment Checkpoints for the Week

## Weekly Assessment

Use pp. 103–108 of *Weekly Tests* to check:

✔  **Phonics** Prefixes *pre-, mid-, over-, out-, bi-, de-*

✔  **Comprehension** Fact and Opinion

✔ Review **Comprehension** Cause and Effect

✔ **Selection Vocabulary**

| attic | customer | spare |
|-------|----------|-------|
| board | labeled | stamps |
| chores | | |

Weekly Tests

## Differentiated Assessment

**A**
**Advanced**

Use pp. 103–108 of *Fresh Reads for Fluency and Comprehension* to check:

✔  **Comprehension** Fact and Opinion

✔ Review **Comprehension** Cause and Effect

✔ **Fluency** Words Correct Per Minute

**OL**
**On-Level**

**SI**
**Strategic Intervention**

Fresh Reads for Fluency and Comprehension

## Managing Assessment

Use *Assessment Handbook* for:

✔ **Weekly Assessment Blackline Masters for Monitoring Progress**

✔ **Observation Checklists**

✔ **Record-Keeping Forms**

✔ **Portfolio Assessment**

Assessment Handbook

# TEACHER NOTES

## DAY 1   Differentiate Vocabulary

- **Word Knowledge** Amazing Words
- **Read** "Rocks and More Rocks"
- **Inquiry** Identify Questions

"Rocks and More Rocks"
pp. 48–49

## DAY 2   Differentiate Comprehension

- **Word Knowledge** Selection Vocabulary
- **Access Text** Read *Rocks in His Head*
- **Inquiry** Investigate

## DAY 3   Differentiate Close Reading

- **Word Knowledge** Develop Vocabulary
- **Close Reading** Read *Rocks in His Head*
- **Inquiry** Investigate

## DAY 4   Differentiate Vocabulary

- **Word Knowledge** Amazing Words
- **Read** "Marvelous Marble Mania"
- **Inquiry** Organize

## DAY 5   Differentiate Reteaching

- **Conventions** Possessive Pronouns
- **Reread** "Rocks and More Rocks" or Leveled Readers
- **Inquiry** Communicate

Teacher Guides and Student pages can be found in the Leveled Reader Database.

 Place English Language Learners in the groups that correspond to their reading abilities.
**If...** students need scaffolding and practice,
**then...** use the ELL Notes on the instructional pages.

## Independent Practice

**Independent Practice Stations**

See pp. 86h and 86i for Independent Stations.

**Pearson Trade Book Library**

See the Leveled Reader Database for lesson plans and student pages.

**Reading Street Digital Path**

Independent Practice Activities are available in the Digital Path.

**Independent Reading**

See p. 86i for independent reading suggestions.

**On-Level**

## Common Core State Standards

**Literature 3.** Describe characters in a story (e.g., their traits, motivations, or feelings) and explain how their actions contribute to the sequence of events. **Literature 4.** Determine the meaning of words and phrases as they are used in text, distinguishing literal from nonliteral language. **Informational Text 1.** Ask and answer questions to demonstrate understanding of a text, referring explicitly to the text as the basis for the answers. **Foundational Skills 4.** Read with sufficient accuracy and fluency to support comprehension. **Language 4.a.** Use sentence-level context as a clue to the meaning of a word or phrase.

## ① Build Word Knowledge
### Practice Amazing Words

**DEFINE IT** Elicit the definition for the word *hobby* from students. Ask: How would you describe a hobby to another student? (Possible response: something a person likes to do) Clarify or give a definition when necessary. Continue with the words *project* and *murmur.*

**Team Talk** **TALK ABOUT IT** Have partners internalize meanings. Ask: How can you pair the Amazing Words together in a sentence? (Possible response: "I need a hobby or project," I murmured, "so I have something to do on Saturdays.") Allow time for students to play with the words. Review the concept map with students. Discuss other words they can add to the concept map.

### Independent Reading Options

**Trade Book Library**

**e𝗦𝗧𝗥𝗘𝗘𝗧 𝗜𝗡𝗧𝗘𝗥𝗔𝗖𝗧𝗜𝗩𝗘**
www.ReadingStreet.com

Teacher Guides are available on the Leveled Reader Database.

## ② Text-Based Comprehension
### Read

**READ ALOUD "Rocks and More Rocks"** Have partners read "Rocks and More Rocks" from *Reading Street Sleuth* on pp. 48–49.

**ACCESS TEXT** Discuss the Sleuth Work section with students before they work on it. Remind students that they can use these steps with other texts they read.

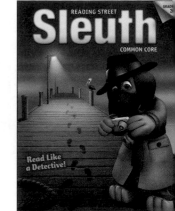

**Gather Evidence** Have partners take notes of text evidence. Invite students to share the evidence they found in the story.

**Ask Questions** Talk together about the skill of interviewing. Point out that reporters ask two types of questions: one answered with facts and one answered with opinions. Have students share their questions and identify them as factual or opinion based.

**Make Your Case** Encourage students who took the same side on the issue to share the reasons they cited. Talk about the characteristics of convincing evidence and reasons.

**ELL**

**If...** students need more scaffolding and practice with **Vocabulary, then...** use the activities on pp. DI•67–DI•68 in the Teacher Resources section on SuccessNet.

 On-Level

# Build Word Knowledge
## Practice Selection Vocabulary

| | | | |
|---|---|---|---|
| attic | board | chores | customer |
| labeled | spare | stamps | |

**DEFINE IT** Discuss the definition for the word *chores* with students. Ask: How would you describe chores to another student? (Possible response: small tasks or easy jobs that you have to do regularly) Continue with the remaining words.

**Team Talk** **TALK ABOUT IT** Have pairs use the selection vocabulary in sentences to internalize meaning. Ask: How can you pair the selection vocabulary together in a sentence? (Possible response: Our chore was to label and put stamps on all the envelopes.) Allow time for students to play with the words and then share their sentences.

# Read
## Rocks in His Head

If you read *Rocks in His Head* during whole group time, then use the following instruction.

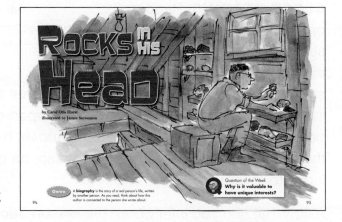

**ACCESS TEXT** Reread the text on p. 99. Ask questions to check understanding. Why did people think that the narrator's father wouldn't care about the stock market? (He had no money in the stock market.) What did the narrator's father mean by "I think bad times are coming"? (He figured that a lot of people in the country would lose money and jobs because of what happened in the stock market.)

Have students identify sections from today's reading that they did not completely understand. Reread them aloud and clarify misunderstandings.

If you are reading *Rocks in His Head* during small group time, then return to pp. 96–99a to guide the reading.

---

**eStreet Interactive**
www.ReadingStreet.com

**Pearson eText**
- Student Edition
- Leveled Reader Database
- *Reading Street Sleuth*

---

## More Reading for Group Time

**ON-LEVEL**

**Reviews**
- Fact and Opinion
- Inferring
- Selection Vocabulary

Use this suggested Leveled Reader or other text at students' instructional level.

**eStreet Interactive**
www.ReadingStreet.com

Use the Leveled Reader Database for lesson plans and student pages for *Fun with Hobbies and Science!*

**SMALL GROUP TIME**

## Common Core State Standards

**Informational Text 3.** Describe the relationship between a series of historical events, scientific ideas or concepts, or steps in technical procedures in a text, using language that pertains to time, sequence, and cause/effect. **Language 1.i.** Produce simple, compound, and complex sentences. **Language 4.a.** Use sentence-level context as a clue to the meaning of a word or phrase. **Also Foundational Skills 4.**

## ① Build Word Knowledge
### Develop Vocabulary

**REREAD FOR VOCABULARY** Reread paragraph 9 on p. 103. Introduce: Let's read this paragraph to find out what *mineralogist* means. To help students understand the word *mineralogist,* ask questions related to the context, such as: What are minerals? Why did Mrs. Johnson want the narrator's father to work in her museum? Have students use online sources to find out more information about a mineralogist.

## ② Read
### *Rocks in His Head*

If you read *Rocks in His Head* during whole group time, then use the following instruction.

**CLOSE READING** Read pp. 100–101. Have students search though the text to find the main events in this part of the

selection. Have students work with a partner to make a list of the main events in the order that they occur. (people stopped coming for gas; narrator's father packs up his things; friends help him move; he moves his family to a house that's falling apart; he fixes up the house; he puts his rocks in the attic; he looks for a job)

Ask: What can you infer about the reason people stopped coming to the gas station? (They didn't have money for gas or time to play chess. They didn't have jobs and had to spend time looking for work.) Why do you think the narrator's father leaves the gas station? Why does he move his family into a house that is old and run down? (Since many people were out of work and nobody was buying gas, his business failed. This meant his family couldn't afford to keep the house they had and had to move to one that was cheaper and not as nice.)

If you are reading *Rocks in His Head* during small group time, then return to pp. 100–105a to guide the reading.

If... students need more scaffolding and practice with the **Main Selection, then...** use the activities on p. DI•72 in the Teacher Resources section on SuccessNet.

 **On-Level**

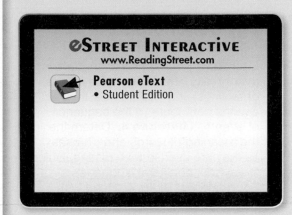

# 1 Build Word Knowledge
## Practice Amazing Words

| hobby | ornament | project | descendant |
|---|---|---|---|
| leftover | forge | murmur | compartment |
| ancestor | | | |

**Team Talk** **LANGUAGE DEVELOPMENT** Have partners practice building more complex sentences. Display a sentence starter and have students add oral phrases or clauses using the Amazing Words. For example: My ancestors _____. (My ancestors made ornaments / that were forged with care / and made from leftover odds and ends.) Guide students to add at least three phrases or clauses per sentence.

# 2 Read
## "Marvelous Marble Mania"

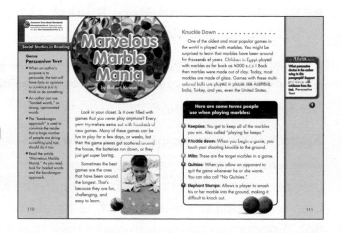

**BEFORE READING** Read aloud the information about persuasive texts on p. 110. Have students preview "Marvelous Marble Mania" and set a purpose for reading.

• How is a persuasive text different from a biography? (It tries to convince you of something instead of providing information about someone.)

• What does this author want to persuade you to do? (admire or play with marbles)

**DURING READING** Have students read along with you.

• How is this persuasive text organized? (It's organized by topic.)

• How is this persuasive text similar to and different from a biography? (Both may try to convince a reader. However, a biography usually tells a story.)

**AFTER READING** Have students share their reaction to "Marvelous Marble Mania." Then have them write and present a one- or two-minute persuasive talk about a favorite hobby of theirs from note cards.

**SMALL GROUP TIME**

## Independent Reading Options

**Trade Book Library**

**eStreet Interactive**
www.ReadingStreet.com

Teacher Guides are available on the Leveled Reader Database.

*Rocks in His Head* **SG•37**

## Common Core State Standards

**Literature 3.** Describe characters in a story (e.g., their traits, motivations, or feelings) and explain how their actions contribute to the sequence of events. **Literature 4.** Determine the meaning of words and phrases as they are used in text, distinguishing literal from nonliteral language. **Foundational Skills 4.** Read with sufficient accuracy and fluency to support comprehension. **Writing 2.** Write informative/explanatory texts to examine a topic and convey ideas and information clearly. **Language 4.** Determine or clarify the meaning of unknown and multiple-meaning words and phrases based on grade 3 reading and content, choosing flexibly from a range of strategies.

## More Reading for Group Time

**ON-LEVEL**

**Reviews**
- Fact and Opinion
- Inferring
- Selection Vocabulary

Use this suggested Leveled Reader or other text at students' instructional level.

### eStreet Interactive
www.ReadingStreet.com

Use the Leveled Reader Database for lesson plans and student pages for *Fun with Hobbies and Science!*

 **On-Level**

## ① Build Word Knowledge
### Practice Possessive Pronouns

**IDENTIFY** Choral read the bottom of p. 109 with students and discuss the function of possessive pronouns, explaining that they tell who or what owns something, such as *The backpack is his*. Have partners reread the model biography to find examples of how the author used possessive pronouns. Encourage students to use the student model biography on the same page to practice. Allow time for students to discuss their examples and correct any misunderstandings.

## ② Text-Based Comprehension
### Read

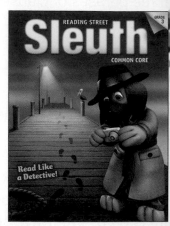

**REREAD "Rocks and More Rocks"** Have partners reread "Rocks and More Rocks."

**EXTEND UNDERSTANDING** Talk together about Patrick's rock collection and what he is learning from having such a collection.

**PERFORMANCE TASK • Prove It!** Have students work with a partner. Have them choose something that people collect. Have pairs research the item and then write a list of three to five tips for starting and maintaining such a collection. Encourage partners to make their tips easy to follow and fact based.

**COMMUNICATE** Have small groups share their tips for collecting. Invite the audience to ask followup questions.

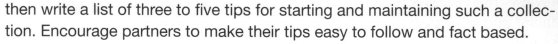

**Strategic Intervention**

# 1 Build Word Knowledge
## Reteach Amazing Words

Repeat the definition of the word. We learned that *hobby* means something a person likes to do. Then use the word in a sentence. Sometimes a hobby turns into a real job.

**Team Talk** **TALK ABOUT IT** Have partners take turns using the word *hobby* in a sentence. Continue this routine to practice the Amazing Words *project* and *murmur*. Review the concept map with students. Discuss other words they can add to the concept map.

> **Corrective feedback** | **If...** students need more practice with the Amazing Words, **then...** use visuals from the Student Edition or online sources to clarify meaning.

# 2 Text-Based Comprehension
## Read

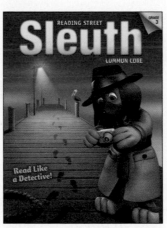

**READ "Rocks and More Rocks"** Have students track the print as you read "Rocks and More Rocks" from *Reading Street Sleuth* on pp. 48–49.

**ACCESS TEXT** Discuss the Sleuth Work section with students and provide support as needed as they work on it. Remind students that they can use these steps with other texts they read.

**Gather Evidence** Talk together about the evidence students found in the story. Make a list of words, phrases, and sentences that are considered evidence.

**Ask Questions** Talk together about the skill of interviewing. Invite students to pretend to ask Mrs. Simpson one question that requires a factual answer and one question that would allow her to share an opinion.

**Make Your Case** Have students choose a side to the issue. Encourage students who took the same side on the issue to make note of their reasons for their opinions. Remind students of the characteristics of convincing evidence and reasons.

---

### eSTREET INTERACTIVE
www.ReadingStreet.com

**Pearson eText**
- Student Edition
- Leveled Reader Database
- *Reading Street Sleuth*

**SMALL GROUP TIME**

### More Reading for Group Time

**CONCEPT LITERACY**
**Practice**
Concept Words

**BELOW-LEVEL**
**Reviews**
- Fact and Opinion
- Inferring
- Selection Vocabulary

Use these suggested Leveled Readers or other text at students' instructional level.

### eSTREET INTERACTIVE
www.ReadingStreet.com

Use the Leveled Reader Database for lesson plans and student pages for *I Collect Rocks* and *Grandpa's Rock Kit*.

*Rocks in His Head*   **SG•39**

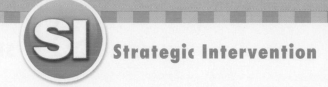

## Strategic Intervention

### © Common Core State Standards

**Informational Text 1.** Ask and answer questions to demonstrate understanding of a text, referring explicitly to the text as the basis for the answers. **Informational Text 3.** Describe the relationship between a series of historical events, scientific ideas or concepts, or steps in technical procedures in a text, using language that pertains to time, sequence, and cause/effect. **Language 4.a.** Use sentence-level context as a clue to the meaning of a word or phrase.

## 1 Build Word Knowledge
### Reteach Selection Vocabulary

**DEFINE IT** Describe *customer* to a friend. Give a definition when necessary. Restate the word in student-friendly terms and clarify meaning with a visual. *Customer* means a person who buys things.

| | | | |
|---|---|---|---|
| attic | board | chores | customer |
| labeled | spare | stamps | |

**Team Talk** **TALK ABOUT IT** Have you been a customer? Where? Turn and talk to your partner about this. Allow time for partners to discuss. Ask for examples. Rephrase students' examples for usage when necessary or to correct misunderstandings. Continue with the remaining words.

**Corrective feedback** | **If...** students need more practice with selection vocabulary, **then...** use the *Envision It! Pictured Vocabulary Cards*.

## 2 Read
### *Rocks in His Head*

If you read *Rocks in His Head* during whole group time, then use the instruction below.

**ACCESS TEXT** Reread the text on p. 99. Ask questions to check understanding. What happened to the stock market? (It "fell," which meant many people in the country were losing money.) What did the narrator's father mean by, "I think bad times are coming." (He thought that a lot of people would lose money and jobs.) What happened when the bad times came? (People couldn't afford to buy cars or fix them.)

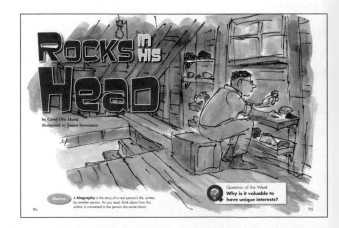

Have students identify sections they did not understand. Reread them aloud. Clarify the meaning of each section to build understanding.

If you are reading *Rocks in His Head* during small group time, then return to pp. 96–99a to guide the reading.

### Independent Reading Options

**Trade Book Library**

**eStreet Interactive**
www.ReadingStreet.com

Teacher Guides are available on the Leveled Reader Database.

**Strategic Intervention**

# 1 Build Word Knowledge
## Develop Vocabulary

**REREAD FOR VOCABULARY** Reread paragraph 9 on p. 103. Introduce: Let's read this paragraph to find out what *mineralogist* means. To help students understand the word *mineralogist,* ask questions related to the context, such as: What are minerals? Why did Mrs. Johnson want the narrator's father to work at the museum? What types of things would he do?

> **Corrective feedback** | **If...** students have difficulty understanding the word *mineralogist,*
> **then...** guide students to use online sources to find more information.

**eStreet Interactive**
www.ReadingStreet.com

**Pearson eText**
• Student Edition

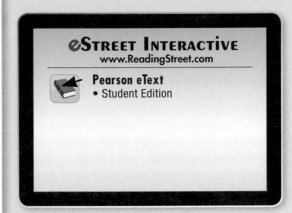

# 2 Read
## Rocks in His Head

If you read *Rocks in His Head* during whole group time, then use the instruction below.

**CLOSE READING** Read pp. 100–101. Have students search though the text to find time references that help to tell

the sequence of the events in the story. As a class, make a list of these words and phrases in the order they occur. *(Then, One day, When, in no time, before, after, spent a lot of time, On rainy days when, Sometimes)*

Now let's use the times we listed to retell what happened in this part of the story. (People stopped coming to the gas station. The narrator's father packs his things. His friends move him in a truck. Then he and his family move into an old house. Before he fixes up the house, he puts his rocks in the attic. After he fixes the house, he spends time with his rocks. He spends a lot of time looking for a job. On rainy days, he goes to the science museum.)

If you are reading *Rocks in His Head* during small group time, then return to pp. 100–105a to guide the reading.

**ELL**

**If...** students need more scaffolding and practice with the **Main Selection, then...** use the activities on p. DI•72 in the Teacher Resources section on SuccessNet.

**SMALL GROUP TIME**

## Strategic Intervention

### Common Core State Standards

**Foundational Skills 4.** Read with sufficient accuracy and fluency to support comprehension. **Writing 2.** Write informative/explanatory texts to examine a topic and convey ideas and information clearly. **Language 1.a.** Explain the function of nouns, pronouns, verbs, adjectives, and adverbs in general and their functions in particular sentences. **Language 1.i.** Produce simple, compound, and complex sentences.

# 1 Build Word Knowledge
## Review Amazing Words

| | | | |
|---|---|---|---|
| hobby | ornament | project | descendant |
| leftover | forge | murmur | compartment |
| ancestor | | | |

**Team Talk** **LANGUAGE DEVELOPMENT** Have partners practice building more complex sentences. Display a sentence starter and have students add oral phrases or clauses using the Amazing Words. For example: My ancestors _____. (My ancestors' hobby was / to make ornaments / from leftover scraps of wood.) Guide students to add at least two phrases or clauses per sentence.

**Corrective feedback** | **If...** students have difficulty using Amazing Words orally, **then...** review the meaning of each of the words.

# 2 Read
## "Marvelous Marble Mania"

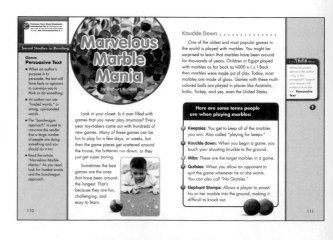

**BEFORE READING** Read aloud the information about persuasive texts on p. 110. Persuasive texts use facts and opinions to try to convince you to think or act in a certain way. What are some persuasive texts that you see in your everyday life? (newspaper and magazine advertisements, billboards, ads on the sides of buses) Read the rest of the panel. Then have students read the introduction.

**DURING READING** Have students perform a choral reading of the selection. As they read, write the following words on the board: *fun, challenging, easy to learn.* Where do you see these words in the text? Are these words facts or opinions? How do you know?

**AFTER READING** Have students share their reactions. Then guide students through the Reading Across Texts and Writing Across Texts activities.

**If...** students need more scaffolding and practice with **Amazing Words, then...** use the Routine on pp. xxxvi–xxxvii in the *ELL Handbook.*

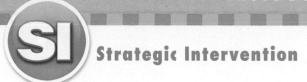

**Strategic Intervention**

## 1 Build Word Knowledge

### Review Possessive Pronouns

**IDENTIFY** Choral read the bottom of p. 109 with students to review possessive pronouns. Have partners reread the model biography on p. 109 to find examples of how the author used possessive pronouns. Have students use the student model biography on that page to practice. Allow time for students to discuss their examples and correct any misunderstandings.

## 2 Text-Based Comprehension

### Read

**REREAD "Rocks and More Rocks"** Have partners reread "Rocks and More Rocks" with partners alternating paragraphs.

**EXTEND UNDERSTANDING** Talk together about students' experiences with collecting things. Have students make connections between Patrick's rock collecting experiences and their own.

**PERFORMANCE TASK • Prove It!** Have students work with a partner. Have them choose something that people collect. Have pairs research the item and then write a list of three to five tips for starting and maintaining such a collection. Remind students to number their tips so readers can easily follow along.

**COMMUNICATE** Have partners share their tips with small groups. Invite listeners to summarize what they learned from each other.

**SMALL GROUP TIME**

### More Reading for Group Time

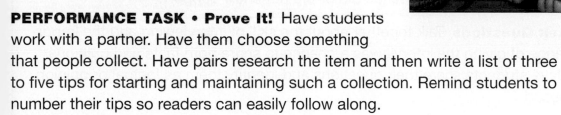

**CONCEPT LITERACY**

**Practice**
Concept Words

**BELOW-LEVEL**

**Reviews**
• Fact and Opinion
• Inferring
• Selection Vocabulary

Use these suggested Leveled Readers or other text at students' instructional level.

Use the Leveled Reader Database for lesson plans and student pages for *I Collect Rocks* and *Grandpa's Rock Kit*.

**A** Advanced

## ① Build Word Knowledge

### Extend Amazing Words

[Team Talk] Have pairs of students define *hobby*. Discuss other names for *hobby*. (*pastime, project*) Continue with *project* and *murmur*.

## ② Text-Based Comprehension

### Read

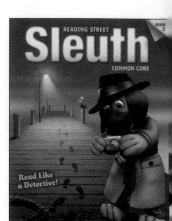

**READ "Rocks and More Rocks"** Have students read "Rocks and More Rocks" from *Reading Street Sleuth* on pp. 48–49.

**ACCESS TEXT** Discuss the Sleuth Work section with students before they work on it. Remind students that they can use these steps with other texts they read.

**Gather Evidence** Have students take notes of text evidence. Invite students to share the evidence and talk about how this evidence did or did not show support.

**Ask Questions** Talk together about the skill of interviewing and the importance of giving the interviewee a chance to share both facts and opinions. Have students share their questions and identify them as factual or opinion based.

**Make Your Case** Have students share their paragraphs, pointing out the convincing evidence from the story that supports their side of the issue. If time permits, have students rank their evidence from most convincing to least.

## ③ Inquiry: Extend Concepts

**IDENTIFY QUESTIONS** Have students think about questions they have about unique interests and use these questions to explore a potential new interest or hobby. Have students create a plan to start this hobby. Throughout the week, they will gather information. On Day 5, they will present what they have learned.

**If...** students need more scaffolding and practice with **Vocabulary, then...** use the activities on pp. DI•67–DI•68 in the Teacher Resources section on SuccessNet.

**A** Advanced

# 1 Build Word Knowledge

## Extend Selection Vocabulary

**Team Talk** Have partners use the selection vocabulary in sentences to internalize their meanings. Have students use as many of the words as they can while making sure the sentence is grammatically correct.

| | | |
|---|---|---|
| attic | board | chores |
| customer | labeled | spare |
| stamps | | |

# 2 Read

## Rocks in His Head

If you read *Rocks in His Head* during whole group time, then use the instruction below.

**ACCESS TEXT** Reread the text on p. 99. Have students list the facts and then any opinions that appear in the selection. (Facts: The stock market fell. The narrator's father didn't have money in the market. Bad times did come. The narrator's father played chess or hunted for rocks when business was slow. Opinions: People didn't think the narrator's father would care about the stock market. The narrator's father said he might have rocks in his head. He thought bad times would come.)

Ask: What can you infer about the narrator's father from this passage? (He wasn't that interested in money, because he didn't invest in the market. He was smart. He predicted bad times were coming, and they did.)

If you are reading *Rocks in His Head* during small group time, then return to pp. 96–99a to guide the reading.

# 3 Inquiry: Extend Concepts

**INVESTIGATE** Encourage students to use materials at their independent reading levels or student-friendly search engines to identify relevant and credible sites to gather information about a new interest or hobby. Have students consider how they will present their information.

**SMALL GROUP TIME**

### More Reading for Group Time

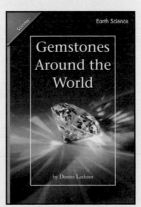

**ADVANCED**

**Reviews**
• Fact and Opinion
• Inferring

Use this suggested Leveled Reader or other text at students' instructional level.

**eSTREET INTERACTIVE**
www.ReadingStreet.com

Use the Leveled Reader Database for lesson plans and student pages for *Gemstones Around the World.*

**A** Advanced

## Common Core State Standards

**Informational Text 3.** Describe the relationship between a series of historical events, scientific ideas or concepts, or steps in technical procedures in a text, using language that pertains to time, sequence, and cause/effect. **Informational Text 6.** Distinguish their own point of view from that of the author of a text. **Language 4.a.** Use sentence-level context as a clue to the meaning of a word or phrase.

## 1 Build Word Knowledge
### Develop Vocabulary

**REREAD FOR VOCABULARY** Reread paragraph 9 on p. 103. Let's read this paragraph to find out what *mineralogist* means. Discuss meaning and context with students.

## 2 Read

### *Rocks in His Head*

If you read *Rocks in His Head* during whole group time, then use the instruction below.

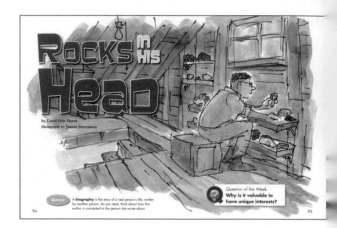

**CLOSE READING** Read pp. 100–101. Have students create a T-chart with the heads **Cause** and **Effect** and list them in the order they occur. (Cause: Many people are out of work. Effect: People stop buying gas and other services. Cause: People aren't buying gas. Effect: The narrator's father moves out of the gas station. Cause: The father isn't making any money. Effect: He moves his family into a run-down house. Cause: The father is out of work. Effect: The father spends lots of time looking for jobs. Cause: Sometimes it's rainy and he can't find any work. Effect: The father goes to the science museum.)

Ask: What can you infer about the father's life based on this information? (He didn't seem like an anxious person. He tried to find work, but he also always found time for what he was really interested in.)

If you are reading *Rocks in His Head* during small group time, then return to pp. 100–105a to guide the reading.

## Independent Reading Options

**Trade Book Library**

**eSTREET INTERACTIVE**
www.ReadingStreet.com
Teacher Guides are available on the Leveled Reader Database.

## 3 Inquiry: Extend Concepts

**INVESTIGATE** Provide time for students to investigate their topics in books or online. If necessary, help them locate information that is focused on their topics.

**If...** students need more scaffolding and practice with the **Main Selection,** **then...** use the activities on p. DI•72 in the Teacher Resources section on SuccessNet.

 **Advanced**

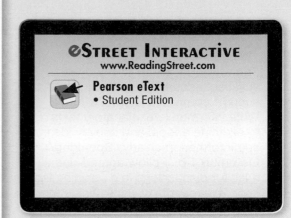
**eSTREET INTERACTIVE**
www.ReadingStreet.com

**Pearson eText**
• Student Edition

# ① Build Word Knowledge

## Extend Amazing Words and Selection Vocabulary

| | | | |
|---|---|---|---|
| hobby | ornament | project | descendant |
| leftover | forge | murmur | compartment |
| ancestor | | | |

| | | |
|---|---|---|
| attic | board | chores |
| customer | labeled | spare |
| stamps | | |

**Team Talk** Have partners practice building more complex sentences. Display a sentence starter and have students add oral phrases or clauses using the Amazing Words and the selection vocabulary. Guide students to add at least three phrases or clauses per sentence.

# ② Read

## "Marvelous Marble Mania"

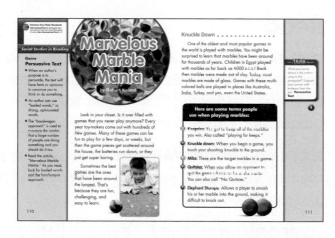

**BEFORE READING** Have students read the panel information on persuasive text on p. 110. Then have students use the text features—including the headings, photographs, and illustrations—to set a purpose for reading.

**DURING READING** Have students read the selection. Point out that a persuasive text tries to convince a reader to hold a certain opinion or to do something. How is this persuasive text organized differently from the biography you just read? (It is organized according to ideas. The biography is organized chronologically.) As they read, have students note elements of persuasive text.

**AFTER READING** Have students discuss Reading Across Texts. Then have them complete the Writing Across Texts activity independently.

# ③ Inquiry: Extend Concepts

**ORGANIZE INFORMATION** Provide time for students to organize their information into a format that will effectively communicate their findings to their audience. Provide any necessary materials or computer time.

**SMALL GROUP TIME**

---

**Independent Reading Options**

**Trade Book Library**

**eSTREET INTERACTIVE**
www.ReadingStreet.com

Teacher Guides are available on the Leveled Reader Database.

**A** Advanced

## Common Core State Standards

**Foundational Skills 4.** Read with sufficient accuracy and fluency to support comprehension. **Writing 2.** Write informative/explanatory texts to examine a topic and convey ideas and information clearly. **Speaking/Listening 1.b.** Follow agreed-upon rules for discussions (e.g., gaining the floor in respectful ways, listening to others with care, speaking one at a time about the topics and texts under discussion).

## More Reading for Group Time

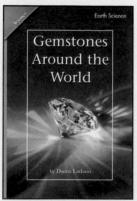

Earth Science

Gemstones Around the World

by Donna Latham

**ADVANCED**

**Reviews**
- Fact and Opinion
- Inferring

Use this suggested Leveled Reader or other text at students' instructional level.

### eSTREET INTERACTIVE
www.ReadingStreet.com

Use the Leveled Reader Database for lesson plans and student pages for *Gemstones Around the World.*

## 1 Build Word Knowledge
### Extend Possessive Pronouns

**IDENTIFY AND EXTEND** Choral read the bottom of p. 109 with students and have them explain the function of possessive pronouns, providing an example, such as *her notebook, our house,* or *its tail,* to help them along. Have partners reread the model biography to find examples of how the author used possessive pronouns. Encourage students to use the student biography on the same page to practice. Allow time for students to discuss their examples and correct any misunderstandings.

## 2 Text-Based Comprehension
### Read

**REREAD "Rocks and More Rocks"** Have small groups reread the selection. Have small groups discuss how Patrick might weed out some of his rocks before Mrs. Simpson stops by.

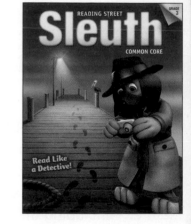

**EXTEND UNDERSTANDING** Talk together about the new information students learned about rocks and rock collecting.

**PERFORMANCE TASK • Prove It!** Have students work with a partner. Have them choose something that people collect. Have pairs research the item and then write a list of three to five tips for starting and maintaining such a collection. Remind students to write their tips in a clear, focused way. Discuss how opinions may or may not belong in a list of tips.

**COMMUNICATE** Have small groups share their tips for collecting. Invite the audience to point out tips that seem easy to follow and tips that may be more difficult to follow.

## 3 Inquiry: Extend Concepts

**COMMUNICATE** Have students share their inquiry projects on new interests with the rest of the class. Provide the following tips for presenting.

- Match your tone of voice and your pitch to your content.
- Make eye contact with the audience and point to visuals as you speak.
- Speak slowly and pause briefly after key points.

## This Week's Target Skills and Strategies

| Target Skills and Strategies |  Common Core State Standards for English Language Arts | Indiana Academic Standards for English Language Arts |
|---|---|---|
| **Phonics and Spelling** Skill: Suffixes *-er, -or, -ess, -ist* | **CCSS Foundational Skills 3.a.** Identify and know the meaning of the most common prefixes and derivational suffixes. **(Also CCSS Language 2.e.)** | **IN 3.1.8** Use knowledge of prefixes and suffixes to determine the meaning of words. |
| **Text-Based Comprehension** Skill: Fact and Opinion | **CCSS Informational Text 1.** Ask and answer questions to demonstrate understanding of a text, referring explicitly to the text as the basis for the answers. | **IN 3.2.2** Ask questions and support answers by connecting prior knowledge with literal information from the text. **(Also IN 3.2.3)** |
| Strategy: Questioning | **CCSS Informational Text 1.** Ask and answer questions to demonstrate understanding of a text, referring explicitly to the text as the basis for the answers. **(Also CCSS Informational Text 3.)** | **IN 3.2.2** Ask questions and support answers by connecting prior knowledge with literal information from the text. **(Also IN 3.2.3)** |
| **Vocabulary** Skill: Multiple-Meaning Words Strategy: Context Clues | **CCSS Language 4.** Determine or clarify the meaning of unknown and multiple-meaning word and phrases based on *grade 3 reading and content,* choosing flexibly from a range of strategies. **(Also CCSS Language 4.a.)** | **IN 3.1.6** Use sentence and word context to find the meaning of unknown words. **(Also IN 3.1.9)** |
| **Fluency** Skill: Appropriate Phrasing | **CCSS Foundational Skills 4.** Read with sufficient accuracy and fluency to support comprehension. | **IN 3.1.3** Read aloud grade-level-appropriate literary and informational texts fluently and accurately and with appropriate timing, change in voice, and expression. |
| **Listening and Speaking** Sportscast | **CCSS Speaking/Listening 4.** Report on a topic or text, tell a story, or recount an experience with appropriate facts and relevant, descriptive details, speaking clearly at an understandable pace. | The Indiana Academic Standards for Listening and Speaking are not currently assessed on ISTEP+ assessments. Educators and students should implement the Common Core Standards for Speaking and Listening as soon as possible. |
| **Six-Trait Writing** Trait of the Week: Organization | **CCSS Writing 4.** With guidance and support from adults, produce writing in which the development and organization are appropriate to task and purpose. **(Also CCSS Writing 3.a., CCSS Language 3.)** | **IN 3.4.9** Organize related ideas together within a paragraph to maintain a consistent focus. |
| **Writing** Autobiography | **CCSS Writing 3.** Write narratives to develop real or imagined experiences or events using effective technique, descriptive details, and clear event sequences. **(Also CCSS Writing 3.a.)** | **IN 3.5.1** Write narratives. |
| **Conventions** Skill: Contractions | **CCSS Language 3.** Use knowledge of language and its conventions when writing, speaking, reading, or listening. **(Also CCSS Language 1.)** | **IN 3.6** Students write using Standard English conventions appropriate to this grade level. |

## This Week's Cross-Curricular Standards and Resources

### Cross-Curricular Indiana Academic Standards for Social Studies

**Social Studies**
**IN 3.1.7** Distinguish between fact and fiction in historical accounts by comparing documentary sources on historical figures and events with fictional characters and events in stories.

### Reading Street Sleuth

*Women in the Olympics*
pp. 50–51

Follow the path to close reading using the Super Sleuth tips:

- Gather Evidence

- Ask Questions

- Make Your Case

- Prove it!

### More Reading in Science and Social Studies

Concept Literacy

Below Level

On Level

Advanced

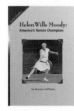

ELL

ELD

ISBN-13: 978-0-328-73390-3   ISBN-10: 0-328-73390-3

# Your 90-Minute Reading Block

| | Whole Group | Formative Assessment | Small Group  OL On Level  SI Strategic Intervention  A Advanced | Daily Independent Options |
|---|---|---|---|---|
| | | How do I make my small groups flexible? | What are my other students reading and learning every day in Small Groups? | What do my other students do when I lead Small Groups? |
| **DAY 1** | **Content Knowledge** Build Oral Language/Vocabulary  **Phonics/Word Analysis**  **Read Decodable Reader**  **Text-Based Comprehension**  **Selection Vocabulary**  **Research and Inquiry** Step 1–Identify and Focus Topic  **Spelling Pretest** Connect to Phonics/Word Analysis | **Monitor Progress** Check Oral Vocabulary | **Differentiate Vocabulary**  **Build Word Knowledge**  OL Practice Amazing Words  SI Reteach Amazing Words  A Extend Amazing Words  OL SI A Text-Based Comprehension  Read *Reading Street Sleuth*, pp. 50–51 or Leveled Readers  A Inquiry Project  E L L Access Vocabulary | ★ **Independent Reading** © Suggestions for this week's independent reading:  • A high-quality magazine article about rock collecting  • *Torchlight,* by Carol Otis Hurst  • Another biography by a favorite author  **Book Talk** Foster critical reading and discussion skills through independent and close reading.  Students should focus on discussing one or more of the following:  • Key Ideas and Details  • Craft and Structure  • Integration of Ideas |
| **DAY 2** | **Content Knowledge** Build Oral Language/Vocabulary  **Phonics/Word Analysis**  **Vocabulary Skill**  **Text-Based Comprehension** **Read** Main Selection, using Access Text Notes  **Research and Inquiry** Step 2–Navigate/Search  **Spelling** Connect to Phonics/Word Analysis | **Monitor Progress** Formative Assessment: Check Word Reading | **Differentiate Comprehension**  **Build Word Knowledge**  OL Practice Selection Vocabulary  SI Reteach Selection Vocabulary  A Extend Selection Vocabulary  OL SI A Access Text  Read *America's Champion Swimmer: Gertrude Ederle*  A Inquiry Project  E L L Access Comprehension Skill |  **Pearson eText** • Student Edition • Decodable Readers • Leveled Readers |
| **DAY 3** | **Content Knowledge** Build Oral Language/Vocabulary  **Phonics/Word Analysis**  **Read Decodable Passage**  **Text-Based Comprehension** **Read** Main Selection, using Close Reading Notes  **Fluency**  **Research and Inquiry** Step 3–Analyze Information  **Spelling** Connect to Phonics/Word Analysis | **Monitor Progress** Check Retelling | **Differentiate Close Reading**  OL SI **Reread to Develop Vocabulary**  A **Reread to Extend Vocabulary**  OL SI A **Close Reading**  Read *America's Champion Swimmer: Gertrude Ederle*  A Inquiry Project  E L L Access Main Selection |  **Trade Book Library**   **Materials from School or Classroom Library** |
| **DAY 4** | **Content Knowledge** Build Oral Language/Vocabulary  **Phonics/Word Analysis**  **Read Decodable Passage**  **Read Content Area Paired Selection with Genre Focus**  **Let's Learn It!** Vocabulary/Fluency/Listening and Speaking  **Research and Inquiry** Step 4–Synthesize  **Spelling** Connect to Phonics/Word Analysis | **Monitor Progress** Check Fluency | **Differentiate Vocabulary**  **Build Word Knowledge**  OL Develop Language Using Amazing Words  SI Review/Discuss Amazing Words  A Extend Amazing Words and Selection Vocabulary  OL SI A Text-Based Comprehension  Read "Women Athletes"  A Inquiry Project  E L L Access Amazing Words | **Independent Stations Practice Last Week's Skills**  ★ Focus on these activities when time is limited.  **Word Wise** ★ **Word Work** **Read for Meaning** ★ **Let's Write!** **Words to Know** **Get Fluent** |
| **DAY 5** | **Content Knowledge** Build Oral Language/Vocabulary  **Text-Based Comprehension**  **Vocabulary Skill**  **Phonics/Word Analysis**  **Assessment** Fluency, Comprehension  **Research and Inquiry** Step 5–Communicate  **Spelling Test** Connect to Phonics/Word Analysis | **Monitor Progress** Formative Assessment: Check Oral Vocabulary  **Monitor Progress** Fluency; Comprehension | **Differentiate Reteaching**  OL **Practice Contractions**  SI **Review Contractions**  A **Extend Contractions**  OL SI A **Text-Based Comprehension**  Reread *Reading Street Sleuth*, pp. 50–51 or Leveled Readers  A Inquiry Project  E L L Access Conventions and Writing | |

## Assessment Resources

Common Core Weekly Tests, pp. 109–114

Common Core Fresh Reads for Fluency and Comprehension, pp. 109–114

Common Core Unit 4 Benchmark Test

Common Core Success Tracker, ExamView, and Online Lesson Planner

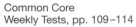

## Teaching the Common Core State Standards This Week

The Common Core State Standards for English Language Arts are divided into strands for **Reading** (including **Foundational Skills**), **Writing**, **Speaking and Listening**, and **Language**. The chart below shows some of the content you will teach this week, strand by strand. Turn to this week's 5-Day Planner on pages 116d–116e to see how this content is taught each day.

## Reading Strand

- **Phonics/Word Analysis:** Suffixes *-er, -or, -ess, -ist*
- **Text-Based Comprehension:** Fact and Opinion; Questioning
- **Fluency:** Appropriate Phrasing
- **Literary Terms:** Word Choice
- **Genre:** Main Selection: Biography; Paired Selection: Online Directories

## Common Core State Standards for English Language Arts

## Writing Strand

- **Writing Mini-Lesson:** Autobiography
- **Trait:** Organization
- **Look Back and Write:** Text Evidence

## Speaking and Listening Strand

- **Content Knowledge:** Build Oral Language
- **Listening and Speaking:** Sportscast
- **Research and Inquiry**

## Language Strand

- **Oral Vocabulary: Amazing Words** *ordinary, imagination, assemble, magnificent, organize, erect, suspend, accompany, provision, spectacle*
- **Vocabulary:** Multiple-Meaning Words; Context Clues
- **Selection Vocabulary:** *drowned, strokes, medals, current, continued, stirred, celebrate*
- **Academic Vocabulary:** *contraction, apostrophe, word choice, biography, subhead*
- **Conventions:** Contractions
- **Spelling:** Suffixes *-er, -or, -ess, -ist*

# Text-Based Comprehension

## Text Complexity Measures

Use the rubric to familiarize yourself with the text complexity of **America's Champion Swimmer: Gertrude Ederle**.

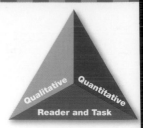

### Bridge to Complex Knowledge

| Quantitative Measures | | |
|---|---|---|
| | **Lexile** | 750L |
| | **Average Sentence Length** | 10.45 |
| | **Word Frequency** | 3.62 |

| Qualitative Measures | | |
|---|---|---|
| | **Levels of Meaning** | understand biographies; understand the writer's motivation |
| | **Structure** | events in order chronologically; simple graphics |
| | **Language Conventionality and Clarity** | literal, clear, conventional language |
| | **Theme and Knowledge Demands** | text assumes no prior knowledge; experiences described are uncommon |

| Reader and Task Suggestions | |
|---|---|
| | **FORMATIVE ASSESSMENT** Based on assessment results, use the **Reader and Task Suggestions** in Access Main Selection to scaffold the selection or support independence for students as they read **America's Champion Swimmer: Gertrude Ederle**. |

| READER AND TASK SUGGESTIONS | |
|---|---|
| **Preparing to Read the Text** | **Leveled Tasks** |
| • Review skills and strategies for understanding multiple-meaning words.<br>• Review the text structure of a biography.<br>• Remind students that biographies often contain dates and famous events. Tell them to adjust their reading rate to better understand what is happening and when. | • **Levels of Meaning • Analysis** Students may find it difficult to understand why the writer chose Gertrude Ederle as a subject. As they read, have students note Gertrude's accomplishments and abilities.<br>• **Structure** If students have difficulty following the events in the selection, have them look at the illustrations and match them to what is happening in the text. |

**Recommended Placement** Both the qualitative and quantitative measures suggest this text should be placed in the Grade 2–3 text complexity band, which is where both the Common Core State Standards and *Scott Foresman Reading Street* have placed it.

# Focus on Common Core State Standards ©

**Main Selection, pp. 124–139**

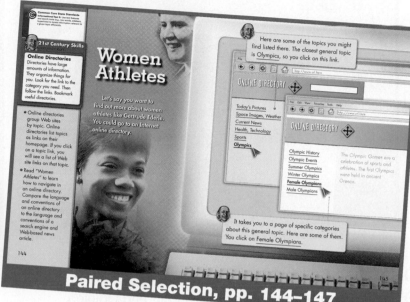

**Paired Selection, pp. 144–147**

## Text-Based Comprehension

**Fact and Opinion**
CCSS Informational Text 1.

**Questioning**
CCSS Informational Text 1.,
CCSS Informational Text 3.

## Fluency

**Appropriate Phrasing**
CCSS Foundational Skills 4.

## Writing and Conventions

**Trait:** Organization
CCSS Writing 3.a., CCSS Writing 4.

**Writing Mini-Lesson:** Autobiography
CCSS Writing 3.a.

**Conventions:** Contractions
CCSS Language 1., CCSS Language 3.

## Oral Vocabulary

### Amazing Words

| | |
|---|---|
| ordinary | erect |
| imagination | suspend |
| assemble | accompany |
| magnificent | provision |
| organize | spectacle |

CCSS Language 6.

## Selection Vocabulary

**Multiple-Meaning Words**
CCSS Language 4.

**Context Clues**
CCSS Language 4., CCSS Language 4.a.

| | |
|---|---|
| celebrate | medals |
| continued | strokes |
| current | stirred |
| drowned | |

## Phonics and Spelling

**Suffixes -er, -or, -ess, -ist**
CCSS Foundational Skills 3.a.,
CCSS Language 2.e.

| | |
|---|---|
| dentist | tourist |
| editor | organist |
| artist | lioness |
| hostess | shipper |
| actress | chemist |
| swimmer | investor |
| seller | conductor |
| tutor | |

**Challenge Words**

| | |
|---|---|
| announcer | commuter |
| pharmacist | pianist |
| journalist | |

## Listening and Speaking

**Media Literacy:** Sportscast
CCSS Speaking/Listening 4.

# Preview Your Week

*What unique traits does it take to be the first to do something?*

**Main Selection, pp. 124–139**

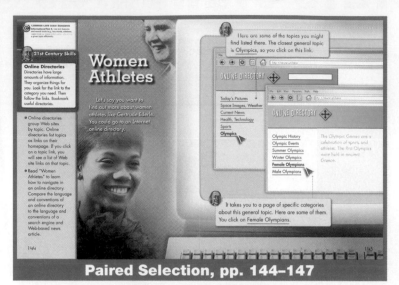

**Paired Selection, pp. 144–147**

**Genre:** Biography

🔊 **Vocabulary:** Multiple-Meaning Words

🔊 **Text-Based Comprehension:** Fact and Opinion

**21st Century Skills:** Online Directories

# Build Content Knowledge

Zoom in on ©

**Time for SOCIAL STUDIES**

### KNOWLEDGE GOALS
Students will understand that being first takes

- bravery
- imagination
- willingness to work hard
- determination

### THIS WEEK'S CONCEPT MAP
Develop a concept-related graphic organizer like the one below over the course of this week.

### BUILD ORAL VOCABULARY
This week, students will acquire the following academic vocabulary/domain-specific words.

**Amazing Words**

| | | |
|---|---|---|
| ordinary | organize | accompany |
| imagination | erect | provision |
| assemble | suspend | spectacle |
| magnificent | | |

**OPTIONAL CONCEPT-BASED READING** Use the Digital Path to access readers offering different levels of text complexity.

Concept Literacy

Below-Level

On-Level

Advanced

ELL

ELD

# This Week's Digital Resources

## eSTREET INTERACTIVE
### www.ReadingStreet.com

### Get Ready to Read

 **Concept Talk Video**   Use this video on the Digital Path to introduce and demonstrate the weekly concept of being first.

 **Pearson eText**   Read the eText of the Student Edition pages on Pearson SuccessNet for comprehension and fluency support.

 **Envision It! Animations**   Use this vibrant animation on the Digital Path to explain the target comprehension skill, Fact and Opinion.

### Read and Comprehend

 **Journal**   Use the Word Bank on the Digital Path to have students write sentences using this week's selection vocabulary words.

 **Background Building Audio CD**   This audio CD provides important background information about being first to help students read and comprehend the weekly texts.

 **Pearson eText**   Read the eText of the main selection, *America's Champion Swimmer: Gertrude Ederle,* and the paired selection, "Women Athletes," with audio support on Pearson SuccessNet.

 **Vocabulary Activities**   A variety of interactive vocabulary activities on the Digital Path help students practice selection vocabulary and concept-related words.

 **Story Sort**   Use the Story Sort Activity on the Digital Path after reading *America's Champion Swimmer: Gertrude Ederle* to involve students in summarizing.

### Language Arts

 **Grammar Jammer**   Present an inviting animation on the Digital Path to provide an engaging grammar lesson that will hold students' attention.

**Pearson eText**   Find the Student Edition eText of the Let's Write It! and Let's Learn It! pages with audio support on Pearson SuccessNet.

## Additional Resources

 **Teacher Resources DVD-ROM** Use the following resources on the TR DVD or on Pearson SuccessNet throughout the week:

- Amazing Word Cards
- Reader's and Writer's Notebook
- Writing Transparencies
- Daily Fix-It Transparencies
- Scoring Rubrics
- Grammar Transparencies
- ELL Support
- Let's Practice It!
- Graphic Organizers
- Vocabulary Cards

## This Week's Skills

**Phonics/Word Analysis**
Suffixes *-er, -or, -ess, -ist*

**Comprehension**
◉ **Skill:** Fact and Opinion
◉ **Strategy:** Questioning

**Language**
◉ **Vocabulary:** Multiple-Meaning Words
**Conventions:** Contractions

**Fluency**
Appropriate Phrasing

**Writing**
Autobiography

# 5-Day Planner

## DAY 1

### Get Ready to Read

**Content Knowledge** 116j
Oral Vocabulary: *ordinary, imagination, assemble, magnificent*

**Monitor Progress**
Check Oral Vocabulary

**Phonics/Word Analysis** 118a
◉ Suffixes *-er, -or, -ess, -ist*
**READ** Decodable Reader 19A
Reread for Fluency

### Read and Comprehend

**Text-Based Comprehension** 120a
◉ Fact and Opinion
◉ Questioning

**Fluency** 120–121
Appropriate Phrasing

**Selection Vocabulary** 121a
*celebrate, continued, current, drowned, medals, stirred, strokes*

### Language Arts

**Research and Inquiry** 121b
Identify and Focus Topic

**Spelling** 121c
Suffixes *-er, -or, -ess, -ist*, Pretest

**Conventions** 121d
Contractions

**Handwriting** 121d
Cursive Letters *r* and *s*

**Writing** 121e
Autobiography

## DAY 2

### Get Ready to Read

**Content Knowledge** 122a
Oral Vocabulary: *organize, erect*

**Phonics/Word Analysis** 122c
◉ Suffixes *-er, -or, -ess, -ist*

**Monitor Progress**
Check Word Reading

**Literary Terms** 122d
Word Choice

### Read and Comprehend

**Vocabulary Skill** 122e
◉ Multiple-Meaning Words

**Fluency** 122–123
Appropriate Phrasing

**Text-Based Comprehension**
124–125
**READ** *America's Champion Swimmer: Gertrude Ederle*—1st Read

### Language Arts

**Research and Inquiry** 131b
Navigate/Search

**Conventions** 131c
Contractions

**Spelling** 131c
Suffixes *-er, -or, -ess, -ist*

**Writing** 131d
Autobiography

## DAY 3

### Get Ready to Read

**Content Knowledge** 132a
Oral Vocabulary: *suspend, accompany*

**Word Analysis** 132c
Fluent Word Reading
**DECODE AND READ**
Decodable Practice Passage 19B

### Read and Comprehend

**Text-Based Comprehension** 132e
Check Understanding
**READ** *America's Champion Swimmer: Gertrude Ederle*—2nd Read
Monitor Progress Check Retelling

**Fluency** 141b
Appropriate Phrasing

### Language Arts

**Research and Study Skills** 141c
Bar Graphs

**Research and Inquiry** 141d
Analyze Information

**Conventions** 141e
Contractions

**Spelling** 141e
Suffixes -er, -or, -ess, -ist

**Writing** 143–143
Autobiography

## DAY 4

### Get Ready to Read

**Content Knowledge** 144a
Oral Vocabulary: *provision, spectacle*

**Phonics/Word Analysis** 144c
Review Prefixes
Fluent Word Reading
**DECODE AND READ**
Decodable Practice Passage 19C

### Read and Comprehend

**21st Century Skills** 144g
Online Directories
**READ** "Women Athletes"—Paired Selection

**Fluency** 148–149
Appropriate Phrasing
Monitor Progress Check Fluency

**Vocabulary Skill** 149a
Multiple-Meaning Words

**Listening and Speaking** 149a
Media Literacy: Sportscast

### Language Arts

**Research and Inquiry** 149b
Synthesize

**Conventions** 149c
Contractions

**Spelling** 149c
Suffixes -er, -or, -ess, -ist

**Writing** 149d
Autobiography

## DAY 5

### Get Ready to Read

**Content Knowledge** 149f
Review Oral Vocabulary
Monitor Progress
Check Oral Vocabulary

### Read and Comprehend

**Text-Based Comprehension** 149h
Review Fact and Opinion

**Vocabulary Skill** 149h
Review Multiple-Meaning Words

**Phonics/Word Analysis** 149i
Review Suffixes -er, -or, -ess, -ist

**Literary Terms** 149i
Review Word Choice

**Assessment** 149j, 149l
Monitor Progress
Fluency; Fact and Opinion

### Language Arts

**Research and Inquiry** 149n
Communicate

**Spelling** 149o
Suffixes -er, -or, -ess, -ist, Test

**Conventions** 149o
Contractions

**Writing** 149p
Autobiography

**Wrap Up Your Week!** 149q

# Access for All

## What do I do in group time?
It's as easy as 1-2-3!

**1** TEACHER-LED SMALL GROUPS → **2** INDEPENDENT PRACTICE STATIONS → **3** INDEPENDENT READING

## Small Group Time

### © Bridge to Common Core

**SKILL DEVELOPMENT**
- Suffixes *-er, -or, -ess, -ist*
- Fact and Opinion
- Questioning
- Multiple-Meaning Words

**DEEP UNDERSTANDING**
**This Week's Knowledge Goals**
Students will understand that being first takes
- bravery
- imagination
- willingness to work hard
- determination

## **1** Small Group Lesson Plan

|  | DAY 1 Differentiate Vocabulary | DAY 2 Differentiate Comprehension |
|---|---|---|
| **OL On-Level** pp. SG•50–SG•54 | **Build Word Knowledge** Practice Amazing Words **Text-Based Comprehension** Read *Reading Street Sleuth,* pp. 50–51 or Leveled Readers | **Build Word Knowledge** Practice Selection Vocabulary **Access Text** Read *America's Champion Swimmer: Gertrude Ederle* |
| **SI Strategic Intervention** pp. SG•55–SG•59 | **Build Word Knowledge** Reteach Amazing Words **Text-Based Comprehension** Read *Reading Street Sleuth,* pp. 50–51 or Leveled Readers | **Build Word Knowledge** Reteach Selection Vocabulary **Access Text** Read *America's Champion Swimmer: Gertrude Ederle* |
| **A Advanced** pp. SG•60–SG•64 | **Build Word Knowledge** Extend Amazing Words **Text-Based Comprehension** Read *Reading Street Sleuth,* pp. 50–51 or Leveled Readers | **Build Word Knowledge** Extend Selection Vocabulary **Access Text** Read *America's Champion Swimmer: Gertrude Ederle* |
| **Independent Inquiry Project** | Identify Questions | Investigate |
| **ELL** If... students need more scaffolding and practice with... | **Vocabulary,** then... use the activities on DI•92–DI•93 in the Teacher Resources section on SuccessNet. | **Comprehension Skill,** then... use the activities on page DI•96 in the Teacher Resources section on SuccessNet. |

## Build Text-Based Comprehension

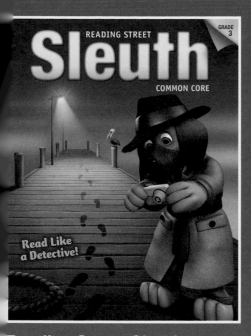

### Reading Street Sleuth

- Provides access to grade-level text for all students
- Focuses on finding clues in text through close reading
- Builds capacity for complex text

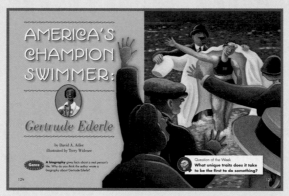

*America's Champion Swimmer: Gertrude Ederle*

### Optional Leveled Readers

| Concept Literacy | Below-Level | On-Level | Advanced | ELL | ELD |
|---|---|---|---|---|---|

---

| **DAY 3** | **DAY 4** | **DAY 5** |
|---|---|---|
| **Differentiate Close Reading** | **Differentiate Vocabulary** | **Differentiate · Reteaching** |
| **Reread to Develop Vocabulary** **Close Reading** Read *America's Champion Swimmer: Gertrude Ederle* | **Build Word Knowledge** Develop Language Using Amazing Words **Text-Based Comprehension** Read "Women Athletes" | **Practice Contractions** **Text-Based Comprehension** Reread *Reading Street Sleuth,* pp. 50–51 or Leveled Readers |
| **Reread to Develop Vocabulary** **Close Reading** Read *America's Champion Swimmer: Gertrude Ederle* | **Build Word Knowledge** Review/Discuss Amazing Words **Text-Based Comprehension** Read "Women Athletes" | **Review Contractions** **Text-Based Comprehension** Reread *Reading Street Sleuth,* pp. 50–51 or Leveled Readers |
| **Reread to Extend Vocabulary** **Close Reading** Read *America's Champion Swimmer: Gertrude Ederle* | **Build Word Knowledge** Extend Amazing Words and Selection Vocabulary **Text-Based Comprehension** Read "Women Athletes" | **Extend Contractions** **Text-Based Comprehension** Reread *Reading Street Sleuth,* pp. 50–51 or Leveled Readers |
| Investigate | Organize | Communicate |
| **Main Selection,** **then...** use the activities on page DI•97 in the Teacher Resources section on SuccessNet. | **Amazing Words,** **then...** use the Routine on pp. xxxvi–xxxvii in the *ELL Handbook.* | **Conventions and Writing,** **then...** use the activities on pp. DI•99–DI•100 in the Teacher Resources section on SuccessNet. |

# ② Independent Stations

## Practice Last Week's Skills

⭐ Focus on these activities when time is limited.

---

## WORD WISE

**Spell and use words in sentences.**

**OBJECTIVES**

• Spell words with prefixes *pre-, mid-, over-, out-, bi-,* and *de-.*

**MATERIALS**

• *Word Wise* Flip Chart Activity 19, teacher-made word cards, dictionary, paper and pencils

 **Letter Tile Drag and Drop**

● Students list one word with each prefix *pre-, mid-, over-, out-, bi-,* and *de-,* and use each word in a sentence.

▲ Students list two words with each prefix *pre-, mid-, over-, out-, bi-,* and *de-,* and use each word in a sentence.

■ Students list two words with each prefix *pre-, mid-, over-, out-, bi-,* and *de-,* and use each word in a sentence. Students add other such words to the list.

---

## WORD WORK

**Identify and pronounce words.**

**OBJECTIVES**

• Identify and pronounce words with prefixes *pre-, mid-, over-, out-, bi-,* and *de-.*

**MATERIALS**

• *Word Work* Flip Chart Activity 19, teacher-made word cards, paper and pencils

 **Letter Tile Drag and Drop**

● Students read aloud ten words with the prefixes, group them by prefix, and then list other words with the prefixes.

▲ Students place twelve words with the prefixes in a six-column chart, and then add words on their own.

■ Students place fifteen words with the prefixes in a six-column chart, and then add words on their own.

---

## LET'S WRITE!

**Write a biography.**

**OBJECTIVES**

• Write a biography about someone you know.

**MATERIALS**

• *Let's Write!* Flip Chart Activity 19, paper and pencils

 **Grammar Jammer**

● Students write a short biography of someone they know and admire, including interesting facts and details.

▲ Students write a biography of someone they know and admire, including interesting facts and details, and using complete sentences.

■ Students write a biography of someone they know and admire, including interesting facts and details, and combining short sentences.

---

## WORDS TO KNOW

**Determine word meanings.**

**OBJECTIVES**

• Identify the meanings of multiple-meaning words.

**MATERIALS**

• *Words to Know* Flip Chart Activity 19, teacher-made word cards, dictionary, paper and pencils

 **Vocabulary Activities**

● Students look up three words with multiple meanings. They write two sentences for each word to show its different meanings.

▲ Students look up four words with multiple meanings. They write two sentences for each word to show its different meanings.

■ Students look up five words with multiple meanings. They write at least two sentences for each word to show its different meanings.

## Manage the Stations

Use these management tools to set up and organize your Practice Stations:

Practice Station Flip Charts

Classroom Management Handbook for Differentiated Instruction Practice Stations, p. 37

### READ FOR MEANING

**Use text-based comprehension tools.**

#### OBJECTIVES

• Identify fact and opinion in expository text.

#### MATERIALS

• *Read for Meaning* Flip Chart Activity 19, Leveled Readers, paper and pencils

 **Pearson eText**
  • Leveled eReaders

 **Envision It! Animations**

● Students read a book and write one sentence telling a fact from the text and one telling an opinion.

▲ Students read a book and write two sentences telling two facts from the text and two sentences giving two opinions.

■ Students read a book and write one paragraph describing facts from the text and one paragraph describing the opinions.

## 3 Independent Reading ©

Students should select appropriately complex texts to read and write about independently every day before, during, and after school.

Suggestions for this week's independent reading:
  • A high-quality magazine article about rock collecting
  • *Torchlight,* by Carol Otis Hurst
  • Another biography by a favorite author

**BOOK TALK** Have partners discuss their independent reading for the week. Tell them to refer to their Reading Logs and paraphrase what each selection was about. Then have students focus on discussing one or more of the following:

#### Key Ideas and Details
  • What are some of the main ideas in the text? How do you know?
  • Summarize the events in the text.

#### Craft and Structure
  • How is the information in the text organized?
  • What facts are presented about the topic? What opinions?

#### Integration of Ideas
  • Make three inferences based on the information presented in the text.
  • Compare this book to others you have read.

### GET FLUENT

**Practice fluent reading.**

#### OBJECTIVES

• Read aloud with expression.

#### MATERIALS

• *Get Fluent* Flip Chart Activity 19, Leveled Readers

 **Pearson eText**
  • Leveled eReaders

● Students choose a partner and practice reading with correct expression from a Concept Literacy Reader or a Below-Level Reader.

▲ Students choose a partner and practice reading with correct expression from an On-Level Reader.

■ Students choose a partner and practice reading with correct expression from an Advanced Reader.

 **Pearson eText**
  • Student Edition
  • Decodable Readers
  • Leveled Readers

 **Trade Book Library**

 **School or Classroom Library**

# DAY 1
## at a Glance

### Materials

- Student Edition
- Reader's and Writer's Notebook
- Decodable Reader

---

## ⓒ Bridge to Common Core

**INTEGRATION OF KNOWLEDGE/IDEAS**
This week, students will read, write, and talk about unique traits.

**Texts This Week**
- "A First in Space: Ellen Ochoa"
- "Swim!"
- "Learn to Swim"
- *America's Champion Swimmer: Gertrude Ederle*
- "Women Athletes"

**Social Studies Knowledge Goals**
Students will understand that being first takes
- bravery
- imagination
- willingness to work hard
- determination

---

# Street Rhymes!

*Study hard and practice. Try to do your best—
in a race or spelling bee or when you take a test.
If you want to be first in something that you do—
concentrate and focus. Always see it through!*

- To introduce this week's concept, read aloud the poem several times and ask students to join you.

# Content Knowledge

## Unique Traits

**CONCEPT TALK** To further explore the unit concept of One of a Kind, this week students will read, write, and talk about what unique traits it takes to be the first to do something. Write the Question of the Week *What unique traits does it take to be the first to do something?* on the board.

## Build Oral Language

**TALK ABOUT UNIQUE TRAITS** Have students turn to pp. 116–117 in their Student Editions. Look at each of the photos. Then use the prompts to guide discussion and create a concept map.

- Why is a picture of George Washington on this page? (He was the first president.) What unique traits do you think George Washington had? (He was a strong leader; he was smart, honest, and inspiring.) Let's add *Leadership* to our concept map.

- Neil Armstrong was the first person on the moon. What are some unique traits of astronauts? (Possible responses: They are brave, intelligent, and organized.) Let's add *Bravery* to our concept map.

- What unique traits do swimmers competing in a race have? (Possible responses: They use imagination and determination to help them win races.) Let's add *Determination* and *Imagination* to the concept map.

Common Core State Standards
Speaking/Listening 1.c. Ask questions
to check understanding of information
presented, stay on topic, and link their
comments to the remarks of others.
Also Language 6.

Oral Vocabulary

## Let's Talk About

**Being First**

- Ask questions about bravery, imagination, and determination.
- Pose and answer questions about what it takes to be first at something.
- Discuss historical firsts.

READING STREET ONLINE
CONCEPT TALK VIDEO
www.ReadingStreet.com

You've learned 1 7 7 Amazing Words so far this year!

116   117

Student Edition, pp. 116–117

**CONNECT TO READING** Tell students that this week they will be reading about people who were the first to achieve something. Throughout the week, encourage students to add concept-related words to this week's concept map. Encourage students to ask relevant questions about things they don't understand.

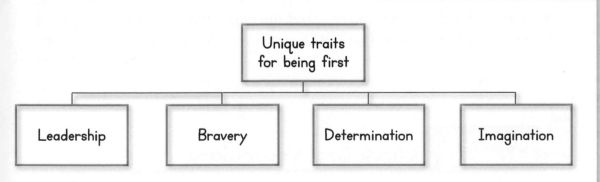

Unique traits for being first

Leadership | Bravery | Determination | Imagination

**eStreet Interactive**
www.ReadingStreet.com

**Pearson eText**
- Student Edition

**Concept Talk Video**

## ELL

**Preteach Concepts** Use the Day 1 instruction on ELL Poster 19 to build knowledge and oral vocabulary.

**ELL Support** Additional ELL support and modified instruction is provided in the *ELL Handbook* and in the ELL Support lessons found on the *Teacher Resources DVD-ROM*.

*Gertrude Ederle* **116–117**

**Speaking/Listening 1.d.** Explain their own ideas and understanding in light of the discussion. **Language 4.** Determine or clarify the meaning of unknown and multiple-meaning word and phrases based on grade 3 reading and content, choosing flexibly from a range of strategies. **Language 6.** Acquire and use accurately grade-appropriate conversational, general academic, and domain-specific words and phrases, including those that signal spatial and temporal relationships (e.g., *After dinner that night we went looking for them*). Also **Speaking/Listening 1., Language 4.a.**

## Amazing Words

You've learned | 1 | 7 | 7 | words so far.

You'll learn | 0 | 1 | 0 | words this week!

| | |
|---|---|
| ordinary | erect |
| imagination | suspend |
| assemble | accompany |
| magnificent | provision |
| organize | spectacle |

# Content Knowledge

## Build Oral Vocabulary

**INTRODUCE AMAZING WORDS** "A First in Space: Ellen Ochoa" on p. 117b is about the first Hispanic-American female in space. Tell students to listen for this week's Amazing Words—*ordinary, imagination, assemble,* and *magnificent*—as you read the Teacher Read Aloud on p. 117b.

### Amazing Words  Robust Vocabulary Routine

1. **Introduce** Write the word *imagination* on the board. Have students say the word aloud with you. In "A First in Space: Ellen Ochoa," we learn that Ochoa had a vivid *imagination* as a child. Does the author include any context clues for this word? Supply a student-friendly definition.

2. **Demonstrate** Have students answer questions to demonstrate understanding. How is daydreaming a way of using your *imagination*? How do you know if someone has a good *imagination*?

3. **Apply** Ask students to give a personal example of *imagination*.

4. **Display the Word** Run your hand under the syllables *i-mag-i-na-tion* as you read the word.

See p. OV•4 to teach *ordinary, assemble,* and *magnificent*.

Routines Flip Chart

**AMAZING WORDS AT WORK** Reread "A First in Space: Ellen Ochoa" aloud. As students listen, have them notice how the Amazing Words are used in context. To build oral vocabulary, lead the class in a discussion about the Amazing Words' meanings. Remind students to ask and answer questions.

**MONITOR PROGRESS**  Check Oral Vocabulary

During discussion, listen for students' use of Amazing Words.

**If...** students are unable to use the Amazing Words in discussion,

**then...** use the Oral Vocabulary Routine in the Routines Flip Chart to demonstrate words in different contexts.

# Teacher Read Aloud

**MODEL FLUENCY** As you read "A First in Space: Ellen Ochoa," model appropriate phrasing by grouping words in a meaningful way and paying attention to punctuation cues.

# A First in Space: Ellen Ochoa

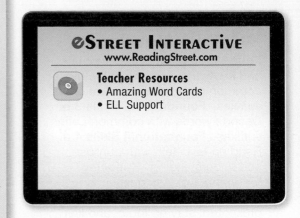
When Dr. Ellen Ochoa was growing up, few women dreamed of going into space. Ellen was different, though. She was no ordinary woman!

The first American woman did not go into space until 1983. In 1993 Ellen Ochoa reached a goal that was truly a first. She became the first Hispanic-American woman in space.

Ellen Ochoa was born on May 10, 1958, in Los Angeles. Her interest in exploring space started at a young age. Her vivid imagination helped her dream of the day when she could go into space. Ellen also had a great desire to learn. She studied hard in school. Math and science were her favorite subjects.

Ellen's combined love of math and science grew. It helped her decide what to study in college. She majored in physics at San Diego State University, where she graduated in 1980. Physics is a special branch of science that deals with changes in matter. But one degree wasn't enough for Ellen. She received a master of science degree in 1981 and a doctorate in electrical engineering in 1985. Both of these degrees were from Stanford University.

Along with her keen interest in science and her brilliant mind, Ellen had an intense curiosity about everything she came in contact with. This led her to invent a tool that helped find flaws in the production of a variety of small manufacturing parts. She later helped assemble other tools that would become helpful in the science field.

Although remaining an inventor could have led to a magnificent career, Ellen wanted more. She saw a way to combine her scientific knowledge with her long-time interest in space exploration. In 1990 she was selected by NASA (National Aeronautics and Space Administration) to join the astronaut program. She became an astronaut in 1991.

After a few years of serving in several positions at NASA, the big day finally came. Ellen's childhood dream became a reality! In April 1993 she went into space on the Space Shuttle *Discovery*. Ellen became the first Hispanic-American woman in space.

During the nine-day mission on the *Discovery*, Ellen and the rest of the crew performed many tasks. The *Discovery* mission was the first of several space flights for Ellen. Her roles on the other space flights varied. Since her first flight, she has logged hundreds of hours in space.

Throughout the years, Ellen has received a number of awards, including a Distinguished Service Medal. One of Ellen's highest achievements was to help develop the International Space Station.

To this day, Ellen Ochoa still plays a major role in space exploration.

**ELL Support for Read Aloud** Use the modified Read Aloud on p. DI•94 of the ELL Support lessons on the *Teacher Resources DVD-ROM* to prepare students to listen to "A First in Space: Ellen Ochoa."

**Support Listening Comprehension** To build background knowledge, preview new vocabulary and support understanding of complex text with visuals from the Student Edition and online sources.

 **Common Core State Standards**

**Foundational Skills 3.a.** Identify and know the meaning of the most common prefixes and derivational suffixes. **Foundational Skills 3.b.** Decode words with common Latin suffixes. **Foundational Skills 4.a.** Read on-level text with purpose and understanding. **Speaking/ Listening 1.c.** Ask questions to check understanding of information presented, stay on topic, and link their comments to the remarks of others. **Language 2.e.** Use conventional spelling for high-frequency and other studied words and for adding suffixes to base words (e.g., *sitting, smiled, cries, happiness*).

## Skills Trace

**⊙ Suffixes *-er, -or, -ess, -ist***
**Introduce** U4W4D1
**Practice** U4W4D3; U4W4D4
**Reteach/Review** U4W4D5; U4W5D4
**Assess/Test** Weekly Test U4W4
Benchmark Test U4
**KEY:** U=Unit   W=Week   D=Day

## Vocabulary Support

You may wish to explain the meanings of these words.

**actress** a female who acts

**hostess** a woman who receives another person as her guest

**countess** the wife of a count or an earl

**flutist** a person who plays the flute

**pianist** a person who plays the piano

# Word Analysis

## Teach/Model

### ⊙ Suffixes *-er, -or, -ess, -ist*

**CONNECT** Connect today's lesson to previously learned prefixes *mid-* and *pre-*. Write *preview* and *midpoint*. You can already read words like these. Each is a base word with a prefix. Read these words. Today you'll learn to spell and read words with suffixes.

**MODEL** Write *painter*. *Painter* is a two-syllable word formed from the base word *paint* and the ending, or suffix, *-er*. Point out each word part, read the parts, and then read the word. Often suffixes like *-er* change how a base word is used. For example, *painter* names a person who paints. Write *visitor, player, collector, princess,* and *harpist*. Model how to read each word by covering the suffix, reading the base word (*visit, play, collect, prince, harp*), reading the suffix, and reading the whole word. Discuss how the suffix changes the meanings of the base words.

**GROUP PRACTICE** Continue the process. This time have students read the words with you. Identify the suffix in each word and tell how it changes the meaning of the base word. Point out the spelling changes.

| | | | | | |
|---|---|---|---|---|---|
| artist | swimmer | seller | editor | actress | builder |
| hostess | sailor | tourist | countess | writer | farmer |

**REVIEW** What do you know about reading words with suffixes? When you recognize a suffix, cover the suffix, read the base word first, read the suffix, and then read the whole word.

## Guide Practice

**MODEL** Have students turn to p. 118 in their Student Editions. Each word on this page has a suffix. The first word has the suffix *-er*. I cover the suffix and read the base word *teach*. Adding the suffix *-er* gives me *teacher*.

**GROUP PRACTICE** For each word in Words I Can Blend, ask students to identify the base word and the suffix and then read the whole word.

| Corrective feedback | **If...** students have difficulty reading a word, **then...** model reading the parts and then the whole word, and then ask students to read it with you. |
|---|---|

**Envision It!** Suffixes to Know

painter
-er
lioness
-ess
violinist
-ist
sailor
-or

**READING STREET ONLINE
SOUND-SPELLING CARDS**
www.ReadingStreet.com

### Phonics
## Suffixes -er, -or, -ess, -ist

### Words I Can Blend

**teacher**
**inventor**
**actress**
**artist**
**visitor**

### Sentences I Can Read

1. My teacher told us about the great inventor Thomas Edison.
2. I don't have one favorite actress.
3. Last week a famous artist was a visitor at our school.

## I Can Read!

I am kind of a dreamer. I often imagine what my life will be like when I grow up. Each day I imagine I am something different.

For example, one day I am a famous inventor, the next a writer or sailor. I love music, so sometimes I pretend I am a flutist or pianist in an orchestra. And, of course, sometimes I imagine life as a princess.

I guess this is all practice for when I decide what kind of work I will do, as an office worker, a doctor, or maybe even an actress.

**You've learned**
## Suffixes -er, -or, -ess, -ist

118    119

**Student Edition, pp. 118–119**

# Apply

**READ WORDS IN ISOLATION** After students can successfully combine the word parts to read the words on p. 118 in their Student Editions, point to words in random order and ask students to read them naturally.

**READ WORDS IN CONTEXT** Have students read each of the sentences on p. 118. Have them identify words in the sentences that have suffixes.

**Team Talk** Pair students and have them take turns reading each of the sentences aloud.

Chorally read the I Can Read! passage on p. 119 with students. Then have them read the passage aloud to themselves.

**ON THEIR OWN** For additional practice, use *Reader's and Writer's Notebook,* p. 280.

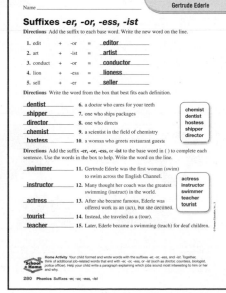

Reader's and Writer's Notebook, p. 280

**ELL**

**Pronunciation** Assist students with the articulation of suffixes. Focus on mouth positions when saying words such as *teacher* and *hostess*.

**Language Transfer** In Spanish, *-er* is pronounced like *air*, such as *better* and *faster* as *be-tair* and *fas-tair*. Pronounce these words and have students pronounce them after you.

*Gertrude Ederle* **118–119**

### Common Core State Standards

**Foundational Skills 3.a.** Identify and know the meaning of the most common prefixes and derivational suffixes. **Foundational Skills 3.d.** Read grade-appropriate irregularly spelled words. **Language 2.e.** Use conventional spelling for high-frequency and other studied words and for adding suffixes to base words (e.g., *sitting, smiled, cries, happiness*). **Also Literature 3., Foundational Skills 4.**

# Decodable Reader 19A

If students need help, then...

## Read *Teller, Tailor, Seller, Sailor*

**READ WORDS IN ISOLATION** Have students turn to p. 37 of *Decodable Practice Readers 3.2.* Have students read each word.

Have students read the high-frequency words *are, people, do, a, what, said, you, the, of, two, wants, watched, their, should, they, to, would,* and *your* on the first page.

**PREVIEW** Have students read the title and preview the story. Tell them that they will read words with suffixes.

**READ WORDS IN CONTEXT** Pair students for reading and listen as they read. One student begins. Students read the entire story, switching readers after each page. Partners reread the story. This time the other student begins. Make sure students are monitoring their accuracy when they decode words.

Decodable Practice Reader 19A

**eSTREET INTERACTIVE**
www.ReadingStreet.com

**Pearson eText**
• Decodable Reader

**Interactive Sound-Spelling Cards**

| Corrective feedback | **If...** students have difficulty decoding a word, **then...** refer them to the *Sound-Spelling Cards* to identify the word parts. Have them read the word parts individually and then together to say the word. |
|---|---|

• What is the new word?

• Is the new word a word you know?

• Does it make sense in the story?

**CHECK DECODING AND COMPREHENSION** Have students retell the story to include characters, setting, and events. Then have students find words in the story that have suffixes. Students should supply *teacher, artist, actress, editors, conductors, driver, writer, inventor, firefighter,* and *chemist.*

# Reread for Fluency

**REREAD DECODABLE READER** Have students reread *Decodable Practice Reader 19A* to develop automaticity decoding words with suffixes.

**Routine** | **Oral Rereading**

**1. Read** Have students read the entire book orally.

**2. Reread** To achieve optimal fluency, students should reread the text three or four times.

**3. Corrective Feedback** Listen as students read. Provide corrective feedback regarding their fluency and decoding.

Routines Flip Chart

**ELL**

**Leveled Support: Suffixes**

**Beginning** Write several words with suffixes from the *Decodable Practice Reader* on the board, such as *teacher, artist, actress,* and *editors.* Point to each word as you say it aloud. Then underline the letters that spell the suffix. Have students repeat the words with you. Repeat the procedure with *conductors, driver, inventor,* and *chemist.*

**Intermediate** After reading, have students find pairs of words with the same suffix. For example: *teacher* and *driver; artist* and *chemist; editor* and *conductor.*

**Advanced** After reading the story, have students choose four or five words with suffixes and write a sentence for each word.

## Common Core State Standards

**Informational Text 1.** Ask and answer questions to demonstrate understanding of a text, referring explicitly to the text as the basis for the answers. **Informational Text 8.** Describe the logical connection between particular sentences and paragraphs in a text (e.g., comparison, cause/effect, first/second/third in a sequence). **Foundational Skills 4.** Read with sufficient accuracy and fluency to support comprehension.

## Skills Trace

### Fact and Opinion

**Introduce** U4W3D1; U4W4D1; U6W1D1

**Practice** U1W4D2; U4W4D5; U6W1D5

**Reteach/Review** U4W3D5; U4W4D5; U6W1D5

**Assess/Test** Weekly Tests U4W3; U4W4; U6W1
Benchmark Test U4

**KEY:** U=Unit   W=Week   D=Day

## Comprehension Support

Students may also turn to pp. EI•7 and EI•23 to review the skill and strategy if needed.

# Text-Based Comprehension

## Fact and Opinion
## Questioning

**READ** Remind students of the weekly concept—Unique Traits. Have studen read "Swim!" on p. 121.

**Think Aloud** **MODEL A CLOSE READ** Have students follow along as you read th second paragraph of "Swim!" I see the word *best* in the first sentence This is a clue word that indicates an opinion or judgment. I cannot prove this statement true or false. The other sentences are facts. I can check in a reference book to verify that these statements are true. As I read the thir paragraph, I asked myself why people do not get hurt when swimming. I reread the second paragraph and thought about my own knowledge. There is little or no impact when you are swimming. You cannot twist an ankle or break an arm in the water. Have students review the strategy of questioning on p. EI•23 of the Student Edition.

**TEACH** Have students read p. 120. Explain that the skill of fact and opinion and the strategy of questioning are tools they can use to deepen and demon strate understanding. Review the bulleted items and explanations on p. 120. Then have students finish reading "Swim!" on their own. After they read, hav them use a graphic organizer like the one on p. 120 and identify statements o fact and opinion from the passage.

**GUIDE PRACTICE** Have students reread "Swim!" using the callouts as guides. Then ask volunteers to respond to the questions in the callouts, citing specific examples from the text to support their answers.

**Skill** an encyclopedia
**Strategy** How can you have fun while swimming? You can read on to see if the author answers the question.

**APPLY** Use *Reader's and Writer's Notebook,* p. 281 for additional practice with fact and opinion.

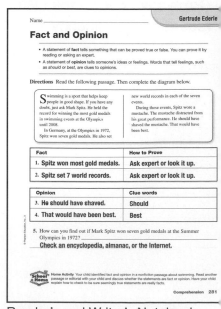

Reader's and Writer's Notebook, p. 281

Common Core State Standards
Informational Text 1. Ask and answer
questions to demonstrate understanding of
a text, referring explicitly to the text as the
basis for the answers.

**Envision It!** Skill Strategy

**Skill**

Fact and Opinion

**Strategy**

Questioning

READING STREET ONLINE
ENVISION IT! ANIMATIONS
www.ReadingStreet.com

**Comprehension Skill**

## Fact and Opinion

- A statement of fact can be proved true or false.
- A statement of opinion cannot be proved true or false. It is a belief or judgment.
- Use what you learned about fact and opinion and a chart like the one below as you read "Swim!" Then write a short paragraph about swimmers.

| Statement | Fact? How Can It Be Checked? | Opinion? What Are Clue Words? |
|---|---|---|
| | | |
| | | |

**Comprehension Strategy**

## Questioning

As you read, ask questions. Questioning helps you identify what you don't understand. Continue to read to find an answer to your question. You can ask literal questions about details in a selection. You can ask interpretive and evaluative questions that you have to think about and answer on your own.

120

# Swim!

Exercise is important for good health. When people do not exercise, their muscles become soft and weak.

Swimming is one of the best ways to exercise. When swimming, you must move against the water. This makes muscles stronger. It takes more energy to move through water than it does through air. So swimming helps people lose fat. All this also helps your heart get and stay strong.

Many people get hurt playing soccer, football, or basketball. Not in swimming! It's one of the safest ways to exercise.

Swimming is also a great way to have fun while you exercise. You can cool off on a hot summer day and play water games with your friends. Swimming races are an exciting way to beat the heat.

If you do not know how to swim, you should learn how—now!

**Skill** What reference could you use to see whether these statements are true?

**Strategy** What questions can you ask about swimming as a way to have fun? How can you answer your questions?

**Your Turn!**

⏸ **Need a Review?** See the *Envision It! Handbook* for help with fact and opinion and questioning.

▶ **Ready to Try It?** As you read *America's Champion Swimmer: Gertrude Ederle*, use what you've learned about fact and opinion and questioning.

121

# Model Fluent Reading

**APPROPRIATE PHRASING** Have students listen as you read paragraph 2 of "Swim!" with appropriate phrasing. Explain that you will group phrases together then pause, using punctuation to help you.

**Routine** Oral Rereading

1. **Select a Passage** Use paragraph 2 of "Swim!"

2. **Model** Have students listen as you read with appropriate phrasing.

3. **Guide Practice** Have students read along with you.

4. **On Their Own** For optimal fluency, students should reread three or four times with appropriate phrasing.

5. **Corrective Feedback** Listen as students read. Provide feedback about their phrasing and attention to punctuation.

Routines Flip Chart

## eSTREET INTERACTIVE
www.ReadingStreet.com

📖 **Pearson eText**
- Student Edition

🎬 **Envision It! Animations**

💿 **Teacher Resources**
- Reader's and Writer's Notebook

**ELL**

**Fact and Opinion** Provide oral practice by having students state facts and opinions about this week's weather. Then write these sentences on the board and read them aloud. Have students identify whether each sentence is a fact or an opinion and then support their answers.

- Everyone likes to swim.
- Swimming is fun.
- Swimming makes you stronger.

# DAY 1

**Ⓒ Common Core State Standards**

**Writing 7.** Conduct short research projects that build knowledge about a topic. **Speaking/Listening 1.** Engage effectively in a range of collaborative discussions (one-on-one, in groups, and teacher led) with diverse partners on grade 3 topics and texts, building on others' ideas and expressing their own clearly. **Speaking/Listening 1.c.** Ask questions to check understanding of information presented, stay on topic, and link their comments to the remarks of others. **Language 4.** Determine or clarify the meaning of unknown and multiple-meaning word and phrases based on grade 3 reading and content, choosing flexibly from a range of strategies. **Also Speaking/Listening 1.d., Writing 8.**

# Selection Vocabulary

Use the following routine to introduce this week's tested selection vocabulary.

**celebrate** to do something special in honor of a special person or day

**continued** kept up; kept on going

**current** a flow or stream of water

**drowned** died or caused to die under water or other liquid because of lack of air to breathe

**medals** pieces of metal, like coins, that are given as prizes or rewards

**stirred** mixed something by moving it around with a spoon or stick

**strokes** single, complete movements made over and over again

**SEE IT/SAY IT** Write *medal*. Scan across the word with your finger as you say it: *me-dal.*

**HEAR IT** Use the word in a sentence. A war hero often receives a *medal* for bravery.

**DEFINE IT** Elicit definitions from students. How would you describe to another student what *medal* means? Clarify or give a definition when necessary. Yes, it means "a prize" or "a reward." Restate the meaning of the word in student-friendly terms. So, *medal* means a prize or reward made from metal.

**Team Talk** Do you think that a *medal* is a valuable thing to have? Turn and talk to your partner about this. Be prepared to explain your answer. Allow students time to discuss. Ask for examples. Rephrase their examples for usage when necessary or to correct misunderstandings.

**MAKE CONNECTIONS** Have students discuss the word. Have you ever received a *medal* or known someone who received a *medal*? Turn and talk to your partner about this. Then be prepared to share. Have students share. Rephrase their ideas for usage when necessary or to correct misunderstandings.

**RECORD** Have students write the word and its meaning.

Continue this routine to introduce the remaining words in this manner.

**Corrective feedback** | **If...** students are having difficulty understanding, **then...** review the definitions in small groups.

# Research and Inquiry

## Step 1 Identify and Focus Topic

**TEACH** Discuss the Question of the Week: *What unique traits does it take to be the first to do something?* Tell students they will research female athletes and their unique traits. They will present their findings as a biography to the class on Day 5.

**Think Aloud**

**MODEL** I'll start by brainstorming a list of questions about female athletes and their traits. First, I'll think about female athletes, though I will only write about one. I watched women compete in the Olympic Games. I also like to watch women play in tennis tournaments. Some possible questions could be: *What were their childhoods like? When did they begin the sport? How much time do they dedicate to playing and practicing the sport?*

**GUIDE PRACTICE** After students have brainstormed inquiry questions, explain that tomorrow they will conduct an online search of their questions. Help students identify keywords that will guide their search.

**ON THEIR OWN** Have students work individually, in pairs, or in small groups to write an inquiry question.

## eStreet Interactive
www.ReadingStreet.com

**Teacher Resources**
- Envision It! Pictured Vocabulary Cards
- Tested Vocabulary Cards

## 21st Century Skills
**Internet Guy** *Don Leu*

### Weekly Inquiry Project

| STEP 1 | Identify and Focus Topic |
|--------|--------------------------|
| STEP 2 | Navigate/Search |
| STEP 3 | Analyze Information |
| STEP 4 | Synthesize |
| STEP 5 | Communicate |

**ELL**

**Multilingual Vocabulary** Students can apply knowledge of their home languages to acquire new English vocabulary by using the Multilingual Vocabulary Lists (*ELL Handbook*, pp. 433–444).

**ELL**

**If...** students need more scaffolding and practice with **Vocabulary, then...** use the activities on pp. DI•92–DI•93 in the Teacher Resources section on SuccessNet.

## Day 1 SMALL GROUP TIME • Differentiate Vocabulary, p. SG•49

| **OL** On-Level | **SI** Strategic Intervention | **A** Advanced |
|-----------------|-------------------------------|----------------|
| • **Practice Vocabulary** Amazing Words | • **Reteach Vocabulary** Amazing Words | • **Extend Vocabulary** Amazing Words |
| • **Read** *Reading Street Sleuth*, pp. 50–51 | • **Read** *Reading Street Sleuth*, pp. 50–51 | • **Read** *Reading Street Sleuth*, pp. 50–51 |
| | | • **Introduce** Inquiry Project |

**Common Core State Standards**

**Language 1.** Demonstrate command of the conventions of standard English grammar and usage when writing or speaking. **Language 2.** Demonstrate command of the conventions of standard English capitalization, punctuation, and spelling when writing. **Language 2.e.** Use conventional spelling for high-frequency and other studied words and for adding suffixes to base words (e.g., *sitting, smiled, cries, happiness*). **Also Language 4.b., 4.c.**

# Spelling Pretest

## Suffixes -er, -or, -ess, -ist

**INTRODUCE** Explain that words with the suffixes *-er, -or, -ess,* and *-ist* are formed by combining a root word with a suffix.

**PRETEST** Say each word, read the sentence, and repeat the word.

| | | |
|---|---|---|
| 1. dentist | The **dentist** cleaned my teeth. |
| 2. editor | The **editor** chose this week's news stories. |
| 3. artist | The **artist** was well-known. |
| 4. hostess | It takes skill to be a good **hostess.** |
| 5. actress | This **actress** performed on stage and in film. |
| 6. swimmer | Gertrude Ederle was a champion **swimmer.** |
| 7. seller | Are you the **seller** of this bike? |
| 8. tutor | Sue's older sister works as a math **tutor.** |
| 9. tourist | I would like to be a **tourist** in the city. |
| 10. organist | Do you know the **organist?** |
| 11. lioness | A female lion is a **lioness.** |
| 12. shipper | The **shipper** packed our dishes carefully. |
| 13. chemist | A **chemist** makes interesting substances. |
| 14. investor | An **investor** put money into the company. |
| 15. conductor | The **conductor** checks everyone's tickets. |

### Challenge words

| | |
|---|---|
| 16. announcer | The **announcer** called out the winning number. |
| 17. pharmacist | You can ask the **pharmacist** for your prescription. |
| 18. journalist | A **journalist** reports the news. |
| 19. commuter | The **commuter** took the train into the city. |
| 20. pianist | The concert featured a young, talented **pianist.** |

**SELF-CORRECT** Have students self-correct their pretests by rewriting misspelled words.

**ON THEIR OWN** Use *Let's Practice It!* p. 247 on the *Teacher Resources DVD-ROM.*

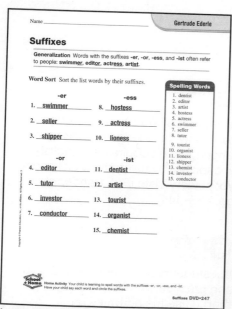

Let's Practice It! TR DVD•247

# Conventions

## Contractions

**MAKE CONNECTIONS** To focus attention on contractions, have students volunteer to share sentences about sports or other outdoor activities in which they participate. Their sentences should include at least one contraction. Have other students identify the two words that make up each contraction.

**TEACH** Display Grammar Transparency 19, and read aloud the explanation and examples in the box. Point out the contractions *we've* and *won't*.

**MODEL** Model writing the correct form of the contraction including placement of the apostrophe, and the two words from which the contraction is formed to complete items 1 and 2. Show how the contraction is formed from the original two words.

**GUIDE PRACTICE** Guide students to complete items 3 and 4. Remind them to identify the words from which the contraction is formed. Record the correct responses on the transparency.

**APPLY** Have students read sentences 5–7 on the transparency and write the contraction to correctly complete each sentence.

### Contractions

A **contraction** is a word made by putting two words together. When words are joined in a contraction, an apostrophe is used to show where a letter or letters have been left out.
- Some contractions combine a pronoun and a verb: *I + will = I'll; they + will = they'll; she + is = she's; it + is = it's; they + have = they've; you + are = you're.*
- Some contractions combine a verb and *not: has + not = hasn't; had + not = hadn't; was + not = wasn't; did + not = didn't; could + not = couldn't, should + not = shouldn't.*
- Some contractions combine two verbs: *should + have = should've; could + have = could've; would + have = would've.*

**Contractions** <u>We've</u> gone swimming every day, but we <u>won't</u> go tomorrow.

**Directions** Write the contraction in each sentence. Then write the words that make up the contraction.

1. Swimming was popular in ancient Greece, and it's still popular today.
   <u>it's; it is</u>
2. Swimmers began competing in the 1896 Olympics, and they've competed ever since.
   <u>they've; they have</u>
3. Women didn't compete in the Olympics until 1912.
   <u>didn't; did not</u>
4. Women should've competed sooner than 1912.
   <u>should've; should have</u>

**Directions** Write the contraction for the underlined words.

5. I see that <u>you are</u> reading about Natalie Coughlin, my favorite athlete.
6. I <u>had not</u> heard of Janet Evans, who competed in 1988.
7. I <u>could have</u> read about Fanny Durack all afternoon.

you're
hadn't
could've

Unit 4 America's Champion Swimmer: Gertrude Ederle          Grammar **19**

Grammar Transparency 19, TR DVD

## Daily Fix-It

1. Isnt Brian the best swimer on the team? *(Isn't; swimmer)*
2. He gos to the pool for a work out every morning. *(goes; workout)*

## Academic Vocabulary ©

A **contraction** is formed by joining two separate words and using a punctuation mark called an **apostrophe** (') to indicate a missing letter or letters.

# Handwriting

**MODEL LETTER FORMATION AND SPACING** Display the cursive lowercase letters *r* and *s*. Follow the stroke instruction pictured to model letter formation. Explain that writing legibly means letters are spaced correctly. Point out that the strokes forming *r* and *s* should be joined properly. Model writing this sentence smoothly: *Vanessa tries to write to her sister.* Make sure the letters are spaced properly and that strokes are joined correctly.

**GUIDE PRACTICE** Have students write these sentences: *Is your brother inside his bedroom? Her bassoon sounds rather sharp.* Circulate around the room, guiding students.

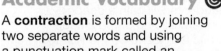

### ELL

**Conventions** Have students work in pairs to practice using contractions correctly. The first partner says a sentence using two separate words, and the second partner repeats the sentence using the proper contraction. Then partners switch roles. Ask students to practice the following: *I will/I'll; had not/hadn't; could have/could've.*

*Gertrude Ederle* **121d**

## Common Core State Standards

**Writing 3.** Write narratives to develop real or imagined experiences or events using effective technique, descriptive details, and clear event sequences. **Writing 3.a.** Establish a situation and introduce a narrator and/or characters; organize an event sequence that unfolds naturally. **Writing 4.** With guidance and support from adults, produce writing in which the development and organization are appropriate to task and purpose.

 **Bridge to Common Core**

### TEXT TYPES AND PURPOSES

This week students write an autobiography that tells about the author's life.

### Narrative Writing

Through reading and discussion, students will gain a deeper understanding of the unique traits it takes to be the first to do something. They will use this knowledge from the texts to write and support their autobiographies.

Through the week, students will improve the range and content of their writing through daily mini-lessons.

### 5-Day Plan

| DAY 1 | Read Like a Writer |
| --- | --- |
| DAY 2 | Developing Main Ideas |
| DAY 3 | Writing Trait: Organization |
| DAY 4 | Revise: Adding |
| DAY 5 | Proofread |

# Writing Zoom in on ©

## Autobiography

**Mini-Lesson** | **Read Like a Writer**

■ **Introduce** This week you will write an **autobiography.** An autobiography tells about the author's life and experiences by using the first-person point of view and vivid descriptive details.

**Genre**  Autobiography

**Trait**  Organization

**Mode**  Narrative

■ **Examine Model Text** Let's read an example of an autobiography that tells us about the author's life. Have students read "My Autobiography" on p. 282 of their *Reader's and Writer's Notebook.*

■ **Key Features** An autobiography tells the story of the writer's own life. Have students underline three sentences in the writing model that tell you that this story is about the author's own life.

An autobiography may cover a person's entire life or just one part of it. Do you think that the model, "My Autobiography," is about the author's entire life, or just one part? How can you tell? (Since it is short, I think "My Autobiography" is about just one part of the author's life.)

Writers use the first-person point of view to write their autobiographies. They use words such as *I* or *me* to show the first-person point of view. Ask students to circle three examples of words that show the use of the first-person point of view in "My Autobiography." Discuss how these words help the reader understand the author's viewpoint.

Reader's and Writer's Notebook, p. 282

## Review Key Features

Review the key features of an autobiography with students. You may want to post the key features in the classroom so that students can refer to the features while working on their autobiographies.

### Key Features of an Autobiography

- tells the story of a person's own life
- may cover a person's whole life or only part of it
- written in first person

## Routine    Quick Write for Fluency    Team Talk

**1. Talk** Have students discuss the key features of autobiographies in pairs.

**2. Write** Each student writes a few sentences defining an autobiography.

**3. Share** Partners read their sentences to one another.

Routines Flip Chart

**eStreet Interactive**
www.ReadingStreet.com

**Teacher Resources**
- Reader's and Writer's Notebook
- Let's Practice It!

**ELL**

**Leveled Support: Read Like a Writer**

**Beginning** Have students read the first two paragraphs of "My Autobiography" aloud. Have them practice with a partner until they can read the paragraphs fluently.

**Intermediate** Ask students to circle any unfamiliar words in "My Autobiography." Have them guess the meanings of the words from context and then confirm their guesses in a dictionary.

**Advanced** Have students suppose that they are going to interview the author of "My Autobiography." Ask them to prepare three questions to ask the author.

# Wrap Up Your Day!

✔ **Content Knowledge** Reread "Street Rhymes!" on p. 116j to students. Ask them what they learned today about the unique traits it takes to be the first to do something.

✔ **Oral Vocabulary** Have students use the Amazing Words they learned in context sentences.

✔ **Homework** Send home this week's Family Times newsletter on *Let's Practice It!* pp. 248–249 on the *Teacher Resources DVD-ROM.*

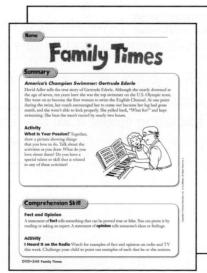

Let's Practice It!
TR DVD•248–249

**Preview DAY 2**

Tell students that tomorrow they will read about a famous female swimmer.

### Materials
- Student Edition
- Reader's and Writer's Notebook

## Common Core State Standards

**Speaking/Listening 1.** Engage effectively in a range of collaborative discussions (one-on-one, in groups, and teacher-led) with diverse partners on grade 3 topics and texts, building on others' ideas and expressing their own clearly. **Speaking/Listening 1.d.** Explain their own ideas and understanding in light of the discussion. **Language 6.** Acquire and use accurately grade-appropriate conversational, general academic, and domain-specific words and phrases, including those that signal spatial and temporal relationships (e.g., *After dinner that night we went looking for them*). **Also Speaking/Listening 1.c., Language 4.**

# Content Knowledge

## Unique Traits

**EXPAND THE CONCEPT** Remind students of the weekly concept question, *What unique traits does It take to be the first to do something?* Tell students that today they will begin reading *America's Champion Swimmer: Gertrude Ederle.* As they read, encourage students to think about this championship swimmer's unique traits.

# Build Oral Language

**TALK ABOUT SENTENCES AND WORDS** Reread these sentences from the Read Aloud, "A First in Space: Ellen Ochoa."

*Her interest in exploring space started at a young age. Her vivid imagination helped her dream of the day when she could go into space.*

- What does *imagination* mean? (the power to create new ideas or pictures in the mind)
- What words in the sentence helped you understand what *imagination* means? (dream of the day)
- How did Ellen use her imagination to keep her interest in space alive? (She pictured what it would be like when she could finally go into space.)
- What does *vivid* mean? (strong and clear)
- What are synonyms for *vivid* that the author could have used? Have students share their suggestions.

**Team Talk** Have students turn to a partner and discuss the following question. Then ask them to share their responses.

- What is the shortest version of these sentences you can make without changing the basic meaning? (Possible response: She dreamed about exploring space from the time she was a child.)

# Build Oral Vocabulary

**Robust Vocabulary Routine**

1. **Introduce** Write the Amazing Word *organize* on the board. Have students say it aloud with you. Relate *organize* to the photographs on pp. 116–117 and "A First in Space: Ellen Ochoa." Why would an astronaut need to *organize* his or her training? Why would it take many people to *organize* an astronaut's mission in space? Have students determine the definition of the word. (To *organize* is to arrange things in a certain order.)

2. **Demonstrate** Have students answer questions with appropriate detail to demonstrate understanding. How do you *organize* your day? How do you *organize* supplies when you work on a school project?

3. **Apply** Have students apply their understanding. What are some synonyms and antonyms for the word *organize?*

4. **Display the Word** Run your hand under the word as you emphasize the syllables *or-gan-ize.* Have students say the word.

See p. OV•4 to teach *erect.*

Routines Flip Chart

**ADD TO THE CONCEPT MAP** Use the photos on pp. 116–117 and the Read Aloud, "A First in Space: Ellen Ochoa," to talk about the Amazing Words *ordinary, imagination, assemble,* and *magnificent.* Add the words to the concept map to develop students' knowledge of the topic. Discuss the following questions. Remind students to ask relevant questions and answer with appropriate detail. Encourage students to build on others' ideas when they answer.

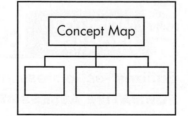

Concept Map

- Why might it be good to have a *magnificent imagination?*
- Are most biographies about *ordinary* people or extraordinary people? Why?
- Why is it important to follow directions when you *assemble* something?

**eSTREET INTERACTIVE**
www.ReadingStreet.com

**Teacher Resources**
• Amazing Word Cards

## Amazing Words

| | |
|---|---|
| ordinary | erect |
| imagination | suspend |
| assemble | accompany |
| magnificent | provision |
| organize | spectacle |

## Access for All

**SI** **Strategic Intervention**
Have students explain how they organize their time during the day.

**A** **Advanced**
Tell students to think about what would happen if their community were to erect a statue of a local hero. Have them write a paragraph identifying the person and describing the statue.

 **Connect to Social Studies**

**Early 1900s** Explain that the events in the selection took place in the early 1900s. Use this opportunity to discuss the terms *year, decade,* and *century.*

**ELL**

**Reinforce Vocabulary** Use the Day 2 instruction on ELL Poster 19 to teach lesson vocabulary and the lesson concept.

*Gertrude Ederle* **122b**

**Common Core State Standards**

**Foundational Skills 3.b.** Decode words with common Latin suffixes. **Foundational Skills 4.** Read with sufficient accuracy and fluency to support comprehension. **Language 3.a.** Choose words and phrases for effect. **Language 4.b.** Determine the meaning of the new word formed when a known affix is added to a known word (e.g., *agreeable/disagreeable, comfortable/ uncomfortable, care/careless, heat/ preheat*). **Language 5.b.** Identify real-life connections between words and their use (e.g., describe people who are *friendly* or *helpful*).

# Word Analysis

## 👆 Suffixes *-er, -or, -ess, -ist*

**Review** Review the suffixes *-er, -or, -ess,* and *-ist,* pointing out that suffixes are added to the ends of base words.

**READ WORDS IN ISOLATION** Have the class read these words. Then point to the words in random order and ask students to read them quickly.

| | | | |
|---|---|---|---|
| speaker | visitor | waitress | tourist |
| actress | realist | inventor | golfer |

**Corrective feedback** | Model reading the base word and then the suffix, and then ask students to read the word with you.

**READ WORDS IN CONTEXT** Have the class read these sentences.

**Team Talk** Have pairs take turns reading the sentences naturally.

The **countess** bowed before the **princess.**

The **artist** painted a picture of the **sailor.**

The **pitcher** threw the ball to the **catcher.**

 **MONITOR PROGRESS** Check Word Reading

**Suffixes *-er, -or, -ess, -ist***

**FORMATIVE ASSESSMENT** Write the following words and have the class read them. Notice which words students miss. Call on individuals to read some of the words.

| | | | | |
|---|---|---|---|---|
| printer | cleaner | tutor | leader | **Spiral Review** Row 2 reviews words with digraphs *sh, th, ch*. |
| duchess | shipper | thinker | checker ← | |
| seller | resell | reader | reread ← | Row 3 contrasts words with prefixes and suffixes. |

**If...** students cannot read words with suffixes at this point,

**then...** use the Day 1 Word Analysis lesson on p. 118a to reteach suffixes. Use words from the *Decodable Practice Passages* (or Reader). Continue to monitor students' progress using other instructional opportunities during the week. See the Skills Trace on p. 118a.

# Literary Terms

## Word Choice

**TEACH** Tell students that writers use specific words and phrases to communicate clearly. No matter what type of writing an author is doing, word choice is important to communicate meaning.

**Think Aloud** **MODEL** Let's look at "Swim!" and analyze the author's word choice. Let's look for words that describe. In the first paragraph, the author says your muscles can become "soft and weak" without exercise. *Soft* and *weak* are examples of descriptive words the author chose. Do you think these are good descriptive words? Why or why not? (Possible response: Yes, they describe muscles.)

**GUIDE PRACTICE** Read the fourth paragraph of "Swim!" and analyze the author's word choice. Point out the descriptive phrases "hot summer day" and "exciting way to beat the heat."

**ON THEIR OWN** Have students analyze the author's word choice in "Learn to Swim."

**eStreet Interactive**
www.ReadingStreet.com

**Pearson eText**
• Student Edition

## Academic Vocabulary ⓒ

**word choice** how an author avoids using the same words over and over and chooses interesting, vivid, and specific words to make his or her meaning clear and keep the attention of his or her audience

# DAY 2

## Common Core State Standards

**Foundational Skills 4.** Read with sufficient accuracy and fluency to support comprehension. **Language 4.** Determine or clarify the meaning of unknown and multiple-meaning word and phrases based on grade 3 reading and content, choosing flexibly from a range of strategies. **Language 4.a.** Use sentence-level context as a clue to the meaning of a word or phrase.

## Selection Vocabulary

**celebrate** to do something special in honor of a special person or day

**continued** kept up; kept on going

**current** a flow or stream of water

**drowned** died or caused to die under water or other liquid because of lack of air to breathe

**medals** pieces of metal, like coins, that are given as prizes or rewards

**stirred** mixed something by moving it around with a spoon or stick

**strokes** single, complete movements made over and over again

 **Bridge to Common Core**

### VOCABULARY ACQUISITION AND USE

Students can determine the correct definition and meanings of unfamiliar words by using context clues, helping them acquire a broad range of general academic and domain-specific words. By consulting a dictionary or glossary to clarify definitions, they demonstrate independence in gathering vocabulary knowledge on their own.

## Vocabulary Support

Refer students to *Words!* on p. W•10 in the Student Edition for additional practice.

# Vocabulary Skill

## Multiple-Meaning Words

**READ** Have students read "Learn to Swim" on p. 123. Use the vocabulary skill and strategy as tools to build comprehension.

**TEACH CONTEXT CLUES** Tell students that a multiple-meaning word is a word that has several definitions given within a dictionary listing for the word. Explain that using the strategy of context clues can help students decide which meaning the author intended.

Write on the board: *"Always swim with a buddy" is a safety rule we follow at the pool.*

 **MODEL** I read the word *rule*. I know *rule* can have more than one meaning. I think "Always swim with a buddy" is a context clue that helps me figure out which meaning to use. In this sentence, *rule* means "what to do and not do."

**GUIDE PRACTICE** Write this sentence on the board: *The first step is to learn to float, bob, and tread water.* Have students determine the multiple-meanings of *step* and *tread* using context clues. For additional support, use *Envision It! Pictured Vocabulary Cards* or *Tested Vocabulary Cards*.

**ON THEIR OWN** Reread "Learn to Swim" on p. 123. Have students use context clues to write a definition for *step*. For additional practice use *Reader's and Writer's Notebook,* p. 283.

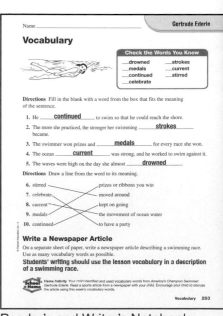

Reader's and Writer's Notebook, p. 283

Common Core State Standards
**Language 4.a.** Use sentence-level context as a clue to the meaning of a word or phrase. Also Language 4.

**Envision It!** Words to Know

celebrate

current

medals

continued
drowned
stirred
strokes

**READING STREET ONLINE**
**VOCABULARY ACTIVITIES**
www.ReadingStreet.com

Vocabulary Strategy for

## 🎯 Multiple-Meaning Words

**Context Clues** You may read a word that doesn't make sense in a sentence. The word may have another meaning. For example, *safe* can mean "free from harm" or "a metal box for storing money and valuables."

**1.** Try the meaning of the word that you know. Does it make sense in the sentence?

**2.** If not, perhaps the word has another meaning. Read on and look at the words around it to figure out another meaning.

**3.** Try the new meaning in the sentence. Does it make sense?

Read "Learn to Swim" on page 123. Look for words that can have more than one meaning. Use nearby words to figure out a new meaning.

**Words to Write** Reread "Learn to Swim." Think about another sport or activity you know. Write an article about it, including the rules for safety. Use words from the Words to Know list in your article.

122

## LEARN TO SWIM

Some people swim for exercise, some swim in races, and some swim for fun. But no matter the reason, everyone should learn how to swim. People have drowned because they couldn't swim.

The first step is to learn to float, bob, and tread water. Then learn to swim the basic strokes—front crawl, backstroke, breaststroke, and sidestroke. These are different ways of moving through the water quickly.

Take your time when you're learning to swim. You're not trying to win medals in the Olympics. You do want to coordinate your arms, legs, and breathing.

Even after you know how to swim, never swim where there is no lifeguard. Ocean tides can pull you under, a river's current can sweep you away, and weather can cause problems too. One swimmer continued to swim after it started to rain. High winds stirred up the water. Luckily, a boater helped the swimmer back to shore.

So, celebrate the beginning of your life-long swimming adventure. Everyone into the pool!

**Your Turn!**

⏸ **Need a Review?** For additional help with context clues and multiple-meaning words, see *Words!*

▶ **Ready to Try It?** Read *America's Champion Swimmer: Gertrude Ederle,* pp. 124–139.

123

**Student Edition, pp. 122–123**

# Reread for Fluency

**APPROPRIATE PHRASING** Read the first paragraph of "Learn to Swim" aloud, modeling appropriate phrasing. Tell students that you are using commas and end punctuation to help you know when to pause after reading a phrase.

**Routine** Oral Rereading

**1. Select a Passage** Use the first paragraph of "Learn to Swim."

**2. Model** Have students listen as you read with appropriate phrasing.

**3. Guide Practice** Have students read along with you.

**4. On Their Own** For optimal fluency, students should reread three or four times with appropriate phrasing.

**5. Corrective Feedback** Listen as students read. Provide feedback about their phrasing and attention to punctuation.

Routines Flip Chart

**eSTREET INTERACTIVE**
www.ReadingStreet.com

📖 **Pearson eText**
• Student Edition

✋ **Vocabulary Activities**

✋ **Journal**

💿 **Teacher Resources**
• Envision It! Pictured Vocabulary Cards
• Tested Vocabulary Cards
• Reader's and Writer's Notebook

**Access for All**

🆂ℹ **Strategic Intervention**

Have students verify the meaning of *current* in a dictionary.

© **Common Core State Standards**

**Informational Text 10.** By the end of the year, read and comprehend informational texts, including history/social studies, science, and technical texts, at the high end of the grades 2–3 text complexity band independently and proficiently. **Foundational Skills 3.** Know and apply grade-level phonics and word analysis skills in decoding words. **Foundational Skills 4.a.** Read on-level text with purpose and understanding. **Also Informational Text 7.**

© **Bridge to Common Core**

**CRAFT AND STRUCTURE**

Students analyze the structure of a biography and how its components relate to each other and the whole. As students preview the selection and prepare to read, they come to see how knowledge of point-of-view will help them better understand the text.

**Academic Vocabulary** ©

**biography** a true story about a real person's life

**Strategy Response Log**

Have students use p. 25 in the *Reader's and Writer's Notebook* to review and use the strategy of questioning.

# Text-Based Comprehension
## Introduce Main Selection

Student Edition, pp. 124–125

**GENRE** A **biography** is a genre that tells about a real person's life. It is written by another person in the third-person point of view, using pronouns such as *she, he,* and *they*. A biography may cover a person's whole life or only a single incident.

**PREVIEW AND PREDICT** Have students read the title of the selection and the names of the author and illustrator. Have them use key words in the title and the illustrations to predict what they think the selection will be about.

**PURPOSE** By analyzing *America's Champion Swimmer: Gertrude Ederle,* a biography, students will gain knowledge of the unique traits it takes to be the first to do something.

# Access Main Selection

## READER AND TASK SUGGESTIONS

| Preparing to Read the Text | Leveled Tasks |
|---|---|
| • Review skills and strategies for understanding multiple-meaning words.<br><br>• Review the text structure of a biography.<br><br>• Remind students that biographies often contain dates and famous events. Tell them to adjust their reading rate to better understand what is happening and when. | • **Analysis** Students may find it difficult to understand why the writer chose Gertrude Ederle as a subject. As they read, have students note Gertrude's accomplishments and abilities.<br><br>• **Structure** If students have difficulty following the events in the selection, have them look at the illustrations and match them to what is happening in the text. |

See Text Complexity Measures for *America's Champion Swimmer: Gertrude Ederle* on the tab at the beginning of this week.

**READ** Tell students that today they will read *America's Champion Swimmer: Gertrude Ederle* for the first time. Use the Read for Understanding routine.

### Routine   Read for Understanding ©

Deepen understanding by reading the selection multiple times.

1. **First Read**—If students need help, then use the **Access Text** notes to help them clarify understanding.

2. **Second Read**—Use the **Close Reading** notes to help students draw knowledge from the text.

---

## Day 2   SMALL GROUP TIME • Differentiate Comprehension, p. SG•49

| OL On-Level | SI Strategic Intervention | A Advanced |
|---|---|---|
| • **Practice** Selection Vocabulary<br>• **Read** *America's Champion Swimmer: Gertrude Ederle* | • **Reteach** Selection Vocabulary<br>• **Read** *America's Champion Swimmer: Gertrude Ederle* | • **Extend** Selection Vocabulary<br>• **Read** *America's Champion Swimmer: Gertrude Ederle*<br>• **Investigate** Inquiry Project |

---

### eSTREET INTERACTIVE
www.ReadingStreet.com

**Pearson eText**
• Student Edition

**AudioText CD**

**Teacher Resources**
• Reader's and Writer's Notebook

**Background Building Audio CD**

---

### Access for All

**A** Advanced

Have students learn about the lives of women in the early 1900s. Students should share their findings with the class.

---

**Build Background** To build background, review the selection summary in English (*ELL Handbook* p. 139). Use the Retelling Cards to provide visual support for the summary.

---

**ELL**

If... students need more scaffolding and practice with the **Comprehension Skill, then...** use the activities on pp. DI•96 in the Teacher Resources section on SuccessNet.

**1ST READ**

# Access Text © If students need help, then...

**FACT AND OPINION** Write these sentences on the board. Have students determine which is a fact and which is an opinion: *Gertrude Ederle was born in 1906. People felt a woman's place was in the home.*

(Think Aloud) **MODEL** I can check whether the first sentence is a fact by looking in an encyclopedia or on the Internet. It can be proved true or false. The word *felt* in the second sentence tells me that this might be an opinion, a belief, which cannot be proved true or false.

**2ND READ**

# Close Reading ©

**FACT AND OPINION • TEXT EVIDENCE** Find one statement of fact from page 126 and use the information on the page to give one statement of opinion. How do you know it is a fact? Why is it an opinion? (*Gertrude Ederle was born on October 23, 1906,* is a fact. It can be proven true or false. *It wasn't fair that women could not vote in 1906* is an opinion. That is the way I feel about something. It cannot be proven true or false.)

In 1906 women were kept out of many clubs and restaurants. In most states they were not allowed to vote. Many people felt a woman's place was in the home.

But Gertrude Ederle's place was in the water.

Gertrude Ederle was born on October 23, 1906. She was the third of six children and was raised in New York City, where she lived in an apartment next to her father's butcher shop. Her family called her Gertie. Most everyone else called her Trudy.

126

**Student Edition, p. 126**

**ON THEIR OWN** Have students reread pp. 126–127 to find more statements of fact about Gertrude Ederle. Ask students what conclusions they
can draw based on those facts. For additional practice see *Let's Practice
It!* p. 250 on the *Teacher Resources DVD-ROM*.

Trudy spent her early years playing on the sidewalks
of New York. It wasn't until she was seven that she
had her first adventure in the water. While visiting her
grandmother in Germany, Trudy fell into a pond and
nearly drowned.

After that near disaster, Trudy's father was determined
to teach her to swim. For her first lesson, he tied one end
of a rope to Trudy's waist and held on to the other end. He
put Trudy into a river and told her to paddle like a dog.

Trudy mastered the dog paddle. She joined her older
sister Margaret and the other children in the water and
copied their strokes. Soon Trudy swam better than any
of them.

127

**Student Edition, p. 127**

**EVALUATION** What do you think the author means when he says that
Gertrude Ederle's "place was in the water"? (He's saying that she was
born to be a swimmer, not someone who was going to stay at home,
no matter what other people thought.)

**Common Core
State Standards**

**Informational Text 1.** Ask and
answer questions to demonstrate
understanding of a text, referring
explicitly to the text as the basis for
the answers. **Informational Text 4.**
Determine the meaning of general
academic and domain-specific words
and phrases in a text relevant to a
grade 3 topic or subject area.
**Also Informational Text 6., 8.**

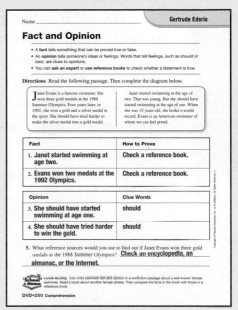

Let's Practice It!
TR DVD•250

**Access for All**

**SI** Strategic Intervention

To aid comprehension, help students
locate New York, New Jersey, Paris,
Germany, and the English Channel
on a world map. Explain that these
locations are important in the
biography. Have students refer to
the map as they read.

**Activate Prior Knowledge** Create
a word web with "Swimming" in the
center hub. Work with students to add
words that tell what they know about
swimming. We're going to read about
how Gertrude Ederle learned to swim.
What do you know about swimming?
What can happen if you do not know
how to swim? What do you do when
you swim?

*Gertrude Ederle* **127a**

## 1ST READ

## Access Text © *If students need help, then...*

**Review** **GENERALIZE** Remind students that a generalization is a statement that is true for many examples. Have students make a generalization about the English Channel after reading p. 129.

**Think Aloud** **MODEL** The clue word *many* on page 129 helps me recognize a generalization about the English Channel. After reading more information in the text, I can generalize that many people fail when trying to swim across the Channel. Several details support my generalization. One is that the English Channel was the "ultimate challenge."

## 2ND READ

## Close Reading ©

**GENERALIZE • TEXT EVIDENCE**
What are two details that support the generalization that Gertrude Ederle was courageous? (In paragraph 3 on p. 128, it says she attempted and succeeded at being the first woman to swim from lower Manhattan to Sandy Hook, New Jersey. In paragraph 3 on p. 129, the author says she was determined to swim the English Channel even though only five men and no women had ever done it successfully.)

From that summer on, it was hard to keep Trudy out of the water. She *loved* to swim. At the age of thirteen she became a member of the New York Women's Swimming Association and took lessons there.

At fifteen Trudy won her first big race.

The next year, she attempted to be the first woman to swim the more than seventeen miles from lower Manhattan to Sandy Hook, New Jersey. When Trudy slowed down, her sister Margaret yelled, "Get going, lazybones!" And Trudy did. She finished in just over seven hours. And she beat the men's record.

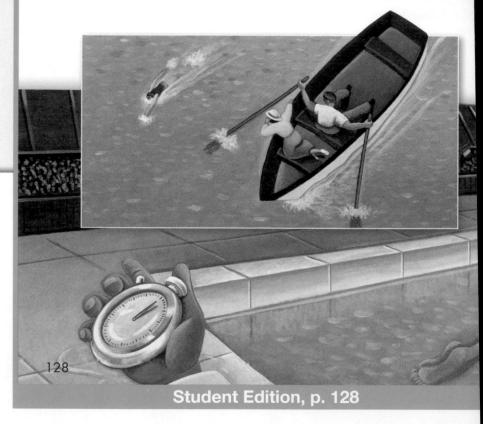

128

**Student Edition, p. 128**

**ON THEIR OWN** Have students make or identify other generalizations from the selection. For additional practice with generalizing, use *Let's Practice It!* p. 251 on the *Teacher Resources DVD-ROM.*

> People were beginning to notice Gertrude Ederle. Newspapers described her as courageous, determined, modest, and poised. They called her the most perfect swimmer. Trudy's mother said she was "just a plain home girl."
>
> In 1924 this "plain home girl" was good enough to make the U.S. Olympic team. Trudy won three medals at the games in Paris. Her team won more points than all the other countries' swimming teams combined.
>
> By 1925 Trudy had set twenty-nine U.S. and world records. She was determined to take on the ultimate challenge: the English Channel. Many had tried to swim the more-than-twenty-mile-wide body of cold, rough water that separates England from France. But only five men—and no women—had ever made it all the way across.

129

**Student Edition, p. 129**

**INFERENCE** Why did Trudy's sister, Margaret, yell and call her "lazy-bones" while Trudy swam? (Margaret probably knew Trudy well. She knew yelling at her and calling her names would motivate Trudy. It may have worked since Trudy beat the men's record for the swim.)

## Common Core State Standards

**Informational Text 1.** Ask and answer questions to demonstrate understanding of a text, referring explicitly to the text as the basis for the answers. **Informational Text 6.** Distinguish their own point of view from that of the author of a text.

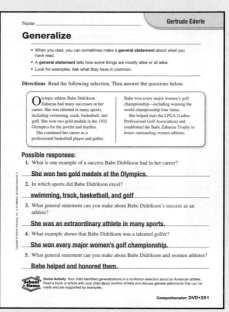

Let's Practice It! TR DVD•251

## Access for All

 **Strategic Intervention**

The first paragraph on p. 129 uses the words *courageous, determined, modest,* and *poised* to describe Trudy. Help students find synonyms and examples for each word.

**A** **Advanced**

Have students learn more about swimming the English Channel and write down these facts. Then have students write an opinion sentence based on each fact they found.

**ELL**

**Vocabulary** Focus students' attention on the term *lazybones* in the last paragraph on p. 128. *Lazybones* is a word people use when someone is being lazy, not moving quickly, or sleeping a lot. Ask students to describe a time when they felt like a "lazybones."

**Questioning** Read aloud the last paragraph on p. 129. What questions could you ask about this paragraph? Have students share their questions and how they might find the answers.

*Gertrude Ederle* **129a**

## Access Text ©  *If students need help, then...*

### ⊙ MULTIPLE-MEANING WORDS

Write this sentence from the selection on the board. *For almost nine hours she fought the strong current.* Have students read the sentence and use context to determine the meaning of the word *current*.

**Think Aloud** **MODEL** When I read the word *current,* I think of the meaning "up-to-date." But this meaning doesn't make sense here. So I look at the words around it. The words *Trudy stepped into the water* and *fighting a strong current* help me understand that *current* means "the flow of water" in this sentence.

**ON THEIR OWN** Have students use context to determine the correct meaning of the word *matter* in the second paragraph on p. 130 (to be important). For additional practice use *Reader's and Writer's Notebook,* p. 287.

## Close Reading ©

**ANALYSIS** What two meanings can you think of for the word *Channel?* (a band of frequency on a TV or radio; a wide passage of water) Use context clues to tell the meaning of the word *Channel* on page 130, paragraph 2. (When I look for context clues within the sentence, I see the word *swim.* This tells me that the meaning of *Channel* in the sentence is "a wide passage of water.")

Many people were sure Trudy couldn't do it. A newspaper editorial declared that Trudy wouldn't make it and that women must admit they would "remain forever the weaker sex."

It didn't matter to Trudy what people said or wrote. She was going to swim the Channel.

Early in the morning on August 18, 1925, Trudy stepped into the water at Cape Gris-Nez, France, the starting point for the swim. For almost nine hours she fought the strong current. Then, when Trudy had less than seven miles to go, her trainer thought she had swallowed too much water and pulled her, crying, from the sea.

Trudy did not give up her dream. She found a new trainer, and a year later, on Friday, August 6, 1926, she was ready to try again.

130

**Student Edition, p. 130**

**CHECK PREDICTIONS** Have students look back at the predictions they made earlier and discuss whether they were accurate. Then have students preview the rest of the selection and either adjust their predictions accordingly or make new predictions.

Trudy wore a red bathing cap and a two-piece bathing suit and goggles that she and her sister Margaret had designed. To protect her from the icy cold water, Margaret coated Trudy with lanolin and heavy grease. The greasing took a long time—too long for Trudy. "For heaven's sake," she complained. "Let's get started."

If you want to teach this selection in two sessions, stop here.

If you want to continue reading this selection, turn to p. 132–133.

**Student Edition, p. 131**

**DRAW CONCLUSIONS • TEXT EVIDENCE** What conclusion can you draw from the fact that Trudy found a new trainer after her first trainer pulled her from the sea? What in the text supports your idea? (She was not going to give up. The text on p. 130, paragraph 4, says that on Friday, August 6, 1926, she was ready to try again.)

## Common Core State Standards

**Informational Text 1.** Ask and answer questions to demonstrate understanding of a text, referring explicitly to the text as the basis for the answers. **Language 4.a.** Use sentence-level context as a clue to the meaning of a word or phrase.

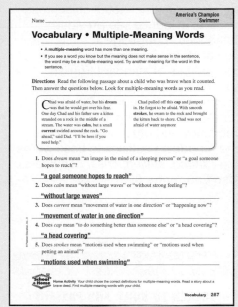

Reader's and Writer's Notebook, p. 287

## Access for All

**SI Strategic Intervention**

Arrange students in small groups, providing a topic for each, such as swimming and coaching. Have students write statements of fact and opinion about their topic. Groups can share their statements. Other groups can decide which statements are fact and which are opinions.

**A Advanced**

Have students discuss Trudy's character traits. Ask them to consider how these traits have helped her achieve success so far in the selection.

## ELL

**Sentence Structure** Some sentences on pp. 130–131 have complex sentence structures and may be difficult for students to comprehend. For these sentences, read them aloud with students and paraphrase the content.

**Common Core State Standards**

**Foundational Skills 3.a.** Identify and know the meaning of the most common prefixes and derivational suffixes. **Writing 7.** Conduct short research projects that build knowledge about a topic. **Writing 8.** Recall information from experiences or gather information from print and digital sources; take brief notes on sources and sort evidence into provided categories. **Language 1.** Demonstrate command of the conventions of standard English grammar and usage when writing or speaking. **Language 2.e.** Use conventional spelling for high-frequency and other studied words and for adding suffixes to base words (e.g., *sitting, smiled, cries, happiness*). **Also Language 3.**

## Bridge to Common Core

### RESEARCH TO BUILD AND PRESENT KNOWLEDGE

Students create research plans and begin to gather relevant information about their biographies. They conduct Internet searches using their inquiry questions, consulting other sources, and assessing the credibility of each one. This process enables students to demonstrate an understanding of the subject under investigation. As students access online information, they should always note their sources for a Works Cited page.

# Research and Inquiry

## Step 2 | Navigate/Search

**TEACH** Have students generate a plan for gathering relevant information for their biography. Students should search the Internet using their inquiry questions and keywords from Day 1. Explain that students should search for and collect information from multiple sources of oral and written information, including interviews. For example, students might download and listen to an audio file of an interview with their chosen female athlete.

**Think Aloud** **MODEL** I first searched for American women in the Olympics. I found a Web site I plan on using for one source. I also want to include information from an interview, so I searched for *Interviews with women athletes*. I found several interviews. One of them is an audio file. I will download it and listen to the interview.

**GUIDE PRACTICE** Have students continue their review of Web sites they identified. Remind students to differentiate among facts and opinions as they read about their chosen athlete. Tell students to take simple notes about their findings as they conduct their research.

**ON THEIR OWN** Have students write down Web addresses, authors, and the dates the Web sites were last updated, and create a Works Cited page.

# Conventions

## Contractions

**TEACH** Write *we* and *are* on the board. Ask students to name the contraction formed by putting these words together. (we're) Repeat for *did* and *not,* and *should* and *have.*

**GUIDE PRACTICE** Have students review something they have written to see if they can replace any words with contractions. Write the contractions named by students.

Have students look for and read aloud contractions found in *America's Champion Swimmer.* Ask them to identify the two words from which each contraction is formed. (*wasn't,* p. 127; *couldn't, wouldn't, didn't,* p. 130; *Let's,* p. 131; *it's, didn't,* p. 132; *couldn't,* p. 134)

**ON THEIR OWN** For additional practice, use *Reader's and Writer's Notebook,* p. 284.

# Spelling

## Suffixes -er, -or, -ess, -ist

**TEACH** Remind students that their spelling words for this week have the suffixes *-er, -or, -ess,* and *-ist.* Remind students that the suffixes *-er, -or,* and *-ist* often mean "someone who is or does something." The suffix *-ess* means "a female who does something." Also remind students that the base may be a word part, a word root, or a word that has had a spelling change, such as doubling the *m* in *swimmer.*

**GUIDE PRACTICE** Have students write each spelling word and underline the suffix.

**ON THEIR OWN** For additional practice, use *Reader's and Writer's Notebook,* p. 285.

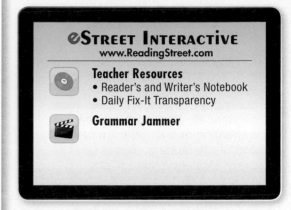

**eSTREET INTERACTIVE**
www.ReadingStreet.com

**Teacher Resources**
• Reader's and Writer's Notebook
• Daily Fix-It Transparency

**Grammar Jammer**

## Daily Fix-It

3. The swimmer jump into the pool with a spelash. *(jumps or jumped; splash)*

4. A tuter will helped her with some strokes. *(tutor; help)*

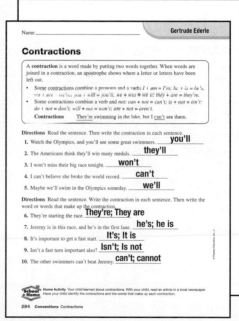

Reader's and Writer's Notebook, pp. 284–285

**Conventions** To provide students with practice on contractions, use the modified grammar lessons in the *ELL Handbook* and *Grammar Jammer* online at: www.ReadingStreet.com

## Common Core State Standards

**Writing 3.** Write narratives to develop real or imagined experiences or events using effective technique, descriptive details, and clear event sequences. **Writing 3.a.** Establish a situation and introduce a narrator and/or characters; organize an event sequence that unfolds naturally. **Writing 3.c.** Use temporal words and phrases to signal event order. **Writing 4.** With guidance and support from adults, produce writing in which the development and organization are appropriate to task and purpose. **Writing 8.** Recall information from experiences or gather information from print and digital sources; take brief notes on sources and sort evidence into provided categories.

# Writing
## Zoom in on ©

## Autobiography

### Writing Trait: Organization

**INTRODUCE THE PROMPT** Remind students that they will be writing an autobiography this week. Review the key features of an autobiography. Remind students that they should think about these features as they plan their writing. Then explain that they will begin the writing process for an autobiography today. Read aloud the writing prompt.

### Writing Prompt

Think about your own life and experiences. Now write an autobiography.

**Think Aloud** **SELECT A TOPIC** To help choose the main topics for your autobiography, let's think about some of the most important experiences in your life. Display a story sequence chart, and use it to model planning your writing. I will begin my autobiography by including information about when I was born. I can include details about the time and place. Write information about birth date and birthplace in the first box of the chart. Ask students what other events in someone's life might be good to include in an autobiography. Fill in the chart with their examples and discuss them.

**GATHER INFORMATION** Remind students that they can do research by looking at journals or talking to family members to help them think of more ideas for their autobiography. Remind them to keep this chart as the students will refer back to it tomorrow as they draft. Suggest that they use time-order words as they write about the events.

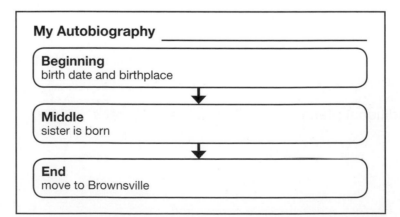

**My Autobiography** _____

**Beginning**
birth date and birthplace

↓

**Middle**
sister is born

↓

**End**
move to Brownsville

**Corrective feedback** Circulate around the room and talk briefly with students who are having trouble completing the chart. Ask students to consider what experiences in their life have been most important.

## Mini-Lesson | Developing Main Ideas

### eStreet Interactive
www.ReadingStreet.com

**Teacher Resources**
- Reader's and Writer's Notebook
- Graphic Organizer

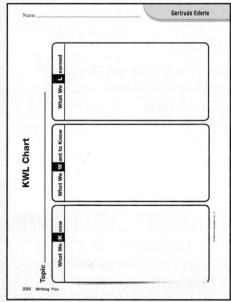

■ The main topics of your autobiography will be the central ideas of your paragraphs. You can develop these ideas by using a KWL chart. I might want to remember more information about my best friend. **On the board, make a KWL chart. In the K column, I write down what I know:** *Cassandra was my best friend, and she lived next door.* **Fill in the K column.**

■ Now I think about what I want to know to fill in details. I want to know how Cassandra and I first met. So I put that in the W column. **Fill in the W column of the chart.** When I find out, either by remembering or by looking in my journal, I put the information in the L column.

Have students fill out their own KWL charts using the form on p. 286 of their *Reader's and Writer's Notebook.*

## Routine | Quick Write for Fluency | Team Talk

**1. Talk** Students discuss their chosen main events in pairs.

**2. Write** Each student writes a paragraph summarizing his or her main events.

**3. Share** Partners read their paragraphs to one another.

Routines Flip Chart

Reader's and Writer's Notebook,
p. 286

# Wrap Up Your Day!

✔ **Content Knowledge** *What did you learn about Gertrude Ederle?*

✔ **Text-Based Comprehension** *What facts and opinions did the author include in this part of the story?*

### Preview DAY 3

Tell students that tomorrow they will read more about how Gertrude Ederle makes history.

### Materials

- Student Edition
- Reader's and Writer's Notebook
- Retelling Cards
- Decodable Reader

## Common Core State Standards

**Speaking/Listening 1.** Engage effectively in a range of collaborative discussions (one-on-one, in groups, and teacher-led) with diverse partners on grade 3 topics and texts, building on others' ideas and expressing their own clearly. **Speaking/Listening 1.c.** Ask questions to check understanding of information presented, stay on topic, and link their comments to the remarks of others. **Also Speaking/Listening 1.a., Language 6.**

# Content Knowledge

Zoom in on

## Unique Traits

**EXPAND THE CONCEPT** Remind students of the weekly concept question, *What unique traits does it take to be the first to do something?* Discuss how the question relates to *America's Champion Swimmer: Gertrude Ederle.* Encourage students to think about what unique traits it would take to swim the English Channel.

## Build Oral Language

**TALK ABOUT SENTENCES AND WORDS** Reread sentences from Student Edition p. 127.

*Trudy mastered the dog paddle. She joined her older sister Margaret and the other children in the water and copied their strokes.*

- What does *mastered* mean? (to become an expert in)
- What does *strokes* mean? (single movements done again and again)
- What were Margaret and the other children doing in the water? (They were swimming.)
- Why was Trudy copying their strokes? (to learn how to swim)

**Team Talk** Have students work with a partner to combine the sentences into one. Encourage students to use sequence words or conjunctions.

# Build Oral Vocabulary

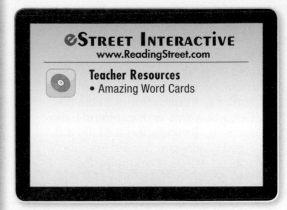

**eSTREET INTERACTIVE**
www.ReadingStreet.com

**Teacher Resources**
• Amazing Word Cards

### Amazing Words    Robust Vocabulary Routine

**1. Introduce** Write the word *suspend* on the board. Have students say it with you. Yesterday we read that Trudy had to *suspend* her attempt to swim the English Channel. Have students determine a definition of *suspend*. (To *suspend* is to stop something for a period of time.)

**2. Demonstrate** Have students work in student-led groups to answer questions to demonstrate understanding. Why did Trudy have to *suspend* her attempt to swim the English Channel? (Her trainer thought she had swallowed too much water, so he pulled her from the water.)

**3. Apply** Have students apply their understanding. Have you ever had to *suspend* an activity you were working on? Why? For how long?

**4. Display the Word** Students can decode the sounds in *suspend* and blend them.

See p. OV•4 to teach *accompany*.

Routines Flip Chart

### Amazing Words

| | |
|---|---|
| ordinary | erect |
| imagination | suspend |
| assemble | accompany |
| magnificent | provision |
| organize | spectacle |

**ADD TO THE CONCEPT MAP** Use illustrations and topic sentences to review pp. 126–131 of *America's Champion Swimmer: Gertrude Ederle.* Discuss the Amazing Words *organize* and *erect.* Add these and other concept-related words to the concept map. Use the following questions to develop students' understanding of the concept. Remind students to ask and answer questions with appropriate detail and to give suggestions based on the ideas of others.

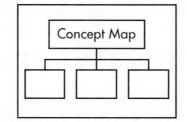

Concept Map

• Trudy *organized* her time and training. Why is it important to *organize* your time when working to achieve a goal?

• To stand *erect* means to stand tall, as if proud. Why would you stand *erect* if you are working to achieve a goal?

**Expand Vocabulary** Use the Day 3 instruction on ELL Poster 19 to help students expand vocabulary.

© **Common Core State Standards**
Foundational Skills 3.a. Identify and know the meaning of the most common prefixes and derivational suffixes. **Foundational Skills 3.b.** Decode words with common Latin suffixes. **Foundational Skills 3.d.** Read grade-appropriate irregularly spelled words. **Language 2.e.** Use conventional spelling for high-frequency and other studied words and for adding suffixes to base words (e.g., *sitting, smiled, cries, happiness*). **Language 4.b.** Determine the meaning of the new word formed when a known affix is added to a known word (e.g., *agreeable/disagreeable, comfortable/uncomfortable, care/careless, heat/preheat*). **Also Foundational Skills 3.**

# Word Analysis

## ⟳ Suffixes *-er, -or, -ess, -ist*

**MODEL WORD SORTING** Write *-er, -or, -ess,* and *-ist* as headings in a four-column chart. Now we are going to sort words. We'll put words with the suffix *-er* in the first column. Words with the suffix *-or* will go in the second column. Words with the suffix *-ess* will go in the third column, and words with the suffix *-ist* will go in the fourth column. I will start. Write *countess* and model how to read it, using the routine on p. 118a. *Countess* is made up of the word *count* and the suffix *-ess,* so I'll write *countess* in the third column. Model reading *dentist* and *inventor* in the same way.

**GUIDE PRACTICE** Use the practice words from the activities on 118a for the word sort. Point to a word. Have students read the word, identify its parts, and tell where it should be written on the chart.

**Corrective feedback** | For corrective feedback, model reading the base word and then the suffix.

| -er | -or | -ess | -ist |
|---|---|---|---|
| swimmer | inventor | countess | dentist |
| seller | editor | actress | artist |
| writer | sailor | hostess | tourist |
| builder | | | |
| farmer | | | |

## Fluent Word Reading

**MODEL** Write *rancher.* I know that *-er* is a suffix. I know the base word *ranch.* I can put the parts together to read *rancher.*

**GUIDE PRACTICE** Write the words below. Look for the word parts you know. When I point to the word, we'll read it together. Allow one second per word part previewing time for the first reading.

| dancer | collector | duchess | guitarist | visitor | settler |
|---|---|---|---|---|---|

**ON THEIR OWN** Have students read the list above three or four times, until they can read one word per second.

# Decodable Passage 19B

students need help, then...

## Read *Spring Show*

**READ WORDS IN ISOLATION** Have students turn to p. 45 in *Decodable Practice Readers 3.2* and find the first list of words. Each word in this list has a suffix. Let's decode and read these words. Be sure that students identify the base word and suffix in each word.

Next, have students read the high-frequency words.

**PREVIEW** Have students read the title and preview the story. Tell them that they will read words with suffixes.

**READ WORDS IN CONTEXT** Chorally read the story along with students. Have students identify words in the story that have suffixes. Make sure that students are monitoring their accuracy when they decode words.

**Team Talk** Pair students and have them take turns reading the story aloud to each other. Monitor students as they read to check for proper pronunciation and appropriate pacing.

**eStreet Interactive**
www.ReadingStreet.com

**Pearson eText**
• Decodable Reader

### Access for All

**A** **Advanced**

Challenge more advanced students to read words containing both a prefix and a suffix. They should isolate the prefix, then the suffix, and then identify the base word. Next, they should blend the syllables in sequence to read the whole word.

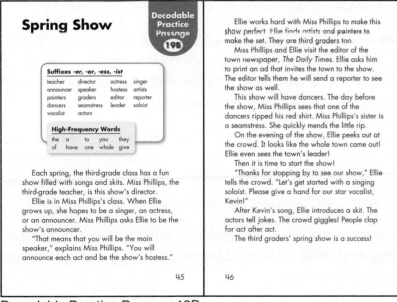

**Spring Show**

Decodable Practice Passage **19B**

**Suffixes -er, -or, -ess, -ist**

| | | | |
|---|---|---|---|
| teacher | director | actress | singer |
| announcer | speaker | hostess | artists |
| painters | graders | editor | reporter |
| dancers | seamstress | leader | soloist |
| vocalist | actors | | |

**High-Frequency Words**

| | | | | |
|---|---|---|---|---|
| the | a | to | you | they |
| of | have | one | whole | give |

Each spring, the third-grade class has a fun show filled with songs and skits. Miss Phillips, the third-grade teacher, is this show's director.

Ellie is in Miss Phillips's class. When Ellie grows up, she hopes to be a singer, an actress, or an announcer. Miss Phillips asks Ellie to be the show's announcer.

"That means that you will be the main speaker," explains Miss Phillips. "You will announce each act and be the show's hostess."

45

Ellie works hard with Miss Phillips to make this show perfect. Ellie finds artists and painters to make the set. They are third graders too.

Miss Phillips and Ellie visit the editor of the town newspaper, *The Daily Times.* Ellie asks him to print an ad that invites the town to the show. The editor tells them he will send a reporter to see the show as well.

This show will have dancers. The day before the show, Miss Phillips sees that one of the dancers ripped his red shirt. Miss Phillips's sister is a seamstress. She quickly mends the little rip.

On the evening of the show, Ellie peeks out at the crowd. It looks like the whole town came out! Ellie even sees the town's leader!

Then it is time to start the show!

"Thanks for stopping by to see our show," Ellie tells the crowd. "Let's get started with a singing soloist. Please give a hand for our star vocalist, Kevin!"

After Kevin's song, Ellie introduces a skit. The actors tell jokes. The crowd giggles! People clap for act after act.

The third graders' spring show is a success!

46

Decodable Practice Passage 19B

## Common Core State Standards

**Informational Text 2.** Determine the main idea of a text; recount the key details and explain how they support the main idea. **Informational Text 3.** Describe the relationship between a series of historical events, scientific ideas or concepts, or steps in technical procedures in a text, using language that pertains to time, sequence, and cause/effect. **Informational Text 10.** By the end of the year, read and comprehend informational texts, including history/social studies, science, and technical texts, at the high end of the grades 2–3 text complexity band independently and proficiently. **Also Informational Text 7.**

## Strategy Response Log

Have students write questions about Trudy's swimming career in *America's Champion Swimmer: Gertrude Ederle* on p. 25 in the *Reader's and Writer's Notebook.*

# Text-Based Comprehension
## Check Understanding

**Student Edition, pp. 124–125**

**If...** you chose to read *America's Champion Swimmer: Gertrude Ederle* in two parts,

**then...** use the following questions to monitor students' understanding of the selection. Encourage students to cite evidence from the text.

**EVALUATION** What conclusion can you draw about Trudy's father from facts presented in the text? How can you support your conclusion? I can conclude that Trudy's father was a wise man. I know this because of the fact that after Trudy's near disaster, he taught her to swim. (p. 127)

**ANALYSIS** Trudy's mother calls her a "plain home girl." How do you know which meaning of *plain* the author intends? The author uses *plain* to mean simple and ordinary. I know because of the context. Everyone calls Trudy the "most perfect swimmer," but her mother calls her "plain." (p. 129)

**RETELL** Have students retell *America's Champion Swimmer: Gertrude Ederle,* referring to details in the text. Have them summarize information in the text in a logical order.

| Corrective feedback | **If...** students leave out important details, **then...** have students look back through the illustrations in the selection. |

**READ** Use the **Access Text** and **Close Reading** notes to finish reading *America's Champion Swimmer: Gertrude Ederle.*

**...** you followed the Read for Understanding routine below,

**hen...** ask students to retell the selection before you reread *America's Champion Swimmer: Gertrude Ederle*.

**RETELL** Have students retell *America's Champion Swimmer: Gertrude Ederle,* referring to details in the text. Have them summarize information in the text in a logical order.

| **Corrective feedback** | **If...** students leave out important details, **then...** have students look back through the illustrations in the selection. |

**READ** Return to p. 126–127 and use the **2nd Read/Close Reading** notes to reread *America's Champion Swimmer: Gertrude Ederle.*

# Read Main Selection

**Routine** Read for Understanding ©

Deepen understanding by reading the selection multiple times.

1. **First Read**—If students need help, then use the **Access Text** notes to help them clarify understanding.

2. **Second Read**—Use the **Close Reading** notes to help students draw knowledge from the text.

**Check Retelling** To support retelling, review the multilingual summary for *America's Champion Swimmer: Gertrude Ederle* with the appropriate Retelling Cards to scaffold understanding.

## Day 3 SMALL GROUP TIME • Differentiate Close Reading, p. SG•49

| **OL** On-Level | **SI** Strategic Intervention | **A** Advanced |
|---|---|---|
| • **Reread** to Develop Vocabulary<br>• **Read** *America's Champion Swimmer: Gertrude Ederle* | • **Reread** to Develop Vocabulary<br>• **Read** *America's Champion Swimmer: Gertrude Ederle* | • **Reread** to Extend Vocabulary<br>• **Read** *America's Champion Swimmer: Gertrude Ederle*<br>• **Investigate** Inquiry Project |

**If...** students need more scaffolding and practice with the **Main Selection, then...** use the activities on p. DI•97 in the Teacher Resources section on SuccessNet.

## Access Text © *If students need help, then...*

**⟳ QUESTIONING** Tell students that asking questions can improve their understanding of a text. Have students read the last sentence of the second paragraph on p. 132. Ask what question they might ask.

**(Think Aloud) MODEL** I wonder why reporters and photographers would follow Trudy. I think the author might have told me this information to help me understand how important the swim was. No woman in history had accomplished Trudy's goal of swimming the English Channel.

## Close Reading ©

**SYNTHESIS** What other questions might you ask about these pages? See if a partner can help you answer each question. (Who sailed on the boat the *Alsace?* Why was it important for Trudy's family to accompany her? Did having her family there make a difference to Trudy?)

**⟳ FACT AND OPINION • TEXT EVIDENCE** What is one statement of fact and one statement of opinion from pages 132–133? (Fact: In paragraph 2, it says that Trudy's father, sister, and trainer were on a tugboat. Opinion: In paragraph 1, Trudy says that the water is cold.)

Finally, at a little past seven in the morning, she stepped into the water. "Gee, but it's cold," Trudy said.

Trudy's father, her sister Margaret, her trainer, and a few other swimmers were on board a tugboat named *Alsace.* The boat would accompany Trudy to make sure she didn't get lost in the fog and was safe from jellyfish, sharks, and the Channel's powerful currents. There was a second boat, too, with reporters and photographers on board.

As the *Alsace* bobbed up and down in the choppy water, Margaret wrote in chalk on the side of the boat, "This way, Ole Kid." She drew an arrow that pointed to England.

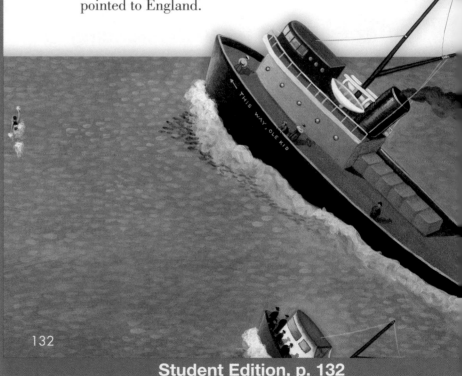

132

**Student Edition, p. 132**

**ON THEIR OWN** Have students read pp. 132–133 and ask and answer literal, interpretive, and evaluative questions to seek clarification. Have students support their answers with evidence from the text and make corrections and adjustments as needed.

To entertain Trudy, Margaret and some of the others sang American songs, including "The Star-Spangled Banner" and "East Side, West Side." Trudy said the songs kept her "brain and spirit good."

At first the sea was calm.

Trudy swam so fast that her trainer was afraid she would tire herself out. He ordered her to slow down.

Trudy refused.

At about ten-thirty in the morning, Trudy had her first meal. She floated on her back and ate chicken and drank beef broth. A while later, she ate chocolate and chewed on sugar cubes. Then she swam on.

THIS WAY, OLE KID

133

**Student Edition, p. 133**

**ANALYSIS** Did Margaret's singing have the effect on Trudy that she hoped for? How do you know? (Yes, Trudy kept swimming and said the singing kept her "brain and spirit good.")

## Common Core State Standards

**Informational Text 1.** Ask and answer questions to demonstrate understanding of a text, referring explicitly to the text as the basis for the answers. **Informational Text 3.** Describe the relationship between a series of historical events, scientific ideas or concepts, or steps in technical procedures in a text, using language that pertains to time, sequence, and cause/effect. **Also Speaking/Listening 1.c.**

### Access for All

**A** Advanced

Have students find out about *Alsace*. Have them discuss the significance of the ship's name.

### Connect to Science

**Fog Formation** Fog is a cloud touching the ground. It usually forms overnight when the air cools to a temperature near the dew point, and the water vapor in the air condenses into water droplets.

### ELL

**Questioning** Read aloud the second paragraph on p. 132. Model using the questioning strategy to deepen comprehension. There were parts of the paragraph I did not understand. I will ask my questions, then reread to find the answer. How many boats were there? There were two. Who was on each boat? Trudy's father, sister, trainer, and other swimmers were on the first boat. Reporters and photographers were on the second boat. What other questions can I ask about the paragraph?

*Gertrude Ederle* **133a**

**1ST READ**

## Access Text © If students need help, then...

**⊙ FACT AND OPINION** After students have read pp. 134–135, have them list two statements of fact from the pages. Ask them how they would confirm that the facts are true.

**Think Aloud** **MODEL** I see that by six o'clock the waves were twenty feet high. I could check an Internet site to verify this fact. The author also says thousands of people waited to greet Trudy. I could also verify this information by looking in a book or on the Internet.

At about one-thirty in the afternoon, it started to rain. A strong wind stirred the water. For a while, Trudy would swim forward a few feet only to be pulled back twice as far.

By six o'clock the tide was stronger. The waves were twenty feet high. The rough water made the people aboard the *Alsace* and the news boat seasick.

Trudy's trainer was sure she couldn't finish the swim. He told her to give up.

"No, no," Trudy yelled over the sound of the waves. She kept swimming.

In the next few hours, the rain and wind became stronger and the sea rougher. At times the rough water pulled the boats away, out of Trudy's sight. She was scared. It was eerie being out there all alone.

Now Trudy began to have trouble kicking in the water. When the *Alsace* came close again, Trudy said her left leg had become stiff. Her trainer was frightened for her. He yelled, "You must come out."

134

**Student Edition, p. 134**

**2ND READ**

## Close Reading ©

**⊙ FACT AND OPINION • TEXT EVIDENCE** What was Trudy's opinion of her accomplishment? (She had succeeded and all women would be proud.) What detail from the selection supports the opinion? (In paragraph 5 on p. 135, Trudy said, "All the women of the world will celebrate.")

**SYNTHESIS** What is one generalization you can make about the English Channel? (It is a cold, rough body of water that can change very quickly.)

**REREAD CHALLENGING TEXT** Have students reread p. 134 to better understand the description of the conditions Trudy was swimming in. Have them list the adjectives the author uses.

**ON THEIR OWN** Ask students to draw conclusions about the statements of fact they identified and support their assertions with textual information. Then have students reread the two pages and look for two statements of opinion.

### Common Core State Standards

**Informational Text 2.** Determine the main idea of a text; recount the key details and explain how they support the main idea. **Informational Text 8.** Describe the logical connection between particular sentences and paragraphs in a text (e.g., comparison, cause/effect, first/second/third in a sequence).

"What for?" Trudy shouted, and kept swimming.

Trudy continued to fight the tide and the constant stinging spray of water in her face. She knew she would either swim the Channel or drown.

As Trudy neared Kingsdown, on the coast of England, she saw thousands of people gathered to greet her. They lit flares to guide her to shore.

At about nine-forty at night, after more than fourteen hours in the water, Trudy's feet touched land. Hundreds of people, fully dressed, waded into the water to greet her. When she reached the shore, her father hugged Trudy and wrapped her in a warm robe.

"I knew if it could be done, it had to be done, and I did it," Trudy said after she got ashore. "All the women of the world will celebrate."

### Access for All

**SI** Strategic Intervention

Have students work in pairs to reread pp. 134–135, identifying when comprehension breaks down. Have them record questions and reread to find the answer.

### Connect to Science
**Swimming in Current**
Swimming in a strong current can propel or slow a swimmer. A current has an effect on a swimmer's motion much like a force such as a pull or push.

135

**Student Edition, p. 135**

**ANALYSIS** How do you form a summary? Summarize the important points on pp. 129–130 in the order they happened. (I know that a summary presents the main ideas, so I can look for topic sentences and important dates as I read. Trudy's first attempt to cross the English Channel was on August 18, 1925. She did not make it. She tried again on August 6, 1926, and was successful.)

### ELL

**Vocabulary** Some vocabulary in the selection may be difficult for students to understand. Explain unfamiliar words and phrases such as *stirred the water, seasick, eerie,* and *stinging spray.*

## Access Text © If students need help, then...

### ◉ MULTIPLE-MEANING WORDS

Ask students to use context clues to determine the meaning of the word *beat* in the first paragraph on p. 136. (to do better than others in a competition)

**Think Aloud** **MODEL** I know the word *beat* has more than one meaning. I can use context clues to figure out which meaning the author intends. The first sentence gives Trudy's time for swimming the Channel. If she *beat* men's records, I know the author means she had the best record.

**ON THEIR OWN** Have students use context clues to determine the meaning of the word *called* in the first paragraph on p. 136. Have students monitor and adjust their comprehension as they figure out the meaning of the word.

## Close Reading ©

**ANALYSIS** The word *record* has multiple meanings. It can be pronounced different ways, too, according to the meaning. Which meaning and pronunciation does the author intend in the first paragraph on page 136? (The author intends for the word *record* to mean "the best done so far," such as the fastest time for completing something. The pronunciation is REHK uhrd.)

Trudy swam the Channel in just fourteen hours and thirty-one minutes. She beat the men's record by almost two hours. In newspapers across the world, Trudy's swim was called history-making. Reporters declared that the myth that women are the weaker sex was "shattered and shattered forever."

Trudy sailed home aboard the SS *Berengaria*. After six days at sea, the ship entered New York Harbor.

Two airplanes circled and tipped their wings to greet Trudy. People on boats of all kinds rang their bells and tooted their horns to salute her. Foghorns sounded.

136

**Student Edition, p. 136**

**ANALYSIS** Help students generate text-based questions by providing the following question stem: In the selection, what did Trudy do when _____?

**DEVELOP LANGUAGE** Have students reread the first paragraph on p. 136. What does the word *shattered* mean here? What else can be *shattered?*

Trudy climbed into an open car for a parade up lower Broadway. An estimated two million people, many of them women, stood and cheered. They threw scraps of newspaper, ticker tape, pages torn from telephone books, and rolls of toilet paper.

When her car arrived at the New York city hall, Mayor Jimmy Walker praised Trudy for her courage, grace, and athletic prowess. "American women," he said, "have ever added to the glory of our nation."

**Student Edition, p. 137**

**ANALYSIS** What effect do the words *rang* and *tooted* have in the last paragraph on page 136? (They help the reader experience the celebration.)

**MONITOR AND CLARIFY • TEXT EVIDENCE** Reread to find the answers to these questions, citing page numbers as references in the text. Where did Trudy begin the swim? (France, p. 130) Where did she end? (England, p. 135) Where was Trudy's celebration parade? (New York, p. 137)

## Common Core State Standards

**Informational Text 3.** Describe the relationship between a series of historical events, scientific ideas or concepts, or steps in technical procedures in a text, using language that pertains to time, sequence, and cause/effect. **Language 3.** Use knowledge of language and its conventions when writing, speaking, reading, or listening. **Language 3.a.** Choose words and phrases for effect. **Language 4.a.** Use sentence-level context as a clue to the meaning of a word or phrase.

## Access for All

**SI** Strategic Intervention

After students read the first paragraph on p. 137, discuss how visualization can help them understand the events. Students may not be familiar with ticker tape. Explain that ticker tape refers to small pieces of paper, sometimes called confetti.

Point out the italicized *Berengaria* on p. 136. Explain that ship titles are written in italics.

**1ST READ**

## Access Text © *If students need help, then…*

◉ **QUESTIONING** Remind students that they ask questions to help monitor comprehension and understand what they have read.

**MODEL** After I finish reading, I ask myself questions to help me understand things I'm not sure of. The text says that President Calvin Coolidge sent a message that was read at the ceremony. I wonder why he did that. The President wanted everyone to know that he thought this was a very important event.

**2ND READ**

## Close Reading ©

**ANALYSIS** Read the last sentence on page 139. How does this show the author's opinion of Trudy? (This shows how the author thinks Trudy is a role model for all girls and women.)

**CROSS-TEXT EVALUATION**
**Use a Strategy to Self-Check** How did the Read Aloud, "A First in Space: Ellen Ochoa," help you understand this selection?

138

**Student Edition, p. 138**

**SYNTHESIS • TEXT EVIDENCE** Using what you learned in this selection, identify some of the unique traits it takes to be first at something. Have students cite examples from the text to support their responses.

**CHECK PREDICTIONS** Have students return to the predictions they made earlier and use illustrations to confirm whether they were accurate.

President Calvin Coolidge sent a message that was read at the ceremony. He called Trudy "America's Best Girl." And she was. Gertrude Ederle had become a beacon of strength to girls and women everywhere.

139

**Student Edition, p. 139**

**SYNTHESIS** What are some important facts and details in the selection? (Trudy Ederle lived in a time when women were not seen as equal to men. She almost drowned but then learned to swim. She beat records and swam in the Olympics. On her second attempt, she swam the English Channel, breaking the previous record. She became a role model.)

## Common Core State Standards

**Informational Text 2.** Determine the main idea of a text; recount the key details and explain how they support the main idea. **Informational Text 7.** Use information gained from illustrations (e.g., maps, photographs), and the words in a text to demonstrate understanding of the text (e.g., where, when, why, and how key events occur). **Also Informational Text 9., 10.**

## Access for All

**SI** **Strategic Intervention**

Have students work in pairs to reread pp. 132–139, asking literal, interpretive, and evaluative questions to deepen understanding.

**A** **Advanced**

Remind students that when reading a biography, it is important to differentiate between facts and the author's opinion of the person. Have students make a list of important ideas from the selection, separating the author's opinions and factual information.

**ELL**

**Metaphor** Point out the phrase "beacon of strength" on p. 139. Guide students in using context to understand the meaning of the metaphor.

*Gertrude Ederle* **139a**

Common Core State Standards
Informational Text 1. Ask and answer questions to demonstrate understanding of a text, referring explicitly to the text as the basis for the answers. Also Informational Text 2., Writing 8.

**Envision It!** Retell

READING STREET ONLINE
STORY SORT
www.ReadingStreet.com

140

## Think Critically

1. How would you feel about the challenge of swimming all the way across the English Channel? **Text to Self**

2. David Adler writes many biographies. Explain the difference in point of view between a biography and autobiography. How would this biography have been different if it were an autobiography? **Think Like an Author**

3. This biography is full of facts and also several statements of opinion. Write a sentence that tells your opinion of this biography. Support your opinion with evidence from the text. **Fact and Opinion**

4. What questions do you have about swimmers who beat records and make history? Write a literal, an interpretive, and an evaluative question.
   **Questioning**

5. **Look Back and Write** Look back at the question on page 125. Write about Gertrude Ederle and how she surprised the world by being first. Provide evidence to support your answer.
   **Key Ideas and Details • Text Evidence**

### Meet the Author
# DAVID ADLER

David Adler has written almost two hundred books! He was the first person to write a book about Gertrude Ederle. "I read every newspaper and magazine story I could find about her," he says. Some newspapers said a woman could never swim the English Channel.

Mr. Adler has five brothers and sisters. "My parents encouraged each of us to be an individual. As a child I was known as the family artist." Paintings and drawings he did then still hang in his parents' home.

"I've always been a dreamer," Mr. Adler says. He recently spoke with his fourth-grade teacher. She remembered the time she went to the principal. "What should I do with Adler?" she asked. "He's always dreaming."

"Leave him alone," the principal said. "Maybe one day he'll become a writer."

**Read more books by David Adler.**

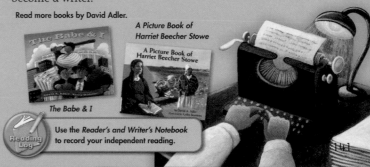

*A Picture Book of Harriet Beecher Stowe*

*The Babe & I*

Use the *Reader's and Writer's Notebook* to record your independent reading.

**Student Edition, pp. 140–141**

---

## Common Core State Standards

**Informational Text 1.** Ask and answer questions to demonstrate understanding of a text, referring explicitly to the text as the basis for the answers. **Also Informational Text 2., 6, Writing 2., 2.b., 4., 10., Speaking/Listening 4., Language 3.**

### Bridge to Common Core

**RANGE OF READING AND LEVEL OF TEXT COMPLEXITY**

To increase students' capacity for reading and comprehending complex texts independently and proficiently, have them read other informational texts by David Adler or about the social studies topic, unique traits. After students read closely for a sustained period of time, they should record their reading in their Reading Logs.

## Think Critically

1. **TEXT TO SELF** I like to swim, but I would be scared to swim that far.

2. **THINK LIKE AN AUTHOR** A biography uses the third-person point of view. An autobiography uses the first-person point of view. If this were an autobiography, it would be written by Gertrude Ederle in the first-person point of view.

3. **FACT AND OPINION** This biography is inspiring to people of all ages and abilities. The text supports my opinion because it is about different stages of Trudy's life.

4. **QUESTIONING** Have any swimmers beat Trudy's records? What kind of people are swimmers who try to beat records? Would they make good role models?

5. **LOOK BACK AND WRITE • TEXT EVIDENCE** To build writing fluency, allow 10–15 minutes.

## Scoring Rubric  Look Back and Write

**TOP-SCORE RESPONSE** A top-score response uses text evidence to tell about how Gertrude Ederle surprised the world by being first.

**A top-score response should include:**

- The English Channel is more than twenty miles wide and is cold and rough.
- Only five men and no women had ever swum all the way across the English Channel.
- Trudy failed on her first attempt to swim the English Channel, but she surprised the world when she succeeded on her second try.

# Retell

Have students work in pairs to retell the selection, using the retelling strip in the Student Edition or the Story Sort as prompts. Monitor students' retellings.

## Scoring Rubric  Expository Retelling

| | 4 | 3 | 2 | 1 |
|---|---|---|---|---|
| **Connections** | Makes connections and generalizes beyond the text | Makes connections to other events, texts, or experiences | Makes a limited connection to another event, text, or experience | Makes no connection to another event, text, or experience |
| **Author's Purpose** | Elaborates on author's purpose | Tells author's purpose with some clarity | Makes some connection to author's purpose | Makes no connection to author's purpose |
| **Topic** | Describes the main topic | Identifies the main topic with some details early in retelling | Identifies the main topic | Retelling has no sense of topic |
| **Important Ideas** | Gives accurate information about events, steps, and ideas using details and key vocabulary | Gives accurate information about events, steps, and ideas with some detail and key vocabulary | Gives limited or inaccurate information about events, steps, and ideas | Gives no information about events, steps, and ideas |
| **Conclusions** | Draws conclusions and makes inferences to generalize beyond the text | Draws conclusions about the text | Is able to tell some learnings about the text | Is unable to draw conclusions or make inferences about the text |

**Don't Wait Until Friday**

## MONITOR PROGRESS  Check Retelling

**If...** students have difficulty retelling,

**then...** use the Retelling Cards/Story Sort to scaffold their retellings.

---

**eSTREET INTERACTIVE**
www.ReadingStreet.com

**Pearson eText**
- Student Edition

**Story Sort**

### Plan to Assess Retelling

- ☐ **Week 1** Strategic Intervention
- ☐ **Week 2** Advanced
- ☐ **Week 3** Strategic Intervention
- ☑ **This week assess On-Level students.**
- ☐ **Week 5** Assess any students you have not yet checked during this unit.

### Meet the Author

Have students read about author David Adler on p. 141. Ask them how he shares his research findings in *America's Champion Swimmer: Gertrude Ederle.*

### Read Independently

Have students enter their independent reading into their Reading Logs.

**Common Core State Standards**

**Informational Text 7.** Use information gained from illustrations (e.g., maps, photographs), and the words in a text to demonstrate understanding of the text (e.g., where, when, why, and how key events occur). **Foundational Skills 4.** Read with sufficient accuracy and fluency to support comprehension. **Foundational Skills 4.a.** Read on-level text with purpose and understanding.

# Fluency

## Appropriate Phrasing

**MODEL FLUENT READING** Have students turn to p. 132 of *America's Champion Swimmer: Gertrude Ederle*. Have students follow along as you read this page. Tell them to listen for pauses between phrases. Explain that you will look at the punctuation in the sentences to help you decide when to pause.

**GUIDE PRACTICE** Have students follow along as you read the page again. Ask questions to be sure students comprehend the text. Then have them reread the page as a group without you until they read with appropriate phrasing and with no mistakes. Ask questions to be sure students comprehend the text. Continue in the same way on p. 133.

| Corrective feedback | **If...** students are having difficulty reading with the right phrasing, **then...** prompt them as follows:<br>• Are there commas to tell me that a group of words belong together?<br>• Are there groups of words that should be read together?<br>• Try to read groups of words, not word-by-word. |
| --- | --- |

# Reread for Fluency

**Routine** Oral Rereading

1. **Select a Passage** For *America's Champion Swimmer: Gertrude Ederle*, use p. 134.

2. **Model** Have students listen as you read p. 134 with appropriate phrasing.

3. **Guide Practice** Have students read along with you.

4. **On Their Own** For optimal fluency, students should reread three or four times with appropriate phrasing.

5. **Corrective Feedback** Listen as students read. Provide feedback about their phrasing and encourage them to remember to pause for commas and periods as they read.

Routines Flip Chart

# Research and Study Skills

## Bar Graphs

**TEACH** Review with students that **bar graphs** are useful for comparing data. Ask students what kind of texts use graphs. Students may mention textbooks, newspapers, magazines, or almanacs. Show a graph from a content area text and use it to explain the following information:

- A bar graph shows data, or information, in visual form. The title and labels tell what information the graph shows and compares.

- A bar graph uses bars that go up and down (vertical) or bars that go across (horizontal) to compare amounts, groups, or things over a period of time.

Provide small groups of students with examples of bar graphs. Have each group show its bar graph to the class and explain what it shows.

**GUIDE PRACTICE** Discuss these questions:

How do you know what information a bar graph shows? (The title and labels tell you what the bar graph is about.)

How do you read a bar graph? (Once you know what information the graph shows, you read each label at the bottom and follow each up the left side of the graph.)

After groups describe their bar graphs, ask specific questions about the data.

**ON THEIR OWN** Have students review the instructions and complete p. 288 of the *Reader's and Writer's Notebook*.

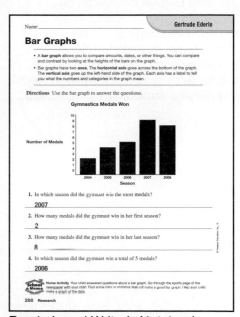

Reader's and Writer's Notebook,
p. 288

 **Common Core State Standards**

**Writing 7.** Conduct short research projects that build knowledge about a topic. **Writing 8.** Recall information from experiences or gather information from print and digital sources; take brief notes on sources and sort evidence into provided categories. **Language 1.** Demonstrate command of the conventions of standard English grammar and usage when writing or speaking. **Language 2.** Demonstrate command of the conventions of standard English capitalization, punctuation, and spelling when writing. **Language 2.e.** Use conventional spelling for high-frequency and other studied words and for adding suffixes to base words (e.g., *sitting, smiled, cries, happiness*).

# Research and Inquiry

## Step 3 Analyze Information

**TEACH** Tell students that today they will analyze their findings and may need to change the focus of their original inquiry question.

**Think Aloud** **MODEL** Now that I've done research, I need to analyze what I've found. I have gathered a lot of facts about women who were Olympic athletes, but I need to find additional information. I've also collected a lot of opinions from different sources. I need to make sure I distinguish among the facts and opinions. I now need to narrow my focus. What part of this athlete's accomplishments do I want to focus on? For example, I could include basic facts about Wilma Rudolph. She was the first American woman to win three gold medals in the Olympics.

**GUIDE PRACTICE** Have students analyze their findings. They may need to refocus or narrow their inquiry question. Remind students that sorting their findings into categories can help them see where they lack information.

**ON THEIR OWN** Provide categories for students' research, such as *childhood, training,* and *achievements.* Have students organize their notes into the provided categories.

# Conventions

## Contractions

**REVIEW** Remind students that this week they learned about contractions.

- A contraction is a word made by putting two words together.

- When two words are joined in a contraction, an apostrophe shows where a letter or letters have been left out.

**CONNECT TO ORAL LANGUAGE** Have the class complete these sentence frames by replacing the underlined words with either the correct contraction or the word parts.

> I <u>will not</u> swim today. (won't)
>
> I <u>can't</u> wait to race. (cannot)

**ON THEIR OWN** For additional support, use Let's Practice It! p. 252 on the *Teacher Resources DVD-ROM*.

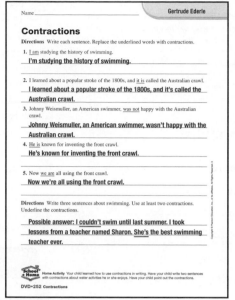

Let's Practice It!
TR DVD•252

## Access for All

**SI Strategic Intervention**

If students do not understand contractions, have partners use word cards. On one set of cards, make pairs of words. On the other set of cards, show each contraction. Have partners match the two words to their contracted form.

## Daily Fix-It

5. Didnt you learn the backstroke.
   *(Didn't; backstroke?)*

6. He do the backstroke in races but the crawl is faster. *(does; races,)*

# Spelling

## Suffixes *-er, -or, -ess, -ist*

**FREQUENTLY MISSPELLED WORDS** The words *who, once,* and *one* are words that students often misspell. These words are difficult because the sound /w/ can be spelled in different ways. Think carefully before you write these words. Have students practice writing these words by writing sentences using each one.

**ON THEIR OWN** For additional practice, use *Reader's and Writer's Notebook,* p. 289.

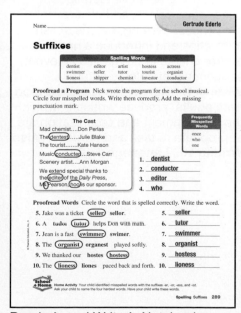

Reader's and Writer's Notebook, p. 289

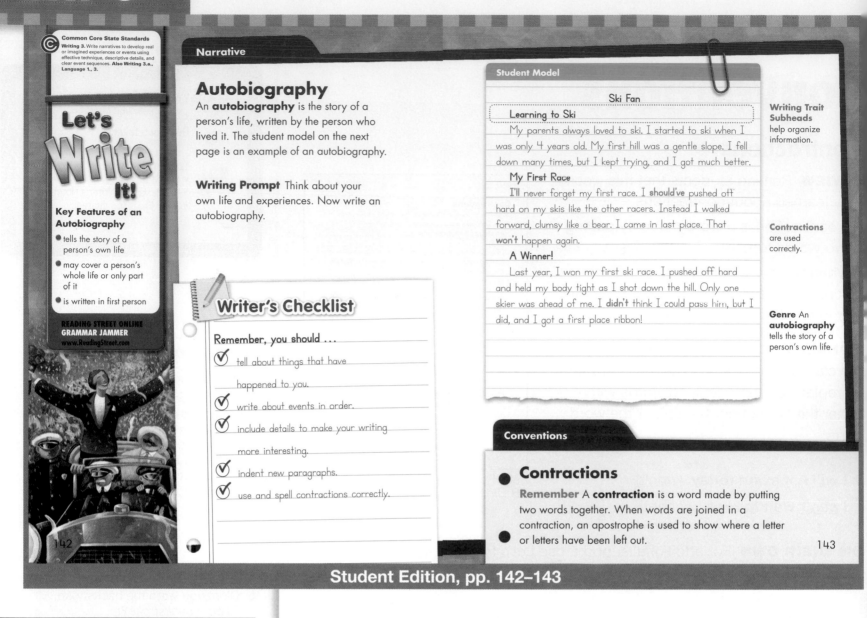

**Common Core State Standards**
Writing 3. Write narratives to develop real or imagined experiences or events using effective technique, descriptive details, and clear event sequences. **Also Writing 3.a., Language 1., 3.**

**Narrative**

## Autobiography

An **autobiography** is the story of a person's life, written by the person who lived it. The student model on the next page is an example of an autobiography.

**Writing Prompt** Think about your own life and experiences. Now write an autobiography.

**Student Model**

### Ski Fan

#### Learning to Ski

My parents always loved to ski. I started to ski when I was only 4 years old. My first hill was a gentle slope. I fell down many times, but I kept trying, and I got much better.

#### My First Race

I'll never forget my first race. I **should've** pushed off hard on my skis like the other racers. Instead I walked forward, clumsy like a bear. I came in last place. That **won't** happen again.

#### A Winner!

Last year, I won my first ski race. I pushed off hard and held my body tight as I shot down the hill. Only one skier was ahead of me. I **didn't** think I could pass him, but I did, and I got a first place ribbon!

**Writing Trait Subheads** help organize information.

**Contractions** are used correctly.

**Genre** An **autobiography** tells the story of a person's own life.

### Writer's Checklist

Remember, you should ...

- ☑ tell about things that have happened to you.
- ☑ write about events in order.
- ☑ include details to make your writing more interesting.
- ☑ indent new paragraphs.
- ☑ use and spell contractions correctly.

**Conventions**

- **Contractions**

  **Remember** A **contraction** is a word made by putting two words together. When words are joined in a contraction, an apostrophe is used to show where a letter or letters have been left out.

142    143

**Student Edition, pp. 142–143**

**Common Core State Standards**

**Writing 3.** Write narratives to develop real or imagined experiences or events using effective technique, descriptive details, and clear event sequences. **Writing 3.a.** Establish a situation and introduce a narrator and/or characters; organize an event sequence that unfolds naturally. **Writing 4.** With guidance and support from adults, produce writing in which the development and organization are appropriate to task and purpose. **Also Writing 10., Language 1., 3.**

# Let's Write It!

**WRITE AN AUTOBIOGRAPHY** Use pp. 142–143 in the Student Edition. Direct students to read the key features of an autobiography that appear on p. 142. Remind students that they can refer to the information in the Writer's Checklist as they write their own autobiographies.

Read the student model on p. 143. Point out the paragraph organization as well as the first-person point of view in the model.

**CONNECT TO CONVENTIONS** Remind students that contractions are formed from two words, using an apostrophe to show where a letter or letters are omitted. Point out the correct use of contractions in the model.

# Writing

## Autobiography

**Writing Trait: Organization**

**DISPLAY RUBRIC** Display Scoring Rubric 19 from the *Teacher Resources DVD-ROM* and go over the criteria for each trait under each score. Then, using the model in the Student Edition, choose students to explain why the model should score a 4 for one of the traits. If a student offers that the model should score below 4 for a particular trait, the student should offer support for that response. Remind students that this is the rubric that will be used to evaluate the autobiography they write.

### Scoring Rubric   Autobiography

|  | **4** | **3** | **2** | **1** |
|---|---|---|---|---|
| **Focus/Ideas** | Clear, focused autobiography with many supporting details | Most ideas in autobiography clear and supported | Some ideas in autobiography clear or off-topic | Autobiography with no clarity or development |
| **Organization** | Organized logically into paragraphs; follows a clear sequence | Organized logically, with generally strong paragraphs; sequence is fairly clear | Attempt to organize into paragraphs, but not clearly; weak sequence | No apparent organizational pattern in use of paragraphs or sequence |
| **Tone** | Engaging; shows writer's feeling about subject | Evident voice connecting with reader | Weak voice | Flat writing with no identifiable voice |
| **Word Choice** | Vivid, precise word choice | Accurate word choice | Limited or repetitive word choice | Incorrect or very limited word choice |
| **Sentences** | Varied sentences in logical progression | Not as varied; order mostly logical | Too many similar sentences | Many fragments and run-ons |
| **Conventions** | Excellent control and accuracy; contractions used correctly | Good control, few errors; contractions mostly used correctly | Weak control; contractions used incorrectly | Serious errors that obscure meaning |

**STORY SEQUENCE CHART** Have students refer to the story sequence chart they worked on yesterday. If their charts are not complete, have them reflect on their own experiences and take notes in order to finish their charts.

**WRITE** You will be using your story sequence chart as you write the paragraphs for the first draft of your autobiography. When you are drafting, don't worry if your autobiography does not sound exactly the way you want it. You will have a chance to revise it tomorrow.

## Access for All

**SI** Strategic Intervention

Ask students to pay attention to any places where they become confused as they read the student model. Then suggest that they reread to help clarify their understanding.

**Professional Development** Teachers need "to plan instructional activities that give students opportunities to use the new forms and modes of expression to which they are being exposed." —L. Wong Fillmore and Catherine E. Snow

**Common Core State Standards**

**Writing 3.a.** Establish a situation and introduce a narrator and/or characters; organize an event sequence that unfolds naturally. **Writing 3.c.** Use temporal words and phrases to signal event order. **Writing 4.** With guidance and support from adults, produce writing in which the development and organization are appropriate to task and purpose. **Also Writing 3.**

---

**Ⓒ Bridge to Common Core**

### RANGE OF WRITING

As students progress through the writing project, they routinely write for a range of tasks and purposes. In this lesson, they learn to use paragraphs effectively as they organize and develop first drafts of their autobiographies.

---

# Writing

## Autobiography

**Mini-Lesson** | **Writing Trait: Organization**

■ **Introduce** Explain that prose writing is organized into paragraphs. Each paragraph should develop one main idea with supporting details. Also point out that writers indent paragraphs to show the transition from one to the next. Display the Drafting Tips to students. Remind them that the focus of drafting is to get their ideas down in an organized way. Then display Writing Transparency 19A.

> ### My First Pet
>
> I wanted pet for a long time. My parents said that I could have one. They asked me what kind of pet I wanted. I am quiet and like to sit by the window. So, I thought Id ask for a cat. My sister is alergic to cat hair. So I asked for a rabbit instead.
>
> **At the Pet Store**
> We went to the pet store to pick out my rabbit. In the cage at the store, there were a bunch of rabbits. They were cute. I picked one out.
> The man took it out of the cage and handed it to me. Its fur was nice. He told me how to feed it and take care of it.
>
> **Fluffy's New Home**
> On the way home, my mom asked me what my rabbit's name was. I said its name was Fluffy. Now Fluffy lives with my family and me. I feed Fluffy carrots and rabbit food, and change her water every day. I'm so glad to finally have a pet of my own!
>
> Unit 4 America's Champion Swimmer: Gertrude Ederle    Writing: Model **19A**

Writing Transparency 19A, TR DVD

### Drafting Tips

✔ Use the sequence of events as they happened to organize your draft.

✔ Write your autobiography in the first person, using the pronoun *I*.

✔ Don't worry about grammar or mechanics while drafting. You can fix any mechanical errors at the proofreading stage.

 **Think Aloud** **MODEL** I'm going to write the first paragraph of my autobiography, *My First Pet*. I want to get my ideas on paper in an organized way. I won't worry about revising or proofreading, since those steps come later in my writing process. I want to make sure that my paragraphs are each organized around a single main idea.

Point to the bold subheads in *My First Pet*. Explain that the subheads are used to clearly label the sections in the autobiography.

Have students use the drafting tips to guide them in developing their drafts. Remind them to organize each of their paragraphs around a single main idea. Suggest that they use time-order words and transition words to keep the events in the correct sequence.

**eSTREET INTERACTIVE**
www.ReadingStreet.com

**Teacher Resources**
• Writing Transparency

## Routine | Quick Write for Fluency | Team Talk

1. **Talk** Pairs talk about the important events in their lives that they are writing about.

2. **Write** Each student writes a paragraph about an important event in his or her life, using contractions.

3. **Share** Partners check each other's paragraphs for correct use of contractions.

Routines Flip Chart

### Access for All

 **Advanced**
Have students read a short magazine article, focusing on the way it uses paragraphs. Ask them to underline the topic sentence of each paragraph.

### Academic Vocabulary ©
A **subhead** labels a section of a piece of writing.

# Wrap Up Your Day!

✔ **Content Knowledge** Have students discuss the challenges Gertrude Ederle faced as she swam the English Channel.

✔ **Text-Based Comprehension** *How could you tell that this story really happened?* Encourage students to cite examples from the text.

**Preview DAY 4**

Tell students that tomorrow they will read about a famous Olympian.

### Materials

- Student Edition
- Reader's and Writer's Notebook
- Decodable Reader

## (c) Common Core State Standards

**Speaking/Listening 1.a.** Come to discussions prepared, having read or studied required material; explicitly draw on that preparation and other information known about the topic to explore ideas under discussion.
**Speaking/Listening 1.c.** Ask questions to check understanding of information presented, stay on topic, and link their comments to the remarks of others. **Language 6.** Acquire and use accurately grade-appropriate conversational, general academic, and domain-specific words and phrases, including those that signal spatial and temporal relationships (e.g., *After dinner that night we went looking for them*). **Also Speaking/Listening 1.**

# Content Knowledge

## Unique Traits

**EXPAND THE CONCEPT** Remind students of the weekly concept question, *What unique traits does it take to be the first to do something?* Have students discuss how the unique traits of great women athletes enable them to achieve their goals.

## Build Oral Language

**Team Talk** **TALK ABOUT SENTENCES AND WORDS** Have students reread these sentences from p. 136.

*In newspapers across the world, Trudy's swim was called history-making. Reporters declared that the myth that women are the weaker sex was "shattered and shattered forever."*

- What is *history-making?* How can a person make history? (A person can make history by doing something that has never been done before.) How did Trudy make history? (Trudy made history by being the first woman to swim across the English Channel.)
- What is a *myth?* (A *myth* is a legend or a story that is not real.) Is saying that no woman could swim the English Channel a *myth* or a fact? (It is a *myth* because Trudy showed that it could be done.)

# Build Oral Vocabulary

## Amazing Words
### Robust Vocabulary Routine

1. **Introduce** Write the Amazing Word *provision* on the board. Have students say it aloud with you. During Trudy's second attempt to swim the English Channel, Margaret brought *provisions* for Trudy. Have students determine a definition of *provision*. (A *provision* is something provided to meet a need.)

2. **Demonstrate** Have students answer questions to demonstrate understanding. What *provisions* would you need if you were going on a trip in the desert? (water, food)

3. **Apply** Have students apply their understanding. List *provisions* you might need in different situations, such as *provisions* for an astronaut in space or a mountain climber.

4. **Display the Word** Point out the different sound-spellings in the word as you read it.

See p. OV•4 to teach *spectacle*.

Routines Flip Chart

**ADD TO THE CONCEPT MAP** Use the illustrations and topic sentences to review pp. 132–139 of *America's Champion Swimmer: Gertrude Ederle*. Discuss the Amazing Words *suspend* and *accompany*. Add these and other concept-related words to the concept map. Use the following questions to develop

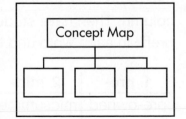

Concept Map

students' understanding of the concept. Remind students to ask and answer questions with appropriate detail and to build on other students' answers.

- Have you ever had to *suspend* something you were working on? Why might an athlete *suspend* other activities while training?

- Many people accompanied Trudy as she swam the English Channel. When do you need someone to *accompany* you? Why does a coach *accompany* an athlete?

**eSTREET INTERACTIVE**
www.ReadingStreet.com

**Teacher Resources**
- Amazing Word Cards
- Reader's and Writer's Notebook

## Amazing Words

| | |
|---|---|
| ordinary | erect |
| imagination | suspend |
| assemble | accompany |
| magnificent | provision |
| organize | spectacle |

## Strategy Response Log

Have students complete p. 25 in the *Reader's and Writer's Notebook*. Then have students work with a partner to answer their questions.

### ELL

**Produce Oral Language** Use the Day 4 instruction on ELL Poster 19 to extend and enrich language.

## Common Core State Standards

**Foundational Skills 3.** Know and apply grade-level phonics and word analysis skills in decoding words. **Foundational Skills 3.a.** Identify and know the meaning of the most common prefixes and derivational suffixes. **Language 2.e.** Use conventional spelling for high-frequency and other studied words and for adding suffixes to base words (e.g., *sitting, smiled, cries, happiness*). **Also Foundational Skills 3.d.**

---

Name _____  Gertrude Ederle

**Prefixes**

Directions  Add the prefix **pre-, de-, mid-, over-, out-,** or **bi-** to each base word. Write the new word on the line.

| | | | | |
|---|---|---|---|---|
| 1. pre- | + | fix | = | prefix |
| 2. bi- | + | cycle | = | bicycle |
| 3. over- | + | pay | = | overpay |
| 4. pre- | + | paid | = | prepaid |
| 5. out- | + | guess | = | outguess |
| 6. de- | + | frost | = | defrost |
| 7. over- | + | sleep | = | oversleep |
| 8. mid- | + | night | = | midnight |
| 9. out- | + | shine | = | outshine |
| 10. bi- | + | monthly | = | bimonthly |
| 11. mid- | + | summer | = | midsummer |
| 12. de- | + | claw | = | declaw |

Directions  Match one of the words you wrote above to each definition. Write the word on the line.

11. to shine more brightly than   outshine
12. the middle of the night   midnight
13. machine with two wheels   bicycle
14. pay too much   overpay
15. paid for beforehand   prepaid
16. remove the claws from   declaw

**Home Activity** Your child wrote words with the prefixes pre- (prepaid), mid- (midnight), over- (oversleep), out- (outshine), de- (declaw), and bi- (bicycle). Read an article about Olympic athletes to your child. Have him or her look for words with prefixes. Together, predict what each word might mean and then look it up in a dictionary.

Prefixes DVD•253

Let's Practice It! TR DVD•253

---

# Word Analysis

## Review Prefixes

**REVIEW SOUND-SPELLINGS** To review prefixes *pre-, mid-, over-, out-, bi-,* and *de-,* write these words: *preview, midnight, overpriced, outbid, bicycle, deactivate.* We studied words like these last week. What do you know about decoding words with prefixes? (Identify the base word and the prefix. Then combine the two parts to read the word.) Have students read the words. Then review what each prefix means: *pre-,* before; *mid-,* middle; *over-,* too much; *out-,* surpassing; *bi-,* two; *de-,* not, opposite. Use the base word and prefix to figure out what each word means. (*preview*–"view before," *midnight*–"middle of the night," *overpriced*–"priced too much," *outbid*–"bid higher," *bicycle*–"cycle with two wheels," *deactivate*–"to not activate")

> **Corrective feedback**
>
> **If...** students are unable to identify the prefix and figure out what each word means,
> **then...** refer them to *Sound-Spelling Cards* 150, 151, 156, 159, 160, and 161.

**GUIDE PRACTICE** Draw a six-column chart. When I say a word, listen for the prefix. Hold up the number of fingers to tell me which prefix you hear and the column to place the word in: *overdue, outbid, decode, pre-owned, mid-summer, bifocal, defuse, prepaid, midstream, overbite, bimonthly, outclass, prerecord, overdid, midweek, outdo, dehumidify, biannual, overjoyed, out-dated, prequel, derail, midwest, biped.* Write each word in the appropriate column. Then have students read the words. Ask volunteers to underline the prefix in each word and tell the word's meaning.

| 1 pre- | 2 mid- | 3 over- | 4 out- | 5 bi- | 6 de- |
|---|---|---|---|---|---|
| pre-owned | midsummer | overdue | outbid | bifocal | decode |
| prepaid | midstream | overbite | outclass | bimonthly | defuse |
| prerecord | midweek | overdid | outdo | biannual | dehumidify |
| prequel | midwest | overjoyed | outdated | biped | derail |

**ON THEIR OWN** For additional practice, use *Let's Practice It!* p. 253 on the *Teacher Resources DVD-ROM.*

# Fluent Word Reading

## Spiral Review

**READ WORDS IN ISOLATION** Display these words. Tell students that they can already decode some words on this list. Explain that they should know other words because they appear often in reading.

Have students read the list three or four times until they can read at the rate of two to three seconds per word.

### Word Reading

| | | | | |
|---|---|---|---|---|
| feet | early | their | scarves | the |
| disturb | men's | world | workout | watched |
| have | worm | children | certain | shirts |
| earth | elves | of | mice | dirty |

| Corrective feedback | **If...** students have difficulty reading whole words, **then...** have them use sound-by-sound blending for decodable words or chunking for words that have word parts, or have them say and spell high-frequency words. |
|---|---|
| | **If...** students cannot read fluently at a rate of two to three seconds per word, **then...** have pairs practice the list until they can read it fluently. |

**eSTREET INTERACTIVE**
www.ReadingStreet.com

**Teacher Resources**
• Let's Practice It!

**Interactive Sound-Spelling Cards**

## Access for All

**SI** Strategic Intervention

To assist students having difficulty with prefixes, focus on only one prefix at a time. Write words with the prefix *pre-* on separate cards. Have students identify the prefix and the base word and then combine the parts to read the word. Discuss what the prefix means and how it changes the meaning of the word. Repeat using words with the prefixes *mid-, over-, out-, bi-,* and *de-.*

## Spiral Review

These activities review

• previously taught high-frequency words *their, watched, have, of, the.*

• irregular plurals; *r*-controlled vowels spelled *ear, or, er, ir, ur.*

**Fluent Word Reading** Have students listen to a more fluent reader say the words. Then have them repeat the words.

*Gertrude Ederle*  **144d**

**Common Core State Standards**

**Foundational Skills 3.a.** Identify and know the meaning of the most common prefixes and derivational suffixes. **Foundational Skills 3.d.** Read grade-appropriate irregularly spelled words. **Language 2.e.** Use conventional spelling for high-frequency and other studied words and for adding suffixes to base words (e.g., *sitting, smiled, cries, happiness*).

# Fluent Word Reading

**READ WORDS IN CONTEXT** Display these sentences. Call on individuals to read a sentence. Then randomly point to review words and have students read them. To help you monitor word reading, high-frequency words are underlined and decodable words are italicized.

**MONITOR PROGRESS** Sentence Reading

It is too *early* to disturb <u>the</u> *children.*
After the *workout,* the *men's feet* were *dirty.*
I'm *certain* there are millions <u>of</u> *mice* in our *world.*
<u>The</u> *elves* <u>have</u> bright red *scarves* to match <u>their</u> *shirts.*
We <u>watched</u> the *worm* tunnel into a mound <u>of</u> *earth.*

**If...** students are unable to read an underlined high-frequency word,

**then...** read the word for them and spell it, having them echo you.

**If...** students have difficulty reading an italicized decodable word,

**then...** guide them in using sound-by-sound blending or chunking.

# Reread for Fluency

Have students reread the sentences to develop automaticity decoding words.

**Routine** Oral Rereading

**1. Read** Have students read all the sentences orally.

**2. Reread** To achieve optimal fluency, students should reread the sentences three or four times.

**3. Corrective Feedback** Listen as students read. Provide corrective feedback regarding their fluency and decoding.

Routines Flip Chart

# Decodable Passage 19C

students need help, then...

## Read *A Princess or Not?*

**READ WORDS IN ISOLATION** Have students turn to p. 47 in *Decodable Practice Readers 3.2* and find the first list of words. Each word in this list has a suffix. Let's decode and read these words. Be sure that students identify the base word and suffix in each word.

Next, have students read the high-frequency words.

**PREVIEW** Have students read the title and preview the story. Tell them that they will read words with suffixes.

**READ WORDS IN CONTEXT** Chorally read the story along with students. Have students identify words in the story that have suffixes. Make sure that students are monitoring their accuracy when they decode words.

**Team Talk** Pair students and have them take turns reading the story aloud to each other. Monitor students as they read to check for proper pronunciation and appropriate pacing.

**eSTREET INTERACTIVE**
www.ReadingStreet.com

**Pearson eText**
• Decodable Reader

## Access for All

**A** Advanced

Have students write their own sentences using some of the decodable words found in the sentences on p. 144e.

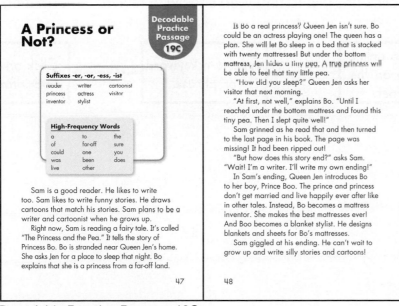

Decodable Practice Passage 19C

**Common Core State Standards**

**Informational Text 5.** Use text features and search tools (e.g., key words, sidebars, hyperlinks) to locate information relevant to a given topic efficiently. **Writing 6.** With guidance and support from adults, use technology to produce and publish writing (using keyboarding skills) as well as to interact and collaborate with others.

 **Bridge to Common Core**

**KEY IDEAS AND DETAILS**

Searching the Internet to learn about women athletes will lead students to Web sites and links that provide information explicitly. By reading the Web pages closely, students will be able to determine the central ideas and summarize the main ideas and key details of the information presented.

# 21st Century Skills

## Online Directories

**INTRODUCE** Explain to students that technology is all around us. Tell them that online directories are one type of technology we use today. Ask students to share what they already know about online directories, such as what they are and how they work.

**DISCUSS** Discuss with students how the Internet has changed the way we find information. For example, ask: How can you use the Internet to learn about a famous female athlete? (type her name in a search engine) Explain: Before the Internet, available information was more limited. You could read only what was available in the library. Review steps to locate information on the Internet. Then explain that an online directory can help us locate information. An online directory groups Web sites by topics.

**GROUP PRACTICE** Display a graphic organizer like the one below. Ask the following questions to help students complete the organizer:

• How can you find an online directory? (search the Internet)

• How can an online directory help you find information? (You type in a keyword and click on links to find Web sites with relevant information.)

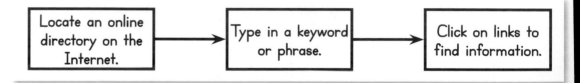

Locate an online directory on the Internet. → Type in a keyword or phrase. → Click on links to find information.

eSTREET INTERACTIVE
www.ReadingStreet.com

Teacher Resources
• Graphic Organizer

**Team Talk** Have students work in pairs to list the benefits of using an online directory when searching for information on the Internet. Ask them to share their lists with the class.

**READ** Tell students that they will now read about using an online directory to locate information about women athletes. Have the class think about times when using an online directory would be helpful.

## Day 4 SMALL GROUP TIME • Differentiate Vocabulary, p. SG•49

| OL On-Level | SI Strategic Intervention | A Advanced |
|---|---|---|
| • **Develop** Language Using Amazing Words | • **Review/Discuss** Amazing Words | • **Extend** Amazing Words and Selection Vocabulary |
| • **Read** "Women Athletes" | • **Read** "Women Athletes" | • **Read** "Women Athletes" |
| | | • **Organize** Inquiry Project |

 **ELL**

**If...** students need more scaffolding and practice with the **Amazing Words,**
**then...** use the Routine on pp. xxxvi–xxxvii in the *ELL Handbook.*

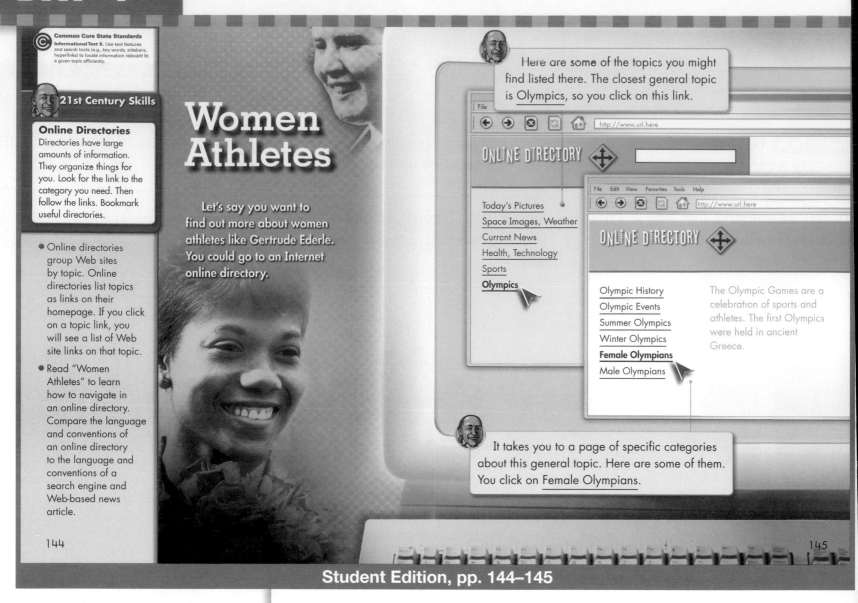

Common Core State Standards
**Informational Text 5.** Use text features and search tools (e.g., key words, sidebars, hyperlinks) to locate information relevant to a given topic efficiently.

**21st Century Skills**

**Online Directories**
Directories have large amounts of information. They organize things for you. Look for the link to the category you need. Then follow the links. Bookmark useful directories.

- Online directories group Web sites by topic. Online directories list topics as links on their homepage. If you click on a topic link, you will see a list of Web site links on that topic.

- Read "Women Athletes" to learn how to navigate in an online directory. Compare the language and conventions of an online directory to the language and conventions of a search engine and Web-based news article.

## Women Athletes

Let's say you want to find out more about women athletes like Gertrude Ederle. You could go to an Internet online directory.

Here are some of the topics you might find listed there. The closest general topic is Olympics, so you click on this link.

ONLINE DIRECTORY

Today's Pictures
Space Images, Weather
Current News
Health, Technology
Sports
**Olympics**

ONLINE DIRECTORY

Olympic History
Olympic Events
Summer Olympics
Winter Olympics
**Female Olympians**
Male Olympians

The Olympic Games are a celebration of sports and athletes. The first Olympics were held in ancient Greece.

It takes you to a page of specific categories about this general topic. Here are some of them. You click on Female Olympians.

144     145

**Student Edition, pp. 144–145**

## Common Core State Standards

**Informational Text 3.** Describe the relationship between a series of historical events, scientific ideas or concepts, or steps in technical procedures in a text, using language that pertains to time, sequence, and cause/effect. **Informational Text 5.** Use text features and search tools (e.g., key words, sidebars, hyperlinks) to locate information relevant to a given topic quickly and efficiently.

## Access Text ©

**TEACH 21st Century Skills: Online Directories** Have students preview "Women Athletes" on pp. 144–147. Have them look at the online directory and the steps the user took to reach the article about Wilma Rudolph. Discuss how the design of an online directory makes it easy to navigate. Have students find the list of topics and the list of categories on p. 145. Then ask: Why did the user click on Olympics on the first screen?

> **Corrective feedback**
> **If...** students are unable to explain why the user clicked on Olympics,
> **then...** use the model to guide students in using online directories.

**eSTREET INTERACTIVE**
www.ReadingStreet.com

**Pearson eText**
• Student Edition

**Think Aloud** **MODEL** An online directory gives different topics. The user is searching for women athletes, so she clicked on Olympics, assuming there would be a link for women athletes within that topic.

**N THEIR OWN** Have students work in pairs to use an online directory to find information about female athletes who have set world records.

# Close Reading

**EVALUATION • TEXT EVIDENCE** In an online directory, what happens with each click of the mouse? Are the results more general or more specific? (more specific) What clues in the text tell you that? (The first screen shows a list of several topics not related to each other. The second screen shows only topics related to the Olympics.)

**SYNTHESIS** What questions should you ask yourself when deciding which link to click on? (What information do I want to find? What kinds of Web sites am I likely to find within each link?)

## Access for All

 **Strategic Intervention**
Guide students in navigating the online directory in the Student Edition. Discuss each link and why only certain ones are relevant to the search.

**A** **Advanced**
Have students select another topic from the online directory and list possible Web sites it would contain.

**Evaluating Web Sites** Remind students that they should evaluate written information for its relevance. Direct students to look at the online directory on p. 145. Ask: Which link would you click if you wanted to find out the score of an important football game? (sports) When might you click on the link for Health, Technology? (Possible response: when you want to find information about staying healthy or using a computer)

*Gertrude Ederle* **145a**

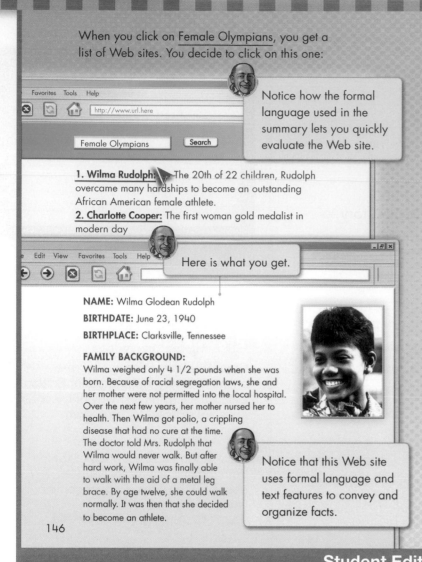

When you click on Female Olympians, you get a list of Web sites. You decide to click on this one:

Favorites  Tools  Help

http://www.url.here

Female Olympians      Search

**Notice how the formal language used in the summary lets you quickly evaluate the Web site.**

**1. Wilma Rudolph:** The 20th of 22 children, Rudolph overcame many hardships to become an outstanding African American female athlete.
**2. Charlotte Cooper:** The first woman gold medalist in modern day

Edit  View  Favorites  Tools  Help

**Here is what you get.**

**NAME:** Wilma Glodean Rudolph

**BIRTHDATE:** June 23, 1940

**BIRTHPLACE:** Clarksville, Tennessee

**FAMILY BACKGROUND:**
Wilma weighed only 4 1/2 pounds when she was born. Because of racial segregation laws, she and her mother were not permitted into the local hospital. Over the next few years, her mother nursed her to health. Then Wilma got polio, a crippling disease that had no cure at the time. The doctor told Mrs. Rudolph that Wilma would never walk. But after hard work, Wilma was finally able to walk with the aid of a metal leg brace. By age twelve, she could walk normally. It was then that she decided to become an athlete.

**Notice that this Web site uses formal language and text features to convey and organize facts.**

146

File  Edit  View  Favorites  Tools  Help

http://www.url.here

**ACHIEVEMENTS:** In high school, she became a basketball star. She set state records for scoring. She led her team to a state championship. Then she became a track star, going to her first Olympic Games in 1956. She won a bronze medal in the 4 x 4 relay.

On September 7, 1960, in Rome, Wilma became the first American woman to win three gold medals in the Olympics. She won the 100-meter dash and the 200-meter dash, and ran anchor on the 400-meter relay team.

**If you wanted to see a video of Wilma, you could look for a documentary about her life.**

**for more practice**

**Get Online!**
www.ReadingStreet.com
Use online directories to find out about women athletes.

**21st Century Skills Online Activity**
Log on and follow the step-by-step directions for using online directories to find more about women athletes.

147

**Student Edition, pp. 146–147**

## Common Core State Standards

**Informational Text 1.** Ask and answer questions to demonstrate understanding of a text, referring explicitly to the text as the basis for the answers. **Informational Text 5.** Use text features and search tools (e.g., key words, sidebars, hyperlinks) to locate information relevant to a given topic efficiently. **Foundational Skills 3.** Know and apply grade-level phonics and word analysis skills in decoding words. **Foundational Skills 4.a.** Read on-level text with purpose and understanding. **Also Informational Text 10., Language 3.b.**

# Access Text ©

**TEACH 21st Century Skills: Online Directories** Remind students that an online directory provides a list to Web sites about a topic. Clicking on a Web site will take you directly to it. Then ask: What other female athlete could the reader have read about?

| Corrective feedback | **If...** students are unable to identify the other Web site, **then...** use the model to guide students in reading the online directory. |

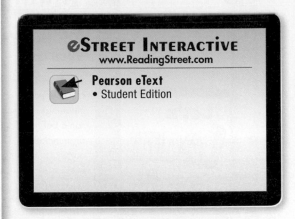

**MODEL** When the user clicked on Female Olympians, she got a list of Web sites. I can see Wilma Rudolph. This is the first Web site. The second one I see is Charlotte Cooper. If the user clicked on her name, the online directory would take the user to a Web site about Charlotte Cooper.

**ON THEIR OWN** Have students practice using online directories to gain information about other female athletes.

# Close Reading ©

**EVALUATION • TEXT EVIDENCE** Does the Web site about Wilma Rudolph provide facts or opinions? (The Web site presents facts about Rudolph.) Does the text state that the site uses formal or informal language to convey and organize facts? (The site uses formal language.)

**SYNTHESIS** What generalization can you make about using an online directory? (Most online directories help you locate information in just a few clicks.)

# Get Online!
## Online Directory

**FOR MORE PRACTICE** Show students how to locate the Web site www.ReadingStreet.com by clicking on the appropriate links. Be sure that they follow the step-by-step directions for using an online directory. Discuss with students how an online directory can help them locate information quickly. Ask students to compare and contrast the language and conventions of an online directory to the language and conventions of a search engine or Web-based news article. Make sure students understand how communication changes when moving from one genre of media to another.

## Access for All

**SI Strategic Intervention**
Help students navigate an online directory and a search engine. Show them how they are alike and how they are different.

**A Advanced**
Have students use an online directory to locate information about Charlotte Cooper.

**Reading a Web Site** Discuss the Web site shown on pp. 146–147 with students. Discuss each heading and the information it contains. For example, ask: What information would you find in the section called Family Background? (information about Rudolph's childhood)

*Gertrude Ederle* **147a**

Common Core State Standards
Language 4.a. Use sentence-level context as a clue to the meaning of a word or phrase. **Also Foundational Skills 4., Speaking/Listening 4., Language 4.**

## Let's Learn It!

READING STREET ONLINE
ONLINE STUDENT EDITION
www.ReadingStreet.com

## Vocabulary

### Multiple-Meaning Words

**Context Clues** Multiple-meaning words are spelled the same but have different meanings. Homographs are spelled the same but have different meanings and pronunciations. Use context clues to figure out what meaning or pronunciation to use.

**Practice It!** Write sentences for two multiple-meaning words and two homographs. Switch sentences with a partner. Write down the different meanings and pronunciations for each word using the context of the sentence. Use a dictionary if necessary.

## Fluency

### Appropriate Phrasing

Notice the different lengths of sentences when you read. Paying attention to the rhythm of sentences makes the story flow more smoothly.

**Practice It!** With your partner, practice reading page 130. Remember to pause at commas and other punctuation. Read with rhythm to give meaning to the events in the story.

148

## Listening and Speaking

When giving a presentation, speak loudly and clearly.

### Sportscast

A sports announcer describes the action of a sports event in a sportscast. Expression is important when reporting.

**Practice It!** Prepare and deliver a three-minute TV sportscast that includes news about Gertrude Ederle's swim. Choose two additional sports events to describe in your sportscast. Discuss how using video would change the descriptions.

### Tips

**Listening ...**
• Draw conclusions about how design influences the message.

**Speaking ...**
• Determine your purpose for speaking.
• Use visual and sound aids.

**Teamwork ...**
• Ask and answer questions about how using sound and video changes communication in a sportscast.

149

**Student Edition, pp. 148–149**

### Common Core State Standards

**Speaking/Listening 1.b.** Follow agreed-upon rules for discussions (e.g., gaining the floor in respectful ways, listening to others with care, speaking one at a time about the topics and texts under discussion). **Speaking/Listening 4.** Report on a topic or text, tell a story, or recount an experience with appropriate facts and relevant, descriptive details, speaking clearly at an understandable pace. **Language 4.a.** Use sentence-level context as a clue to the meaning of a word or phrase. **Also Foundational Skills 3., 4.b., Language 3., 3.b., 4.**

# Fluency

## Appropriate Phrasing

**GUIDE PRACTICE** Use the Student Edition activity as an assessment tool. Make sure the reading passage is at least 200 words in length. As students read aloud with partners, walk around to make sure their phrasing is appropriate and that they use punctuation as a guide.

Don't Wait Until Friday **MONITOR PROGRESS** **Check Fluency**

**FORMATIVE ASSESSMENT** As students reread, monitor their progress toward their individual fluency goals.

Current Goal: 95–105 words correct per minute.
End-of-Year Goal: 120 words correct per minute.

**If...** students cannot read fluently at a rate of 95–105 words correct per minute,

**then...** have students practice with text at their independent levels.

# Vocabulary

## Multiple-Meaning Words

**TEACH MULTIPLE-MEANING WORDS • CONTEXT CLUES** Write the following sentences on the board: *Please close the door. The post office is close to the school.* Have students name the word that appears in each sentence. Point out and say aloud the different pronunciations. Explain that words that are spelled the same but have two different sounds and meanings are called homographs.

**GUIDE PRACTICE** Have students identify the homographs in the following sentences: *The usher will lead you to your seat. Timmy broke the lead on his pencil.*

**ON THEIR OWN** Ask students to list and write the meanings of several homographs and multiple-meaning words. Have students use a dictionary to copy down the different pronunciations.

# Listening and Speaking

## Media Literacy: Sportscast

**TEACH** Tell students that sportscasters often write what they are going to say. Students should record facts about Gertrude Ederle's historic swim. They should also make notes about two or more sports they want to talk about. Remind students that spoken communication in a sportscast may be less formal than a written presentation on the same topic.

**GUIDE PRACTICE** As students are preparing their sportscast, walk around the room, making sure students are considering the length of their sportscast. Remind students to listen attentively, speak coherently with appropriate rate, volume, enunciation, and conventions of language, and make eye contact with one another.

**ON THEIR OWN** Have students practice presenting their sportscast with a partner.

**Sportscast**

Remind students that they should be aware of their posture and body language when presenting their sportscast. Additionally, students should use notes or other memory aids to help them deliver their sportscast.

 **Bridge to Common Core**

**PRESENTATION OF KNOWLEDGE/IDEAS**

As students present their sportscasts, they should adapt their speech to emulate a TV sportscaster who is communicating with at-home viewers. They should use appropriate phrasing and present their sportscasts in an organized fashion. Students should make and use notes as they present information and findings on their topics so listeners can follow the line of reasoning.

**ELL**

**Practice Pronunciation** Assist pairs of students by modeling the correct pronunciation of the homographs in the lesson.

*Gertrude Ederle* **149a**

**Writing 8.** Recall information from experiences or gather information from print and digital sources; take brief notes on sources and sort evidence into provided categories. **Language 1.** Demonstrate command of the conventions of standard English grammar and usage when writing or speaking. **Language 2.** Demonstrate command of the conventions of standard English capitalization, punctuation, and spelling when writing. **Also Foundational Skills 3.a., Language 2.e., Writing 6.**

# Research and Inquiry

## Step 4 Synthesize

**TEACH** Have students synthesize their research findings and results. Review how to choose relevant information from a number of sources and organize it logically. Students should organize their notes into provided categories about their athlete, such as *childhood, training,* and *achievements*. Suggest that students use a chart to sort their information into categories.

**GUIDE PRACTICE** Have students use a word processing program to prepare for their presentations on Day 5. Remind them to use a large enough font so that they can read it while standing in front of the class.

**ON THEIR OWN** Have students continue organizing and combining their research findings as they plan the presentations of their biographies.

# Conventions

## Contractions

**TEST PRACTICE** Remind students that grammar skills, such as contractions, are often assessed on important tests.

Contractions are formed by combining two words.

An apostrophe is used to show where a letter or letters have been omitted.

**ON THEIR OWN** For additional practice, use *Reader's and Writer's Notebook,* p. 290.

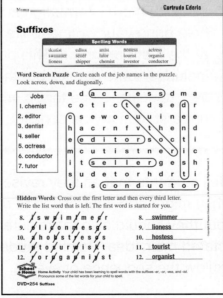

Reader's and Writer's Notebook, p. 290

# Spelling

## Suffixes *-er, -or, -ess, -ist*

**PRACTICE SPELLING STRATEGY** Supply pairs of students with index cards on which the spelling words have been written. Have one student read a word while the other writes it. Then have students switch roles. Have them use the cards to check their spelling and correct any misspelled words.

**ON THEIR OWN** For additional practice, use *Let's Practice It!* p. 254 on the *Teacher Resources DVD-ROM.*

Let's Practice It! TR DVD•254

## eSTREET INTERACTIVE
www.ReadingStreet.com

**Teacher Resources**
- Reader's and Writer's Notebook
- Let's Practice It!
- Daily Fix-It Transparency

## Daily Fix-It

7. Hurry, or you'll miss you're swimming leson. *(your; lesson)*

8. Julia and her left really erly. *(she; early)*

## Bridge to Common Core

**CONVENTIONS OF STANDARD ENGLISH**
As students identify, form, and use contractions, they are demonstrating command of the conventions of standard English. Your guidance will help them use correct grammar, usage, and spelling to convey meaning when they speak and write.

## Write Guy *by Jeff Anderson*

### Teaching Trait-by-Trait: Focus

In a writing conference, choose one aspect of a student's draft, not many things. This will help the student more than trying to think about multiple writing traits at once. Maybe there is one skill at this student's growing edge of knowledge that I can help him improve. I'd hate to see that lost in a swarm of my other comments.

# Writing Zoom in on ©

## Autobiography

**Mini-Lesson** | **Revise: Adding**

■ Yesterday we wrote autobiographies about our own lives and experiences. Today we will revise our drafts. The goal is to make your writing clearer, more interesting, and more informative.

■ Display Writing Transparency 19B. Remind students that revising does not include corrections of grammar and mechanics. Tell them that this will be done during the lesson as they proofread their work. Then introduce the revising strategy of adding.

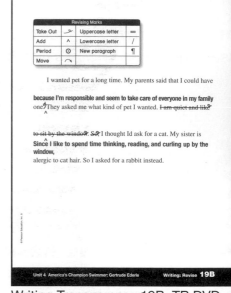

Writing Transparency 19B, TR DVD

■ When you revise, ask yourself, *What can I add to my draft to make my writing clearer, more interesting, and more vivid?* The revising strategy of adding is the one in which more information is added to help bring your writing to life. Let's look at the first paragraph. This paragraph includes some details, but they are not very specific. Since this is an autobiography, I want to make sure the reader understands my personality. I'll need to add some more vivid details here.

Tell students that as they revise, they should not only look for places where they might add information to make their descriptions clearer and more vivid, but they should also make sure that each paragraph has a single, clearly stated main idea. Remind students to use time-order words to help the reader follow the sequence of events.

### Revising Tips

✔ Use sensory language and comparisons to make your descriptions more vivid.

✔ Add information to support the central idea and make your writing more detailed.

**PEER CONFERENCING • PEER REVISION** Have students work in groups of three on peer revision. Each member of the group should write two questions on the draft of each of the other group members. Ask students to focus on asking questions that will help to make the details in the draft clearer and more vivid.

Have students revise their drafts using their group members' questions from Peer Revision, as well as the key features of an autobiography to guide them. Be sure that students are using the revising strategy of adding.

**Corrective feedback** | Circulate around the room to monitor students and confer with them as they revise. Remind students correcting errors that they will have time to edit tomorrow. They should be working on content and organization today.

## Routine  Quick Write for Fluency  [Team Talk]

1. **Talk** Pairs discuss what they read about Gertrude Ederle in *America's Champion Swimmer*.

2. **Write** Each student writes a paragraph telling what he or she learned.

3. **Share** Partners read each other's paragraphs and check for paragraph structure and vivid details.

Routines Flip Chart

**E L L**

**Writing: Support Revision** Suggest that students read their drafts aloud. Have them identify any places in their draft where they become confused while reading. Then have them revise those places to make their drafts clearer.

# Wrap Up Your Day!

✔ **Content Knowledge** *What did you learn about Wilma Rudolph?*

✔ **Oral Vocabulary** Monitor students' use of oral vocabulary as they respond: *When people* assemble *for an Olympic event, do they expect* something *ordinary or* something *magnificent?*

✔ **Text Features** Ask students how graphics helped them understand the selection.

**Preview DAY 5**

Remind students to think about Wilma Rudolph's unique traits.

### Materials

- Student Edition
- Weekly Test
- Reader's and Writer's Notebook

### © Bridge to Common Core

**INTEGRATION OF KNOWLEDGE/IDEAS**
This week, students have integrated content presented in diverse media and analyzed how different texts address similar topics. They have developed knowledge about unique traits to expand the unit topic of One of a Kind.

**Social Studies Knowledge Goals**
Students have learned that being first takes

- bravery
- imagination
- willingness to work hard
- determination

# Content Knowledge

## Unique Traits

**REVIEW THE CONCEPT** Have students look back at the reading selections to find examples that best demonstrate unique traits for being first.

## Build Oral Language

**REVIEW AMAZING WORDS** Display and review this week's concept map. Remind students that this week they have learned ten Amazing Words related to being first. Have students use the Amazing Words and the concept map to answer the question *What unique traits does it take to be the first to do something?*

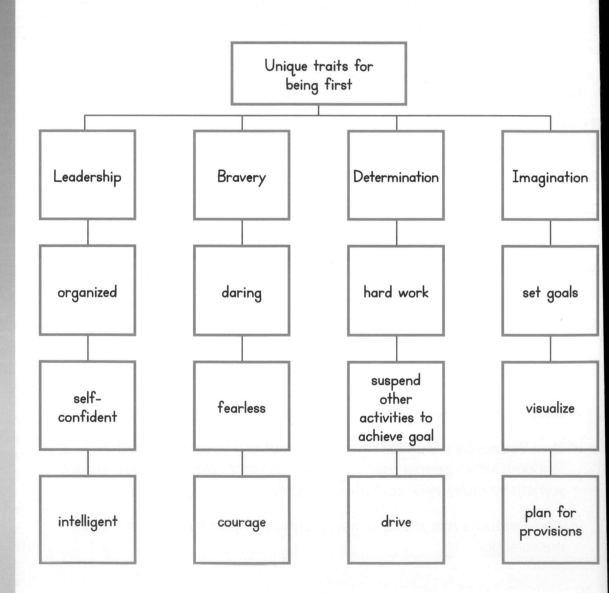

# Build Oral Vocabulary

**Team Talk** **CONNECT TO AMAZING IDEAS** Have pairs of students discuss how the Question of the Week connects to the question for this unit of study: *What does it mean to be unique?* Tell students to use the concept map and what they have learned from this week's discussions and reading selections to form an Amazing Idea—a realization or "big idea" about One of a Kind. Remind partners to answer questions with appropriate detail and to give suggestions that build on each other's ideas. Then ask pairs to share their Amazing Ideas with the class.

Amazing Ideas might include these key concepts:

• Someone who is unique does not follow the crowd or try to be like everyone else.

• Being unique is not always easy.

• If you are unique, people like you for who you are.

**WRITE ABOUT IT** Have students write a few sentences about their Amazing Idea, beginning with "This week I learned . . ."

## eStreet Interactive
www.ReadingStreet.com

Concept Talk Video

Teacher Resources
• Amazing Word Cards

Story Sort

## Amazing Words

| | |
|---|---|
| ordinary | erect |
| imagination | suspend |
| assemble | accompany |
| magnificent | provision |
| organize | spectacle |

It's Friday

**MONITOR PROGRESS** **Check Oral Vocabulary**

**FORMATIVE ASSESSMENT** Have individuals use this week's Amazing Words to describe a unique person. Monitor students' abilities to use the Amazing Words and note which words you need to reteach.

**If...** students have difficulty using the Amazing Words,

**then...** reteach using the Oral Vocabulary Routine, pp. 117a, 122b, 132b, 144b, OV•4.

 **ELL**

**Check Concepts and Language** Use the Day 5 instruction on ELL Poster 19 to monitor students' understanding of the lesson concept.

**Concept Map** Work with students to add new words to the concept map.

Zoom in on ©

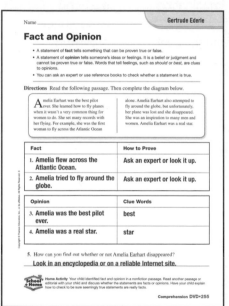

Let's Practice It! TR DVD•255

## Selection Vocabulary

**celebrate** to do something special in honor of a special person or day

**continued** kept up; kept on going

**current** a flow or stream of water

**drowned** died or caused to die under water or other liquid because of lack of air to breathe

**medals** pieces of metal, like coins, that are given as prizes or rewards

**stirred** mixed something by moving it around with a spoon or stick

**strokes** single, complete movements made over and over again

# Text-Based Comprehension

## Review ⊙ Fact and Opinion

**TEACH** Remind students that statements of fact can be proven true or false and that statements of opinion tell someone's ideas or feelings. For additional support have students review p. EI•7 on fact and opinion.

**GUIDE PRACTICE** Have student pairs find an example of a statement of opinion and an example of a statement of fact in *America's Champion Swimmer: Gertrude Ederle.* Then have pairs explain how the statement of fact can be proven true or false. Ask them to identify a word or words that help identify the statement of opinion.

**ON THEIR OWN** For additional practice, use *Let's Practice It!* p. 255 on the *Teacher Resources DVD-ROM.*

# Vocabulary Skill

## Review ⊙ Multiple-Meaning Words

**TEACH** Remind students to use context to help them distinguish among multiple-meaning words.

**GUIDE PRACTICE** Write the following sentence on the board and review how to use context to determine the meaning of the word *end. Cami counted fifty strokes as she swam from one end of the pool to the other.*

**ON THEIR OWN** Have students write two sentences for the word *current.* The word should have a different meaning in each sentence. Partners can trade sentences and identify the context clues that help them determine which meaning of the word *current* is being used.

# Word Analysis

## Review 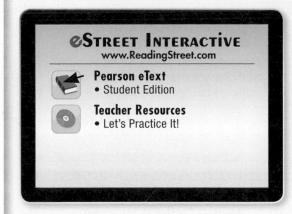 Suffixes

**TEACH** Write the following sentences on the board. Have students read each one, first quietly to themselves and then aloud as you track the print.

1. The violinist watched the conductor.
2. The visitor asked the waitress for a special menu.
3. The actor and actress were performers in a play.
4. The cyclist pedaled after the leader of the group.
5. The explorer presented his discoveries to the princess.

**GUIDE PRACTICE** Have students discuss with a partner which words have suffixes, and ask them to identify the suffixes. Then call on individuals to share with the class.

# Literary Terms

## Review Word Choice

**TEACH** Have students reread pp. 132–133 of *America's Champion Swimmer: Gertrude Ederle.* Remind students that authors use specific words to communicate meaning.

**GUIDE PRACTICE** Point out exact words and phrases on p. 132, such as *powerful currents* and *choppy water.* Discuss how these words help readers form a picture of the setting and events in their mind. Ask students to think about how readers' comprehension might be different without these words and phrases. Have students point out other examples of exact words.

**ON THEIR OWN** Have students make a two-column chart with the headings *word choice* and *effect.* Ask them to use the chart to analyze the author's word choice on p. 133.

## Common Core State Standards

**Foundational Skills 4.** Read with sufficiet accuracy and fluency to support comprehension.

### Plan to Assess Fluency

☐ **Week 1** Advanced

☐ **Week 2** Strategic Intervention

☐ **Week 3** On-Level

☑ **This week assess Strategic Intervention students.**

☐ **Week 5** Assess any students you have not yet checked during this unit.

Set individual goals for students to enable them to reach the year-end goal.

• Current Goal: 95–105 WCPM

• Year-End Goal: 120 WCPM

# Assessment

## Monitor Progress

**FLUENCY** Make two copies of the fluency passage on p. 149k. As the student reads the text aloud, mark mistakes on your copy. Also mark where the student is at the end of one minute. To figure words correct per minute (WCPM), subtract the number of mistakes from the total number of words read in one minute.

**RATE**

| Corrective feedback | **If...** students cannot read fluently at a rate of 95–105 WCPM, **then...** make sure they practice with text at their independent reading level. Provide additional fluency practice by pairing nonfluent readers with fluent readers. **If...** students already read at 120 WCPM, **then...** have them read a book of their choice independently. |
|---|---|

## ELL

**If...** students need more scaffolding and practice with **Conventions and Writing, then...** use the activities on pp. DI•99–DI•100 in the Teacher Resources section on SuccessNet.

**Day 5   SMALL GROUP TIME • Differentiate Reteaching, p. SG•49**

| **OL On-Level** | **SI Strategic Intervention** | **A Advanced** |
|---|---|---|
| • **Practice** Contractions<br>• **Reread** *Reading Street Sleuth,* pp. 50–51 | • **Review** Contractions<br>• **Reread** *Reading Street Sleuth,* pp. 50–51 | • **Extend** Contractions<br>• **Reread** *Reading Street Sleuth,* pp. 50–51<br>• **Communicate** Inquiry Project |

# The Duck Olympics

|  |  |
|---|---|
| Henry always dreamed of swimming in the Duck Olympics. He | 10 |
| practiced his strokes every day. Sometimes the ocean current was very | 21 |
| strong. Once he almost drowned. | 26 |

|  |  |
|---|---|
| Jerry was also trying out for the Olympics. | 34 |

|  |  |
|---|---|
| "You'll never be able to win because your feet are too small," Jerry | 47 |
| told Henry. | 49 |

|  |  |
|---|---|
| Henry didn't need to be reminded of his problem. | 58 |

|  |  |
|---|---|
| "I'm still going to try," Henry replied. | 65 |

|  |  |
|---|---|
| "Why bother? It's a waste of your time," Jerry said. | 75 |

|  |  |
|---|---|
| All his life, Henry was always in last place. It was true that his feet | 90 |
| were very small for a duck, but why shouldn't he try? | 101 |

|  |  |
|---|---|
| Henry's teacher Bert helped Henry improve his strokes. | 109 |

|  |  |
|---|---|
| "Keep kicking your feet," he would shout. | 116 |

|  |  |
|---|---|
| Henry listened to everything Bert said. Bert had trained many other | 127 |
| ducks. One even made it to the Olympics. | 135 |

|  |  |
|---|---|
| Henry continued practicing. Another swimmer would have given | 143 |
| up a long time ago. | 148 |

|  |  |
|---|---|
| When the day of the tryouts came, Henry was nervous. Other | 159 |
| ducks had their instructors pushing them too. | 166 |

|  |  |
|---|---|
| "On your mark, get ready, swim!" shouted the head duck. | 176 |

|  |  |
|---|---|
| Henry moved his feet faster than he ever did before. He zoomed | 188 |
| past Jerry and swam straight to the finish line. | 197 |

|  |  |
|---|---|
| "You made it to the Olympics!" shouted Bert. | 205 |

|  |  |
|---|---|
| Henry quacked for joy. | 209 |

**MONITOR PROGRESS**

• Check Fluency

##  Common Core State Standards

**Informational Text 1.** Ask and answer questions to demonstrate understanding of a text, referring explicitly to the text as the basis for the answers.

# Assessment

## Monitor Progress

For a written assessment of Suffixes, Fact and Opinion, and Selection Vocabulary, use Weekly Test 19, pp. 109–114.

**◉ FACT AND OPINION** Use "Bessie Coleman" on p. 149m to check students' understanding of fact and opinion.

1. Why was it surprising that Bessie became a pilot? Support your conclusion with evidence from the text. **She was raised during a time when African American women did not have many opportunities. Flying schools in the United States would not even teach an African American to fly.**

2. Is this sentence a statement of fact or a statement of opinion? "She shocked Americans." How do you know it might be a fact or an opinion? **It is an opinion. It is the author's feeling or judgment that Bessie's flying shocked Americans. It cannot be proved true or false.**

3. Name two facts that you learned about Bessie Coleman from this passage. **Bessie was eight years old when the Wright Brothers flew the first airplane. Bessie learned to fly in France.**

> **Corrective feedback** | **If...** students are unable to answer the comprehension questions,
> **then...** use the Reteach lesson in *First Stop.*

# Bessie Coleman

When the Wright Brothers invented and flew the first airplane in 1903, Bessie Coleman was eight years old. There wasn't TV or radio then, and poor families like Bessie's probably didn't see a newspaper regularly. So it is likely that Bessie didn't know about the Wright Brothers' success immediately.

But when she did finally hear about it, what did Bessie think? Did she realize that she might fly too someday? That idea may have seemed impossible then.

Bessie came from a large, poor Texas family. Both of her parents had been slaves when they were young. Most of her brothers and sisters still worked in cotton fields.

Bessie was smart. She was good at math. She even went to college for a year. In those days, most African Americans didn't get that chance. Did Bessie think about flying while she was in college?

During World War I, two of Bessie's brothers were soldiers. In 1919, they told her about women pilots in France. Their stories gave Bessie a goal. She would become a pilot!

Yet in 1919, no American flying school would teach an African American woman to fly. That didn't stop Bessie. She found a way to get to France, thousands of miles away! There she learned to fly.

When she returned to America, Bessie flew in air shows. She shocked Americans. There was great prejudice against women and African Americans then. At first, many people didn't believe that Bessie was really a pilot. But then they saw her fly!

**MONITOR PROGRESS** • Fact and Opinion

© **Common Core State Standards**

**Writing 2.** Write informative/explanatory texts to examine a topic and convey ideas and information clearly. **Writing 7.** Conduct short research projects that build knowledge about a topic. **Speaking/Listening 1.b.** Follow agreed-upon rules for discussions (e.g., gaining the floor in respectful ways, listening to others with care, speaking one at a time about the topics and texts under discussion). **Speaking/Listening 3.** Ask and answer questions about information from a speaker, offering appropriate elaboration and detail. **Speaking/Listening 6.** Speak in complete sentences when appropriate to task and situation in order to provide requested detail or clarification. **Language 2.e.** Use conventional spelling for high-frequency and other studied words and for adding suffixes to base words (e.g., *sitting, smiled, cries, happiness*). **Also Speaking/Listening 4., Language 1.**

# Research and Inquiry

## Step 5 Communicate

**PRESENT IDEAS** Have students share their inquiry results by presenting their information and giving a brief talk on their research.

**SPEAKING** Remind students how to be good speakers and how to communicate effectively with their audience.

• Speak clearly.

• Speak at an appropriate volume and pace.

• Use correct sentence structure.

• Make eye contact with the audience.

**LISTENING** Remind students of these tips for being a good listener.

• Wait until the speaker has finished before raising your hand to ask a relevant question or to make a comment.

• Be polite, even if you disagree.

**LISTEN TO IDEAS** Have students listen attentively to the various talks on their research. Have them make pertinent comments, closely related to the topic.

# Spelling Test

## Suffixes -er, -or, -ess, -ist

To administer the spelling test, refer to the directions, words, and sentences on p. 121c.

# Conventions

## Contractions

**MORE PRACTICE** Remind students that contractions are formed by combining two words. An apostrophe shows the location of the omitted letter or letters.

**GUIDE PRACTICE** Have students work in pairs to practice the contractions *he's, they've, wasn't, haven't, should've,* and *could've.* The first partner should say a sentence containing the contraction, and then the second partner should say a different sentence containing the original two words.

**ON THEIR OWN** Write these sentences. Have students look back in *America's Champion Swimmer: Gertrude Ederle* to find the correct contractions to fill in the blanks. Remind them that contractions are formed by combining two words. Students should complete *Let's Practice It!* p. 256 on the *Teacher Resources DVD-ROM.*

1. **Many people thought Trudy _____ swim the English Channel.** (couldn't)

2. **It _____ matter to Trudy what people said.** (didn't)

3. **"_____ get started," Trudy said.** (Let's)

4. **The boat made sure she _____ get lost.** (didn't)

5. **Trudy's trainer was sure that she _____ finish the swim.** (couldn't)

**eStreet Interactive**
www.ReadingStreet.com

**Teacher Resources**
- Let's Practice It!
- Daily Fix-It Transparency

## Daily Fix-It

9. Beths race is next, and her coatch is talking to her. *(Beth's; coach)*

10. The winer will go to the finals in new york. *(winner; New York)*

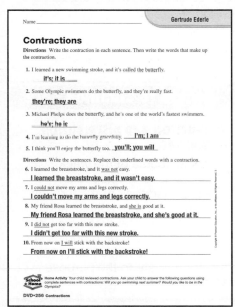

Let's Practice It! TR DVD•256

## Common Core State Standards

**Writing 5.** With guidance and support from peers and adults, develop and strengthen writing as needed by planning, revising, and editing. **Language 1.** Demonstrate command of the conventions of standard English grammar and usage when writing or speaking. **Language 2.** Demonstrate command of the conventions of standard English capitalization, punctuation, and spelling when writing. **Language 2.e.** Use conventional spelling for high-frequency and other studied words and for adding suffixes to base words (e.g., *sitting, smiled, cries, happiness*).

### Teacher Note

**Writing Self-Evaluation** Make copies of the Writing Self-Evaluation Guide on p. 39 of the *Reader's and Writer's Notebook.*

 **Bridge to Common Core**

#### PRODUCTION AND DISTRIBUTION OF WRITING

Over the course of the week, students have developed and strengthened their drafts through planning, revising, editing, and rewriting. The final drafts are clear and coherent autobiographies in which the organization and style are appropriate to the purpose and audience.

# Writing

## Autobiography

**REVIEW REVISING** Remind students that yesterday they revised their autobiographies, paying particular attention to paragraph organization and use of vivid details. Today they will proofread their compositions.

## Mini-Lesson | Proofread

### Proofread for Contractions

■ **Teach** When we proofread, we look closely at our work, searching for errors in mechanics such as spelling, capitalization, punctuation, and grammar. Today we will focus on contractions.

■ **Model** Let's look at a paragraph from the autobiography we started yesterday. Display Writing Transparency 19C. Explain that you will look for errors in the use of contractions. I see a problem in the fourth sentence. This sentence contains the contraction *Id.* This contraction is formed from the two words *I would,* so I need an apostrophe to mark the place where the letters are left out. I should change *Id* to *I'd.* Explain to students that they should reread their autobiographies several times, each time looking for different types of errors: spelling, punctuation, capitalization, and grammar.

Writing Transparency 19C, TR DVD

**PROOFREAD** Display the Proofreading Tips. Ask students to proofread their compositions, using the Proofreading Tips and paying particular attention to contractions. Circulate around the room answering students' questions. When students have finished editing their own work, have pairs proofread one another's autobiography. Then have students create a final draft.

### Proofreading Tips

✔ Be sure that all contractions are used correctly.

✔ Check for correct spelling, capitalization, punctuation, and grammar.

✔ Use correct indentation when beginning new paragraphs in your autobiography.

**eSTREET INTERACTIVE**
www.ReadingStreet.com

**Teacher Resources**
• Writing Transparency
• Reader's and Writer's Notebook

**PRESENT** Give students two options for presenting: an oral presentation to the class or a bound pamphlet. For oral presentations, encourage students to use gestures to act out the events that they are describing. Students creating bound pamphlets should find or make appropriate illustrations for their autobiography as well as a cover page. When students have finished, have each student complete the Writing Self-Evaluation Guide.

## Routine — Quick Write for Fluency — Team Talk

1. **Talk** Pairs discuss what they learned about writing this week.

2. **Write** Each partner writes a few sentences summarizing what he or she learned.

3. **Share** Each partner reads the sentences to the other.

Routines Flip Chart

# Wrap Up Your Week!

## Unique Traits

What unique traits does it take to be the first to do something?

 **Think Aloud** In *America's Champion Swimmer: Gertrude Ederle* and "Women Athletes," we learned about the unique traits of some famous women athletes.

**Team Talk** Have students recall their Amazing Ideas about one of a kind and use these ideas to help them demonstrate their understanding of the Question of the Week.

Next Week's Concept
## Unique Behaviors of Animals

What behaviors are unique to different animals?

**Poster Preview** Prepare students for next week by using Week 5 ELL Poster 20. Read the Talk-Through to introduce the concept and vocabulary. Ask students to identify and describe actions in the art.

**Selection Summary** Send home the summary of the next week's selection, *Fly, Eagle, Fly!,* in English and in students' home languages, if available in the *ELL Handbook.* They can read the summary with family members.

What behaviors are unique to different animals? Tell students that next week they will be reading about an eagle that thinks it is a chicken.

**Preview Next Week**

# Assessment Checkpoints for the Week

## Weekly Assessment

Use pp. 109–114 of *Weekly Tests* to check:

✔ **Phonics/Word Analysis** Suffixes *-er, -or, -ess, -ist*

✔  **Comprehension** Fact and Opinion

✔ **Review Comprehension** Generalize

✔ **Selection Vocabulary**

| | |
|---|---|
| celebrate | medals |
| continued | stirred |
| current | strokes |
| drowned | |

Weekly Tests

## Differentiated Assessment

**Advanced**

Use pp. 109–114 of *Fresh Reads for Fluency and Comprehension* to check:

✔  **Comprehension** Fact and Opinion

✔ **Review Comprehension** Generalize

✔ **Fluency** Words Correct Per Minute

**OL**
**On-Level**

**SI**
**Strategic Intervention**

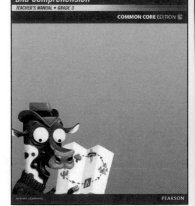

Fresh Reads for Fluency and Comprehension

## Managing Assessment

Use *Assessment Handbook* for:

✔ **Weekly Assessment Blackline Masters for Monitoring Progress**

✔ **Observation Checklists**

✔ **Record-Keeping Forms**

✔ **Portfolio Assessment**

Assessment Handbook

# TEACHER NOTES

## DAY 1 Differentiate Vocabulary

- **Word Knowledge** Amazing Words
- **Read** "Women in the Olympics"
- **Inquiry** Identify Questions

"Women in the Olympics"
pp. 50–51

## DAY 2 Differentiate Comprehension

- **Word Knowledge** Selection Vocabulary
- **Access Text** Read *America's Champion Swimmer: Gertrude Ederle*
- **Inquiry** Investigate

## DAY 3 Differentiate Close Reading

- **Word Knowledge** Develop Vocabulary
- **Close Reading** Read *America's Champion Swimmer: Gertrude Ederle*
- **Inquiry** Investigate

## DAY 4 Differentiate Vocabulary

- **Word Knowledge** Amazing Words
- **Read** "Women Athletes"
- **Inquiry** Organize

## DAY 5 Differentiate Reteaching

- **Conventions** Contractions
- **Reread** "Women in the Olympics" or Leveled Readers
- **Inquiry** Communicate

Teacher Guides and Student pages can be found in the Leveled Reader Database.

 Place English Language Learners in the groups that correspond to their reading abilities.
**If...** students need scaffolding and practice,
**then...** use the ELL Notes on the instructional pages.

## Independent Practice

**Independent Practice Stations**

See pp. 116h and 116i for Independent Stations.

**Pearson Trade Book Library**

See the Leveled Reader Database for lesson plans and student pages.

**Reading Street Digital Path**

Independent Practice Activities are available in the Digital Path.

**Independent Reading**

See p. 116i for independent reading suggestions.

## © Common Core State Standards

**Informational Text 1.** Ask and answer questions to demonstrate understanding of a text, referring explicitly to the text as the basis for the answers. **Foundational Skills 4.** Read with sufficient accuracy and fluency to support comprehension. **Language 4.** Determine or clarify the meaning of unknown and multiple-meaning words and phrases based on grade 3 reading and content, choosing flexibly from a range of strategies. **Also Language 6.**

## Independent Reading Options

**Trade Book Library**

**eSTREET INTERACTIVE**
www.ReadingStreet.com

Teacher Guides are available on the Leveled Reader Database.

### ELL

**If...** students need more scaffolding and practice with **Vocabulary, then...** use the activities on pp. DI•92–DI•93 in the Teacher Resources section on SuccessNet.

## OL On-Level

# ① Build Word Knowledge
## Practice Amazing Words

**DEFINE IT** Elicit the definition for the word *imagination* from students. Ask: How would you describe *imagination* to another student? (Possible response: Imagination is the ability to create new images in the mind.) Clarify or give a definition when necessary. Continue with the words *magnificent* and *ordinary*.

**Team Talk** **TALK ABOUT IT** Have students internalize meanings. Ask: How can you pair the Amazing Words together in a sentence? (Possible response: Use your imagination to turn an ordinary day into a magnificent day.) Allow time for students to play with the words. Review the concept map with students. Discuss other words they can add to the concept map.

# ② Text-Based Comprehension
## Read

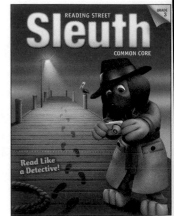

**READ ALOUD "Women in the Olympics"** Have partners read "Women in the Olympics" from *Reading Street Sleuth* on pp. 50–51.

**ACCESS TEXT** Discuss the Sleuth Work section with students before they work on it. Remind students that they can use these steps with other texts they read.

**Gather Evidence** Have partners work together to note evidence in the text. Invite partners to share this evidence as you make a master list. Discuss whether the evidence was fact or opinion.

**Ask Questions** Have partners share their questions with each other. Talk together about where students might look to find the answers to their questions. If time permits, have partners choose one to research further.

**Make Your Case** Have students discuss their opinions, sharing convincing reasons for those opinions. Encourage students to use facts from the text or other sources that may also support their opinions.

On-Level

# 1 Build Word Knowledge

## Practice Selection Vocabulary

| | | | |
|---|---|---|---|
| celebrate | continued | current | drowned |
| medals | stirred | strokes | |

**DEFINE IT** Discuss the definition for the word *current* with students. Ask: How would you describe a current to another student? (Possible response: A current is a flow or stream of water.) Continue with the remaining words.

**Team Talk** **TALK ABOUT IT** Have pairs use the selection vocabulary in sentences to internalize meaning. Ask: How can you pair the selection vocabulary together in a sentence? (Possible response: The swimmer's strong strokes saved her from being drowned by the current.) Allow time for students to play with the words and then share their sentences.

# 2 Read

## America's Champion Swimmer: Gertrude Ederle

If you read *America's Champion Swimmer: Gertrude Ederle* during whole group time, then use the following instruction.

**ACCESS TEXT** Reread the last paragraph on p. 129 and the first two paragraphs on p. 130. Ask questions to check understanding. What was Trudy determined to do? (swim the English Channel) Why did most people think that Trudy would never be able to accomplish this? (She was a woman. No woman had made it across the English Channel. In those days, most people thought of women as the "weaker sex.")

Have students identify sections from today's reading that they did not completely understand. Reread them aloud and clarify misunderstandings.

If you are reading *America's Champion Swimmer: Gertrude Ederle* during small group time, then return to pp. 126–131a to guide the reading.

**SMALL GROUP TIME**

## More Reading for Group Time

Biography

*Great Women in U.S. History*

by Megan Litwin
illustrated by Aleksey Ivanov

**ON-LEVEL**

### Reviews
• Fact and Opinion
• Questioning
• Selection Vocabulary

Use this suggested Leveled Reader or other text at students' instructional level.

Use the Leveled Reader Database for lesson plans and student pages for *Great Women in U.S. History*.

**OL** On-Level

## Common Core State Standards

**Informational Text 3.** Describe the relationship between a series of historical events, scientific ideas or concepts, or steps in technical procedures in a text, using language that pertains to time, sequence, and cause/effect. **Informational Text 5.** Use text features and search tools (c.g., kcy words, sidebars, hyperlinks) to locate information relevant to a given topic efficiently. **Language 4.a.** Use sentence-level context as a clue to the meaning of a word or phrase. **Also Language 6.**

## ① Build Word Knowledge

### Develop Vocabulary

**REREAD FOR VOCABULARY** Reread the second paragraph on p. 132. Introduce: Let's read this paragraph to find out what *accompany* means. To help students understand the word *accompany,* ask questions related to the context, such as: Where will the tugboat be as Trudy swims the channel? What is its purpose? Have students use a dictionary or thesaurus to find out more information about the word *accompany.*

## ② Read

### America's Champion Swimmer: Gertrude Ederle

If you read *America's Champion Swimmer: Gertrude Ederle* during whole group time, then use the following instruction.

**CLOSE READING** Read pp. 134–135. Have students note questions they have and things they wonder about as they read though the text. Then have them make a list of their questions in the order that they occur. (How could Trudy keep swimming when the waves were so high? Why didn't she give up? How long will she be able to keep swimming? How did she feel when she saw the flares lit up along the shore? Why did she think women everywhere would celebrate her victory?)

Ask: How does asking questions help you understand what you're reading? (It makes you think more carefully about the content and makes you focus on what might happen next.)

If you are reading *America's Champion Swimmer: Gertrude Ederle* during small group time, then return to pp. 132–139a to guide the reading.

**If...** students need more scaffolding and practice with the **Main Selection,** **then...** use the activities on p. DI•97 in the Teacher Resources section on SuccessNet.

 On-Level

# 1 Build Word Knowledge

## Practice Amazing Words

| | | | |
|---|---|---|---|
| ordinary | erect | imagination | suspend |
| assemble | accompany | magnificent | provision |
| organize | spectacle | | |

**Team Talk** **LANGUAGE DEVELOPMENT** Have students practice building more complex sentences. Display a sentence starter and have students add oral phrases or clauses using the Amazing Words. For example: The students _____. (The students were organized, / and they carefully assembled the provisions / that would accompany them on the trip.) Guide students to add at least three phrases or clauses per sentence.

# 2 Read

## "Women Athletes"

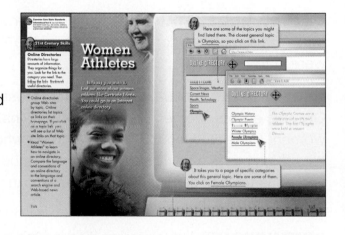

**BEFORE READING** Read aloud the information about online directories on p. 144. Explain that online directories can help students find information for research papers. Have students preview "Women Athletes" and set a purpose for reading. Ask: What features do you see that are different from stories you have read? (topics and headings) Why are some words in red type? (so the reader can easily find important or interesting parts)

**DURING READING** Have students read along with you while tracking the print. Ask:

- How is an online directory organized? (in broad topics and specific categories)

- How is this online information similar to and different from a biography? (This online information tells about someone's life like a biography, but it is briefer and lacks a beginning, middle, and end.)

**AFTER READING** Have students write a paragraph comparing and contrasting Wilma Rudolph and Gertrude Ederle. Then have students complete the Get Online! activity.

eStreet Interactive
www.ReadingStreet.com

Pearson eText
• Student Edition

SMALL GROUP TIME

## Independent Reading Options

**Trade Book Library**

eStreet Interactive
www.ReadingStreet.com

Teacher Guides are available on the Leveled Reader Database.

## On-Level

### Common Core State Standards

**Informational Text 1.** Ask and answer questions to demonstrate understanding of a text, referring explicitly to the text as the basis for the answers. **Foundational Skills 4.** Read with sufficient accuracy and fluency to support comprehension. **Writing 1.** Write opinion pieces on topics or texts, supporting a point of view with reasons. **Language 4.** Determine or clarify the meaning of unknown and multiple-meaning words and phrases based on grade 3 reading and content, choosing flexibly from a range of strategies. **Also Speaking/ Listening 1.d.**

## 1 Build Word Knowledge

### Practice Contractions

**IDENTIFY** Choral read the bottom of p. 143 with students and discuss contractions. Have partners reread the model autobiography to find examples of how the author used contractions. Encourage students to use the model student autobiography on the same page to practice. Allow time for students to discuss their examples and correct any misunderstandings.

## 2 Text-Based Comprehension

### Read

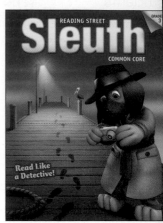

**REREAD "Women in the Olympics"** Have partners reread "Women in the Olympics."

**EXTEND UNDERSTANDING** Talk together about modern Olympics in comparison to how the Olympics were in the past.

**PERFORMANCE TASK • Prove It!** In most Olympic events, women compete only against women. Have students debate as a group whether they think this is a good idea. Encourage students to make a list of the pros and cons to each side of the issue. They can then use this list to support their opinions during the debate.

**COMMUNICATE** Have groups discuss the most compelling arguments debated. Invite students to tell why they found certain opinions to be more compelling than others.

### More Reading for Group Time

**ON-LEVEL**

**Reviews**
• Fact and Opinion
• Questioning
• Selection Vocabulary

Use this suggested Leveled Reader or other text at students' instructional level.

### eSTREET INTERACTIVE
www.ReadingStreet.com

Use the Leveled Reader Database for lesson plans and student pages for *Great Women in U.S. History.*

**SI** Strategic Intervention

# 1 Build Word Knowledge

## Reteach Amazing Words

Repeat the definition of the word *imagination.* We learned that *imagination* is the ability to create new images in the mind. Then use the word in a sentence. Use your *imagination* to turn a regular day into a great day.

**Team Talk** **TALK ABOUT IT** Have students take turns using the word *imagination* in a sentence. Continue this routine to practice the Amazing Words *magnificent* and *ordinary*. Review the concept map with students. Discuss other words they can add to the concept map.

**Corrective feedback** | **If...** students need more practice with the Amazing Words, **then...** use visuals from the Student Edition or online sources to clarify meaning.

# 2 Text-Based Comprehension

## Read

**REREAD "Women in the Olympics"** Have students track the print as you read "Women in the Olympics" from *Reading Street Sleuth* on pp. 50–51.

**ACCESS TEXT** Discuss the Sleuth Work section with students and provide support as needed as they work on it. Remind students that they can use these steps with other texts they read.

**Gather Evidence** Remind students that facts can be proven true or false. Have partners work together to note evidence in the text. Invite partners to identify their evidence as fact or opinion.

**Ask Questions** Have partners write and share their questions with each other. Talk together about where students might look to find the answers to their questions. Invite students to share what part of the text triggered their questions.

**Make Your Case** Have students choose a side and discuss their opinions. Remind them to share convincing reasons for those opinions. Encourage students to use facts from the text or other sources that may also support their opinions.

**eSTREET INTERACTIVE**
www.ReadingStreet.com

**Pearson eText**
• Leveled Reader Database
• *Reading Street Sleuth*

## More Reading for Group Time

**CONCEPT LITERACY**
**Practice**
Concept Words

**BELOW-LEVEL**
**Reviews**
• Fact and Opinion
• Questioning
• Selection Vocabulary

Use these suggested Leveled Readers or other text at students' instructional level.

**eSTREET INTERACTIVE**
www.ReadingStreet.com

Use the Leveled Reader Database for lesson plans and student pages for *Women Who Were First!* and *Across the English Channel.*

**Strategic Intervention**

## Common Core State Standards

**Informational Text 3.** Describe the relationship between a series of historical events, scientific ideas or concepts, or steps in technical procedures in a text, using language that pertains to time, sequence, and cause/effect. **Foundational Skills 4.** Read with sufficient accuracy and fluency to support comprehension. **Language 4.** Determine or clarify the meaning of unknown and multiple-meaning words and phrases based on grade 3 reading and content, choosing flexibly from a range of strategies. **Language 4.a.** Use sentence-level context as a clue to the meaning of a word or phrase. **Also Informational Text 1.**

## 1 Build Word Knowledge
### Reteach Selection Vocabulary

**DEFINE IT** Describe *strokes* to a friend. Give a definition when necessary. Restate the word in student-friendly terms and clarify meaning with a visual.

| | | | |
|---|---|---|---|
| celebrate | continued | current | drowned |
| medals | stirred | strokes | |

**Team Talk** **TALK ABOUT IT** Have you used strokes to do something? Turn and talk to your partner about this. Rephrase students' examples for usage when necessary or to correct misunderstandings. Continue with the remaining words.

**Corrective feedback** | **If...** students need more practice with selection vocabulary, **then...** use the *Envision It! Pictured Vocabulary Cards.*

## 2 Read
### *America's Champion Swimmer: Gertrude Ederle*

If you read *America's Champion Swimmer: Gertrude Ederle* during whole group time, then use the instruction below.

**ACCESS TEXT** Reread the last paragraph on p. 129 and the first two paragraphs on p. 130. Ask questions to check understanding. What was Trudy determined to do? (swim the English Channel) Why did she want to do this? (No woman had ever done it.) Why did most people think that Trudy would never succeed? (In those days, most people thought of women as the "weaker sex.")

Have students identify sections they did not understand. Reread them aloud. Clarify the meaning of each section to build understanding.

If you are reading *America's Champion Swimmer: Gertrude Ederle* during small group time, then return to pp. 126–131a to guide the reading.

## Independent Reading Options

**Trade Book Library**

**eSTREET INTERACTIVE**
www.ReadingStreet.com

Teacher Guides are available on the Leveled Reader Database.

**Strategic Intervention**

# 1 Build Word Knowledge

## Develop Vocabulary

**REREAD FOR VOCABULARY** Reread the second paragraph on p. 132.
Introduce: Let's read this paragraph to find out what *accompany* means. To
help students understand the word *accompany,* ask questions related to the
context, such as: What is Trudy doing? Who is on the tugboat? Where will the
tugboat be as Trudy is swimming? What is its purpose?

**Corrective feedback** | **If...** students have difficulty understanding the word *accompany,*
**then...** guide students to use a dictionary or thesaurus.

# 2 Read

## America's Champion Swimmer: Gertrude Ederle

If you read *America's Champion Swimmer: Gertrude Ederle* during whole group time, then use the instruction below.

**CLOSE READING** Read pp. 134–135. Have students search though the text
to find time references that help to explain the sequence of the events in the
story. As a class, make a list of these words and phrases in the order they
occur. (At about one-thirty in the afternoon, For a while, By six o'clock, In the
next few hours, At times, Now, When)

Now let's use the times we listed to retell what happened in this part of the
story. (It started to rain at one-thirty in the afternoon. A strong wind stirred
up the water and made it hard for Trudy to swim forward. By six o'clock the
waves were twenty feet high. Her trainer wanted her to quit, but she said no.
In the next few hours, the sea got rougher and pulled the boats away from
Trudy. She was scared. Then her leg got stiff and she had trouble kicking. Her
trainer told her to come out of the water.)

If you are reading *America's Champion Swimmer: Gertrude Ederle* during
small group time, then return to pp. 132–139a to guide the reading.

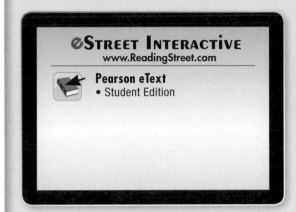

**eSTREET INTERACTIVE**
www.ReadingStreet.com

**Pearson eText**
• Student Edition

**SMALL GROUP TIME**

**If...** students need more scaffolding
and practice with the **Main Selection,**
**then...** use the activities on p. DI•97
in the Teacher Resources section on
SuccessNet.

## Strategic Intervention

### Common Core State Standards

**Informational Text 5.** Use text features and search tools (e.g., key words, sidebars, hyperlinks) to locate information relevant to a given topic efficiently. **Foundational Skills 4.** Read with sufficient accuracy and fluency to support comprehension. **Writing 1.** Write opinion pieces on topics or texts, supporting a point of view with reasons. **Language 3.** Use knowledge of language and its conventions when writing, speaking, reading, or listening. **Also Writing 10., Speaking/Listening 1., 1.d., Language 6.**

## ① Build Word Knowledge

### Review Amazing Words

| | | | |
|---|---|---|---|
| ordinary | erect | imagination | suspend |
| assemble | accompany | magnificent | provision |
| organize | spectacle | | |

**Team Talk** **LANGUAGE DEVELOPMENT** Have students practice building more complex sentences. Display a sentence starter and have students add oral phrases or clauses using the Amazing Words. For example: The kids _____. (The kids assembled / by the bus / and packed provisions for the trip.) Guide students to add at least two phrases or clauses per sentence.

**Corrective feedback** | **If...** students have difficulty using Amazing Words orally, **then...** review the meaning of each of the words.

## ② Read

### "Women Athletes"

**BEFORE READING** Read aloud the information about online directories on p. 144. An online directory is like a table of contents or an index. It can help you find information about a topic. This selection will explain a search for information about women athletes.

Read the rest of the panel. Then have students find the cursor on each reproduced computer screen and read the name of the link that was chosen.

**DURING READING** Have students perform a choral reading of the selection. When you get to the article about Wilma Rudolph, point out the subheads. Subheads can help you locate specific information quickly. What are the subheads in this article? (They are Name, Birthdate, Birthplace, Family Background, and Achievements.)

**AFTER READING** Have students share their reactions to the selection. Then guide them through the Get Online! activity.

**If...** students need more scaffolding and practice with **Amazing Words, then...** use the Routine on pp. xxxvi–xxxvii in the *ELL Handbook.*

**SI** **Strategic Intervention**

# 1 Build Word Knowledge

## Review Contractions

**IDENTIFY** Choral read the bottom of p. 143 with students to review contractions. Have partners reread the model autobiography on p. 143 to find examples of how the author used contractions. Allow time for students to discuss their examples and correct any misunderstandings.

# 2 Text-Based Comprehension

## Read

**REREAD "Women in the Olympics"** Have partners reread "Women in the Olympics," alternating paragraphs.

**EXTEND UNDERSTANDING** Talk together about how women were treated early on in Olympic history. Have students identify facts that tell about this.

**PERFORMANCE TASK • Prove It!** In most Olympic events, women compete only against women. Have students debate as a group whether they think this is a good idea. Encourage students to make a list of at least three pros and three cons to each side of the issue. They can then use this list to support their opinions during the debate.

**COMMUNICATE** Have groups discuss how the debate went. Talk together about the notion that there is no winner in a debate. Remind students that it is important to not only share their opinions but also convincing reasons.

**SMALL GROUP TIME**

## More Reading for Group Time

**CONCEPT LITERACY**
**Practice**
Concept Words

**BELOW-LEVEL**
**Reviews**
• Fact and Opinion
• Questioning
• Selection Vocabulary

Use these suggested Leveled Readers or other text at students' instructional level.

Use the Leveled Reader Database for lesson plans and student pages for *Women Who Were First!* and *Across the English Channel.*

**A** Advanced

## ① Build Word Knowledge

### Extend Amazing Words

**Team Talk** Have students define *imagination*. Discuss other words associated with *imagination*. (*fantasy, originality*) Continue with *magnificent* and *ordinary*.

## ② Text-Based Comprehension

### Read

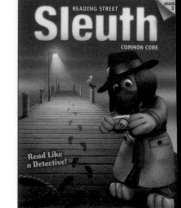

**READ "Women in the Olympics"** Have students read "Women in the Olympics" from *Reading Street Sleuth* on pp. 50–51.

**ACCESS TEXT** Discuss the Sleuth Work section with students before they work on it. Remind students that they can use these steps with other texts they read.

**Gather Evidence** Have students note evidence in the text. Invite them to share their evidence, discussing whether or not it is factual.

**Ask Questions** Talk together about the questions students asked. Have students share where they might look to find the answer to at least one of their questions.

**Make Your Case** Have students share their opinions, noting convincing reasons to support those opinions. Encourage students to use facts from the text to support their opinions.

## ③ Inquiry: Extend Concepts

**IDENTIFY QUESTIONS** Have students think about questions they have about the qualities it takes to be the first person to do something. Ask them to select an historical figure who became the first to do something and write a profile about that person's qualities. Throughout the week, they will gather information. On Day 5, they will present what they have learned using pictures and a presentation about that person's life.

**If...** students need more scaffolding and practice with **Vocabulary, then...** use the activities on pp. DI•92–DI•93 in the Teacher Resources section on SuccessNet.

 **Advanced**

# 1 Build Word Knowledge

## Extend Selection Vocabulary

**Team Talk** Have partners use the selection vocabulary in sentences to inter-alize their meanings. Have students use as many of the words as they can while making sure the sentence is grammatically correct. (Possible response: he day after the big meet, the team continued to celebrate winning five medals.) Continue with additional selection vocabulary words.

| | | | |
|---|---|---|---|
| celebrate | continued | current | drowned |
| medals | stirred | strokes | |

# 2 Read

## America's Champion Swimmer: Gertrude Ederle

If you read *America's Champion Swimmer: Gertrude Ederle* during whole group time, then use the instruction below.

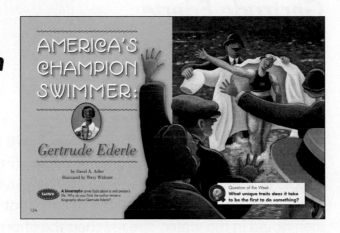

**ACCESS TEXT** Reread the last paragraph on p. 129 and the first two paragraphs on p. 130. Discuss the similarities and differences in the information provided. (Similar: Both pages tell how Trudy is determined to swim the English Channel. Different: Page 129 contains mostly facts about Trudy's records, a description of the channel, and who a listing who had made it across. Page 130 contains mostly opinions, including a newspaper editorial and the common belief that she couldn't do it.)

If you are reading *America's Champion Swimmer: Gertrude Ederle* during small group time, then return to pp. 126–131a to guide the reading.

# 3 Inquiry: Extend Concepts

**INVESTIGATE** Encourage students to identify relevant and credible sites to gather information about personal qualities. Have students consider how they will present their information.

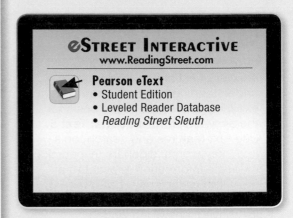

**eStreet Interactive**
www.ReadingStreet.com

**Pearson eText**
• Student Edition
• Leveled Reader Database
• *Reading Street Sleuth*

## More Reading for Group Time

**ADVANCED**

**Reviews**
• Fact and Opinion
• Questioning

Use this suggested Leveled Reader or other text at students' instructional level.

**eStreet Interactive**
www.ReadingStreet.com

Use the Leveled Reader Database for lesson plans and student pages for *Changing Times: Women in the Early Twentieth Century.*

**SMALL GROUP TIME**

## A Advanced

## 1 Build Word Knowledge
### Develop Vocabulary

**REREAD FOR VOCABULARY** Reread the last paragraph on p. 137. Let's read this paragraph to find out what *prowess* means. (superior ability, skill) Discuss meaning and context with students.

## 2 Read
### America's Champion Swimmer: Gertrude Ederle

If you read *America's Champion Swimmer: Gertrude Ederle* during whole group time, then use the instruction below.

**CLOSE READING** Read pp. 134–136. Have students list statements of fact and statements of opinion from the pages. (Facts: The water was so rough the people on the tugboat were seasick. The waves were sometimes twenty feet high. Trudy continued to fight the twenty-foot waves and the tide. After fourteen hours in the water, she reached the shore. Opinions: All the women of the world would celebrate. The myth that women were the weaker sex was "shattered and shattered forever." )

Ask: What conclusion can you draw from the facts you recorded? (Trudy faced enormous obstacles during her swim but her determination and skill as a swimmer allowed her to overcome them.) What conclusion can you draw from the opinions you recorded? (Some people saw her accomplishment as a great achievement for women everywhere.)

If you are reading *America's Champion Swimmer: Gertrude Ederle* during small group time, then return to pp. 132–139a to guide the reading.

## 3 Inquiry: Extend Concepts

**INVESTIGATE** Provide time for students to investigate their historical figure in books or online. If necessary, help them locate information that is focused on their topics.

---

## C Common Core State Standards

**Informational Text 1.** Ask and answer questions to demonstrate understanding of a text, referring explicitly to the text as the basis for the answers. **Informational Text 5.** Use text features and search tools (e.g., key words, sidebars, hyperlinks) to locate information relevant to a given topic efficiently. **Language 3.** Use knowledge of language and its conventions when writing, speaking, reading, or listening. **Also Writing 7., 8., Language 6.**

## Independent Reading Options

**Trade Book Library**

### eStreet Interactive
www.ReadingStreet.com

Teacher Guides are available on the Leveled Reader Database.

## ELL

**If...** students need more scaffolding and practice with the **Main Selection, then...** use the activities on p. DI•97 in the Teacher Resources section on SuccessNet.

**A** Advanced

eStreet Interactive
www.ReadingStreet.com

Pearson eText
• Student Edition

# Build Word Knowledge

## Extend Amazing Words and Selection Vocabulary

| | | |
|---|---|---|
| ordinary | erect | imagination |
| suspend | assemble | accompany |
| magnificent | provision | organize |
| spectacle | | |

| | | |
|---|---|---|
| celebrate | continued | current |
| drowned | medals | stirred |
| strokes | | |

**Team Talk** Have students practice building more complex sentences. Display a sentence starter and have students add oral phrases or clauses using the Amazing Words and the selection vocabulary. For example: The group _____. (The group assembled to celebrate their medals / and enjoy a magnificent lunch / that was organized by their friends and family.) Guide students to add at least three phrases or clauses per sentence.

# 2 Read

## "Women Athletes"

**BEFORE READING** Have students read the panel information on online directories on p. 144. Then have students use the text features to set a purpose for reading "Women Athletes."

**DURING READING** Point out that the user begins with a list of general topics and then clicks on links to find specific information. How is an online directory different from a biography? (With the directory, the user chooses which information to access, while the reader of the biography usually reads the information from beginning to end.)

**AFTER READING** Have students complete the Get Online! activity.

# 3 Inquiry: Extend Concepts

**ORGANIZE INFORMATION** Provide time for students to organize their information into a format that will effectively communicate the life of their historical figure to their audience. Provide any necessary materials, such as poster board, markers and other supplies, or computer time.

**SMALL GROUP TIME**

### Independent Reading Options

**Trade Book Library**

**eStreet Interactive**
www.ReadingStreet.com

Teacher Guides are available on the Leveled Reader Database.

## Common Core State Standards

**Foundational Skills 4.** Read with sufficient accuracy and fluency to support comprehension. **Writing 1.** Write opinion pieces on topics or texts, supporting a point of view with reasons. **Speaking/Listening 4.** Report on a topic or text, tell a story, or recount an experience with appropriate facts and relevant, descriptive details, speaking clearly at an understandable pace.

## More Reading for Group Time

**ADVANCED**

**Reviews**
• Fact and Opinion
• Questioning

Use this suggested Leveled Reader or other text at students' instructional level.

### eStreet Interactive
www.ReadingStreet.com

Use the Leveled Reader Database for lesson plans and student pages for *Changing Times: Women in the Early Twentieth Century.*

**A** Advanced

# 1 Build Word Knowledge

## Extend Contractions

**IDENTIFY AND EXTEND** Choral read the bottom of p. 143 with students and have them explain the form and function of contractions. Have partners reread the model autobiography to find examples of how the author used contractions. Encourage students to use the model autobiography on the same page to practice. Allow time for students to discuss their examples and correct any misunderstandings.

# 2 Text-Based Comprehension

## Read

**REREAD "Women in the Olympics"** Have small groups reread the selection. Have small groups discuss how it might have felt to be a women athlete in early Olympic games.

**EXTEND UNDERSTANDING** Talk together about the modern woman athlete and how she compares to the early woman athlete.

**PERFORMANCE TASK • Prove It!** In most Olympic events, women compete only against women. Have students debate as a group whether they think this is a good idea. Encourage students to list their convincing reasons along with supportive evidence.

**COMMUNICATE** Have groups discuss how their debate went. Remind students that no one is a winner. Have them describe the experience they had debating.

# 3 Inquiry: Extend Concepts

**COMMUNICATE** Have students share their inquiry projects on their historical figures with the rest of the class. Provide the following tips for presenting.

• Match your tone of voice and your pitch to your content.

• Speak loudly and clearly.

• Make eye contact with the audience and point to visuals as you speak.

# Indiana Common Core Edition

## This Week's Target Skills and Strategies

| Target Skills and Strategies |  Common Core State Standards for English Language Arts | Indiana Academic Standards for English Language Arts |
|---|---|---|
| **Phonics and Spelling**<br>Skill: Syllables VCCCV | **CCSS Foundational Skills 3.c.** Decode multisyllable words (e.g., *supper, chimpanzee, refrigerator, terrible, frightening*). **(Also CCSS Language 2.f.)** | **IN 3.1.2** Read words with several syllables. |
| **Text-Based Comprehension**<br>Skill: Cause and Effect | **CCSS Informational Text 3.** Describe the relationship between a series of historical events, scientific ideas or concepts, or steps in technical procedures in a text, using language that pertains to time, sequence, and cause/effect. **(Also CCSS Informational Text 1.)** | **IN 3.2.8** Distinguish between cause and effect and between fact and opinion in informational text. |
| Strategy: Monitor and Clarify | **CCSS Informational Text 1.** Ask and answer questions to demonstrate understanding of a text, referring explicitly to the text as the basis for the answers. | **IN 3.2.2** Ask questions and support answers by connecting prior knowledge with literal information from the text. **(Also IN 3.2.3)** |
| **Vocabulary**<br>Skill: Unknown Words<br>Strategy: Dictionary/Glossary | **CCSS Language 4.** Determine or clarify the meaning of unknown and multiple-meaning word and phrases based on *grade 3 reading and content,* choosing flexibly from a range of strategies. **(Also CCSS Language 4.d.)** | **IN 3.1.7** Use a dictionary to learn the meaning and pronunciation of unknown words. |
| **Fluency**<br>Skill: Rate | **CCSS Foundational Skills 4.b.** Read on-level prose and poetry orally with accuracy, appropriate rate, and expression on successive readings. | **IN 3.1.3** Read aloud grade-level-appropriate literary and informational texts fluently and accurately and with appropriate timing, change in voice, and expression. |
| **Listening and Speaking**<br>Book Review | **CCSS Speaking/Listening 1.a.** Come to discussions prepared, having read or studied required material; explicitly draw on that preparation and other information known about the topic to explore ideas under discussion. | The Indiana Academic Standards for Listening and Speaking are not currently assessed on ISTEP+ assessments. Educators and students should implement the Common Core Standards for Speaking and Listening as soon as possible. |
| **Six-Trait Writing**<br>Trait of the Week: Word Choice | **CCSS Writing 3.c.** Use temporal words and phrases to signal event order. | **IN 3.5.1** Write narratives. |
| **Writing**<br>Summary | **CCSS Writing 3.a.** Establish a situation and introduce a narrator and/or characters; organize an event sequence that unfolds naturally. **(Also CCSS Writing 5.)** | **IN 3.5.1** Write narratives. |
| **Conventions**<br>Skill: Prepositions | **CCSS Language 1.** Demonstrate command of the conventions of standard English grammar and usage when writing or speaking. | **IN 3.6** Students write using Standard English conventions appropriate to this grade level. |

## This Week's Cross-Curricular Standards and Resources

### Cross-Curricular Indiana Academic Standards for Social Studies

**Social Studies**
**IN 3.3.7** Describe how climate and the physical characteristics of a region affect the vegetation and animal life living there.
**IN 3.3.11** Identify and describe the relationship between human systems and physical systems and the impact they have on each other.

### Reading Street Sleuth

*Communicating Without Words*
pp. 52–53

Follow the path to close reading using the Super Sleuth tips:

- Gather Evidence
- Ask Questions
- Make Your Case
- Prove it!

### More Reading in Science and Social Studies

Concept Literacy    Below Level    On Level

Advanced    ELL    ELD

ISBN-13: 978-0-328-73390-3    ISBN-10: 0-328-73390-3

# Your 90-Minute Reading Block

| | **Whole Group** | **Formative Assessment** | **Small Group** OL On Level  SI Strategic Intervention  A Advanced | **Daily Independent Options** |
|---|---|---|---|---|
| | | How do I make my small groups flexible? | What are my other students reading and learning every day in Small Groups? | What do my other students do when I lead Small Groups? |
| **DAY 1** | **Content Knowledge**<br>Build Oral Language/Vocabulary<br>**Phonics/Word Analysis**<br>**Read Decodable Reader**<br>**Text-Based Comprehension**<br>**Selection Vocabulary**<br>**Research and Inquiry**<br>Step 1–Identify and Focus Topic<br>**Spelling Pretest**<br>Connect to Phonics/Word Analysis | **Monitor Progress**<br>Check Oral Vocabulary | *Differentiate Vocabulary*<br>**Build Word Knowledge**<br>OL Practice Amazing Words<br>SI Reteach Amazing Words<br>A Extend Amazing Words<br>OL SI A **Text-Based Comprehension**<br>Read *Reading Street Sleuth*, pp. 52–53 or Leveled Readers<br>A Inquiry Project<br>ELL Access Vocabulary | ⭐ **Independent Reading** ©<br>Suggestions for this week's independent reading:<br>• *A Picture Book of Harry Houdini*, by David A. Adler<br>• An information-rich Web site about Gertrude Ederle<br>• A book about women athletes |
| **DAY 2** | **Content Knowledge**<br>Build Oral Language/Vocabulary<br>**Phonics/Word Analysis**<br>**Vocabulary Skill**<br>**Text-Based Comprehension**<br>**Read** Main Selection, using Access Text Notes<br>**Research and Inquiry**<br>Step 2–Navigate/Search<br>**Spelling**<br>Connect to Phonics/Word Analysis | **Monitor Progress**<br>Formative Assessment: Check Word Reading | *Differentiate Comprehension*<br>**Build Word Knowledge**<br>OL Practice Selection Vocabulary<br>SI Reteach Selection Vocabulary<br>A Extend Selection Vocabulary<br>OL SI A **Access Text**<br>Read *Fly, Eagle, Fly!: An African Tale*<br>A Inquiry Project<br>ELL Access Comprehension Skill | **Book Talk**<br>Foster critical reading and discussion skills through independent and close reading.<br>Students should focus on discussing one or more of the following:<br>• Key Ideas and Details<br>• Craft and Structure<br>• Integration of Ideas |
| **DAY 3** | **Content Knowledge**<br>Build Oral Language/Vocabulary<br>**Phonics/Word Analysis**<br>**Read Decodable Passage**<br>**Text-Based Comprehension**<br>Read Main Selection, using Close Reading Notes<br>**Fluency**<br>**Research and Inquiry**<br>Step 3–Analyze Information<br>**Spelling**<br>Connect to Phonics/Word Analysis | **Monitor Progress**<br>Check Retelling | *Differentiate Close Reading*<br>OL SI **Reread to Develop Vocabulary**<br>A **Reread to Extend Vocabulary**<br>OL SI A **Close Reading**<br>Read *Fly, Eagle, Fly!: An African Tale*<br>A Inquiry Project<br>ELL Access Main Selection |  **Pearson eText**<br>• Student Edition<br>• Decodable Readers<br>• Leveled Readers<br><br> **Trade Book Library** |
| **DAY 4** | **Content Knowledge**<br>Build Oral Language/Vocabulary<br>**Phonics/Word Analysis**<br>**Read Decodable Passage**<br>**Read Content Area Paired Selection with Genre Focus**<br>**Let's Learn It!**<br>Vocabulary/Fluency/Listening and Speaking<br>**Research and Inquiry**<br>Step 4–Synthesize<br>**Spelling**<br>Connect to Phonics/Word Analysis | **Monitor Progress**<br>Check Fluency | *Differentiate Vocabulary*<br>**Build Word Knowledge**<br>OL Develop Language Using Amazing Words<br>SI Review/Discuss Amazing Words<br>A Extend Amazing Words and Selection Vocabulary<br>OL SI A **Text-Based Comprehension**<br>Read "Purple Coyote"<br>A Inquiry Project<br>ELL Access Amazing Words |  **Materials from School or Classroom Library**<br><br>**Independent Stations**<br>Practice Last Week's Skills<br>⭐ Focus on these activities when time is limited.<br><br>**Word Wise**<br>**Word Work**<br>⭐ **Read for Meaning**<br>**Let's Write!**<br>**Words to Know**<br>⭐ **Get Fluent** |
| **DAY 5** | **Content Knowledge**<br>Build Oral Language/Vocabulary<br>**Text-Based Comprehension**<br>**Vocabulary Skill**<br>**Phonics/Word Analysis**<br>**Assessment**<br>Fluency, Comprehension<br>**Research and Inquiry**<br>Step 5–Communicate<br>**Spelling Test**<br>Connect to Phonics/Word Analysis | **Monitor Progress**<br>Formative Assessment: Check Oral Vocabulary<br><br>**Monitor Progress**<br>Fluency; Comprehension | *Differentiate Reteaching*<br>OL **Practice Prepositions**<br>SI **Review Prepositions**<br>A **Extend Prepositions**<br>OL SI A **Text-Based Comprehension**<br>Reread *Reading Street Sleuth*, pp. 52–53 or Leveled Readers<br>A Inquiry Project<br>ELL Access Conventions and Writing | |

## Assessment Resources

Common Core
Weekly Tests, pp. 115–120

Common Core Fresh Reads for Fluency
and Comprehension, pp. 115–120

Common Core
Unit 4 Benchmark Test

Common Core Success Tracker,
ExamView, and Online Lesson Planner

## Teaching the Common Core State Standards This Week

The Common Core State Standards for English Language Arts are divided into strands for **Reading** (including **Foundational Skills**), **Writing**, **Speaking and Listening**, and **Language**. The chart below shows some of the content you will teach this week, strand by strand. Turn to this week's 5-Day Planner on pages 150d–150e to see how this content is taught each day.

### Reading Strand

- **Phonics/Word Analysis:** Syllables VCCCV
- **Text-Based Comprehension:** Cause and Effect; Monitor and Clarify
- **Fluency:** Rate

- **Literary Terms:** Sensory Details
- **Genre:** Main Selection: Folk Tale; Paired Selection: Trickster Tale

### Common Core State Standards for English Language Arts

### Writing Strand

- **Writing Mini-Lesson:** Summary
- **Trait:** Word Choice
- **Look Back and Write:** Text Evidence

### Speaking and Listening Strand

- **Content Knowledge:** Build Oral Language
- **Listening and Speaking:** Book Review
- **Research and Inquiry**

### Language Strand

- **Oral Vocabulary: Amazing Words** *armor, agile, snout, protrude, extraordinary, scenery, pesky, unfurl, coil, intersection*
- **Vocabulary:** Unknown Words; Dictionary/Glossary
- **Selection Vocabulary:** *scrambled, gully, echoed, valley, reeds, clutched, thatch*

- **Academic Vocabulary:** *syllable, transition words, preposition, prepositional phrase, transitional word, folk tale, outline, limericks, free verse poems, imagery, rhyming poems*
- **Conventions:** Prepositions
- **Spelling:** Syllables VCCCV

# Text-Based Comprehension

## Text Complexity Measures

Use the rubric to familiarize yourself with the text complexity of *Fly Eagle, Fly!: An African Tale*.

## Bridge to Complex Knowledge

| Quantitative Measures | Lexile | 730L |
|---|---|---|
| | **Average Sentence Length** | 11.18 |
| | **Word Frequency** | 3.65 |

| Qualitative Measures | Levels of Meaning | understand the elements of folk tales; figurative language; simile |
|---|---|---|
| | **Structure** | simple; conventional structure |
| | **Language Conventionality and Clarity** | clear language; close alignment between pictures and text |
| | **Theme and Knowledge Demands** | cultural experience different from most readers |

| Reader and Task Suggestions | **FORMATIVE ASSESSMENT** Based on assessment results, use the **Reader and Task Suggestions** in Access Main Selection to scaffold the selection or support independence for students as they read *Fly Eagle, Fly!: An African Tale*. |
|---|---|

| READER AND TASK SUGGESTIONS | |
|---|---|
| **Preparing to Read the Text** | **Leveled Tasks** |
| • Review using a dictionary to find the meanings, syllable divisions, and pronunciations of unfamiliar words.<br>• Review the features of a folk tale.<br>• Remind students to adjust their reading rate as they encounter challenging vocabulary and concepts. | • **Theme and Knowledge Demands** If students have difficulty understanding the setting of this folk tale and the culture of its characters, have them name things in the picture on pp. 162–163 that provide clues that the story does not take place in the United States.<br>• **Structure** Many students may not have difficulty with the simple structure and clear language of this folk tale. Have students identify what happens first, next, and last and the conflict in the story. |

**Recommended Placement** Both the qualitative and quantitative measures suggest this text should be placed in the Grade 2–3 text complexity band, which is where both the Common Core State Standards and *Scott Foresman Reading Street* have placed it.

# Focus on Common Core State Standards ©

Folk tales are stories or legends from other lands and are handed down from one generation to the next. Where is this story from?

**Genre**

Question of the Week
**What behaviors are unique to different animals?**

**Main Selection, pp. 158–171**

**Paired Selection, pp. 176–181**

---

## Text-Based Comprehension

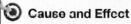 **Cause and Effect**
CCSS Informational Text 1.,
CCSS Informational Text 3.

**Monitor and Clarify**
CCSS Informational Text 1.

## Fluency

**Rate**
CCSS Foundational Skills 4.b.

## Writing and Conventions

**Trait:** Word Choice
CCSS Writing 3.c.

**Writing Mini-Lesson:** Summary
CCSS Writing 3.a., CCSS Writing 5.

**Conventions:** Prepositions
CCSS Language 1.

---

## Oral Vocabulary

### Amazing Words

| | |
|---|---|
| armor | scenery |
| agile | pesky |
| snout | unfurl |
| protrude | coil |
| extraordinary | intersection |

CCSS Language 6.

## Selection Vocabulary

**Unknown Words**
CCSS Language 4.,
CCSS Language 4.d.

**Dictionary/Glossary**
CCSS Language 4.d.

| | |
|---|---|
| clutched | scrambled |
| echoed | thatch |
| gully | valley |
| reeds | |

---

## Phonics and Spelling

**Syllables VCCCV**
CCSS Foundational Skills 3.c.,
CCSS Language 2.f.

| | |
|---|---|
| monster | pilgrim |
| surprise | contrast |
| hundred | explode |
| complete | district |
| control | address |
| sample | substance |
| instant | children |
| inspect | |

**Challenge Words**

| | |
|---|---|
| merchant | curtsy |
| embrace | contract |
| purchase | |

## Listening and Speaking

**Book Review**
CCSS Speaking/Listening 1.a.

---

*Fly, Eagle, Fly!* **150a**

# Preview Your Week

*What behaviors are unique to different animals?*

**Main Selection, pp. 158–171**

**Genre:** Folk Tale

**Vocabulary:** Unknown Words

**Text-Based Comprehension:** Cause and Effect

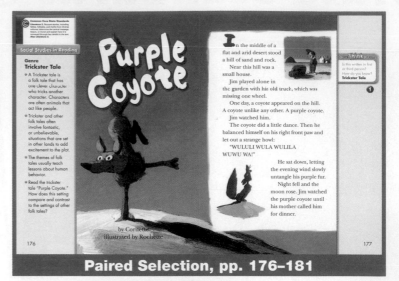

**Paired Selection, pp. 176–181**

**Social Studies in Reading**

**Genre:** Trickster Tale

# Build Content Knowledge

 Zoom in on ©

 **TIME FOR Science**

### KNOWLEDGE GOALS

Students will understand that some animals

- have lures on their heads
- blend in with their surroundings
- change colors

### THIS WEEK'S CONCEPT MAP

Develop a concept-related graphic organizer like the one below over the course of this week.

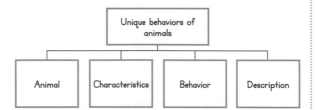

Unique behaviors of animals

| Animal | Characteristics | Behavior | Description |

### BUILD ORAL VOCABULARY

This week, students will acquire the following academic vocabulary/domain-specific words.

#### Amazing Words

| armor | extraordinary | unfurl |
| agile | scenery | coil |
| snout | pesky | intersection |
| protrude | | |

**OPTIONAL CONCEPT-BASED READING** Use the Digital Path to access readers offering different levels of text complexity.

Concept Literacy | Below-Level | On-Level | Advanced | ELL | ELD

# This Week's Digital Resources

## eStreet Interactive
### www.ReadingStreet.com

### Get Ready to Read

 **Concept Talk Video** Use this video on the Digital Path to preface and introduce the weekly concept of unique animal behaviors.

 **Pearson eText** Read the eText of the Student Edition pages on Pearson SuccessNet for comprehension and fluency support.

 **Envision It! Animations** Use this colorful animation on the Digital Path to explain the target comprehension skill, Cause and Effect.

### Read and Comprehend

 **Journal** Use the Word Bank on the Digital Path to have students write sentences using this week's selection vocabulary words.

 **Background Building Audio CD** This audio CD provides essential background information about unique animal behaviors to help students read and comprehend the weekly texts.

 **Pearson eText** Read the eText of the main selection, *Fly, Eagle, Fly!: An African Tale*, and the paired selection, "Purple Coyote," with audio support on Pearson SuccessNet.

 **Vocabulary Activities** A variety of interactive vocabulary activities on the Digital Path help students practice selection vocabulary and concept-related words.

 **Story Sort** Use the Story Sort Activity on the Digital Path after reading *Fly, Eagle, Fly!: An African Tale* to involve students in summarizing.

### Language Arts

 **Grammar Jammer** Pick a valuable animation on the Digital Path to provide an engaging grammar lesson that will draw students' attention.

**Pearson eText** Find the Student Edition eText of the Let's Write It! and Let's Learn It! pages with audio support on Pearson SuccessNet.

## Additional Resources

 **Teacher Resources DVD-ROM** Use the following resources on the TR DVD or on Pearson SuccessNet throughout the week:

- Amazing Word Cards
- Reader's and Writer's Notebook
- Writing Transparencies
- Daily Fix-It Transparencies
- Scoring Rubrics
- Grammar Transparencies
- ELL Support
- Let's Practice It!
- Graphic Organizers
- Vocabulary Cards

## This Week's Skills

### Phonics/Word Analysis
- Syllables VCCCV

### Comprehension
- **Skill:** Cause and Effect
- **Strategy:** Monitor and Clarify

### Language
- **Vocabulary:** Unknown Words
- **Conventions:** Prepositions

### Fluency
Rate

### Writing
Summary

# 5-Day Planner

## DAY 1

### Get Ready to Read

**Content Knowledge** 150j
Oral Vocabulary: *armor, agile, snout, protrude*

> **Monitor Progress**
> Check Oral Vocabulary

**Phonics/Word Analysis** 152a
- Syllables VCCCV
**READ** Decodable Reader 20A
Reread for Fluency

### Read and Comprehend

**Text-Based Comprehension** 154a
- Cause and Effect
- Monitor and Clarify

**Fluency** 154–155
Rate

**Selection Vocabulary** 155a
*clutched, echoed, gully, reeds, scrambled, thatch, valley*

### Language Arts

**Research and Inquiry** 155b
Identify and Focus Topic

**Spelling** 155c
Syllables VCCCV, Pretest

**Conventions** 155d
Prepositions

**Handwriting** 155d
Cursive Letter *f*

**Writing** 155e
Summary

## DAY 2

### Get Ready to Read

**Content Knowledge** 156a
Oral Vocabulary: *extraordinary, scenery*

**Phonics/Word Analysis** 156c
- Syllables VCCCV

> **Monitor Progress**
> Check Word Reading

**Literary Terms** 156d
Sensory Details

### Read and Comprehend

**Vocabulary Skill** 156e
- Unknown Words

**Fluency** 156–157
Rate

**Text-Based Comprehension** 158–159
**READ** *Fly, Eagle, Fly!: An African Tale*—1st Read

### Language Arts

**Research and Inquiry** 167b
Navigate/Search

**Conventions** 167c
Prepositions

**Spelling** 167c
Syllables VCCCV

**Writing** 167d
Summary

# DAY 3

## Get Ready to Read

**Content Knowledge** 168a
Oral Vocabulary: *pesky, unfurl*

**Phonics/Word Analysis** 168c
Syllables VCCCV
Fluent Word Reading
**DECODE AND READ**
Decodable Practice Passage 20B

## Read and Comprehend

**Text-Based Comprehension** 168e
Check Understanding
**READ** *Fly, Eagle, Fly!: An African Tale*—2nd Read
Monitor Progress Check Retelling

**Fluency** 173b
Appropriate Rate

## Language Arts

**Research and Study Skills** 173c
Outlining and Summarizing

**Research and Inquiry** 173d
Analyze Information

**Conventions** 173e
Prepositions

**Spelling** 173e
Syllables VCCCV

**Writing** 174–175
Summary

# DAY 4

## Get Ready to Read

**Content Knowledge** 176a
Oral Vocabulary: *coil, intersection*

**Phonics/Word Analysis** 176c
Review Suffixes
Fluent Word Reading
**DECODE AND READ**
Decodable Practice Passage 20C

## Read and Comprehend

**Genre** 176g
Trickster Tale
**READ** "Purple Coyote"—Paired Selection

**Fluency** 182–183
Appropriate Rate
Monitor Progress Check Fluency

**Vocabulary Skill** 183a
Unknown Words

**Listening and Speaking** 183a
Book Review

## Language Arts

**Research and Inquiry** 183b
Synthesize

**Conventions** 183c
Prepositions

**Spelling** 183c
Syllables VCCCV

**Writing** 183d
Summary

# DAY 5

## Get Ready to Read

**Content Knowledge** 183f
Review Oral Vocabulary
Monitor Progress
Check Oral Vocabulary

## Read and Comprehend

**Text-Based Comprehension** 183h
Review Cause and Effect

**Vocabulary Skill** 183h
Review Unknown Words

**Phonics/Word Analysis** 183i
Review Syllables VCCCV

**Literary Terms** 183i
Review Sensory Details

**Assessment** 183j, 183l
Monitor Progress
Fluency; Cause and Effect

## Language Arts

**Research and Inquiry** 183n
Communicate

**Spelling** 183o
Syllables VCCCV, Test

**Conventions** 183o
Prepositions

**Writing** 183p
Summary

**Wrap Up Your Week!** 183q

# Access for All

## What do I do in group time?
It's as easy as 1-2-3!

**①** TEACHER-LED SMALL GROUPS → **②** INDEPENDENT PRACTICE STATIONS → **③** INDEPENDENT READING

## Small Group Time

### C Bridge to Common Core

**SKILL DEVELOPMENT**
- Syllables VCCCV
- Cause and Effect
- Monitor and Clarify
- Unknown Words

**DEEP UNDERSTANDING**
**This Week's Knowledge Goals**
Students will understand that some animals
- have lures on their heads
- blend in with their surroundings
- change colors

## ① Small Group Lesson Plan

| | DAY 1 | DAY 2 |
|---|---|---|
| | **Differentiate Vocabulary** | **Differentiate Comprehension** |
| **OL On-Level** pp. SG•66–SG•70 | **Build Word Knowledge** Practice Amazing Words **Text-Based Comprehension** Read *Reading Street Sleuth*, pp. 52–53 or Leveled Readers | **Build Word Knowledge** Practice Selection Vocabulary **Access Text** Read *Fly, Eagle, Fly!: An African Tale* |
| **SI Strategic Intervention** pp. SG•71–SG•75 | **Build Word Knowledge** Reteach Amazing Words **Text-Based Comprehension** Read *Reading Street Sleuth*, pp. 52–53 or Leveled Readers | **Build Word Knowledge** Reteach Selection Vocabulary **Access Text** Read *Fly, Eagle, Fly!: An African Tale* |
| **A Advanced** pp. SG•76–SG•80 | **Build Word Knowledge** Extend Amazing Words **Text-Based Comprehension** Read *Reading Street Sleuth*, pp. 52–53 or Leveled Readers | **Build Word Knowledge** Extend Selection Vocabulary **Access Text** Read *Fly, Eagle, Fly!: An African Tale* |
| **Independent Inquiry Project** | Identify Questions | Investigate |
| **ELL** If... students need more scaffolding and practice with... | **Vocabulary,** then... use the activities on pp. DI•117–DI•118 in the Teacher Resources section on SuccessNet. | **Comprehension Skill,** then... use the activities on p. DI•121 in the Teacher Resources section on SuccessNet. |

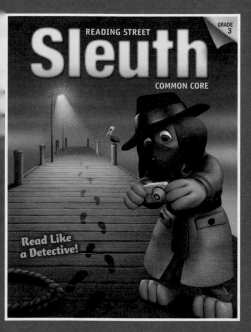

**READING STREET** GRADE 3

# Sleuth

COMMON CORE

Read Like a Detective!

### Reading Street Sleuth

- Provides access to grade-level text for all students
- Focuses on finding clues in text through close reading
- Builds capacity for complex text

## Build Text-Based Comprehension (Zoom in on ©)

*Fly, Eagle, Fly!*

Folk Tales are stories or legends from other lands and are handed down from one generation to the next. Where is this story from?

**Genre**

**Question of the Week**
What behaviors are unique to different animals?

*Fly, Eagle, Fly!*

### Optional Leveled Readers

| Concept Literacy | Below-Level | On-Level | Advanced | ELL | ELD |

| DAY 3 | DAY 4 | DAY 5 |
|---|---|---|
| **Differentiate Close Reading** | **Differentiate Vocabulary** | **Differentiate Reteaching** |
| **Reread to Develop Vocabulary** **Close Reading** Read *Fly, Eagle, Fly!: An African Tale* | **Build Word Knowledge** Develop Language Using Amazing Words **Text-Based Comprehension** Read "Purple Coyote" | **Practice Prepositions** **Text-Based Comprehension** Reread *Reading Street Sleuth*, pp. 52–53 or Leveled Readers |
| **Reread to Develop Vocabulary** **Close Reading** Read *Fly, Eagle, Fly!: An African Tale* | **Build Word Knowledge** Review/Discuss Amazing Words **Text-Based Comprehension** Read "Purple Coyote" | **Review Prepositions** **Text-Based Comprehension** Reread *Reading Street Sleuth*, pp. 52–53 or Leveled Readers |
| **Reread to Extend Vocabulary** **Close Reading** Read *Fly, Eagle, Fly!: An African Tale* | **Build Word Knowledge** Extend Amazing Words and Selection Vocabulary **Text-Based Comprehension** Read "Purple Coyote" | **Extend Prepositions** **Text-Based Comprehension** Reread *Reading Street Sleuth*, pp. 52–53 or Leveled Readers |
| Investigate | Organize | Communicate |
| **Main Selection,** **then...** use the activities on p. DI•122 in the Teacher Resources section on SuccessNet. | **Amazing Words,** **then...** use the Routine on pp. xxxvi–xxxvii in the *ELL Handbook*. | **Conventions and Writing,** **then...** use the Grammar Transition Lessons on pp. 312–386 in the *ELL Handbook*. |

# ②Independent Stations

## Practice Last Week's Skills

★ Focus on these activities when time is limited.

---

## WORD WISE

### Spell and use words in sentences.

#### OBJECTIVES

• Spell words with suffixes -er, -or, -ess, and -ist.

#### MATERIALS

• *Word Wise* Flip Chart Activity 20, teacher-made word cards, dictionary, paper and pencils

 **Letter Tile Drag and Drop**

● Students place ten words with the suffixes in a four-column chart and then use one of each in a sentence.

▲ Students place twelve words with the suffixes in a four-column chart and then use two of each in a sentence.

■ Students place fifteen words with the suffixes in a four-column chart and then use three of each in a sentence.

---

## WORD WORK

### Identify and pronounce words.

#### OBJECTIVES

• Identify and pronounce words with suffixes -er, -or, -ess, and -ist.

#### MATERIALS

• *Word Work* Flip Chart Activity 20, teacher-made word cards, paper and pencils

 **Letter Tile Drag and Drop**

● Students read aloud and group ten words by suffix, and then list other words with the suffixes. Students circle the suffix in each word.

▲ Students read aloud and group twelve words by suffix, and then list other words with the suffixes.

■ Students read aloud and group fifteen words by suffix, and then list other words with the suffixes.

---

## LET'S WRITE!

### Write in a genre or style.

#### OBJECTIVES

• Write an autobiography telling about your life.

#### MATERIALS

• *Let's Write!* Flip Chart Activity 20, paper and pencils

 **Grammar Jammer**

● Students write a short autobiography that tells about some of the important events in their life.

▲ Students write an autobiography, using a separate paragraph for each event they relate.

■ Students write an autobiography, using a separate paragraph for each event, being sure to vary sentence structure.

---

## WORDS TO KNOW

### Determine word meanings.

#### OBJECTIVES

• Determine the meanings of multiple-meaning words.

#### MATERIALS

• *Words to Know* Flip Chart Activity 20, teacher-made word cards, dictionary, paper and pencils

 **Vocabulary Activities**

● Students look up three words with multiple meanings. They write two sentences for each word to show its different meanings.

▲ Students look up four words with multiple meanings. They write two sentences for each word to show its different meanings.

■ Students look up five words with multiple meanings. They write at least two sentences for each word to show its different meanings.

## Manage the Stations

Use these management tools to set up and organize your Practice Stations:

Practice Station Flip Charts

Classroom Management Handbook for Differentiated Instruction Practice Stations, p. 38

---

 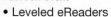 

### READ FOR MEANING

**Use text-based comprehension tools.**

#### OBJECTIVES
• Identify fact and opinion in expository text.

#### MATERIALS
• *Read for Meaning* Flip Chart Activity 20, Leveled Readers, paper and pencils

 **Pearson eText**  **Envision It! Animations**
• Leveled eReaders

● Students read a book and write one sentence telling a fact from the text and one telling an opinion.

▲ Students read a book, write two sentences telling two facts from the text, and then write two sentences giving two opinions.

■ Students read a book and write one paragraph describing facts from the text and one paragraph describing the opinions.

---

### GET FLUENT

**Practice fluent reading.**

#### OBJECTIVES
• Read aloud with appropriate phrasing.

#### MATERIALS
• *Get Fluent* Flip Chart Activity 20, Leveled Readers

 **Pearson eText**
• Leveled eReaders

● Students choose a partner and practice reading with appropriate phrasing from a Concept Literacy Reader or a Below-Level Reader.

▲ Students choose a partner and practice reading with appropriate phrasing from an On-Level Reader.

■ Students choose a partner and practice reading with appropriate phrasing from an Advanced Reader.

---

## 3 Independent Reading

Students should select appropriately complex texts to read and write about independently every day before, during, and after school.

Suggestions for this week's independent reading:
• *A Picture Book of Harry Houdini,* by David A. Adler
• An information-rich Web site about Gertrude Ederle
• A book about women athletes

---

**BOOK TALK**  Have partners discuss their independent reading for the week. Tell them to refer to their Reading Logs and paraphrase what each selection was about. Then have students focus on discussing one or more of the following:

**Key Ideas and Details**
• What are some of the main ideas in the text? How do you know?
• Summarize the events in the text.

**Craft and Structure**
• How is the information in the text organized?
• What facts are presented about the topic? What opinions?

**Integration of Ideas**
• Ask three questions about the subject and look for answers in the text.
• Compare this book to others you have read.

---

 **Pearson eText**
• Student Edition
• Decodable Readers
• Leveled Readers

 **Trade Book Library**

 **School or Classroom Library**

### Materials

- Student Edition
- Reader's and Writer's Notebook
- Decodable Reader

---

## Ⓒ Bridge to Common Core

**INTEGRATION OF KNOWLEDGE/IDEAS**

This week, students will read, write, and talk about unique animal behaviors.

**Texts This Week**

- "Where Are the Alligators?"
- "Birds of Prey"
- "Eagle Watching"
- *Fly, Eagle, Fly!: An African Tale*
- "Purple Coyote"

**Science Knowledge Goals**

Students will understand that some animals

- have lures on their heads
- blend in with their surroundings
- change colors

---

# Street Rhymes!

An armadillo has a shell.
A pig will use its snout to smell.
A snake will coil on the ground.
The cheetah's fastest all around!

- To introduce this week's concept, read aloud the poem several times and ask the students to join you.

# Content Knowledge  Zoom in on Ⓒ

## Unique Animal Behaviors

**CONCEPT TALK** To further explore the unit concept of One of a Kind, this week students will read, write, and talk about behaviors that are unique to different animals. Write the Question of the Week on the board, *What behaviors are unique to different animals?*

# Build Oral Language

**TALK ABOUT UNIQUE ANIMAL BEHAVIORS** Have students turn to pp. 150–151 in their Student Editions. Look at each of the photos. Then use the prompts to guide discussion and create a concept map.

- What do bats look like? What do they do? (Bats have long snouts and wings. They hang upside down.) Let's begin the concept map with *Animal, Characteristics,* and *Behavior. Characteristics* are what an animal looks like. *Behaviors* are the ways an animal acts.

- What is the lizard doing? (It is balancing on a branch.) What word can you use to describe its actions? (You could call its action *agile.*) Every animal's behavior can be described using an adjective. Let's add *Description* to the map.

Oral Vocabulary

Common Core State Standards
Speaking/Listening 1.c. Ask questions to check understanding of information presented, stay on topic, and link their comments to the remarks of others. Also Language 6.

## Let's Talk About

### Unique Animal Behaviors

- Describe unique animals.
- Pose and answer questions about why animals exhibit unique behaviors.
- Discuss what behaviors are unique to specific animals.

**READING STREET ONLINE
CONCEPT TALK VIDEO**
www.ReadingStreet.com

You've learned
**1 8 7**
Amazing Words ☆
so far this year!

150

151

Student Edition, pp. 150–151

**CONNECT TO READING** Tell students that this week they will be reading about unique behaviors of different animals. Encourage students to add concept-related words to this week's concept map.

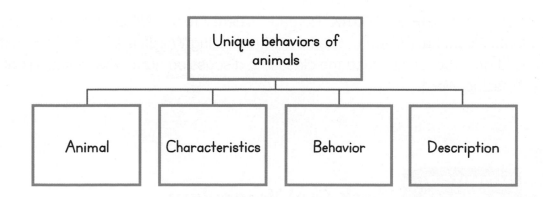

Unique behaviors of animals

Animal | Characteristics | Behavior | Description

**eSTREET INTERACTIVE**
www.ReadingStreet.com

**Pearson eText**
- Student Edition

**Concept Talk Video**

ELL

**Preteach Concepts** Use the Day 1 instruction on ELL Poster 20 to assess and build background knowledge, develop concepts, and build oral vocabulary.

**ELL Support Additional** ELL support and modified instruction is provided in the *ELL Handbook* and in the ELL Support lessons on the *Teacher Resources DVD-ROM*.

*Fly, Eagle, Fly!* **150–151**

## Amazing Words

You've learned ⑴⑻⑺ words so far.

You'll learn ⓪①⓪ words this week!

| | |
|---|---|
| armor | scenery |
| agile | pesky |
| snout | unfurl |
| protrude | coil |
| extraordinary | intersection |

# Content Knowledge

## Build Oral Vocabulary

**INTRODUCE AMAZING WORDS** "Where Are the Alligators?" on p. 151b is about American alligators and their behaviors. Tell students to listen for this week's Amazing Words—*armor, agile, snout,* and *protrude*—as you read the Teacher Read Aloud on p. 151b.

## Amazing Words  Robust Vocabulary Routine

1. **Introduce** Write the word *armor* on the board. Have students say the word aloud with you. In "Where Are the Alligators?" we learn about animals that look like lizards in a suit of *armor*. What does *armor* mean? Supply a student-friendly definition. *Armor* is any kind of protective covering for the body, such as the shell of an armadillo.

2. **Demonstrate** Have students answer questions to demonstrate understanding. What is *armor* usually made of? How is an alligator's skin like *armor?*

3. **Apply** Have students give examples of the ways *armor* protects.

4. **Display the Word** Run your hand under the syllables *ar-mor* as you read the word. Have students say the word again.

See p. OV•5 to teach *agile, snout,* and *protrude*.

Routines Flip Chart

**AMAZING WORDS AT WORK** Reread "Where Are the Alligators?" aloud. As students listen, have them notice how the Amazing Words are used in context. To build oral vocabulary, lead the class in a discussion about the meanings of the Amazing Words.

 **MONITOR PROGRESS** Check Oral Vocabulary

During discussion, listen for students' use of Amazing Words.

**If...** students are unable to use the Amazing Words in discussion,

**then...** use the Oral Vocabulary Routine in the Routines Flip Chart to demonstrate words in different contexts.

# Teacher Read Aloud

**MODEL FLUENCY** As you read "Where Are the Alligators?" model appropriate rate by reading at a speed that will improve the listener's comprehension.

# Where Are the Alligators?

**eSTREET INTERACTIVE**
www.ReadingStreet.com

**Teacher Resources**
• Amazing Word Cards
• ELL Support

What looks like a lizard in a suit of armor? The American alligator! The American alligator is one of the largest reptiles in the world. Most grow to about 10 feet long and weigh about 500 pounds. But some male alligators can be twice that length and weigh twice as much!

American alligators live in only a few states. Most live in Florida and Louisiana, but they can live in Texas too. Alligators in Texas live in the Rio Grande, a river. Most of the alligators in Florida live in swamps and rivers in an area called the Everglades.

American alligators are excellent swimmers. They have agile bodies, so they move easily through water. The snout and tail of an alligator are the perfect shapes for digging holes in the bottoms of swamps and rivers. The alligators dig out plants they find to make the holes deeper. They push the mud to the side to make the holes wider. Some gator holes are as small as bathtubs. Others can be as large as swimming pools!

Alligators use these holes mostly for shelter. When the weather gets too cold, they stay in the holes and sleep. And when the weather gets too dry, and the rivers and swamps become too shallow, then the alligators stay in their holes until it rains again and the water level rises.

What makes an alligator different from a crocodile? Well, for one thing, they live in different places. It is very rare to find a crocodile in any of America's rivers. Crocodiles live mostly in the Nile River in Egypt and in other areas of Africa.

Alligators look different from crocodiles too. For one thing, alligators have snouts that are short and rounded, while crocodiles have long and pointed snouts. Also, crocodiles have big teeth that protrude upward from their bottom jaws. An alligator's teeth protrude downward from the top. Alligators have about 80 teeth, and they are very sharp! When they lose a tooth, another grows in its place.

For many, many years, American alligators were in danger of disappearing. People hunted them, and many were killed. But other people worked hard to save the alligators. Today no one can hunt alligators because there are laws that protect them.

Now that alligators are protected, there are many more around. You can find them in water and you can find them on land. You might see them lying in the sun by a riverbank. You might see their snouts sticking out of the water. Alligators breathe air, so they swim close to the surface. You might hear an alligator, too, especially if it is angry. Alligators roar like lions and sound very fierce!

**Discuss the Read Aloud** Have small groups of students discuss what they already know about alligators. Use the following conversation starters: *Where do alligators live? How would you describe an alligator to a friend? Share answers with the group. Use pictures from the Student Edition to provide visual support.*

**Support Read Aloud** Use the modified Read Aloud from the ELL Support Lessons (p. DI•119) on the *Teacher Resources DVD-ROM.*

**Common Core State Standards**

**Foundational Skills 3.c.** Decode multisyllable words. **Language 2.f.** Use spelling patterns and generalizations (e.g., word families, position-based spellings, syllable patterns, ending rules, meaningful word parts) in writing words.

## Skills Trace

**Syllables VCCCV**

**Introduce** U4W5D1
**Practice** U4W5D3; U4W5D4
**Reteach/Review** U4W5D5; U5W1D5
**Assess/Test** Weekly Test U4W5
Benchmark Test U4
**KEY:** U=Unit   W=Week   D=Day

## Vocabulary Support

You may wish to explain the meanings of these words.

**complex** hard to understand

**merchant** someone who buys and sells goods for a living

**contrast** to compare two things to show their differences

## Academic Vocabulary

**syllable** a word part that contains a single vowel sound

# Word Analysis

## Teach/Model

### Syllables VCCCV

**CONNECT** Connect today's lesson to previously learned syllabication patterns CVC and VCCV. Write *super* and *supper*. You already can read words like these. Read these words. Today you'll learn to spell and read words with the syllabication pattern VCCCV.

**MODEL** Write *pilgrim*. When I say the word *pilgrim,* I hear two syllables. I see two vowels. Identify each vowel by writing *V* below it. I see three consonants between the vowels: *l, g, r*. Identify each consonant by writing *C* below it. Divide the word into syllables. *(pil-grim)* I divide the syllables between the *l* and *g* because *gr* is a blend and should not be split. I put the parts, or syllables, together to read the whole word: *pilgrim*. Write *surprise, farther, monster, mischief, dolphin,* and *hungry.* Model how to read each word by identifying the vowels and the consonants in the VCCCV pattern. Discuss how to divide the words into syllables. Remind students to not split blends or digraphs.

**GUIDE PRACTICE** Have students read each word with you. Identify the VCCCV pattern, divide the word into syllables, and then read the word.

| | | | | |
|---|---|---|---|---|
| complex | sample | explore | merchant | address |
| contrast | inspect | central | purchase | simple |

**REVIEW** What do you know about reading words with the syllable pattern VCCCV? Identify the VCCCV pattern. Then divide between the blend or digraph and the other consonant.

## Guide Practice

**MODEL** Have students turn to p. 152 in their Student Editions. Each word on this page has the VCCCV pattern. In the first word, the letters *u, n, d, r, e* make the VCCCV pattern. I know *dr* is a blend. I divide the word between the *n* and *d*, and say the syllables together to read *hundreds*.

**GROUP PRACTICE** For each word in Words I Can Blend, ask students to identify the VCCCV pattern, divide the word into syllables, and say the word.

> **Corrective feedback** | **If...** students have difficulty reading a word, **then...** model reading the parts and then the whole word, and then ask students to read it with you.

Envision It! Sounds to Know

sandwich

VCCCV

**READING STREET ONLINE
SOUND-SPELLING CARDS**
www.ReadingStreet.com

**Phonics**

 **Syllable Pattern VCCCV**

### Words I Can Blend

# hundreds
# children
# complete
# explain
# instead

### Sentences I Can Read

1. Hundreds of children go to school in my town.
2. Did you complete the test?
3. Explain why we are going tomorrow instead of today.

152

 I Can Read!

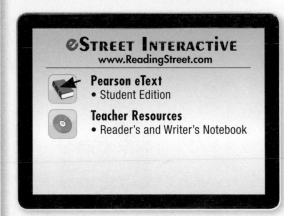

Children in my apartment complex have a concrete area where we play. Sometimes we complain that there simply is not enough room there, but we get constant use out of it anyway.

A man came to inspect the area last week. He explained they are going to destroy the old playground and improve the area. That's what Mom said, anyway.

I can't wait until it is complete and we have an outstanding new place to play.

**You've learned**
 Syllable Pattern VCCCV

153

# Apply

**READ WORDS IN ISOLATION** After students can successfully decode the words on p. 152 in their Student Editions, point to words in random order and ask students to read them naturally.

**READ WORDS IN CONTEXT** Have students read each of the sentences on p. 152. Have them identify words with the VCCCV syllable pattern.

**Team Talk** Pair students and have them take turns reading each of the sentences aloud.

Chorally read the I Can Read! passage on p. 153 with the students. Then have them read the passage to themselves.

**ON THEIR OWN** For additional practice, use the *Reader's and Writer's Notebook*, p. 291.

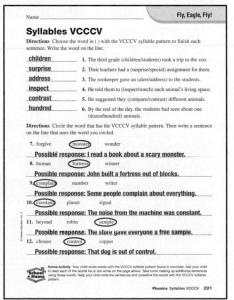

Reader's and Writer's Notebook, p. 291

 eSTREET INTERACTIVE
www.ReadingStreet.com

**Pearson eText**
• Student Edition

**Teacher Resources**
• Reader's and Writer's Notebook

**ELL**

**Language Transfer** Consonant blends with *l* and *r* are difficult for speakers of some Asian languages. Pronounce each syllable in VCCCV words and have students practice pronouncing them after you.

*Fly, Eagle, Fly!* **152–153**

### Common Core State Standards

**Foundational Skills 3.** Know and apply grade-level phonics and word analysis skills in decoding words. **Foundational Skills 3.c.** Decode multisyllable words. **Foundational Skills 3.d.** Read grade-appropriate irregularly spelled words. **Language 2.f.** Use spelling patterns and generalizations (e.g., word families, position-based spellings, syllable patterns, ending rules, meaningful word parts) in writing words. **Also Foundational Skills 4.**

# Decodable Reader 20A

If students need help, then...

## Read *Miss Mildred's Ostrich*

**READ WORDS IN ISOLATION** Have students turn to p. 49 of *Decodable Practice Readers 3.2.* Have students read each word.

Have students read the high-frequency words *friends, a, very, they, to, you, were, one, would, was, into, do,* and *want* on the first page.

**PREVIEW** Have students read the title and preview the story. Tell them that they will read words with the syllable pattern VCCCV.

**READ WORDS IN CONTEXT** Pair students for reading and listen as they read. One student begins. Students read the entire story, switching readers after each page. Partners reread the story. This time the other student begins. Make sure students are monitoring their accuracy when they decode words.

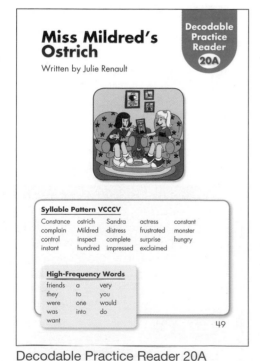

Decodable Practice Reader 20A

**eSTREET INTERACTIVE**
www.ReadingStreet.com

**Pearson eText**
• Decodable Reader

**Interactive Sound-Spelling Cards**

| **Corrective feedback** | **If...** students have difficulty decoding a word, **then...** refer them to the *Sound-Spelling Cards* to identify the word parts. Have them read the word parts individually and then together to say the word. |
|---|---|

• What is the new word?

• Is the new word a word you know?

• Does it make sense in the story?

**CHECK DECODING AND COMPREHENSION** Have students retell the story to include characters, setting, and events. Then have students find words in the story that have the syllabication pattern VCCCV. Students should supply *Constance, ostrich, Sandra, actress, constant, complain, Mildred, distress, frustrated, monster, control, inspect, complete, surprise, hungry, instant, hundred, impressed, exclaimed*.

# Reread for Fluency

**REREAD DECODABLE READER** Have students reread *Decodable Practice Reader 20A* to develop automaticity decoding words with the VCCCV syllable pattern.

| **Routine** | Oral Rereading |  |
|---|---|---|

1. **Read** Have students read the entire book orally.

2. **Reread** To achieve optimal fluency, students should reread the text three or four times.

3. **Corrective Feedback** Listen as students read. Provide corrective feedback regarding their fluency and decoding.

Routines Flip Chart

**ELL**

**Syllables VCCCV**

**Beginning** Write on the board several words with the VCCCV syllable pattern from the *Decodable Practice Reader*. Point to each word as you say it aloud. Then identify the letters that make the VCCCV syllable pattern by writing *V* under and *C* under. Identify blends and model how to divide each word. Have students say the syllables and then put the parts together to say the word with you.

**Intermediate** After reading, have students find words with the VCCCV syllable pattern, write them, and draw a line between the syllables.

**Advanced** After reading, have students choose 4–5 VCCCV syllable pattern words and write a sentence for each word.

### ⓒ Common Core State Standards

**Informational Text 3.** Describe the relationship between a series of historical events, scientific ideas or concepts, or steps in technical procedures in a text, using language that pertains to time, sequence, and cause/effect. **Foundational Skills 4.b.** Read on-level prose and poetry orally with accuracy, appropriate rate, and expression on successive readings. **Also Informational Text 1.**

## Skills Trace

**⚫ Cause and Effect**

**Introduce** U3W5D1; U4W5DI; U6W2D1

**Practice** U3W5D2; U3W5D3; U4W3D2; U4W5D3; U5W1D2; U6W2D2; U6W2D3; U6W4D2; U6W4D3

**Reteach/Review** U3W5D5; U4W5D5; U6W2D5

**Assess/Test** Weekly Tests U3W5; U4W5; U6W2
Benchmark Tests U6

**KEY:** U=Unit   W=Week   D=Day

## Academic Vocabulary ⓒ

**transition words** words like *because, so,* and *then* that show how one idea or event relates to another

## Comprehension Support

Students may also turn to pp. EI•3 and EI•21 to review the skill and strategy if needed.

# Text-Based Comprehension

## ⚫ Cause and Effect
## ⚫ Monitor and Clarify

**READ** Remind students of the weekly concept—Unique Animal Beheviors. Have students read "Birds of Prey" on p. 155.

### MODEL A CLOSE READ

**Think Aloud** Demonstrate close reading for students. Today we read about eagles. Have students follow along as you read. In the last sentence of the first paragraph, I see the clue word *because*. I know that the cause comes after that word. The cause is that eagles have large pupils. What effect do the large pupils have? (Eagles can spot their prey from long distances.) When I read about how eagles build their nests in tall trees or on cliffs, I wondered why they didn't build them closer to the ground. I reread to clarify my understanding. Now I understand that eagles build their nests in high places to protect the young chicks.

**TEACH** Have students read p. 154. Explain that the skill of cause and effect and the strategy of monitoring and clarifying are tools they can use to help deepen their understanding of a text. Then have students look back at "Birds of Prey." After they read, have them use a graphic organizer like the one on p. 154 and identify causes and effects from the passage.

**GUIDE PRACTICE** Have students reread "Birds of Prey" using the callouts as guides. Then ask volunteers to respond to the questions in the callouts, citing specific examples from the text to support their answers.

**Skill** *Because;* eagles can spot prey from long distances because of their large pupils.
**Strategy** Have students reread any portion of the selection they don't understand.

**APPLY** Use *Reader's and Writer's Notebook,* p. 292, for additional practice with cause and effect.

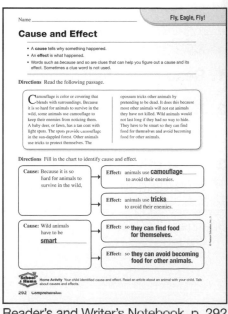

Reader's and Writer's Notebook, p. 292

Common Core State Standards
Informational Text 3. Describe the relationship between a series of historical events, scientific ideas or concepts, or steps in technical procedures in a text, using language that pertains to time, sequence, and cause/effect.
Also Informational Text 1.

**Envision It!** | Skill Strategy

**Skill**

Cause and Effect

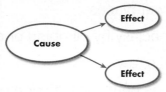

**Strategy**

Monitor and Clarify

**READING STREET ONLINE
ENVISION IT! ANIMATIONS
www.ReadingStreet.com**

Comprehension Skill

## Cause and Effect

- A cause tells why something happened.
- An effect is what happened.
- *Because* and *so* are clue words that show a cause-and-effect relationship.
- Use what you learned about cause and effect and a graphic organizer like the one below to read "Birds of Prey." Then use your graphic organizer to write a paragraph that explains the cause-and-effect relationship.

Cause → Effect
Cause → Effect

Comprehension Strategy

## Monitor and Clarify

Good readers think about what they are reading. They stop reading when they are confused and try to figure out what's wrong. When you are confused, go back and reread to help clarify your understanding.

# Birds of Prey

Eagles are large birds of prey that are members of the falcon family. Like all birds of prey, eagles have very large hooked beaks, strong legs, and powerful talons or claws. Another advantage that eagles have is their keen eyesight. Eagles can spot their prey from very long distances because they have large pupils.

Eagles are different from many other birds of prey. They are larger, have a more powerful build, and have heavier heads and bills. Most eagles are larger than any other birds of prey apart from vultures.

Eagles build their nests in tall trees or on high cliffs so that their young chicks are protected from other animals. In recent years, eagles have fallen prey to their environment. Many eagles have moved away from the heavily populated areas in the United States or disappeared entirely because of human expansion.

**Skill** What clue word is in this paragraph? What cause and effect does it show?

**Strategy** Are you having trouble understanding how eagles are different from other birds of prey? Go back and reread this paragraph aloud.

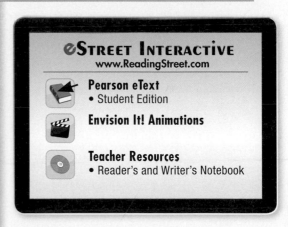

**Your Turn!**

⏸ **Need a Review?** See the *Envision It! Handbook* for help with cause and effect and monitoring and clarifying.

▶ **Ready to Try It?** As you read *Fly, Eagle, Fly!*, use what you've learned about cause and effect and monitoring and clarifying to understand the text.

154

155

**Student Edition, pp. 154–155**

# Model Fluent Reading

**RATE** Have students listen as you read paragraphs 1–3 of "Birds of Prey" at the appropriate rate. Explain that as the excitement builds, your rate increases to reflect the feeling of the text.

**Routine** Paired Reading

1. **Select a Passage** For "Birds of Prey," use the whole passage.

2. **Reading 1** Students read the entire passage, switching readers at the end of each paragraph.

3. **Reading 2** Partners reread the passage. This time the other student begins.

4. **Reread** For optimal fluency, have partners continue to read three or four times.

5. **Corrective Feedback** Listen as students read. Provide feedback about their rate and encourage them to adjust rate to reflect the feeling of the text.

Routines Flip Chart

**eStreet Interactive**
www.ReadingStreet.com

**Pearson eText**
• Student Edition

**Envision It! Animations**

**Teacher Resources**
• Reader's and Writer's Notebook

**ELL**

**Cause and Effect** Write on the board: *"The baby bird wanted to grow up so she tried to fly. The bird fell because she wasn't ready to fly."* Circle the words *so* and *because*. Then ask volunteers to help you label the cause and the effect in each sentence. Make sure students understand that the cause comes before the word *so* and after the word *because*.

## Common Core
## State Standards

**Writing 7.** Conduct short research projects that build knowledge about a topic. **Language 4.** Determine or clarify the meaning of unknown and multiple-meaning word and phrases based on grade 3 reading and content, choosing flexibly from a range of strategies. **Also Language 6.**

# Selection Vocabulary

Use the following routine to introduce this week's tested selection vocabulary.

**clutched** grasped something tightly

**echoed** the repeating of a sound caused by its reflecting off a hard surface

**gully** a ditch made by heavy rains or running water

**reeds** tall grasses that grow in wet places

**scrambled** made your way, especially by climbing or crawling quickly

**thatch** roofing material made of straw

**valley** an area of low land that lies between hills or mountains

**SEE IT/SAY IT** Write *clutched.* Scan across the word with your finger as you say it: *clutched*

**HEAR IT** Use the word in a sentence. She *clutched* my hand during the scary parts of the movie.

**DEFINE IT** Elicit definitions from students. How would you tell a friend what the word *clutched* means? Clarify or give a definition when necessary. Yes, it means "grabbed tightly." Restate the word in student-friendly terms. So *clutched* means to grab or hold onto something tightly.

 Do people usually *clutch* someone or something in good or bad situations? Why might you *clutch* someone or something? Turn and talk to your partner about this. Be prepared to explain your answer. Allow students time to discuss. Ask for examples. Rephrase their examples for usage when necessary or to correct misunderstandings.

**MAKE CONNECTIONS** Have students discuss the word. Have you ever *clutched* something or someone? Why? Turn and talk to your partner about this. Then be prepared to share. Have students share. Rephrase their ideas for usage when necessary or to correct misunderstandings.

**RECORD** Have students write the word and its meaning.

Continue this routine to introduce the remaining words in this manner.

> **Corrective feedback** | **If...** students are having difficulty understanding, **then...** review the definitions in small groups.

# Research and Inquiry

## Step 1 | Identify and Focus Topic

**TEACH** Discuss the Question of the Week: *What behaviors are unique to different animals?* Tell students they will research the instincts and behaviors of a chosen animal and write a journal article about it. They will present their findings to the class on Day 5.

**Think Aloud** **MODEL** I would like to learn more about bears. I'll start by brainstorming a list of questions about bears. I know they hibernate, but I don't know when or why or what they do to prepare for hibernation. Some possible questions could be *When do bears hibernate? Why do they hibernate? When do bears prepare for hibernation?*

**GUIDE PRACTICE** After students have brainstormed inquiry questions, explain that tomorrow they will conduct research using their questions. Help students identify keywords that will guide their search. Tell students they will write an outline later in the week.

**ON THEIR OWN** Have students work individually, in pairs, or in small groups to write an inquiry question.

---

**eSTREET INTERACTIVE**
www.ReadingStreet.com

**Teacher Resources**
- Envision It! Pictured Vocabulary Cards
- Tested Vocabulary Cards

---

**21st Century Skills**
**Internet Guy** *Don Leu*

**Weekly Inquiry Project**

| STEP 1 | Identify and Focus Topic |
|--------|--------------------------|
| STEP 2 | Navigate/Search |
| STEP 3 | Analyze Information |
| STEP 4 | Synthesize |
| STEP 5 | Communicate |

**ELL**

**Multilingual Vocabulary** Students can apply knowledge of their home languages to acquire new English vocabulary by using the Multilingual Vocabulary Lists (*ELL Handbook*, pp. 433–444).

**ELL**

**If...** students need more scaffolding and practice with **Vocabulary, then...** use the activities on pp. DI•117–DI•118 in the Teacher Resources section on SuccessNet.

---

## Day 1 | SMALL GROUP TIME • Differentiate Vocabulary, p. SG•65

| **OL** On-Level | **SI** Strategic Intervention | **A** Advanced |
|---|---|---|
| • **Practice Vocabulary** Amazing Words | • **Reteach Vocabulary** Amazing Words | • **Extend Vocabulary** Amazing Words |
| • **Read** *Reading Street Sleuth,* pp. 52–53 | • **Read** *Reading Street Sleuth,* pp. 52–53 | • **Read** *Reading Street Sleuth,* pp. 52–53 |
| | | • **Introduce** Inquiry Project |

## Common Core State Standards

**Language 1.** Demonstrate command of the conventions of standard English grammar and usage when writing or speaking. **Language 2.** Demonstrate command of the conventions of standard English capitalization, punctuation, and spelling when writing. **Language 2.f.** Use spelling patterns and generalizations (e.g., word families, position-based spellings, syllable patterns, ending rules, meaningful word parts) in writing words.

# Spelling Pretest

## Syllables VCCCV

**INTRODUCE** Tell students to think of words that have the spelling pattern VCCCV. This week we will spell words with the spelling pattern VCCCV.

**PRETEST** Say each word, read the sentence, and repeat the word.

| | | |
|---|---|---|
| 1. | monster | I was a **monster** for Halloween. |
| 2. | surprise | Your **surprise** made me happy. |
| 3. | hundred | Review the notes one **hundred** times. |
| 4. | complete | Make sure you **complete** your chores. |
| 5. | control | Please **control** the volume of your voice. |
| 6. | sample | Here is a free **sample** of our new CD. |
| 7. | instant | We will be back in an **instant.** |
| 8. | inspect | They **inspect** the elevator twice a year. |
| 9. | pilgrim | A **pilgrim** is a kind of traveler. |
| 10. | contrast | Her clean room is a sharp **contrast** to her sister's dirty room. |
| 11. | explode | Fireworks **explode,** so never play with them. |
| 12. | district | What voting **district** are you in? |
| 13. | address | Who do I **address** the envelope to? |
| 14. | substance | Yeast is a **substance** used in baking. |
| 15. | children | A lot of **children** are on the playground. |

### Challenge Words

| | | |
|---|---|---|
| 16. | merchant | The **merchant** sells toys and books. |
| 17. | embrace | Molly and her mother **embrace** each morning. |
| 18. | purchase | I will **purchase** a new backpack at the store. |
| 19. | curtsy | The girl did a **curtsy** at the end of her performance. |
| 20. | contract | The men signed a **contract** to build the new office. |

**SELF-CORRECT** Have students self-correct their pretests by rewriting misspelled words.

**ON THEIR OWN** Use *Let's Practice It!* page 257 on the *Teacher Resources DVD-ROM.*

---

Name _____    **Fly, Eagle, Fly!**

**Syllable Patterns VCCCV**

**Generalization** Words with VCCCV syllable patterns divide after the first consonant: mon ster.

**Word Sort** Sort the list words according to whether or not you already know how to spell them. Write every word.

| words I know how to spell | words I'm learning how to spell |
|---|---|
| 1. Answers will vary. | 9. Answers will vary. |
| 2. _____ | 10. _____ |
| 3. _____ | 11. _____ |
| 4. _____ | 12. _____ |
| 5. _____ | 13. _____ |
| 6. _____ | 14. _____ |
| 7. _____ | 15. _____ |
| 8. _____ | |

**Spelling Words**
1. monster
2. surprise
3. hundred
4. complete
5. control
6. sample
7. instant
8. inspect
9. pilgrim
10. contrast
11. explode
12. district
13. address
14. substance
15. children

**Home Activity** Your child is learning words with VCCCV (vowel-consonant-consonant-consonant-vowel) syllable patterns. Have your child study each word in the second column on this page, write the word, cover the word, and write it again.

**Syllable Patterns VCCCV DVD•257**

Let's Practice It! TR DVD•257

# Conventions

## Prepositions

**MAKE CONNECTIONS** Ask volunteers to describe the location of objects in the room. Point out the prepositions they use to describe locations.

**TEACH** Display Grammar Transparency 20, and read aloud the explanation and examples in the box.

**MODEL** Model combining the sentences to complete items 1–2.

**GUIDE PRACTICE** Guide students to complete item 3. Remind them to find the prepositional phrase and insert it in the combined sentence. Record the correct responses on the transparency.

**APPLY** Have students read sentences 4–5 on the transparency and choose the correct preposition to complete each sentence.

Grammar Transparency 20, TR DVD

# Handwriting

**MODEL LETTER FORMATION, SLANTING, AND SPACING** Display the lowercase cursive letter *f*. Follow the stroke instruction pictured to model letter formation.

Explain that writing legibly means that the letters slant the same way and that there should be more space between words than between letters in a word. Model writing this sentence: *I flew first class to find my friends in France.*

**GUIDE PRACTICE** Have students write the following: *fifteen fireflies, fifty frogs,* and *funny fish.*

---

## Daily Fix-It

1. Tamara and me couldnt find Dad's coin with an eagle's picture. *(I; couldn't)*
2. Its worth a lot of mony. *(It's; money)*

## Academic Vocabulary

A **preposition** is a word that shows a relationship between a noun and another word.

A **prepositional phrase** is the combination of a preposition and the noun to which it relates.

## ELL

**Leveled Support: Prepositions** Write the following prepositions on the board: *on, under, above, in, behind, between.*

**Beginning** Use an object such as a book to demonstrate each preposition. For example, put the book on a desk and say *The book is* **on** *the desk.*

**Intermediate** Have students work with a partner to draw pictures to show the meaning of each preposition.

**Advanced** Have students use each preposition in a sentence.

**Supporting Handwriting** Provide extra practice writing lowercase cursive letter *f* with words such as *fluffy, fearful,* and *flavorful.*

**Common Core State Standards**

**Writing 3.a** Establish a situation and introduce a narrator and/or characters; organize an event sequence that unfolds naturally. **Writing 3.c.** Use temporal words and phrases to signal event order.

 **Bridge to Common Core**

### TEXT TYPES AND PURPOSES

This week students will write two summaries to practice writing for tests. They will adapt the form, organization, and content of their writing to communicate clearly to an external audience.

### Narrative Writing

Through reading and discussing, students will gain a deeper understanding of the unique behaviors of animals. They will use this knowledge from the texts to write summaries that develop experiences using effective, well-chosen details and well-structured event sequences.

Throughout the week, students will improve their range and content of writing through daily mini-lessons.

### 5-Day Plan

| DAY 1 | Read Like a Writer |
|-------|--------------------|
| DAY 2 | Writing Trait: Time-Order Transition Words |
| DAY 3 | Evaluation |
| DAY 4 | Using Strong Verbs |
| DAY 5 | Revise: Conventions |

# Writing

## Summary

**Mini-Lesson** | **Writing for Tests: Read Like a Writer**

■ **Introduce** This week you will write a summary. A summary is a short retelling of a piece of writing, such as an article or a story.

| Genre | Summary |
|-------|---------|
| Trait | Word Choice |
| Mode | Narrative |

■ **Examine Model Text** Let's read an example of a summary written in response to a writing prompt on a test. Have students read "Summary of Why the Dog Wags His Tail" on p. 293 of their *Reader's and Writer's Notebook.*

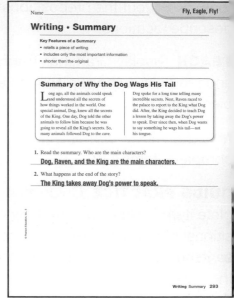

Reader's and Writer's Notebook, p. 293

■ **Key Features** A summary is shorter than the original story, and it includes only the most important information. Ask students to identify some of the most important information from the story in the model.

Summaries are usually presented in a logical order. Time-order transition words are used to help explain the order of events. Have students circle the time-order transition words in the passage.

## Review Key Features

Review the key features of summaries with students. You may want to post the key features in the classroom for students to refer to as they work on their summaries.

### Key Features of a Summary

- retells a piece of writing
- includes only the most important information
- is shorter than the original writing

**Routine** **Quick Write for Fluency** Team Talk

**1. Talk** Have pairs take a few minutes to discuss the features of a summary.

**2. Write** Each person writes one sentence about one of the features.

**3. Share** Partners share their sentences with one another.

Routines Flip Chart

**eSTREET INTERACTIVE**
www.ReadingStreet.com

**Teacher Resources**
- Reader's and Writer's Notebook
- Let's Practice It!

## Academic Vocabulary

A **transitional word** is a word that helps explain the order of events.

## ELL

**Retelling** Have students practice orally retelling a story.

**Beginning** Give students a story map and have them sketch what happened in the beginning, middle, and end of the story. Have them use their story map to guide their retelling.

**Intermediate** Have students use brief sentences to retell the story.

# Wrap Up Your Day!

✔ **Content Knowledge** Reread "Street Rhymes!" on p. 150j to students. Ask them what they learned this week about being one of a kind.

✔ **Oral Vocabulary** Have students use the Amazing Words they learned in context sentences.

✔ **Homework** Send home this week's Family Times newsletter on *Let's Practice It!* pp. 258–259 on the *Teacher Resources DVD-ROM.*

Let's Practice It!
TR DVD•258–259

**Preview DAY 2**

Tell students that tomorrow they will read about an animal with a unique behavior.

# DAY 2
## at a Glance

### Materials
- Student Edition
- Reader's and Writer's Notebook

### Common Core State Standards

**Speaking/Listening 1.** Engage effectively in a range of collaborative discussions (one-on-one, in groups, and teacher-led) with diverse partners on grade 3 topics and texts, building on others' ideas and expressing their own clearly. **Also Language 6.**

# Content Knowledge

## Unique Animal Behaviors

**EXPAND THE CONCEPT** Remind students of the weekly concept question, *What behaviors are unique to different animals?* Tell students that today they will begin reading *Fly, Eagle, Fly!: An African Tale.* As they read, encourage students to think about behaviors that are unique to different animals.

## Build Oral Language

**TALK ABOUT SENTENCES AND WORDS** Reread sentences from the Read Aloud, "Where Are the Alligators?"

*They have agile bodies, so they move easily through the water. The snout and tail of an alligator are the perfect shapes for digging holes in the bottom of swamps and rivers.*

- What does the word *agile* mean? Use the context clues to help you determine the meaning. (able to move easily)
- Why is it important that an alligator is agile? (Being able to move easily in water would make it a good swimmer.)
- Why does the author describe the alligator's tail and snout? (to show how these features make it unique)

**Team Talk** Have students turn to a partner and discuss the following question. Then ask them to share their responses.

- What is the most important characteristic of an alligator? Why? (Possible response: It is most important for an alligator to have a tail and snout that are perfect for digging holes in the bottoms of swamps and rivers. Alligators use these holes for shelter.)

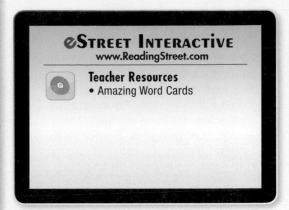
# Build Oral Vocabulary

## Amazing Words — Robust Vocabulary Routine

1. **Introduce** Write the Amazing Word *extraordinary* on the board. Have students say it aloud with you. Relate *extraordinary* to the photographs on pp. 150–151 and "Where Are the Alligators?" What makes each animal picture *extraordinary*? What behaviors of alligators are *extraordinary*? Have students determine the definition of the word. (Something that is *extraordinary* is very unusual and deserves attention.)

2. **Demonstrate** Have students answer questions to demonstrate understanding. Some bats hang upside down to sleep. Why is that *extraordinary*? What *extraordinary* behavior or characteristic does your favorite animal have?

3. **Apply** Have students apply their understanding by using the word in a personal context.

4. **Display the Word** Run your hand under the word as you emphasize the syllables *ex-traor-di-nar-y.* Have students say the word.

See p. OV•5 to teach *scenery.*

Routines Flip Chart

## Amazing Words

| | |
|---|---|
| armor | scenery |
| agile | pesky |
| snout | unfurl |
| protrude | coil |
| extraordinary | intersection |

**ADD TO THE CONCEPT MAP** Use the photos on pages 150–151 and the Read Aloud, "Where Are the Alligators?" to discuss the unique behaviors of animals, and talk about the Amazing Words *armor, agile, snout,* and *protrude.* Add these and other concept-related words to the concept map to develop students' knowledge of the topic. Discuss the photos and vocabulary to generate questions about the topic. Encourage students to build on others' ideas when they answer. Add some of the words generated in discussion to the concept map, including the Amazing Words *extraordinary* and *scenery.*

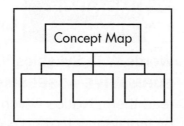

Concept Map

• Does the word *snout* describe a characteristic or a behavior? Explain your answer.

• What kind of behavior could be described as *agile*?

• If an animal has skin like *armor,* what purpose would it serve?

**Reinforce Vocabulary** Use the Day 2 instruction on ELL Poster 20 to teach lesson vocabulary and the lesson concept.

**Cognates** Spanish-speaking students might find it helpful to connect the Amazing Word *extraordinary* to the Spanish cognate *extraordinario.*

# Word Analysis

## Syllables VCCCV

### Common Core State Standards

**Literature 4.** Determine the meaning of words and phrases as they are used in a text, distinguishing literal from nonliteral language. **Foundational Skills 3.c.** Decode multisyllable words. **Language 5.** Demonstrate understanding of word relationships and nuances in word meanings.

**REVIEW** Review the syllable pattern VCCCV, reminding students that when dividing words into syllables, they should not split blends or digraphs.

**READ WORDS IN ISOLATION** Display these words. Have the class read the words. Then point to the words in random order and ask students to read them quickly.

| | | |
|---|---|---|
| district | address | complain |
| control | purchase | extreme |
| further | dolphin | |

**Corrective feedback** | Model identifying the VCCCV syllabication pattern, reading the syllables and then reading the word. Then ask students to read the word with you.

**READ WORDS IN CONTEXT** Display these sentences. Have the class read the sentences.

**Team Talk** Have pairs take turns reading the sentences naturally.

The **children** got into a lot of **mischief.**

The **monster** liked to eat ham **sandwiches.**

My uncle is **employed** at an **orchard.**

**Don't Wait Until Friday**

**MONITOR PROGRESS** Check Word Reading

**Words With Syllables VCCCV**

**FORMATIVE ASSESSMENT** Write the following words and have the class read them. Notice which words students miss during the group reading. Call on individuals to read some of the words.

| explain | improve | simply | instruct | **Spiral Review** |
|---|---|---|---|---|
| super | supper | hoper | hopper | Row 2 reviews words with VCV and VCCV patterns. |
| subject | abstain | captive | although | Row 3 contrasts words with VCCV and VCCCV patterns. |

**If...** students cannot read words with the VCCCV syllable pattern at this point,

**then...** use the Day 1 Word Analysis lesson on p. 152a to reteach the VCCCV syllable pattern. Use words from the *Decodable Practice Passages* (or Reader). Continue to monitor students' progress using other instructional opportunities during the week. See the Skills Trace on p. 152a.

# Literary Terms

## Sensory Details

**TEACH** Tell students that sensory details are words that help the reader see, smell, taste, hear, or feel what is described. Writers use sensory details to bring things and events to life for readers. Sensory details appear in all kinds of writing: nonfiction, fiction, and poetry.

**Think Aloud** **MODEL** Listen as I read this sentence from "Eagle Watching." *The eagles swooped over the reeds and thatch . . .* What sense does the sentence appeal to—sight, smell, hearing, taste, or touch? (sight) Which words make you "see" what happened? (The words *swooped, reeds, and thatch* help the reader "see" what happened.)

**GUIDE PRACTICE** Read aloud p. 160 of *Fly, Eagle, Fly!: An African Tale.* Pause at the end of each paragraph and have students identify the senses to which the descriptions appeal. Ask volunteers to share what they imagined as you read.

**ON THEIR OWN** Have students read p. 161, paying attention to the sensory details the author uses to bring the story to life.

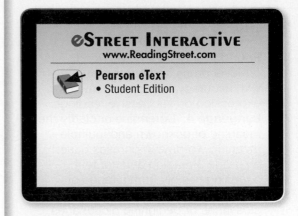

**eStreet Interactive**
www.ReadingStreet.com

**Pearson eText**
• Student Edition

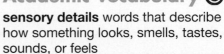

## Academic Vocabulary

**sensory details** words that describe how something looks, smells, tastes, sounds, or feels

## Common Core State Standards

**Foundational Skills 4.b.** Read on-level prose and poetry orally with accuracy, appropriate rate, and expression on successive readings. **Language 4.** Determine or clarify the meaning of unknown and multiple-meaning words and phrases based on grade 3 reading and content, choosing flexibly from a range of strategies. **Language 4.d.** Use glossaries or beginning dictionaries, both print and digital, to determine or clarify the precise meaning of key words and phrases.

## Selection Vocabulary

**clutched** grasped something tightly

**echoed** the repeating of a sound caused by its reflecting off a hard surface

**gully** a ditch made by heavy rains or running water

**reeds** tall grasses that grow in wet places

**scrambled** made your way, especially by climbing or crawling quickly

**thatch** roofing material made of straw

**valley** an area of low land that lies between hills or mountains

### Bridge to Common Core

**VOCABULARY ACQUISITION AND USE**

Students need to learn and use various strategies to determine or clarify the meanings of unknown and multiple-meaning words. If they cannot analyze the structure of a word or use context clues to determine its meaning, they must know how to utilize general and specialized reference materials in order to identify the definition of a word. All of these strategies expand students' knowledge of vocabulary.

## Vocabulary Support

Refer students to *Words!* on p. W•14 in the Student Edition for additional practice.

# Vocabulary Skill

## Unknown Words

**READ** Have students read "Eagle Watching" on p. 157. Use the vocabulary skill and strategy as tools to build comprehension.

**TEACH DICTIONARY/GLOSSARY USE** Explain to students that if they are not able to use word parts or context to determine the meaning of unknown words, they should use a dictionary or glossary. Remind students that dictionaries give the meaning, syllabication, and pronunciation of words.

**Think Aloud**

**MODEL** Write on the board: *Loud eagle cries often echoed across the valley.* I can't figure out the meaning of *echoed* from the context. When I look up *echoed* in a dictionary, I see that it means that a sound is "repeated because it reflects off a surface." Now I understand that the cries of the eagles were repeated off the sides of the hills that made the valley. Dictionaries and glossaries divide each word into syllables and show the pronunciation of each word in parentheses.

**GUIDE PRACTICE** Write this sentence on the board: *Rashid scrambled to the front of the line for lunch.* Have students try to determine the meaning of the word *scrambled* from context clues. If they cannot determine the meaning, have them use a dictionary or glossary to find the definition. Have students tell the number of syllables and the pronunciation of *scrambled,* as well. For additional support, use *Envision It! Pictured Vocabulary Cards* or *Tested Vocabulary Cards.*

**ON THEIR OWN** Have students reread "Eagle Watching" on p. 157. Have students use a dictionary to determine the meanings of the lesson vocabulary. For additional practice use *Reader's and Writer's Notebook,* p. 294.

Reader's and Writer's Notebook, p. 294

Common Core State Standards
Language 4.d. Use glossaries or beginning dictionaries, both print and digital, to determine or clarify the precise meaning of key words and phrases. Also Language 4.

**Envision It!** Words to Know

gully

reeds

valley

clutched
echoed
scrambled
thatch

**READING STREET ONLINE
VOCABULARY ACTIVITIES**
www.ReadingStreet.com

156

Vocabulary Strategy for

## ▶ Unknown Words

**Dictionary/Glossary** You can use a dictionary or glossary to find the meaning, syllable division, and pronunciation of an unknown word.

1. Find the entry word and pronunciation in the dictionary or glossary.

2. Look at the pronunciation key and each syllable to pronounce the word correctly.

3. Read all of the definitions. Which meaning best fits the sentence?

4. Try that meaning in the sentence. If it doesn't make sense, try another meaning of the word.

Read "Eagle Watching" on page 157. Use a dictionary or glossary to find the meanings, syllable divisions, and pronunciations of the Words to Know.

**Words to Write** Reread "Eagle Watching." What kind of animals are you interested in studying? Write about your interest. Use words from the Words to Know list in your answer.

# Eagle Watching

José and his father scrambled up the side of the gully. Near the top of the gully was their favorite eagle-watching spot. José and his father looked for the bald eagles that lived in the area. First, they used their binoculars to scan the tops of the trees. Eagles usually perch in high places so that they can look for food. Next, José and his father listened for the eagles. Loud eagle cries often echoed across the valley.

In the valley below where José and his father hid was a large lake. The eagles swooped over the reeds and thatch along the lake's edge, skimmed over the surface, and dipped down and snatched fish out of the water. Then the eagles flew away with the fish clutched in their sharp talons, or claws. They carried the fish back to their nests, high in the tall trees or on the cliffs. It was an amazing sight, and José never got tired of watching it.

**Your Turn!**

⏸ **Need a Review?** For help with using a dictionary or glossary to find the meanings of unknown words, see *Words!*

▶ **Ready to Try It?** Read *Fly, Eagle, Fly!* on pp. 158–171.

157

**Student Edition, pp. 156–157**

# Reread for Fluency

**RATE** Read paragraph 1 of "Eagle Watching," keeping an even rate. Tell students that your rate reflects the content.

## Routine    Paired Reading                    **Team Talk**

1. **Select a Passage** For "Eagle Watching," use the whole passage.

2. **Reading 1** Students read the entire passage, switching readers at the end of each paragraph.

3. **Reading 2** Partners reread the passage. This time the other student begins.

4. **Reread** For optimal fluency, students should continue to read three or four times.

5. **Corrective Feedback** Listen as students read. Encourage them to adjust rate based on the content of the selection.

Routines Flip Chart

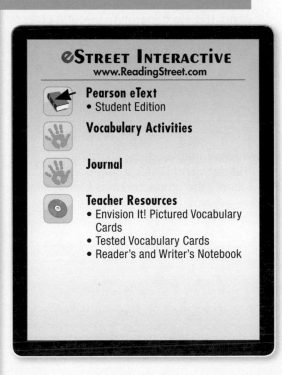

# *e*STREET INTERACTIVE
www.ReadingStreet.com

**Pearson eText**
• Student Edition

**Vocabulary Activities**

**Journal**

**Teacher Resources**
• Envision It! Pictured Vocabulary Cards
• Tested Vocabulary Cards
• Reader's and Writer's Notebook

**Common Core State Standards**

**Literature 2.** Recount stories, including fables, folktales, and myths from diverse cultures; determine the central message, lesson, or moral and explain how it is conveyed through key details in the text. **Also Literature 10.**

---

 **Bridge to Common Core**

### CRAFT AND STRUCTURE

Students analyze the structure of the selection and how its components relate to each other and the whole when they examine its genre. As they preview the title and illustrations and prepare to read, they come to see how purpose shapes the content and style of the text.

---

### Academic Vocabulary ©

**folk tale** a story created by an anonymous person and passed from generation to generation through oral storytelling until a collector or writer puts it into written form

---

### Strategy Response Log

Have students use p. 26 in the *Reader's and Writer's Notebook* to identify the characteristics of folk tales.

---

# Text-Based Comprehension
## Introduce Main Selection

**Student Edition, pp. 158–159**

**GENRE** Explain that **folk tales** are stories that are created by anonymous storytellers and handed down orally from generation to generation until someone records them. Often there are several versions of one folk tale. Folk tales express themes about human nature, often through animals. Characters usually aren't well developed, but instead represent an aspect of human nature or are used to move the plot along.

**PREVIEW AND PREDICT** Have students preview the title and illustrations to predict what the selection will be about.

**PURPOSE** By analyzing *Fly, Eagle, Fly!,* a folk tale, students will gain knowledge about the unique behaviors of animals.

# Access Main Selection

| READER AND TASK SUGGESTIONS | |
|---|---|
| **Preparing to Read the Text** | **Leveled Tasks** |
| • Review using a dictionary to find the meanings, syllable divisions, and pronunciations of unfamiliar words.<br><br>• Review the features of a folk tale.<br><br>• Remind students to adjust their reading rate as they encounter challenging vocabulary and concepts. | • **Theme and Knowledge Demands** If students have difficulty understanding the setting of this folk tale and the culture of its characters, have them name things in the picture on pp. 162–163 that provide clues that the story does not take place in the United States.<br><br>• **Structure** Many students may have difficulty with the simple structure and clear language of this folk tale. Have these students identify what happens first, next, and last and the conflict in the story. |

See Text Complexity Measures for *Fly, Eagle, Fly!* on the tab at the beginning of this week.

**READ** Tell students that today they will read *Fly, Eagle, Fly!* for the first time. Use the Read for Understanding routine.

## Routine    Read for Understanding ©

Deepen understanding by reading the selection multiple times.

1. **First Read**—If students need support, then use the **Access Text** notes to help them clarify understanding.

2. **Second Read**—Use the **Close Reading** notes to help students draw knowledge from the text.

| **Day 2**  SMALL GROUP TIME • Differentiate Comprehension, p. SG•65 | | |
|---|---|---|
|  **On-Level** | **Strategic Intervention** |  **Advanced** |
| • **Practice** Selection Vocabulary<br>• **Read** *Fly, Eagle, Fly!* | • **Reteach** Selection Vocabulary<br>• **Read** *Fly, Eagle, Fly!* | • **Extend** Selection Vocabulary<br>• **Read** *Fly, Eagle, Fly!*<br>• **Investigate** Inquiry Project |

**eStreet Interactive**
www.ReadingStreet.com

 **Pearson eText**
• Student Edition

 **AudioText CD**

 **Teacher Resources**
• Reader's and Writer's Notebook

 **Background Building Audio CD**

## Access for All

**A** Advanced

Have students share with partners one of their favorite folk tales, explaining the plot and describing the main idea of the tale.

**ELL**

**Build Background** To build background, review the selection summary in English (*ELL Handbook*, p. 145). Use the Retelling Cards to provide visual support for the summary.

**If...** students need more scaffolding and practice with the **Comprehension Skill, then...** use the activities on p. DI•121 in the Teacher Resources section on SuccessNet.

1ST READ

## Access Text © If students need help, then...

⊙ **CAUSE AND EFFECT** Explain that a cause is *why* something happens and an effect is *what* happens. Why does the farmer go to the valley and river-bed? (He needs to find the lost calf.)

**MODEL** (Think Aloud) In the first sentence on p. 160, I read that the farmer went "to search for a lost calf." I know that "what happened" is the farmer goes out to search. Is that the cause or the effect? **(effect)** If I ask myself why that happened, I know that the calf getting lost causes him to conduct a search.

**ON THEIR OWN** Have students reread pp. 160–161 to identify and further understand cause-and-effect relationships. For additional practice, use *Let's Practice It!* p. 260 on the *Teacher Resources DVD-ROM.*

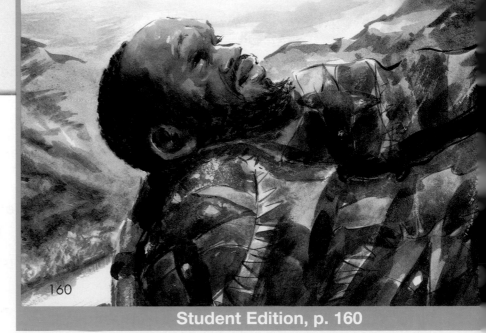

A farmer went out one day to search for a lost calf. The little herd boys had come back without it the evening before. And that night there had been a terrible storm.

He went to the valley and searched. He searched by the riverbed. He searched among the reeds, behind the rocks, and in the rushing water.

He wandered over the hillside and through the dark and tangled forests where everything began, then out again along the muddy cattle tracks.

He searched in the long thatch grass, taller than his own head. He climbed the slopes of the high mountain with its rocky cliffs rising to the sky. He called out all the time, hoping that the calf might hear, but also because he felt so alone. His shouts echoed off the cliffs. The river roared in the valley below.

160

**Student Edition, p. 160**

2ND READ

## Close Reading ©

**SYNTHESIS** What makes the story seem like a folk tale so far? (The characters don't have names, and the animals seem to be important to the plot of the story.)

**REREAD CHALLENGING TEXT** Have students reread the last paragraph on p. 160 to clarify the emotions the farmer is experiencing. Students may need help understanding his helpless, lonely feelings that foreshadow a future action of his.

**DEVELOP LANGUAGE** Have students reread the first paragraph on p. 161. *What does the word* gully *mean? Where might you see a* gully?

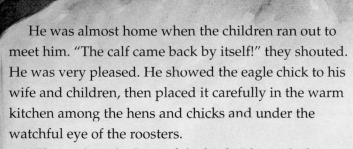

He climbed up a gully in case the calf had huddled there to escape the storm. And that was where he stopped. For there, on a ledge of rock, close enough to touch, he saw the most unusual sight—an eagle chick, very young, hatched from its egg a day or two before and then blown from its nest by the terrible storm.

He reached out and cradled it in both hands. He would take it home and care for it. And home he went, still calling, calling in case the calf might hear.

He was almost home when the children ran out to meet him. "The calf came back by itself!" they shouted. He was very pleased. He showed the eagle chick to his wife and children, then placed it carefully in the warm kitchen among the hens and chicks and under the watchful eye of the roosters.

"The eagle is the king of the birds," he said, "but we shall train it to be a chicken."

161

**Student Edition, p. 161**

**ANALYSIS • TEXT EVIDENCE** How does the storyteller describe the eagle chick? Cite details from the tale. ("very young, hatched from its egg a day or two before and then blown from its nest.")

**Common Core State Standards**

**Literature 1.** Ask and answer questions to demonstrate understanding of a text, referring explicitly to the text as the basis for the answers. **Also Literature 3.**

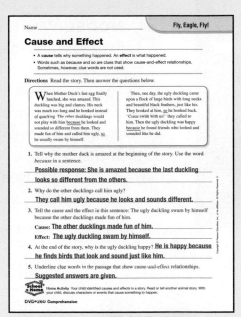

Let's Practice It! TR DVD•260

**Connect to Science**

**Fledglings** Often fledglings, or small birds that are just learning to fly, seem as if they need human intervention. However, experts agree that these creatures have the best chance of survival if they are left alone. The mother bird will watch over them and continue to feed and protect them even after they are out of the nest.

**ELL**

**Activate Prior Knowledge** Remind students of your discussion about eagles and their behavior. What do you know about chickens? Do eagles and chickens behave the same or differently? Will the farmer have problems teaching the eagle to be a chicken? Have students talk to partners about the differences between eagles and chickens.

*Fly, Eagle, Fly!* **161a**

## Access Text © If students need help, then...

⊙ **MONITOR AND CLARIFY** Have students read p. 162 and look at the illustrations on pp. 162 and 163. Ask students why the eagle is living among the chickens and acting like them. (The farmer planned to teach the eagle to be a chicken.)

**(Think Aloud)** **MODEL** When I read about the eagle acting like a chicken, I am confused. To clarify, I will return to page 161 and reread the last two paragraphs. What plan does the farmer have for the eagle? (He wants to teach it to be a chicken.) Do the eagle's actions make sense now? (yes)

So the eagle lived among the chickens, learning their ways. His children called their friends to see the strange bird. For as it grew, living on the bits and pieces put out for the chickens, it began to look quite different from any chicken they had ever seen.

## Close Reading ©

**INFERENCE • TEXT EVIDENCE** Why does the eagle start acting like the chickens? Cite evidence from the text. (The farmer places the eagle with the chickens, so it learns the way chickens behave. We learn this from the last two paragraphs on p. 161 and the first sentence on p. 162.)

162

**Student Edition, p. 162**

**ON THEIR OWN** Have students reread p. 162 and have them generate questions to clarify the text. Have students use text evidence to support, adjust, or correct their comprehension.

163

**Student Edition, p. 163**

**SYNTHESIS • TEXT EVIDENCE** Reread page 162 and look at the illustration on pages 162 and 163. What reaction do people have when they see the eagle? (People are laughing.) What information helps you understand why people have this reaction? (The text on p. 162 says it looks "quite different from any chicken they had ever seen.")

**Common Core State Standards**

**Literature 1.** Ask and answer questions to demonstrate understanding of a text, referring explicitly to the text as the basis for the answers. **Literature 3.** Describe characters in a story (e.g., their traits, motivations, or feelings) and explain how their actions contribute to the sequence of events.

**ELL**

**Vocabulary: Multiple Meanings** Read aloud the first sentence on p. 162. The word *ways* can mean "different paths or routes." It can also mean "certain behaviors or actions." Reread the sentence with students and ask which definition fits on this page.

*Fly, Eagle, Fly!* **163a**

## 1ST READ

## Access Text © If students need help, then...

**Review** DRAW CONCLUSIONS Ask students why they think the eagle refuses to fly.

**Think Aloud** **MODEL** I know it is the eagle's nature to fly, but so far in the story, the farmer has let the chickens raise the eagle. The eagle thinks it is a chicken, and the chickens don't fly. Therefore, I think the eagle refuses to fly because it has never seen the chickens do it.

## 2ND READ

## Close Reading ©

**INFERENCE • TEXT EVIDENCE**
Have students reread p. 164. What does the farmer conclude about the eagle? (He concludes that it is a chicken because it walks, talks, eats, and thinks like a chicken.)

**EVALUATION • TEXT EVIDENCE**
Why does the friend want to prove the eagle is an eagle? Use facts and details from the story to support your answer. (On p. 165, he says, "You belong not to the earth but to the sky. Fly, Eagle, fly!" The friend believes the eagle is going against its nature by staying on the ground all the time.)

One day a friend dropped in for a visit. He and the farmer sat at the door of the kitchen hut. The friend saw the bird among the chickens. "Hey! That's not a chicken. It's an eagle!"

The farmer smiled at him and said, "Of course it's a chicken. Look—it walks like a chicken, it talks like a chicken, it eats like a chicken. It *thinks* like a chicken. Of course it's a chicken."

But the friend was not convinced. "I will show you that it is an eagle," he said.

"Go ahead," said the farmer.

164

**Student Edition, p. 164**

**ON THEIR OWN** Have students reread pp. 164–165 and use evidence from the text to draw a conclusion about a character or event in the story. For additional practice with drawing conclusions, use *Let's Practice It!* p. 261 on the *Teacher Resources DVD-ROM.*

The farmer's children helped his friend catch the bird. It was fairly heavy but he lifted it above his head and said: "You are not a chicken but an eagle. You belong not to the earth but to the sky. Fly, Eagle, fly!"

The bird stretched out its wings as the farmer and his family had seen it do before. But it looked about, saw the chickens feeding, and jumped down to scratch with them for food.

"I told you it was a chicken," the farmer said, and roared with laughter.

165

**Student Edition, p. 165**

**ANALYSIS • TEXT EVIDENCE** What details on page 165 make you see, feel, hear, taste, or smell? (The words *roared with laughter* appeal to the sense of hearing and sight. They create an image of a man doubling over with laughter.)

**Literature 1.** Ask and answer questions to demonstrate understanding of a text, referring explicitly to the text as the basis for the answers. **Literature 3.** Describe characters in a story (e.g., their traits, motivations, or feelings) and explain how their actions contribute to the sequence of events. **Also Literature 4.**

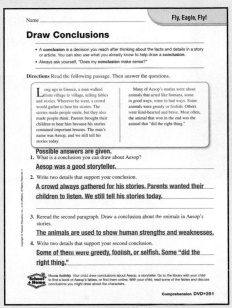

Let's Practice It! TR DVD•261

### Access for All

Ⓐ **Advanced**

Challenge students to draw conclusions about the farmer based on his actions, words, and thoughts. What can you conclude about the farmer based on his plan to teach the eagle—the king of birds—to be a chicken?

🄴🄻🄻

**Build Academic Vocabulary**
Supply meanings for the supporting Academic Vocabulary as needed. For example: Sensory details are words that describe things you see, hear, taste, feel, or smell. Write on the board several basic words that appeal to the senses, such as *sweet, green, soft, scream, flowery,* and have students identify the sense to which each word appeals.

## Access Text © If students need help, then...

**◉ MONITOR AND CLARIFY** After students read pp. 166–167, ask them why the friend is so determined to prove that the eagle is actually an eagle. Tell students to pay special attention to the friend's words.

**(Think Aloud) MODEL** At first, I thought the friend wanted to prove the farmer wrong. But he repeatedly tells the bird it is an eagle and explains that it belongs to the sky, not the earth. I think he is determined to help the eagle realize what it really is and where it actually belongs.

**ON THEIR OWN** Have students reread pp. 166–167 and practice fix-up strategies to help them monitor, adjust, and correct their understanding of the story.

## Close Reading ©

**INFERENCE • TEXT EVIDENCE**

Where does the friend take the eagle? Why do you think he does this? Cite evidence from the text to support your response. (He takes the bird to the top of the tallest hut. On p. 166, the friend says he wants to prove to the farmer that the bird is an eagle and not a chicken. He hopes that being up high will seem familiar to the bird and inspire it to fly.)

Next day the friend was back. "Farmer," he said, "I will prove to you that this is no chicken but an eagle. Bring me a ladder." With the large bird under one arm, he struggled up the slippery thatch of the tallest hut.

The farmer doubled over with laughter. "It eats chicken food. It thinks like a chicken. It *is* a chicken." The friend, swaying on top of the hut, took the eagle's head, pointed it to the sky, and said: "You are not a chicken but an eagle. You belong not to the earth but to the sky. Fly, Eagle, fly!"

**Student Edition, p. 166**

**CHECK PREDICTIONS** Have students look back at the predictions they made earlier and discuss whether they were accurate. Then have students preview the rest of the selection and either adjust their predictions accordingly or make new predictions.

Again the great bird stretched out its wings. It trembled and the claws that clasped his hand opened. "Fly, Eagle, fly!" the man cried.

But the bird scrambled out of his hands, slid down the thatch, and sailed in among the chickens.

There was much laughter.

Very early next morning, on the third day, the farmer's dogs began to bark. A voice was calling outside in the darkness. The farmer ran to the door. It was his friend again. "Give me one more chance with the bird," he begged.

"Do you know the time? It's long before dawn. Are you crazy?"

"Come with me. Fetch the bird."

Reluctantly the farmer went into the kitchen, stepping over his sleeping children, and picked up the bird, which was fast asleep among the chickens. The two men set off, disappearing into the darkness.

167

**Student Edition, p. 167**

If you want to teach this selection in two sessions, stop here.

If you want to continue reading this selection, turn to page 168–169.

**ANALYSIS** Help students generate text-based questions by providing the following question stem: In the selection, what did the eagle do when _____?

 **Common Core State Standards**

**Literature 1.** Ask and answer questions to demonstrate understanding of a text, referring explicitly to the text as the basis for the answers. **Literature 3.** Describe characters in a story (e.g., their traits, motivations, or feelings) and explain how their actions contribute to the sequence of events. **Also Literature 10.**

## Access for All

**SI** Strategic Intervention

Have students work in small groups to summarize the main events of the selection. From their summaries, determine whether they need to apply fix-up strategies to improve comprehension.

**A** Advanced

Have students work in pairs to investigate the natural habitats and behaviors of eagles. Have students present their findings to the class, using visuals to add interest to their presentations.

**Oral Language: Intonation** Tell students that the intonation of dialogue is determined by the end punctuation. Point out that intonation signals questions, exclamations, and statements. Demonstrate reading different types of sentences from p. 167. Have students identify them as questions, exclamations, or statements based on intonation.

**Monitor and Clarify** Tell students they should keep asking themselves questions to make sure they understand the story. Write these questions: *Whom or what is the story about? Where does the story take place? What happens in the beginning, middle, and end?*

*Fly, Eagle, Fly!* **167a**

**Common Core State Standards**

**Writing 8.** Recall information from experiences or gather information from print and digital sources; take brief notes on sources and sort evidence into provided categories. **Language 1.** Demonstrate command of the conventions of standard English grammar and usage when writing or speaking. **Language 2.f.** Use spelling patterns and generalizations (e.g., word families, position-based spellings, syllable patterns, ending rules, meaningful word parts) in writing words.

 **Bridge to Common Core**

**RESEARCH TO BUILD AND PRESENT KNOWLEDGE**

On Day 2 of the weeklong research project, students gather relevant information based on their focused questions from Day 1. They consult informational texts as well as digital sources to find information that helps them find specific, useful information. This process enables students to demonstrate an understanding of the subject under investigation.

# Research and Inquiry

## Step 2 Navigate/Search

**TEACH** Have students generate a research plan for gathering relevant information about their topics. Suggest that students search encyclopedias—either print, electronic, or online versions—using their inquiry questions and keywords. Tell them to skim and scan each book or site for information that helps answer their inquiry question or leads them to specific information that will be useful. Bolded or italicized words may be clues to the kind of information the Web site source provides. Have students look for visual aids such as photographs, illustrations, graphs, and diagrams. Remind students to take notes as they gather information.

**Think Aloud** **MODEL** While looking for information on bears and hibernation, I found that black bears start preparing for hibernation in the summer by eating carbohydrate-rich diets. I will use keywords from this information, such as *diets*, to lead me to more specific information. One fact I found explains that bears eat a lot of berries.

**GUIDE PRACTICE** Have students continue their review of sources they identified. Tell them to make sure to skim and scan for further keywords that might lead to more information. Remind students that they can use graphic organizers and outlines to take simple notes. As students access online information, they should note their sources for a Works Cited page.

**ON THEIR OWN** Have students sort their notes into an organizer as they prepare their journal entry. Suggest that they organize their notes by main ideas and supporting details.

# Conventions

## Prepositions

**TEACH** Write *An eagle flew* and *An eagle flew from the tall trees* on the board. Point out the preposition *from.* A preposition shows a relationship between a noun or pronoun and the other words in a sentence. Underline *from the tall trees.* This is a prepositional phrase, which is a group of words that begins with a preposition and ends with a noun or pronoun.

**GUIDE PRACTICE** Have students complete the sentence frames orally by adding a prepositional phrase.

> Eagles fly _____.
>
> Chickens scratch _____.
>
> Farmers plant _____.

**ON THEIR OWN** For additional practice, use the *Reader's and Writer's Notebook,* p. 295.

# Spelling

## Syllables VCCCV

**TEACH** Remind students that their spelling words for this week have the syllable pattern VCCCV. Model how to spell the word *surprise.* First, write the letter *s.* Then write the first vowel, *u.* Write the group of three consonants, *rpr,* and the last vowel, *i.* Finally, write the last letters, *se.*

**GUIDE PRACTICE** Have students write each spelling word and identify and underline the VCCCV syllable pattern in it.

**ON THEIR OWN** For additional practice, use the *Reader's and Writer's Notebook,* p. 296.

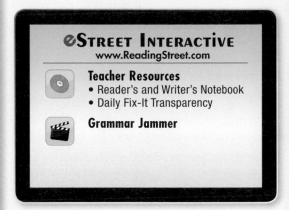

**eSTREET INTERACTIVE**
www.ReadingStreet.com

**Teacher Resources**
• Reader's and Writer's Notebook
• Daily Fix-It Transparency

**Grammar Jammer**

## Daily Fix-It

3. The bald eagle live high on top the cliff. *(lives; top of)*

4. It seems like the bigest bird in the wirld. *(biggest; world)*

## Academic Vocabulary

**outline** a plan that shows how research information is organized

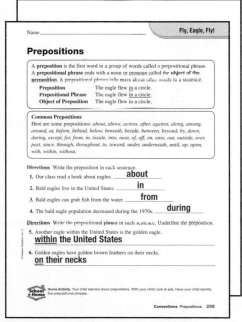

Reader's and Writer's Notebook, pp. 295–296

**Conventions** To provide students with practice on prepositions, use the modified grammar lessons in the *ELL Handbook* and the Grammar Jammer online at: www.ReadingStreet.com

© **Common Core State Standards**

**Writing 3.c.** Use temporal words and phrases to signal event order.

# Writing

## Summary

**INTRODUCE THE PROMPT** Remind students that yesterday they learned about the key features of a summary. Tell them today they will practice writing for tests by creating a summary that addresses the prompt. Read aloud the writing prompt.

### Writing Prompt

Think about a tale you know well. Now write a summary of the plot, telling the events in time order.

| Mini-Lesson | Writing for Tests: Time-Order Transition Words |
| --- | --- |

- When we write summaries, we want to include only the most important information. We also want to present that information in the order that it happens in the story.

- Explain that a story sequence chart can help students identify the important parts of a story in the order that they happen. Display a story sequence chart and complete it with a well-known story as the example. Discuss what happened first in the story, and write the most important information in the first Events box. Then identify two more important events and write them in the next two Events boxes. Then discuss what happens last in the story and write the information in the last Events box.

- Many summaries include time-order transition words. Time-order transition words help us organize our writing and reading. The words tell when things happened or in what order. Examples of time-order transition words include *first, then, next, last, meanwhile,* and *finally.*

**DISCUSS RUBRIC** Discuss the scoring rubric found on p. 297 in the *Reader's and Writer's Notebook*. Go over the criteria for each trait under each score. Remind students that this is the rubric that will be used to evaluate the summaries they write.

**SAMPLE TEST** Direct students to get paper and pencil ready to take a writing test. Display the writing prompt for students and give them appropriate time to write to it. Remind students to allow themselves a couple of minutes after writing to reread what they've written and make changes or additions.

## Routine  Quick Write for Fluency  Team Talk

**1. Talk** Have pairs discuss time-order transition words.

**2. Write** Have students write two to three sentences using time-order transition words.

**3. Share** Have students read their own writing to their partner.

Routines Flip Chart

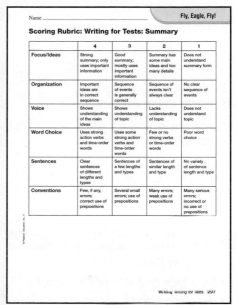

Reader's and Writer's Notebook, p. 297

# Wrap Up Your Day!

✔ **Content Knowledge** *What did you learn about how the farmer's friend tried to prove that the eagle was not a chicken?*

✔ **Text-Based Comprehension** *What caused the farmer and his family to laugh when the man tried to get the eagle to fly? How can you figure out what the words* claws *and* clasped *mean?*

**Preview DAY 3**

Tell students that tomorrow they will read more about the man and his attempts to make the eagle fly.

## Common Core State Standards

**Speaking/Listening 1.** Engage effectively in a range of collaborative discussions (one-on-one, in groups, and teacher-led) with diverse partners on grade 3 topics and texts, building on others' ideas and expressing their own clearly. **Language 6.** Acquire and use accurately grade-appropriate conversational, general academic, and domain-specific words and phrases, including those that signal spatial and temporal relationships (e.g., *After dinner that night we went looking for them*).

# Content Knowledge

## Unique Animal Behaviors

**EXPAND THE CONCEPT** Remind students of the weekly concept question, *What behaviors are unique to different animals?* Tell students that today they will read more about the eagle and the chickens. Encourage students to think about the unique behavior of the eagle.

# Build Oral Language

**TALK ABOUT SENTENCES AND WORDS** Reread sentences from Student Edition page 160, *Fly, Eagle, Fly!*

*He called out all the time, hoping that the calf might hear, but also because he felt so alone. His shouts echoed off the cliffs. The river roared in the valley below.*

- What does the word *echoed* mean? (sound that bounced back)
- What is so extraordinary about the area that would make his voice echo? (He is in the cliffs over a valley. The sound of his voice bounces off the cliffs so he can hear his words echoed back.)
- What is another word for *echoed?* (repeated)

**Team Talk** Have students work with a partner to replace key words in the sentences with synonyms. Use the following sentence frames.

**He _____ out all the time, hoping that the calf might hear, but also because he felt so alone. His shouts _____ off the cliffs. The river roared in the _____ below.**

# Build Oral Vocabulary

## Amazing Words    Robust Vocabulary Routine

1. **Introduce** Write the word *pesky* on the board. Have students say it with you. Yesterday, we read about a farmer who trains an eagle to be a chicken. His *pesky* friend tries to prove him wrong and teach the eagle to fly. Have students determine the definition of *pesky*. (A *pesky* person is troublesome or irritating.)

2. **Demonstrate** Have students answer questions to demonstrate understanding. Why might chickens be thought of as *pesky*? (They make a mess or are in the way.)

3. **Apply** Have students apply their understanding by listing possible synonyms of *pesky*.

4. **Display the Word** Point out the CVC syllable *pes,* and the ending, *-ky.* Say the word and have students repeat.

See p. OV•5 to teach *unfurl.*

Routines Flip Chart

**ADD TO THE CONCEPT MAP** Discuss the Amazing Words *extraordinary* and *scenery.* Add these and other concept-related words to the concept map. Use the following questions to develop students' understanding of the concept.

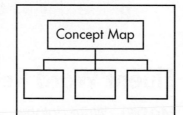

- What animal behavior or characteristic do you think is *extraordinary*?

- How could the *scenery* and environment affect an animal's behavior?

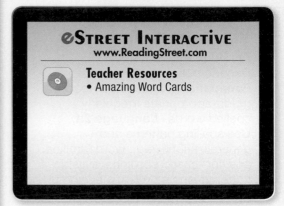

**eSTREET INTERACTIVE**
www.ReadingStreet.com

**Teacher Resources**
• Amazing Word Cards

## Amazing Words

| | |
|---|---|
| armor | scenery |
| agile | pesky |
| snout | unfurl |
| protrude | coil |
| extraordinary | intersection |

**ELL**

**Expand Vocabulary** Use the Day 3 instruction on ELL Poster 20 to help students expand vocabulary.

 **Common Core State Standards**

**Foundational Skills 3.c.** Decode multisyllable words. **Foundational Skills 3.d.** Read grade-appropriate irregularly spelled words. **Language 2.f.** Use spelling patterns and generalizations (e.g., word families, position-based spellings, syllable patterns, ending rules, meaningful word parts) in writing words.

# Word Analysis

## ⊙ Syllables VCCCV

**MODEL WORD BUILDING** Now we are going to build words with the syllabication pattern VCCCV. Write *central* and identify the VCCCV pattern. Watch me change the vowel *e* in the first syllable to the vowel *o,* and the vowel *a* in the second syllable to the vowel *o.* Model how to pronounce the new word *control*.

**GUIDE PRACTICE** Write *hardly* and have the class decode it with you. Remind students that the letter *y* is sometimes considered a vowel. Have students spell *hardly* with their letter tiles. Monitor students' work.

> **Corrective feedback** | Model the correct spelling and have students correct their tiles.

- Change the *h* to *p* and the *d* to *t*. Say the new word.

| p | a | r | t | l | y |
|---|---|---|---|---|---|

- Change the vowel *a* to the vowel *o*. Say the new word.

| p | o | r | t | l | y |
|---|---|---|---|---|---|

- Change the vowel *o* to the vowel *e*. Say the new word.

| p | e | r | t | l | y |
|---|---|---|---|---|---|

## Fluent Word Reading

**MODEL** Write *dolphin*. I can identify the VCCCV pattern in *dolphin*. I divide the word between the *l* and *p,* say each syllable, and put the parts together to say *dolphin*.

**GUIDE PRACTICE** Write the words below. Look for the word parts you know. When I point to the word, we'll read it together. Allow one second per word part previewing time for the first reading.

| huddle | contract | orphan | explain | enclose | complain |
|---|---|---|---|---|---|

**ON THEIR OWN** Have students read the list above three or four times, until they can read one word per second.

# Decodable Passage 20B

If students need help, then...

## Read *Manfred's Monsters*

**READ WORDS IN ISOLATION** Have students turn to p. 57 in *Decodable Practice Readers 3.2* and find the first list of words. Each word in this list has the VCCCV syllabication pattern. Let's read these words. Be sure that students identify the correct pattern.

Next, have students read the high-frequency words.

**PREVIEW** Have students read the title and preview the story. Tell them that they will read words with the VCCCV syllable pattern.

**READ WORDS IN CONTEXT** Chorally read the story along with the students. Have students identify words in the story that have the VCCCV syllable pattern. Make sure that students are monitoring their accuracy when they decode words.

**Team Talk** Pair students and have them take turns reading the story aloud to each other. Monitor students as they read to check for proper pronunciation and appropriate pacing.

**eSTREET INTERACTIVE**
www.ReadingStreet.com

**Pearson eText**
• Decodable Reader

**Letter Tile Drag and Drop**

## Access for All

**A** Advanced

Have students come up with their own addition and deletion questions and build new words.

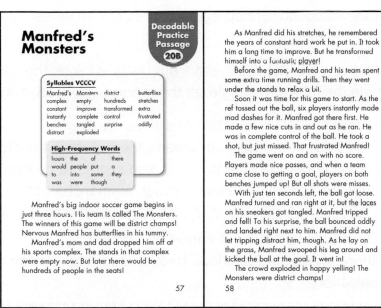

## Manfred's Monsters

**Decodable Practice Passage 20B**

### Syllables VCCCV

| | | | |
|---|---|---|---|
| Manfred's | Monsters | district | butterflies |
| complex | empty | hundreds | stretches |
| constant | improve | transformed | extra |
| instantly | complete | control | frustrated |
| benches | tangled | surprise | oddly |
| distract | exploded | | |

### High-Frequency Words

| | | | |
|---|---|---|---|
| hours | the | of | there |
| would | people | put | a |
| to | into | some | they |
| was | were | though | |

Manfred's big indoor soccer game begins in just three hours. His team is called The Monsters. The winners of this game will be district champs! Nervous Manfred has butterflies in his tummy.

Manfred's mom and dad dropped him off at his sports complex. The stands in that complex were empty now. But later there would be hundreds of people in the seats!

57

As Manfred did his stretches, he remembered the years of constant hard work he put in. It took him a long time to improve. But he transformed himself into a fantastic player!

Before the game, Manfred and his team spent some extra time running drills. Then they went under the stands to relax a bit.

Soon it was time for this game to start. As the ref tossed out the ball, six players instantly made mad dashes for it. Manfred got there first. He made a few nice cuts in and out as he ran. He was in complete control of the ball. He took a shot, but just missed. That frustrated Manfred!

The game went on and on with no score. Players made nice passes, and when a team came close to getting a goal, players on both benches jumped up! But all shots were misses.

With just ten seconds left, the ball got loose. Manfred turned and ran right at it, but the laces on his sneakers got tangled. Manfred tripped and fell! To his surprise, the ball bounced oddly and landed right next to him. Manfred did not let tripping distract him, though. As he lay on the grass, Manfred swooped his leg around and kicked the ball at the goal. It went in!

The crowd exploded in happy yelling! The Monsters were district champs!

58

Decodable Practice Passage 20B

**Common Core State Standards**
**Literature 1.** Ask and answer questions to demonstrate understanding of a text, referring explicitly to the text as the basis for the answers. **Literature 2.** Recount stories, including fables, folktales, and myths from diverse cultures; determine the central message, lesson, or moral and explain how it is conveyed through key details in the text.

**Strategy Response Log**

Have students revisit p. 26 in the *Reader's and Writer's Notebook* to add more information about folk tales.

# Text-Based Comprehension
## Check Understanding

Student Edition, pp. 158–159

**If...** you chose to read *Fly, Eagle, Fly!* in two parts,
**then...** use the following questions to monitor students' understanding of pp. 158–167 of the selection. Encourage students to cite evidence from the text.

**SYNTHESIS** How are each of the friend's attempts to teach the eagle to fly similar? *Each time, he raises the eagle off the ground.* (pp. 165, 166)

**EVALUATION** What folk tale characteristics does *Fly, Eagle, Fly!* have? *Fly, Eagle, Fly!* has characters that move, or create, the events in the story, but we don't know much about the characters. It also seems to be expressing an important message about human nature through animal characters.

**Corrective feedback**  **If...** students leave out important details,
**then...** have students look back through the illustrations in the selection.

**READ** Use the **Access Text** and **Close Reading** notes to finish reading *Fly, Eagle, Fly!*

**If...** you followed the Read for Understanding routine below,
**then...** ask students to retell the selection before you reread *Fly, Eagle, Fly!*

**RETELL** Have students retell the story of *Fly, Eagle, Fly!* using time-order transition words and details.

> **Corrective feedback** | **If...** students leave out important details,
> **then...** have students look back through the illustrations in the selection.

**READ** Return to p. 160–161 and use the **2nd Read/Close Reading** notes to reread *Fly, Eagle, Fly!*

# Read Main Selection

**Routine** | **Read for Understanding** ©

Deepen understanding by reading the selection multiple times.

1. **First Read**— If students need support, then use the **Access Text** notes to help them clarify understanding.

2. **Second Read**—Use the **Close Reading** notes to help students draw knowledge from the text.

**ELL**

**Check Retelling** To support retelling, review the multilingual summary for *Fly, Eagle, Fly!* with the appropriate Retelling Cards to scaffold understanding.

**Day 3** | **SMALL GROUP TIME • Differentiate Close Reading, p. SG•65**

| **OL On-Level** | **SI Strategic Intervention** | **A Advanced** |
|---|---|---|
| • **Reread** to Develop Vocabulary | • **Reread** to Develop Vocabulary | • **Reread** to Extend Vocabulary |
| • **Read** *Fly, Eagle, Fly!* | • **Read** *Fly, Eagle, Fly!* | • **Read** *Fly, Eagle, Fly!* |
| | | • **Investigate** Inquiry Project |

**ELL**

**If...** students need more scaffolding and practice with the **Main Selection,**
**then...** use the activities on p. DI•122 in the Teacher Resources section on SuccessNet.

# Access Text © If students need help, then...

**UNKNOWN WORDS** Have students use a dictionary to determine the meaning of the word *veld* in the last paragraph on p. 168.

**Think Aloud** **MODEL** When I look up *veld* in the dictionary, I look first at the guide words to find the right page. *Veld* comes between words that start with *va* and *vi*. The definition of *veld* is "open country in South Africa, with grass or bushes but few trees." Does that make sense here? Yes, it does.

# Close Reading ©

**EVALUATION • TEXT EVIDENCE**

Have students reread p. 168. Where is the friend taking the eagle? Why do you think they need to go there at night? Cite details from the text to support your answer. (He is taking the eagle to the mountains where the farmer found it. They go at night so "our eagle may see the sun rise over the mountain and follow it into the sky where it belongs.")

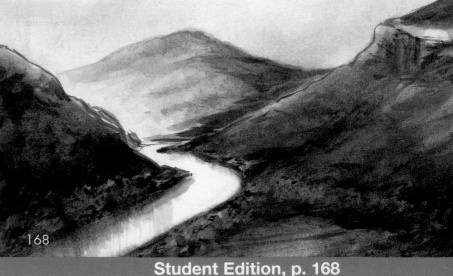

"Where are we going?" asked the farmer sleepily.

"To the mountains where you found the bird."

"And why at this ridiculous time of the night?"

"So that our eagle may see the sun rise over the mountain and follow it into the sky where it belongs."

They went into the valley and crossed the river, the friend leading the way. The bird was very heavy and too large to carry comfortably, but the friend insisted on taking it himself.

"Hurry," he said, "or the dawn will arrive before we do!"

The first light crept into the sky as they began to climb the mountain. Below them they could see the river snaking like a long, thin ribbon through the golden grasslands, the forest, and the veld, stretching down toward the sea. The wispy clouds in the sky were pink at first and then began to shimmer with a golden brilliance.

168

**Student Edition, p. 168**

**ON THEIR OWN** Have students find the word *crevices* (p. 169) in a dictionary and figure out the meaning of the word. (narrow splits or cracks) For additional practice, use *Reader's and Writer's Notebook,* p. 298.

Sometimes their path was dangerous as it clung to the side of the mountain, crossing narrow shelves of rock and taking them into dark crevices and out again. They were both panting, especially the friend who was carrying the bird.

169

**Student Edition, p. 169**

**ANALYSIS** How does the friend's plan to go to the mountain relate to his other attempts to teach the eagle to fly? (He wants to bring it to a high place. The mountain is higher than the roof.)

## Common Core State Standards

**Literature 3.** Describe characters in a story (e.g., their traits, motivations, or feelings) and explain how their actions contribute to the sequence of events. **Also Literature 1., Language 4., 4.d.**

## Access for All

 **Strategic Intervention**

Tell students that *insisted* means "to state or demand something despite disagreement" and "to request urgently." Read the sentence on p. 168 and ask students which meaning fits best in this context.

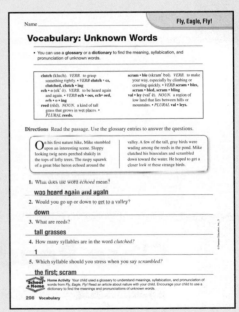

Reader's and Writer's Notebook, p. 298

**Monitor and Clarify** Read p. 168 and model monitoring and clarifying: I don't understand why they are taking such a long journey with the bird. I will review the page. I see that the friend says the bird will see the sun and follow it into the sky where the bird belongs. That's why they are climbing so high. He wants to take the bird to the top of the mountain to teach it to fly. Have students review or reread to clarify understanding as needed.

## Access Text © If students need help, then...

**⊙ CAUSE AND EFFECT** Ask students to tell what happens at the end of the story and to identify why it happens.

**MODEL** At the end, the eagle flies away. That is the effect of the farmer's friend trying to help the bird understand where it belongs, which is the cause.

**ON THEIR OWN** Have students reread p. 171 and identify the cause of the farmer being quiet.

**CROSS-TEXT EVALUATION**
**Use a Strategy to Self-Check** How did "Eagle Watching" on p. 157 help you understand this selection?

170

**Student Edition, p. 170**

## Close Reading ©

**SYNTHESIS** What message does the folk tale express through the actions of the characters and the events? How can you apply that message to your life? (The folk tale expresses the idea that we all have a true nature and that we just need to find that nature to "soar." If we really know ourselves, we can be our best by simply being who we are and doing what we do.)

**SYNTHESIS • TEXT EVIDENCE** Using what you learned in this selection, tell about the unique behaviors of animals such as eagles and chickens. Have students cite examples from the text to support their responses.

**CHECK PREDICTIONS** Have students return to the predictions they made earlier and confirm whether they are accurate.

 **Common Core State Standards**

**Literature 1.** Ask and answer questions to demonstrate understanding of a text, referring explicitly to the text as the basis for the answers. **Literature 2.** Recount stories, including fables, folktales, and myths from diverse cultures; determine the central message, lesson, or moral and explain how it is conveyed through key details in the text. **Also Literature 10.**

At last he said, "This will do." He looked down the cliff and saw the ground thousands of feet below. They were very near the top.

Carefully the friend carried the bird onto a ledge of rock. He set it down so that it looked toward the east, and began talking to it.

The farmer chuckled. "It talks only chickens' talk."

But the friend talked on, telling the bird about the sun, how it gives life to the world, how it reigns in the heavens, giving light to each new day.

"Look at the sun, Eagle. And when it rises, rise with it. You belong to the sky, not to the earth."

At that moment the sun's first rays shot out over the mountain, and suddenly the world was ablaze with light.

The golden sun rose majestically, dazzling them. The great bird stretched out its wings to greet the sun and feel the life-giving warmth on its feathers. The farmer was quiet. The friend said, "You belong not to the earth, but to the sky. Fly, Eagle, fly!"

He clambered back to the farmer.

All was silent. Nothing moved. The eagle's head stretched up; its wings stretched outwards; its legs leaned forward as its claws clutched the rock.

And then, without really moving, feeling the updraft of a wind more powerful than any man or bird, the great eagle leaned forward and was swept upward, higher and higher, lost to sight in the brightness of the rising sun, never again to live among the chickens.

171

**Student Edition, p. 171**

**ANALYSIS • TEXT EVIDENCE** What does the friend tell the eagle about the sun? (On p. 171, he says the sun gives life and lights each day. He tells the eagle to rise with the rising sun.)

## Access for All

**SI** Strategic Intervention

When students finish the selection, ask them to tell a partner what *Fly, Eagle, Fly!* is about. Have them explain its important points in four or five sentences.

**A** Advanced

Have students identify the theme of the folk tale and write it in their own words. Then have them describe a time when they applied the theme in their own lives.

**Homonyms** Tell students that some words have the same pronunciation and spelling but have different meanings. Point out the word *rose* in paragraph 7 on p. 171. Explain that *rose* can be the name of a flower and it can also mean "the past tense of *rise*." Read the sentence aloud. Help students determine the meaning of the word.

Common Core State Standards
Literature 1. Ask and answer questions to demonstrate understanding of a text, referring explicitly to the text as the basis for the answers. Also Literature 2., Writing 8.

## Envision It! | Retell

READING STREET ONLINE
STORY SORT
www.ReadingStreet.com

172

## Think Critically

1. The author writes this folk tale about the journey of returning the eagle to the mountain. Have you ever read another folk tale about a journey? What was the setting? Compare and contrast both folk tales. Text to Text

2. *Fly, Eagle, Fly!* is a folk tale and has a lesson to teach. What lesson do you think the author is trying to teach? **Think Like an Author**

3. Why do you think the eagle acted like a chicken? Cause and Effect

4. Look back through the selection. What parts did you reread to help you understand? What parts did you visualize? What background knowledge did you use? What questions did you ask yourself? Monitor and Clarify

5. **Look Back and Write** Look back at pages 162–165. Write about why everyone thought the eagle was a chicken. Provide evidence to support your answer. **Key Ideas and Details • Text Evidence**

**Meet the Illustrator**

## Niki Daly

Niki Daly was born in Cape Town, South Africa, and he lives there today. His picture books have won awards all over the world.

Mr. Daly uses watercolors with pen or pencil to create his lively pictures. For his books, Mr. Daly says he first watches people. Then he draws his characters many times, "until they become as real as the people around me."

As a child, Mr. Daly read a lot of comic books. They taught him to tell stories through pictures. In his books, Mr. Daly tries to show children of all races in South Africa. Mr. Daly also likes to write songs. He has even recorded two albums.

Read more books by Niki Daly.

*Jamela's Dress*

*Old Bob's Brown Bear*

Use the *Reader's and Writer's Notebook* to record your independent reading.

Reading Log

173

---

**Student Edition, pp. 172–173**

---

## Common Core State Standards

Literature 1. Ask and answer questions to demonstrate understanding of a text, referring explicitly to the text as the basis for the answers. Also Literature 2., Writing 8., 10., Speaking/Listening 4, Language 3.

### Bridge to Common Core

**RANGE OF READING AND LEVEL OF TEXT COMPLEXITY**

To increase students' capacity for reading and comprehending complex texts independently and proficiently, have them read other folk tales or read books about the unique behaviors of animals. After students read closely for a sustained period of time, they should record their reading in their Reading Logs.

# Think Critically

1. **TEXT TO TEXT** I read *Johnny Appleseed.* The settings are both outdoors. *Fly, Eagle, Fly!* takes place in Africa, and *Johnny Appleseed* is set in the United States.

2. **THINK LIKE AN AUTHOR** The author is trying to teach the lesson that we need to be true to our own nature, even if others try to change us.

3. **CAUSE AND EFFECT** The eagle acted like a chicken because the farmer trained it to live like a chicken and that's all it knew.

4. **MONITOR AND CLARIFY** I reread to learn why the eagle chick was alone. I visualized the eagle soaring. I asked why the friend talked to the eagle.

5. **LOOK BACK AND WRITE • TEXT EVIDENCE** To build writing fluency, allow 10–15 minutes.

## Scoring Rubric   Look Back and Write

**TOP-SCORE RESPONSE** A top-score response uses details to tell why everyone believed the eagle was a chicken.

**A top-score response should include:**

• a description and explanation of people's reactions, including the farmer's

• a description of the friend's protest and reasons for his attempts

• an explanation for the people's reasoning.

# Retell

Have students work in pairs to retell the selection, using the retelling strip in the Student Edition or the Story Sort as prompts. Monitor student's retellings.

## Scoring Rubric   Narrative Retelling

|  | 4 | 3 | 2 | 1 |
|---|---|---|---|---|
| **Connections** | Makes connections and generalizes beyond the text | Makes connections to other events, stories, or experiences | Makes a limited connection to another event, story, or experience | Makes no connection to another event, story, or experience |
| **Author's Purpose** | Elaborates on author's purpose | Tells author's purpose with some clarity | Makes some connection to author's purpose | Makes no connection to author's purpose |
| **Characters** | Describes the main character(s) and any character development | Identifies the main character(s) and gives some information about them | Inaccurately identifies some characters or gives little information about them | Inaccurately identifies the characters or gives no information about them |
| **Setting** | Describes the time and location | Identifies the time and location | Omits details of time or location | Is unable to identify time or location |
| **Plot** | Describes the problem, goal, events, and ending using rich detail | Tells the problem, goal, events, and ending with some errors that do not affect meaning | Tells parts of the problem, goal, events, and ending with gaps that affect meaning | Retelling has no sense of story |

**Don't Wait Until Friday**

## MONITOR PROGRESS   Check Retelling

**If...** students have difficulty retelling,

**then...** use the Retelling Cards/Story Sort to scaffold their retellings.

**eSTREET INTERACTIVE**
www.ReadingStreet.com

**Pearson eText**
• Student Edition

**Story Sort**

## Plan to Assess Retelling

☐ **Week 1** Strategic Intervention
☐ **Week 2** Advanced
☐ **Week 3** Strategic Intervention
☐ **Week 4** On-Level
☑ **This week assess any students you have not yet checked during this unit.**

## Meet the Illustrator

Have students read about illustrator Niki Daly on p. 173. Ask them how he uses his drawing talents to bring *Fly, Eagle, Fly!* to life for readers.

## Read Independently

Have students enter their independent reading information into their Reading Logs.

**Common Core State Standards**

**Foundational Skills 4.b.** Read on-level prose and poetry orally with accuracy, appropriate rate, and expression on successive readings. **Writing 2.a.** Introduce a topic and group related information together; include illustrations when useful to aiding comprehension. **Also Informational Text 2., Foundational Skills 4.**

# Fluency

## Appropriate Rate

**MODEL FLUENT READING** Have students turn to p. 169 of *Fly, Eagle, Fly!* Have students follow along as you read the page. Tell them to listen to how fast you read and to pay attention to your pauses and how they correlate to punctuation and content.

**GUIDE PRACTICE** Have students follow along as you read the page again. Then have them reread the page as a group without you until they read with the appropriate rate and with no mistakes. Continue in the same way for p. 171.

| Corrective feedback | **If...** students are having difficulty reading at the correct rate, **then...** prompt them as follows: |
| --- | --- |
| | • Do you think you need to slow down or read more quickly? |
| | • Read the sentence more quickly. Now read it more slowly. Which helps you understand what you are reading? |
| | • Tell me the sentence. Read it at the rate that would help me understand it. |

# Reread for Fluency

**Routine** Paired Reading

1. **Select a Passage** For *Fly, Eagle, Fly!*, use p. 167.

2. **Reading 1** Students read the entire passage, switching readers at the end of each paragraph.

3. **Reading 2** Partners reread the passage. This time the other student begins.

4. **Reread** For optimal fluency, have partners continue to read three or four times.

5. **Corrective Feedback** Listen as students read. Provide feedback about their rate and encourage them to adjust their rate based on punctuation and content.

Routines Flip Chart

# Research and Study Skills

## Outlining and Summarizing

**TEACH** Tell students that good readers summarize to check their understanding of a text. When students summarize nonfiction, they tell the main ideas in their own words. When they summarize fiction, they tell what happened in a story. Outlines, like summaries, list the main ideas of a text. However, outlines are visually organized to show the main ideas and the details that support those ideas. Outlines can be used to better understand a text and to organize students' own writing. Draw a basic outline:

I. Main idea

    A. Important detail

        1. Support

- A summary tells the main idea or ideas of a nonfiction text. It leaves out unimportant details. For a story, a summary tells what happened, listing the main events, the goals of the characters, how they tried to reach them, and whether they were successful.

- An outline visually organizes main ideas and supporting details. It can be used to map a text or to organize writing.

**GUIDE PRACTICE** What should you include in a summary of a story? (an explanation of the main events, goals of the characters, and how they reached them) Why would an outline help you with your own writing? (It allows you to organize your main ideas and make sure you have enough support for each idea.)

**ON THEIR OWN** Have students review and complete p. 299 of the *Reader's and Writer's Notebook*.

**eStreet Interactive**
www.ReadingStreet.com

**Teacher Resources**
- Reader's and Writer's Notebook

## Access for All

 **Advanced**

Have students read a magazine or encyclopedia article about animal instincts. Challenge them to write a two- to three-sentence summary of the article.

---

Name _____     *Fly, Eagle, Fly!*

**Outlining and Summarizing**

Summarizing refers to finding the most important ideas about a topic or text. You can summarize what you read or what you learn in class. One way to summarize is by making an outline. An outline shows a main idea and details, as in the one shown below.

**An Endangered Animal—The African Elephant**

I. Size
  A. Weight
    1. 7,000 to 16,000 pounds
    2. Males larger
  B. Height and Length
    1. 10 to 13 ft high
    2. 20 to 24 ft long

II. Diet—Vegetation
  A. Grasses
  B. Leaves
  C. Fruit

III. Habitat—Africa
  A. Forest
  B. Grassland

**Directions** Write the words from the box in the outline. Use the outline above as a guide.

| Habitat | Deer | 45 to 80 pounds | Rabbits | Wetlands |

**The Red Wolf**

I. Size
  A. 4 1/2 to 5 1/2 ft long
  B. Weight
    1. **45 to 80 pounds**
    2. Males larger
II. **Habitat**
  A. Forests
  B. Mountains
  C. **Wetlands**

III. Diet
  A. Mainly small animals
    1. Rodents
    2. **Rabbits**
  B. Others
    1. Insects
    2. Berries
    3. **Deer**

**School + Home Home Activity** Your child learned how to make an outline to summarize ideas. Give your child information about a familiar topic. Include at least three main ideas and several details about the main ideas. Help him or her organize these ideas in an outline.

Research Outlining and Summarizing **299**

Reader's and Writer's Notebook, p. 299

---

**Summarize** Give English learners the opportunity to practice their summarizing skills orally. Ask them to tell you the main things that happened in *Fly, Eagle, Fly!* Invite students to illustrate their summaries to further solidify understanding.

## Common Core State Standards

**Writing 8.** Recall information from experiences or gather information from print and digital sources; take brief notes on sources and sort evidence into provided categories. **Language 1.** Demonstrate command of the conventions of standard English grammar and usage when writing or speaking. **Language 2.f.** Use spelling patterns and generalizations (e.g., word families, position-based spellings, syllable patterns, ending rules, meaningful word parts) in writing words.

# Research and Inquiry

## Step 3 Analyze Information

**TEACH** Tell students that once they gather information, they need to summarize the information in their own words and then consider whether it has led them to a better question or to a specific area of inquiry.

**Think Aloud** **MODEL** Originally, I thought that learning about when bears start preparing for hibernation would be the most important, but I learned from my research that how they prepare for hibernation is both well documented and fascinating. I will refocus my inquiry question to include information from my online research. Now my inquiry question is *How do bears prepare for hibernation?*

**GUIDE PRACTICE** Have students analyze their findings. They may need to refocus their inquiry question to better fit the information they found. Remind students that if they have difficulty improving their focus, they can ask a reference librarian or a local expert for guidance.

Remind students that they can add to their graphic organizers and outlines as they research.

**ON THEIR OWN** Have students write brief summaries of the information they gathered and share their summaries with partners. Have partners pose questions that arise from the summaries to further direct investigation.

# Conventions

## Prepositions

**REVIEW** Remind students that this week they learned about prepositions.

A preposition shows a relationship between a noun or pronoun and the other words in a sentence.

A prepositional phrase is a group of words that begins with a preposition. It ends with a noun or pronoun called the object of the preposition.

**CONNECT TO ORAL LANGUAGE** Write the following sentences, and have students complete each sentence with a prepositional phrase.

> Gary walked _____.
>
> I followed it _____.
>
> A little bird flew _____.

**ON THEIR OWN** For additional support, use *Let's Practice It!* page 262 on the *Teacher Resources DVD-ROM.*

Let's Practice It! TR DVD•262

# Spelling

## Syllables VCCCV

**FREQUENTLY MISSPELLED WORDS** The words *Christmas* and *went* are words that students often misspell. These words are difficult because of the syllable pattern. Tell students to think carefully before they write these words. Have students practice writing the words *Christmas* and *went* by writing sentences using each word. Ask pairs of students to exchange sentences and check for any misspellings.

**ON THEIR OWN** For additional support, use the *Reader's and Writer's Notebook,* p. 300.

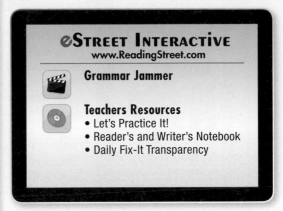

eStreet Interactive
www.ReadingStreet.com

**Grammar Jammer**

**Teachers Resources**
• Let's Practice It!
• Reader's and Writer's Notebook
• Daily Fix-It Transparency

## Access for All

**SI Strategic Intervention**

Create sentences to describe the location of classroom objects. Example: *The books are on the bookshelves. The Word Wall is beside the window.* On blank index cards, write the subject and verb of each sentence (e.g., *The books are*). On separate cards, write the prepositional phrase (e.g., *on the bookshelves*). Mix the cards and have students match the cards to make sentences.

## Daily Fix-It

5. Jamal has saw a movie bout eagloo. *(seen; about)*

6. They builds nests with sticks and leafs. *(build; leaves)*

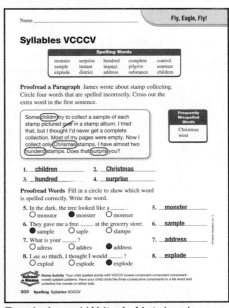

Reader's and Writer's Notebook, p. 300

Common Core State Standards
**Writing 3.a.** Establish a situation and introduce a narrator and/or characters; organize an event sequence that unfolds naturally. **Also Writing 3.c., Language 1.**

## Let's Write It!

**Key Features of a Summary**

- retells a piece of writing
- includes only the most important information
- shorter than the original

**READING STREET ONLINE**
**GRAMMAR JAMMER**
**www.ReadingStreet.com**

174

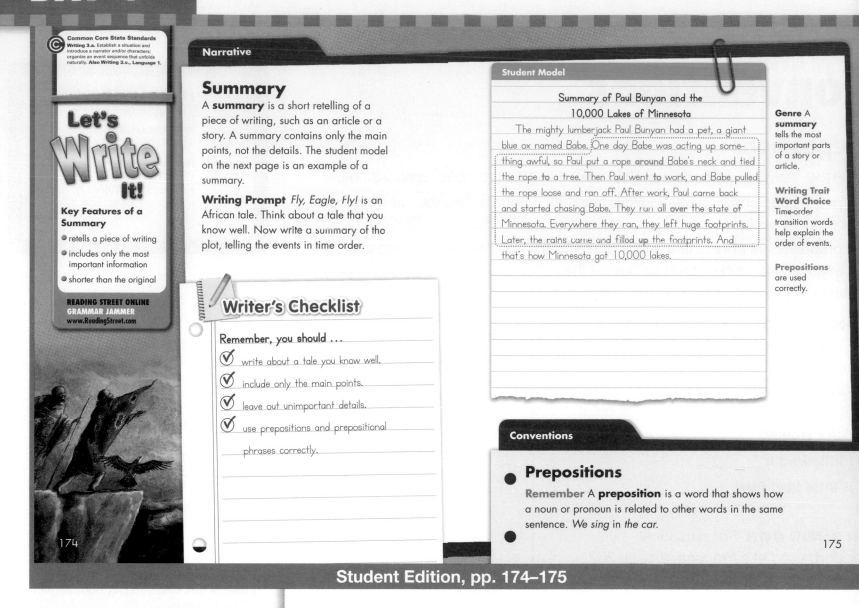

**Narrative**

### Summary

A **summary** is a short retelling of a piece of writing, such as an article or a story. A summary contains only the main points, not the details. The student model on the next page is an example of a summary.

**Writing Prompt** *Fly, Eagle, Fly!* is an African tale. Think about a tale that you know well. Now write a summary of the plot, telling the events in time order.

#### Writer's Checklist

Remember, you should ...

- ☑ write about a tale you know well.
- ☑ include only the main points.
- ☑ leave out unimportant details.
- ☑ use prepositions and prepositional phrases correctly.

**Student Model**

Summary of Paul Bunyan and the
10,000 Lakes of Minnesota

The mighty lumberjack Paul Bunyan had a pet, a giant blue ox named Babe. One day Babe was acting up something awful, so Paul put a rope around Babe's neck and tied the rope to a tree. Then Paul went to work, and Babe pulled the rope loose and ran off. After work, Paul came back and started chasing Babe. They ran all over the state of Minnesota. Everywhere they ran, they left huge footprints. Later, the rains came and filled up the footprints. And that's how Minnesota got 10,000 lakes.

**Genre** A **summary** tells the most important parts of a story or article.

**Writing Trait Word Choice** Time-order transition words help explain the order of events.

**Prepositions** are used correctly.

**Conventions**

### Prepositions

**Remember** A **preposition** is a word that shows how a noun or pronoun is related to other words in the same sentence. *We sing* in *the car.*

175

**Student Edition, pp. 174–175**

## Common Core State Standards

**Language 1.** Demonstrate command of the conventions of standard English grammar and usage when writing or speaking. **Language 3.** Use knowledge of language and its conventions when writing, speaking, reading, or listening. **Also Writing 3.a., Writing 4.**

## Let's Write It!
### Write a Summary

**WRITE A SUMMARY** Use pp. 174–175 in the Student Edition. Direct students to read the key features of a summary that appear on p. 174. Remind students that they can refer to the information in the Writer's Checklist as they write their own summaries.

Read the student model on p. 175. Point out the key features of summaries in the model.

**CONNECT TO CONVENTIONS** Remind students that prepositions show a relationship between a noun or pronoun and the other words in a sentence. Point out the correct use of prepositions in the model.

# Writing

## Summary

### Writing for Tests: Summary

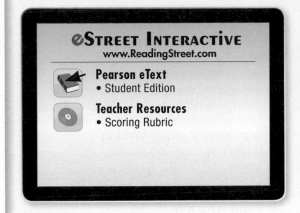

**e STREET INTERACTIVE**
www.ReadingStreet.com

**Pearson eText**
• Student Edition

**Teacher Resources**
• Scoring Rubric

**DISPLAY RUBRIC** Have students return to the scoring rubric from p. 297 of the *Reader's and Writer's Notebook* that you reviewed on Day 2. Go over the criteria for each trait under each score. Then explain to students that they will use this rubric to evaluate the summaries they wrote yesterday.

## Scoring Rubric Summary

| | 4 | 3 | 2 | 1 |
|---|---|---|---|---|
| **Focus/Ideas** | Strong summary; only uses important information | Good summary; mostly uses important information | Summary has some main ideas and too many details | Does not understand summary form |
| **Organization** | Important ideas are in correct sequence | Sequence of events is generally correct | Sequence of events isn't always clear | No clear sequence of events |
| **Voice** | Shows understanding of the main ideas | Shows understanding of topic | Lacks understanding of topic | Does not understand topic |
| **Word Choice** | Uses strong action verbs and time-order words | Uses some strong action verbs and time-order words | Few or no strong verbs or time-order words | Poor word choice |
| **Sentences** | Clear sentences of different lengths and types | Sentences of a few lengths and types | Sentences of similar length and type | No variety of sentence length and type |
| **Conventions** | Few, if any, errors; correct use of prepositions | Several small errors; use of prepositions | Many errors; weak use of prepositions | Many serious errors; incorrect or no use of prepositions |

**Prepositions** Have students practice understanding the meaning of prepositions by playing a question game using prepositions as clues. For example, "Is it on the desk?"

**Common Core State Standards**

**Writing 2.a.** Introduce a topic and group related information together; include illustrations when useful to aiding comprehension. **Writing 3.c.** Use temporal words and phrases to signal event order. **Writing 5.** With guidance and support from peers and adults, develop and strengthen writing as needed by planning, revising, and editing. **Also Language 5.b.**

### Bridge to Common Core

**RANGE OF WRITING**

Throughout the week, students progress through the writing process as they continue to write for a range of tasks and purposes. In this lesson, they evaluate their own summary writing based on a rubric. This will help students focus on the task and purpose of the writing.

# Writing

## Summary

### Mini-Lesson    Writing for Tests: Evaluation

■ **Introduce** Explain that when you evaluate writing with a rubric, you are evaluating different traits in the writing. Have students read aloud a few of the six traits in the rubric.

■ **Evaluate a Trait** Tell students that they will evaluate their sample writing test based on one of the six traits in the rubric. We will focus on trait 2, organization. Remind students that the information presented in the summary should be in the correct sequence. According to the rubric, we want to make sure that the information summarized is in the correct sequence. In your summary, you should have first written about what happens first in the story. Then you should have written about the events that happen next and what happens at the end.

■ **Apply Scoring** Have students review their summaries to make sure that the important ideas are in the correct sequence. Then, using the rubric as a guide, have them assess their organization on a scale from 4 to 1.

Direct students to continue evaluating their summaries based on the other five traits on the rubric. Remind students that they may receive different number scores for each of the different traits, but that is all right. Lower or higher scores for different traits can help them see where their strengths lie and where they might need to focus more attention and effort.

## Writing Trait: Word Choice

As students review their writing, remind them to use words and phrases such as *one day, then,* and *next week,* to show time-order. The words are called transition words, and they help readers understand when each event occurs. Have partners review their summaries to look for time-order transition words, o help sequence the information in the correct order.

**Routine** | **Quick Write for Fluency**  Team Talk

1. **Talk** Pairs talk about why presenting information in the correct sequence is important.

2. **Write** Students write one to two sentences using prepositional phrases to explain why presenting information in the correct sequence is important.

3. **Share** Students read their sentences to their partner. Partners check each other's writing for correct use of prepositional phrases.

Routines Flip Chart

**ELL**

**Sequence** Give students photographs, drawings, or images from a magazine of something that happens in sequence. Then have them use the pictures to tell about the sequence of events.

# Wrap Up Your Day!

✔ **Content Knowledge** Have students discuss what unique behaviors helped the eagle fly away.

✔ **Text-Based Comprehension** *What finally caused the eagle to fly away?*

**Preview DAY 4**

Tell students that tomorrow they will read about a coyote with some unique traits and behaviors.

*Fly, Eagle, Fly!* **175c**

# DAY 4
## at a Glance

### Materials

- Student Edition
- Reader's and Writer's Notebook
- Decodable Reader

## ⓒ Common Core State Standards

**Speaking/Listening 1.** Engage effectively in a range of collaborative discussions (one-on-one, in groups, and teacher-led) with diverse partners on grade 3 topics and texts, building on others' ideas and expressing their own clearly. **Also Language 5.a., 6.**

# Content Knowledge

## Unique Animal Behaviors

**EXPAND THE CONCEPT** Remind students of the weekly concept question, *What behaviors are unique to different animals?* Have students discuss the unique behaviors of the animals they have read about.

## Build Oral Language

[Team Talk] **TALK ABOUT SENTENCES AND WORDS** Have students reread the last paragraph of *Fly, Eagle, Fly!* on page 171 of the Student Edition.

*And then, without really moving, feeling the updraft of a wind more powerful than any man or bird, the great eagle leaned forward and was swept upward, higher and higher, lost to sight in the brightness of the rising sun, never again to live among the chickens.*

- This is one paragraph, but it is also one long sentence. How many commas are in this sentence? **(6)** Sometimes authors choose to write long sentences like this. If we read this sentence with a short pause at each comma, but without taking a breath, what feeling does the length of the sentence add to the ending of the story? **(If we read it without taking a breath, it seems to add to the suspense of the eagle's final decision.)**

- How would this ending be different if it had been written in several short sentences instead of one long one? **Have students turn to a partner and share their ideas.**

- What is the importance of the eagle being "lost to sight in the brightness of the sun"? **(The sun is large and great, and the eagle seems to be flying toward it. The eagle is large and great too, and it belongs in the sky like the sun.)**

# Build Oral Vocabulary

## Amazing Words
### Robust Vocabulary Routine

1. **Introduce** Write the Amazing Word *coil* on the board. Have students say it aloud with you. We read about the friend and the farmer climbing a road that *coils* around and up a mountain. What was the road like? (It was winding and steep. It wrapped around the mountain.) Have students provide a definition. (Something that *coils* winds in circles.)

2. **Demonstrate** Have students answer questions to demonstrate understanding. What kind of animal *coils* itself? (snake)

3. **Apply** Have students apply their understanding. Why might a snake *coil* itself?

4. **Display the Word** Point out the vowel sound-spelling in the word *coil* as you read it.

See p. OV•5 to teach *intersection*.

Routines Flip Chart

**ADD TO THE CONCEPT MAP** Discuss the Amazing Words *pesky* and *unfurl*. Add these and other concept-related words to the concept map. Use the following questions to develop students' understanding of the concept.

- What animals do you think are *pesky*? Why?
- What kind of things might *unfurl*? What animals might need to *unfurl*?

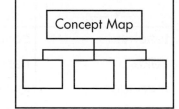
Concept Map

**eSTREET INTERACTIVE**
www.ReadingStreet.com
**Teacher Resources**
- Amazing Word Cards
- Reader's and Writer's Notebook

## Amazing Words

| | |
|---|---|
| armor | scenery |
| agile | pesky |
| snout | unfurl |
| protrude | coil |
| extraordinary | intersection |

## Strategy Response Log

Have students review the characteristics of a folk tale on p. 26 of the *Reader's and Writer's Notebook*. Then have them compare *Fly, Eagle, Fly!* to another example of a folk tale they have read or know about.

**ELL**

**Produce Oral Language** Use the Day 4 instruction on ELL Poster 20 to extend and enrich language.

**Common Core State Standards**

**Foundational Skills 3.a.** Identify and know the meaning of the most common prefixes and derivational suffixes. **Foundational Skills 3.b.** Decode words with common Latin suffixes. **Also Foundational Skills 4.b.**

# Word Analysis

**Review** Suffixes *-er, -or, -ess, -ist*

**REVIEW SUFFIXES** To review suffixes *-er, -or, -ess,* and *-ist,* write *golfer, sculptor, heiress,* and *tourist.* You studied words like these last week. What do you know about how to read a word with a suffix? (Cover the suffix, read the base word, and then uncover the suffix and read the parts together.) Have students identify the suffixes and read the words. Review with students that the suffixes *-er, -or, -ess,* and *-ist* mean "one who does something," so they change the base word's meaning to "one who does (base word)." Have students discuss the meaning of each word.

> **Corrective feedback** | If students are unable to identify the suffix and tell the meaning of each word, refer them to *Sound-Spelling Cards* 165, 166, 171, and 176.

**GUIDE PRACTICE** Display a four-column chart. When I say a word, listen for the suffix. Hold up the number of fingers to tell me which suffix you hear and the column to place the word in: *cyclist, collector, actress, teacher, narrator, baker, manager, duchess, lioness, flutist, investor, internist, defender, shepherdess, machinist, auditor.* Write each word in the appropriate column. Then have students read the words. Ask volunteers to identify the suffix and tell the meaning of the word.

| 1 *-er* | 2 *-or* | 3 *-ess* | 4 *-ist* |
|---------|---------|----------|----------|
| teacher | collector | actress | cyclist |
| baker | narrator | duchess | flutist |
| manager | investor | lioness | internist |
| defender | auditor | shepherdess | machinist |

**ON THEIR OWN** For additional practice, use *Let's Practice It!* p. 263 on the *Teacher Resources DVD-ROM.*

---

Name _____     *Fly, Eagle, Fly!*

**Suffixes**

**Directions** Add the suffix **-er, -or, -ess,** or **-ist** to each base word. Write the new word on the line. (HINT: you may have to change the spelling of the base word.)

1. teach   +   -er   =   __teacher__
2. invent   +   -or   =   __inventor__
3. lion   +   -ess   =   __lioness__
4. science   +   -ist   =   __scientist__
5. write   +   -er   =   __writer__
6. actor   +   -ess   =   __actress__
7. type   +   -ist   =   __typist__
8. create   +   -or   =   __creator__

**Directions** Match one of the words in the box to each definition. Write the word on the line.

| artist   counselor   empress   speaker |

9. person who speaks   __speaker__
10. person who creates art   __artist__
11. female ruler of an empire   __empress__
12. one who gives counsel   __counselor__

**Home Activity** Your child wrote words with the suffixes -er (teacher), -or (visitor), -ess (lioness), and -ist (tourist). Read an article about the bald eagle with your child. Have your child point out words with suffixes and tell you what they mean.

Suffixes DVD•263

Let's Practice It! TR DVD•263

# Fluent Word Reading

## Spiral Review

**READ WORDS IN ISOLATION** Display these words. Tell students that they can already decode some words on this list. Explain that they should know other words on the list because they appear often in reading.

Have students read the list three or four times until they can read at the rate of two to three seconds per word.

### Word Reading

| stars | pretest | said | port | for |
|---|---|---|---|---|
| decorate | roared | midnight | to | overtime |
| their | biweekly | short | before | precut |
| storm | decode | chores | they | watched |

| | |
|---|---|
| **Corrective feedback** | **If...** students have difficulty reading whole words, **then...** have them use sound-by-sound blending for decodable words or chunking for words that have word parts, or have them say and spell high-frequency words. |
| | **If...** students cannot read fluently at a rate of two to three seconds per word, **then...** have pairs practice the list until they can read it fluently. |

## Spiral Review

These activities review

• previously taught high-frequency words *watched, to, said, their, they.*

• *r*-controlled vowels (*ar, or, ore, oar*); prefixes (*pre-, mid-, over-, bi-, de-*).

**Fluent Word Reading** Have students listen to a more fluent reader say the words. Then have them repeat the words.

**Common Core State Standards**

**Foundational Skills 3.b.** Decode words with common Latin suffixes. **Foundational Skills 3.d.** Read grade-appropriate irregularly spelled words. **Foundational Skills 4.b.** Read on-level prose and poetry orally with accuracy, appropriate rate, and expression on successive readings.

# Fluent Word Reading

**READ WORDS IN CONTEXT** Display these sentences. Call on individuals to read a sentence. Then randomly point to review words and have students read them. To help you monitor word reading, high-frequency words are underlined and decodable words are italicized.

**MONITOR PROGRESS** **Sentence Reading**

We <u>watched</u> the ship leave the *port* at *midnight.*
<u>They</u> finished <u>their</u> *chores* after studying for the *biweekly pretest.*
The *stars* shone *for* a *short* time *before* the *storm roared* in.
He worked *overtime* <u>to</u> *decode* the message.
Mom <u>said</u> to *decorate* the *precut* tree.

**If...** students are unable to read an underlined high-frequency word,

**then...** read the word for them and spell it, having them echo you.

**If...** students have difficulty reading an italicized decodable word,

**then...** guide them in using sound-by-sound blending or chunking.

# Reread for Fluency

Have students reread the sentences to develop automaticity decoding words.

**Routine** **Oral Rereading**

1. **Read** Have students read all the sentences orally.

2. **Reread** To achieve optimal fluency, students should reread the sentences three or four times.

3. **Corrective Feedback** Listen as students read. Provide corrective feedback regarding their fluency and decoding.

Routines Flip Chart

# Decodable Passage 20C

If students need help, then...

## Read *Winston's Complex Costume*

**READ WORDS IN ISOLATION** Have students turn to p. 59 in *Decodable Practice Readers 3.2* and find the first list of words. Each word in this list has the VCCCV syllabication pattern. Let's read these words. Be sure that students identify the VCCCV syllable pattern.

Next, have students read the high-frequency words.

**PREVIEW** Have students read the title and preview the story. Tell them that they will read words with the VCCCV syllable pattern.

**READ WORDS IN CONTEXT** Chorally read the story along with the students. Have students identify words in the story that have the VCCCV syllable pattern. Make sure that students are monitoring their accuracy when they decode words.

(**Team Talk**) Pair students and have them take turns reading the story aloud to each other. Monitor students as they read to check for proper pronunciation and appropriate pacing.

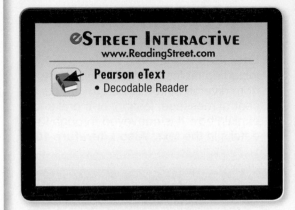

**eSTREET INTERACTIVE**
www.ReadingStreet.com

**Pearson eText**
• Decodable Reader

## Access for All

**A** Advanced

Have students write their own sentences using some of the decodable words found in the sentences on p. 176e.

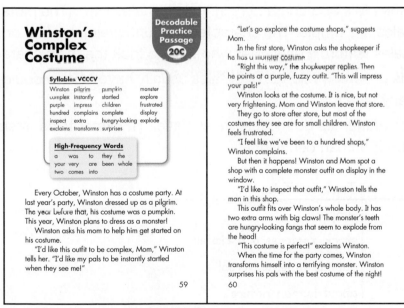

**Winston's Complex Costume**

Decodable Practice Passage 20C

**Syllables VCCCV**

| Winston | pilgrim | pumpkin | monster |
| complex | instantly | startled | explore |
| purple | impress | children | frustrated |
| hundred | complains | complete | display |
| inspect | extra | hungry-looking | explode |
| exclaims | transforms | surprises | |

**High-Frequency Words**

| a | was | to | they | the |
| your | very | are | been | whole |
| two | comes | into | | |

Every October, Winston has a costume party. At last year's party, Winston dressed up as a pilgrim. The year before that, his costume was a pumpkin. This year, Winston plans to dress as a monster!

Winston asks his mom to help him get started on his costume.

"I'd like this outfit to be complex, Mom," Winston tells her. "I'd like my pals to be instantly startled when they see me!"

59

"Let's go explore the costume shops," suggests Mom.

In the first store, Winston asks the shopkeeper if he has a monster costume.

"Right this way," the shopkeeper replies. Then he points at a purple, fuzzy outfit. "This will impress your pals!"

Winston looks at the costume. It is nice, but not very frightening. Mom and Winston leave that store.

They go to store after store, but most of the costumes they see are for small children. Winston feels frustrated.

"I feel like we've been to a hundred shops," Winston complains.

But then it happens! Winston and Mom spot a shop with a complete monster outfit on display in the window.

"I'd like to inspect that outfit," Winston tells the man in this shop.

This outfit fits over Winston's whole body. It has two extra arms with big claws! The monster's teeth are hungry-looking fangs that seem to explode from the head!

"This costume is perfect!" exclaims Winston.

When the time for the party comes, Winston transforms himself into a terrifying monster. Winston surprises his pals with the best costume of the night!

60

Decodable Practice Passage 20C

**Common Core State Standards**

**Literature 2.** Recount stories, including fables, folktales, and myths from diverse cultures; determine the central message, lesson, or moral and explain how it is conveyed through key details in the text. **Also Literature 10.**

### Ⓒ Bridge to Common Core

**KEY IDEAS AND DETAILS**

Examining the structure of the trickster tale genre enables students to determine what the text says explicitly and cite textual evidence to support conclusions. By reading the text closely, students can determine the central ideas and summarize key details, making logical inferences about lessons or morals.

 **Science in Reading**

## Trickster Tale

**INTRODUCE** Explain to students that what we read is structured differently depending on the author's reasons for writing and what kind of information he or she wishes to convey. Different types of texts are called genres. Tell them that the trickster tale is one type of genre.

**DISCUSS THE GENRE** Ask students what they know about trickster tales. Then discuss the elements of trickster tales with students. A trickster tale is a kind of folk tale. Like folk tales, trickster tales have simple plots and undeveloped characters, and they share a lesson about human nature. The characters are sometimes animals that act like humans. The settings are often outside time—they could be anywhere at any time. A trickster tale is special because it has a character who tries to trick the main character.

**GROUP PRACTICE** Display a two-column chart like the one below. In the first column, list literary elements. In the second, record a brief description of how each appears in trickster tales. Ask the following questions. Remind students to answer questions with appropriate detail.

- What are the plots and characters in trickster tales like? (The plots of trickster tales are simple. The characters are undeveloped, flat, or stock. Trickster tales feature a character who tries to trick the main character.)

- What kinds of settings do trickster tales usually have? (They could be anywhere at any time.)

- What kinds of themes do trickster tales have? (Trickster tales often teach lessons about human behavior.)

| Trickster Tales | |
|---|---|
| plot | simple |
| characters | stock, features a trickster |
| settings | outside time, universal |
| themes | about human nature |

**Team Talk** Have students work in pairs to review other elements of folk tales with which they are familiar. Have them list additional elements in the chart.

**READ** Tell students that they will now read a trickster tale about a coyote that has turned purple. Have students think about what they might learn from a trickster tale.

**eStreet Interactive**
www.ReadingStreet.com

**Teachers Resources**
• Graphic Organizer

---

**Day 4 SMALL GROUP TIME • Differentiate Vocabulary, p. SG•65**

| **OL** On-Level | **SI** Strategic Intervention | **A** Advanced |
|---|---|---|
| • **Develop** Language Using Amazing Words | • **Review/Discuss** Amazing Words | • **Extend** Amazing Words and Selection Vocabulary |
| • **Read** "Purple Coyote" | • **Read** "Purple Coyote" | • **Read** "Purple Coyote" |
| | | • **Organize** Inquiry Project |

**ELL**

**If...** students need more scaffolding and practice with the **Amazing Words,**
**then...** use the Routine on pp. xxxvi–xxxvii in the *ELL Handbook.*

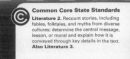

**Common Core State Standards**
Literature 2. Recount stories, including fables, folktales, and myths from diverse cultures; determine the central message, lesson, or moral and explain how it is conveyed through key details in the text. Also Literature 3.

## Social Studies in Reading

**Genre**
**Trickster Tale**

- A Trickster tale is a folk tale that has one clever character who tricks another character. Characters are often animals that act like people.

- Trickster and other folk tales often involve fantastic, or unbelievable, situations that are set in other lands to add excitement to the plot.

- The themes of folk tales usually teach lessons about human behavior.

- Read the trickster tale "Purple Coyote." How does this setting compare and contrast to the settings of other folk tales?

# Purple Coyote

by Cornette
illustrated by Rochette

176

In the middle of a flat and arid desert stood a hill of sand and rock.

Near this hill was a small house.

Jim played alone in the garden with his old truck, which was missing one wheel.

One day, a coyote appeared on the hill. A coyote unlike any other. A purple coyote.

Jim watched him.

The coyote did a little dance. Then he balanced himself on his right front paw and let out a strange howl:

"WULULI WULA WULILA WUWU WA!"

He sat down, letting the evening wind slowly untangle his purple fur.

Night fell and the moon rose. Jim watched the purple coyote until his mother called him for dinner.

Let's **Think** About...

Is this written in first or third person? How do you know?
**Trickster Tale**

1

177

**Student Edition, pp. 176–177**

**Common Core State Standards**

**Literature 2.** Recount stories, including fables, folktales, and myths from diverse cultures; determine the central message, lesson, or moral and explain how it is conveyed through key details in the text. **Literature 6.** Distinguish their own point of view from that of the narrator or those of the characters. **Also Literature 3., 9., 10.**

# Access Text ©

**TEACH Trickster Tale** Have students read the information about trickster tales and preview pp. 176–177 of "Purple Coyote." Point out that a trickster tale is a type of folk tale. Ask: What is "fantastic" about the coyote? (He is purple.) What about the story is unexpected? (He sings.)

> **Corrective feedback**
> **If...** students are unable to identify the fantastic and unexpected elements of the story,
> **then...** use the model to guide students in answering the questions.

**eSTREET INTERACTIVE**
www.ReadingStreet.com

**Pearson eText**
• Student Edition

**Think Aloud** **MODEL** On page 176, I learn that trickster tales often have fantastic characters and unexpected events. I know that coyotes aren't usually purple. In fact, I don't know of any purple animals. The coyote's color is fantastic. When I preview the page, I see his song in all capital letters. Coyote howls don't sound like that, so his howl is unexpected.

**ON THEIR OWN** Have students record other unexpected or fantastic events as they read pp. 176–177.

# Close Reading ©

**ANALYSIS • TEXT EVIDENCE** Reread the first paragraph on p. 177. Is the desert setting like most deserts you have read about? Explain. (Yes; it is flat, arid, and sandy.)

**SYNTHESIS** Does the setting remind you of the setting in a myth you have read? How are the settings alike and different? (This story and "How the Desert Tortoise Got Its Shell" both take place in a desert. In this folk tale, the flat and arid desert stands on a hill of sand and rock. In the myth "How the Desert Tortoise Got Its Shell," there are many desert plants and a dry riverbed in addition to the sand.)

# Genre

**LET'S THINK ABOUT...** As you read "Purple Coyote," use Let's Think About in the Student Edition to help students focus on the features of a trickster tale.

The tale is written in the third person because it uses the words *Jim, he,* and *his*. If it were written in the first person, it would use words such as *I, me,* and *mine*.

## Access for All

**SI** Strategic Intervention

Remind students that when they compare, they tell how things are alike. When they contrast, they tell how things are different. Write these clue words on the board: *Compare: similar, like, same; Contrast: unlike, differ, different.*

**A** Advanced

Write the word *universal* on the board. Explain that it means something can apply to all situations. Have students discuss in small groups the qualities of folk tales and trickster tales that make them universal.

## Academic Vocabulary ©

**folk tale** a fictional story that is a traditional tale handed down from one generation to another

**Cognates** Spanish students may better understand the fantastic element of the trickster tale if you introduce the cognate for the title— *Coyote Púrpura.* Ask: What is unusual about a purple coyote?

The next day, Jim didn't play with his truck, which had lost a second wheel.

He went to wait for the coyote at the bottom of the hill.

The purple coyote appeared. He did his little dance, balanced himself on his right front paw, and let out his "WULULI WULA WULILA WUWU WA!"

Jim climbed up the hill.

It wasn't very hard, as the hill was neither high nor steep.

He went up to the animal, greeted him and asked, "Why are you purple? That's not normal for a coyote!"

"I won't tell you!" answered the coyote.

"Why not?"

"Because it's a secret! But you can ask me questions if you want."

Jim thought hard. He looked the purple coyote straight in the eyes and asked, "Did you eat too many blueberries?"

"I never eat blueberries," the coyote replied.

Every afternoon, the purple coyote returned to the hill, did his little dance, balanced himself on his right front paw, and howled:

"WULULI WULA WULILA WUWU WA!"

Every afternoon, Jim joined the coyote, greeted him, and asked him a question. "Did you put purple dye on your fur?"

"No," answered the coyote.

"Were you born purple?"

"No."

"Did you catch purple-itis?"

"No."

"Did you catch purple fever?"

"No."

The days went by. Jim began to lose patience.

"I don't care if I never find out why you're purple!" he shouted at the coyote.

Let's **Think** About...

What details in the plot make it a fantastic situation? **Trickster Tale**

**2**

178

Let's **Think** About...

Who do you think is the clever character? Who will be tricked? Why? **Trickster Tale**

**3**

179

**Student Edition, pp. 178–179**

## Common Core State Standards

**Literature 2.** Recount stories, including fables, folktales, and myths from diverse cultures; determine the central message, lesson, or moral and explain how it is conveyed through key details in the text. **Literature 7.** Explain how specific aspects of a text's illustrations contribute to what is conveyed by the words in a story (e.g., create mood, emphasize aspects of a character or setting). **Also Literature 3.**

# Access Text ©

**TEACH Trickster Tale** Have students preview the illustrations, the questions, and the text on pp. 178–179. Have students use the information they gather to make predictions about what will happen on these pages.

**Corrective feedback** | **If...** students are not able to make predictions, **then...** use the model to guide the thinking process.

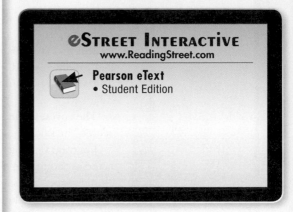

**MODEL** When I look at the pictures, I see the boy walking up the hill toward the coyote. I think he will talk to the coyote. I think the boy wants to find out why the coyote does that silly song and dance. Since this story is a trickster tale, I think the coyote will talk back.

**ON THEIR OWN** Have students record their predictions based on the clues they found during previewing. Then, when they finish, have them revisit their predictions to see whether they were accurate.

# Close Reading

**EVALUATION** Why do you think the coyote refuses to tell the boy why he is purple? (He wants the boy to guess why he is purple because he wants to trick the boy.)

**SYNTHESIS • TEXT EVIDENCE** How are the plots in *Fly, Eagle, Fly!* and "Purple Coyote" alike? What do the characters in each tale do to solve their problems? Cite evidence from the two texts to support your answer. (The plots are alike because the characters repeat actions to solve the problem. In *Fly, Eagle, Fly!* the friend tries three times to get the eagle to fly. In "Purple Coyote," the boy asks question after question to find out why the coyote is purple.)

# Genre

**LET'S THINK ABOUT...** features of a trickster tale.

▶ The coyote couldn't have been purple, stood on one paw, sung his song, or talked back. Also, the boy could not have approached the coyote.

▶ The coyote is the clever character. The boy will be tricked because the coyote seems like he has a plan.

## Access for All

 **Strategic Intervention**

Explain that students must think about all of the elements of the story, including the genre, to put together information to form conclusions. Have students work with partners to list evidence that will help them conclude why the coyote doesn't want to tell the boy his secret.

**A** **Advanced**

Have students write about the similarities and differences between *Fly, Eagle, Fly!* and "Purple Coyote." Tell students to think about the general attributes of the texts to make their comparisons.

**Build Academic Vocabulary** Have pairs of students practice using key words, such as *similar, like, unlike,* and *different,* to compare and contrast the plots of *Fly, Eagle, Fly!* and "Purple Coyote."

Let's **Think** About...

How is this Coyote similar to the Coyote in the myth "Catch It and Run"? **Trickster Tale**

④

In his anger, he thought about not coming up the hill anymore, but his curiosity was too strong.

"Tell me instead why you do that dance and why you howl in that funny way," he asked.

The coyote smiled. "That's my second secret," he said.

Jim tried very hard to keep calm. He acted as though he didn't care. "That's a stupid secret," he said. "Anyone can dance and howl like that! Look!"

Jim did a little dance, then leaned over on his right arm and howled a piercing "WULULI WULA WULILA WUWU WA!"

All at once, Jim turned purple.

180

As for the coyote, he got his color back. He was once again the color of desert and sand.

"Well done!" said the coyote. "You've discovered my two secrets in one try! You've given me back my natural color. Now I can leave. Goodbye, Jim!"

He disappeared into the vast desert.

Jim was now all purple and all by himself.

Night had fallen on the hill when a little raccoon came up to him.

"Hello," the raccoon said.

"Hello!" replied the purple kid.

"Did you see?" said Jim. "I'm purple all over."

"Yes," said the small animal.

"It's my secret," Jim went on.

"Do you want to find out why?"

"No."

181

Let's **Think** About...

Explain the interaction between Jim and the coyote. What changes did they undergo? **Trickster Tale**

⑤

Let's **Think** About...

Summarize the theme and supporting details from the story in your own words. What does this show about human behavior? **Trickster Tale**

⑥

Let's **Think** About...

**Reading Across Texts** Compare and contrast the settings in the two folk tales, *Fly, Eagle, Fly!* and "Purple Coyote." How are they alike and different?

**Writing Across Texts** Make a Venn diagram that compares and contrasts the settings in each of these folk tales.

**Student Edition, pp. 180–181**

---

© **Common Core State Standards**

**Literature 2.** Recount stories, including fables, folktales, and myths from diverse cultures; determine the central message, lesson, or moral and explain how it is conveyed through key details in the text. **Also Literature 3., 7., 9.**

# Access Text ©

**TEACH Trickster Tale** Have students preview pp. 180–181. Ask: How has the purple coyote tricked the boy?

> **Corrective feedback** | **If...** students have difficulty answering the question, **then...** use the model to guide students' thinking.

**MODEL** When I preview these pages, I look at the illustrations. I see that now the coyote is a normal color and the boy is purple. I think the coyote tricked the boy so that he could return to his normal color.

**ON THEIR OWN** Have students finish the selection and discuss what the coyote did to trick the boy.

# Close Reading ©

**SYNTHESIS** When is it good to be curious? (when you want to find out how something works or you want to learn more about someone)

**EVALUATION** What kind of character is the raccoon? (He is smart and knows how to stay out of trouble.)

# Genre

**LET'S THINK ABOUT...** features of a trickster tale.

Both coyotes are very clever, and they trick other characters to get their way.

At first Jim was nice to the coyote when he kept asking why the coyote was purple. But after a while, Jim lost patience and shouted at the coyote.

The theme is that curiosity can cause trouble. The boy is curious about the coyote, so he ignores his common sense and tries to uncover the coyote's secret. In the end, his curiosity hurts him. This tale shows that sometimes people don't know when to stop asking questions.

# Reading and Writing Across Texts

Have students review *Fly, Eagle, Fly!: An African Tale* and make notes about the setting. Then have them make notes about the setting of "Purple Coyote." Instruct students to review these notes to find similarities and differences between the two settings. Then have students record their notes about the setting in a Venn diagram. Challenge students to write a brief paragraph that compares and contrasts the settings of these folk tales.

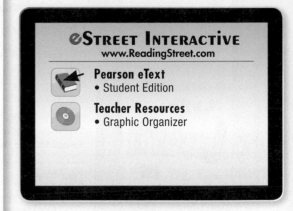

**eStreet Interactive**
www.ReadingStreet.com

**Pearson eText**
• Student Edition

**Teacher Resources**
• Graphic Organizer

**Connect to Social Studies**

**Coyote the Trickster** The coyote often appears in Native American folk tales as a trickster. In these stories, he interacts with people or other animals as a cunning, greedy, vain, foolish, and powerful character.

**Theme** Help students identify theme by asking: What lesson did you learn from this story? Have students state the theme in their own words with the sentence starter *I learned that . . . .*

**Common Core State Standards**
Language 4.d. Use glossaries or beginning dictionaries, both print and digital, to determine or clarify the precise meaning of key words and phrases. Also Foundational Skills 4.b., Speaking/Listening 1.a., Language 4.

## Let's Learn It!

READING STREET ONLINE
ONLINE STUDENT EDITION
www.ReadingStreet.com

## Vocabulary

### Unknown Words

**Dictionary/Glossary** Use a dictionary or glossary to find the meanings of unknown words. The words are listed in alphabetical order and shown with their syllable divisions, pronunciations, and meanings. Choose the meaning that fits the context of the text you are reading.

**Practice It!** Use a dictionary to look up *shimmer, brilliance,* and *majestically* from *Fly, Eagle, Fly!* Write down the definitions and pronunciations of the words as they are used in the story.

## Fluency

### Rate

The rate at which you read can depend on your interest or familiarity with the topic. You can improve your rate by reading a selection more than once. You can also speed up or slow down when you read aloud to match the mood of the story.

**Practice It!** With a partner, practice reading aloud *Fly, Eagle, Fly!* pages 160–161. Read the pages a second time. Did your rate improve? Does reading faster or slower help make your reading more interesting?

182

## Listening and Speaking

*Make contributions and keep the discussion going.*

Get Ready For Middle School

### Book Review

A book review tells your opinion about a book. It should focus on themes, the author's purpose for writing, and what effect the book might have on readers.

**Practice It!** Follow directions for presenting a book review in a group. Discuss your reactions to the story, and decide if you would recommend it to friends. Present your review to the class.

### Tips

**Listening ...**
- Face the speakers.
- Draw conclusions about what the speakers say.

**Speaking ...**
- Use appropriate persuasive techniques.
- Use appropriate emotional clues.
- Use prepositions and prepositional phrases correctly.

**Teamwork ...**
- Ask and answer questions with detailed information.
- Give suggestions for why others may or may not like the book.

183

**Student Edition, pp. 182–183**

## Common Core State Standards

**Language 4.d.** Use glossaries or beginning dictionaries, both print and digital, to determine or clarify the precise meaning of key words and phrases. **Speaking/Listening 1.a.** Come to discussions prepared, having read or studied required material; explicitly draw on that preparation and other information known about the topic to explore ideas under discussion. **Speaking/Listening 1.b.** Follow agreed-upon rules for discussions (e.g., gaining the floor in respectful ways, listening to others with care, speaking one at a time about the topics and texts under discussion). **Also Foundational Skills 4.b., Speaking/Listening 1.c., Language 4.**

# Fluency

## Appropriate Rate

**GUIDE PRACTICE** Use the Student Edition activity as an assessment tool. Make sure the reading passage is at least 200 words in length. As students read aloud with partners, walk around to make sure their rate is appropriate and that it changes to reflect content and punctuation.

**Don't Wait Until Friday**

**MONITOR PROGRESS** Check Fluency

**FORMATIVE ASSESSMENT** As students reread, monitor progress toward their individual fluency goals. Current Goal: 95–105 words correct per minute. End-of-Year Goal: 120 words correct per minute.

**If...** students cannot read fluently at a rate of 95–105 words correct per minute, **then...** have students practice with text at their independent levels.

# Vocabulary Skill

## ⊙ Unknown Words

**TEACH UNKNOWN WORDS • DICTIONARY/GLOSSARY** Write these sentences on the board: *The scientist proved his brilliance when he made that major discovery. The brilliance of the afternoon sun nearly blinded us.*

Remind students that a word may have more than one definition. When they look up a word in the dictionary or glossary, they need to look at the context of the word to determine which definition the author intended.

**GUIDE PRACTICE** Have students look up *brilliance, shimmer,* and *majestically* in a dictionary or glossary. Help them use the context of the story to determine the intended meaning for each word.

**ON THEIR OWN** Walk around the room, making sure students are able to locate the words in a dictionary or glossary and identify their intended meanings. Have students identify the number of syllables in each word and use the pronunciation key to help them figure out how to say each word correctly.

# Listening and Speaking

## Book Review

**TEACH** Tell one member of each group that when group members review a book, they need to tell their reaction to the story and whether they would recommend it to a friend. Explain that when they present their reviews, they should speak coherently with appropriate rate, volume, enunciation, and conventions of language, and they should make eye contact with their audience.

**GUIDE PRACTICE** Have each chosen group member restate to the group the oral instructions for how to review a book and how to deliver the review. Encourage group members to listen attentively, to ask and answer questions, and to provide suggestions that build upon the ideas of others.

**ON THEIR OWN** Have group members follow the multistep oral instructions to prepare and give their book reviews.

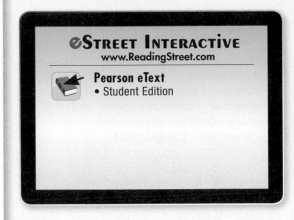

## Book Review

Reiterate to students that book reviews are a way to express an opinion. Remind students that when giving an opinion, they need to provide reasons and support for that opinion. They should cite evidence from the actual text being reviewed in order to support their opinions in this case.

## ©) Bridge to Common Core

### PRESENTATION OF KNOWLEDGE/ IDEAS

As students give their book reviews, they present information, opinions, and supporting evidence so listeners can follow the line of reasoning and the organization. Students listen attentively, to ask and answer questions, and to provide suggestions that build upon the ideas of others.

## ELL

**Unknown Words** After students find the word in the dictionary, assist them by helping them identify synonyms of the words to replace in context. For example, in the first sentence, replace *brilliance* with both *skill* and *light,* and then have students raise their hands to indicate which meaning is intended.

 **Common Core State Standards**

**Writing 8.** Recall information from experiences or gather information from print and digital sources; take brief notes on sources and sort evidence into provided categories. **Language 1.** Demonstrate command of the conventions of standard English grammar and usage when writing or speaking. **Language 2.f.** Use spelling patterns and generalizations (e.g., word families, position-based spellings, syllable patterns, ending rules, meaningful word parts) in writing words.

# Research and Inquiry

## Step 4 Synthesize

**TEACH** Have students synthesize their research findings and results. Students should use their summaries to help write their journal entries. Suggest that students might also find that their graphic organizers are a helpful reference source when writing their journal entries.

**GUIDE PRACTICE** Have students review their graphic organizers and summaries to prepare to write their journal entries. If students are using illustrations, suggest that they use drawing paper for the illustrations and then paste the illustrations into their journals.

**ON THEIR OWN** Have students write a brief explanation of their research findings. Then have them organize and combine information for their presentation.

# Conventions

## Prepositions

**TEST PRACTICE** Remind students that grammar skills, such as prepositions, are often assessed on important tests. Remind students that a preposition shows the relationship between a noun or pronoun and the other words in the sentence. A prepositional phrase adds more important details by telling exactly where something occurs or how things are related.

**ON THEIR OWN** For additional practice, use *Reader's and Writer's Notebook,* p. 301.

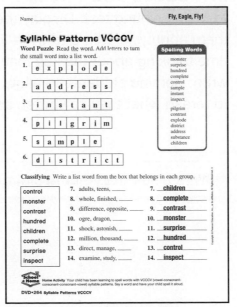

Reader's and Writer's Notebook, p. 301

# Spelling

## Syllables VCCCV

**PRACTICE SPELLING STRATEGY** Give pairs of students index cards on which the spelling words have been written. Have one student read a word while the other writes it. Then have students switch roles. Have them use the cards to check their spelling and correct any misspelled words.

**ON THEIR OWN** For additional practice, use *Let's Practice It!* p. 264 on the *Teacher Resources DVD-ROM.*

Let's Practice It! TR DVD•264

**eSTREET INTERACTIVE**
www.ReadingStreet.com

**Teachers Resources**
- Reader's and Writer's Notebook
- Let's Practice It!
- Daily Fix-It Transparency

## Daily Fix-It

**7.** The eagle is diveing into a Pond. *(diving; pond)*

**8.** The childrens were interested of the eagle's dives. *(children; in)*

## Ⓒ Bridge to Common Core

### CONVENTIONS OF STANDARD ENGLISH

As students correctly use prepositions and spell words with the syllable pattern VCCCV, they are demonstrating command of the conventions of standard English. Your guidance will help them use correct grammar, usage, and spelling to convey meaning when they speak and write.

**Common Core State Standards**

**Language 1.** Demonstrate command of the conventions of standard English grammar and usage when writing or speaking. **Language 3.a.** Choose words and phrases for effect. **Also Language 1.a., 1.b.**

---

**Write Guy** by *Jeff Anderson*

**Powerful Words, Powerful Verbs**

If students have trouble distinguishing complete sentences from fragments, have them ask this question: "Who or what did something? What did that person or thing do?" Students can have fun making a complete statement by adding together subject *(David)* and powerful verbs *(laughed, talked, punched)*: *David laughed*.

# Writing

## Summary

**REVIEW** Remind students that yesterday, they evaluated their summaries using a writing rubric. Tell them that they will again practice writing for tests by writing another summary based on a new prompt.

| **Mini-Lesson** | **Writing for Tests: Using Strong Verbs** |
| --- | --- |

■ Discuss the importance of word choice in writing. Strong verbs can create sounds or images for a reader. Using strong verbs in your writing will make it more interesting and lively. As you write, think about how you can use strong verbs to make your writing better.

■ Write the following sentence on the board: *Emily walked home from school*. Model how to improve the sentence with strong verbs. The verb *walked* does not tell me much. I can use a different verb in the sentence to show exactly how Emily walked home from school. The sentence *Emily strolled home from school* is more specific. It tells the reader exactly how Emily walked.

---

**INTRODUCE NEW PROMPT** Direct students to get paper and pencil ready to take a writing test. Display the new writing prompt for students and allow them appropriate time to write to the prompt. Tell students to spend some time thinking about the key features of the writing product before beginning to write. Remind students to allow themselves a couple of minutes after writing to reread what they've written and make changes or additions.

### Writing Prompt

Write a summary of the plot of your favorite animated movie.

**Routine** | **Quick Write for Fluency** | **Team Talk**

**1. Talk** Pairs discuss how to use stronger verbs when writing sentences.

**2. Write** Students write one sentence using the verb *ran;* they then write two other sentences replacing the word *ran* with stronger verbs, such as *sprinted, jogged,* or *dashed*.

**3. Share** Students share what they wrote with their partners and each checks the other's writing for strong verb choices.

Routines Flip Chart

**Word Choice** Pair an English learner with a proficient English speaker to discuss pictures of people or animals in books or magazines. Have them use strong verbs to describe what the people or animals are doing.

# Wrap Up Your Day!

✔ **Content Knowledge** Have students discuss why the coyote was purple.

✔ **Oral Vocabulary** Monitor students' use of oral vocabulary as they respond to this question: *What extraordinary scenery would you see in a desert?*

✔ **Text Features** Discuss how the illustrations help students understand the text.

**Preview DAY 5**

Remind students to think about what it means to be unique.

### Materials

- Student Edition
- Weekly Test
- Reader's and Writer's Notebook

## Bridge to Common Core

**INTEGRATION OF KNOWLEDGE/IDEAS**

This week, students have integrated content presented in diverse media and analyzed how different texts address similar topics. They have developed knowledge about unique animal behaviors to expand the unit topic of One of a Kind.

**Science Knowledge Goals**

Students have learned that some animals

- have lures on their heads
- blend in with their surroundings
- change colors

# Content Knowledge

## Unique Animal Behaviors

**REVIEW THE CONCEPT** Have students look back at the reading selections to find examples that best demonstrate unique animal behaviors.

## Build Oral Language

**REVIEW AMAZING WORDS** Display and review this week's concept map. Remind students that this week they have learned ten Amazing Words related to unique animal behaviors. Have students use the Amazing Words and the concept map to answer the Question of the Week, *What behaviors are unique to different animals?*

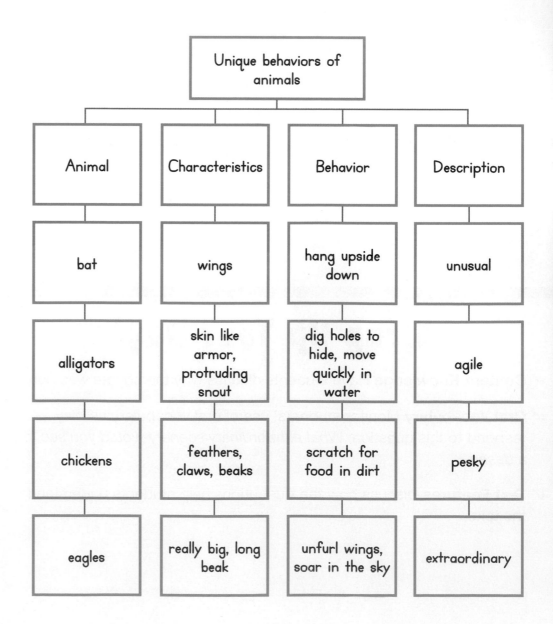

# Build Oral Vocabulary

**Team Talk** **CONNECT TO AMAZING IDEAS** Have pairs of students discuss how the Question of the Week connects to the question for this unit of study: *What does it mean to be unique?* Tell students to use the concept map and what they have learned from this week's discussions and reading selections to form an Amazing Idea—a realization or "big idea" about being One of a Kind. Remind partners to pose and answer questions with appropriate detail and to give suggestions that build on each other's ideas. Then ask pairs to share their Amazing Ideas with the class.

Amazing Ideas might include these key concepts:

- Even when we act like others, we each still have qualities that are special to us alone.
- Sometimes animals' behaviors are unique, but their outcome is the same.
- The way animals and people act, as well as the way they look, makes them unique.

**WRITE ABOUT IT** Have students write a few sentences about their Amazing Idea, beginning with "This week I learned . . ."

## MONITOR PROGRESS   Check Oral Vocabulary

**FORMATIVE ASSESSMENT** Have individuals use this week's Amazing Words to describe unique animal behaviors. Monitor students' abilities to use the Amazing Words and note which words you need to reteach.

**If...** students have difficulty using the Amazing Words,

**then...** reteach using the Oral Vocabulary Routine on pp. 151a, 156b, 168b, 176b, OV•5.

## Amazing Words

| | |
|---|---|
| armor | scenery |
| agile | pesky |
| snout | unfurl |
| protrude | coil |
| extraordinary | intersection |

**Check Concepts and Language**
Use the Day 5 instruction on ELL Poster 20 to monitor students' understanding of the lesson concept.
**Concept Map** Work with students to add new words to the concept map.

Zoom in on ©

## © Common Core State Standards

**Speaking/Listening 1.** Engage effectively in a range of collaborative discussions (one-on-one, in groups, and teacher-led) with diverse partners on grade 3 topics and texts, building on others' ideas and expressing their own clearly. **Language 4.d.** Use glossaries or beginning dictionaries, both print and digital, to determine or clarify the precise meaning of key words and phrases. **Also Literature 4., Foundational Skills 3.c., Language 4.a.**

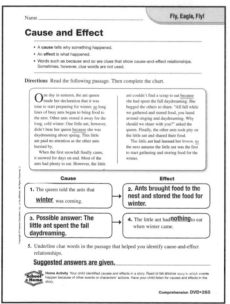

Let's Practice It! TR DVD•265

## Selection Vocabulary

**clutched** grasped something tightly

**echoed** the repeating of a sound caused by its reflecting off a hard surface

**gully** a ditch made by heavy rains or running water

**reeds** tall grasses that grow in wet places

**scrambled** made your way, especially by climbing or crawling quickly

**thatch** roofing material made of straw

**valley** an area of low land that lies between hills or mountains

# Text-Based Comprehension

## Review ☉ Cause and Effect

**TEACH** Review the definition of cause and effect on p. 154. Remind students that words such as *because* and *so* signal cause-and-effect relationships. For additional support have students review p. EI•3 on cause and effect.

**GUIDE PRACTICE** Have partners identify an example of cause and effect in "Birds of Prey" on p. 155. Then have pairs tell which of the events is a cause and which is an effect. Have students explain, using the words *so* or *because*.

**ON THEIR OWN** For additional practice with cause and effect, use *Let's Practice It!* page 265 on the *Teacher Resources DVD-ROM*.

# Vocabulary Skill

## Review ☉ Unknown Words

**TEACH** Remind students to use a dictionary or glossary to help them understand the meanings of unknown words.

**GUIDE PRACTICE** Review with students how to find the correct meaning of *huddled* using a dictionary or glossary. Explain that there may be more than one definition for the word. Remind students that they can also find the number of syllables and the pronunciation for a word.

**ON THEIR OWN** Have students write sentences for the lesson vocabulary words. Tell students to be sure to include context clues to indicate the intended definition of the word. Invite volunteers to share their sentences with the class. Have students tell how they used the dictionary or glossary to determine the number of syllables and the pronunciation of each word.

# Word Analysis

## Review ⟳ Syllables VCCCV

**TEACH** Write the following sentences on the board. Have students read each one, first quietly to themselves and then aloud as you track the print.

1. Should I explain why you don't walk on wet concrete?

2. All of the partners have contracts to sell the orchard's apples.

3. My conscience stopped me from making the purchase.

4. We attended a surprise function at the district office.

5. One hundred dolphins were simply having fun.

**Team Talk** Have students discuss with a partner which words have the VCCCV syllable pattern. Ask them to identify the syllables and read the words. Then call on individuals to share with the class.

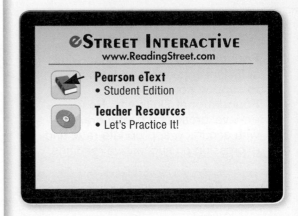

**eSTREET INTERACTIVE**
www.ReadingStreet.com

**Pearson eText**
• Student Edition

**Teacher Resources**
• Let's Practice It!

# Literary Terms

## Review Sensory Details

**TEACH** Have students reread pp. 164–167 of *Fly, Eagle, Fly!* Remind students that sensory details help them see, hear, taste, smell, or feel the thing the author describes.

**GUIDE PRACTICE** Read aloud p. 167 to students. Tell them to close their eyes and pay attention to what they imagine as you read. Discuss how the author uses sensory details to create vivid images and which senses those details address.

**ON THEIR OWN** Have students make a concept web with *Sensory details* listed in the center circle and each of the five senses listed in the outer circles. Then have students record words and details from the story in the circles with the appropriate senses.

**Articulation Tip** If students have trouble pronouncing blends and digraphs in VCCCV syllable patterns, demonstrate how to pronounce them by slowly repeating words. Have students practice saying them until they develop confidence.

**Sensory Details** Reinforce the connection between words and senses by asking students to interact with the text. Read the first sentence on p. 167, *Again the great bird stretched out its wings.* Then ask students to mimic the action. If necessary, show them by stretching out your arms. Continue the exercise with the next sentence, having students demonstrate trembling.

*Fly, Eagle, Fly!* **183i**

### © Common Core State Standards

**Foundational Skills 4.** Read with sufficient accuracy and fluency to support comprehension.
**Foundational Skills 4.b.** Read on-level prose and poetry orally with accuracy, appropriate rate, and expression on successive readings.

## Plan to Assess Fluency

- ☐ **Week 1** Advanced
- ☐ **Week 2** Strategic Intervention
- ☐ **Week 3** On-Level
- ☐ **Week 4** Strategic Intervention
- ☑ **This week assess any students you have not yet checked during this unit.**

Set individual goals for students to enable them to reach the year-end goal.

- Current Goal: 95–105 WCPM
- Year-End Goal: 120 WCPM

# Assessment

## Monitor Progress

**FLUENCY** Make two copies of the fluency passage on p. 183k. As the student reads the text aloud, mark mistakes on your copy. Also mark where the student is at the end of one minute. To check the student's comprehension of the passage, have him or her retell what was read.

To figure words correct per minute (WCPM), subtract the number of mistakes from the total number of words read in one minute.

**RATE**

| Corrective feedback | **If...** students cannot read fluently at a rate of 95–105 WCPM, **then...** make sure they practice with text at their independent reading level. Provide additional fluency practice by pairing nonfluent readers with fluent readers. |
| | **If...** students already read at 120 WCPM, **then...** they do not need to reread three or four times. |

**If...** students need more scaffolding and practice with **Conventions and Writing,**
**then...** use the Grammar Transition Lessons on pp. 312–386 in the *ELL Handbook*.

## Day 5   SMALL GROUP TIME • Differentiate Reteaching, p. SG•65

| **OL** On-Level | **SI** Strategic Intervention | **A** Advanced |
|---|---|---|
| • **Practice** Prepositions<br>• **Reread** *Reading Street Sleuth*, pp. 52–53 | • **Review** Prepositions<br>• **Reread** *Reading Street Sleuth*, pp. 52–53 | • **Extend** Prepositions<br>• **Reread** *Reading Street Sleuth*, pp. 52–53<br>• **Communicate** Inquiry Project |

# Bats Are Special

Andy and Dora were exploring the valley with their parents when    11

it started to rain.    15

"Let's look for a place to stay dry," Mom said.    25

"There's a cave just over the gully," Dad added.    34

"Aren't bats in caves?" Dora asked in a frightened voice.    44

"You shouldn't be afraid of bats. They're really cool," Andy replied.    55

"How cool can they be? They can't even see!" Dora exclaimed.    66

"Are you kidding? Bats can't see color, but they can see in the    79

dark better than you or I," Andy said. "They also use echoes to help    93

them hunt for insects," Andy added.    99

"What about vampire bats?" Dora asked.    105

"They can be found in Mexico, Central America, and South    115

America," Andy answered. "Unlike Dracula, they need only about    124

2 tablespoons of blood a day. That amount doesn't hurt the animal it    137

takes the blood from," Andy added.    143

"Did you know that the smallest bat weighs less than a penny?"    155

Mom said.    157

"I'd like to see one of those," Dora said excitedly.    167

"You'd have to go to Thailand. They're called bumblebee bats,"    177

her father added.    180

"Let's hurry to the cave," Dora said as she scrambled ahead.    191

"I thought you were afraid," Andy shouted.    198

"Not anymore! Bats are too special to be afraid of," Dora laughed.    210

**MONITOR PROGRESS**    • Check Fluency

 **Common Core State Standards**

**Informational Text 1.** Ask and answer questions to demonstrate understanding of a text, referring explicitly to the text as the basis for the answers.

# Assessment

## Monitor Progress

For a written assessment of Syllables VCCCV, Cause and Effect, and Selection Vocabulary, use Weekly Test 20, pages 115–120.

**CAUSE AND EFFECT** Use "Armadillos" on p. 183m to check students' understanding of cause and effect.

**1.** What did you learn from the passage? (I learned about armadillos' features and their habits.)

**2.** What causes an armadillo to pull its legs under its armor to hide? Is there a clue word to help you identify the cause? (Being frightened causes it to hide. The clue word is *because*.)

**3.** If an armadillo is really frightened, what will it likely do? (It will jump up to scare the attacker or might even fight with its claws.)

> **Corrective feedback** | **If...** students are unable to answer the comprehension questions,
> **then...** use the Reteach lesson in *First Stop*.

# Armadillos

Are you curious about armadillos? These weird-looking critters are covered with big, tough scales. They even have scales on their faces and long, skinny tails. The scales look like armor that ancient knights wore. Armadillos need to protect themselves, so they use their armor. They quickly pull their legs under the armor and hide when they are frightened.

What happens when you poke an armadillo hiding in its armor? It usually fakes being dead. But if you scare it enough, it might jump straight up and scare you back.

Most of the day, armadillos stay in burrows because they are shy and do not want to be seen. A burrow is a hole or tunnel. Armadillos have sharp claws that help them to dig burrows and to catch food. They also use their claws to fight anything that attacks them. Armadillos will fight only when hiding, jumping, or playing dead doesn't work.

Armadillos come out at night to hunt for dinner. They eat bugs, small animals, and some plants. Some armadillos also eat small worms that live in dead, rotting animals! Yuck! Armadillos have a strong sense of smell, so they use it to find food in the dark night. Rotting animals must be easy to smell.

How big do armadillos grow? The kind found in the United States can be 30 inches long. There are giant armadillos in South America that grow five feet long and can weigh over 60 pounds. That's as big as some dogs!

**MONITOR PROGRESS**    • Cause and Effect

# DAY 5

## Common Core State Standards

**Speaking/Listening 4.** Report on a topic or text, tell a story, or recount an experience with appropriate facts and relevant, descriptive details, speaking clearly at an understandable pace. **Language 1.** Demonstrate command of the conventions of standard English grammar and usage when writing or speaking. **Language 2.f.** Use spelling patterns and generalizations (e.g., word families, position-based spellings, syllable patterns, ending rules, meaningful word parts) in writing words. **Also Speaking/ Listening 1.b.**

# Research and Inquiry

## Step 5 Communicate

**PRESENT IDEAS** Have students share their inquiry results by presenting their journals and giving a brief talk on their research. Have students display any outlines and graphic organizers they created on Days 2 and 3.

**SPEAKING** Remind students how to be good speakers and how to communicate effectively with their audience.

• Speak coherently, using an appropriate rate and volume.

• Maintain eye contact with the audience.

• Respond to relevant questions with appropriate details.

**LISTENING** Review with students these tips for being a good listener.

• Listen attentively without interrupting the speaker.

• Jot down relevant questions and ask them after the speaker finishes.

• Be polite, even if you disagree.

**LISTEN TO IDEAS** Have students listen attentively to the various journal presentations. Have them make pertinent comments, closely related to the topic.

# Spelling Test

## Syllables VCCCV

To administer the spelling test, refer to the directions, words, and sentences on page 155c.

# Conventions

## Prepositions

**MORE PRACTICE** Remind students that prepositions show a relationship between a noun or pronoun and the other words in a sentence. A preposition is the first word in a group of words called a prepositional phrase. A prepositional phrase ends with a noun or pronoun and adds important detail to writing.

**GUIDE PRACTICE** Have students add a preposition to complete the sentence frames.

> My cat is _____ the chair. (on, behind)
>
> Marta is sitting _____ Jeff and Kara. (between)
>
> The bird flew _____ the sky. (across, through)

**ON THEIR OWN** Write these sentences. Have students look back in *Fly, Eagle, Fly!* to find the correct preposition to fill in each blank. Students should complete *Let's Practice It!* page 266 on the *Teacher Resources DVD-ROM*.

> 1. He searched _____ the riverbed. (by)
> 2. He searched _____ the reeds, _____ the rocks, and _____ the rushing water. (among, behind, in)
> 3. He wandered _____ the hillside. (over)
> 4. His shouts echoed _____ the cliffs. (off)

**eSTREET INTERACTIVE**
www.ReadingStreet.com

**Teacher Resources**
- Let's Practice It!
- Daily Fix-It Transparency

## Daily Fix-It

9. An eagle sudenly appeared on the Ridge. *(suddenly; ridge)*
10. The eagles flight took us by suprise. *(eagle's; surprise)*

Name _____  Fly, Eagle, Fly!

**Prepositions**

Directions Write the prepositional phrase in each sentence. Underline the preposition.

1. A chicken has a comb on its head.
**on its head**

2. The comb is located above the beak.
**above the beak**

3. Each type of chicken has a different comb.
**of chicken**

4. The one with the zigzag comb is a White Leghorn rooster.
**with the zigzag comb**

Directions Choose the preposition in ( ) that makes sense in each sentence. Write the sentence.

5. Chickens and eagles are different ___ one another. (above, from)
**Chickens and eagles are different from one another.**

6. Chickens fly only ___ short distances. (for, below)
**Chickens fly only for short distances.**

7. Eagles can soar high ___ the sky. (off, in)
**Eagles can soar high in the sky.**

8. Chickens often live ___ farms. (on, out)
**Chickens often live on farms.**

Home Activity Your child reviewed prepositions. Ask your child to use sentences with prepositional phrases to answer these questions: Where do you do your homework? When do you do your homework?

DVD•266 Prepositions

Let's Practice It! TR DVD•266

*Fly, Eagle, Fly!* **183o**

© **Common Core State Standards**

**Writing 10.** Write routinely over extended time frames (time for research, reflection, and revision) and shorter time frames (a single sitting or a day or two) for a range of discipline-specific tasks, purposes, and audiences. **Language 1.** Demonstrate command of the conventions of standard English grammar and usage when writing or speaking. **Also Writing 5.**

## Teacher Note

**Writing Self-Evaluation** Make copies of the Writing Self-Evaluation Guide on p. 39 of the *Reader's and Writer's Notebook* and hand out to students.

© **Bridge to Common Core**

### PRODUCTION AND DISTRIBUTION OF WRITING

Throughout the week, students developed writing in which organization and style were appropriate to the task, purpose, and audience. Given opportunities to practice writing for shorter time frames, students expand their range and ability of writing.

# Writing

## Summary

**REVIEW** Remind students that yesterday they learned more about the key features of summaries and wrote to a second prompt. Today they will evaluate their writing from yesterday.

| **Mini-Lesson** | **Writing for Tests: Revise** |
|---|---|

■ Yesterday we wrote a summary of the plot of our favorite animated movie. Part of effectively writing for tests is using some of the test-taking time to revise and edit what we've written. The goal is to make the writing as clear as possible. Today we will focus on making sure we used prepositions and prepositional phrases correctly.

■ Remind students that prepositional phrases add important details to writing by telling exactly where something occurs or how two things are related. Some words can be prepositions or not, depending on their use in a sentence. Remind them that a preposition is part of a phrase and is followed by a noun or a pronoun. It cannot stand alone. Write these sentences on the board: *The eagle flew <u>down</u>. The eagle flew <u>down</u> the mountain. Down* is not a preposition in the first sentence. *Down* is a preposition in the second sentence.

Look for places where you have used or could use a prepositional phrase. Remind students of some common prepositions, such as *of, for, on, down, at,* and so on. Tell students to make sure that their prepositional phrases make sense and that they include both a preposition and an appropriate noun.

**DISPLAY** Display the following Revising Tips for students.

### Revising Tips

✔ Make sure that you include prepositions that make sense in your summary.

✔ Review your writing to make sure that it is clear and focused.

✔ Check that your prepositional phrases are appropriate to the summary.

**EVALUATE** Have students spend a few minutes editing and revising the sample test-writing piece they wrote on Day 4. When students have finished editing, have them use the Scoring Rubric from their *Reader's and Writer's Notebook,* p. 297 that they used in Day 3. This time they should use it to evaluate the sample test-writing they just revised.

**Routine** | **Quick Write for Fluency** | **Team Talk**

1. **Talk** Pairs discuss what they learned about writing summaries.

2. **Write** Students write a paragraph explaining three things they learned about writing summaries.

3. **Share** Partners read one another's paragraphs.

Routines Flip Chart

# Wrap Up Your Week!

## Unique Animal Behaviors

What behaviors are unique to different animals?

**Think Aloud** In *Fly, Eagle, Fly!* and "Purple Coyote," we learned about unique animal behaviors.

**Team Talk** Have students recall their Amazing Ideas about unique animal behaviors and use these ideas to help them demonstrate their understanding of the Question of the Week.

Concept for Unit 5 Week 1
## Cultures and Clothing

How does culture influence the clothes we wear?

**Poster Preview** Prepare students for Unit 5 Week 1 by using Unit 5 Week 1 ELL Poster 21. Read the Talk-Through to introduce the concept and vocabulary. Ask students to identify and describe actions in the art.

**Selection Summary** Send home the summary of the Unit 5 Week 1 selection, *Suki's Kimono,* in English and in students' home languages, if available in the *ELL Handbook.* They can read the summary with family members.

How does culture influence the clothes we wear? Tell students that in Unit 5 Week 1 they will read about a girl whose culture influences her choice in clothes.

**Preview Unit 5, Week 1**

## Poetry

- **Limericks** are humorous, often silly, poems told in five lines. The first, second, and fifth lines rhyme and have matching beats. The third and fourth lines are shorter, rhyme, and have matching beats.

- **Free verse poems** express powerful emotions and images using comparisons and sensory language, and don't use **rhyme patterns** or a regular **rhythm**, or **cadence**.

- **Rhyming poems** have rhyming words at the ends of their lines and sometimes within lines. They may use vivid **imagery** too.

### LIMERICKS

#### by Edward Lear

There was a Young Lady whose nose,
Was so long that it reached to her toes;
So she hired an Old Lady,
Whose conduct was steady,
To carry that wonderful nose.

There was an Old Man of Apulia,
Whose conduct was very peculiar;
He fed twenty sons,
Upon nothing but buns,
that whimsical Man of Apulia.

### Written at the Po-Shan Monastery

#### by Hsin Ch'i-chi
#### translated by Irving Y. Lo

I would rather be myself:
Why pretend being someone else?
Having traveled everywhere, I've returned to farming.
One pine, one bamboo, is a real friend;
Mountain birds, mountain flowers are my brothers.

**Let's Think About...**
What are the characteristics of the limericks, and how do they create imagery?

**1**

**Let's Think About...**
What are the characteristics of the free verse poem, and how do they create imagery?

**2**

184    185

**Student Edition, pp. 184–185**

### Academic Vocabulary

**limericks** silly, short poems told in five lines per verse

# Poetry

## Limericks

**TEACH** Review the definition of limericks on p. 184. Remind students that limericks are usually silly or funny and might contain some repetitive words. Limericks always have five lines in a verse, specific lines that rhyme, and a specific number of beats per line. Read the first verse of "Limericks" aloud, tapping your hand on a table for each of the beats. Point out that the number of beats does NOT match the number of words in the limerick.

**GUIDE PRACTICE** Write the second verse of the poem "Limericks" on the board. Number each line 1 through 5. Then ask volunteers to name the numbers of the lines that rhyme (1, 2, and 5; 3 and 4). Ask other volunteers to count the number of beats in each line. Then ask a volunteer to find an example of repetition in the limerick.

**ON THEIR OWN** Have students take turns reading "Limericks" aloud. Tell students to pay attention to the rhyming patterns and beat as they read. Point out that sometimes the rhymes are forced as in *lady* and *steady*.

## Free Verse Poems

**TEACH** Review the definition of free verse poems on p. 184. Remind students that free verse poems do not rhyme, nor do they have cadence, or a regular rhythm. Free verse poems sound more like everyday speech and often express a strong emotion.

**GUIDE PRACTICE** Make a two-column chart with the headings "Limericks" and "Po-Shan Monastery." Fill in the chart by asking about characteristics of limericks and free verse poems. Make sure to include questions about rhyme, cadence, and repetition.

**ON THEIR OWN** Have students write a free verse poem about a funny or interesting person they know. Have them share their poems with the rest of the class.

## Imagery

**TEACH** Review the idea that authors use imagery to help their readers see, hear, feel, smell, and touch what is happening in the poem. Point out that imagery can be found in limericks and free verse poems, and note that it is the author's choice of words that helps the readers create pictures in their minds.

**GUIDE PRACTICE** Have students discuss the imagery in the poems on pp. 184–185. Ask them to identify specific phrases that helped them create pictures in their minds.

**ON THEIR OWN** Have partners practice reading each poem several times.

## Let's Think About...

The limericks have a specific length and rhyming pattern shared by all limericks. They use sensory words that create imagery for the reader. In the first limerick, we can "see" the long nose that hangs down to the girl's toes. In the second limerick, we can "smell" and "taste" the buns that the man feeds to his sons.

The free verse poem contains no rhymes and has no rhythm. It sounds like the writer is just speaking to the reader. The imagery is created by the writer's choice of words. We can "see" the trees, birds, and flowers that are his companions.

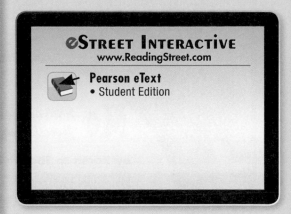

### Academic Vocabulary

**free verse poems** poems that express strong emotions without rhyme or rhythm

**imagery** descriptive language in a poem or story that helps the reader see, hear, feel, smell, and touch what is happening

### Access for All

**SI** Strategic Intervention

Read a number of different short poems to students (including limericks). Have students pick out the poems that are limericks. Have them explain what makes the poem a limerick.

**A** Advanced

Have student pairs write their own limericks and read them to the rest of the class. Suggest topics that students might write about, such as people they've met, places they've been to, or fun things they've done.

**Rhyming Words** Make sure English language learners understand rhyme by writing the following on the board: *fish/wish, dream/team,* and *bumper/jumper*. Have students identify the parts of the words that sound the same. Then ask students to name other words that rhyme.

**Me** With apologies to Joyce Kilmer ("Trees")

**by Karen Jo Shapiro**

I think that I will never see,
another person just like me.

Someone who has my color hair,
and picks the kind of clothes I wear.

Someone who thinks the thoughts I think,
and drinks the drinks I like to drink.

Who walks and talks my special way,
and plays the games I choose to play.

So many kinds of folks I see,
but only I can be a ME.

186

**BY MYSELF**
**by Eloise Greenfield**

When I'm by myself
And I close my eyes
I'm a twin
I'm a dimple in a chin
I'm a room full of toys
I'm a squeaky noise
I'm a gospel song
I'm a gong
I'm a leaf turning red
I'm a loaf of brown bread
I'm a whatever I want to be
An anything I care to be
And when I open my eyes
What I care to be
Is me

187

**Student Edition, pp. 186–187**

## Common Core State Standards

**Literature 10.** By the end of the year, read and comprehend literature, including stories, dramas, and poetry, at the high end of the grades 2–3 text complexity band independently and proficiently. **Foundational Skills 4.b.** Read on-level prose and poetry orally with accuracy, appropriate rate, and expression on successive readings. **Also Literature 5.**

## Academic Vocabulary ©

**rhyming poems** poems with rhyming words at the ends of their lines and sometimes within their lines

# Poetry

## Rhyming Poems

**TEACH** Remind students that rhyme occurs when two or more words have the same ending sounds. Have students supply examples. Then explain that a poet sometimes builds a poem out of pairs of rhyming lines, which are called couplets.

**GUIDE PRACTICE** Have students identify the rhymes in each of the couplets in "Me." Then have them notice that the couplets are of different lengths, but each pair has the same number of beats.

**ON THEIR OWN** Ask students to write a short rhyming poem that uses couplets. You may want to narrow their choices by suggesting topics such as pets, favorite foods, or something they are good at. Encourage students to include imagery in their poems by using words that appeal to the senses.

# Close Reading ©

**ANALYSIS** How does the rhythm of rhyming couplets affect the way you read "Me"? (The lines have a rhythm, so once you get in the groove, the couplets are easy to read. Also, after you read the first line and know what the last word is, you can anticipate what the rhyming word might be in the next line.)

**ANALYSIS** How is the rhyming pattern of the poem "Me" different than the rhyming pattern of a limerick? (In the poem "Me," the rhyming pattern is rhyming couplets, but in a limerick, there is a fifth line that rhymes with the first two lines.)

**SYNTHESIS • TEXT EVIDENCE** Reread "By Myself." What kind of poem is it? Explain your answer. (The poem starts off as a free verse poem because the first two lines do not rhyme. But after that, it uses rhyming couplets. Since most of the lines of the poem are like that, it is a rhyming poem.)

# Practice Fluent Reading

**EXPRESSION** Have partners take turns reading "Me" aloud. Before they begin, have them discuss the main feeling, or emotion, expressed in the poem. For example, does it express wonder, joy, pride, love, or something else? Then have students attempt to show this feeling as they read. After students finish, have them listen to the AudioText of the poem. What emotion does the reader express? Does it echo the one they tried to express in their own readings?

# Writing Poetry

Have students write their own poems modeled on "By Myself." Students can use that poem's first two and last five lines and then supply their own endings to lines 3–10. When students have finished, invite them to read their works aloud.

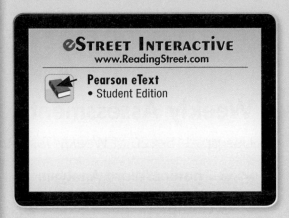

## Access for All

**SI** Strategic Intervention

Have students make a list of the rhyming words found in the poems on pp. 186–187 to start a rhyming journal. Ask them to write other words that rhyme with the words on their list and add to it whenever they hear or think of another rhyming word.

**A** Advanced

Point out that the poem "Me" used the rhyming scheme (couplets) and cadence of a famous poem that begins *I think that I shall never see/ A poem lovely as a tree*. Ask students to find another poem that they like and use its rhyming scheme and cadence to write their own versions, like the author of "Me" did.

**Monitor Understanding** Read "Me" and "By Myself" aloud. Make sure students understand who the poems are about and what message the authors are trying to give the reader. Have students look back at the text to clarify their understanding if necessary.

# Assessment Checkpoints for the Week

## Weekly Assessment

Use pp. 115–120 of *Weekly Tests* to check:

✔ ◉ **Phonics/Word Analysis** Syllables VCCCV

✔ ◉ **Comprehension Skill** Cause and Effect

✔ Review **Comprehension Skill** Draw Conclusions

✔ **Selection Vocabulary**

| clutched | gully | scrambled | valley |
|---|---|---|---|
| echoed | reeds | thatch | |

Weekly Tests

## Differentiated Assessment

**Advanced**

**On-Level**

**Strategic Intervention**

Use pp. 115–120 of *Fresh Reads for Fluency and Comprehension* to check:

✔ ◉ **Comprehension Skill** Cause and Effect

✔ Review **Comprehension Skill** Draw Conclusions

✔ **Fluency** Words Correct Per Minute

Fresh Reads for Fluency and Comprehension

## Managing Assessment

Use *Assessment Handbook* for:

✔ **Weekly Assessment Blackline Masters for Monitoring Progress**

✔ **Observation Checklists**

✔ **Record-Keeping Forms**

✔ **Portfolio Assessment**

Assessment Handbook

# TEACHER NOTES

## DAY 1 Differentiate Vocabulary

- **Word Knowledge** Amazing Words
- **Read** "Communicating Without Words"
- **Inquiry** Identify Questions

"Communicating Without Words"
pp. 52–53

## DAY 2 Differentiate Comprehension

- **Word Knowledge** Selection Vocabulary
- **Access Text** Read *Fly, Eagle, Fly!*
- **Inquiry** Investigate

## DAY 3 Differentiate Close Reading

- **Word Knowledge** Develop Vocabulary
- **Close Reading** Read *Fly, Eagle, Fly!*
- **Inquiry** Investigate

## DAY 4 Differentiate Vocabulary

- **Word Knowledge** Amazing Words
- **Read** "Purple Coyote"
- **Inquiry** Organize

## DAY 5 Differentiate Reteaching

- **Conventions** Prepositions
- **Reread** "Communicating Without Words" or Leveled Readers
- **Inquiry** Communicate

Teacher Guides and Student pages can be found in the Leveled Reader Database.

Place English Language Learners in the groups that correspond to their reading abilities.
**If...** students need scaffolding and practice,
**then...** use the ELL Notes on the instructional pages.

## Independent Practice

**Independent Practice Stations**

See pp. 150h and 150i for Independent Stations.

**Pearson Trade Book Library**

See the Leveled Reader Database for lesson plans and student pages.

**Reading Street Digital Path**

Independent Practice Activities are available in the Digital Path.

**Independent Reading**

See p. 150i for independent reading suggestions.

**OL** On-Level

## 1 Build Word Knowledge

### Practice Amazing Words

**DEFINE IT** Elicit the definition for the word *armor* from students. Ask: How would you describe *armor* to another student? (Possible response: Armor is a covering worn to protect the body.) Clarify or give a definition when necessary. Continue with the words *snout* and *protrude*.

**Team Talk** **TALK ABOUT IT** Have pairs internalize meanings. Ask: How can you pair the Amazing Words together in a sentence? (Possible response: A long black snout protruded from the animal's scaly armor.) Allow time for students to play with the words. Review the concept map with students. Discuss other words they can add to the concept map.

## 2 Text-Based Comprehension

### Read

**READ ALOUD "Communicating Without Words"** Have partners read "Communicating Without Words" from *Reading Street Sleuth* on pp. 52–53.

**ACCESS TEXT** Discuss the Sleuth Work section with students before they work on it. Remind students that they can use these steps with other texts they read.

**Gather Evidence** Have partners work together to list details from the text. Invite students to share an interesting detail.

**Ask Questions** Have students share the questions they asked. Talk together about the sources students may use to find answers to their questions. If time permits, have partners research the answer to one of their questions.

**Make Your Case** Encourage students to revisit the text to identify evidence that supports their opinions. Have students share their opinion and the evidence that supports it.

---

### Sidebar

**©** **Common Core State Standards**

**Literature 1.** Ask and answer questions to demonstrate understanding of a text, referring explicitly to the text as the basis for the answers. **Informational Text 2.** Determine the main idea of a text; recount the key details and explain how they support the main idea. **Foundational Skills 4.** Read with sufficient accuracy and fluency to support comprehension. **Speaking/Listening 1.** Engage effectively in a range of collaborative discussions (one-on-one, in groups, and teacher-led) with diverse partners on grade 3 topics and texts, building on others' ideas and expressing their own clearly. **Language 4.** Determine or clarify the meaning of unknown and multiple-meaning words and phrases based on grade 3 reading and content, choosing flexibly from a range of strategies.

**Independent Reading Options**

**Trade Book Library**

**e**STREET INTERACTIVE
www.ReadingStreet.com

Teacher Guides are available on the Leveled Reader Database.

**If...** students need more scaffolding and practice with **Vocabulary, then...** use the activities on pp. DI•117–DI•118 in the Teacher Resources section on SuccessNet.

 On-Level

# 1 Build Word Knowledge
## Practice Selection Vocabulary

| | | | |
|---|---|---|---|
| clutched | echoed | gully | reeds |
| scrambled | thatch | valley | |

**DEFINE IT** Discuss the definition for the word *reeds* with students. Ask: How would you describe reeds to another student? (Possible response: Reeds are tall grasses that grow in wet places.) Continue with the remaining words.

**Team Talk** **TALK ABOUT IT** Have pairs use the selection vocabulary in sentences to internalize meaning. Ask: How can you pair the selection vocabulary together in a sentence? (Possible response: Jared clutched his lost turtle as he scrambled out of the reeds.) Allow time for students to play with the words and then share their sentences.

# 2 Read
## *Fly, Eagle, Fly!*

If you read *Fly, Eagle, Fly!* during whole group time, then use the following instruction.

**ACCESS TEXT** Reread p. 167. Ask questions to check understanding. What is the farmer's friend trying to get the eagle to do? (fly from the rooftop) Why does the eagle slide back to the ground to be with the chickens? (It was raised as a chicken since it was a little chick and doesn't know how to behave any differently. It probably has never flown.)

Have students identify sections from today's reading that they did not completely understand. Reread them aloud and clarify misunderstandings.

If you are reading *Fly, Eagle, Fly!* during small group time, then return to pp. 160–167a to guide the reading.

## eStreet Interactive
www.ReadingStreet.com

**Pearson eText**
• Student Edition
• Leveled Reader Database
• *Reading Street Sleuth*

SMALL GROUP TIME

## More Reading for Group Time

**ON-LEVEL**

**Reviews**
• Cause and Effect
• Monitor and Clarify
• Selection Vocabulary

Use this suggested Leveled Reader or other text at students' instructional level.

## eStreet Interactive
www.ReadingStreet.com

Use the Leveled Reader Database for lesson plans and student pages for *Buddy Ran Away*.

*Fly, Eagle, Fly!* **SG•67**

**On-Level**

**Common Core State Standards**

**Literature 1.** Ask and answer questions to demonstrate understanding of a text, referring explicitly to the text as the basis for the answers. **Literature 2.** Recount stories, including fables, folktales, and myths from diverse cultures; determine the central message, lesson, or moral and explain how it is conveyed through key details in the text. **Language 1.** Demonstrate command of the conventions of standard English grammar and usage when writing or speaking. **Language 4.d.** Use glossaries or beginning dictionaries, both print and digital, to determine or clarify the precise meaning of key words and phrases. **Also Language 4.**

## ① Build Word Knowledge
### Develop Vocabulary

**REREAD FOR VOCABULARY** Reread the paragraph on p. 169. Introduce: Let's read this paragraph to find out what *crevices* means. To help students understand the word *crevices,* ask questions related to the context, such as: Why is the path the men are walking on so dangerous? What do the words *into* and *out again* in this paragraph tell you about the word *crevices?* Have students use a dictionary or thesaurus to find out more information about *crevices.*

## ② Read
### Fly, Eagle, Fly!

If you read *Fly, Eagle, Fly!* during whole group time, then use the following instruction.

**CLOSE READING** Read p. 171. Have students monitor their understanding of the text by asking themselves questions about parts that are not clear as they read. Have students work with partners to make a list of questions in the order they occur. (What does the farmer's friend mean by, "This will do"? Why did the friend face the bird toward the east? Why did the farmer say, "It talks only chickens' talk"? Why did the friend keep saying that the bird belonged to the sky, not to the earth?)

Ask: Why do you think the eagle would never live among chickens again? (Once the eagle flies, experiencing life as it is meant to, it would never want to go back to living on the ground again.)

If you are reading *Fly, Eagle, Fly!* during small group time, then return to pp. 168–171a to guide the reading.

**If...** students need more scaffolding and practice with the **Main Selection, then...** use the activities on p. DI•122 in the Teacher Resources section on SuccessNet.

OL On-Level

**eSTREET INTERACTIVE**
www.ReadingStreet.com

**Pearson eText**
• Student Edition

# 1 Build Word Knowledge

## Practice Amazing Words

| | | | |
|---|---|---|---|
| armor | scenery | agile | pesky |
| snout | unfurl | protrude | coil |
| extraordinary | intersection | | |

**Team Talk** **LANGUAGE DEVELOPMENT** Have partners practice building more complex sentences. Display a sentence starter and have students add oral phrases or clauses using the Amazing Words. For example: The _____ scenery. (The extraordinary scenery included purple flowers / that were coiled / around a fence / and a swan unfurling its wings.) Guide students to add at least three phrases or clauses per sentence.

# 2 Read

## "Purple Coyote"

**BEFORE READING** Read aloud the information on p. 176. Have students preview "Purple Coyote" and set a purpose for reading. Ask:

• Based on the information in the side column, what would you expect this story to be about? (a person or animal playing a trick on another person or animal)

• How would you expect the animals in this tale to act? (The information says that animals in folk tales often act like people. The coyote will probably be able to talk.)

**DURING READING** Have students read along with you. Ask:

• Who are the characters mentioned on the first few pages? (Jim and the purple coyote)

• Why do you think the coyote behaves so strangely? (He will probably try to trick Jim.)

**AFTER READING** Have students share their reaction to "Purple Coyote." Then have them create and act out a trickster tale explaining how a school rule came to be.

### Independent Reading Options

**Trade Book Library**

**eSTREET INTERACTIVE**
www.ReadingStreet.com

Teacher Guides are available on the Leveled Reader Database.

**SMALL GROUP TIME**

**On-Level**

## Common Core State Standards

**Informational Text 2.** Determine the main idea of a text; recount the key details and explain how they support the main idea. **Foundational Skills 4.** Read with sufficient accuracy and fluency to support comprehension. **Writing 7.** Conduct short research projects that build knowledge about a topic. **Speaking/Listening 1.** Engage effectively in a range of collaborative discussions (one-on-one, in groups, and teacher-led) with diverse partners on grade 3 topics and texts, building on others' ideas and expressing their own clearly. **Language 4.** Determine or clarify the meaning of unknown and multiple-meaning words and phrases based on grade 3 reading and content, choosing flexibly from a range of strategies.

## More Reading for Group Time

**ON-LEVEL**

**Reviews**
- Cause and Effect
- Monitor and Clarify
- Selection Vocabulary

Use this suggested Leveled Reader or other text at students' instructional level.

### eStreet Interactive
www.ReadingStreet.com

Use the Leveled Reader Database for lesson plans and student pages for *Buddy Ran Away*.

# 1 Build Word Knowledge
## Practice Prepositions

**IDENTIFY** Choral read the bottom of p. 175 with students and explain the function of prepositions, guiding them to see what the words *on, in,* and *at* have in common. Have partners reread the model summary to find examples of how the author used each preposition. Encourage students to use the student model summary on the same page to practice. Allow time for students to discuss their examples and correct any misunderstandings.

# 2 Text-Based Comprehension
## Read

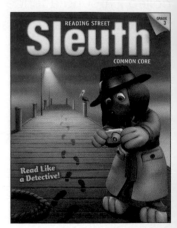

**REREAD "Communicating Without Words"** Have partners reread "Communicating Without Words."

**EXTEND UNDERSTANDING** Talk together about animals that use touch to communicate with each other. Invite students to talk about how humans use touch to communicate.

**PERFORMANCE TASK • Prove It!** Have students research an animal and how it communicates. Then have students create animal communication trading cards on index cards. Students can write the name of the animal and how it communicates on one side and draw a picture of the animal on the other side. Point out that information on the trading card should be factual.

**COMMUNICATE** Have students share their trading cards with each other. Invite students to share other facts that could be added to the trading cards for each animal.

 **Strategic Intervention**

# 1 Build Word Knowledge
## Reteach Amazing Words

Repeat the definition of the word *armor*. We learned that armor is a covering worn to protect the body. Then use the word in a sentence. Knights wore suits of armor to protect themselves during battle.

**Team Talk** **TALK ABOUT IT** Have pairs take turns using the word *armor* in a sentence. Continue this routine to practice the Amazing Words *snout* and *protrude*. Review the concept map with students. Discuss other words they can add to the concept map.

> **Corrective feedback** | **If...** students need more practice with the Amazing Words, **then...** use visuals from the Student Edition or online sources to clarify meaning.

# 2 Text-Based Comprehension
## Read

**READ "Communicating Without Words"** Have students track the print as you read the selection from *Reading Street Sleuth* on pp. 52–53.

**ACCESS TEXT** Discuss the Sleuth Work section with students and provide support as needed as they work on it. Remind students that they can use these steps with other texts they read.

**Gather Evidence** Talk together about ways in which animals communicate. Have partners revisit the text and work together to list details about animal communication. Invite students to share an interesting detail from the text.

**Ask Questions** Talk together about the three ways animals communicate, according to the article. Have students choose one of those methods to write questions about. Invite students to share the questions they asked. Discuss the sources students may use to find answers to their questions.

**Make Your Case** Talk together and make connections between how animals and people communicate. Then have students work with a partner to find evidence from the text that supports their opinions.

---

**SMALL GROUP TIME**

## More Reading for Group Time

**CONCEPT LITERACY**
**Practice**
Concept Words

**BELOW-LEVEL**
**Reviews**
• Cause and Effect
• Monitor and Clarify
• Selection Vocabulary

Use these suggested Leveled Readers or other text at students' instructional level.

Use the Leveled Reader Database for lesson plans and student pages for *What Can Animals Do?* and *Swimming Like Buck*.

**Strategic Intervention**

##  Common Core State Standards

**Literature 1.** Ask and answer questions to demonstrate understanding of a text, referring explicitly to the text as the basis for the answers. **Literature 2.** Recount stories, including fables, folktales, and myths from diverse cultures; determine the central message, lesson, or moral and explain how it is conveyed through key details in the text. **Language 4.a.** Use sentence-level context as a clue to the meaning of a word or phrase. **Also Language 4.**

## ① Build Word Knowledge
### Reteach Selection Vocabulary

**DEFINE IT** Describe *thatch* to a friend. Give a definition when necessary. Restate the word in student-friendly terms and clarify meaning with a visual. *Thatch* means roofing material made of straw. Page 166 shows a thatch roof.

| | | | |
|---|---|---|---|
| clutched | echoed | gully | reeds |
| scrambled | thatch | valley | |

**Team Talk** **TALK ABOUT IT** Have you seen a roof made of thatch? Turn and talk to your partner about this. Rephrase students' examples for usage when necessary or to correct misunderstandings.

> **Corrective feedback** | **If...** students need more practice with selection vocabulary, **then...** use the *Envision It! Pictured Vocabulary Cards*.

## ② Read
### Fly, Eagle, Fly!

If you read *Fly, Eagle, Fly!* during whole group time, then use the instruction below.

**ACCESS TEXT** Reread p. 167. Ask questions to check understanding. Who is the man in this passage? (the farmer's friend) What is the farmer's friend trying to get the eagle to do? (fly from the rooftop) Why is he doing this? (He wants to prove that it's an eagle, not a chicken.) Why does the eagle slide back to the ground to be with the chickens? (It was raised as a chicken since it was a little chick and doesn't know how to behave any differently. It probably has never flown.)

Have students identify sections they did not understand. Reread them aloud. Clarify the meaning of each section to build understanding.

If you are reading *Fly, Eagle, Fly!* during small group time, then return to pp. 160–167a to guide the reading.

**Independent Reading Options**

**Trade Book Library**

**eStreet Interactive**
www.ReadingStreet.com

Teacher Guides are available on the Leveled Reader Database.

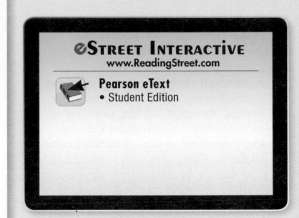

**eSTREET INTERACTIVE**
www.ReadingStreet.com

**Pearson eText**
• Student Edition

## SI Strategic Intervention

# 1 Build Word Knowledge

## Develop Vocabulary

**REREAD FOR VOCABULARY** Reread the paragraph on p. 169. Introduce: Let's read this paragraph to find out what *crevices* means. To help students understand the word *crevices,* ask questions related to the context, such as: Where are the men walking? Why is the path so dangerous? What do the words *into* and *out again* tell you about the word *crevices*? Why are the *crevices* dark?

> **Corrective feedback** | **If...** students have difficulty understanding the word *crevices,* **then...** guide students to use a dictionary or thesaurus to find more information.

# 2 Read

## *Fly, Eagle, Fly!*

If you read *Fly, Eagle, Fly!* during whole group time, then use the instruction below.

**CLOSE READING** Read pp. 168–169. Have students create a three-column chart on the board with the heads **Characters, Setting,** and **Plot.** Have students search the text for the information. Fill out the chart as a class. (Characters: farmer, farmer's friend, eagle; Setting: a valley, the mountain, early in the morning; Plot: The farmer's friend wants to take the eagle to the mountain so it can fly away. He wants to get there before the sun rises.)

Now let's use the information in our chart to retell what happened in this part of the story. (The farmer's friend takes the farmer and the eagle back to the mountain where it came from. He thinks it belongs there and wants it to fly. They cross the valley early in the morning. The friend hurries so they can get there before the sun comes up. They start climbing the mountain as it becomes light. The path is sometimes dangerous, and both men are tired.)

If you are reading *Fly, Eagle, Fly!* during small group time, then return to pp. 168–171a to guide the reading.

**SMALL GROUP TIME**

## ELL

**If...** students need more scaffolding and practice with the **Main Selection, then...** use the activities on p. DI•122 in the Teacher Resources section on SuccessNet.

**SI** Strategic Intervention

## © Common Core State Standards

**Literature 2.** Recount stories, including fables, folktales, and myths from diverse cultures; determine the central message, lesson, or moral and explain how it is conveyed through key details in the text. **Foundational Skills 4.** Read with sufficient accuracy and fluency to support comprehension. **Writing 7.** Conduct short research projects that build knowledge about a topic. **Language 1.** Demonstrate command of the conventions of standard English grammar and usage when writing or speaking.

## ❶ Build Word Knowledge
### Review Amazing Words

| | | | |
|---|---|---|---|
| armor | scenery | agile | pesky |
| snout | unfurl | protrude | coil |
| extraordinary | intersection | | |

**Team Talk** **LANGUAGE DEVELOPMENT** Have students practice building more complex sentences. Display a sentence starter and have students add on oral phrases or clauses using the Amazing Words. For example: The puppy unfurled _____. (The puppy unfurled its blanket / and put its wet snout on my arm.) Guide students to add at least two phrases or clauses per sentence.

> **Corrective feedback** | **If...** students have difficulty using Amazing Words orally, **then...** review the meaning of each of the words.

## ❷ Read
### "The Purple Coyote"

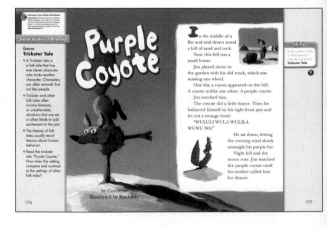

**BEFORE READING** Read aloud the information about the trickster tale on p. 176. A trickster tale is a folk tale in which one character fools others. Like other folk tales, trickster tales entertain and also show how people and animals behave. As I read, I will try to figure out which animal is the trickster. Read the rest of the panel. Then have students read the introduction to the selection.

**DURING READING** Have students perform a choral reading of the selection. Encourage them to create different voices for the coyote, the boy, and the raccoon. How can we make the coyote sound tricky? How should the raccoon sound—smart, sarcastic, or bored? How should the boy sound?

**AFTER READING** Have students share their reactions to the selection. Then guide them through the Reading Across Texts and Writing Across Texts activities.

**If...** students need more scaffolding and practice with **Amazing Words, then...** use the Routine on pp. xxxvi–xxxvii in the *ELL Handbook.*

**Strategic Intervention**

# 1 Build Word Knowledge
## Review Prepositions

**IDENTIFY** Choral read the bottom of p. 175 with students to review prepositions. Have partners reread the model summary on p. 175 to find examples of how the author used each preposition. Have students use the student model summary on that page to practice. Allow time for students to discuss their examples and correct any misunderstandings.

# 2 Text-Based Comprehension
## Read

**REREAD "Communicating Without Words"** Have partners reread "Communicating Without Words" with partners alternating paragraphs.

**EXTEND UNDERSTANDING** Talk together about animals that use sound to communicate with each other. Have students identify the animals discussed in the article plus additional examples of other animals that communicate using sound.

**PERFORMANCE TASK • Prove It!** Have students research an animal and how it communicates. Then have students create animal communication trading cards on index cards. Students can write the name of the animal and how it communicates on one side and draw a picture of the animal on the other side. Encourage students to name one additional fact for the animal they have chosen.

**COMMUNICATE** Have students share their trading cards with each other. Invite students to summarize the way each animal communicates.

### More Reading for Group Time

**CONCEPT LITERACY**
**Practice**
Concept Words

**BELOW-LEVEL**
**Reviews**
• Cause and Effect
• Monitor and Clarify
• Selection Vocabulary

Use these suggested Leveled Readers or other text at students' instructional level.

*e*STREET INTERACTIVE
www.ReadingStreet.com

Use the Leveled Reader Database for lesson plans and student pages for *What Can Animals Do?* and *Swimming Like Buck.*

**SMALL GROUP TIME**

**A** Advanced

## Common Core State Standards

**Literature 2.** Recount stories, including fables, folktales, and myths from diverse cultures; determine the central message, lesson, or moral and explain how it is conveyed through key details in the text. **Foundational Skills 4.** Read with sufficient accuracy and fluency to support comprehension. **Speaking/Listening 1.** Engage effectively in a range of collaborative discussions (one-on-one, in groups, and teacher-led) with diverse partners on grade 3 topics and texts, building on others' ideas and expressing their own clearly. **Language 4.** Determine or clarify the meaning of unknown and multiple-meaning words and phrases based on grade 3 reading and content, choosing flexibly from a range of strategies.

## ❶ Build Word Knowledge

### Extend Amazing Words

**Team Talk** Have pairs of students define *armor*. Discuss synonyms for *armor*. (*shielding, metal plating*) How is metal plating different from armor? (Metal plating is used for military equipment, like ships and tanks. *Armor* refers to protection for people or animals.) Continue with *snout* and *protrude*.

## ❷ Text-Based Comprehension

### Read

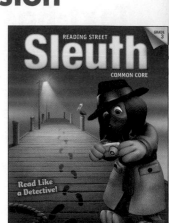

**READ "Communicating Without Words"** Have students read "Communicating Without Words" from *Reading Street Sleuth* on pp. 52–53.

**ACCESS TEXT** Discuss the Sleuth Work section with students before they work on it. Remind students that they can use these steps with other texts they read.

**Gather Evidence** Have students list details from the text. Invite them to share their details.

**Ask Questions** Have students share the questions they asked and what sources they may use to find answers to their questions. If time permits, have students research the answer to one of their questions.

**Make Your Case** Have students revisit the text to find evidence that supports their opinion. Have them share this evidence.

## ❸ Inquiry: Extend Concepts

**IDENTIFY QUESTIONS** Have students think about questions they have about birds and use these questions to select a bird to study. Have them research both its learned and instinctive behaviors, such as feeding, grooming, communication, and interactions with other birds, animals, and humans. Throughout the week, they will gather information. On Day 5, they will present what they have learned.

**If...** students need more scaffolding and practice with **Vocabulary, then...** use the activities on pp. DI•117–DI•118 in the Teacher Resources section oon SuccessNet.

A Advanced

# 1 Build Word Knowledge

## Extend Selection Vocabulary

**Team Talk** Have partners use the selection vocabulary in sentences to internalize their meanings. Have students use as many of the words as they can while making sure the sentence is grammatically correct.

| | | |
|---|---|---|
| clutched | echoed | gully |
| reeds | scrambled | thatch |
| valley | | |

# 2 Read

## Fly, Eagle, Fly!

If you read *Fly, Eagle, Fly!* during whole group time, then use the instruction below.

**ACCESS TEXT** Reread p. 167. Discuss what can be inferred about the two characters from the information provided in this part of the story. (The farmer is someone who prefers to let things be how they are and would rather not try to change things. He has no great expectations of the eagle and not much curiosity either. Maybe he has too many kids to feed to worry about a bird. The farmer's friend, however, is determined to restore the eagle to its rightful place in the world. He takes great risks to pursue something he really believes in.)

Ask: Why do you think people laughed when the eagle landed back on the ground with the chickens? (They probably thought that the farmer's friend looked really silly when he failed again to get the eagle to fly.)

If you are reading *Fly, Eagle, Fly!* during small group time, then return to pp. 160–167a to guide the reading.

# 3 Inquiry: Extend Concepts

**INVESTIGATE** Encourage students to use materials at their independent reading levels or student-friendly search engines to identify relevant and credible sites to gather information about bird behavior. Have students consider how they will present their information.

**eStreet Interactive**
www.ReadingStreet.com

**Pearson eText**
• Student Edition
• Leveled Reader Database
• *Reading Street Sleuth*

**SMALL GROUP TIME**

## More Reading for Group Time

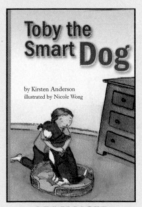

**ADVANCED**

**Reviews**
• Cause and Effect
• Monitor and Clarify

Use this suggested Leveled Reader or other text at students' instructional level.

**eStreet Interactive**
www.ReadingStreet.com

Use the Leveled Reader Database for lesson plans and student pages for *Toby the Smart Dog*.

**A** Advanced

## Common Core State Standards

**Literature 1.** Ask and answer questions to demonstrate understanding of a text, referring explicitly to the text as the basis for the answers. **Literature 2.** Recount stories, including fables, folktales, and myths from diverse cultures; determine the central message, lesson, or moral and explain how it is conveyed through key details in the text. **Language 1.** Demonstrate command of the conventions of standard English grammar and usage when writing or speaking. **Also Language 4.**

## ➊ Build Word Knowledge
### Develop Vocabulary

**REREAD FOR VOCABULARY** Reread the paragraph on p. 169. Let's read this paragraph to find out what *crevices* means. Discuss meaning and context with students.

## ➋ Read
### *Fly, Eagle, Fly!*

If you read *Fly, Eagle, Fly!* during whole group time, then use the instruction below.

**CLOSE READING** Read p. 171. Have students create a T-chart with the heads **Questions** and **Answers.** Have students read through the text to create questions and answers that help them evaluate the text. (1. Why does the friend set the eagle down so it is facing the east? He wanted the eagle to see the dazzling sight of the sun. 2. Why does the farmer say that the eagle "talks only chickens' talk"? His friend has begun talking to the bird, and the farmer is mocking him. 3. Why does the friend talk to the eagle? He's trying to get the eagle to understand where it belongs. 4. Why does the farmer grow quiet as the sun rises? Perhaps he is surprised the eagle is stretching out its great wings. 5. Why is the eagle "swept upward" instead of flying off on its own? The wind is a symbol of the power of nature, and it has taken the eagle to its true place in the world.)

Ask: How does the author use the character of the farmer's friend in fulfilling his purpose in writing the story? (The author has written a folk tale. He uses the farmer's friend to reveal the moral of the story.)

If you are reading *Fly, Eagle, Fly!* during small group time, then return to pp. 168–171a to guide the reading.

### Independent Reading Options

**Trade Book Library**

**𝑒STREET INTERACTIVE**
www.ReadingStreet.com

Teacher Guides are available on the Leveled Reader Database.

**ELL**

**If...** students need more scaffolding and practice with the **Main Selection, then...** use the activities on p. DI•122 in the Teacher Resources section on SuccessNet.

## ➌ Inquiry: Extend Concepts

**INVESTIGATE** Provide time for students to investigate their topics in books or online. If necessary, help them locate information that is focused on their topics.

**Advanced**

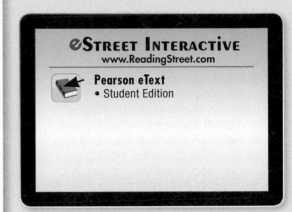

**eSTREET INTERACTIVE**
www.ReadingStreet.com

**Pearson eText**
• Student Edition

# 1 Build Word Knowledge

## Extend Amazing Words and Selection Vocabulary

| | | |
|---|---|---|
| armor | scenery | agile |
| pesky | snout | unfurl |
| protrude | coil | extraordinary |
| intersection | | |

| | | |
|---|---|---|
| clutched | echoed | gully |
| reeds | scrambled | thatch |
| valley | | |

**Team Talk** Have partners practice building more complex sentences. Display a sentence starter and have students add oral phrases or clauses using the Amazing Words and the selection vocabulary. Guide students to add at least three phrases or clauses per sentence.

# 2 Read

## "Purple Coyote"

**BEFORE READING** Have students read the panel information on trickster tales on p.176. Then have students use the text features, including the time line and statistics, to set a purpose for reading. After that, have students read "Purple Coyote" on their own.

**DURING READING** Point out that a trickster tale tells why people or animals behave as they do. What does this trickster tale seem to say about humans? (We're not as smart as we think we are!) As they read, have students think about other trickster tales they've read.

**AFTER READING** Have students discuss Reading Across Texts. Then have them complete the Writing Across Texts activity independently.

# 3 Inquiry: Extend Concepts

**ORGANIZE INFORMATION** Provide time for students to organize their information into a format that will effectively communicate their findings to their audience. Provide any necessary materials or computer time.

**SMALL GROUP TIME**

**Independent Reading Options**

**Trade Book Library**

**eSTREET INTERACTIVE**
www.ReadingStreet.com

Teacher Guides are available on the Leveled Reader Database.

**A** Advanced

**Common Core State Standards**

**Foundational Skills 4.** Read with sufficient accuracy and fluency to support comprehension. **Writing 7.** Conduct short research projects that build knowledge about a topic. **Speaking/Listening 1.a.** Come to discussions prepared, having read or studied required material; explicitly draw on that preparation and other information known about the topic to explore ideas under discussion.

**More Reading for Group Time**

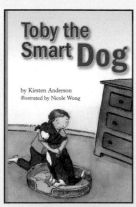

**ADVANCED**

**Reviews**
• Cause and Effect
• Monitor and Clarify

Use this suggested Leveled Reader or other text at students' instructional level.

**eSTREET INTERACTIVE**
www.ReadingStreet.com

Use the Leveled Reader Database for lesson plans and student pages for *Toby the Smart Dog*.

# ① Build Word Knowledge
## Extend Prepositions

**IDENTIFY AND EXTEND** Prepositions Choral read the bottom of p. 175 with students and have them explain the function of prepositions. Help students indicate that prepositions show position, direction, time, or location. Have partners reread the model summary to find examples of how the author used each preposition. Encourage students to use the student model summary on the same page to practice. Allow time for students to discuss their examples and correct any misunderstandings.

# ② Text-Based Comprehension
## Read

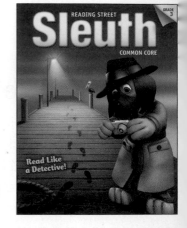

**REREAD "Communicating Without Words"**
Have small groups reread the selection. Have them discuss how peacocks and fireflies are alike in their communication methods.

**EXTEND UNDERSTANDING** Talk together about animals that use visuals to communicate with each other. Have students identify the animals discussed in the article plus additional examples of other animals that communicate using visuals.

**PERFORMANCE TASK • Prove It!** Have students research an animal and how it communicates. Then have students create animal communication trading cards on index cards. Students can write the name of the animal and how it communicates on one side and draw a picture of the animal on the other side. Invite students to create a bullet list of facts about the animal.

**COMMUNICATE** Have students share their trading cards with each other. Encourage students to trade their cards and ask questions that may lead to further research.

# ③ Inquiry: Extend Concepts

**COMMUNICATE** Have students share their inquiry projects on bird behavior with the rest of the class. Provide tips for presenting.

# One of a Kind

## What does it mean to be unique?

During this week, you may wish to:

☑ Choose content to **review** based on progress monitoring

☑ Focus on **target skills** or use the **flexible plan** to adjust instruction

☑ Provide opportunities for interacting with texts by using **model text** in the *Reader's* and *Writer's Notebook*

☑ Develop students' understanding of genre and text structure using the **Strategy Response Log** in the *Reader's* and *Writer's Notebook*

| DAY 1 | DAY 2 | DAY 3 | DAY 4 | DAY 5 |
|---|---|---|---|---|
| REVIEW WEEK 1 | REVIEW WEEK 2 | REVIEW WEEK 3 | REVIEW WEEK 4 | REVIEW WEEK 5 |
| **The Man Who Invented Basketball** | **Hottest, Coldest, Highest, Deepest** | **Rocks in His Head** | **America's Champion Swimmer: Gertrude Ederle** | **Fly, Eagle, Fly!: An African Tale** |
| How do talents make someone unique? | What makes nature's record holders unique? | Why is it valuable to have unique interests? | What unique traits does it take to be the first to do something? | What behaviors are unique to different animals? |
| • **Amazing Words** *mock, idle, potential, ecstatic, thrill, audition, necessary, result, succeed, rise, verge* | • **Amazing Words** *evergreens, lumber, competitors, plunged, valuable, champ, sprinter, acrobat, weaken, ranger* | • **Amazing Words** *hobby, project, leftover, murmur, ancestor, ornament, descendant, forge, compartment* | • **Amazing Words** *ordinary, imagination, assemble, magnificent, organize, erect, suspend, accompany, provision, spectacle* | • **Amazing Words** *armor, agile, snout, protrude, extraordinary, scenery, pesky, unfurl, coil, intersection* |
| **Text-Based Comprehension** Generalize; Summarize | **Text-Based Comprehension** Graphic Sources; Important Ideas | **Text-Based Comprehension** Fact and Opinion; Inferring | **Text-Based Comprehension** Fact and Opinion; Questioning | **Text-Based Comprehension** Cause and Effect; Monitor and Clarify |
| **Phonics** Irregular Plurals | **Phonics** *r*-Controlled Vowels | **Phonics** Prefixes *pre-, mid-, over-, out-, bi-, de-* | **Phonics** Suffixes *-er, -or, -ess, -ist* | **Phonics** Syllables VCCCV |
| **Vocabulary** Unfamiliar Words; Context Clues | **Vocabulary** Unknown Words; Dictionary/Glossary | **Vocabulary** Multiple-Meaning Words; Context Clues | **Vocabulary** Multiple-Meaning Words; Context Clues | **Vocabulary** Unknown Words; Dictionary/Glossary |
| • **Fluency** Accuracy | • **Fluency** Appropriate Phrasing and Punctuation Cues | • **Fluency** Expression | • **Fluency** Appropriate Phrasing | • **Fluency** Rate |
| • **Conventions** Singular and Plural Pronouns | • **Conventions** Subject and Object Pronouns | • **Conventions** Possessive Pronouns | • **Conventions** Contractions | • **Conventions** Prepositions |
| • **Spelling** Irregular Plurals | • **Spelling** *r*-Controlled Vowels | • **Spelling** Prefixes *pre-, mid-, over-, out-, bi-, de-* | • **Spelling** Suffixes *-er, -or, -ess, -ist* | • **Spelling** Syllables VCCCV |

Optional **UNIT 4 Review**

# Preview Your Week

*What does it mean to be unique?*

## DAY 1

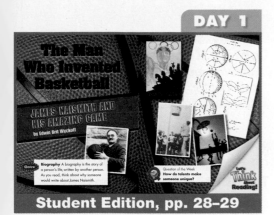

**Student Edition, pp. 28–29**

**Genre:** Biography
**Phonics:** Irregular Plurals
**Text-Based Comprehension:** Generalize

## DAY 2

**Student Edition, pp. 62–63**

**Genre:** Expository Text
**Phonics:** *r*-Controlled Vowels
**Text-Based Comprehension:** Graphic Sources

## DAY 3

**Student Edition, pp. 94–95**

**Genre:** Biography
**Phonics:** Prefixes *pre-, mid-, over-, out-, bi-, de-*
**Text-Based Comprehension:** Fact and Opinion

## DAY 4

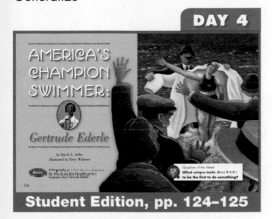

**Student Edition, pp. 124–125**

**Genre:** Biography
**Phonics:** Suffixes *-er, -or, -ess, -ist*
**Text-Based Comprehension:** Fact and Opinion

## DAY 5

**Student Edition, pp. 158–159**

**Genre:** Folk Tale
**Phonics:** Syllables VCCCV
**Text-Based Comprehension:** Cause and Effect

## Reinforce Content Knowledge

What does it mean to be unique?

| How do talents make someone unique? | What makes nature's record holders unique? | Why is it valuable to have unique interests? | What unique traits does it take to be the first to do something? | What behaviors are unique to different animals? |

# 5-Day Planner

## DAY 1 Review Week 1

### Get Ready to Read

**Content Knowledge** UR•6
Oral Vocabulary: *mock, idle, potential, ecstatic, thrill, audition, necessary, result, succeed, rise, verge*

### Read and Comprehend

**Text-Based Comprehension**
UR•8–13
 Generalize

**Vocabulary Skill** UR•10–13
 Unfamiliar Words

**Fluency** UR•13
Accuracy

### Language Arts

**Phonics/Word Analysis** UR•14
 Irregular Plurals

**Spelling** UR•14
Irregular Plurals

**Conventions** UR•15
Singular and Plural Pronouns

**Wrap Up Week 1 Review!** UR•15

## DAY 2 Review Week 2

### Get Ready to Read

**Content Knowledge** UR•16
Oral Vocabulary: *evergreen, lumber, competitor, plunge, valuable, champ, sprinter, acrobat, weaken, ranger*

### Read and Comprehend

**Text-Based Comprehension**
UR•18–23
 Graphic Sources

**Vocabulary Skill** UR•20–23
 Unknown Words

**Fluency** UR•23
Appropriate Phrasing

### Language Arts

**Word Analysis** UR•24
 *r*-Controlled Vowels

**Spelling** UR•24
*r*-Controlled Vowels

**Conventions** UR•25
Subject and Object Pronouns

**Wrap Up Week 2 Review!** UR•25

## DAY 3 Review Week 3

### Get Ready to Read

**Content Knowledge** UR•26
Oral Vocabulary: *hobby, project, leftover, murmur, ancestor, ornament, descendant, forge, compartment*

### Read and Comprehend

**Text-Based Comprehension**
UR•28–33
◉ Fact and Opinion

**Vocabulary Skill** UR•30–33
◉ Multiple-Meaning Words

**Fluency** UR•33
Read with Expression

### Language Arts

**Word Analysis** UR•34
◉ Prefixes *pre-, mid-, over-, out-, bi-, de-*

**Spelling** UR•34
Prefixes *pre-, mid-, over-, out-*

**Conventions** UR•35
Possessive Pronouns

**Wrap Up Week 3 Review!** UR•35

## DAY 4 Review Week 4

### Get Ready to Read

**Content Knowledge** UR•36
Oral Vocabulary: *ordinary, imagination, assemble, magnificent, organize, erect, suspend, accompany, provision, spectacle*

### Read and Comprehend

**Text-Based Comprehension**
UR•38–43
◉ Fact and Opinion

**Vocabulary Skill** UR•40–43
◉ Multiple-Meaning Words

**Fluency** UR•43
Read with Appropriate Phrasing

### Language Arts

**Phonics** UR•44
◉ Suffixes *-er, -or, -ess, -ist*

**Spelling** UR•44
Suffixes *-er, -or, -ess, -ist*

**Conventions** UR•45
Contractions

**Wrap Up Week 4 Review!** UR•45

## DAY 5 Review Week 5

### Get Ready to Read

**Content Knowledge** UR•46
Oral Vocabulary: *armor, agile, snout, protrude, extraordinary, scenery, pesky, unfurl, coil, intersection*

### Read and Comprehend

**Text-Based Comprehension**
UR•48–53
◉ Cause and Effect

**Vocabulary Skill** UR•50–53
◉ Unknown Words

**Fluency** UR•53
Read with Appropriate Rate

### Language Arts

**Phonics** UR•54
◉ Syllables VCCCV

**Spelling** UR•54
Syllables VCCCV

**Conventions** UR•55
Prepositions

**Wrap Up Week 5 Review!** UR•55

# Access for All
## Small Group Lesson Plan
Focus on these activities when time is limited.

| | DAY 1 Review Week 1 | DAY 2 Review Week 2 |
|---|---|---|
| | **pages UR·6–UR·15** | **pages UR·16–UR·25** |
| **OL On-Level** | **Review**<br>★• Generalize<br>• Unfamiliar Words<br>• Read with Accuracy<br>★• Quick Write for Fluency | **Review**<br>★• Graphic Sources<br>• Unknown Words<br>• Read with Appropriate Phrasing<br>★• Quick Write for Fluency |
| **SI Strategic Intervention** | **Reteach and Review**<br>• Content Knowledge<br>• Oral Vocabulary<br>★• Irregular Plurals<br>★• Generalize<br>• Unfamiliar Words<br>• Read with Accuracy<br>• Spelling<br>★• Singular and Plural Pronouns<br>★• Quick Write for Fluency | **Reteach and Review**<br>• Content Knowledge<br>• Oral Vocabulary<br>★• r-Controlled Vowels<br>★• Graphic Sources<br>• Unknown Words<br>• Read with Appropriate Phrasing<br>• Spelling<br>★• Subject and Object Pronouns<br>★• Quick Write for Fluency |
| **A Advanced** | **Extend**<br>★• Generalize<br>• Unfamiliar Words<br>★• Quick Write for Fluency | **Extend**<br>★• Graphic Sources<br>• Unknown Words<br>★• Quick Write for Fluency |
| **ELL** | **Reteach and Review**<br>• Content Knowledge<br>• Oral Vocabulary<br>• ELL Poster<br>★• Irregular Plurals<br>★• Generalize<br>• Unfamiliar Words<br>• Read with Accuracy<br>• Spelling<br>★• Singular and Plural Pronouns<br>★• Quick Write for Fluency | **Reteach and Review**<br>• Content Knowledge<br>• Oral Vocabulary<br>• ELL Poster<br>★• r-Controlled Vowels<br>★• Graphic Sources<br>• Unknown Words<br>• Read with Appropriate Phrasing<br>• Spelling<br>★• Subject and Object Pronouns<br>★• Quick Write for Fluency |

## DAY 3 Review Week 3

**pages UR•26–UR•35**

**Review**
- ★ Fact and Opinion
- Multiple-Meaning Words
- Read with Expression
- ★ Quick Write for Fluency

**Reteach and Review**
- Content Knowledge
- Oral Vocabulary
- ★ Prefixes *pre-, mid-, over-, out-, bi-, de-*
- ★ Fact and Opinion
- Multiple-Meaning Words
- Read with Expression
- Spelling
- ★ Possessive Pronouns
- ★ Quick Write for Fluency

**Extend**
- ★ Fact and Opinion
- Multiple-Meaning Words
- ★ Quick Write for Fluency

**Reteach and Review**
- Content Knowledge
- Oral Vocabulary
- ELL Poster
- ★ Prefixes *pre-, mid-, over-, out-, bi-, de-*
- ★ Fact and Opinion
- Multiple-Meaning Words
- Read with Expression
- Spelling
- ★ Possessive Pronouns
- ★ Quick Write for Fluency

## DAY 4 Review Week 4

**pages UR•36–UR•45**

**Review**
- ★ Fact and Opinion
- Multiple-Meaning Words
- Read with Appropriate Phrasing
- ★ Quick Write for Fluency

**Reteach and Review**
- Content Knowledge
- Oral Vocabulary
- ★ Suffixes *-er, -or, -ess, -ist*
- ★ Fact and Opinion
- Multiple-Meaning Words
- Read with Appropriate Phrasing
- Spelling
- ★ Contractions
- ★ Quick Write for Fluency

**Extend**
- ★ Fact and Opinion
- Multiple-Meaning Words
- ★ Quick Write for Fluency

**Reteach and Review**
- Content Knowledge
- Oral Vocabulary
- ELL Poster
- ★ Suffixes *-er, -or, -ess, -ist*
- ★ Fact and Opinion
- Multiple-Meaning Words
- Read with Appropriate Phrasing
- Spelling
- ★ Contractions
- ★ Quick Write for Fluency

## DAY 5 Review Week 5

**pages UR•46–UR•55**

**Review**
- ★ Cause and Effect
- Unknown Words
- Read with Appropriate Rate
- ★ Quick Write for Fluency

**Reteach and Review**
- Content Knowledge
- Oral Vocabulary
- ★ Syllables VCCCV
- ★ Cause and Effect
- Unknown Words
- Read with Appropriate Rate
- Spelling
- ★ Prepositions
- ★ Quick Write for Fluency

**Extend**
- ★ Cause and Effect
- Unknown Words
- ★ Quick Write for Fluency

**Reteach and Review**
- Content Knowledge
- Oral Vocabulary
- ELL Poster
- ★ Syllables VCCCV
- ★ Cause and Effect
- Unknown Words
- Read with Appropriate Rate
- Spelling
- ★ Prepositions
- ★ Quick Write for Fluency

## Content Knowledge

### Talents

**REVISIT THE CONCEPT** Today students will explore how the question for this unit of study connects to *The Man Who Invented Basketball*. Remind students of the Question of the Week, *How do talents make someone unique?*

## Build Oral Language

**DISCUSS BEING ONE OF A KIND** Remind students of the question for this unit of study, *What does it mean to be unique?* Use the prompts and the concept map from Week 1 to discuss what it means to be unique and how our talents can make us unique.

- What kinds of results can a person get by using his or her unique talents?
- How is every person unique?
- In what way could a talent make someone unique?

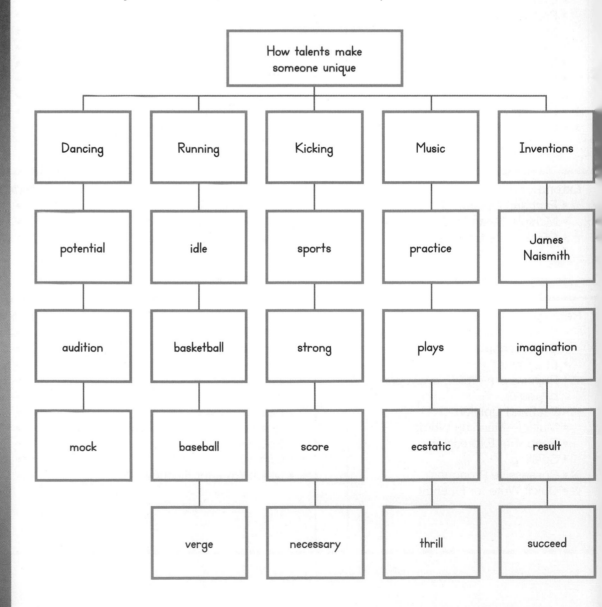

---

**Content Knowledge**
Review Oral Vocabulary

**Text-Based Comprehension**
Review Generalize

**Selection Vocabulary**
Review Unfamiliar Words

**Fluency**
Accuracy

**Phonics/Word Analysis**
Review Irregular Plurals

**Spelling**
Review Irregular Plurals

**Conventions**
Review Singular and Plural Pronouns

**Writing**
Quick Write for Fluency

### Materials

- Student Edition
- Retelling Cards
- Reader's and Writer's Notebook
- Sound-Spelling Cards

---

### Common Core State Standards

**Speaking/Listening 1.** Engage effectively in a range of collaborative discussions (one-on-one, in groups, and teacher-led) with diverse partners on grade 3 topics and texts, building on others' ideas and expressing their own clearly. **Language 6.** Acquire and use accurately grade-appropriate conversational, general academic, and domain-specific words and phrases, including those that signal spatial and temporal relationships (e.g., *After dinner that night we went looking for them*).

# Build Oral Vocabulary

**REVIEW AMAZING WORDS** Display the Amazing Words for *The Man Who Invented Basketball.* Remind students that the words are related to the week's concept.

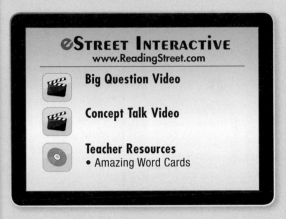

## Amazing Words

### Robust Vocabulary Routine

1. **Review** Ask students for definitions of the words, starting at the top of the list. Listen for accurate definitions. Prompt students to connect the words to the unit concept of One of a Kind whenever possible.

2. **Demonstrate** Have students use two or more Amazing Words in the same sentence. Guide the discussion by providing an example that shows the meaning of each word. *An audition is a way to show your talent and potential.* Follow this pattern to the end of the list, covering as many of the eleven words as possible.

3. **Apply** Assign the words in random order and have students come up with new sentences for them. *To show you are becoming more comfortable using these Amazing Words, think up more new sentences for them.*

Routines Flip Chart

**AMAZING WORDS AT WORK** Have students use the Retelling Cards/Story Sort for *The Man Who Invented Basketball* to talk about the Amazing Words.

**CONNECT TO READING** Tell students that today they will be rereading passages from *The Man Who Invented Basketball* and reading "Margie Goldstein, Rider of the Year." As they read, ask students to think about how talents can make someone unique.

## Amazing Words

| | |
|---|---|
| mock | necessary |
| idle | result |
| potential | succeed |
| ecstatic | rise |
| thrill | verge |
| audition | |

## ELL

**Build Background** Use ELL Poster 16 to review the Week 1 lesson concept and to practice oral language. Point out and read the question: *How do talents make someone unique?*

**3**

Let's **Think** About...

Can you visualize how to play the game of duck on a rock? **Visualize**

Let's **Think** About...

How do you think James will use duck on a rock years later in his life? **Predict**

**4**

The best game in town was called duck on a rock. One player, the guard, would put a rock about the size of his fist on top of a great big rock near the blacksmith shop. The other boys threw stones at the "duck" to knock it off the big rock. If they missed, they had to pick up their stones before the guard could tag them. It sounds easy, but it is not. The pitch could be soft, but it had to be perfectly aimed. When a player missed the duck, there was a lot of running, shouting, and laughing. James would remember duck on a rock years later when it would be very important to him.

James and his friends used this big rock to play their favorite game, duck on a rock.

### THE DROPOUT

James was great at sports. He also worked hard on the family farm. He did not work hard at school, though, and his grades were never very good. He wanted to grow up fast and be a man with a job. When he was fifteen, he left school and worked as a lumberjack.

32

He cut down trees for almost five years. Then he decided to change his life.

James had a plan. He wanted to go back to high school and finish fast. His next step would be college. In 1883, James entered McGill University in Montreal, Canada.

When James was home for a visit, his brother, Robbie, had a terrible pain in his side. They all thought it was just a stomachache. It was actually a very bad infection. Robbie died a few hours later. A doctor could have helped him. Knowing Robbie might have been saved stayed in James's mind every day of his life.

In 1887, James graduated from McGill University after studying Hebrew and philosophy. Hebrew is an ancient language that many ministers study. Philosophy teaches people to think about life. James had a lot to think about.

Let's **Think** About...

How would you summarize some of the things James had to think about? Support your answer with information from the text. **Summarize**

**5**

33

**Student Edition, pp. 32–33**

## Common Core State Standards

**Informational Text 2.** Determine the main idea of a text; recount the key details and explain how they support the main idea. **Informational Text 8.** Describe the logical connection between particular sentences and paragraphs in a text (e.g., comparison, cause/effect, first/second/third in a sequence).

# Access Text

**REVIEW**  **GENERALIZE** Review making generalizations on p. 24. Remind students that a generalization tells how some things are all alike or mostly alike. Students can use several examples to come up with a generalization.

**GUIDE PRACTICE** Read aloud the first paragraph on p. 32 and have students identify a generalization. (The best game in town was called duck on a rock.) What is a generalization you can make from the details in this paragraph about how people felt when playing duck on a rock? People always had a good time playing it.

**ON THEIR OWN** Have pairs of students reread pp. 32–35 and use the information on these pages to make a generalization about James's attitude toward hard work.

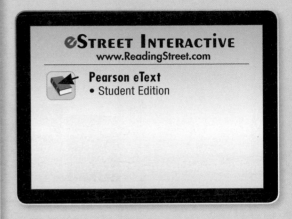

# Close Reading ©

**SYNTHESIS • TEXT EVIDENCE** James Naismith used his memories of the game duck on a rock to help him invent basketball. How are the two games alike? In both games, a "soft pitch" is the best way to aim. Neither game involves teams of men banging into each other and into walls.

**SYNTHESIS • TEXT EVIDENCE** Use the information from pages 32–33 to make a generalization about James Naismith. James Naismith experienced many things before he graduated from college.

**EVALUATION** Why did James Naismith invent basketball? He invented basketball because people needed a fun game that could be played indoors. What do you think people today owe James Naismith for inventing the game? We owe him appreciation for inventing a game that so many people enjoy playing and watching.

## Access for All

**SI Strategic Intervention**

For students having difficulty creating accurate general statements, have them choose between an accurate and an inaccurate general statement. Discuss why students chose one over the other. For example, "James Naismith never loved sports" versus "James Naismith always loved sports."

**A Advanced**

Discuss with students how some general statements can be too extreme and are therefore inaccurate. Direct students to generate one accurate and one inaccurate general statement. For example, "James never got good grades" and "James always hated school."

### TOUGH LOVE AND A TOUGH LIFE

Winter in Canada can be very hard. Icy wind sweeps down from the north. Rivers freeze solid. Crossing them can be scary and dangerous.

James Naismith turned eleven in 1872. He was old enough to know where the river near his home became safe, solid ice. But he took a shortcut he had never tried before. His team of horses pulled his wagon onto the frozen river. Their feet pounded the ice. Then one heavy hoof slammed through the sheet of ice. James jumped off the wagon and landed in the water. Grabbing the horses by their reins, he pulled hard. Slowly he forced them to the other side of the river.

James looked around. He saw his uncle Peter Young watching him from behind some trees. But his uncle had not helped him. Uncle Peter wanted James to learn to solve problems by himself and not to take foolish chances. It was a tough lesson.

> **Let's Think About...**
> Read the second paragraph. What do you think the biography will be about? Support your prediction with evidence from the text. **Predict**
>
> **1**

**James grew up near Almonte, Ontario, in Canada.**

James was born on November 6, 1861, near Almonte, Ontario, which is in Canada. When he was almost nine, his father, John Naismith, came down with deadly typhoid fever. So they would not catch the disease, James, his sister, Annie, and brother, Robbie, were taken to their grandmother's home. A few days later, their father died. Two weeks later, their mother, Margaret, died of the same disease. A short time later, their grandmother Annie Young died of old age.

That left Uncle Peter to take care of the children in Bennie's Corners, near Almonte. The village had a schoolhouse, a blacksmith shop, a store, and lots of other kids to play with.

The children had lots of fun with very little money. When James needed ice skates, he made them. Then he raced out onto the frozen swimming hole like a champion skater.

> **Let's Think About...**
> How would you describe the early part of James Naismith's childhood? Use information from the text and maintain a logical order.
> **Summarize**
>
> **2**

30                                                                                      31

**Student Edition, pp. 30–31**

---

## Ⓒ Common Core State Standards

**Informational Text 2.** Determine the main idea of a text; recount the key details and explain how they support the main idea. **Informational Text 8.** Describe the logical connection between particular sentences and paragraphs in a text (e.g., comparison, cause/effect, first/second/third in a sequence). **Language 4.** Determine or clarify the meaning of unknown and multiple-meaning word and phrases based on grade 3 reading and content, choosing flexibly from a range of strategies. **Language 4.a.** Use sentence-level context as a clue to the meaning of a word or phrase.

## Access Text Ⓒ

**REVIEW 🔊 UNFAMILIAR WORDS** Have students use context to determine the relevant meanings of unfamiliar words. Review the instruction on p. 26. Remind students that they should look at context clues to see if the author has included any clues as to the new word's meaning.

**GUIDE PRACTICE** Point out the word *reins* on p. 30. Have students identify clues that might help them understand the word. Point out that the text shows that reins are connected to horses. James pulls on them, and with the reins, James controls the horses. Then work with students to help determine the meaning of the word.

**ON THEIR OWN** Use *Let's Practice It!* p. 270 on the *Teacher Resources DVD-ROM* for additional practice with unfamiliar words.

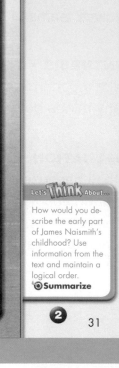

Name _____

**Unit 4 Week 1 Interactive Review**

### Vocabulary

| basketball | disease | freeze | guard |
| popular | sports | study | terrible |

**Directions** Write a word from the box to complete each sentence.

1. The loud noise gave Grace a ___terrible___ headache.
2. The ___guard___ kept the gold safe.
3. Frank was sick for two weeks with a ___disease___.
4. We all like to sing the ___popular___ song.
5. If it gets any colder outside, the lake will ___freeze___.
6. Meg likes to run and play many ___sports___.
7. The students must ___study___ hard to pass the test.
8. The player threw the ___basketball___ into the air.

**Directions** Write the word from the box that goes with each definition.

9. really bad ___terrible___
10. a person who watches over or protects something ___guard___
11. turn into ice ___freeze___
12. to spend time learning, usually by reading ___study___
13. a problem in the body; sickness ___disease___
14. a game played on a court where two teams try to throw a ball through a raised hoop ___basketball___
15. liked by many people ___popular___
16. games in which people use their bodies ___sports___

**Home Activity** Your child used words from *The Men Who Invented Basketball* to complete sentences and match definitions. Have your child write a story about playing sports using as many of the vocabulary words as possible.

DVD•270 **Vocabulary**

**Let's Practice It! TR DVD•270**

**eSTREET INTERACTIVE**
www.ReadingStreet.com

**Pearson eText**
• Student Edition

**Teacher Resources**
• Let's Practice It!

## Close Reading ©

**DEVELOP LANGUAGE** Write the following sentences on the board: "James felt *jittery* crossing the ice. He was nervous that it would crack." Then have students guess the meaning of the word *jittery.* Have them explain what context clue helped them figure out the word's meaning. ("worried"; the word *nervous* in the next sentence)

**ANALYSIS • TEXT EVIDENCE** Have students identify a generalization in the first paragraph of p. 30. (Winters in Canada can be very hard.)

**ANALYSIS** What event from his past made James want to become a doctor? James remembered his brother dying without any help. It made him want to become a doctor to help people.

**INFERENCE** James drove a team of horses in the snow when he was eleven and made his own ice skates to go skate on the frozen pond. What do these details tell you about the kind of person James was as a child? The details tell me that James could do a lot of difficult things. He was skillful and a problem-solver.

### Access for All

**SI** Strategic Intervention

Write the following sentence on the board: *One heavy hoof* <u>*slammed*</u> *through the sheet of ice.* Then create a three-column chart on the board. Write the underlined word in the left column. As a class, discuss context clues. Write these in the middle column. Move on to students' ideas about the meaning of the word. Write these in the right-hand column. Then test whether the different ideas make sense in the sentence.

**A** Advanced

Have students use unfamiliar words that the class has defined to write their own sentences. Tell students to include context clues that hint at their meanings.

*weiveR tinU lanoitpO*

---

Name_____

**Read** the story. **Answer** the questions.

### Margie Goldstein, Rider of the Year

"Margie, you're too little to control those big horses."

"Margie, your legs aren't long enough! Maybe you should stick to ponies."

"Margie, don't try to jump that horse. He's too dangerous! The best rider at this stable is afraid to get on his back!"

Young Margie Goldstein heard comments like these all the time. Growing up in Wellington, Florida, she lived near huge horse farms and riding arenas. She loved animals and she thought she would love to ride horses, but her parents said no. They knew how dangerous horses could be. They knew how much lessons cost. They knew how much time it would take to become a good rider.

Wellington is the home of some major American horse shows. Champion riders come from all over the world to compete there. Junior riders test their skills against other children and young people their age. Young Margie Goldstein longed to be one of them.

But at first, Margie had to be content taking care of other people's dogs and cats. She spent hours and hours in stables, taking care of other people's horses, too. People would give her saddles and bridles in exchange for her work. The owner of the stable paid her in extra riding time instead of money.

Margie Goldstein had a hidden gift that even she didn't know about at first. Besides being a fine athlete, she "had a way with animals." That means that she somehow earned their trust right away. Maybe it was her soft voice or the quiet way she walked into their stall. Maybe it was the way she used her hands and legs to communicate when she was in the saddle.

Comprehension DVD•271

---

Name_____

Whatever it was, some of the most difficult ponies and horses responded to her. It wasn't easy, and Goldstein broke a lot of bones along the way. Soon, though, people noticed she had a special talent with horses. When a horse trusts its rider, the two of them become a team, and then they can do just about anything.

As an adult, Margie Goldstein is still shorter than most other riders, but nothing stops her. She has been <u>Rider of the Year,</u> an <u>all-time money winner,</u> and also an <u>Olympic champion.</u> She's still riding today at the very highest levels of show jumping.

1. Underline the best generalization of what people thought about young Margie Goldstein's riding ability.

   <u>She would never be good enough.</u>

   Horses are too dangerous.

   Only tall people can be good riders.

2. Underline details in the selection that support this generalization: Margie Goldstein is one of the very best riders. **Suggested answers are underscored in the text.**

3. Make a generalization about these details: A horse can jump over stone walls, hedges, fences, and many other obstacles.

   **Possible response: Horses jump over many, many different obstacles.**

 **School + Home** **Home Activity** Your child made generalizations about information in a biography. Name three objects or animals that are the same in some way, such as cardinal, blue jay, and crow. Have your child make a generalization about them, such as *All birds have two legs* or *all birds have beaks*.

DVD•272 Comprehension

Let's Practice It! TR DVD•271–272

---

## Common Core State Standards

**Informational Text 2.** Determine the main idea of a text; recount the key details and explain how they support the main idea. **Informational Text 3.** Describe the relationship between a series of historical events, scientific ideas or concepts, or steps in technical procedures in a text, using language that pertains to time, sequence, and cause/effect. **Informational Text 8.** Describe the logical connection between particular sentences and paragraphs in a text (e.g., comparison, cause/effect, first/second/third in a sequence). **Language 4.** Determine or clarify the meaning of unknown and multiple-meaning word and phrases based on grade 3 reading and content, choosing flexibly from a range of strategies. **Language 4.a.** Use sentence-level context as a clue to the meaning of a word or phrase. **Also Foundational Skills 4.**

# Access Text ©

Have students read "Margie Goldstein, Rider of the Year" and respond to the questions.

**REVIEW ● GENERALIZE • TEXT EVIDENCE** Provide details from the text that support this generalization: Margie Goldstein is one of the very best riders. She has been Rider of the Year, an all-time money winner, and an Olympic champion.

Remind students of generalizing clue words such as *all, always, never, most, many, some, sometimes,* and *usually.* Have students look for some of these clue words in the text.

**REVIEW ● SUMMARIZE** Have students summarize information in the text while maintaining meaning and logical order. How would you summarize this story in two or three sentences? Margie Goldstein had a way with animals. She loved horses. She became a very good rider.

**REVIEW UNFAMILIAR WORDS** Use context to determine the relevant meanings of unfamiliar words. In Question 3, the author uses the word *obstacles.* What context clues could you use to help you figure out what this word means? The sentence says that horses jump over water, fences, rock walls, and other *obstacles.* Fences and rock walls and water are all things in the horse's way, so I think that *obstacles* means "things that are in the way."

If students are familiar with the word *obstacles,* find a different word and work with students to use context to understand what the word means. Such words might include *stables* and *arenas.*

**REVIEW GENERALIZE** Make a generalization about these details: A horse can jump over stone walls, hedges, fences, and many other obstacles. Horses can jump over many different obstacles.

# Reread for Fluency

**MODEL FLUENT READING** Help students read aloud grade-level appropriate text fluently, with accuracy and comprehension. Remind students that when they read, it is important to read with accuracy in order to understand what they are reading. Model reading the first paragraph of "Margie Goldstein, Rider of the Year" on p. 271 aloud with accuracy. Have students track the print as you read.

## Routine | Paired Reading

1. **Select a Passage** Pair students and have them read "Margie Golstein, Rider of the Year."

2. **Reading 1** Students read the entire story, switching readers at the end of each paragraph.

3. **Reading 2** Partners reread the story. This time the other student begins.

4. **Reread** For optimal fluency, have partners continue to read three or four times.

5. **Corrective Feedback** Listen to students read and provide corrective feedback regarding their accuracy.

Routines Flip Chart

## Common Core State Standards

**Language 1.** Demonstrate command of the conventions of standard English grammar and usage when writing or speaking. **Language 1.a.** Explain the function of nouns, pronouns, verbs, adjectives, and adverbs in general and their functions in particular sentences. **Language 1.b.** Form and use regular and irregular plural nouns. **Language 2.e.** Use conventional spelling for high-frequency and other studied words and for adding suffixes to base words (e.g., *sitting, smiled, cries, happiness*).

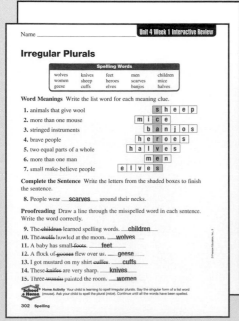

Let's Practice It! TR DVD•269

Reader's and Writer's Notebook, pp. 302–303

# Word Analysis

**REVIEW ⊚ IRREGULAR PLURALS** Review irregular plurals using *Sound-Spelling Card* 140.

Use *Let's Practice It!* p. 269 on the *Teacher Resources DVD-ROM*.

**READ WORDS IN CONTEXT** Point out that students know how to read these words. Have students read the sentences together. Allow several seconds previewing time for the first reading.

Have students complete items 10–14. Then have students read the sentences they wrote aloud.

> **Corrective feedback**
>
> **If...** students have difficulty reading irregular plurals, **then...** guide them in using the word parts strategy. Have students read each sentence repeatedly until they can read the sentences fluently.

# Spelling

**REVIEW IRREGULAR PLURALS** Write *halves, wolves,* and *mice.* Point out that these words are plurals. Remind students that they have learned how to spell irregular plurals.

**SPELLING STRATEGY** Review irregular plurals by having students follow the spelling strategy for spelling these words.

> **Step 1: Mark the letters that give you a problem.**
>
> **Step 2: Find words you know with the same letters.**
>
> **Step 3: Use your problem words and the word you know in a sentence.**

**ON THEIR OWN** Use p. 302 of the *Reader's and Writer's Notebook* for additional practice with irregular plurals.

# Conventions

**REVIEW SINGULAR AND PLURAL PRONOUNS** Review **singular pronoun** and **plural pronoun** with students.

**GUIDE PRACTICE** Read the following sentences. Have students identify the pronouns.

1. Thanks for reading **us** a funny story.

2. **It** made the class laugh out loud.

**ON THEIR OWN** For additional practice use *Reader's and Writer's Notebook,* p. 303.

## Routine   Quick Write for Fluency   Team Talk

1. **Talk** Pairs discuss the information in the sports time lines in *The Man Who Invented Basketball* and "My Turn at Bat."

2. **Write** Students write short time lines about their own experience playing sports, using singular and plural pronouns.

3. **Share** Partners read each other's time lines, checking for the correct use of singular and plural pronouns.

Routines Flip Chart

## eStreet Interactive
www.ReadingStreet.com

**Teacher Resources**
• Reader's and Writer's Notebook
• Let's Practice It!

**Interactive Sound-Spelling Card**

## Writing Workshop
Use the writing process lesson on pp. WP•1–WP•10 for this week's writing instruction.

# Wrap Up Week 1 Review!

✔ **Content Knowledge** How did James Naismith's talents make him unique?

✔ **Generalize** What makes a sport enjoyable to play?

✔ **Unfamiliar Words** How can you determine what an unfamiliar word means?

✔ **Homework** Send home this week's Family Times newsletter on *Let's Practice It!* pp. 218–219 on the *Teacher Resources DVD-ROM.*

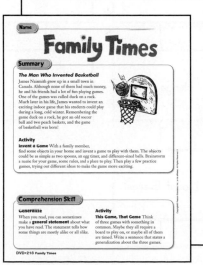

Let's Practice It!
TR DVD•218–219

Preview
DAY 2

Tell students that tomorrow they will review *Hottest, Coldest, Highest, Deepest.*

# Review
## Week 2

### Materials

- Student Edition
- Retelling Cards
- Reader's and Writer's Notebook
- Sound-Spelling Cards

### Ⓒ Common Core State Standards

**Speaking/Listening 1.** Engage effectively in a range of collaborative discussions (one-on-one, in groups, and teacher-led) with diverse partners on grade 3 topics and texts, building on others' ideas and expressing their own clearly. **Language 6.** Acquire and use accurately grade-appropriate conversational, general academic, and domain-specific words and phrases, including those that signal spatial and temporal relationships (e.g., *After dinner that night we went looking for them*).

# Content Knowledge

## Nature's Record Holders

**REVISIT THE CONCEPT** Today students will explore how the question for this unit of study connects to *Hottest, Coldest, Highest, Deepest.* Remind students of the Question of the Week, *What makes nature's record holders unique?*

## Build Oral Language

**DISCUSS BEING ONE OF A KIND** Remind students of the question for this unit of study, *What does it mean to be unique?* Use the prompts and the concept map from Week 2 to discuss what it means to be unique in nature.

- How can you tell if something in nature is unique?
- Is one way of being unique the best way? Why or why not?
- How can an evergreen tree be unique?

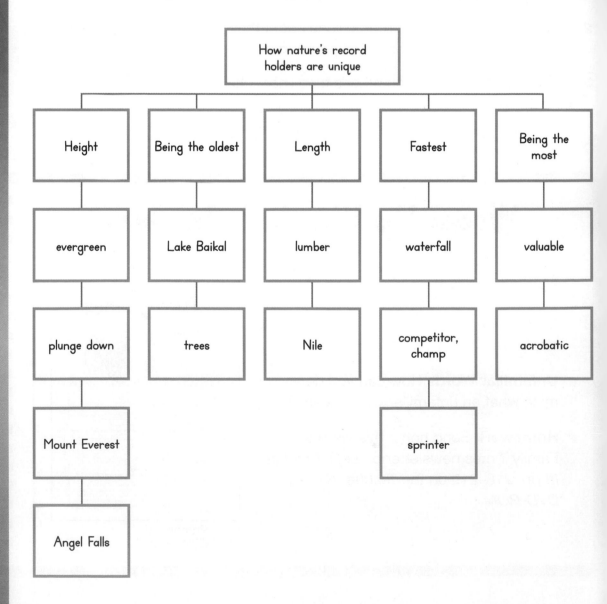

# Build Oral Vocabulary

**REVIEW AMAZING WORDS** Display the Amazing Words for *Hottest, Coldest, Highest, Deepest.* Remind students that the words are related to the week's concept.

## Amazing Words  Robust Vocabulary Routine

1. **Review** Ask students for definitions of the words, starting at the top of the list. Listen for accurate definitions. Prompt students to connect the words to the unit concept of One of a Kind whenever possible.

2. **Demonstrate** Have students use two or more Amazing Words in the same sentence. Guide the discussion by providing an example that shows the meaning of each word. *The ranger* who guided our park tour gave us *valuable* tips for staying on the marked trails. Follow this pattern to the end of the list, covering as many of the ten words as possible.

3. **Apply** Assign the words in random order and have students come up with more sentences for them. To show that you are becoming more comfortable using these Amazing Words, think up more new sentences for them.

Routines Flip Chart

**AMAZING WORDS AT WORK** Have students use the Retelling Cards/Story Sort for *Hottest, Coldest, Highest, Deepest* to talk about the Amazing Words.

**CONNECT TO READING** Tell students that today they will be rereading passages from *Hottest, Coldest, Highest, Deepest* and reading "Ban the Penny?" As they read, ask students to think about what it means to be unique.

**eStreet Interactive**
www.ReadingStreet.com

**Big Question Video**

**Concept Talk Video**

**Teacher Resources**
• Amazing Word Cards

## Amazing Words

| | |
|---|---|
| evergreen | champ |
| lumber | sprinter |
| competitor | acrobat |
| plunge | weaken |
| valuable | ranger |

**ELL**

**Build Background** Use ELL Poster 17 to review the Week 2 lesson concept and to practice oral language. Point out and read that question: *What makes nature's record holders unique?*

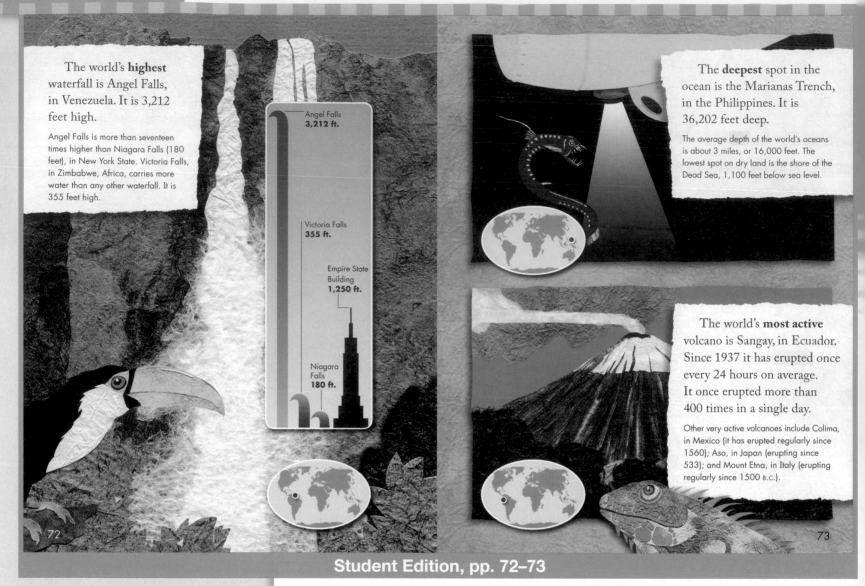

The world's **highest** waterfall is Angel Falls, in Venezuela. It is 3,212 feet high.

Angel Falls is more than seventeen times higher than Niagara Falls (180 feet), in New York State. Victoria Falls, in Zimbabwe, Africa, carries more water than any other waterfall. It is 355 feet high.

Angel Falls
**3,212 ft.**

Victoria Falls
**355 ft.**

Empire State Building
**1,250 ft.**

Niagara Falls
**180 ft.**

The **deepest** spot in the ocean is the Marianas Trench, in the Philippines. It is 36,202 feet deep.

The average depth of the world's oceans is about 3 miles, or 16,000 feet. The lowest spot on dry land is the shore of the Dead Sea, 1,100 feet below sea level.

The world's **most active** volcano is Sangay, in Ecuador. Since 1937 it has erupted once every 24 hours on average. It once erupted more than 400 times in a single day.

Other very active volcanoes include Colima, in Mexico (it has erupted regularly since 1560); Aso, in Japan (erupting since 533); and Mount Etna, in Italy (erupting regularly since 1500 B.C.).

72

73

**Student Edition, pp. 72–73**

## © Common Core State Standards

**Informational Text 7.** Use information gained from illustrations (e.g., maps, photographs) and the words in a text to demonstrate understanding of the text (e.g., where, when, why, and how key events occur).

# Access Text ©

**REVIEW** 🔎 **GRAPHIC SOURCES** Review the definition of graphic sources on p. 58. Remind students that graphic sources are ways of showing information visually. Explain that maps and charts are two kinds of graphic sources. Remind students that looking at graphic sources before they read can help them predict what the text will be about.

**GUIDE PRACTICE** Point to the graph on p. 72. Have students tell what information the chart displays visually. Ask whether Victoria Falls is taller or shorter than the Empire State Building.

**ON THEIR OWN** Have students use the information in the chart to make a list of the heights of Angel Falls, Victoria Falls, Niagara Falls, and the Empire State Building in order from lowest to highest.

## Close Reading ©

**SYNTHESIS** Look at the chart on page 72. Where on the chart would you expect to see a waterfall that is 1,000 feet high? between Angel Falls and Victoria Falls

**EVALUATION** How does showing the Empire State Building next to Angel Falls in the graphic help you visualize the height of the falls? The Empire State building is a very tall skyscraper. But Angel Falls is shown as being much higher than the top of the building. The chart helps me imagine how very high the falls must be.

**EVALUATION** How do you think knowing about nature's record holders helps scientists? Scientists can use information about extreme places to learn about other places that are similar, but not as extreme.

**eStreet Interactive**
www.ReadingStreet.com

**Pearson eText**
• Student Edition

### Access for All

**SI** **Strategic Intervention**
Scaffold students' discussion of the chart on p. 72 by providing a simple chart with a picture of a six-inch pencil, a ruler, and a yardstick, each labeled with its height. Ask students to tell which item is tallest and to explain how they used the chart to answer the question.

**A** **Advanced**
Have students create another book page about the most extreme temperature change in the United States in one day, which occurred in Browning, Montana, between January 23 and 24, 1916. During a 24-hour period, the temperature went from 44°F to –56°F. Encourage students to include an illustration, a map, and a chart.

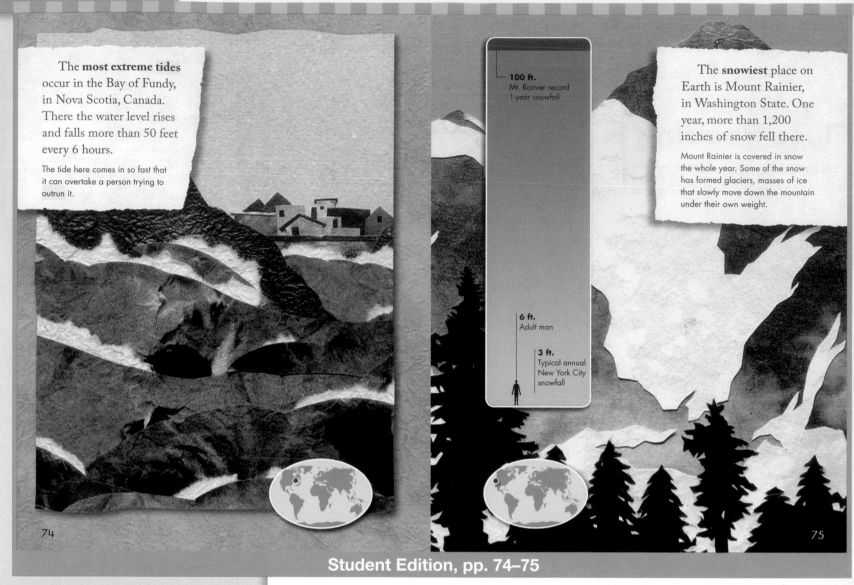

The **most extreme tides** occur in the Bay of Fundy, in Nova Scotia, Canada. There the water level rises and falls more than 50 feet every 6 hours.

The tide here comes in so fast that it can overtake a person trying to outrun it.

100 ft.
Mt. Rainier record
1-year snowfall

6 ft.
Adult man

3 ft.
Typical annual
New York City
snowfall

The **snowiest** place on Earth is Mount Rainier, in Washington State. One year, more than 1,200 inches of snow fell there.

Mount Rainier is covered in snow the whole year. Some of the snow has formed glaciers, masses of ice that slowly move down the mountain under their own weight.

74

75

**Student Edition, pp. 74–75**

## Common Core State Standards

**Informational Text 7.** Use information gained from illustrations (e.g., maps, photographs) and the words in a text to demonstrate understanding of the text (e.g., where, when, why, and how key events occur). **Language 4.** Determine or clarify the meaning of unknown and multiple-meaning word and phrases based on grade 3 reading and content, choosing flexibly from a range of strategies. **Language 4.d.** Use glossaries or beginning dictionaries, both print and digital, to determine or clarify the precise meaning of key words and phrases.

# Access Text ©

**REVIEW ⦿ UNKNOWN WORDS** Review the strategy for finding the meanings of unknown words on p. 60. Remind students that if they come across an unknown word when they read, they can use a dictionary or glossary to determine the meaning, syllabication, and pronunciation of the word.

**GUIDE PRACTICE** Point to the word *tide* on p. 74 and have students use a dictionary or glossary to find its pronunciation, syllabication, and meaning.

**ON THEIR OWN** Use *Let's Practice It!* p. 274 on the *Teacher Resources DVD-ROM* for additional practice with unknown words.

---

Name _____                        Unit 4 Week 2 Interactive Review

**Vocabulary**

Check the Words You Know

___average    ___erupted    ___tides
___depth      ___outrun     ___waterfalls
___deserts    ___peak

**Directions** Write the meaning of the underlined word on the line.

1. Cactus plants grow in <u>deserts</u>.
   **dry areas that have little rain**

2. The waters in the sea rise and fall with the <u>tides</u>.
   **rising and falling of water**

3. We could hear the rushing waters of the <u>waterfalls</u>.
   **a stream of water that falls from a high place**

4. A rabbit can <u>outrun</u> a turtle.
   **run faster than**

5. What is the <u>depth</u> of this swimming pool at the deep end?
   **deepness**

6. On an <u>average</u> day, the pizza place sells 100 pizzas.
   **usual**

7. The volcano <u>erupted</u> and threw out lava and rocks.
   **blew up**

8. The explorer climbed all the way to the <u>peak</u> of the mountain.
   **highest point, top**

**Directions** On a separate sheet of paper, write a short paragraph about a place you would like to visit or explore. Use as many vocabulary words as possible. Circle the vocabulary words you used.
   **Check students' writing to make sure some vocabulary words were used.**

**Home Activity** Your child defined and used words from *Hottest, Coldest, Highest, Deepest*. With your child, visit the library or go online to the Web to find out about some of the plants and animals that live in the desert, and how they have adapted to life without much water.

DVD•274 Vocabulary

Let's Practice It! TR DVD•274

## Close Reading ©

**DEVELOP LANGUAGE** Some of the words you read have endings that are not shown in the dictionary. How can you figure out which part of the word to use? What word would you look up to find the meaning of *snowiest* on page 75? I can look for the base word first and then see if I need to include an ending. For *snowiest,* the base word is *snow,* but I can tell it is describing something so I want the word as an adjective; I will look up *snowy.*

**SYNTHESIS** How does seeing the typical annual New York City snowfall in the chart on page 75 help you understand the record snowfall in one year on Mount Rainier? The amount of annual snowfall in New York City is very small compared to the amount of snow that fell in one year on Mount Rainier. Comparing the two snowfalls helps me understand how much snow fell on Mount Rainier in a year.

**INFERENCE** We read on page 74 that the Bay of Fundy has the most extreme tides. What might happen to boats in the bay at low tide? The boats in the bay might be on dry ground or stuck in very shallow water.

**EVALUATION • TEXT EVIDENCE** Which would be more impressive to see: the extreme tides in the Bay of Fundy or Mount Rainier, the snowiest place on Earth? Explain your response, using information from the text in your answer. Seeing the tide in the Bay of Fundy would be impressive because of how quickly it comes in. The text says that the tide comes in "so fast that it can overtake a person trying to outrun it."

### eStreet Interactive
www.ReadingStreet.com

**Pearson eText**
• Student Edition

**Teacher Resources**
• Let's Practice It!

## Access for All

**SI Strategic Intervention**
Review clues that help students understand which part of speech to look up when defining an unknown word: a noun names a person, place, or thing; a verb shows action; an adjective tells more about a noun; an adverb tells more about a verb.

**A Advanced**
Give students nine cards. Have them each choose (or assign) three words from the selection. Have them write each word on one card, its definition on another, and the pronunciation and syllabication on another. Have students mix up the cards and give them to a partner to sort. Then have students use the words in sentences that show understanding of meaning.

Name_____

**Read** the story. **Answer** the questions.

## Ban the Penny?

Look in the junk drawer in your home. Are there pennies scattered at the bottom? If so, yours is not the only drawer containing loose pennies. There are many pennies that do not get spent in this country. They often end up stored in jars in people's homes or at the bottom of their drawers.

One reason that pennies do not get spent is because nothing costs a penny anymore. Pennies are mostly used to make change, and so people end up with the extra coins in their pockets or purses.

Some people believe that the United States should stop making pennies because they are so little used. But the other, more important reason is that the penny has become more expensive to make.

The penny is made up of a mixture of zinc and copper. These metals have become much more expensive. It now costs more to make a penny than the coin is worth. This is also true of the nickel. People who want to ban the penny say that the U.S. would save a lot of money if it did not make pennies anymore.

What about the video game that is priced $9.98? The price would probably be changed to $10.00. Something that was $5.02 would probably cost $5.00. In some ways, this change could make buying things simpler.

**Home Activity** Your child used a chart to learn about the cost of making pennies and other coins. Have your child explain to you how to tell which coins cost more to make than they are worth.

Comprehension DVD•275

---

Name_____

The penny still has many supporters. People say that things would be more expensive without the penny. They argue that people with little money would be hurt if the nickel was the coin with the least value. They also point out that many people still do use pennies.

When it comes down to it, most people seem to like the penny. They want to keep it around for now, even if it is expensive to make. Maybe they would miss seeing Abe Lincoln's face in their change purse!

| The Cost of Making Coins | |
|---|---|
| Coin | Cost |
| Penny | 1.23 cents |
| Nickel | 5.73 cents |
| Dime | 2.99 cents |
| Quarter | 7.03 cents |
| Sacajawea dollar | 15.89 cents |

1. What does the chart show?

   **It shows the cost of making some different kinds of money.**

2. Look at the chart. Which coins cost more to make than they are worth?

   **the penny and the nickel**

3. Look at the chart. Which coin costs the most to make?

   **the Sacajawea dollar**

DVD•276 Comprehension

Let's Practice It! TR DVD•275–276

---

## Common Core State Standards

**Informational Text 2.** Determine the main idea of a text; recount the key details and explain how they support the main idea. **Informational Text 5.** Use text features and search tools (e.g., key words, sidebars, hyperlinks) to locate information relevant to a given topic efficiently. **Informational Text 7.** Use information gained from illustrations (e.g., maps, photographs) and the words in a text to demonstrate understanding of the text (e.g., where, when, why, and how key events occur). **Language 4.** Determine or clarify the meaning of unknown and multiple-meaning word and phrases based on grade 3 reading and content, choosing flexibly from a range of strategies. **Language 4.d.** Use glossaries or beginning dictionaries, both print and digital, to determine or clarify the precise meaning of key words and phrases.
**Also Foundational Skills 4.**

# Access Text

Have students read "Ban the Penny?" and respond to the questions.

**REVIEW GRAPHIC SOURCES** What does the chart show? It shows the cost of making some different kinds of coins.

Tell students that the chart uses columns and rows to display information visually. Point to the title "The Cost of Making Coins" and the column heads, *Coin* and *Cost,* and explain that students can use this information to understand what the chart shows.

**REVIEW IMPORTANT IDEAS** What is an important idea in the text? How can you tell? An important idea is that some people think pennies should be banned because it costs more than one cent to make a penny. I can tell because almost every paragraph talks about pennies. I also see that the title says "Ban the Penny?" and the chart shows the cost of making coins, emphasizing how much it costs to make a penny.

**REVIEW** 🔁 **UNKNOWN WORDS** Use a dictionary to find the meaning, syllabication, and pronunciation of *mixture* in paragraph 4 on page 275. Which meaning is correct in this sentence? How do you know? **The correct meaning is "something that has been mixed." I know because it makes sense in the sentence.** How do you pronounce the word? **/miks//chər/ with an accent on the first syllable**

**REVIEW** 🔁 **GRAPHIC SOURCES** Look at the chart. Which coins cost more to make than they are worth? **the penny and the nickel**

Ask students to explain the order in which the coins are listed in the left column. (They are listed from the coin with the lowest monetary value, the penny, to the coin with the highest value, the Sacajawea dollar.)

# Reread for Fluency

**MODEL FLUENT READING** Read the first two paragraphs of "Ban the Penny?" aloud, using punctuation marks to aid in appropriate phrasing. Remind students that phrasing, or grouping words together, helps listeners understand the meanings of spoken words.

## Routine   Oral Rereading

1. **Read** Have students read the first paragraph of "Ban the Penny?" orally.

2. **Reread** To achieve optimal fluency, students should reread the text three or four times.

3. **Corrective Feedback** Listen as students read. Provide corrective feedback about their phrasing, paying special attention to how they use punctuation marks to group words.

Routines Flip Chart

## Common Core State Standards

**Foundational Skills 3.** Know and apply grade-level phonics and word analysis skills in decoding words. **Foundational Skills 4.** Read with sufficient accuracy and fluency to support comprehension. **Language 1.a.** Explain the function of nouns, pronouns, verbs, adjectives, and adverbs in general and their functions in particular sentences. **Language 1.f.** Ensure subject-verb and pronoun-antecedent agreement.

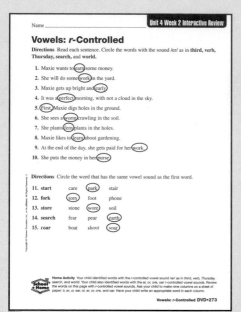

Let's Practice It! TR DVD•273

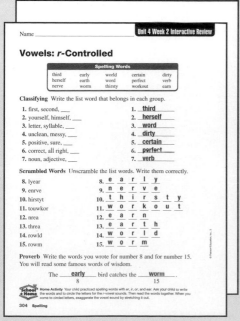

Reader's and Writer's Notebook, pp. 304–305

# Phonics

**REVIEW r-CONTROLLED VOWELS** Review the r-controlled vowel sound /ėr/ spelled *ir, er, ur, ear, or;* /är/ spelled *ar;* and /ôr/ spelled *or, ore, oar,* using *Sound-Spelling Cards* 62, 67, 72, 87, 91, 92, 93, and 104.

Use *Let's Practice It!* p. 273 on the *Teacher Resources DVD-ROM.*

**READ WORDS IN ISOLATION** Point out that students know how to blend the words in items 11–15. Have students read the words in each row together. Allow several seconds previewing time for the first reading.

**READ WORDS IN CONTEXT** Look at sentences 1–10. Point out that there are many words in the sentences that students already know. Have students read the sentences together.

| Corrective feedback | **If...** students have difficulty reading the r-controlled vowel sounds /ėr/, /är/, or /ôr/, **then...** guide them in using sound-by-sound blending. Have students read all the words in each row repeatedly until they can read the words fluently. Then have students read each sentence repeatedly until they can read the sentences fluently. |

# Spelling

**REVIEW r-CONTROLLED VOWELS** Write *thirsty, certain, earn,* and *worm.* Point out the /ėr/ sound. Write *start.* Point out that it has the /är/ sound. Write *horn, sore,* and *board.* Point out the /ôr/ sound. Remind students that they have learned how to spell words with these sounds.

**SPELLING STRATEGY** Review words with r-controlled vowels by having students follow the spelling strategy for spelling these words.

Tell students that even short words can be hard to spell until you discover where they come from. Example: *heard*

The spelling of *heard* makes sense when you remember that *heard* Is the past tense of *hear. Hear* is a meaning helper for *heard.*

**ON THEIR OWN** Use p. 304 of the *Reader's and Writer's Notebook* for additional practice with r-controlled words.

# Conventions

**REVIEW SUBJECT AND OBJECT PRONOUNS** Review **subject pronoun** and **object pronoun** with students.

**GUIDE PRACTICE** Read the sentences. Have students identify each pronoun and say whether it is a subject pronoun or an object pronoun.

1. **I** have visited the Sacramento River. [subject]
2. Mary talked to **us** about her birthday. [object]

**ON THEIR OWN** For additional practice use *Reader's and Writer's Notebook,* p. 305.

| **Routine** | **Quick Write for Fluency** | **Team Talk** |

1. **Talk** Have pairs discuss the amazing places described in *Hottest, Coldest, Highest, Deepest* and "Paul Bunyan and the Great Lakes."

2. **Write** Students write a few sentences describing one of these amazing places. Students should include subject and object pronouns in their sentences.

3. **Share** Partners read their sentences to each other, making sure that subject and object pronouns are used correctly.

Routines Flip Chart

### *e*STREET INTERACTIVE
#### www.ReadingStreet.com

**Teacher Resources**
• Reader's and Writer's Notebook
• Let's Practice It!

**Interactive Sound-Spelling Cards**

## Writing Workshop

Use the writing process lesson on pp. WP•1–WP•10 for this week's writing instruction.

# Wrap Up Week 2 Review!

✔ **Content Knowledge** What makes Mount Everest unique?

✔ **Graphic Sources** What can you learn about rivers from the graphics in *Hottest, Coldest, Highest, Deepest?*

✔ **Unknown Words** Where can you find the meanings of words you don't know?

## Preview DAY 3

Tell students that tomorrow they will review *Rocks in His Head.*

# Review
## Week 3

### Materials
- Student Edition
- Retelling Cards
- Reader's and Writer's Notebook
- Sound-Spelling Cards

### Ⓒ Common Core State Standards

**Speaking/Listening 1.** Engage effectively in a range of collaborative discussions (one-on-one, in groups, and teacher-led) with diverse partners on grade 3 topics and texts, building on others' ideas and expressing their own clearly. **Language 6.** Acquire and use accurately grade-appropriate conversational, general academic, and domain-specific words and phrases, including those that signal spatial and temporal relationships (e.g., *After dinner that night we went looking for them*).

# Content Knowledge

## Unique Interests

**REVISIT THE CONCEPT** Today students will explore how the question for this unit of study connects to *Rocks in His Head.* Remind students of the Question of the Week, *Why is it valuable to have unique interests?*

## Build Oral Language

**DISCUSS BEING ONE OF A KIND** Remind students of the question for this unit of study, *What does it mean to be unique?* Use the prompts and the concept map from Week 3 to discuss how being unique can be valuable.

- Who are some people you think are unique? What is unique about them?
- What can having a unique hobby add to a person's life?
- What might a person with unique interests have to offer to others?

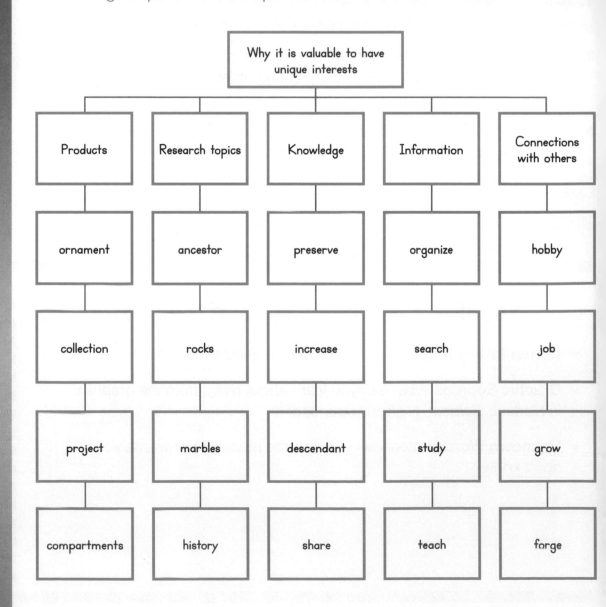

# Build Oral Vocabulary

**REVIEW AMAZING WORDS** Display the Amazing Words for *Rocks in His Head*. Remind students that the words are related to the week's concept.

## Robust Vocabulary Routine

1. **Review** Ask students for definitions of the words, starting at the top of the list. Listen for accurate definitions. Prompt students to connect the words to the unit concept of One of a Kind whenever possible.

2. **Demonstrate** Have students use two or more Amazing Words in the same sentence. Guide the discussion by providing an example that shows the meaning of each word. *People sometimes decorate using ornaments that they create from leftover scraps of material.* Follow this pattern to the end of the list, covering as many of the nine words as possible.

3. **Apply** Assign the words in random order and have students come up with more new sentences for them. *To show that you are becoming more comfortable using these Amazing Words, think up more new sentences for them.*

Routines Flip Chart

**AMAZING WORDS AT WORK** Have students use the Retelling Cards/Story Sort for *Rocks in His Head* to talk about the Amazing Words.

**CONNECT TO READING** Tell students that today they will be rereading passages from *Rocks in His Head* and reading "First Woman in Space." As they read, ask students to think about how unique interests are valuable.

## eSTREET INTERACTIVE
www.ReadingStreet.com

**Big Question Video**

**Concept Talk Video**

**Teacher Resources**
• Amazing Word Cards

## Amazing Words

| | |
|---|---|
| hobby | ornament |
| project | descendant |
| leftover | forge |
| murmur | compartment |
| ancestor | |

**ELL**

**Build Background** Use ELL Poster 18 to review the Week 3 lesson concept and to practice oral language. Point out and read the question: *Why is it valuable to have unique interests?*

He had to build more shelves for the rocks, up the west wall of the station.

Then people stopped coming for gas. They stopped coming to play chess, and they even stopped coming to look at the rocks and minerals. They were all too busy looking for work.

One day my father picked up the chess set and carefully packed it in a big box. He took down each mineral, wrapped it in newspaper, and carefully placed it in a wooden box.

When his friends came with a truck to help us move, they said, "Watch out for those wooden boxes. He's got rocks in his boxes, now."

"Yessir," said my father. "That's just what I got in there. Take a look at this one."

The house we moved to was old and falling apart. My father said he'd have it fixed up in no time.

But before he started in on the repairs, we had to take those rocks up to the attic, where he'd already built tiny little wooden shelves.

My father did fix up the old house, and after he finished each repair, he went up to the attic with his rocks. He spent a lot of time reading about rocks, too.

100

"If you think those rocks are ever going to do you any good," said my mother, "you've got rocks in your head."

"Maybe I have," said my father. "Maybe I have." He reached into his pocket. "Take a look at this one."

My father spent a lot of time looking for any job he could find. Most jobs lasted only a day or two.

On rainy days when my father could find no other work, he'd take the bus to the science museum. They had a whole room full of glass cases containing many rocks. Sometimes he'd spend the whole day in that room.

101

**Student Edition, pp. 100–101**

## Common Core State Standards

**Informational Text 1.** Ask and answer questions to demonstrate understanding of a text, referring explicitly to the text as the basis for the answers. **Informational Text 3.** Describe the relationship between a series of historical events, scientific ideas or concepts, or steps in technical procedures in a text, using language that pertains to time, sequence, and cause/effect.

# Access Text ©

**REVIEW © FACT AND OPINION** Review the definitions of fact and opinion on p. 90. Remind students that a statement of fact can be proved true or false. An opinion gives someone's thoughts or feelings. Tell students that they can draw conclusions about statements of fact by looking for clues in the text.

**GUIDE PRACTICE** Point out that in the last paragraph on p. 101 the narrator says that the science museum had "a whole room full of glass cases containing many rocks." Ask students what conclusion they can draw from this statement of fact. Have them support their answer with textual evidence.

**ON THEIR OWN** Have students look back at *Rocks in His Head* on pp. 100–101 and find one statement of fact and one opinion.

**eStreet Interactive**
www.ReadingStreet.com

**Pearson eText**
• Student Edition

# Close Reading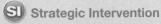

**ANALYSIS**  Reread page 101. What is one statement of fact about how the father supported the family? What opinion can you make about the father? Statement of Fact: The father took any job he could find to support his family. Opinion: By working at any job he could find, he showed a strong sense of responsibility.

**ANALYSIS • TEXT EVIDENCE**  What details on page 100 let you know that the father really cared about his rocks? He built shelves to display them; he wrapped each rock in newspaper when they moved.

**SYNTHESIS**  Why do you think the father keeps studying rocks even when he is having a hard time finding a job? What can people learn from his example? By studying rocks, he is continuing to learn about things that interest him, even though his job situation is stalled. His example shows that keeping up with a hobby can help people get through hard times.

## Access for All

**SI** Strategic Intervention

Have students make a T-chart with the head *Facts* in the left column and the head *Opinions* in the right column. Tell students to list facts and opinions as they read.

**A** Advanced

Ask students if they agree with the narrator's mother that rocks will never do the father "any good." Have them predict whether the father's unique interest in rocks will help him advance in life.

One afternoon he looked up to see a lady standing beside him. "I've seen you here before," she said.

"I come here a lot," he said. "I guess I've got rocks in my head."

"Tell me what you're looking for," she said.

"I'm looking for rocks that are better than mine," he said.

"How many did you find?" she asked.

"Ten," he said.

The lady looked around at the hundreds of rocks, in all those glass cases. "Only ten?"

"Maybe eleven," he said.

He smiled. She did, too.

"You *have* got rocks in your head," she said. "I'm Grace Johnson, the director of this museum. These rocks have come from all over the world."

"So have mine," said my father. He reached into his pocket. "Take a look at this one," he said.

"Did you study rocks at college?" she asked.

"Couldn't afford to go to college," he said.

"Let me see the rest of your rocks," she said.

Mrs. Johnson got out her big Packard touring car, and my father got in. They drove to our house.

"Where are the rocks?" she asked.

"Up here," said my father, leading the way to the attic. "Watch your step."

Two hours later Mrs. Johnson said, "I can't hire you as a mineralogist. The board won't allow it. But I need a night janitor at the museum. Will you take the job?"

"Will I be cleaning rocks?" he asked.

"Sometimes," she said.

So my father took the job as night janitor at the museum. Before he went home, he'd open some of the mineral cases and scrub some of the rocks with a toothbrush until they sparkled like diamonds.

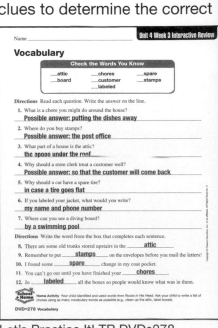

102     103

**Student Edition, pp. 102–103**

---

## Common Core State Standards

**Informational Text 1.** Ask and answer questions to demonstrate understanding of a text, referring explicitly to the text as the basis for the answers. **Informational Text 3.** Describe the relationship between a series of historical events, scientific ideas or concepts, or steps in technical procedures in a text, using language that pertains to time, sequence, and cause/effect. **Language 4.** Determine or clarify the meaning of unknown and multiple-meaning word and phrases based on grade 3 reading and content, choosing flexibly from a range of strategies. **Language 4.a.** Use sentence-level context as a clue to the meaning of a word or phrase.

# Access Text ©

**REVIEW** **MULTIPLE-MEANING WORDS** Review the definition of multiple-meaning words on p. 92. Remind students that when they encounter a multiple-meaning word they can use context clues to determine the correct meaning.

**GUIDE PRACTICE** Point to the word *lot* on p. 102. Ask students to explain how context clues helped them determine the correct meaning of *lot*.

**ON THEIR OWN** Use *Let's Practice It!* p. 278 on the *Teacher Resources DVD-ROM* for additional practice with multiple-meaning words.

Let's Practice It! TR DVD•278

## Close Reading ©

**DEVELOP LANGUAGE** What are two meanings for the word *rest* on page 103? Use context clues to determine the correct meaning in this sentence. *Rest* can mean "to be still or quiet" or "what is left." The word *rocks* in the sentence tells me that the correct meaning here is "what is left."

**ANALYSIS** Look at the first two sentences on page 103. Which sentence states a fact and which sentence states an opinion? How do you know? The first sentence is an opinion, because it can't be proved. The second statement can be proved, so it is a statement of fact.

**INFERENCE** Why does Mrs. Johnson hire the narrator's father as a janitor rather than as a mineralogist? The museum board wanted to hire someone who had studied rocks in college, and the narrator's father hadn't been to college. But Mrs. Johnson can see that the father loves rocks and would be a good addition to the staff at the museum.

**eStreet Interactive**
www.ReadingStreet.com

**Pearson eText**
• Student Edition

**Teacher Resources**
• Let's Practice It!

### Access for All

**SI** Strategic Intervention

Have students work in pairs to identify context clues for multiple-meaning words and determine the correct meaning.

**A** Advanced

Point out that this biography provides many more facts than opinions about its subject, the narrator's father. Have students discuss whether including more opinions would or would not create a more accurate picture of the father.

Name_____

**Read** the story. **Answer** the questions.

### First Woman in Space

Valentina Tereshkova is a *cosmonaut*, the Russian word for *astronaut*. She was born in 1937 in Russia, which was then part of the Soviet Union. Her father drove a tractor and her mother worked in a textile mill. As a girl, Tereshkova enjoyed ordinary sports, such as swimming, but she also had a special interest. She loved to parachute! She became an expert at the sport while she was working in a factory. She even started a parachuting club to get other workers interested.

Tereshkova remembers one day in 1961 very well. That was the day that a Russian man became the first human to travel in space. Tereshkova later called that the most exciting day of her life. It also gave her the idea of applying for the cosmonaut training program. She wrote a letter that described her skill and her many parachute jumps.

At that time, all Russian cosmonauts were men, so imagine Tereshkova's surprise when she was accepted! Of the more than 400 women who applied, she was one of only five who were accepted. <u>She thought she was the luckiest person in the world when she got the news.</u>

Her parachuting skill was one of the main reasons Tereshkova was accepted for cosmonaut training. During the months of training, she made more than 100 parachute jumps. During some of them, she had to wear a space suit!

On June 16, 1963, Tereshkova found herself in a tiny, cramped, one-person space capsule. She was about to become the first

Comprehension DVD•279

---

woman in space. After blasting off, she spent three days alone in space and made 48 orbits around the Earth. That means she traveled about 1.2 million miles in space! She felt sick to her stomach much of the time, but she was still able to take photographs and talk on the radio. At the end of her flight, she ejected herself and parachuted back to Earth.

Before Tereshkova, women had not been allowed to travel in space. Thanks to this brave woman, training programs in the Soviet Union and in the United States began to accept women for space travel. She is a true hero in early space programs.

1. Reread the first paragraph. Write a sentence that states a fact about Valentina Tereshkova's special interest.

**Possible response: She liked to parachute; she started a parachuting club.**

2. Reread the third paragraph. Underline the sentence that states Tereshkova's opinion about being accepted as a cosmonaut.

**Suggested answer is undersored in the text.**

3. The author had the opinion that Valentina Tereshkova is a true hero. Find in the story two facts that support this opinion and write them on the lines below.

**Possible responses: She was the first woman in space, she orbited Earth 48 times by herself. She felt sick to her stomach much of the time, but she was still able to take photographs and talk on the radio.**

**School + Home** Home Activity Your child identified fact and opinion in a nonfiction passage. Choose a topic that you and your child know about, such as a favorite hobby or animal. Take turns telling facts about the topic. Then express opinions about it. Discuss what makes facts and opinions different.

DVD•280 Comprehension

Let's Practice It! TR DVD•279–280

---

## Common Core State Standards

**Informational Text 1.** Ask and answer questions to demonstrate understanding of a text, referring explicitly to the text as the basis for the answers. **Informational Text 3.** Describe the relationship between a series of historical events, scientific ideas or concepts, or steps in technical procedures in a text, using language that pertains to time, sequence, and cause/effect. **Informational Text 6.** Distinguish their own point of view from that of the author of a text. **Foundational Skills 4.** Read with sufficient accuracy and fluency to support comprehension. **Language 4.** Determine or clarify the meaning of unknown and multiple-meaning word and phrases based on grade 3 reading and content, choosing flexibly from a range of strategies. **Language 4.a.** Use sentence-level context as a clue to the meaning of a word or phrase.

UR•32   One of a Kind • Unit 4 • Week 6

## Access Text ©

Have students read "First Woman in Space" and respond to the questions.

**REVIEW ◉ FACT AND OPINION** Reread the first paragraph. Write a sentence that has a statement of fact about Valentina Tereshkova's special interest. She liked to parachute; she started a parachute club.

Tell students that a fact is a statement they can prove to be true or false by looking in a reference book, or by using their own knowledge and experience. An opinion is a personal judgment about something.

**REVIEW ◉ INFERRING** Use information from the text and what you know about people to make an inference about the character traits that helped Valentina Tereshkova become the first woman in space. Tereshkova made more than 100 parachute jumps during training, and even though she felt sick when she was in space, she took pictures and did her job. These details show that she was a courageous, hard-working, and responsible person.

**REVIEW ⦿ MULTIPLE-MEANING WORDS** How do context clues help you determine the appropriate definition of the multiple-meaning word *capsule* in paragraph 5? I know that a capsule is a kind of pill, but that meaning doesn't make sense here. Tereshkova blasts into space inside this capsule, so it must be a part of a space ship.

Review with students that they can look for clues in surrounding text to distinguish among multiple-meaning words.

**REVIEW ⦿ FACT AND OPINION** Reread the third paragraph. Underline the sentence that states Tereshkova's opinion about being accepted as a cosmonaut. She thought she was the luckiest person in the world when she got the news.

Have students identify the clue word that indicates this is an opinion. (the word *thought*)

# Reread for Fluency

**MODEL FLUENT READING** Have students listen as you read the first three paragraphs on p. 279 of "First Woman in Space" with appropriate expression. Explain that you will adjust your voice level to stress important words and phrases.

## Routine | Oral Rereading

1. **Read** Have students read "First Woman in Space" orally.

2. **Reread** To achieve optimal fluency, students should reread three or four times with expression.

3. **Corrective Feedback** Listen as students read. Provide corrective feedback regarding their oral reading, paying special attention to expression.

Routines Flip Chart

## Common Core State Standards

**Foundational Skills 3.a.** Identify and know the meaning of the most common prefixes and derivational suffixes. **Language 1.a.** Explain the function of nouns, pronouns, verbs, adjectives, and adverbs in general and their functions in particular sentences. **Language 2.f.** Use spelling patterns and generalizations (e.g., word families, position-based spellings, syllable patterns, ending rules, meaningful word parts) in writing words.

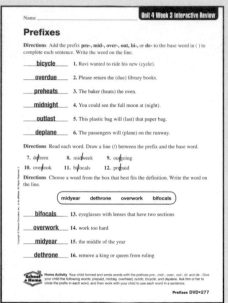

Let's Practice It! TR DVD•277

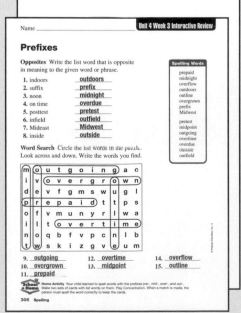

Reader's and Writer's Notebook, pp. 306–307

# Word Analysis

**REVIEW PREFIXES** Review the prefixes *pre-, mid-, over-, out-, bi-,* and *de-* using Sound-Spelling Cards 150, 151, 156, 159, 160, and 161.

Use *Let's Practice It!* p. 277 on the *Teacher Resources DVD-ROM.*

**READ WORDS IN ISOLATION** Point out that students know how to read the words in the box. Have students read the words in the box together. Allow several seconds previewing time for the first reading.

**READ WORDS IN CONTEXT** Point out that there are many words in the sentences that students already know. Have students read the sentences together.

| Corrective feedback | **If...** students have difficulty reading the prefixes *pre-, mid-, over-, out-, bi-,* and *de-,* **then...** guide them in using the word parts strategy. Have students read all the words in the box repeatedly until they can read the words fluently. Then have students read each sentence repeatedly until they can read the sentences fluently. |
| --- | --- |

# Spelling

**REVIEW PREFIXES** Write *midpoint, overgrown, outdoors,* and *preview.* Point out that these words have prefixes. Remind students that they have learned how to spell words with prefixes *pre-, mid-, over-,* and *out-.*

**SPELLING STRATEGY** Review words with prefixes by having students follow the spelling strategy for spelling these words.

> **Step 1: Draw a line between the base word and the prefix.**
>
> **Step 2: Study the word, one part at a time.**

**ON THEIR OWN** Use p. 306 of the *Reader's and Writer's Notebook* for additional practice with spelling words with prefixes.

# Conventions

**REVIEW POSSESSIVE PRONOUNS** Review **possessive pronoun** with students.

**GUIDE PRACTICE** Read the following sentences. Have students identify the possessive pronoun(s) in each sentence.

1. **My** aunt has a collection of pet frogs.
2. **My** brother keeps **his** eyes open for additions to **our** collection.

**ON THEIR OWN** For additional practice use *Reader's and Writer's Notebook,* p. 307.

## Routine | Quick Write for Fluency | Team Talk

1. **Talk** Pairs discuss the objects that are collected in *Rocks in His Head* and "Marvelous Marble Mania."

2. **Write** Students write a paragraph about what they and their friends collect, using possessive pronouns correctly.

3. **Share** Partners read each other's paragraphs, checking for the correct use of possessive pronouns.

Routines Flip Chart

**eStreet Interactive**
www.ReadingStreet.com

**Teacher Resources**
• Reader's and Writer's Notebook
• Let's Practice It!

**Interactive Sound-Spelling Cards**

## Writing Workshop
Use the writing process lesson on pp. WP•1–WP•10 for this week's writing instruction.

# Wrap Up Week 3 Review!

✔ **Content Knowledge** What was valuable about the interest that Carol Otis Hurst's father had in rocks?

✔ **Fact and Opinion** What are some statements of fact or opinion in *Rocks in His Head?*

✔ **Multiple-Meaning Words** How can you determine the meaning of a multiple-meaning word in a sentence?

## Preview DAY 4

Tell students that tomorrow they will review *America's Champion Swimmer: Gertrude Ederle.*

### Materials

- Student Edition
- Retelling Cards
- Reader's and Writer's Notebook
- Sound-Spelling Cards

## Ⓒ Common Core State Standards

**Speaking/Listening 1.** Engage effectively in a range of collaborative discussions (one-on-one, in groups, and teacher-led) with diverse partners on grade 3 topics and texts, building on others' ideas and expressing their own clearly. **Language 6.** Acquire and use accurately grade-appropriate conversational, general academic, and domain-specific words and phrases, including those that signal spatial and temporal relationships (e.g., *After dinner that night we went looking for them*).

# Content Knowledge

## Unique Traits

**REVISIT THE CONCEPT** Today students will explore how the question for this unit of study connects to *America's Champion Swimmer: Gertrude Ederle.* Remind students of the Question of the Week, *What unique traits does it take to be the first to do something?*

# Build Oral Language

**DISCUSS BEING ONE OF A KIND** Remind students of the question for this unit of study, *What does it mean to be unique?* Use the prompts and the concept map from Week 4 to discuss how being unique can help you accomplish your goals.

- How can a person use his or her imagination to set unique goals?
- How can a person's unique talents help him or her achieve a magnificent goal?

# Build Oral Vocabulary

**REVIEW AMAZING WORDS** Display the Amazing Words for *America's Champion Swimmer: Gertrude Ederle.* Remind students that the words are related to the week's concept.

## Amazing Words · Robust Vocabulary Routine

1. **Review** Ask students for definitions of the words, starting at the top of the list. Listen for accurate definitions. Prompt students to connect the words to the unit concept of being One of a Kind whenever possible.

2. **Demonstrate** Have students use two or more Amazing Words in the same sentence. Guide the discussion by providing an example that shows the meaning of each word. *Many people would* suspend *their daily activities to watch a* magnificent spectacle. Follow this pattern to the end of the list, covering as many of the ten words as possible.

3. **Apply** Assign the words in random order and have students come up with more sentences for them. *To show that you are becoming more comfortable using these Amazing Words, think up more new sentences for them.*

Routines Flip Chart

**AMAZING WORDS AT WORK** Have students use the Retelling Cards/Story Sort for *America's Champion Swimmer: Gertrude Ederle* to talk about the Amazing Words.

**CONNECT TO READING** Tell students that today they will be rereading passages from *America's Champion Swimmer: Gertrude Ederle* and reading "Karen Gaffney." As they read, ask students to think about how having unique traits helps people accomplish goals.

**eSTREET INTERACTIVE**
www.ReadingStreet.com

**Big Question Video**

**Concept Talk Video**

**Teacher Resources**
• Amazing Word Cards

## Amazing Words

| | |
|---|---|
| ordinary | erect |
| imagination | suspend |
| assemble | accompany |
| magnificent | provision |
| organize | spectacle |

**ELL**

**Build Background** Use ELL Poster 19 to review the Week 4 lesson concept and to practice oral language. Point out and read the question: *What unique traits does it take to be the first to do something?*

From that summer on, it was hard to keep Trudy out of the water. She *loved* to swim. At the age of thirteen she became a member of the New York Women's Swimming Association and took lessons there.

At fifteen Trudy won her first big race.

The next year, she attempted to be the first woman to swim the more than seventeen miles from lower Manhattan to Sandy Hook, New Jersey. When Trudy slowed down, her sister Margaret yelled, "Get going, lazybones!" And Trudy did. She finished in just over seven hours. And she beat the men's record.

People were beginning to notice Gertrude Ederle. Newspapers described her as courageous, determined, modest, and poised. They called her the most perfect swimmer. Trudy's mother said she was "just a plain home girl."

In 1924 this "plain home girl" was good enough to make the U.S. Olympic team. Trudy won three medals at the games in Paris. Her team won more points than all the other countries' swimming teams combined.

By 1925 Trudy had set twenty-nine U.S. and world records. She was determined to take on the ultimate challenge: the English Channel. Many had tried to swim the more-than-twenty-mile-wide body of cold, rough water that separates England from France. But only five men—and no women—had ever made it all the way across.

128    129

**Student Edition, pp. 128–129**

## Common Core State Standards

**Informational Text 1.** Ask and answer questions to demonstrate understanding of a text, referring explicitly to the text as the basis for the answers. **Informational Text 6.** Distinguish their own point of view from that of the author of a text.

# Access Text ©

**REVIEW FACT AND OPINION** Review the definitions of fact and opinion on p. 120. Remind students that a fact can be proved true or false by checking a reference source. An opinion is a statement of someone's belief. It cannot be proved true or false. You may or may not agree with an opinion.

**GUIDE PRACTICE** Read aloud the first two sentences in the first paragraph on p. 128. Point out the word *loved* in the second sentence. Ask students if the word signifies a fact or an opinion. (opinion) Read aloud the third sentence. Ask students if the sentence can be proved true or false. (yes) Point out that the sentence is a statement of fact.

**ON THEIR OWN** Have students find a statement of fact on p. 129. Ask them to explain how they recognized it. Have students tell what conclusions they can draw from the statement of fact they identified. Ask students to find evidence in the text that supports their conclusion.

## Close Reading ©

**ANALYSIS** How was Trudy's mother's opinion of Trudy different from the public's opinion of Trudy? What conclusion can you draw from that? The public believed Trudy was courageous, determined, modest, and poised. They called her the most perfect swimmer. However, Trudy's mother said she was "just a plain home girl." Trudy's mother was realistic and down to earth.

**INFERENCE** From a young age, Trudy began training seriously, winning her first big race at the age of fifteen. How do you think this training helped Trudy when she reached the Olympics? Trudy's training prepared her to compete in and win difficult races.

**INFERENCE • TEXT EVIDENCE** Do you think Trudy's successful swim from Manhattan to Sandy Hook inspired her to try to swim the English Channel? Use information from the text to support your answer. Yes. Trudy was the first woman to swim from Manhattan to Sandy Hook and she beat the men's record. Doing so probably inspired her to try swimming the English Channel—something no woman had yet done.

### Access for All

**SI** Strategic Intervention

Remind students that facts can be proved true or false. Have students select a fact from the selection. Guide them in using the Internet or another source to verify the fact.

**A** Advanced

Point out that a statement of opinion can be well supported or poorly supported. Have students revisit the selection and assess the support of different opinions.

At about one-thirty in the afternoon, it started to rain. A strong wind stirred the water. For a while, Trudy would swim forward a few feet only to be pulled back twice as far.

By six o'clock the tide was stronger. The waves were twenty feet high. The rough water made the people aboard the *Alsace* and the news boat seasick.

Trudy's trainer was sure she couldn't finish the swim. He told her to give up.

"No, no," Trudy yelled over the sound of the waves. She kept swimming.

In the next few hours, the rain and wind became stronger and the sea rougher. At times the rough water pulled the boats away, out of Trudy's sight. She was scared. It was eerie being out there all alone.

Now Trudy began to have trouble kicking in the water. When the *Alsace* came close again, Trudy said her left leg had become stiff. Her trainer was frightened for her. He yelled, "You must come out."

"What for?" Trudy shouted, and kept swimming.

Trudy continued to fight the tide and the constant stinging spray of water in her face. She knew she would either swim the Channel or drown.

As Trudy neared Kingsdown, on the coast of England, she saw thousands of people gathered to greet her. They lit flares to guide her to shore.

At about nine-forty at night, after more than fourteen hours in the water, Trudy's feet touched land. Hundreds of people, fully dressed, waded into the water to greet her. When she reached the shore, her father hugged Trudy and wrapped her in a warm robe.

"I knew if it could be done, it had to be done, and I did it," Trudy said after she got ashore. "All the women of the world will celebrate."

134        135

**Student Edition, pp. 134–135**

---

## Common Core State Standards

**Informational Text 1.** Ask and answer questions to demonstrate understanding of a text, referring explicitly to the text as the basis for the answers. **Language 4.** Determine or clarify the meaning of unknown and multiple-meaning word and phrases based on grade 3 reading and content, choosing flexibly from a range of strategies. **Language 4.a.** Use sentence-level context as a clue to the meaning of a word or phrase.

# Access Text ©

**REVIEW MULTIPLE-MEANING WORDS** Review the definition of a multiple-meaning word on p. 122. Remind students that using context clues can help them determine the correct meaning of the word.

**GUIDE PRACTICE** Point out the word *flares* in the third paragraph on p. 135. Guide students in using the three steps from p. 122 to determine the correct meaning of the word *flare* in this sentence.

**ON THEIR OWN** Use *Let's Practice It!* p. 282 on the *Teacher Resources DVD-ROM* for additional practice with multiple-meaning words.

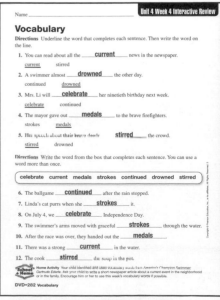

Let's Practice It! TR DVD•282

## Close Reading ©

**DEVELOP LANGUAGE** What meanings can you think of for the word *sting?* Use context clues to tell the meaning of *stinging* on page 135, paragraph 2. *Sting* can mean "to wound with a sharp-pointed part" or it can mean that "something hurts or is painful." When I look for context clues within the sentence, I see the word *fight.* This tells me that something was painful.

**ANALYSIS** What is the author's opinion of Trudy? What details from the selection support your understanding? He admires and respects Trudy. The author includes details about Trudy overcoming a prejudice against women and her lack of swimming skills. He describes the celebration held after she swam the English Channel. The author includes President Coolidge's quotation, "America's Best Girl," and agrees with it.

**SYNTHESIS** This biography is about a woman who overcame challenges to accomplish a goal. Can you think of another text, either fiction or nonfiction, in which someone overcomes a challenge to reach a goal? a biography of Helen Keller

**eStreet Interactive**
www.ReadingStreet.com

**Pearson eText**
• Student Edition

**Teacher Resources**
• Let's Practice It!

### Access for All

**SI** Strategic Intervention
Guide students in using a dictionary to confirm the meaning of a multiple-meaning word.

**A** Advanced
Have students locate three multiple-meaning words within the text and write sentences to illustrate the different meanings of each.

Name _____

**Read** the story. Then follow the directions and answer the questions.

### Karen Gaffney

Karen Gaffney swims laps across the pool. Her short arms are strong, and she speeds across the pool.

"Keep pushing, Karen! Four more laps," her coach calls out.

In many ways, Karen is like any talented swimmer. <u>She trains at least an hour a day.</u> She has been on swim teams. She faces all the challenges of swimming. But Karen Gaffney is a unique athlete who has faced much bigger challenges in her life.

Karen was born with Down syndrome. This condition keeps a person from growing to full size. Many people with Down syndrome have other health problems. Their bones do not grow correctly. They can have heart problems and other illnesses. In the past, many children with Down syndrome did not have a chance to live normal lives.

Karen's parents made sure that she had as many chances as possible. Her dad taught her to swim when she was nine months old. Swimming helped Karen build stronger muscles. Often her parents had to encourage her to float and try new swim strokes. But soon, Karen loved swimming.

As Karen grew, she had problems with her hips. She'd had many surgeries. Karen learned to use her arms a lot in her swimming. She adapted her kick for her weak leg. When Karen walks, she often limps. Swimming is a way for her to move gracefully and quickly.

Comprehension DVD•283

---

Name _____

Karen competed in the Special Olympics. That was a wonderful experience for her. One day she met a swimmer who had crossed the English Channel. Karen thought this sounded like a great challenge, so she joined a team of people who would make the swim. Through the cold water, she completed her part of the race. Karen became the first person with Down syndrome to ever try swimming the English Channel.

Today, Karen is training to swim across Lake Tahoe in California. The lake is twelve miles long. The swim will raise money for Down syndrome research. If she makes it, Karen will have set another record. She will be the first swimmer with Down syndrome to swim across Lake Tahoe. (Karen Gaffney is an inspiration to athletes everywhere.)

1. Underline a sentence in the third paragraph that states a fact about Karen Gaffney. **Possible answers are given.**

2. Draw a circle around a sentence in the last paragraph that states an opinion about Karen Gaffney. **Possible answer is given.**

3. Write your own opinion about Karen Gaffney, based on what you have read in the selection.

   **Possible answers: Karen is very brave. Karen is a really good athlete.**

**Home Activity** Your child identified facts and opinions in a biographical passage. Have your child point out a fact and an opinion in the selection and explain how he or she knows the difference.

DVD•284 Comprehension

Let's Practice It! TR DVD•283–284

---

## Common Core State Standards

**Informational Text 1.** Ask and answer questions to demonstrate understanding of a text, referring explicitly to the text as the basis for the answers. **Informational Text 3.** Describe the relationship between a series of historical events, scientific ideas or concepts, or steps in technical procedures in a text, using language that pertains to time, sequence, and cause/effect. **Foundational Skills 4.** Read with sufficient accuracy and fluency to support comprehension. **Language 4.** Determine or clarify the meaning of unknown and multiple-meaning word and phrases based on grade 3 reading and content, choosing flexibly from a range of strategies. **Language 4.a.** Use sentence-level context as a clue to the meaning of a word or phrase.

## Access Text ©

Have students read "Karen Gaffney" and respond to the questions.

**REVIEW FACT AND OPINION** Look back at the selection. Find one statement of fact and one statement of opinion about Karen Gaffney. Statement of Fact: Karen was born with Down syndrome. Statement of Opinion: Karen Gaffney is an inspiration to athletes everywhere.

Remind students that a fact can be proved true or false. An opinion is a statement of belief. To help students monitor their comprehension, have them tell what conclusions they can draw from the fact they identified.

**REVIEW QUESTIONING** What question might you ask yourself after reading the fourth paragraph? How does having Down syndrome affect Karen's ability to swim?

**REVIEW ◉ MULTIPLE-MEANING WORDS** What meanings can the word *lap* have? to drink, body part formed when sitting, one length of a swimming pool What meaning does the word *laps* have in the first sentence? lengths of a swimming pool How does context help you determine the meaning? The sentence talks about swimming in a pool, so I know the author means lengths of a swimming pool.

**REVIEW ◉ FACT AND OPINION** What is your opinion about Karen Gaffney based on what you read in the selection? Karen is very brave. Karen is a really good athlete.

Have students support their opinion with information in the text. Remind them that others may or may not agree with their opinion. An opinion cannot be proved true or false.

# Reread for Fluency

**MODEL FLUENT READING** Remind students that when they read, it is important to read with appropriate phrasing in order to understand what they are reading. Model reading the first paragraph of "Karen Gaffney" with appropriate phrasing and have students track the print as you read.

## Routine | Paired Reading

1. **Select a Passage** Pair students and have them read "Karen Gaffney."

2. **Reading 1** Students read the entire selection, switching readers at the end of each page.

3. **Reading 2** Partners reread the selection. This time the other student begins.

4. **Reread** For optimal fluency, have partners continue to read three or four times.

5. **Corrective Feedback** Listen to students read and provide corrective feedback regarding their appropriate phrasing.

Routines Flip Chart

## Common Core State Standards

**Foundational Skills 3.a.** Identify and know the meaning of the most common prefixes and derivational suffixes. **Foundational Skills 3.b.** Decode words with common Latin suffixes. **Language 2.e.** Use conventional spelling for high-frequency and other studied words and for adding suffixes to base words (e.g., sitting, smiled, cries, happiness). **Language 3.** Use knowledge of language and its conventions when writing, speaking, reading, or listening.

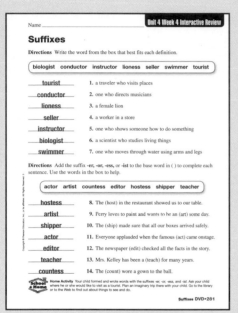

Let's Practice It! TR DVD•281

Reader's and Writer's Notebook,
pp. 308–309

# Word Analysis

**REVIEW SUFFIXES** Review the suffixes -er, -or, -ess, and -ist, using Sound-Spelling Cards 165, 166, 171, and 176.

Use Let's Practice It! p. 281 on the Teacher Resources DVD-ROM.

**READ WORDS IN ISOLATION** Point out that students know how to read the words in the boxes. Have students read the words in the boxes together. Allow several seconds previewing time for the first reading.

**READ WORDS IN CONTEXT** Point out that there are many words in sentences 8–14 that students already know. Have students read the sentences together.

| Corrective feedback | **If...** students have difficulty reading words with the suffixes -er, -or, -ess, and -ist, **then...** guide them in using the word parts strategy. Have students read all the words in the boxes repeatedly until they can read the words fluently. Then have students read each sentence repeatedly until they can read the sentences fluently. |
|---|---|

# Spelling

**REVIEW SUFFIXES** Write seller, actor, actress, and tourist. Point out that these words have suffixes. Remind students that they have learned how to spell words with suffixes -er, -or, -ess, and -ist.

**SPELLING STRATEGY** Review words with suffixes by having students follow the spelling strategy for spelling these words.

> **Step 1: Draw a line between the base word and the suffix.**
>
> **Step 2: Study the word, one part at a time.**

**ON THEIR OWN** Use p. 308 of the Reader's and Writer's Notebook for additional practice with spelling words with suffixes.

# Conventions

**REVIEW CONTRACTIONS** Review **contractions** with students.

**GUIDE PRACTICE** Read the following sentences. Have students identify the contraction in each sentence.

1. I **didn't** know that swimming is an Olympic sport.

2. **I'd** like to be in the Olympics one day.

3. Unfortunately, I **don't** swim very well.

**ON THEIR OWN** For additional practice use *Reader's and Writer's Notebook,* p. 309.

## Routine    Quick Write for Fluency    Team Talk

1. **Talk** Pairs discuss what they learned in the two selections this week about the accomplishments of female athletes.

2. **Write** Each student writes a few sentences summarizing the accomplishments of a particular female athlete, using contractions.

3. **Share** Students read their sentences to their partners, who then check for the correct use of contractions.

Routines Flip Chart

**eSTREET INTERACTIVE**
www.ReadingStreet.com

**Teacher Resources**
• Reader's and Writer's Notebook
• Let's Practice It!

**Interactive Sound-Spelling Cards**

## Writing Workshop
Use the writing process lesson on pp. WP•1–WP•10 for this week's writing instruction.

# Wrap Up Week 4 Review!

✔ **Content Knowledge** What traits helped Gertrude Ederle become the first woman to swim the English Channel?

✔ **Fact and Opinion** What are two statements of fact about Gertrude Ederle that you read in the selection?

✔ **Multiple-Meaning Words** How can parts of speech help you understand the meaning of a multiple-meaning word?

**Preview DAY 5**

Tell students that tomorrow they will review *Fly, Eagle, Fly!: An African Tale.*

### Materials

- Student Edition
- Retelling Cards
- Reader's and Writer's Notebook
- Sound-Spelling Cards

 **Common Core State Standards**

**Speaking/Listening 1.** Engage effectively in a range of collaborative discussions (one-on-one, in groups, and teacher-led) with diverse partners on grade 3 topics and texts, building on others' ideas and expressing their own clearly. **Language 6.** Acquire and use accurately grade-appropriate conversational, general academic, and domain-specific words and phrases, including those that signal spatial and temporal relationships (e.g., *After dinner that night we went looking for them*).

# Content Knowledge

## Unique Animal Behaviors

**REVISIT THE CONCEPT** Today students will explore how the question for this unit of study connects to *Fly, Eagle, Fly!* Remind students of the Question of the Week, *What behaviors are unique to different animals?*

## Build Oral Language

**DISCUSS BEING ONE OF A KIND** Remind students of the question for this unit of study, *What does it mean to be unique?* Use the prompts and the concept map from Week 5 to discuss what makes different animals unique.

- How do the ways animals look, sound, or act make them unique?
- How do animals' extraordinary characteristics make them unique?

# Build Oral Vocabulary

**REVIEW AMAZING WORDS** Display the Amazing Words for *Fly, Eagle, Fly!* Remind students that the words are related to the week's concept.

## Amazing Words    Robust Vocabulary Routine

1. **Review** Ask students for definitions of the words, starting at the top of the list. Listen for accurate definitions. Prompt students to connect the words to the unit concept of One of a Kind whenever possible.

2. **Demonstrate** Have students use two or more Amazing Words in the same sentence. Guide the discussion by providing an example that shows the meaning of each word. *The beautiful scenery in the valley made the view extraordinary.* Follow this pattern to the end of the list, covering as many of the ten words as possible.

3. **Apply** Assign the words in random order and have students come up with more new sentences for them. To show that you are becoming more comfortable using these Amazing Words, think up more new sentences for them.

Routines Flip Chart

**AMAZING WORDS AT WORK** Have students use the Retelling Cards/Story Sort for *Fly, Eagle, Fly!* to talk about the Amazing Words.

**CONNECT TO READING** Tell students that today they will be rereading passages from *Fly, Eagle, Fly!* and reading "The Foolish Mouse." As they read, ask students to think about how animal behaviors are unique.

## eStreet Interactive
www.ReadingStreet.com

- Big Question Video
- Concept Talk Video
- **Teacher Resources**
  - Amazing Word Cards

## Amazing Words

| | |
|---|---|
| armor | scenery |
| agile | pesky |
| snout | unfurl |
| protrude | coil |
| extraordinary | intersection |

**ELL**

**Build Background** Use ELL Poster 20 to review the Week 5 lesson concept and to practice oral language. Point out and read the question: *What behaviors are unique to different animals?*

Next day the friend was back. "Farmer," he said, "I will prove to you that this is no chicken but an eagle. Bring me a ladder." With the large bird under one arm, he struggled up the slippery thatch of the tallest hut.

The farmer doubled over with laughter. "It eats chicken food. It thinks like a chicken. It *is* a chicken."

The friend, swaying on top of the hut, took the eagle's head, pointed it to the sky, and said: "You are not a chicken but an eagle. You belong not to the earth but to the sky. Fly, Eagle, fly!"

166

Again the great bird stretched out its wings. It trembled and the claws that clasped his hand opened. "Fly, Eagle, fly!" the man cried.

But the bird scrambled out of his hands, slid down the thatch, and sailed in among the chickens.

There was much laughter.

Very early next morning, on the third day, the farmer's dogs began to bark. A voice was calling outside in the darkness. The farmer ran to the door. It was his friend again. "Give me one more chance with the bird," he begged.

"Do you know the time? It's long before dawn. Are you crazy?"

"Come with me. Fetch the bird."

Reluctantly the farmer went into the kitchen, stepping over his sleeping children, and picked up the bird, which was fast asleep among the chickens. The two men set off, disappearing into the darkness.

167

**Student Edition, pp. 166–167**

## Common Core State Standards

**Literature 1.** Ask and answer questions to demonstrate understanding of a text, referring explicitly to the text as the basis for the answers. **Literature 2.** Recount stories, including fables, folktales, and myths from diverse cultures; determine the central message, lesson, or moral and explain how it is conveyed through key details in the text.

# Access Text ©

**REVIEW © CAUSE AND EFFECT** Review the meanings of *cause* and *effect* on p. 154. Remind students that a cause is why something happens and an effect is what happens. Tell students that the words *because* and *so* are clues to cause-and-effect relationships. Sometimes an author uses these words, but many times the reader has to figure out the relationship based on the descriptions of events.

**GUIDE PRACTICE** Point out the words of the farmer on p. 166, "It eats chicken food. It thinks like a chicken. It *is* a chicken." Explain that the effect is that the farmer believes the eagle is a chicken. Ask students what causes the farmer to have this belief.

**ON THEIR OWN** Have students write a sentence that tells the cause-and-effect relationship in the above example. Tell students to use the clue word *because* in their sentences.

# Close Reading ©

**EVALUATION** The farmer believes the eagle is a chicken because it thinks like a chicken and acts like a chicken. Are the reasons, or causes, for his belief valid? Why or why not? **No. Just because the eagle acts like a chicken doesn't mean it really is a chicken.**

**SYNTHESIS** In "Eagle Watching," the author describes how eagles act in the wild. In *Fly, Eagle, Fly!,* what effect does the farmer have on the eagle when he takes it home? **He changes its behavior by teaching it to be a chicken.**

**EVALUATION** The eagle is America's national bird, and represents freedom. How does the farmer try to change this representation of the eagle? **He tries to tame it and take away its true nature.**

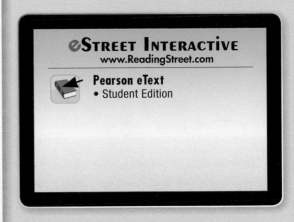

## Access for All

**SI** **Strategic Intervention**

Prior to presenting this Synthesis question to students, review the selection "Eagle Watching," pointing out the descriptions of the ways the birds behave in the wild.

**A** **Advanced**

Have students identify and explain the faulty reasoning behind the farmer's beliefs. Then ask them to come up with a cause-and-effect statement as to why the farmer might feel this way.

At last he said, "This will do." He looked down the cliff and saw the ground thousands of feet below. They were very near the top.

Carefully the friend carried the bird onto a ledge of rock. He set it down so that it looked toward the east, and began talking to it.

The farmer chuckled. "It talks only chickens' talk."

But the friend talked on, telling the bird about the sun, how it gives life to the world, how it reigns in the heavens, giving light to each new day.

"Look at the sun, Eagle. And when it rises, rise with it. You belong to the sky, not to the earth."

At that moment the sun's first rays shot out over the mountain, and suddenly the world was ablaze with light.

The golden sun rose majestically, dazzling them. The great bird stretched out its wings to greet the sun and feel the life-giving warmth on its feathers. The farmer was quiet. The friend said, "You belong not to the earth, but to the sky. Fly, Eagle, fly!"

He clambered back to the farmer.

All was silent. Nothing moved. The eagle's head stretched up; its wings stretched outwards; its legs leaned forward as its claws clutched the rock.

And then, without really moving, feeling the updraft of a wind more powerful than any man or bird, the great eagle leaned forward and was swept upward, higher and higher, lost to sight in the brightness of the rising sun, never again to live among the chickens.

170

171

**Student Edition, pp. 170–171**

## Common Core State Standards

**Literature 1.** Ask and answer questions to demonstrate understanding of a text, referring explicitly to the text as the basis for the answers. **Literature 2.** Recount stories, including fables, folktales, and myths from diverse cultures; determine the central message, lesson, or moral and explain how it is conveyed through key details in the text. **Language 4.** Determine or clarify the meaning of unknown and multiple-meaning word and phrases based on grade 3 reading and content, choosing flexibly from a range of strategies. **Language 4.d.** Use glossaries or beginning dictionaries, both print and digital, to determine or clarify the precise meaning of key words and phrases.

# Access Text ©

**REVIEW © UNKNOWN WORDS** Review the instruction for *unknown words* on p. 156. Remind students that they can use a dictionary or glossary to look up unknown words. They can then choose the meaning that makes the most sense in the context in which the word is used.

**GUIDE PRACTICE** Point out the word *reigns* in the fourth paragraph on p. 171. Help students use a dictionary to look up the word, check its pronunciation, and determine the intended meaning within this context.

**ON THEIR OWN** Use *Let's Practice It!* p. 286 on the *Teacher Resources DVD-ROM* for additional practice with unknown words.

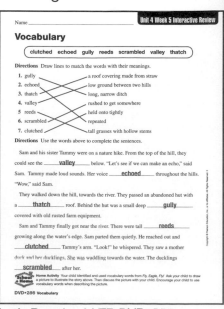

Let's Practice It! TR DVD•286

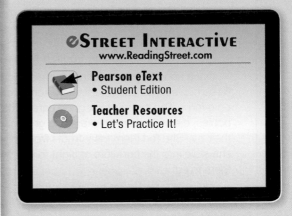

**eStreet Interactive**
www.ReadingStreet.com

**Pearson eText**
• Student Edition

**Teacher Resources**
• Let's Practice It!

## Close Reading ©

**DEVELOP LANGUAGE** Use a dictionary to look up the meaning of the word *clambered* from paragraph 8 on page 171. What does it mean in this context? It means "climbed awkwardly."

**EVALUATION** Would the eagle have ever flown without the farmer's friend taking it to the mountain? Explain. Probably not, because being on the mountaintop at the break of day made the eagle remember its true nature. When it was in the valley with the chickens, it could not realize its true nature.

**SYNTHESIS** What would you say is the message of this folk tale for people? Be true to yourself no matter what.

### Access for All

**SI** Strategic Intervention

Help students look up unknown words in the dictionary, reviewing how to use guide words and pronunciation keys. Then guide them in identifying the definition that fits the context. Suggest they replace the original word in the sentence with its definition. For example, *He climbed awkwardly back to the farmer.*

**A** Advanced

Have small groups of students discuss times when they have found it hard to be true to their beliefs or natures, such as when they experience peer pressure or disagree with the majority of people around them.

Name _____

**Read** the story. **Answer** the questions.

### The Foolish Mouse

Once upon a time, a mother mouse and her three babies, two daughters and a son, lived on a farm. The mother took good care of her babies, cleaning their whiskers and grooming their fur. She fed them tasty treats from the fields. Sometimes she stole into the barn late at night to find a little grain or corn for them to eat.

The baby mice grew fat and bold, thanks to their mother's good care. Soon they were tumbling around in the nest, getting into trouble. If one mouse poked her nose out of the mouse hole to take long, deep breaths of fresh air, another mouse soon followed. Before long, all three were outside in the sunshine!

Mother Mouse was horrified. "Little mice," she scolded, "you must never, ever forget that you are mice. Mice are small, very small. They make an excellent meal for bigger animals like owls, cats, and foxes. Just one careless move and you are no longer a mouse. You are someone's dinner!" Mother Mouse looked stern.

The two daughters listened carefully to their mother. From that day on, they stayed in their mouse hole until dark. Only then did they creep out to look for food, and they never went very far. At the least hint of trouble, they scampered back to safety.

As you might have guessed, their brother was different. He didn't want to act like a coward. "I may not be big, but I'm brave," he boasted to his sisters. "I'm the bravest mouse that ever lived!"

His sisters laughed. "Listen to Momma," they warned him.

---

Brother Mouse set out to prove that it is safe for mice to venture outside in the daytime like many other animals do. When he wanted to take a walk through the garden to enjoy the sights and smells, he did. After all, he was the bravest mouse of all.

Brother Mouse strolled, as bold as you please, down the garden path. He sniffed the breeze with its scents of lilacs and roses. He enjoyed the bright colors of the flowers and clover. He listened to the sounds of birds chirping and bees buzzing. Just as he started to sing his own little song, he heard the quiet swoop of an owl's powerful wings overhead, and then . . .

1. What is the cause, or the reason, the baby mice grew fat and bold?

   <u>Their mother took good care of them.</u>

2. What is the effect of Mother Mouse's warning on her two daughters?

   <u>They were more careful. They went out only after dark.</u>

3. Brother Mouse forgot to behave carefully, like a mouse. What effect do you think that had?

   <u>Possible response: He may have become dinner for an owl.</u>

4. Find another example of cause and effect in the folk tale and write it below.

   <u>Possible response: Because one sister poked her nose out of the mousehole, her sister and brother did too.</u>

**School + Home** **Home Activity** Your child identified cause and effect in a folk tale. A cause is something that causes something else—an effect—to happen. Take turns discussing possible causes and effects in your home. For example, point to a light switch and ask your child to tell a cause and an effect about it.

Let's Practice It! TR DVD•287–288

---

## © Common Core State Standards

**Literature 1.** Ask and answer questions to demonstrate understanding of a text, referring explicitly to the text as the basis for the answers. **Literature 2.** Recount stories, including fables, folktales, and myths from diverse cultures; determine the central message, lesson, or moral and explain how it is conveyed through key details in the text. **Foundational Skills 4.b.** Read on-level prose and poetry orally with accuracy, appropriate rate, and expression on successive readings. **Language 4.** Determine or clarify the meaning of unknown and multiple-meaning word and phrases based on grade 3 reading and content, choosing flexibly from a range of strategies. **Language 4.d.** Use glossaries or beginning dictionaries, both print and digital, to determine or clarify the precise meaning of key words and phrases.

**UR•52** One of a Kind • Unit 4 • Week 6

# Access Text ©

**REVIEW © CAUSE AND EFFECT** What is the cause, or the reason, the baby mice grew fat and bold? Their mother took good care of them.

Remind students that an effect is something that happens and a cause is the reason that something happens. Review that cause and effect is often signaled by clue words. Read the following sentence from the text that contains a cause-and-effect relationship: "The baby mice grew fat and bold, thanks to their mother's good care." Point out that *thanks to* is a clue that means "because of."

**REVIEW © MONITOR AND CLARIFY** The third paragraph begins, "Mother Mouse was horrified." Why is she horrified? Her babies are outside in the daytime, which is not safe.

Tell students to reread and to read further to monitor and clarify their understanding of events in the story.

**REVIEW ⊙ UNKNOWN WORDS** Read the first sentence on page 288. Use a dictionary to determine the meaning of *venture.* It means "to go ahead in spite of danger."

Review with students how to use a dictionary to find the meanings of unknown words. If necessary, help students use guide words to find the term. Remind them that they need to use the context of the word to determine which meaning is intended. Have students find other unknown words and use a dictionary to find their meanings.

**REVIEW ⊙ CAUSE AND EFFECT** Brother Mouse chose to not behave carefully, like his mother said. What effect do you think that had? He may have become dinner for an owl.

Underline the last sentence of the folk tale. Point out that Brother Mouse is not being careful as his mother warned. Then he hears an owl's wings overhead. Help students explain the two events by using a cause-and-effect relationship. Point out that not all cause-and-effect relationships have clue words. Sometimes readers have to infer the connection based on the events.

# Reread for Fluency

**MODEL FLUENT READING** Remind students that when they read, it is important to read at an appropriate rate in order to understand what they are reading. Model reading the first paragraph of "The Foolish Mouse" on p. 287 at an appropriate rate and have students track the print as you read.

## Routine | Paired Reading

1. **Reading 1** Have partners read the entire folk tale "The Foolish Mouse," switching readers at the end of each paragraph.

2. **Reading 2** Partners reread the selection. This time the other student begins.

3. **Reread** For optimal fluency, have partners continue to read three or four times.

4. **Corrective Feedback** Listen to students read. Provide corrective feedback regarding their rate.

Routines Flip Chart

### Common Core State Standards

**Foundational Skills 3.c.** Decode multisyllable words. **Language 1.** Demonstrate command of the conventions of standard English grammar and usage when writing or speaking. **Language 2.f.** Use spelling patterns and generalizations (e.g., word families, position-based spellings, syllable patterns, ending rules, meaningful word parts) in writing words.

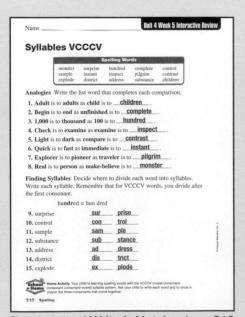

Let's Practice It! TR DVD•285

Reader's and Writer's Notebook, p. 310

# Word Analysis

**REVIEW SYLLABLES VCCCV** Review the syllable pattern VCCCV using *Sound-Spelling Card* 146.

Use *Let's Practice It!* p. 285 on the *Teacher Resources DVD-ROM.*

**READ WORDS IN ISOLATION** Point out that students know how to read these words. Have students read the words with the VCCCV pattern in sentences 1–6 together. Allow several seconds previewing time for the first reading.

**READ WORDS IN CONTEXT** Have students read sentences 1–6 together.

| Corrective feedback | **If...** students have difficulty reading the syllable pattern VCCCV, <br><br> **then...** guide them in using the word parts strategy. Have students read all the words repeatedly until they can read the words fluently. Then have students read each sentence repeatedly until they can read the sentences fluently. |
|---|---|

# Spelling

**REVIEW SYLLABLES VCCCV** Write *instant, partner,* and *address.* Point out that these words have the syllable pattern VCCCV. Remind students that they have learned how to spell words with the syllable pattern VCCCV.

**SPELLING STRATEGY** Review words with the syllable pattern VCCCV by having students follow the spelling strategy for spelling these words.

> **Step 1: Say the word slowly and listen for the syllables.**
>
> **Step 2: Write the word and draw lines between the syllables.**
>
> **Step 3: Study the word syllable by syllable.**

**ON THEIR OWN** Use p. 310 of the *Reader's and Writer's Notebook* for additional practice with the syllable pattern VCCCV.

# Conventions

**REVIEW PREPOSITIONS** Review **preposition** and **prepositional phrase** with students.

**GUIDE PRACTICE** Read the following sentences. Have students identify the preposition in each sentence.

1. I read a folk tale **about** an eagle.
2. The story was **in** my reading book.

**ON THEIR OWN** For additional practice use *Reader's and Writer's Notebook,* p. 311.

---

**Routine** | **Quick Write for Fluency** | **Team Talk**

1. **Talk** Have pairs discuss the special features of the animals in *Fly, Eagle, Fly!* and "Purple Coyote."

2. **Write** Students write a few sentences describing one of these unusual animals, using prepositions correctly.

3. **Share** Partners read each other's sentences and check them for correct use of prepositions.

---

Routines Flip Chart

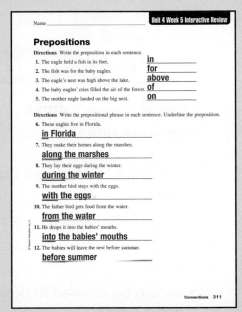

**eStreet Interactive**
www.ReadingStreet.com

**Teacher Resources**
• Reader's and Writer's Notebook
• Let's Practice It!

**Interactive Sound-Spelling Cards**

---

Name _____    Unit 4 Week 5 Interactive Review

**Prepositions**

**Directions** Write the preposition in each sentence.
1. The eagle held a fish in its feet.    in
2. The fish was for the baby eagles.    for
3. The eagle's nest was high above the lake.    above
4. The baby eagles' cries filled the air of the forest.    of
5. The mother eagle landed on the big nest.    on

**Directions** Write the prepositional phrase in each sentence. Underline the preposition.
6. These eagles live in Florida.
   in Florida
7. They make their homes along the marshes.
   along the marshes
8. They lay their eggs during the winter.
   during the winter
9. The mother bird stays with the eggs.
   with the eggs
10. The father bird gets food from the water.
    from the water
11. He drops it into the babies' mouths.
    into the babies' mouths
12. The babies will leave the nest before summer.
    before summer

Conventions 311

Reader's and Writer's Notebook, p. 311

## Writing Workshop
Use pp. WP•1–WP•10 for this week's writing instruction.

---

# Wrap Up Week 5 Review!

✔ **Content Knowledge** What behavior is unique to the eagle in *Fly, Eagle, Fly!: An African Tale*?

✔ **Cause and Effect** What effect did the friend's efforts have on the eagle in the folk tale?

✔ **Unknown Words** How can you find the meanings of unknown words in the dictionary?

**Preview Unit 5**

Use p. 183q to preview Unit 5 Week 1 with students.

# Wrap Up Your Unit!  Zoom in on ©

## Discuss Content Knowledge Gained Through Reading

## What does it mean to be unique?

### WEEK 1

**How do talents make someone unique?**

**Students have learned that people**

- have many kinds of talents
- practice to develop their talents
- should be allowed to develop their talents

### WEEK 2

**What makes nature's record holders unique?**

**Students have learned that nature has**

- unusual appearances
- extreme weather
- extreme events

### WEEK 3

**Why is it valuable to have unique interests?**

**Students have learned that interests**

- are valuable
- lead to learning and research
- lead to a job
- preserve information

## How do people feel about things that are unique?

- They feel that unique things are special and interesting.
- They are drawn to unique things.
- They want to know more about unique things.

Discuss with students the selections they have explored surrounding the idea of what it means to be unique. Throughout discussions, students should support their comments and ideas with evidence from the texts.

## What is unique about the characters, animals, and places in these stories?

- *The Man Who Invented Basketball:* James Naismith used knowledge and skills to invent an indoor game.

- *Hottest, Coldest, Highest, Deepest:* Many places on earth have extreme characteristics.

- *Rocks in His Head:* The author's father has a special rock collection that he is knowledgeable about.

- *America's Champion Swimmer: Gertrude Ederle:* Gertrude has the record of being the first woman to swim across the English Channel.

- *Fly, Eagle, Fly!:* The eagle is trained to behave like a chicken.

## WEEK 4

**What unique traits does it take to be the first to do something?**

**Students have learned that being first takes**

- bravery
- imagination
- willingness to work hard
- determination

## WEEK 5

**What behaviors are unique to different animals?**

**Students have learned that some animals**

- have lures on their heads
- blend in with their surroundings
- change colors

## Talk about being unique.

What is something that makes you unique? (Responses will vary.)

**Team Talk** Have students work in pairs to talk about the Amazing Ideas related to being unique that they discussed each week. Then have students use these ideas to help demonstrate their understanding of the question, *What does it mean to be unique?*

## Amazing Words

**You've learned 197 words this year!**

**You've learned 050 words this unit to use as you talk about being unique.**

# Assessment Checkpoints for the Week

## Unit Assessment

Use Unit 4 *Benchmark Tests* to check:

✔ **Passage Comprehension**

✔ **Phonics**

✔ **Vocabulary Skills**

✔ **Writing Conventions**

✔ **Writing**

✔ **Fluency**

Benchmark Tests

## Managing Assessment

Use *Assessment Handbook* for:

✔ **Weekly Assessment Blackline Masters for Monitoring Progress**

✔ **Observation Checklists**

✔ **Record-Keeping Forms**

✔ **Portfolio Assessment**

Assessment Handbook

## Writing Trait Skills Trace

All of the writing traits taught in Scott Foresman Reading Street are dimensions of good writing. The chart below shows you the writing traits taught each week of the unit. In the column on the right, the criteria to achieve the Indiana Writing Applications Rubric top score are identified. For an overview of the Indiana Writing Applications Rubric and the Language Conventions Rubric, see the back of this page.

| | Writing Trait of the Week/ Weekly Selection | Indiana Writing Applications/Language Conventions Rubric Top Score Point Criteria |
|---|---|---|
| | | A Score Point 6 paper is rare. It fully accomplishes the task and has a distinctive quality that sets it apart as an outstanding performance. |
| **Week 1** | Conventions<br>*The Man Who Invented Basketball*<br><br>**Writing Prompt** *The Man Who Invented Basketball* is about Joseph Naismith, who invented the game of basketball. Write an essay about your favorite sport or game, persuading someone to play it. | There are no errors that impair the flow of communication. Errors that appear will generally be of the first-draft variety; they have a minor impact on the overall communication. |
| **Week 2** | Conventions<br>*Hottest, Coldest, Highest, Deepest*<br><br>**Writing Prompt** Write an imaginative story in which one character tells a riddle to another. | There are no errors that impair the flow of communication. Errors that appear will generally be of the first-draft variety; they have a minor impact on the overall communication. |
| **Week 3** | Sentences<br>*Rocks in His Head*<br><br>**Writing Prompt** *Rocks in His Head* describes a person with a collection. Think about a friend or family member who has an interesting collection. Now write a short biography of that person's life. | **Is the writing fluent and easy to read?**<br>**Does it**<br>• sound natural?<br>• include varied sentence patterns? (Writing may include complex sentence patterns.) |
| **Week 4** | Organization<br>*America's Champion Swimmer: Gertrude Ederle*<br><br>**Writing Prompt** Think about your own life and experiences. Now write an autobiography. | **Does the writing have clear order?**<br>**Does it**<br>• follow a clear sequence with a beginning, a middle, and an end?<br>• have a logical progression of main ideas and support? |
| **Week 5** | Word Choice<br>*Fly, Eagle, Fly!: An African Tail*<br><br>**Writing Prompt** *Fly, Eagle, Fly!* is an African tale. Think about a tale that you know well. Now write a summary of the plot, telling the events in time order. | **Does the writing sample exhibit exceptional word usage?**<br>**Does it**<br>• include dynamic words and provide rich details, strong verbs, and/or vivid descriptions?<br>• demonstrate control of a challenging vocabulary? |

For tips on **Publishing/Presenting** a Problem-Solution Essay, see Step 5 on the Unit 4 Writing Process tab.

## Indiana Writing Resources

Use these resources to build writing skills during and after the teaching of Unit 4.

**Reader's and Writer's Notebook**

**Writing Rubrics and Anchor Papers**

**Digital Resources**
• Online Journal
• Online Writing Transparencies
• Grammar Jammer

**Teacher Resources DVD-ROM**
• Reader's and Writer's Notebook
• Let's Practice It!
• Graphic Organizers
• Writing Transparencies

ISBN-13: 978-0-328-73390-3    ISBN-10: 0-328-73390-3

# Indiana Writing Rubrics

## Indiana Writing Applications Rubric Overview

The released Indiana Writing Applications Rubric Overview can be used to score the Unit 4 Writing Process Problem-Solution Essay on pp. WP•1–WP•10 and other writing assignments.

**Writing Prompt** Write about a problem in your school or community and how that problem might be solved.

**Purpose** Identify a problem and offer a solution

**Audience** Peers, teachers, or other interested adults

| Score Level | Ideas and Content | Organization | Style |
|---|---|---|---|
| | Does the writing sample | Does the writing sample | Does the writing sample |
| 6 | • stay fully focused?<br>• include thorough and complete ideas? | • have clear order? | • exhibit exceptional word usage?<br>• exhibit writing that is fluent and easy to read?<br>• display a strong sense of audience? |
| 5 | • stay focused?<br>• include many relevant ideas? | • have clear order? | • exhibit more than adequate word usage?<br>• exhibit writing that is fluent and easy to read?<br>• display a sense of audience? |
| 4 | • stay mostly focused?<br>• include some relevant ideas? | • have order? | • exhibit adequate word usage?<br>• exhibit writing that is readable?<br>• display some sense of audience? |
| 3 | • exhibit less than minimal focus?<br>• include few relevant ideas? | • have some order? | • exhibit minimal word usage?<br>• exhibit writing that is mostly readable?<br>• display little sense of audience? |
| 2 | • exhibit less than minimal focus?<br>• include few relevant ideas? | • have little order? | • exhibit less than minimal word usage?<br>• exhibit writing that is hard to read?<br>• display little sense of audience? |
| 1 | • have little or no focus?<br>• include almost no relevant ideas? | • have little or no order? | • exhibit less than minimal word usage?<br>• exhibit writing that is hard to read?<br>• display little or no sense of audience? |

NOTE: This chart is only a brief summary of the score points. It is not appropriate to use this summary as the sole tool in scoring student papers.

## Indiana Language Conventions Rubric Overview

| Score Level | Command of Language Skills |
|---|---|
| 4 | In a Score Point 4 paper, there are no errors that impair the flow of communication. Errors that appear will generally be of the first-draft variety; they have a minor impact on the overall communication. |
| 3 | In a Score Point 3 paper, errors are occasional but do not impede the flow of communication; the writer's meaning is not seriously obscured by language errors. |
| 2 | In a Score Point 2 paper, errors are generally frequent and may cause the reader to stop and reread part of the writing. While some aspects of the writing may be more consistently correct than others, the existing errors do impair communication. With a little extra effort on the reader's part, it is still possible to discern most, if not all, of what the writer is trying to communicate. |
| 1 | In a Score Point 1 paper, errors are serious and numerous; they cause the reader to struggle to discern the writer's meaning. Errors are frequently of a wide variety. There may be sections where it is impossible to ascertain what the writer is attempting to communicate. |

# Writing on Reading Street

## DAILY WRITING FOCUS

### Quick Writes for Fluency

- Use the Quick Write routine for **writing on demand**.
- The Quick Write **prompt and routine** extend skills and strategies from daily writing lessons.
- Daily 10-minute **mini-lessons** focus instruction on the **traits** and **craft** of good writing.
- **Writing Traits** are focus/ideas, organization, voice, word choice, sentences, and conventions.
- **Craft** includes drafting strategies, revising strategies, and editing strategies.

## WEEKLY WRITING FOCUS

### Writing Forms and Patterns

- Instruction focuses on a different **product** each week.
- Mini-lessons and models help students learn key features and **organizational patterns**.
- Use **mentor text** every week as a model to exemplify the traits of good writing.
- **Grade 3 Products** include fables, friendly letters, news articles, autobiographies, summaries, realistic fiction, and more.
- **Grade 3 Organizational Patterns** include poetic forms, compare and contrast, main idea and details, narratives, letters, and more.

## UNIT WRITING FOCUS

### Writing Process

- Six **writing process** lessons provide structure to move students through the steps of the writing process.
- One-week and two-week pacing (see the back of this Tab) allows lessons to be used in **Writing Workshops**.
- The **steps of the writing process** are Plan and Prewrite, Draft, Revise, Edit, and Publish and Present.
- **Grade 3 Writing Process Products** include personal narratives, how-to reports, cause-and-effect essays, problem-solution essays, persuasive essays, and research reports.

# Problem-Solution Essay

| PROCESS WRITING STEPS | © COMMON CORE STATE STANDARDS FOR ENGLISH LANGUAGE ARTS | TIPS FOR UNIT 4 PROCESS WRITING |
|---|---|---|
| ① Plan and Prewrite | Writing 1.a., Writing 5. | As students prepare to **prewrite**, remind them to try a range of strategies for thinking of topics. |
| ② Draft | Writing 1., Writing 1.d., Writing 5. | As students **draft** their writing, show them how to use a Problem-Solution graphic organizer to categorize and organize their ideas. |
| ③ Revise | Writing 5. | Before students **revise** their drafts, show them how to use prepositional phrases to add specific details. |
| ④ Edit | Writing 5., Writing 6. | As students **edit** their writing, suggest that they read their writing line by line, checking spelling, punctuation, capitalization, and grammar. |
| ⑤ Publish and Present | Writing 6. | When students are ready to **publish** their writing, have them use the Scoring Rubric to evaluate their own writing. |

# Alternate Pacing Plans for Unit Writing Projects

Sometimes you want to spend more time on writing – perhaps you do a **Writing Workshop.** Below you will find one- or two-week plans for the unit-level writing projects.

| 1-WEEK PLAN | Day 1 | Day 2 | Day 3 | Day 4 | Day 5 |
|---|---|---|---|---|---|
| ① Plan and Prewrite | ■ | ■ | | | |
| ② Draft | | | ■ | | |
| ③ Revise | | | | ■ | |
| ④ Edit | | | | | ■ |
| ⑤ Publish and Present | | | | | ■ |

| 2-WEEK PLAN | Day 1 | Day 2 | Day 3 | Day 4 | Day 5 | Day 6 | Day 7 | Day 8 | Day 9 | Day 10 |
|---|---|---|---|---|---|---|---|---|---|---|
| ① Plan and Prewrite | ■ | ■ | ■ | ■ | | | | | | |
| ② Draft | | | | | ■ | ■ | ■ | | | |
| ③ Revise | | | | | | | | ■ | | |
| ④ Edit | | | | | | | | | ■ | |
| ⑤ Publish and Present | | | | | | | | | | ■ |

# Grade 3 Unit Writing Projects

| UNIT WRITING PROCESS PROJECTS | | UNIT 21ST CENTURY WRITING PROJECTS | |
|---|---|---|---|
| **UNIT 1** | Personal Narrative | **UNIT 1** | E-Pen Pals |
| **UNIT 2** | How-to Report | **UNIT 2** | Story Exchange |
| **UNIT 3** | Cause-and-Effect Essay | **UNIT 3** | Photo Writing |
| **UNIT 4** | Problem-Solution Essay | **UNIT 4** | Classroom Profile |
| **UNIT 5** | Persuasive Essay | **UNIT 5** | E-Newsletter |
| **UNIT 6** | Research Report | **UNIT 6** | Discussion Forum |

You can find all of the Unit 21st Century Writing Projects in the Teacher Resources section on SuccessNet.

**USE RANGE OF STRATEGIES** Encourage students to try a range of strategies for thinking of topics, including these:

✔ With other students, brainstorm problems they know about in their school or community.

✔ Browse through local newspapers or Web sites to generate ideas about problems in the community.

✔ Interview family members or friends about school or local problems they think are a concern.

**NARROW TOPIC** Once you have a list of topics, you need to narrow your choices to one topic. Have students look more closely at their ideas for topics and decide which is the most suitable for the assignment. They might ask: *Do I know enough about this problem to explain it clearly? Can I think of a reasonable solution? Can I describe this problem and solution in two or three paragraphs?*

| Topics | Evaluate |
| --- | --- |
| not enough rain in the area for healthy crops | too difficult; can't think of a reasonable solution |
| buses arriving late to school every day | too simple; not much to explain |
| messy and unused town park ★ | an interesting community problem; can think of a reasonable solution |

**Corrective feedback** | **If...** students have trouble deciding on a topic for their essay, **then...** suggest that they think about this question: *What is something I would like to change in my school or community?*

**Write Guy** *by Jeff Anderson*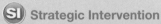
**Use Mentor Texts**
Ask students to recall the problem James Naismith faced in the unit selection *The Man Who Invented Basketball* (traditional outdoor sports could not be played during the winter). Ask students how Naismith solved this problem (invented an indoor sport, basketball). Tell them that they will write an essay in which they describe a problem and its solution.

## Access for All

**SI** Strategic Intervention
For an alternative writing prompt, help students brainstorm some simple problems such as these.
• The car won't start.
• It's raining on the day of the barbecue.
• I lost my lunch money.
Write the list on the board. Have students write about one of the problems and describe a possible solution.

**A** Advanced
For an alternative writing prompt, have students identify a problem in the world beyond their school or community. Invite them to write an essay describing the problem and proposing a solution.

## Common Core State Standards

**Writing 1.a.** Introduce the topic or text they are writing about, state an opinion, and create an organizational structure that lists reasons. **Writing 1.d.** Provide a concluding statement or section. **Writing 5.** With guidance and support from peers and adults, develop and strengthen writing as needed by planning, revising, and editing.

## 1 PREWRITE  Plan and Prewrite

### Mini-Lesson  Planning a First Draft

■ **Use a Problem-Solution Chart** Display Writing Transparency WP24 and read it aloud to students.

 **Think Aloud** **MODEL** This student plans to offer a solution to the problem of her town's messy, unused park. She has categorized her ideas by writing them on this graphic organizer along with a topic sentence that states the central idea or problem and a concluding statement. Now she can start writing a first draft by organizing her facts, details, and explanations or evidence into paragraphs.

■ Have students use *Reader's and Writer's Notebook,* p. 312 to help them plan their first draft. Before you begin writing, use this graphic organizer to categorize and organize ideas about your problem and solution and to plan the paragraphs for your essay.

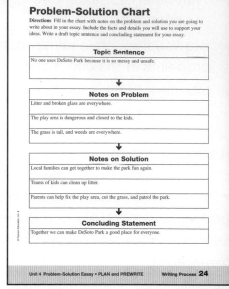

Writing Transparency WP24, TR DVD

Reader's and Writer's Notebook, p. 312

 Draft

**DISPLAY RUBRIC** Display Scoring Rubric WP4 from the *Teacher Resources DVD-ROM*. Review with students the criteria for each trait under each score. Explain that students need to keep these criteria in mind as they develop drafts of their problem-solution essays. Remind them that this is the rubric that will be used to evaluate their problem-solution essays when they are finished.

## Scoring Rubric | Problem-Solution Essay

| | 4 | 3 | 2 | 1 |
|---|---|---|---|---|
| **Focus/Ideas** | Problem-solution essay well focused on one problem and solution | Problem-solution essay generally focused on one problem and solution | Problem-solution essay poorly focused; unclear problem and solution | Problem-solution essay lacking focus; no problem and/or solution |
| **Organization** | Well organized; clear topic sentence, body, concluding statement | Organized, with topic sentence, body, concluding statement | Lacking clear topic sentence, body, concluding statement | Not organized |
| **Voice** | Knowledgeable, confident voice | Generally knowledgeable and convincing | Uncertain voice | No clear voice |
| **Word Choice** | Uses descriptive and persuasive words effectively | Uses some descriptive and persuasive words | Few descriptive or persuasive words | No descriptive or persuasive words |
| **Sentences** | Clear, logical sentences | Reasonably clear, logical sentences | Choppy sentences with lapses in logic | Fragments or run-on sentences |
| **Conventions** | Few, if any, errors | Several minor errors | Frequent errors | Errors that hamper understanding |

**PREPARE TO DRAFT** Have students review the problem-solution charts they worked on earlier. Ask them to make sure that their charts are complete. Encourage them to include facts, details, and explanations or evidence relevant to their topic. You will be using your charts as you write the draft of your essay. Don't worry if your draft doesn't sound exactly the way you want your essay to sound. You will have a chance to revise your draft later.

**Corrective feedback** | **If...** students do not grasp the connection between the Scoring Rubric and their problem-solution essays, **then...** have them help you use the Scoring Rubric to evaluate and score one or more traits of the model problem-solution essay on Writing Transparency WP22.

##  Common Core State Standards

**Writing 1.** Write opinion pieces on topics or texts, supporting a point of view with reasons. **Writing 1.d.** Provide a concluding statement or section. **Writing 5.** With guidance and support from peers and adults, develop and strengthen writing as needed by planning, revising, and editing.

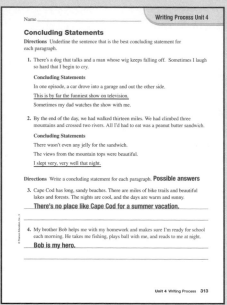

Reader's and Writer's Notebook, p. 313

 **Draft**

### Mini-Lesson    Writing Trait: Organization

■ **Concluding Statements** Display and read aloud Writing Transparency WP25. Ask students what the sentences in each paragraph have in common. Help them think of sentences that sum up the ideas in each paragraph.

> **Think Aloud** **MODEL** When I finish reading a piece of writing, I want to know that I've really reached the end. That's why the last sentence, or concluding statement, is so important. A good concluding statement sums up what the writer has been saying and brings the writing to a satisfying close for readers.

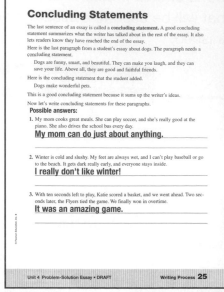

Writing Transparency WP25, TR DVD

■ Have students use *Reader's and Writer's Notebook,* p. 313 to practice selecting and writing concluding statements.

### Tips for Organizing Ideas into Paragraphs

✔ Introduce the problem in the opening paragraph. State your central idea in a clear topic sentence.

✔ Explain your solution to the problem in one or more paragraphs in the body.

✔ Consider beginning your conclusion with a transition word or phrase such as *finally* or *in the end* to let readers know this is the conclusion. End with a concluding statement that sums up your ideas.

**DEVELOP DRAFT** Remind students that the focus of drafting is to get their ideas down in an organized way. Display or photocopy the Tips for Organizing Ideas into Paragraphs for students. Direct them to use what they learned about concluding statements and organizing ideas into paragraphs as they write their drafts.

## 3 Revise

### Mini-Lesson | Writer's Craft: Prepositional Phrases

■ One way to revise writing is to add specific details using prepositional phrases. A prepositional phrase is a group of words that begins with a preposition such as *at, for, in, of, on, to,* or *with*. It can be used to tell what kind, which one, where, when, or how. Discuss this example with students.

**General**   Trash attracts bugs.

**More Specific**   Trash on the picnic table attracts bugs.

The prepositional phrase *on the picnic table* tells which trash. Point out that adding specific details helps make writing clearer and more coherent, which in turn makes it easier for the audience to understand.

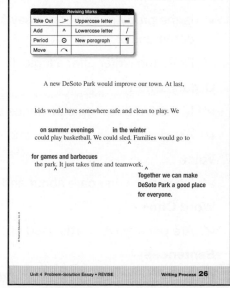

Reader's and Writer's Notebook, p. 314

■ Have students use prepositional phrases to add specific details on *Reader's and Writer's Notebook,* p. 314.

**REVISE MODEL** Display Writing Transparency WP26 and use it to model revising. Point out the revising marks, which students should use when they revise their work. This is part of the problem-solution essay about the messy town park. In the third sentence, the writer added a specific detail with the prepositional phrase *on summer evenings*. It tells when kids could play basketball. The writer also added a concluding statement to wrap up her ideas.

Ask students to point out and explain the other revisions the writer made. (Two prepositional phrases, *in the winter* and *for games and barbecues,* were added to explain when and why activities would take place. Both phrases add specific details to the essay.)

Writing Transparency WP26, TR DVD

### Access for All

**(A) Advanced**

As they revise their work, have students consider ways to improve it.

• Look for places where details would make the writing clearer and more coherent.

• Add prepositional phrases answering the questions *where, when, how, what kind,* or *which one*.

• Try out two or more concluding sentences and choose the one that provides the most satisfying ending.

**ELL**

**Prepositional Phrases** Help students find examples of sentences with one or more prepositional phrases in their reading. Read each example aloud and ask students what detail each prepositional phrase adds to the sentence. Then read the sentence without the prepositional phrase(s) to show students how the sentence changes.

Problem-Solution Essay   **WP•7**

## © Common Core State Standards

**Writing 5.** With guidance and support from peers and adults, develop and strengthen writing as needed by planning, revising, and editing. **Language 1.** Demonstrate command of the conventions of standard English grammar and usage when writing or speaking. **Language 2.** Demonstrate command of the conventions of standard English capitalization, punctuation, and spelling when writing.

---

Name_____ Writing Process Unit 4

**Peer and Teacher Conferencing**
**Problem-Solution Essay**

**Directions** Read your partner's essay. Refer to the Revising Checklist as you write your comments or questions. Offer compliments as well as revision suggestions. Then take turns talking about each other's draft. Give your partner your notes. After you and your teacher talk about your essay, add your teacher's comments to the notes.

### Revising Checklist

**Focus/Ideas**
☐ Is the problem-solution essay focused on one problem in the school or community?
☐ Does the writer offer a logical method of solving the problem?

**Organization**
☐ Is there a clear topic sentence and concluding statement?
☐ Are details of the problem and solution organized in separate paragraphs?

**Voice**
☐ Does the writer show care and understanding of the problem?

**Word Choice**
☐ Are time-order words used effectively in the solution?

**Sentences**
☐ Do prepositional phrases add details to the essay?
☐ Are sentences clear, varied, and logical?

**Things I Thought Were Good** _____

**Things I Thought Could Be Improved** _____

**Teacher's Comments** _____

Unit 4 Writing Process **315**

Reader's and Writer's Notebook,
p. 315

---

## 3 Revise

**REVISE DRAFT** Earlier we wrote drafts of our problem-solution essays. Now we will revise our drafts. When we revise, we try to make our writing clearer and more interesting to our audience.

**PEER CONFERENCING • PEER REVISION** Write the Revising Checklist on the board and review the questions with students. Have pairs exchange drafts and follow the directions for peer and teacher conferencing on *Reader's and Writer's Notebook,* p. 315. Students' revision suggestions might include adding specific details in prepositional phrases to make the writing more coherent and easier for the audience to understand.

Have students revise their problem-solution essays referring to their partner's suggestions and your comments as well as the Revising Checklist and the list of key features of a problem-solution essay (p. WP•1).

> **Corrective feedback**
>
> **If...** students are making spelling, mechanics, and grammar corrections,
> **then...** remind them that they will make those kinds of corrections later when they edit. When they revise, they should be working on the content and organization of their draft.

### Revising Checklist

**Focus/Ideas**

✔ Is the problem-solution essay focused on one problem in the school or community?

✔ Does the writer offer a logical method of solving the problem?

**Organization**

✔ Is there a clear topic sentence as well as a concluding statement?

✔ Are details of the problem and solution organized in separate paragraphs?

**Voice**

✔ Does the writer care about and understand the problem?

**Word Choice**

✔ Are persuasive words used effectively in the solution?

**Sentences**

✔ Do prepositional phrases add details to the essay?

✔ Are sentences clear, varied, and logical?

 **Edit**

## Mini-Lesson | Editing Strategy: Line by Line

■ Suggest that students use this editing strategy as they check their work: Read your writing line by line. As you read each line, check for correct spelling, capitalization, punctuation, and grammar.

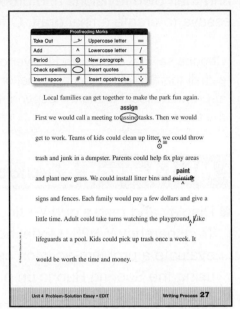

Writing Transparency WP27, TR DVD

■ Display Writing Transparency WP27 and use it to model the editing strategy. Point out the proofreading marks, which students should use when they edit their work. As I check line by line, I see that there are no errors in the first line. In the second line, the writer corrected the spelling of the word *assign*. In the third line, the writer corrected a run-on sentence by adding a period and capitalizing the letter *W*.

■ Ask students to point out and explain the other edits the writer made. (In the fifth line, the verb form *painting* doesn't sound right. The writer changed it to *paint*. In the seventh line, the writer joined the fragment *like lifeguards at a pool* to the preceding sentence, separated by a comma.)

You can create your own rubric, using items from the rubric on p. WP•5 and your own additions or changes, and then have students use it to edit their own drafts. Have them check their drafts for spelling, grammar, and mechanics. Tell them to use proofreading marks to indicate needed corrections.

### Technology Tips

Students who write their problem-solution essays on computers should keep these tips in mind as they edit:

✔ Use the print preview or page layout feature to show how their work will appear on the page before it is printed.

✔ Go to the format or page layout menu to add special features such as borders and shading.

## Write Guy *by Jeff Anderson*
### Finding Fragments

If students have trouble distinguishing complete sentences from fragments while editing their drafts, have them ask these questions: *Who or what did something? What did they do?* If there is no answer to one of these questions, students know their words are a fragment. Help them make a complete sentence by adding a subject or a verb.

**Support Revising and Editing** Invite students to read their drafts aloud to you. Observe whether they note any spelling or grammatical errors by stumbling or self-correcting. Return to those errors and discuss how to correct them. Use the appropriate lessons in the *ELL Handbook* to explicitly teach the English conventions.

## Common Core State Standards

**Writing 6.** With guidance and support from adults, use technology to produce and publish writing (using keyboarding skills) as well as to interact and collaborate with others.

## 5 PUBLISH Publish and Present

**OPTIONS FOR PRESENTING** Have students incorporate peer suggestions and their own revisions and proofreading edits into their problem-solution essays to create a final draft. Offer them two options for presenting their work:

| | |
|---|---|
| Choose several essays and deliver or e-mail them to either the principal or the appropriate local authority, depending on the topics. | Illustrate their essay with "before" and "after" pictures showing the problem and the results of their solution. |

### Mini-Lesson Evaluating Writing

■ Display and read aloud Writing Transparency WP28. Model how to evaluate a problem-solution essay using the Scoring Rubric on p. WP•5.

**Think Aloud MODEL** I would give this problem-solution essay a 4.

It focuses on the problem of the dirty park and a solution for improving it. The essay is organized into a problem paragraph, a solution paragraph, and a conclusion. The writer shows she is concerned about this situation. She uses descriptive details to help readers visualize both the problem and the solution. Sentences are clear, varied, and lively. Spelling, grammar, and mechanics are excellent.

> **Let's Save DeSoto Park**
>
> No one uses Desoto Park because it is so messy and unsafe. Trash is everywhere. Papers blow across the soccer field. Old tires and furniture litter the brook. The playground fence is bent and rusty, and the slide and seesaw are broken. However, we can save the park.
>
> Local families can get together to make the park fun again. First we would call a meeting to assign tasks. Then we would get to work. Teams of kids could clean up litter. We could throw trash and junk in a dumpster. Parents could help fix play areas and plant new grass. We could install litter bins and paint signs and fences. Each family would pay a few dollars and give a little time. Adult could take turns watching the playground, like lifeguards at a pool. Kids could pick up trash once a week. It would be worth the time and money.
>
> A new DeSoto Park would improve our town. At last, kids would have somewhere safe and clean to play. We could play basketball on summer evenings. We could sled in the winter. Families could go to the park for games and barbecues. It just takes time and teamwork. Together we can make DeSoto Park a good place for everyone.
>
> Unit 4 Problem-Solution Essay • PUBLISH and PRESENT    Writing Process **28**

Writing Transparency WP28, TR DVD

■ Have students use the Scoring Rubric to evaluate their problem-solution essays. Encourage them to use the evaluation process to help them identify areas for improvement in their future writing.

# Looking for Teacher Resources and other important information?

Go online to  Pearson SuccessNet

**eStreet Interactive**
www.ReadingStreet.com

## In the *First Stop* on Reading Street, you will find the following information.

- Research into Practice on Reading Street
- Guide to Reading Street
- Assessment on Reading Street
- Customize Writing on Reading Street
- Small Group Instruction on Reading Street

- ELL on Reading Street
- Customize Literacy on Reading Street
- 21st Century Skills on Reading Street
- Teacher Resources for Grade 3
- Index

# Oral Vocabulary for **The Man Who Invented Basketball**

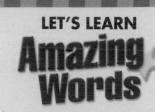

LET'S LEARN
**Amazing Words**

## Oral Vocabulary Routine

**DAY 1**

**idle**

1. **Introduce** *Idle* means "doing nothing, not busy, or not working."
2. **Demonstrate** Jack was *idle* when he should have been doing his homework.
3. **Apply** Have students describe times when they may have been *idle*.
4. **Display the Word** Run your hand under the syllables *i-dle* as you read the word.

**mock**

1. **Introduce** *Mock* means "to laugh at or to make fun of."
2. **Demonstrate** It is unkind to *mock* another person.
3. **Apply** Discuss other meanings of *mock* with students.
4. **Display the Word** Students can decode this word.

**potential**

1. **Introduce** *Potential* means "something possible."
2. **Demonstrate** Annie has the *potential* to be a great singer.
3. **Apply** Have students give other examples of *potential*.
4. **Display the Word** Run your hand under the three syllables *po-ten-tial*.

**DAY 2**

**audition**

1. **Introduce** An *audition* is a hearing to test a person's performance.
2. **Demonstrate** Alex *auditioned* for the school play.
3. **Apply** Have students describe times when a person may need to *audition*.
4. **Display the Word** Have students clap the three syllables *au-di-tion* as you read the word.

**DAY 3**

**result**

1. **Introduce** A *result* is something that happens because of something else.
2. **Demonstrate** The *result* of Tony's fall from the ladder was a broken leg.
3. **Apply** Have students discuss *results*.
4. **Display the Word** Run your hand under the syllables *re-sult* as you read the word.

**DAY 4**

**rise**

1. **Introduce** We *rise* when we get out of bed in the morning.
2. **Demonstrate** Patty usually *rises* from bed at seven in the morning.
3. **Apply** Work with students to find synonyms for *rise*.
4. **Display the Word** Students can blend and decode this word.

**verge**

1. **Introduce** When something is on the *verge,* it means it's about to happen.
2. **Demonstrate** Josh spent too much money and is on the *verge* of being broke.
3. **Apply** Have students think of other situations where they can use the phrase "on the *verge* of" to describe a situation.
4. **Display the Word** Point out that /j/ is spelled *g*.

# Oral Vocabulary for Hottest, Coldest, Highest, Deepest

## Oral Vocabulary Routine

### DAY 1

**lumber**

1. **Introduce** *Lumber* is wood that has been cut into boards or planks to use in building.
2. **Demonstrate** The frames of many homes are built with *lumber.*
3. **Apply** Discuss with students the different uses of *lumber.*
4. **Display the Word** Run your hand under the syllables *lum-ber* as you read the word.

**competitor**

1. **Introduce** A *competitor* is someone who tries hard to win or get something wanted by others.
2. **Demonstrate** There are many *competitors* in a basketball tournament.
3. **Apply** Have students discuss situations in which they compete and who the *competitors* are.
4. **Display the Word** Have students clap the syllables *com-pet-i-tor* as you read the word.

**plunge**

1. **Introduce** *Plunge* can mean "to throw something (or yourself) into something with force" or "to fall or move downward suddenly."
2. **Demonstrate** The day was hot, and Lily *plunged* into the cool lake water.
3. **Apply** Have students use *plunge* in sentences for each meaning of the word.
4. **Display the Word** Students can blend and decode this word.

### DAY 2

**champ**

1. **Introduce** *Champ* is short for *champion.* A *champion* is someone who wins first place in a contest.
2. **Demonstrate** Our team will beat all the others, so we are the *champs!* Ray is a *champ* at chess.
3. **Apply** Have students name someone who is a *champ* at something.
4. **Display the Word** Point out the initial letters and sound /ch/ *ch.* Students can decode this word.

### DAY 3

**acrobat**

1. **Introduce** An *acrobat* is a performer who can do stunts such as somersaults or handstands to entertain others.
2. **Demonstrate** Marcie is a good *acrobat.* She can do cartwheels and somersaults.
3. **Apply** Have students describe other stunts *acrobats* may perform.
4. **Display the Word** Run your hand under the syllables *ac-ro-bat* as you read the word.

### DAY 4

**ranger**

1. **Introduce** A *ranger* is someone whose job is taking care of a national park or forest.
2. **Demonstrate** We met the *ranger* at the entrance to the campgrounds. The forest ranger explained how to prevent forest fires.
3. **Apply** Have students name another job a *ranger* might do at a national park.
4. **Display the Word** Students can decode this word.

## Oral Vocabulary for **Rocks in His Head**

**LET'S LEARN**
**Amazing Words**

## Oral Vocabulary Routine

**DAY 1**

**project**

1. **Introduce** A *project* is a task that needs time and effort to complete.
2. **Demonstrate** I grew sunflower plants as part of a science *project*. Writing my family's history is a huge *project*.
3. **Apply** Ask students to describe a *project* they have recently completed.
4. **Display the Word** Run your hand under the two syllables in *pro-ject* as you read the word.

**leftover**

1. **Introduce** Something that remains unused or uneaten is a *leftover*.
2. **Demonstrate** After Thanksgiving dinner, we made sandwiches from the *leftover* turkey. We took some of the *leftover* cookies and pie home from the party.
3. **Apply** Ask students to complete the sentence: We had *leftover* _____ after the _____.
4. **Display the Word** As you run your hand under the syllables *left-o-ver,* point out the two words in the compound word.

**murmur**

1. **Introduce** To *murmur* is to make a soft, steady sound.
2. **Demonstrate** The mother *murmured* soothing words to the crying baby.
3. **Apply** The breeze *murmured* in the trees.
4. **Display the Word** Run your hand under the syllables *mur-mur* as you read the word.

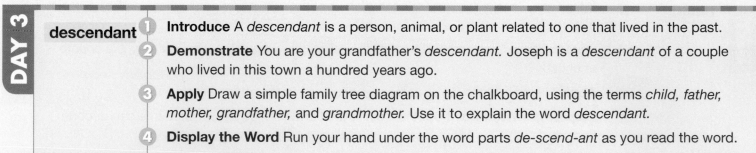

**DAY 3**

**descendant**

1. **Introduce** A *descendant* is a person, animal, or plant related to one that lived in the past.
2. **Demonstrate** You are your grandfather's *descendant*. Joseph is a *descendant* of a couple who lived in this town a hundred years ago.
3. **Apply** Draw a simple family tree diagram on the chalkboard, using the terms *child, father, mother, grandfather,* and *grandmother*. Use it to explain the word *descendant*.
4. **Display the Word** Run your hand under the word parts *de-scend-ant* as you read the word.

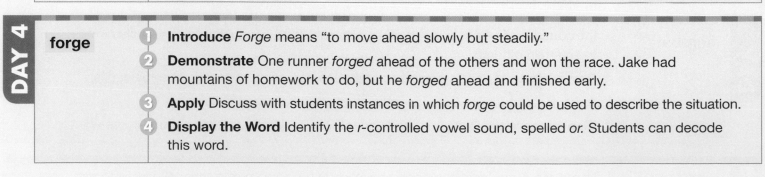

**DAY 4**

**forge**

1. **Introduce** *Forge* means "to move ahead slowly but steadily."
2. **Demonstrate** One runner *forged* ahead of the others and won the race. Jake had mountains of homework to do, but he *forged* ahead and finished early.
3. **Apply** Discuss with students instances in which *forge* could be used to describe the situation.
4. **Display the Word** Identify the *r*-controlled vowel sound, spelled *or*. Students can decode this word.

# Oral Vocabulary for **America's Champion Swimmer: Gertrude Ederle**

**LET'S LEARN**
**Amazing Words**

## Oral Vocabulary Routine

### DAY 1

**ordinary**

1. **Introduce** Something that is usual and not special in any way is *ordinary*.
2. **Demonstrate** We just live in an *ordinary* house. Most of our neighbors are *ordinary* people.
3. **Apply** Have students name a word that means the opposite of *ordinary*. Have them name a word that means almost the same as *ordinary*.
4. **Display the Word** Identify the final *e* sound, spelled *y*. Students can decode the syllables and blend them.

**assemble**

1. **Introduce** *Assemble* means "to gather or come together."
2. **Demonstrate** The whole school *assembled* on the playground to watch the game. Before they left on the hike, the club *assembled* in the park.
3. **Apply** Have students tell when they think a group of people might *assemble*.
4. **Display the Word** Run your hand under the syllables *as-sem-ble* as you read the word.

**magnificent**

1. **Introduce** Something that is *magnificent* is beautiful and splendid.
2. **Demonstrate** President Roosevelt said the Grand Canyon was *magnificent*. Mr. Simmons lives in an old house surrounded by *magnificent* oak trees.
3. **Apply** Have students describe something they think is *magnificent*.
4. **Display the Word** Run your hand under the syllables *mag-nif-i-cent* as you read the word.

### DAY 2

**erect**

1. **Introduce** To *erect* something means "to build something, such as a house or other building."
2. **Demonstrate** They *erected* a new library after the old one burned. Our town *erected* a statue to remember the soldiers who fought in Vietnam.
3. **Apply** Have students tell why they think a town might *erect* a monument.
4. **Display the Word** Run your hand under the syllables *e-rect* as you read the word.

### DAY 3

**accompany**

1. **Introduce** *Accompany* means "to go along with."
2. **Demonstrate** I *accompanied* my mom to the doctor. Bella *accompanied* her friend to school.
3. **Apply** Have students tell when they have *accompanied* a friend or relative somewhere.
4. **Display the Word** Have students clap the syllables in *ac-com-pa-ny*.

### DAY 4

**spectacle**

1. **Introduce** A *spectacle* is an impressive or unusual event.
2. **Demonstrate** The sunset last night was a wonderful *spectacle*. The fireworks made a fabulous *spectacle*.
3. **Apply** Have students name something they think would be a *spectacle*.
4. **Display the Word** Run your hand under the syllables *spec-ta-cle* as you read the word.

## Oral Vocabulary for **Fly, Eagle, Fly!**

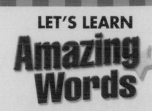
LET'S LEARN
**Amazing Words**

## Oral Vocabulary Routine

**DAY 1**

**agile**

1 **Introduce** A person or animal that is *agile* can move quickly or gracefully.

2 **Demonstrate** A cat is an *agile* animal. The dancers were *agile*.

3 **Apply** Have students name a word that means almost the same as *agile*. Have them name a word that means the opposite of *agile*.

4 **Display the Word** Run your hand under the syllables *ag-ile* as you read the word.

**snout**

1 **Introduce** A *snout* is the part of an animal's face that sticks forward and includes the nose, mouth, and jaws.

2 **Demonstrate** Pigs, dogs, and crocodiles have *snouts*. The dog stuck its *snout* in the hole sniffing out the animal that had been there.

3 **Apply** Have students make a list of other animals that have *snouts*.

4 **Display the Word** Students can decode and blend this word.

**protrude**

1 **Introduce** *Protrude* means "to stick out or thrust forward."

2 **Demonstrate** The long loaf of French bread *protruded* from the grocery bag.

3 **Apply** Work with students to describe things that *protrude*. Students should use the word *protrude* in their descriptions.

4 **Display the Word** Run your hand under the syllables *pro-trude* as you read the word.

**DAY 2**

**scenery**

1 **Introduce** *Scenery* means "the natural surroundings, especially when they are beautiful."

2 **Demonstrate** We enjoyed the *scenery* in the mountains. Harold enjoys painting the *scenery* near the coast.

3 **Apply** Have students describe the *scenery* from the classroom window.

4 **Display the Word** Point out that the letters *sc* spell the /s/ sound in *scenery*.

**DAY 3**

**unfurl**

1 **Introduce** *Unfurl* means "to spread out, shake out, or unfold."

2 **Demonstrate** We will *unfurl* the flag and carry it in the parade. The banner was *unfurled* and hung on the wall.

3 **Apply** Have students demonstrate unfurling a flag or banner. Have them use the word *unfurl* to describe their actions.

4 **Display the Word** Run your hand under the syllables *un-furl* as you read the word.

**DAY 4**

**intersection**

1 **Introduce** The place where two streets or roads cross is an *intersection*.

2 **Demonstrate** This is a busy *intersection*. We are getting a traffic light at this *intersection*.

3 **Apply** Have students tell what they should do when they come to a busy *intersection*. Have them use the word *intersection* in their answers.

4 **Display the Word** Have students clap the syllables in *in-ter-sec-tion*.

## Teacher's Edition

### Text

**KWL Strategy:** The KWL Interactive Reading Strategy was developed and is used by permission of Donna Ogle, National-Louis University, Skokie, Illinois, co-author of *Reading Today and Tomorrow,* Holt, Rinehart & Winston Publishers, 1988. (See also the *Reading Teacher,* February 1986, pp. 564–570.)

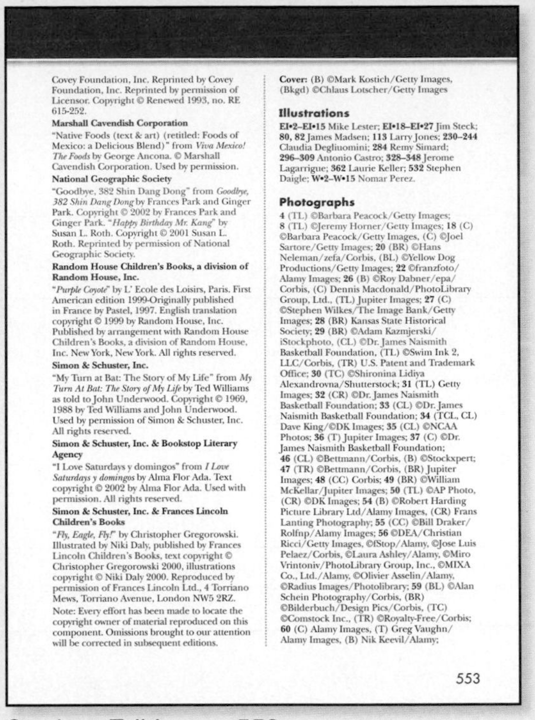

### Photographs

**Cover** (B) ©Mark Kostich/Getty Images, (Bkgd) ©Chlaus Lotscher/Getty Images

Every effort has been made to secure permission and provide appropriate credit for photographic material. The publisher deeply regrets any omission and pledges to correct errors called to its attention in subsequent editions.

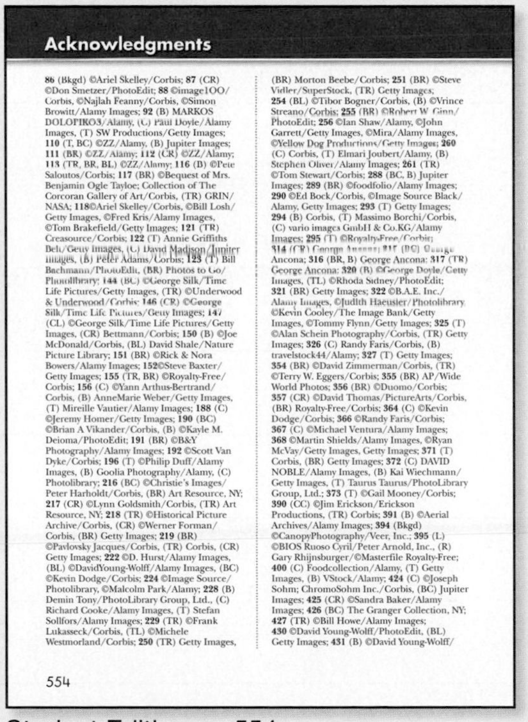

Unless otherwise acknowledged, all photographs are the property of Pearson Education, Inc.

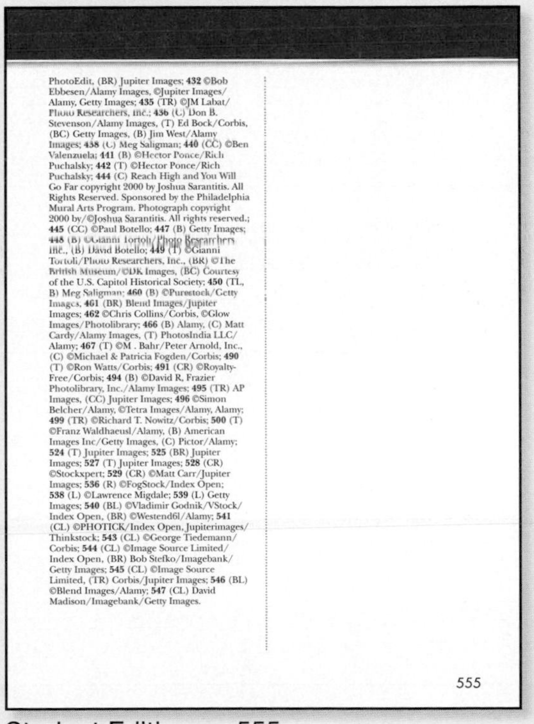

## Student Edition

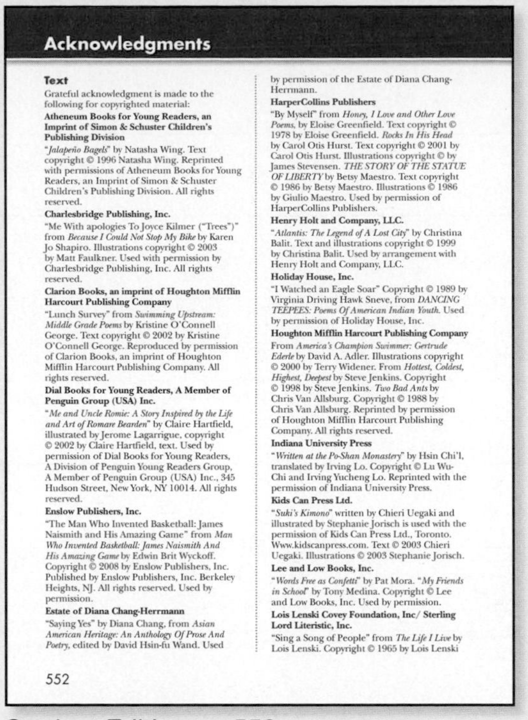

Acknowledgments

**Text**

Grateful acknowledgment is made to the following for copyrighted material:

**Atheneum Books for Young Readers, an Imprint of Simon & Schuster Children's Publishing Division**

"*Jalapeño Bagels*" by Natasha Wing. Text copyright © 1996 Natasha Wing. Reprinted with permissions of Atheneum Books for Young Readers, an Imprint of Simon & Schuster Children's Publishing Division. All rights reserved.

**Charlesbridge Publishing, Inc.**

"Me With apologies To Joyce Kilmer ("Trees")" from *Because I Could Not Stop My Bike* by Karen Jo Shapiro. Illustrations copyright © 2003 by Matt Faulkner. Used with permission by Charlesbridge Publishing, Inc. All rights reserved.

**Clarion Books, an imprint of Houghton Mifflin Harcourt Publishing Company**

"Lunch Survey" from *Swimming Upstream: Middle Grade Poems* by Kristine O'Connell George. Text copyright © 2002 by Kristine O'Connell George. Reproduced by permission of Clarion Books, an imprint of Houghton Mifflin Harcourt Publishing Company. All rights reserved.

**Dial Books for Young Readers, A Member of Penguin Group (USA) Inc.**

"*Me and Uncle Romie: A Story Inspired by the Life and Art of Romare Bearden*" by Claire Hartfield, illustrated by Jerome Lagarrigue, copyright © 2002 by Claire Hartfield, text. Used by permission of Dial Books for Young Readers, A Division of Penguin Young Readers Group, A Member of Penguin Group (USA) Inc., 345 Hudson Street, New York, NY 10014. All rights reserved.

**Enslow Publishers, Inc.**

"The Man Who Invented Basketball: James Naismith and His Amazing Game" from *Man Who Invented Basketball: James Naismith And His Amazing Game* by Edwin Brit Wyckoff. Copyright © 2008 by Enslow Publishers, Inc. Published by Enslow Publishers, Inc. Berkeley Heights, NJ. All rights reserved. Used by permission.

**Estate of Diana Chang-Herrmann**

"Saying Yes" by Diana Chang, from *Asian American Heritage: An Anthology Of Prose And Poetry*, edited by David Hsin-fu Wand. Used by permission of the Estate of Diana Chang-Herrmann.

**HarperCollins Publishers**

"By Myself" from *Honey, I Love and Other Love Poems,* by Eloise Greenfield. Text copyright © 1978 by Eloise Greenfield. *Rocks In His Head* by Carol Otis Hurst. Text copyright © 2001 by Carol Otis Hurst. Illustrations copyright © by James Stevensen. *THE STORY OF THE STATUE OF LIBERTY* by Betsy Maestro. Text copyright © 1986 by Betsy Maestro. Illustrations © 1986 by Giulio Maestro. Used by permission of HarperCollins Publishers.

**Henry Holt and Company, LLC.**

"*Atlantis: The Legend of A Lost City*" by Christina Balit. Text and illustrations copyright © 1999 by Christina Balit. Used by arrangement with Henry Holt and Company, LLC.

**Holiday House, Inc.**

"I Watched an Eagle Soar" Copyright © 1989 by Virginia Driving Hawk Sneve, from *DANCING TEEPEES: Poems Of American Indian Youth.* Used by permission of Holiday House, Inc.

**Houghton Mifflin Harcourt Publishing Company**

From *America's Champion Swimmer: Gertrude Ederle* by David A. Adler. Illustrations copyright © 2000 by Terry Widener. From *Hottest, Coldest, Highest, Deepest* by Steve Jenkins. Copyright © 1998 by Steve Jenkins. *Two Bad Ants* by Chris Van Allsburg. Copyright © 1988 by Chris Van Allsburg. Reprinted by permission of Houghton Mifflin Harcourt Publishing Company. All rights reserved.

**Indiana University Press**

"*Written at the Po-Shan Monastery*" by Hsin Chi'I, translated by Irving Lo. Copyright © Lu Wu-Chi and Irving Yucheng Lo. Reprinted with the permission of Indiana University Press.

**Kids Can Press Ltd.**

"*Suki's Kimono*" written by Chieri Uegaki and illustrated by Stephanie Jorisch is used with the permission of Kids Can Press Ltd., Toronto. Www.kidscanpress.com. Text © 2003 Chieri Uegaki. Illustrations © 2003 Stephanie Jorisch.

**Lee and Low Books, Inc.**

"*Words Free as Confetti*" by Pat Mora. "*My Friends in School*" by Tony Medina. Copyright © Lee and Low Books, Inc. Used by permission.

**Lois Lenski Covey Foundation, Inc/ Sterling Lord Literistic, Inc.**

"Sing a Song of People" from *The Life I Live* by Lois Lenski. Copyright © 1965 by Lois Lenski

552

Student Edition, p. 552

Covey Foundation, Inc. Reprinted by Covey Foundation, Inc. Reprinted by permission of Licensor. Copyright © Renewed 1993, no. RE 615-252.

**Marshall Cavendish Corporation**

"Native Foods (text & art) (retitled: Foods of Mexico: a Delicious Blend)" from *Viva Mexico! The Foods* by George Ancona. © Marshall Cavendish Corporation. Used by permission.

**National Geographic Society**

"Goodbye, 382 Shin Dang Dong" from *Goodbye, 382 Shin Dang Dong* by Frances Park and Ginger Park. Copyright © 2002 by Frances Park and Ginger Park. "*Happy Birthday Mr. Kang*" by Susan L. Roth. Copyright © 2001 Susan L. Roth. Reprinted by permission of National Geographic Society.

**Random House Children's Books, a division of Random House, Inc.**

"*Purple Coyote*" by L' Ecole des Loisirs, Paris. First American edition 1999-Originally published in France by Pastel, 1997. English translation copyright © 1999 by Random House, Inc. Published by arrangement with Random House Children's Books, a division of Random House, Inc. New York, New York. All rights reserved.

**Simon & Schuster, Inc.**

"My Turn at Bat: The Story of My Life" from *My Turn At Bat: The Story of My Life* by Ted Williams as told to John Underwood. Copyright © 1969, 1988 by Ted Williams and John Underwood. Used by permission of Simon & Schuster, Inc. All rights reserved.

**Simon & Schuster, Inc. & Bookstop Literary Agency**

"I Love Saturdays y domingos" from *I Love Saturdays y domingos* by Alma Flor Ada. Text copyright © 2002 by Alma Flor Ada. Used with permission. All rights reserved.

**Simon & Schuster, Inc. & Frances Lincoln Children's Books**

"*Fly, Eagle, Fly!*" by Christopher Gregorowski. Illustrated by Niki Daly, published by Frances Lincoln Children's Books, text copyright © Christopher Gregorowski 2000, illustrations copyright © Niki Daly 2000. Reproduced by permission of Frances Lincoln Ltd., 4 Torriano Mews, Torriano Avenue, London NW5 2RZ.

Note: Every effort has been made to locate the copyright owner of material reproduced on this component. Omissions brought to our attention will be corrected in subsequent editions.

**Cover:** (B) ©Mark Kostich/Getty Images, (Bkgd) ©Chlaus Lotscher/Getty Images

**Illustrations**

**EI•2–EI•15** Mike Lester; **EI•18–EI•27** Jim Steck; **80, 82** James Madsen; **113** Larry Jones; **230–244** Claudia Degliuomini; **284** Remy Simard; **296–309** Antonio Castro; **328–348** Jerome Lagarrigue; **362** Laurie Keller; **532** Stephen Daigle; **W•2–W•15** Nomar Perez.

**Photographs**

**4** (TL) ©Barbara Peacock/Getty Images; **8** (TL) ©Jeremy Horner/Getty Images; **18** (C) ©Barbara Peacock/Getty Images, (C) ©Joel Sartore/Getty Images; **20** (BR) ©Hans Neleman/zefa/Corbis, (BL) ©Yellow Dog Productions/Getty Images; **22** ©franzfoto/Alamy Images; **26** (B) ©Roy Dabner/epa/Corbis, (C) Dennis Macdonald/PhotoLibrary Group, Ltd., (TL) Jupiter Images; **27** (C) ©Stephen Wilkes/The Image Bank/Getty Images; **28** (BR) Kansas State Historical Society; **29** (BR) ©Adam Kazmjerski/iStockphoto, (CL) ©Dr. James Naismith Basketball Foundation, (TL) ©Swim Ink 2, LLC/Corbis, (TR) U.S. Patent and Trademark Office; **30** (TC) ©Shironina Lidiya Alexandrovna/Shutterstock; **31** (TL) Getty Images; **32** (CR) ©Dr. James Naismith Basketball Foundation; **33** (CL) ©Dr. James Naismith Basketball Foundation; **34** (TCL, CL) Dave King/©DK Images; **35** (CL) ©NCAA Photos; **36** (T) Jupiter Images; **37** (C) ©Dr. James Naismith Basketball Foundation; **46** (CL) ©Bettmann/Corbis, (B) ©Stockxpert; **47** (TR) ©Bettmann/Corbis, (BR) Jupiter Images; **48** (CC) Corbis; **49** (BR) ©William McKellar/Jupiter Images; **50** (TL) ©AP Photo, (CR) ©DK Images; **54** (B) ©Robert Harding Picture Library Ltd/Alamy Images, (CR) Frans Lanting Photography; **55** (CC) ©Bill Draker/Rolfnp/Alamy Images; **56** ©DEA/Christian Ricci/Getty Images, ©fStop/Alamy, ©Jose Luis Pelaez/Corbis, ©Laura Ashley/Alamy, ©Miro Vrintoniv/PhotoLibrary Group, Inc., ©MIXA Co., Ltd./Alamy, ©Olivier Asselin/Alamy, ©Radius Images/Photolibrary; **59** (BL) ©Alan Schein Photography/Corbis, (BR) ©Bilderbuch/Design Pics/Corbis, (TC) ©Comstock Inc., (TR) ©Royalty-Free/Corbis; **60** (C) Alamy Images, (T) Greg Vaughn/Alamy Images, (B) Nik Keevil/Alamy;

553

Student Edition, p. 553

Acknowledgments

**86** (Bkgd) ©Ariel Skelley/Corbis; **87** (CR) ©Don Smetzer/PhotoEdit; **88** ©image1OO/Corbis, ©Najlah Feanny/Corbis, ©Simon Browitt/Alamy Images; **92** (B) MARKOS DOLOPIKOS/Alamy, (C) Paul Doyle/Alamy Images, (T) SW Productions/Getty Images; **110** (T, BC) ©ZZ/Alamy, (B) Jupiter Images; **111** (BR) ©ZZ/Alamy; **112** (CR) ©ZZ/Alamy; **113** (TR, BR, BL) ©ZZ/Alamy; **116** (B) ©Pete Saloutos/Corbis; **117** (BR) ©Bequest of Mrs. Benjamin Ogle Tayloe; Collection of The Corcoran Gallery of Art/Corbis, (TR) GRIN/NASA; **118**©Ariel Skelley/Corbis, ©Bill Losh/Getty Images, ©Fred Kris/Alamy Images, ©Tom Brakefield/Getty Images; **121** (TR) Creasource/Corbis; **122** (T) Annie Griffiths Belt/Getty Images, (C) David Madison/Jupiter Images, (B) Peter Adams/Corbis; **123** (T) Bill Bachmann/PhotoEdit, (BR) Photos to Go/Photolibrary; **144** (BC) ©George Silk/Time Life Pictures/Getty Images, (TR) ©Underwood & Underwood/Corbis; **146** (CR) ©George Silk/Time Life Pictures/Getty Images; **147** (CL) ©George Silk/Time Life Pictures/Getty Images, (CR) Bettmann/Corbis; **150** (B) ©Joe McDonald/Corbis, (BL) David Shale/Nature Picture Library; **151** (BR) ©Rick & Nora Bowers/Alamy Images; **152**©Steve Baxter/Getty Images; **155** (TR, BR) ©Royalty-Free/Corbis; **156** (C) ©Yann Arthus-Bertrand/Corbis, (B) AnneMarie Weber/Getty Images, (T) Mireille Vautier/Alamy Images; **188** (C) ©Jeremy Homer/Getty Images; **190** (BC) ©Brian A Vikander/Corbis, (B) ©Kayle M. Deioma/PhotoEdit; **191** (BR) ©B&Y Photography/Alamy Images; **192** ©Scott Van Dyke/Corbis; **196** (T) ©Philip Duff/Alamy Images, (B) Goolia Photography/Alamy, (C) Photolibrary; **216** (BC) ©Christie's Images/Peter Harholdt/Corbis, (BR) Art Resource, NY; **217** (CR) ©Lynn Goldsmith/Corbis, (TR) Art Resource, NY; **218** (TR) ©Historical Picture Archive/Corbis, (CR) ©Werner Forman/Corbis, (BR) Getty Images; **219** (BR) ©Pavlovsky Jacques/Corbis, (TR) Corbis, (CR) Getty Images; **222** ©D. Hurst/Alamy Images, (BL) ©DavidYoung-Wolff/Alamy Images, (BC) ©Kevin Dodge/Corbis; **224** ©Image Source/Photolibrary, ©Malcolm Park/Alamy; **228** (B) Demin Tony/PhotoLibrary Group, Ltd., (C) Richard Cooke/Alamy Images, (T) Stefan Sollfors/Alamy Images; **229** (TR) ©Frank Lukasseck/Corbis, (TL) ©Michele Westmorland/Corbis; **250** (TR) Getty Images, (BR) Morton Beebe/Corbis; **251** (BR) ©Steve Vidler/SuperStock, (TR) Getty Images; **254** (BL) ©Tibor Bogner/Corbis, (B) ©Vrince Streano/Corbis; **255** (BR) ©Robert W. Ginn/PhotoEdit; **256** ©Ian Shaw/Alamy, ©John Garrett/Getty Images, ©Mira/Alamy Images, ©Yellow Dog Productions/Getty Images; **260** (C) Corbis, (T) Elmari Joubert/Alamy, (B) Stephen Oliver/Alamy Images; **261** (TR) ©Tom Stewart/Corbis; **288** (BC, B) Jupiter Images; **289** (BR) ©foodfolio/Alamy Images; **290** ©Ed Bock/Corbis, ©Image Source Black/Alamy, Getty Images; **293** (T) Getty Images; **294** (B) Corbis, (T) Massimo Borchi/Corbis, (C) vario images GmbH & Co.KG/Alamy Images; **295** (T) ©Royalty-Free/Corbis; **314** (CR) George Ancona; **315** (BC) George Ancona; **316** (BR, B) George Ancona; **317** (TR) George Ancona; **320** (B) ©George Doyle/Getty Images, (TL) ©Rhoda Sidney/PhotoEdit; **321** (BR) Getty Images; **322** ©B.A.E. Inc./Alamy Images, ©Judith Haeusler/Photolibrary ©Kevin Cooley/The Image Bank/Getty Images, ©Tommy Flynn/Getty Images; **325** (T) ©Alan Schein Photography/Corbis, (TR) Getty Images; **326** (C) Randy Faris/Corbis, (B) travelstock44/Alamy; **327** (T) Getty Images; **354** (BR) ©David Zimmerman/Corbis, (TR) ©Terry W. Eggers/Corbis; **355** (BR) AP/Wide World Photos; **356** (BR) ©Duomo/Corbis; **357** (CR) ©David Thomas/PictureArts/Corbis, (BR) Royalty-Free/Corbis; **364** (C) ©Kevin Dodge/Corbis; **366** ©Randy Faris/Corbis; **367** (C) ©Michael Ventura/Alamy Images; **368** ©Martin Shields/Alamy Images, ©Ryan McVay/Getty Images, Getty Images; **371** (T) Corbis, (BR) Getty Images; **372** (C) DAVID NOBLE/Alamy Images, (B) Kai Wiechmann/Getty Images, (T) Taurus Taurus/PhotoLibrary Group, Ltd.; **373** (T) ©Gail Mooney/Corbis; **390** (CC) ©Jim Erickson/Erickson Productions, (TR) Corbis; **391** (B) ©Aerial Archives/Alamy Images; **394** (Bkgd) ©CanopyPhotography/Veer, Inc.; **395** (L) ©BIOS Ruoso Cyril/Peter Arnold, Inc., (R) Gary Rhijnsburger/©Masterfile Royalty-Free; **400** (C) Foodcollection/Alamy, (T) Getty Images, (B) VStock/Alamy; **424** (C) ©Joseph Sohm; ChromoSohm Inc./Corbis, (BC) Jupiter Images; **425** (CR) ©Sandra Baker/Alamy Images; **426** (BC) The Granger Collection, NY; **427** (TR) ©Bill Howe/Alamy Images; **430** ©David Young-Wolff/PhotoEdit, (BL) Getty Images; **431** (B) ©David Young-Wolff/

554

Student Edition, p. 554

PhotoEdit, (BR) Jupiter Images; **432** ©Bob Ebbesen/Alamy Images, ©Jupiter Images/Alamy, Getty Images; **435** (TR) ©JM Labat/Photo Researchers, Inc.; **436** (C) Don B. Stevenson/Alamy Images, (T) Ed Bock/Corbis, (BC) Getty Images, (B) Jim West/Alamy Images; **438** (C) Meg Saligman; **440** (CC) ©Ben Valenzuela; **441** (B) ©Hector Ponce/Rich Puchalsky; **442** (T) ©Hector Ponce/Rich Puchalsky; **444** (C) Reach High and You Will Go Far copyright 2000 by Joshua Sarantitis. All Rights Reserved. Sponsored by the Philadelphia Mural Arts Program. Photograph copyright 2000 by/©Joshua Sarantitis. All rights reserved.; **445** (CC) ©Paul Botello; **447** (B) Getty Images; **448** (B) ©Gianni Tortoli/Photo Researchers Inc., (B) David Botello; **449** (T) ©Gianni Tortoli/Photo Researchers, Inc., (BR) ©The British Museum/©DK Images, (BC) Courtesy of the U.S. Capitol Historical Society; **450** (TL, B) Meg Saligman; **460** (B) ©Purestock/Getty Images, **461** (BR) Blend Images/Jupiter Images; **462** ©Chris Collins/Corbis, ©Glow Images/Photolibrary; **466** (B) Alamy, (C) Matt Cardy/Alamy Images, (T) PhotosIndia LLC/Alamy; **467** (T) ©M . Bahr/Peter Arnold, Inc., (C) ©Michael & Patricia Fogden/Corbis; **490** (T) ©Ron Watts/Corbis; **491** (CR) ©Royalty-Free/Corbis; **494** (B) ©David R. Frazier Photolibrary, Inc./Alamy Images; **495** (TR) AP Images, (CC) Jupiter Images; **496** ©Simon Belcher/Alamy, ©Tetra Images/Alamy, Alamy; **499** (TR) ©Richard T. Nowitz/Corbis; **500** (T) ©Franz Waldhaeusl/Alamy, (B) American Images Inc/Getty Images, (C) Pictor/Alamy; **524** (T) Jupiter Images; **525** (BR) Jupiter Images; **527** (T) Jupiter Images; **528** (CR) ©Stockxpert; **529** (CR) ©Matt Carr/Jupiter Images; **536** (R) ©FogStock/Index Open; **538** (L) ©Lawrence Migdale; **539** (L) Getty Images; **540** (BL) ©Vladimir Godnik/VStock/Index Open, (BR) ©Westend6l/Alamy; **541** (CL) ©PHOTICK/Index Open, Jupiterimages/Thinkstock; **543** (CL) ©George Tiedemann/Corbis; **544** (CL) ©Image Source Limited/Index Open, (BR) Bob Stefko/Imagebank/Getty Images; **545** (CL) ©Image Source Limited, (TR) Corbis/Jupiter Images; **546** (BL) ©Blend Images/Alamy; **547** (CL) David Madison/Imagebank/Getty Images.

555

Student Edition, p. 555

# TEACHER NOTES

# TEACHER NOTES

# TEACHER NOTES

# Problem-Solution Essay

## Writing Prompt

Write about a problem in your school or community, and explain how that problem might be solved.

**Purpose** Identify a problem and offer a solution.

**Audience** peers, teachers, or other interested adults

**INTRODUCE GENRE AND PROMPT** In this writing process lesson, you will study a problem-solution essay and use this genre to write a response to the prompt. In a problem-solution essay, a writer describes a problem, or something that he or she thinks needs to be fixed, and a solution for the problem, or a way the problem can be fixed, including reasons why the solution is a good one.

## INTRODUCE KEY FEATURES

### Key Features of a Problem-Solution Essay

- identifies and explains a problem
- offers one or more solutions for the problem
- includes facts and details or evidence to support the solution and to convince readers to accept the solution
- uses descriptive details and persuasive words or opinions to convince readers to accept the solution
- has an introduction, a body, and a conclusion

**Introduce Genre** Show a simple problem, for example, trying to reach something under your desk. Show a way to solve the problem, for example, using a ruler to retrieve the item. Write *problem* and *solution* on the board. Explain that a problem is something that needs to be fixed, and a solution is a way of fixing it. Help students understand that a problem-solution essay describes both a problem and a solution. Discuss the key features of a problem-solution essay that appear on this page.

## Common Core State Standards

**Writing 1.a.** Introduce the topic or text they are writing about, state an opinion, and create an organizational structure that lists reasons. **Writing 1.b.** Provide reasons that support the opinion. **Writing 1.d.** Provide a concluding statement or section. **Writing 5.** With guidance and support from peers and adults, develop and strengthen writing as needed by planning, revising, and editing.

 **Plan and Prewrite**

### Mini-Lesson | Reading Like a Writer

■ **Examine Model Text** Let's look at an example of a student's problem-solution essay that identifies a problem at school and tells how it can be solved. This is an example of the type of essay you might write about a problem in your school or community. Display and read aloud to students "We Need a Longer Recess" on Writing Transparency WP22. Ask them to identify key features of a problem-solution essay in the student model.

■ **Evaluate Model Text** Display and read aloud "Traits of a Good Problem-Solution Essay" on Writing Transparency WP23. Discuss each trait as it is reflected in the model. For Focus/Ideas, ask students to identify the problem and the solution. For Organization, ask them to explain where the problem and the solution are presented in the essay and why they are in that order. Proceed in the same way for each of the remaining traits, defining it when necessary and helping students identify examples of the trait in the model.

---

**We Need a Longer Recess**

Has this ever happened to you? The bell for recess rings. You put on your coat. You line up with everyone else and wait to go out to the playground. Finally, you're outside. You and your friends are deciding what game to play. What happens then? The bell rings, and it's time to go back inside! Our recess at Jefferson Elementary School is too short.

Here is a solution to this problem. Between 8:00 and 8:15 each morning, our principal reads daily messages, but these messages usually take only three or four minutes. For the rest of the time, the students sit at their desks, waiting and talking and fidgeting. It's a waste of time. If we added ten of those fifteen minutes to our morning lessons, recess could start ten minutes earlier, and then we would have time to get some real exercise.

Experts say that kids need regular exercise. It helps us think and learn as well as stay healthy. So spending a little more time on the playground would be good for us.

Unit 4 Problem-Solution Essay ▪ PLAN and PREWRITE    Writing Process **22**

Writing Transparency WP22, TR DVD

---

**Traits of a Good Problem-Solution Essay**

| | |
|---|---|
| **Focus/Ideas** | Essay focuses on one problem and one solution to that problem. Writer provides facts and details to support the solution. |
| **Organization** | Essay's introduction identifies the problem. A body paragraph presents a possible solution. A concluding paragraph sums up the writer's ideas. |
| **Voice** | Voice is informative, entertaining, and persuasive. |
| **Word Choice** | Writer uses descriptive details and persuasive words. |
| **Sentences** | Writer uses a variety of types (statements, questions, exclamations) and structures (simple, compound). |
| **Conventions** | Writer has good control of spelling, grammar, and mechanics. |

Unit 4 Problem-Solution Essay ▪ PLAN and PREWRITE    Writing Process **23**

Writing Transparency WP23, TR DVD

---

**GENERATE IDEAS FOR WRITING** The writing prompt tells you the general topic of your writing: a problem in your school or community and how to solve it. Now you need to think of a specific topic: something at school or in your community that you think is a problem that you can think of a way to solve. First, make a list of as many appropriate topics as you can.

# Looking for Teacher Resources and other important information?

Go online to  **Pearson SuccessNet**

**eStreet Interactive**
www.ReadingStreet.com

In the *First Stop* on Reading Street, you will find the following information.

- Research into Practice on Reading Street
- Guide to Reading Street
- Assessment on Reading Street
- Customize Writing on Reading Street
- Small Group Instruction on Reading Street

- ELL on Reading Street
- Customize Literacy on Reading Street
- 21st Century Skills on Reading Street
- Teacher Resources for Grade 3
- Index

# Looking for Teacher Resources and other important information?

Go online to  Pearson SuccessNet

**eStreet Interactive**
www.ReadingStreet.com

In the *First Stop* on Reading Street, you will find the following information.

- Research into Practice on Reading Street
- Guide to Reading Street
- Assessment on Reading Street
- Customize Writing on Reading Street
- Small Group Instruction on Reading Street

- ELL on Reading Street
- Customize Literacy on Reading Street
- 21st Century Skills on Reading Street
- Teacher Resources for Grade 3
- Index